for

Monica Cooper Elkinton

West Virginia, and indeed the whole world,
is now in the hands of your generation.
May you leave them in better shape
than you inherited them from our generation.

Contents

List of Profiles

Foreword

Ken Hechler

I am delighted both as an environmentalist and as an historian to add my good wishes to the West Virginia Highlands Conservancy for its forty years of dedicated service fighting to protect West Virginia's environment. Fighting is the appropriate word, because it has been a continuous fight. The forces desiring to have a green light to destroy West Virginia have had and still have power, money, and connections. Those of us on the other side have ourselves, our dedication, and the beauty of West Virginia as our weapons.

Along with the Conservancy, and a few other groups, my career as a public servant has been spent fighting for the little guy against most of these same forces. Whether it was timber companies, mining companies, or even the political establishment, the Conservancy has inspired me to research issues, organize politically, and fight for the natural environment. I am proud that I am still able to assist in the latest campaign to obtain more Congressionally-designated wilderness within the Monongahela National Forest. After the 2006 mid-term elections, I am excited by the prospects for the wilderness battle in Congress. I know the people of West Virginia support that too.

As I wrote not too long ago in a piece in *The Charleston Gazette*, of the thousands of votes I cast during my 18 years in Congress, I am proudest of my fight for the health and safety of West Virginia coal miners and protection of our natural environment, particularly my vote for the 1964 Wilderness Act.

Back then the U.S. Forest Service did not take the initiative to consider any part of the Monongahela National Forest for this protection. Rather, West Virginia citizens, led by the Highlands Conservancy, came to me with their own well-thought-out proposals. In 1970, I introduced legislation to designate the Cranberry, Otter Creek, and Dolly

Sods wilderness areas. I was criticized for this too, because these areas were in Congressman Harley Staggers's district. But somebody in Congress from West Virginia needed to step forward. And ultimately, we prevailed, picking up Mr. Staggers' support, and that of both our senators, Jennings Randolph and Robert Byrd.

Well I remember, when attending the annual Forest Festival parade in Elkins, holding a sign that read "Save Dolly Sods, Otter Creek and Cranberry." I think my support of these areas may have led to the parade committee banning political signs. However, they did let me retain the sign on my little red jeep, "Ken Hechler – Your Servant in Congress."

Until my service in the Congress came to an end in 1976, as the Conservancy ended its first decade of existence, I had worked with the leaders and members of the Conservancy on wilderness legislation, repeated efforts to protect the Shavers Fork under the federal Wild and Scenic Rivers system, protecting Canaan Valley, and limiting the abuses of strip mining.

The abuses of mining, especially strip mining, and its big brother, mountaintop-removal mining, have absolutely devastated southern West Virginia. Thank God for the Cindy Ranks, the John McFerrins, and the Julian Martins of the Highlands Conservancy, who have helped bring these abuses to national attention, and enabled local victims in these communities to have the courage to speak out, even at considerable personal risk. This is a life-or-death struggle, and I am pleased the Highlands Conservancy has been and will continue to be involved.

When I became West Virginia Secretary of State in 1985, I might have angered some Conservancy members by taking away your editor of *The Highlands Voice*, Mary Ratliff. But I thought then, and time proved me right, that under Mary's leadership as Deputy Secretary of State, we could reform many of the corrupt election practices that had plagued West Virginia for generations. Together we, and the citizens of West Virginia, cleaned up the election process, which benefits all our citizens, no matter what their interests or political affiliation. I know both Mary and her husband Ray were active members of the Conservancy over many years. Mary also inspired me to continue to join with the Highlands Conservancy to take the lead on environmental issues.

Since leaving Congress, I have tried to address state problems when I could. The Conservancy has kept the heat on mining issues for years, and won some significant reforms, especially Judge Haden's decision on valley fills. You have fought for strong groundwater protection, against out-of-state garbage, and in recent years to save Blackwater Canyon. There never seems to be a shortage of threats: the polluters and exploiters keep seeing a way to make a buck at our expense. The Conservancy has hung in there to protect and preserve our state.

As you celebrate your first forty years, I hope you will enjoy looking back at your well-deserved record of accomplishments. But I hope too that this book will inspire the new generation of West Virginians to pick up where we've left off, and keep fighting!

— Ken

[**Author's Note**] Ken Hechler served in the U.S. House of Representatives from 1959 until 1977, then as West Virginia Secretary of State from 1985 to 2001. In the latter role, as West Virginia's chief election official, he promoted many reforms for clean elections. In 2000, he walked 530 miles with Granny D on her famous trek across the country to promote campaign finance reform, which led to the McCain-Feingold Act. Since leaving public office, he has resumed his writing and lecturing, always on the alert to join the Highlands Conservancy in its continued fight to protect the environment.

Introduction

Mary Wimmer, a leader in the West Virginia Sierra Club, told me that she always felt grounded and inspired by knowing about John Muir. The more she learned of the founder of the Sierra Club, the more inspired she grew and the better able to carry forward Muir's vision.

The West Virginia Highlands Conservancy also has an inspiring origin and history, but not just one dominant personality. The Conservancy's leaders have been all of its organizers, its officers, its newsletter editors, and its issue-oriented activists. This is their story. The story of what they did (and are continuing to do), sprinkled with brief profiles of who they are or were, and perhaps why they are or were so involved.

I remember thinking during the 1980s that the many twists and turns of the effort to save the Canaan Valley from inundation of the Davis Power Project, a story told in Chapter 4, would make a great Ph.D. dissertation topic. In fact, one somewhat naive graduate student began his master's thesis in 1971, thinking he would be able to include the ultimate outcome, only to be well out of graduate school before the eventual realization of the nation's 500th national wildlife refuge was achieved.

When the late Judge Charles Haden II rendered his landmark decision in 1999 outlawing valley fills and therefore ending mountaintop removal mining, at least for a while, I thought the Highlands Conservancy should celebrate that success. But after a quick toast, the activists of that period were back into the trenches working on the new host of issues. These issues required alert, committed West Virginians to counter the raw power of the extractive industries and their friends in government. When there were successes, and there really were many, the celebrations have been fleeting, as the issues of the day have commanded time and energy. Battles were won, but the war was always in doubt, it seemed.

Finally, as has always been the case within the Highlands Conservancy, when something needed to be done, someone needed to volunteer to do it. I realized that if a retrospective was to be written, I needed to step forward. In 2000 I volunteered to organize the Conservancy's thirty-five year history, to be celebrated in 2002.

The Board gave me their encouragement and endorsement. Others told me it was a story that really needed to be told and that no one else was interested or willing to tackle the job. Unfortunately, after an initial organizing flurry, I needed to postpone my involvement for a variety of personal and family reasons. In 2005 I reactivated the project and am now delighted to help celebrate the fortieth anniversary year of the Conservancy.

Between my two spurts of activity, we lost one of the bedrock personalities of the Highlands Conservancy, Sayre Rodman. I remember both Sayre and his wife, Jean, from my first Conservancy event, the 1970 Fall Review in Richwood. And I remember that when I presented my ideas to the Board in 2000, both of them encouraged me to document the Conservancy's history. By then Sayre was in declining health, and I should have realized that the "first generation" of Conservancy founders and leaders were not going to live forever. When Sayre passed away in 2004, I told myself I had better be getting on with this project.

When the American Youth Hostels, a group with many connections to the Conservancy, published its 50th anniversary history, I remember reading it and vicariously meeting the founders and early leaders as if I had been involved myself. In fact, both of my parents had been involved with AYH as young adults, and many of the historical profiles added flesh to what had only been names on Christmas letters that arrived each year throughout my childhood.

This volume is designed to serve several purposes. It is first, and foremost, to celebrate and chronicle the major issues and profile the personalities that have comprised the West Virginia Highlands Conservancy from its organization in 1967 to its fortieth birthday in 2007. I hope those involved will take pride in the successes, remember the challenges, and find strength to continue the struggles. For those who are in the next generation or who read this volume as a supporter but not-yet-an-activist, I hope the inspiration of this parade of Davids, meeting, engaging, and in some cases defeating the parade of Goliaths, will serve as John Muir serves the Sierra Club, as the grounding and inspiring background that informs all future action.

What this book is, and is not:

I can already hear someone saying this is not the full story. True, it is not. This is the story of the West Virginia Highlands Conservancy, but not of all of environmental activism in West Virginia over the past forty years. There were and are many partner organizations, and literally thousands of individual activists that helped achieve virtually all of the successes discussed on the following pages. I have not attempted to outline the complete history of wilderness preservation, of clearcutting, or of strip mine opposition. Indeed, most of those battles have already been chronicled and many of those books are listed as sources or references.

Rather, I have tried to tell the story of the West Virginia Highlands Conservancy and its own involvement in these issues. This is a history of the Conservancy and, through this organization, I hope readers will better understand the issues and where to find additional reference materials and sources.

The selection of issues was very difficult for me. I tried to identify those issues of greatest impact and of long-term involvement by the Conservancy. When necessary, I favored those issues where the Conservancy was a leading player, not just a participating co-sponsor. This latter distinction unfortunately eliminated additional struggles, which in the final analysis, have been left for another discussion. One was the continuing struggle to save the Blackwater Canyon. That struggle began as a major campaign of the Conservancy in the face of the sale of much of the canyon by the Monongahela Power Company to a timber company. The sale threatened this truly beloved "crown jewel" of West Virginia. After successfully growing, both in financial support and in numbers of active supporters, the campaign developed its own organization, Friends of the Blackwater, under the able leadership of Judy Rodd, a former senior vice president of the Conservancy. But while the Conservancy and its members have continued to support these efforts, the Conservancy as a group has not been the leader.

Other coalitions have been omitted from discussion because they have had their own lives outside the Conservancy. One of these has been the West Virginia Environmental Council, a critically important lobbying and monitoring organization in Charleston. Essential to the Conservancy and its ability to promote good legislation or kill harmful legislation, the E-Council has developed into an independent organization with its own history. Thankfully, many of its leaders are or have been active Conservancy members as well.

Finally, although the Highlands Conservancy has experienced an enviable history of internal achievements, I have only grazed that discussion. For example, *The Highlands Voice* has been the glue that has often kept the Conservancy membership informed and involved. Without the valuable record provided by the *Voice* back issues, my research would have truly been impossible. A listing of its editors is included in the appendix. Authors of relevant articles are listed following each chapter.

I have also not followed the internal milestones of the Conservancy's forty years. There are several references to membership levels and spurts of growth, but, besides a short section in Chapter 9, I have left to other discussions the story of the Conservancy's organizational growth and development.

A word about chapter subtitles: I have provided subtitles in an effort to establish markers to important events or subdivisions within chapters. The reader is cautioned, however, that often these threads continue into several later sections before resolution. Since events or issues occurred simultaneously, it was as if several folders were open at the same time.

Acknowledgments

Inevitably in such an undertaking as this there are many people to thank and, inevitably, some will be overlooked by omission. First, the current officers and Board of Directors of the Conservancy have given their encouragement at every step. From initial support when it was only an idea to a recent commitment of financial backing, I have relied upon many of them as well to review draft chapters and provide valuable feedback all through the writing process.

There have been more than a score of individuals who consented to personal and recorded interviews. Most I already knew, but some I met for the first time, letting me associate a personality with what had only previously been a name. To all, I appreciate your time dredging up memories and working me into your busy schedules.

As I traveled from my home in southern Maryland back to West Virginia to conduct my research, I was the recipient of overnight hospitality from several Conservancy leaders. I want to recognize Dave Saville and Barnes Nugent, Hugh and Ruth Rogers, Jean and Buff Rodman, Peter and Marilyn Shoenfeld, and Paul and Cindy Rank in that regard.

Any group's history is open to interpretation, errors of omission and commission and differences of opinion. I have relied heavily on more than twenty different people to read and comment on drafts of chapters. Most of the readers were the major players themselves. Some have reviewed as few as two chapters and Bill McNeel has read every word. To them all, I offer my sincere appreciation. Only they and I will ever know how many errors were caught before publication. For those errors that our best collective reviewing missed, I alone accept full responsibility.

Those who assisted by reading and providing comments were, in alphabetical order: Bob Burrell, Linda Cooper, Rupert Cutler, Monica Elkinton, Lou Greathouse, Julian Martin, John McFerrin, Helen McGinnis, Bill McNeel, Cindy Rank, Buff Rodman, Hugh Rogers, Ruth

Blackwell Rogers, Dave Saville, Marilyn Shoenfeld, Peter Shoenfeld, Bruce Sundquist, Mary Wimmer, Frank Young, and Ed Zahniser.

I am honored that Ken Hechler, a true hero to West Virginia environmentalists, agreed to provide a foreword. Jonathan Jessup's color photography inspires us all, and I knew I wanted his art on the cover. Mike Breiding provided the map of the highlands. To these three, I offer my appreciation also.

When George Parkinson, then Curator of the West Virginia and Regional History Collection at West Virginia University, asked for the records of the West Virginia Highlands Conservancy, he made a pivotal decision. Since then John Cuthbert, Curator, Harold Forbes, Associate Curator, and Michael Ridderbusch, Assistant Curator, have expanded and organized the archive. My ability to retrieve early copies of *The Highlands Voice* and other archival records at WVU has greatly facilitated my research. I can't imagine working on this project without them. From the outset of my project, I made the commitment to them that my notes, drafts, and recordings of interviews would be deposited at WVU as well.

I should also thank several early Conservancy activists — Sue Broughton, Jim Wolf, Bob Burrell, and Nick Zvegintzov — for sharing their personal archival materials. Dave Saville, a later leader, contributed enormously to my research as well.

The search for a publishing partner produced an excellent match. Mary Holliman and her staff at Pocahontas Press have turned a rough draft into the finished product you hold in your hands. I knew they were right when she wrote that she was delighted to help stop mountain-top-removal mining and preserve free-flowing streams. Later she told me she had been active in the Sierra Club some years earlier. Publishers with that perspective are a rare and wonderful find.

My wife, Jan, and our family have both supported this project and, at times, wondered if I had developed a new addiction. Without her support this project simply would not have happened. I also wish to acknowledge both my parents, David and Marian Elkinton, who shared their AYH lives with their sons and who, in later retirement years, each wrote and published genealogical books.

Finally to all supporters, encouragers, and ultimately the readers who realize the need for the occasional look back, this is your book. May you be as inspired as I have been by this story to help continue the fight for the highlands.

A Note on Sources:

The Highlands Voice, the monthly newspaper of the Highlands Conservancy, has been an absolutely indispensable source of information. My earliest drafts cited every reference from the *Voice*, but I was persuaded to omit many of them in favor of readability. In preparation for my research I indexed the thirty-eight years of *Voice* articles, all 6400-plus of them. That index is available in a companion release.

Other sources have included many articles from *The Charleston Gazette*, often reprinted, always with kind permission, in the *Voice*. My personal interviews and correspondence with those intimately involved in the issues have added, or in a few cases corrected, important information.

Any additions or corrections are welcome and should be sent to me at daveelkinton@hotmail.com, or via the Highlands Conservancy's mailing address.

David Elkinton
Huntingtown, Maryland
May 21, 2007

Photographic Highlights
of the First Forty Years

Conservancy Board members

Front row, from left: Geoff Green, Skip Deegan,Charlie Carlson, Don Brannon. 2nd row: Larry George, Linda Winter, Cindy Rank, Lois Rosier. 3rd row: Jeannette Fitzwilliams, Mary Moore Rieffenberger, Jean Rodman, Frank Akers. 4th row: Sayre Rodman, John Purbaugh, unidentified, Joe Rieffenberger, Tom Michael. (photo from *The Highland Voice* archives).

West Virginia Highland Conservancy members met often with state and federal officials over their first forty years.

Top left: Congressman Ken Hechler, left, and Dave Elkinton at the Conservancy Mid-winter Workshop, January 24, 1976.

Middle left: Veteran Conservancy member Don Gasper, left, and Department of Natural Resources director David Callaghan.

Bottom left: Conservancy members Fred Bird, center, and Geoff Green, right, listen to Ava Zeitz of the West Virginia State Highway Department.

Above: Representative John Seiberling and aide, left, discuss Cranberry Wilderness bill with (from left) Bill McNeel, Ed Hamrick, and Larry George.

(These four photos from *The Highland Voice* archives.)

Linda Cooper Elkinton asks a question of President Jimmy Carter, with Governor Rockefeller, Energy Secretary James Schlesinger, and Interior Secretary Cecil Andrus looking on.
Photo by Ellen Snyder.

Core-sampling rig on the Green Mountain Trail, April 22, 1972.
See Chapter Two, pages 36 ff, for a discussion of Judge Maxwell's order that
the Island Creek Coal Company haul its drilling equipment into the Otter
Creek drainage via horseback rather than build a road into an area
potentially to be named Wilderness. Photo by Helen McGinnis.

Cindy Rank and Larry Gibson at Kayford Mountain.
Photo by Jonathan Jessup

Conservancy President Charlie Carlson during his first year in office (photo from *The Highland Voice* archives).

M. Rupert Cutler, left, and Lou Greathouse at a reunion in 2007. Both were key in founding the West Virginia Highlands Conservancy (photo courtesy of Lou Greathouse).

Two boys share a "Save Canaan Valley" T-shirt. Lakin Rosier, whose parents were Conservancy Board members, is the boy on the right. (photo from *The Highlands Voice* archives).

Conservancy member Judy Rodd entertains children at "Nature Skool" during a Conservancy event (photo from *The Highland Voice* archives).

Chapter One

Getting Started:
The Founding of the
West Virginia Highlands Conservancy

During the early and mid-1960s several forces converged that contributed to the formation of what would become the West Virginia Highlands Conservancy. One was the belief among young adults that they
could change the world. In fact some believed they had an obligation to
do so. President Kennedy had challenged that generation when he said,
"Ask not what your country can do for you, but what you can do for your
country." The Peace Corps, VISTA, and later, President Johnson's War on
Poverty, just three of many examples, resulted from that sentiment.

Another factor was an increasing environmental awareness, which
some date from the publication of Rachel Carson's *Silent Spring* in 1962.
Americans were increasingly visiting national parks, organizing hikes and
canoe trips, and learning about the out-of-doors. It would be 1970 before
the enactment of the National Environmental Policy Act and Earth Day,
but the pendulum was swinging in that direction.

In West Virginia, two young professionals were at work with the state
Department of Natural Resources under the conservation-oriented state
administration of Governor Hulett Smith. One was Lou Greathouse,
who had become Superintendent of Holly River State Park in 1958 and,
in 1963, transferred to Charleston as Statewide Recreational Planner.
Within two years a young wildlife biologist named Joe Rieffenberger,
later twice president of the Conservancy, would join him. Two other state
DNR employees who shared common interests with Greathouse and
Rieffenberger were Don Gasper, a fish biologist, and Lee Maynard, who
worked in public affairs.

In a 2007 interview, Greathouse remembered that his assumptions in
planning had included the need to include recreation use in West Vir-

ginia by residents from nearby states and the need to preserve special natural areas, scenic rivers, and wilderness. While at Holly River, he had worked on the congressional bill to establish a national wilderness system (see Chapter 2). During this time he had also developed a close relationship with Joe Hutchison, a professor of Recreation at West Virginia University, and Rupert Cutler of The Wilderness Society in Washington, D.C. Looking back, Greathouse recalled, "The need for a West Virginia Highlands Coalition evolved almost spontaneously in the minds of us all."

In 2007, Cutler remembered his earliest involvement in West Virginia. He remembered working with Bob and Lucille Harrigan on a wilderness support committee in Washington, D.C. He added:

> It was the Harrigans who encouraged me to join them on trips to West Virginia to get acquainted with the back country there. I stayed at their rented farmhouse near Seneca Rocks and hiked with Lou Greathouse, Joe Rieffenberger, Lee Maynard, and others while they [the Harrigans] were canoeing. Of course this was long before the passage of the Eastern Wilderness Areas Act, and we were breaking new ground by suggesting that the back country areas on the Monongahela National Forest should be given formal wilderness status. I hiked in the Cranberry Back Country with Bob Waldrop of the Sierra Club. Lou and I did the Shavers Fork of the Cheat, the dry Gauley River (while Summersville Dam was under construction), and several other places together.
>
> The idea of the West Virginia Highlands Conservancy must have come up as we hiked and sat around Bob Harrigan's farmhouse at night trying to scope out how to save that country from over-development.

As Greathouse worked on developing the first Statewide Comprehensive Outdoor Recreation Plan in West Virginia, spurred on by a requirement in the federal Land and Water Conservation Act of 1965, he recruited others to participate in Governor Smith's Interagency Recreation Council. Greathouse knew that first-hand observation was critical, and frequently led or arranged for "show me" trips to critical or endangered areas across the state, especially in the highlands.

He wrote later:

> In the first resource supply analysis, we divided the state into river basin sub regions, the Potomac, Cheat, Greenbrier, Elk, Little Kanawha, and Ohio. *Further analysis concluded the West Virginia*

Highlands functioned and should be planned as a headwater region as a whole. [Emphasis in the original.]

Various developments and conservation issues were already threatening this region, Greathouse remembered. He specifically cited the Royal Glen Dam near Petersburg, which State Parks Director Kermit McKeever had first told him about in 1962. To raise public awareness of the river valley that would be flooded, Greathouse and Maynard led horseback trips through the Smoke Hole Canyon for five years, taking state leaders and media members. Another issue was clear-cutting, a practice increasingly being used in the Monongahela National Forest (See Chapter 6). The headwaters of Shavers Fork, where Greathouse had spent summers as a youth, and strip mining of coal were also of deep concern. Finally, several proposed highway developments worried this group of conservationists.

Greathouse continued:

> Rupert Cutler made several trips into West Virginia for "Highland Coalition" planning meetings and for exploring remote natural areas in the Highlands with Joe Rieffenberger and me...It became evident to West Virginia leaders (myself, Hutchison, Maynard) and out-of-state leaders (Bob Harrigan [founder of the Petersburg White Water Weekend in 1964], Cutler, Bob Broughton and others) that "we needed them and they needed us" in the West Virginia Highlands Coalition.

Greathouse used the letterhead of the West Virginia Recreation Society, of which he was past president, to invite leaders of a wide number of recreation user groups to a series of meetings. Many of these groups would later become founding sponsors of the West Virginia Highlands Conservancy. Greathouse remembered writing "a proposal for the formation of the West Virginia Highlands Organization. In the main it was very similar to the organization outline of officers, directors at large, organizational directors, and committee chairs that was printed in *The Highlands Voice* forty-three years later. We were careful in the beginning to give a small majority of West Virginia voting directors and committee chairs, to remain a 'West Virginia decision-making organization.'"

Looking back in 2007, Greathouse stressed the collaborative nature of all those involved, no matter their state of residence or recreation interest. Together, they understood that they all needed each other to protect special places they felt were threatened. He added, "The important thing is, after forty-three years, the West Virginia Highlands Conservancy still exists and functions along the objectives of its original purposes. I am amazed and highly gratified. I know this could have never happened without dedicated leaders and volunteers like Tom King, Mr. and Mrs. Max Smith, Bob Burrell, and many others."

Dr. Tom King was a successful dentist in Bridgeport, a prosperous community in north central West Virginia. In the late 1950s and early 60s, as he took his family for weekend canoe trips on the rivers within a few hours drive from home, he had no reason to think his life was about to change. The Monongahela National Forest lay south and east of Bridgeport and contained free-flowing, clean rivers that included all the headwaters of the Potomac River, the Cheat River, and the Greenbrier River. Slightly farther away ran the Youghiogheny and the New, but they were more challenging for his family's canoeing capability.

Gradually King encountered other paddlers and became an active member of the Canoe Cruisers Association, headquartered in Washington, D.C. Many of its members came into the highlands of West Virginia to paddle these same rivers.

When the U.S. Army Corps of Engineers proposed a flood control dam on the South Branch of the Potomac, just upstream from Petersburg, at Royal Glen, the canoeists became politically active. The proposed dam would flood some of their favorite rapids and some extremely scenic river reaches. In 1964 the CCA organized a "white water weekend," based in Petersburg, focusing on the South Branch and the North Fork (of the South Branch). Day-long races, slalom courses, and even an "anything that floats that's not a boat" race on Sunday drew attention to the river in its current beauty, as opposed to the flat, narrow lakes that the Royal Glen dam would create. The next year, the event attracted even more paddlers and spectators. It kept growing. Soon the Petersburg White Water Weekend was drawing thousands of visitors to the area and even was selected as a pre-qualifying event for the 1968 Olympics. Ultimately, it would be discontinued because it became unmanageable.

Meanwhile, other threats to the highlands appeared in the local news, including a proposed parkway across nearby Dolly Sods. People who used these areas wanted a say in their protection. Various ideas were discussed, but everyone agreed on one thing: any political opposition to the dam or other developments, such as highways, would need to be based in West Virginia. The out-of-state weekend paddlers would have minimal political clout.

Before long, Bob Harrigan, a paddler from Washington, D.C., was hosting planning meetings at his camp near Seneca Rocks. Although the idea of a coalition of recreation groups had been discussed for several years, the meetings at Harrigan's camp brought together a group that was ready to implement such a coalition. The idea that eventually emerged was a coalition of outdoor recreation groups, based in West Virginia, but including groups from nearby states as well. The group would be christened the West Virginia Highlands Conservancy, and King would be elected its first president.

The Founding

Max Smith, the first corresponding secretary of the West Virginia Highlands Conservancy, gathered his memories for an article in *The Highlands Voice* in September 1977, marking the tenth anniversary of the Conservancy. He wrote that:

> The Canoe Cruisers Association of Washington, D.C., held their first Annual Whitewater Weekend on the North Fork of the South Branch of the Potomac River between Mouth of Seneca and Petersburg on April 3–5, 1964. At this time some members of the Association were disturbed by reports that a scenic highway was to be built across Dolly Sods.
>
> In the spring of 1965 a meeting was held at Bob Harrigan's camp near Yokum's Motel at Mouth of Seneca. *This was the first meeting for the people who would eventually become the West Virginia Highlands Conservancy.* [Emphasis added]. The various threats to Seneca Rocks-Spruce Knob-Dolly Sods were discussed and it was decided to organize and try to keep these areas in their natural state. A review was planned for that fall in order to publicize the necessity of saving these natural areas. Bob Harrigan acted as Chairman. Here is the roster of that meeting (from memory): Bob Harrigan — Canoe Cruisers, Washington; Dr. Thomas King — Canoe Cruisers, Bridgeport; Rupert Cutler — The Wilderness Society, Washington; Bob and Sue Broughton — Pittsburgh Climbers; Jim Wolfe, Pittsburgh; Bob Burrell, Morgantown [Author's note: Burrell says he was not there]; Joe Rieffenberger — Department of Natural Resources; Jim Johnston — Canoe Cruisers, Washington; Max Smith — West Virginia Wildlife Federation; Sona

Smith — West Virginia Garden Clubs; Bob Waldrop — Sierra Club, Washington; Carl Walker; Lou Greathouse — West Virginia Recreation Society; Joe Hutchison; and Lee Maynard.

More meetings were held through 1965 and 1966. Smith stated that:

> It was decided to organize and become a permanent, on-going organization to act as a watchdog for wilderness areas of West Virginia and to be an activist organization rather than just try to coordinate activities of other outdoor groups. Committees were appointed to write the constitution and bylaws, to select a name, and to plan for the future....The first Mid-Winter Meeting was held at Blackwater Falls Lodge on the last weekend of January 1967. At this meeting we adopted the Constitution and Bylaws, and also accepted the name proposed by Bob Broughton: The West Virginia Highlands Conservancy. Dr. Thomas E. King was elected President, Sona Smith as Secretary-Treasurer, and Maxwell Smith as Corresponding Secretary.
>
> From the very first this group was involved in: scenic roads and parkways; dam construction; unplanned real-estate development; strip mining; water pollution; regional management plan for the Highlands; acquisition of inholdings within the national forest; preservation of wild lands and rivers; and any other matters that affected the Highland Natural Areas.

Bob Broughton took a slightly different slant in an article written shortly after that January meeting. (Smith's article was written ten years later.) According to Broughton's article in the January-February 1967 issue of *The Social Climber*, the newsletter of the Pittsburgh Climbers:

> The West Virginia Highlands Conservancy was formed on January 21, 1967 at a meeting at Blackwater Falls State Park, attended by representatives of a large number of organizations interested in the fate of the Highlands region. The agreed statement of purpose was the preservation and conservation of the natural, scenic, and historic areas of significance within the West Virginia highland region.

Broughton stated that the announced purpose of the meeting was simply to plan the 1967 Highlands Weekend for the following October, but that all those present felt the need for a permanent structure as more immediately necessary.

King was unanimously elected chairman. Others elected were Maxwell Smith as corresponding secretary; Sona (Mrs. Maxwell) Smith as secretary-treasurer; and three directors, representing the "three population centers surrounding the Highlands Region." These were Charles Carlson, of Charleston; Bob Harrigan, of Washington, D.C.; and Bob Broughton of Pittsburgh. Broughton continued by reporting the "unofficial" agreement that all interested organizations would be asked to contribute $10.00 each to cover the initial organizational expenses.

The names of many future battlegrounds were already in the air. Issues identified as in need of careful monitoring included two proposed highway projects. The first, the proposed Highland Scenic Highway, was described as coming down from the Allegheny Front, through Dolly Sods, Flatrock and Roaring Plains, and on south between White's Run and Dry Fork watersheds. The second, the upgrading and straightening of U.S. Route 33 between Elkins and Mouth-of-Seneca (now Seneca Rocks), was described by Broughton as "slicing off huge portions of mountains between Gladys Fork and Laurel Fork rivers, and bringing the road down White's Run valley." Broughton concluded, "It is not too difficult to predict the future appearance of White's Run valley, and Seneca Creek valley, below White's Run."

Broughton finished his article with one of the most articulate statements of the rationale for citizen activism in the cause of wilderness protection:

> We have begun, but will need the help of every reader of this report in order to keep moving. Neither our own club, nor the new West Virginia Highlands Conservancy, wants to or could blindly oppose every new road, gas station, or mine in West Virginia. But we can and must develop an insight into and understanding of the values which are served by planning such developments in a way which will preserve the West Virginia Highlands, and we can and must develop and communicate an understanding of what we hold to be the value and meaning of that wilderness which remains in the area.
>
> For the entire question, as every climber, every caver, every person who has ever been alone in any place that could be called wilderness must know, is one of meaning. The Psalmist has called to us through the ages, "Be still, and know that the Lord he is God." In his world it was in the wilderness that one found the necessary stillness. The meaning of wilderness has changed little since the Psalmist's time. What we find in the wilderness may not be identical with what the Psalmist found; but the need for meaning and purpose in the life of man is not much different now than then. There will always be a need for wilderness, a place where man can find the stillness to come to

terms with meaning and purpose, with himself and with his place in the universe.

Founded as a coalition, representing a variety of groups from garden clubs to hiking and canoeing groups, they shared one thing in common: the Highlands of West Virginia were a special place and no one organization alone could protect them from forces of development.

From their first gathering for a "Highlands Review Weekend" in October 1965, through the many committee meetings, then later at the "Mid-Winter Workshop" held at Blackwater Falls State Park, these activists enjoyed the recreation opportunities of the Highlands of West Virginia, yet they knew they shared another mission. As lovers of a variety of special venues within the Highlands, they shared a concern that forces for economic development might sacrifice the very places they and others loved so much.

Although it would take time to gather and approve the organizational documents, it was clear that, after January 1967, there was agreement on the name and the need to incorporate. Broughton, a law professor at Duquesne University in Pittsburgh, took the lead in the formal organizational development, ultimately developing a constitution and set of bylaws that were eventually adopted. By all accounts it was Broughton who suggested the name should be the West Virginia Highlands Conservancy.

Everyone agreed on the need to get organized, but exactly how to organize was a matter of impassioned discussion. As a coalition of other groups, which could mobilize their collective memberships, the new Conservancy could represent thousands. But there were many voices that preferred the new organization not become a membership-based group, thereby competing for membership dues and energy with its constituent organizations. (Anyone ever involved in building a coalition will recognize this debate.)

In a lengthy letter to the brand-new President Tom King, dated December 20, 1967, Broughton wrote:

> Two basically different concepts have been put forward: (1) The Conservancy should be simply an information exchange, with (in the extreme concept) no effort at meetings to arrive at any kind of consensus, no votes on "policy", no positions taken by the Conservancy as an organization having any identity apart from its members. (2) The Conservancy should be a political action organization; it should lobby

for conservation on its own, acting on the policy positions taken by its members. It may be possible, still, to find a middle ground.

Broughton favored "pattern #2" and explained why. Commenting on the fact that the conservation movement in West Virginia had grown in recent years and "now includes thousands, instead of scores," he continued:

> More importantly, 10 years from now it will be a different kind of a movement than it is now. The demand for "wilderness" 10 years ago was pretty limited because all of us (even near the cities) could get to someplace where we could walk for more than a day without crossing a road or running into civilization. The supply was ample, so the demand was hardly noticed. Now the demand for "wilderness" — relative to the supply — is quite noticeable. Ten years from now it will be enormous. A lot of that increase in demand is coming from the cities.
>
> And that is why, when the job of writing by-laws was given to an outlander, a non-West Virginian, the choice of pattern #2 was almost assured. We don't have a voice in West Virginia, and yet many of us love the highlands and feel a personal stake in their future as strongly as if we were West Virginians. What we need is a voice, not an information exchange. [Emphasis in the original.]

There were other points of view, one held by the then-influential West Virginia Izaak Walton League. Itself a collection of local chapters, the League's bylaws precluded their affiliation with other groups, where it was subject to policy decisions of others. Broughton proposed such groups not be "members" but be "consulted" on matters of policy. He fully understood that dues and classification of membership or affiliation had significant implications. He continued:

> Organizations which are tax-exempt, in the sense that contributions to them are deductible by the contributors, will not, by "active membership" become subject to the sort of reprisals that the Sierra Club has suffered. This is quite an important consideration, since the first big battle the Conservancy tackles is going to be with the combined National Park Service, the National Forest Service, and the Army Corps of Engineers. If any bylaws are adopted, organizations that have 501-C (3) tax-exempt status should not be classified as active members (I believe the Wilderness Society, the Izaak Walton League of West Virginia, and the Audubon Society are in this category.)

It remained, however, until February 1, 1969, before Broughton presented the final bylaws and articles of incorporation with the other founding documents, to be signed by a group of nine incorporators. They were: Dr. Tom King, Charles Carlson, Charles Conrad, Maxwell Smith, Arthur Dunnell, Sara Corrie, Hal Dillon, Robert Broughton, and Carolyn Killoran.

Because of some technical language requirements, the articles of incorporation were not officially recorded by the Secretary of State John D. Rockefeller, IV until January 21, 1970.

The date of the "founding" has been somewhat in dispute.

Apparently the early consensus was that the "official" birth was February 1, 1969, the date when the articles of incorporation were signed. The tenth anniversary was therefore celebrated in 1979. The *Voice* noted that "it was decided to declare 1979 the official birthday," marking ten years since incorporation. That year's Mid-Winter Workshop included a panel with first President Tom King, original *Voice* Editor Bob Burrell, and other early leaders.

For many years, the *Voice* carried a box soliciting new members, which described the Conservancy as "founded in 1969." For some unexplained reason, beginning with the issue of March 1986, the Conservancy was listed as "founded in 1967." This would correspond to the January 1967 date when the decision was made to establish a separate organization, elect officers, and become better organized. In line with this revised view of the date of birth, the twentieth anniversary was celebrated at Cass in 1987 at the annual Fall Review. (By then the Mid-Winter Workshop had been discontinued in favor of the Spring Review.) Five years later, the twenty-fifth anniversary was noted in 1992.

This volume is written for publication in 2007, celebrating the fortieth anniversary from 1967. In the past the Conservancy has been so involved in issues of the day, that it has only briefly taken time to look back and notice its past. One is reminded of a family member who abhors birthdays, preferring instead to look forward.

So successful was the early West Virginia Highlands Conservancy that coalition partners such as the Sierra Club and Wilderness Society, who might have recruited members in this region, yielded to the Highlands Conservancy as their "local" affiliate.

The Fall Highlands Weekend Review

The first Fall Highlands Weekend Review, which was to become a tradition each year thereafter, was held in late October 1965 atop Spruce Knob. Smith remembered it this way:

> It was a cold, wet, miserable day; however the attendance of 350 to 400 persons far exceeded our hopes. After the day's activities there was an evening meeting at Gatewood Management Area on Spruce Mountain. Bob Harrigan had arranged for the meal, and the generator for lights. The meal was an excellent barbecued chicken dinner, which was cooked and eaten in the rain, but enjoyed by all. The meeting later in the Revivalist's Tent was well attended, with the Secretary of the Interior, Stewart Udall, and the U.S. Senator Robert Byrd as main speakers.

In correspondence with the author, Greathouse remembered that night well, referring to it as "the Sermon on the Mount with Senator Byrd." He, Harrigan, Cutler, Hutchison, and Maynard were the primary planners of the review. Maynard, formerly a DNR employee, now with the state Chamber of Commerce, printed the program. According to Greathouse, Hutchison, "calm and thoughtful," was selected to chair the meeting. "We wanted the conservationists' voices to be heard," he recalled, "so five of us spoke before Senator Byrd and he got the message." Greathouse remembered that for ten days before the Spruce Knob meeting, the United States Forest Service in Washington, D.C., had tried to schedule Byrd first on the program.

Cutler, Assistant Executive Director of The Wilderness Society in Washington, D.C., helped distribute the brochures. Others helped spread the word within their outdoor organizations and the mass media. The audience awaited the guest speakers with eager anticipation.

Harrigan, Greathouse, and Cutler were three of the pre-Byrd speakers. Greathouse spoke of the region as "the birthplace of rivers" and what additional "scenic" and "developmental" highways would do to the limited wilderness and scenic rivers.

Cutler spoke just before Byrd. In an article in the *Voice* in 2005, he remembered his role at that 1965 Fall Review:

> I found myself in the role of the "anchor man" of that team of speakers addressing their concerns regarding threats to the Highlands. In the "call and response" speaking style of the late U.S. Senator Hubert Humphrey I did my best to rouse the audience roughly as

follows: "Do you want a Royal Glen Dam? (Nooooo!) Do you want an Appalachian Regional Commission Corridor Highway? (Noooo!) Do you want a Highland Scenic Highway? (Noooo!)" and so forth. We were rocking and rolling, and fervently hoping that our policy-making guests from Washington and Elkins got the message. Following that emotional evening, the organizers concluded they had gotten their new group off to a good start.

As Senator Byrd began, the portable generator failed, plunging all into total darkness. Senator Byrd remarked that was the first time he had ever had the lights turned out on him while speaking. This was not the first, nor the last time the relationship between the activists and the senator would be threatened. Senator Byrd was to play an increasingly important role in virtually all the major issues the Conservancy would address over the next forty years. Naturally during this period his seniority had increased until, by 2007, he was arguably one of the most powerful men in the United States Senate.

Cutler returned to "the wilderness movement" under President Jimmy Carter's administration as Assistant Secretary of Agriculture, 1977–80. During his tenure he was able to direct the United States Forest Service to undertake a comprehensive review of roadless areas (candidates for wilderness protection) called R.A.R.E. II.

The next year, the Fall Review was held nearby, at the Shot Cherry Cabin on Spruce Mountain. According to a letter from Greathouse, written on letterhead of the West Virginia Recreation Society, the Saturday evening meeting was not intended to be a mass meeting, as the year before. Instead it was designed to provide an exchange of views "between the eastern outdoor organizations leadership" on how the Highlands should be developed. It would also be decided whether to make this weekend meeting an annual event. Smith reported in his 1977 article that while the attendance was not as large as in 1965, it was still considered a good crowd and much was accomplished. "I will never forget driving off Spruce Mountain about midnight through the snow!" he remembered.

According to Smith, the 1967 Review, the third in the National Recreation Area, was held October 7–8, and based at the Mouth of Seneca. Since the decision to form as the West Virginia Highlands Conservancy had been made the previous January, this was the first Review under that name. An extensive list of co-sponsors showed how the new Highlands Conservancy had begun to network as a coalition.

Some groups had been founding members, while others were newly involved. They included the Audubon Society of Western Pennsylvania, Brooks Bird Club, Canoe Cruisers of Washington, Explorers Club of Pittsburgh, Tucker County Chapter of the Izaak Walton League, Kanawha Trail Club, Nittany and Pittsburgh Grottoes of the National Speleological Society, West Virginia Chapter of The Nature Conservancy, Pittsburgh Climbers, Potomac Appalachian Trail Club, West Virginia Recreational Society, Atlantic Chapter of the Sierra Club, West Virginia Garden Club, West Virginia Wild Water Association, and The Wilderness Society.

Saturday's day trips included bird banding on Dolly Sods, a float trip through the Trough, a cave trip in the Sinks of Gandy, and a climbing demonstration on Seneca Rocks.

Ironically, several of the leading figures in forming the Conservancy were already moving on to other places. Cutler went to Michigan State University to get a Ph.D. degree, Harrigan became more active nationally and even internationally in river conservation, Maynard became a national leader in Outward Bound, and Greathouse accepted a position as Recreation Planner in Georgia. Greathouse recalled in 2007 that they continued to work together when opportunities arose.

The remaining leadership from within the Highlands Conservancy was strong, despite the absence of several of the key organizers. From the outset, the organization had not been dependent on one or two dominant personalities, but had been a coalition of equal partners. That structure would sustain the West Virginia Highlands Conservancy throughout the next four decades, and distinguish it from some organizations where the loss of a key organizer led to the complete demise of the organization or at least of the group's effectiveness.

The 1967 Review continued the pattern that was to become an annual tradition for the next forty years. The Fall Review Weekend's Saturday night program would spotlight a local issue of interest to Conservancy members. Following the by-now traditional chicken barbecue dinner, an agency presentation was made. This year it was on the Master Plan for the Spruce Knob-Seneca Rocks National Recreation Area. Following Ephe Olliver, Supervisor of the Monongahela National Forest, other speakers, both pro and con, made their comments. The Conservancy had invited United States Senator Jennings Randolph, but in his place, his Legislative Assistant, Phil McGance, attended. Although there was no record that the lights failed that year, what was remembered was that many local residents attended and that the Conservancy became an honest broker between the federal government and local landowners, many of whom feared they would lose property by eminent domain, as the Forest Service developed the Spruce Knob-Seneca Rocks National Recreational Area (see Chapter 6).

Many subsequent Highlands Review Weekends similarly brought Conservancy members, agency representatives and local citizens together to discuss pending issues. Some of these later discussions focused on the Canaan Valley, Corridor H highway, wilderness, Shavers Fork and other rivers, and often the policies of the Monongahela National Forest; virtually all the major issues the Conservancy would address over its first forty years.

Whether by brilliant design or fortuitous accident, the pattern was successful; a Friday evening informal gathering, a Saturday of recreational activities, a Saturday evening group meal, followed by a panel discussion of a current controversial issue, and a Conservancy board of directors meeting on Sunday. All this was held at a camp, state park, or similar facility, and scheduled at the peak of fall scenery. Although there have been large non-Conservancy crowds on occasion, especially if the Saturday evening forum was extremely controversial, there has always been a strong attendance of Conservancy members.

The farthest north Fall Review was one in Morgantown (1999), the farthest west in Sissonville (1998), and the farthest south was Bluestone State Park (1989.) But most have been somewhere within the boundary of the Monongahela National Forest.

In 1983, the Spring Review, patterned on the successful Fall Review, replaced the Mid-Winter Workshop. Since then these two events have punctuated the Conservancy calendar each year. (The board of directors has met the other two quarters, in the absence of a membership event.)

The Highlands Voice

Like King, **Bob Burrell** came into the highlands as a canoe paddler. A microbiologist by training, Burrell had grown up in Ohio, received his Ph.D. from Ohio State, and moved to Morgantown, West Virginia, with his wife and growing family. On weekends he found his way onto many of the same rivers King paddled.

Burrell remembers how few canoe paddlers there were in the early 1960s. "When we saw a car with a canoe on top, we knew who they were. All of the paddlers within a four-state region (West Virginia, Pennsylvania, Maryland, and Virginia) numbered less than fifty," Burrell commented in a 2006 interview. It was natural then that this small community of friends would talk together and consider how their voices could be heard by officials who made decisions that might affect their recreational areas.

In a 1979 column in *The Highlands Voice*, Burrell provided an insight into his motivation. He wrote:

I am a professional biologist who looks around and sees life decaying about him. I have inherited a reverence for life in all its forms from my father, quite aside from any professional interest, and all around me I see the profaning of those living forms. Those forms of life need a spokesman. Their habitat needs a spokesman. Man can speak for himself, but other forms of life and their habitats cannot. I feel I owe it to these forms of life to be their spokesman as sort of an apology for the idiocies perpetrated by other members of my species.

Burrell was a scientist, believed in logical, research-based arguments and liked to write. First as a member of the Scenic Rivers Committee (see Chapter 3), where King tapped him in 1968 to write/edit a newsletter among the river protectionists, then a year later, as editor of the new *Highlands Voice*, Burrell was to leave a lasting mark with his sharp-edged articles and editorials. When he stepped up to become the Conservancy's second president in 1971, he continued to write, this time in a president's column. When he stepped down as president in 1973, he was asked by Ron Hardway, the new editor, to continue a bi-monthly, then in 1974, a monthly column, entitled "Overlook." Therefore, Burrell was a regular writer for the *Voice* from the first issue in March 1969 until his column in November 1978. It is difficult to overstate Burrell's impact in forming much of the founding philosophy and enthusiasm for environmental action that became the signature of the West Virginia Highlands Conservancy.

The first issue of *The Highlands Voice*, a combination WVHC membership newsletter and conservation newspaper, was published in March 1969. Right away, Editor Burrell set the agenda for future issues: a passionate discussion of a wide variety of conservation issues facing the highlands, reports from affiliate organizations, and internal Conservancy reports for the membership.

That initial mimeographed issue contained several seeds that would foreshadow the Conservancy's future. For example, there was a discussion that indicated the Richwood Chapter of the Izaak Walton League was concerned about the large sizes of "even-aged timber management," called clearcutting by the public, of the Monongahela National Forest (see Chapter 6.) Another article discussed the proposed dam on the Gauley River, one of the state's wildest, at Swiss in Nicholas County (see Chapter 3). A report on the recent Mid-Winter Workshop included a resolution passed by the Conservancy's board requesting that the Forest Service manage Dolly Sods and the Red Creek Backwoods Area as wilderness, so that eventual inclusion into the National Wilderness Preservation System would be preserved as an option. Finally, the board endorsed a complete re-routing of the proposed Allegheny Parkway to avoid the Red Creek drainage altogether.

Because of the coalition nature of the Conservancy and the fact that its membership stretched from Baltimore and Washington, D.C., on the east to the Pittsburgh area on the north and to Charleston, West Virginia, on the southwest, members often could not make all meetings and outdoor activities. In addition, the paddlers weren't going to the birding events and the rock climbers weren't members of the garden clubs. With a frequent bi-monthly *Voice*, everyone was kept informed. Only through *The Highlands Voice* was such a coalition possible. Even in this first issue, readers learned Helen McGinnis was leading a hike on Dolly Sods, Charlie Carlson was leading one in the Cranberry Backcountry, and the state legislature was debating a scenic river bill.

The production credits also illustrated a pattern that would prove common in the coming years. Bruce Sundquist, of the American Youth Hostels group in Pittsburgh, and Hal Dillon, a staffer of the West Virginia Department of Natural Resources, both helped write, print, and mail the *Voice*. Carolyn Killoran, wife of another DNR official, was credited as well. The professional expertise of the recreationists from Pittsburgh and Washington, D.C., and the natural resource professionals from the DNR in West Virginia, would together provide much of the early leadership for the Conservancy.

Announced as a quarterly, the *Voice* soon became a bi-monthly, then in 1974, a monthly. Since then it has enjoyed the distinction of being the "conscience of the Highlands."

Sources:

Broughton, Bob
    article in *The Social Climber*, January-February 1967
    letter and attachment to Tom King, December 20, 1967
Burrell, Bob, correspondence with
    article in *The Highlands Voice*, 1979
    interview, June 21, 2006
Cutler, Rupert, correspondence with
    article in *The Highlands Voice*, 2005
Elkinton, Dave, article in *The Highlands Voice*
Greathouse, Lou, correspondence with
    article in *The Highlands Voice*
    interview, April 9, 2007
Harrigan, Lucille, and Bob Harrigan, interview, January 24, 2007
King, Tom, interview, March 30, 2006
Rieffenberger, Joe, interview, March 28, 2007
Rodman, Jean, interview, June 22, 2006
Smith, Max, article in *The Highlands Voice*, September 1977

Chapter Two
The First and Continuing Battle:
Wilderness

Two young professionals, one from California and one from Minnesota, linked together by a fledgling conservation organization through which they could find a broader community of like-minded outdoor enthusiasts, would become pivotal leaders in establishing some of the first federally-protected wilderness areas east of the Mississippi.

Helen McGinnis grew up in northern California, learning from her mother how to collect insects, identify species, and generally enjoy the outdoors. As a student at UC Berkeley, she became active in the University Hiking Club. "All I was really happy doing was being out backpacking in the wilderness areas of the West," she said later, be they the Sierras, the Cascades, the Rockies, or lesser-known areas. After obtaining a master's degree in paleontology, she landed at the Smithsonian Institution in Washington, D.C.

A member of the Sierra Club (founded by northern Californian John Muir, and headed by another Berkeley resident, David Brower, the Sierra Club was primarily a California-based hiking and recreational organization through the early 1960s) since 1957, McGinnis looked up the local chapter in Washington, D.C., and became an active member. In the summer of 1968 McGinnis went on an outing to the Dolly Sods, a barren, windswept high ridge on the Allegheny Front in the Monongahela National Forest. "This area reminded me of the West — open, sweeping vistas, just much smaller," she said later. McGinnis returned for many trips, took notes and photographs, and began to plan a hiking guide to the Dolly Sods area.

At the same time, a young Ph.D. metallurgist from the Midwest had taken a position with U.S. Steel in Pittsburgh. **Bruce Sundquist** became active in both the Sierra Club and the American Youth Hostels. Both had active outings programs, where canoeists, bikers, hikers, and even rock climbers were scheduling weekend trips. Sundquist found himself helping AYH produce canoe guides and hiking guides for areas near Pittsburgh.

As Sundquist began to visit the highlands of West Virginia, a brief three-hour drive away, he met people from other states and a few from West Virginia who were talking about working together to protect special recreation sites they all used.

Sundquist remembers hearing McGinnis give a presentation on Dolly Sods at a very early Mid-Winter Workshop of the West Virginia Highlands Conservancy. He was impressed. McGinnis remembers learning that Sundquist had produced hiking and canoe guides in his basement with a small printing press AYH had bought for that purpose. It was not long before her idea of a Dolly Sods hiking guide and wilderness proposal and his printing press were associated.

In early 1970, McGinnis took a position at the Carnegie Museum in Pittsburgh, and for four years this pair were frequently together at Highlands Conservancy meetings and outings. Then in 1974 McGinnis moved to State College, Pennsylvania, to work on a second master's degree, this time in wildlife management. Except for one visit in the mid-1980s to Dolly Sods, she would be away from West Virginia for twenty-five years.

When she returned to West Virginia in the fall of 2001, McGinnis became an active member of the Eastern Cougar Foundation and an advocate of cougar restoration in eastern wild areas. This was a natural outgrowth of her interest in preserving eastern wilderness because she believed that true wilderness needed top predators. Since 2001, she has authored several articles for *The Highlands Voice* on the movement to document the existence of the cougar in West Virginia.

Sundquist remained in Pittsburgh, moving from U.S. Steel to Westinghouse before retiring to devote more time to his publications and research interests. He has edited and published all eight editions of the *Monongahela National Forest Hiking Guide* (see Chapter 6).

To preserve some portion of the American landscape in a condition relatively "untrammeled by man," has been a dream of many people over many generations. In the 1900s that dream took the form of what came to be called the wilderness movement, often dated from 1924, when Aldo Leopold led the Forest Service to establish the Gila Wilderness, the first official wilderness area. For the next forty years the federal government, by administrative order, established as wilderness portions of federal land. But increasingly, outdoor recreation and natural resource managers and their citizen supporters realized that administrative decisions could always be rescinded.

In 1935 wilderness advocates from both inside and outside government formed The Wilderness Society. Over the next twenty years additional areas were protected, but the need for statutory protection for wilderness became even more obvious. Finally, in 1956 Howard Zahniser, the Society's Executive Secretary since 1945, drafted a bill for Congress and, late that year, it was introduced in both houses. One of its co-sponsors in the United States Senate was Senator William Laird, of West Virginia, a Democratic appointee whose term lasted only from March to November of 1956, when his successor was elected.

But it wasn't until 1964 when both the House and Senate passed the bill. On September 3, 1964, President Lyndon Johnson signed into law the Wilderness Act of 1964. It had taken eight years of lobbying, educating, and public advocacy.

According to Doug Scott, Policy Director of the Campaign for America's Wilderness, whose leadership with the Sierra Club, the Wilderness Society, and CAW had spanned forty years, West Virginia played an important part from the outset of federal legislative protection of wilderness. In Scott's 2004 book, *The Enduring Wilderness*, he chronicled the history of wilderness protection, first nationally, then state-by-state. West Virginia had been among the most active in the eastern United States in the 1960s and '70s and would continue to be a major player in the 2000s.

Scott explained that the 1964 Act made several major changes. For one, it established the national policy to "preserve an enduring resource of wilderness in perpetuity." Second, all federal agencies were mandated to study their holdings and recommend qualifying acreage over the next ten years. Third, Congress itself would approve wilderness designations, instead of an agency's administrative order. And as a down payment, the first 9.1 million acres of statutory wilderness areas began the National Wilderness Preservation System.

According to Scott, a new era of "grassroots organizing" was on its way:

> With the enactment of the Wilderness Act, the Sierra Club, led by Brower and his assistant, Mike McCloskey [who succeeded Brower as Executive Director in 1968], and The Wilderness Society, led by [Stewart] Brandborg and his new assistant executive director, Rupert Cutler, geared up to deal with the hundreds of agency wilderness studies and public hearings required under the Wilderness Act. They had no real choice but to build decentralized capacity to meet this challenge. Grassroots organizing became the new focus, not just for the immediate public hearings but also for the follow-through to build constituent support that would encourage local congressional delegations to back citizen proposals.

This was 1964 and the immediate years thereafter. The first Fall Highlands Weekend Review was the following year, and the same Rupert Cutler was instrumental in organizing it and several of those that followed (see Chapter 1).

Although nothing in the Wilderness Act restricted the areas to be designated wilderness to be located in western United States, and in fact four eastern areas were included in the Act, it soon became the policy of the U.S. Forest Service that all federal land in the east was too scarred by man's activity to qualify. This would be a barrier that West Virginians would find a challenge to overcome.

Scott called this Eastern Wilderness attitude the "Purity Theory":

> By contrast [to other federal agencies], once it became law, the Forest Service chose to ignore all this and adopt their own new interpretation of the act. By the early 1970s the agency was feeling seriously threatened by growing grassroots pressures as activists bypassed the Forest Service to ask Congress to protect "de facto wilderness" — areas in all regions of the country that had never been administratively protected as "primitive areas." Agency leaders felt that congressional expansion of the wilderness system might get out of hand. As a means to help preclude this, they adopted the idea that no areas with evidence of any past human impacts could or should qualify as wilderness under the Wilderness Act. This posture came to be known as the "purity theory." Forest Service leaders chose to bring this issue to a head in 1971, proclaiming that no national forest lands in the eastern half of the United States could even be considered for wilderness designation.

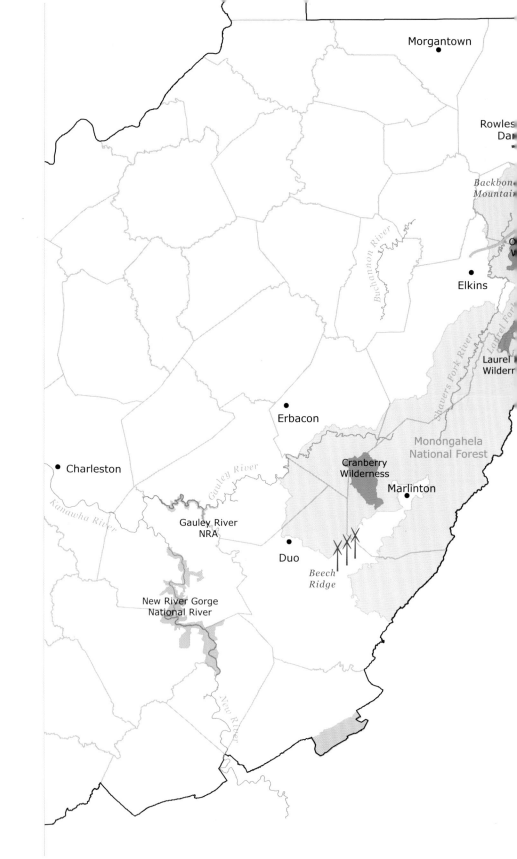

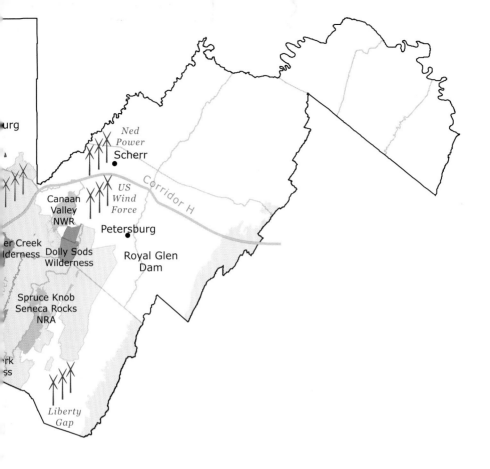

urg

Ned Power
Scherr

US Wind Force

Canaan Valley NWR

Corridor H

Petersburg

er Creek lderness Dolly Sods Wilderness

Royal Glen Dam

Spruce Knob Seneca Rocks NRA

rk ss

Liberty Gap

Map of the West Virginia Highlands

1" equals aprroximately 25 miles

Map produced and donated
by Mike and Betsy Breiding
August 2007

© West Virginia Highlands Conservancy

To gather congressional support for this theory, the Forest Service drafted legislation titled, "Wild Areas East," which would permit some timbering and establish a parallel system to the Wilderness Act. John McGuire, then Associate Chief of the Forest Service, promoted this plan to the Wilderness Conference in Washington, D.C., in 1971, but received a poor reception. In a surprise move, it passed the Senate in 1972, without notice or debate.

As a countermeasure, led by the Wilderness Society, wilderness advocates fashioned the Eastern Wilderness Areas Act, packaging citizen proposals from the East, South, and Midwest. When it was formally introduced in the House in 1973, Rep. John Saylor, of Pennsylvania, an original sponsor nearly a decade earlier of the Wilderness Act, made it clear that he opposed the "purity theory." Senator Henry "Scoop" Jackson, of Washington, and others from both sides of the aisle, also saw the new bill as ending this misinterpretation. Among these was Senator Floyd Haskell, a Colorado Democrat, who would be important later.

Dolly Sods, Otter Creek, and Cranberry

Dolly Sods, Otter Creek, and the Cranberry Back Country were all areas within the Monongahela National Forest. Dolly Sods was a high, windswept, heath-like area along the top of the Allegheny Front on the Grant-Tucker County border, overlooking North Fork Mountain; it provided the visitor a spectacular view east into Virginia. An area near Dolly Sods, called Bear Rocks, was famous for its low-bush huckleberries, amid large rock outcrops. Otter Creek, in nearby Tucker County, was very different. A relatively small watershed, the creek was a series of picturesque waterfalls, linked by a primitive trail network.

The Cranberry Back Country was in Pocahontas County, near the Webster County border. The Back Country had been closed to motorized vehicles, although its trails were favorites of hikers and fishermen. It had also become a black bear management area, where the state Department of Natural Resources conducted black bear research. The primary investigator was Joe Rieffenberger, a Conservancy founder, who would serve as Conservancy president for two separate terms.

Each of these three areas would experience their individual challenges, ultimately overcome barriers to full wilderness protection, and be championed by advocacy committees of their own. Yet each cannot be discussed without acknowledging the intertwining of the three, which culminated in their protection together. Otter Creek and Dolly Sods would achieve protection first, but Cranberry would come later.

As noted earlier, McGinnis began exploring Dolly Sods in the summer of 1968. By the Mid-Winter Workshop of January 1969, reported in the first issue of *The Highlands Voice* in March 1969, the Conservancy was commending the Forest Service for creating the Red Creek Backwoods Area, but this protection still existed by administrative decision only. Various task forces were assembled by the Forest Service to study how these areas might be managed.

A report from that workshop included high praise for McGinnis: "Due to the untiring and very thorough work of Helen McGinnis, who has devoted so much of her time to a study and inventory of this area, a resolution was formulated and adopted."

The resolution both praised the Forest Service for establishing the Red Creek Backwoods Area and recommended that it be expanded, managed to preserve its potential for later inclusion under the Wilderness Act, and specifically be off-limits to strip mining and the feared Allegheny Parkway (see Chapter 4).

From a *Voice* profile in October 2006, McGinnis explained how the idea of Dolly Sods as a potential wilderness area came from several coincidental events:

> Coming to Dolly Sods with a Sierra Club group in the summer of 1968, Helen says it reminded her of her favorite western Wilderness areas, with their open, windswept vistas, yet it was so much smaller. Why wasn't this too a Wilderness area? Through accident, she discovered the Wilderness Society's office, with its informal meeting room where people ate their sack lunches and discussed wilderness strategies near her Smithsonian office. Over many lunches together she developed a close relationship with Rupert Cutler, Assistant Director; Stewart ["Brandy"] Brandborg, Director, and others who were not employed by the Wilderness Society, such as writer Michael Frome and eastern wilderness advocate Ernie Dickerman. Together they encouraged her in thinking about Dolly Sods as a potential wilderness area. It will be remembered that Rupe was instrumental in organizing the first Fall Review on Spruce Knob, and Brandy was there.

By the May 1969 *Voice* issue, Dolly Sods became the subject of President Tom King's "President's Comment":

> A short time ago I accepted Mr. Frederick Dorrell's invitation to sit on an Ad Hoc committee to study the area known as Dolly Sods and

to advise the Forest Service as to its future needs and management. Mr. Dorrell, who is Supervisor of Monongahela National Forest, informed me that the committee would be made up of representatives from government, industry, conservation, and local people who would be affected by any change in the status of the area.

The Forest Service will not be bound by any recommendation on Dolly Sods, but has stated that they will give the most serious consideration to the wishes of the Committee.

Then King added an interesting comment relating this process to that of another federal agency:

This seems to me to be a very sensible way to begin to approach a problem such as Dolly Sods where there are many different interests and opinions. I can't help but think that if the Army Corps of Engineers had chosen this approach to the problem of placing a dam in the Red River Gorge [in eastern Kentucky] the outcome would have been vastly different. The Corps would still have had its dam just as it does today, but the taxpayers would have saved hundreds of thousands of dollars in useless planning and additional thousands which conservationists spent fighting bureaucratic stupidity could have been spent on endangered wildlife or some other worthy purpose. When will people learn to sit down and talk things over before they begin to butt their heads together in futile rage?

A meeting was scheduled for July, a "general meeting – workshop, for all those interested in wilderness preservation in West Virginia." The location would be a large primitive camping area on the top of Cabin Mountain. "We will try to organize the kind of documentation and research for the Cranberry Back Country and Otter Creek that Helen McGinnis did for Red Creek Plains/Dolly Sods," the notice said. Pre-meeting hikes on Dolly Sods were encouraged. The contact given was George Langford, of Pittsburgh.

In the same issue McGinnis reported:

A short illustrated guide to the Dolly Sods area is now available. It contains a map that attempts to show all known formal foot-trails in the region — many not included on other maps — plus easy cross-country routes for hikers, hints for hikers and backpackers, brief descriptions of some leisurely hikes, a list of books and articles on the history and natural history of the region, a discussion of the proposed Dolly Sods Wilderness Area on the north fork drainage of Red Creek and the threats to this wilderness, plus suggestions for action that individuals can take to help preserve the region in a wild, natural condition.

This would become known as *The Hiking Guide and Wilderness Proposal for Dolly Sods*, the first of three. Earlier McGinnis's research fused with Sundquist's offset press, and this was their first joint production.

In the *Voice* of June 1969 there was a report of the ad hoc Wilderness Preservation Committee, which met June 21–22 at "the Roaring Creek Cultural Center, a most imposing edifice not described in any of the tour books or found on any road map." This was the rented house of the Pittsburgh Climbers, up the Roaring Creek hollow, near Onego, and not far from Mouth of Seneca, in Pendleton County. The Climbers rented a series of small houses over many years, using them as weekend base-camps for hikes, ski tours, rock climbs, among other recreational activities. Many small committee meetings would use this house over coming years, including wilderness, river protection, and Davis Power Project sessions.

Elsewhere in that month's *Voice*, a report on the Cranberry recounted a meeting the previous winter with David Francis, president of Princess Coal Company, which had plans to mine under the Cranberry Back Country. Tom King, of the Conservancy, E.M. Olliver, Supervisor of the Monongahela National Forest, a DNR representative, and two Izaak Walton League representatives attended. Although the Forest Service owned the surface rights, Princess owned the mineral rights. The planned mine would be a deep mine, according to Francis, and Zip Little of the IWLA felt that there was little regulatory control expected.

Conservationists found themselves attempting to research the wilderness attributes of both Otter Creek and Cranberry, even though the government did not own the underlying minerals, nor did they for Dolly Sods, for that matter. The first two were thought to involve significant coal reserves, while Dolly Sods was not.

In August's *Voice*, King reported on a recent two-day meeting of the Ad Hoc Committee on Dolly Sods, chaired by new MNF Supervisor Dorrell, who had replaced Olliver. Of the twenty-five members, twenty-two attended. King reported the recommendations included acquisition of inholdings by the federal government, maintenance of the open, heath-like character, and provision of signage and short trails for casual visitors to the area.

Otter Creek Predominates

That October the Highlands Weekend Review included a memorable hike. Wrote King under "President's Comment" in the October 1969 *Highlands Voice*:

> I was almost overwhelmed by the wilderness beauty of the Otter Creek valley, it is an area to which I will return many times in the coming years. Our hike, which was led by Sayre Rodman, attracted one-hundred-nineteen people including our Secretary of State, John D. Rockefeller, IV and his wife. Also in attendance were Angus Peyton, former Commissioner of Commerce, and Mrs. Peyton. Everyone I talked to including the two leaders, just mentioned, agreed that Otter Creek was easily the most beautiful natural area in the State.
>
> The Conservancy is preparing a program to meet problems and threats in this lovely 18,000-acre retreat and you will be hearing more about it elsewhere in *the Highlands Voice*. I hope that every member will lend his hand to help save the "Valley of Opportunity."

In a subsequent article, readers learned of a brochure on Otter Creek prepared by Vic Schmidt and other members of the very effective Wilderness Committee. Based on McGinnis's Dolly Sods *Guide*, the Otter Creek report was both a hiking guide with trails and maps and a case for wilderness protection. There was also a warning of impending threats to Otter Creek from both timbering and coal mining.

In 1970, the third annual Mid-Winter Workshop must have been lively. There were resolutions on clearcutting on the Monongahela National Forest (see Chapter 6), potential dams on the Gauley, Meadow, Greenbrier and New (see Chapter 3), air pollution, and even support for the Environmental Teach-In scheduled for May (which became Earth Day). Burrell wrote, "it was a very active weekend with perhaps more positive action taken at this meeting than any previous one. Conservation meetings are always so paradoxical — so full of disappointment, yet so full of hope."

Burrell then focused on Otter Creek:

> Most of the Board's attention was devoted to Otter Creek. The main program for Saturday afternoon was concerned with the Conservancy's wilderness proposal for this area (see October *Voice*) vs. that of the Forest Service. On paper the Forest Service is supposed to be committed to the multiple-use concept, but it appears that in practice, timber management, sale, and harvest are the prime multiple

uses made of the forest. Conservationists feel that wildlife and recreational values are too often ignored.

The Board discussed ways and laid plans to take appropriate action to obtain wilderness classifications of Otter Creek and other de facto wilderness areas in the Monongahela, feeling that if the multiple use concept is not being used, the Board should take steps to prevent at least a small part of the forest from falling to the woodsman's ax (I am sorry, this is 1970. I should have said, "falling to the woodsman's chain saw").

He also reported that "the Wilderness Committee was assigned the task of researching the Cranberry Backcountry and presenting a resolution at the next board meeting." So now there was a published hiking guide and wilderness proposal for Dolly Sods by McGinnis, a companion volume on Otter Creek by Schmidt, and a potential one on the Cranberry. All of these were published in Sundquist's basement. Such a small organization, just beginning its fourth year, was already publishing a bimonthly mimeographed newsletter and now three hiking guides. These publications were big steps.

By the April 1970 *Voice*, wilderness areas were prominently featured. Langford was soliciting trail information for the Cranberry's research effort. McGinnis reported that the Monongahela Forest staff was completing a management plan for a "Dolly Sods Scenic Area" of about 10,000 acres. She reported the boundaries were carefully drawn to exclude any marketable timber. "Apparently the Forest Service feels it cannot spare any significant acreage of quality forestland from logging anywhere in the region." Conservationists would hear that refrain again.

McGinnis also reported extensively on Otter Creek. DNR wildlife biologists, she reported, "recognize Otter Creek as one of four remote areas in West Virginia large enough to support stable breeding populations of black bears. About fifty to sixty bears inhabit the area." (Cranberry was another such area.) For bear management, the McGowan Mountain Road should be gated, and definitely not extended, which the Forest Service proposed to do, she wrote.

By May's *Voice*, wilderness areas, especially Otter Creek, were still dominating the pages. King's "President's Comments," opened the discussion:

> The Conservancy finds itself today in the unenviable position of having to oppose the wills of two powerful adversaries to preserve the pristine beauty of the Otter Creek basin.

The U.S. Forest Service, which is adamant in their insistence that two thirds of the area should be given over to timber production and that construction of the McGowan mountain road through the headwaters of Otter Creek should be started without a moment's delay. This is the first of our opponents, and the Conservancy has been roundly criticized from several quarters for taking up the Forest Service's valuable time by filing an appeal, as provided by their own regulations, from these decisions which were made without a shred of public participation. We will continue to oppose the Forest Service's stated course of action by any means which is available to us.

Our second adversary is the Island Creek Coal Company which has declared their intention, in recent weeks, of core drilling five sites within the valley to prospect the Sewell coal which underlies much of the area. They are entitled to do this under the law and to construct the necessary roads for moving their equipment from place to place. The law also provides that these roads be approved by the Forest Service in advance and that they be fully restored and reseeded after drilling is complete. The letter from Tony Dorrell to the coal company is most thorough in delineating these responsibilities and I call on every member of the Conservancy to see that they are carried out to the letter. To those of you who are photographers, I urge that you make several trips into Otter Creek this summer for the express purpose of observing these activities of the company…By summer's end we need a complete file on the activities of the coal company within the basin. Remember the coal belongs to Island Creek, but the surface belongs to you! You have as much right to the preservation of your property as they do to theirs.

ITEM: Congressman Ken Hechler of West Virginia has introduced a bill in Congress calling for a wilderness designation for the Otter Creek Basin, the Cranberry Backcountry, and Dolly Sods. The number on the bill is H.R. 17535.

Congressman John P. Saylor of Pennsylvania is expected to intro-duce an omnibus wilderness bill in the near future. It will contain several areas in the west plus the same three in the east contained in Mr. Hechler's bill.

To pause and summarize: first, to protect the potential for future wilderness designation, the Conservancy would oppose further road building by the Forest Service. Second, this was the first indication that Island Creek, mineral owner under the proposed Otter Creek wilderness, intended to prospect their coal. Implied was the possibility that they would find enough that was economically feasible to develop a full-scale coal mine. Third, President King was encouraging citizens to serve as watchdogs throughout the summer. Fourth, and very significantly, at least one West Virginia congressman, Ken Hechler, had introduced legislation to protect all three areas, and Chairman Saylor's omnibus bill "will" contain them. (Not said was that none of these areas were in Hechler's district.)

But that was just the beginning. The next two pages of the *Voice* contained a reprint of an article from the May 17, 1970, Morgantown Sunday *Dominion Post* by Dr. Robert Leo Smith, West Virginia University wildlife biology professor:

> While the West Virginia Highlands Conservancy attacks the Forest Service, the same organization…has been sold a good story by the coal industry. At least they [the Conservancy] play down the effect proposed coal mining would have on Otter Creek and strongly emphasize the damage that would result from logging. They write, "The Island Creek Coal Company, which owns most of the mineral rights in the Basin, plans to take core samples in the near future…A representative of the company has assured the Conservancy members that the coal would be removed by deep mining, and that, except for mine shafts at the mouth of Otter Creek, practically no damage would be done to the surface." What the Highlands Conservancy and most West Virginians don't know is the full story. Island Creek Coal Company plans to make anything the Forest Service might do in the area look like wilderness preservation.

Smith's article included many details. The basin's coal reserve was estimated to be twenty-four million tons of recoverable coal, twenty-two of which are high quality, low sulfur, Sewell. According to Smith, Island Creek wanted to drill five test borings, scattered throughout Otter Creek and, to reach these, build twenty-eight miles of road, twelve feet wide, and sumps twelve feet square would be built at each drilling site to catch waste. Smith continued:

> If minable coal is located by this preliminary method, additional drilling would be necessary. This could involve a prospect hole every mile on a grid over the entire Otter Creek area, each of these would have to be connected by a 12-foot road and each would have one or two sumps. Thus, the entire Otter Creek area would be traversed by a grid of roads a mile apart. Yet the Coal Company assured the Highlands Conservancy members that "except for possible ventilation shafts, there would be no disturbance to the surface.

But this isn't all. Island Creek Coal would build a processing plant at Dry Fork at the mouth of Otter Creek and on the edge of the Otter Creek tract. They would put a road through the lower third of Otter Creek area to the edge of the pioneer area. There they would build an aerial tramway across Otter Creek with a coal tipple and parking lot.

After criticizing the Conservancy for worrying about the McGowan Road extension and preserving Otter Creek's wilderness character, he continued:

> With the outstanding mineral rights, Otter Creek does not stand an outside chance of ever becoming a wilderness area. The Forest Service could well be spending its time more profitably working with the coal companies to modify their plans for the area. If the Highlands Conservancy is really interested in saving the "beauty and wildness of Otter Creek," it and all West Virginians should be working on the coal issue, not the wilderness issue.
>
> What can the Conservancy and the public do? Write the West Virginia Congressional delegation, urging them to secure the mineral rights under Otter Creek. Conservatively, this would require some two million dollars, but it would be well worth the cost…The only way to save Otter Creek is to bring [the mineral rights back together with the surface rights] of the Forest Service.

Despite Smith's strong criticism, Editor Burrell, also a WVU professor, but in the health sciences, added his agreement. Burrell said Smith "has pointed out the real root of many of West Virginia's conservation problems. Next to people pollution, coal mining is the most serious environmental disturbance we have to deal with." From an earlier *Voice*, he reminded readers that the most immediate threat to the Cranberry Back Country was the Princess Coal Company and not the Forest Service. Then Burrell added:

> As long as the people explosion continues (our real problem), as long as there is a public demand for power to run automatic dryers, all electric homes, and TV in every room, as long as our legislators remain insensitive to our environment, and as long as mineral rights are so securely held by such absentee owners, <u>there is not one acre of wild land in West Virginia that can be saved.</u> [Emphasis in original]

Things were moving fast. Not only was the Conservancy advocating and organizing a public campaign for wilderness, but also other issues like clearcutting, blocking dams at Royal Glen and Rowlesburg, the proposed Blue Ridge Power Project on the New River, and supporting Earth Day were all getting attention and requiring effort. 1970 was already a big year. When the Davis Power Project was announced the next month, it would get bigger yet.

Otter Creek in Court

In June 1970, the *Voice's* lead article was titled "Showdown at Otter Creek." It announced that West Virginia Senator Jennings Randolph had introduced S. 3937, designating the same three areas as in Hechler's House bill. Randolph said, "There is a need to protect these areas and to preserve them in their present environment, for the enjoyment of our citizens and future generations. We must act to establish wilderness areas, of which there are only two on the East Coast."

But the last paragraph was a blockbuster:

> Meanwhile the Conservancy sought and was granted a temporary restraining order against the Island Creek Coal Company from cutting roads into the Otter Creek area. Judge Robert E. Maxwell had a hearing and ruled the Conservancy had just cause to restrain the coal company and the Forest Service from such action. Many newspapers throughout the state failed to mention the role of the Conservancy towards this end. Hearings will continue through June and possibly beyond in Elkins on this matter.

This court action by the Conservancy marked the first of perhaps two dozen times over the next thirty-seven years that the Conservancy would use the judicial system as the "court of last resort." Some of the details behind the Otter Creek injunction illustrate the dynamics of joining local West Virginia resource people with expertise from nearby states, a characteristic that has distinguished the Conservancy from its origin to the present day.

> In a 2005 interview, **Fred Anderson** remembered his Conservancy involvement. He and a fellow young attorney, **Jim Moorman**, had renewed their acquaintance as they met in a field near Seneca Rocks. Both were working in Washington, D.C. Moorman invited Anderson to a nearby Highlands Conservancy Fall Review (probably 1968). Over the next several years they attended various Conservancy meetings and became volunteer legal advisers to the Conservancy.

When the Island Creek Coal Company seemed poised to begin the road building, in advance of their core drilling, members of the Conservancy were desperate to preserve the wilderness potential of Otter Creek. Anderson and Moorman researched the brand-new Environmental Policy Act of 1970 and found an opportunity to stop the Forest Service from allowing the roads and drilling. Conservancy President King found "local counsel" in the person of Willis O. Shay, a member of Steptoe and Johnson, a well-known Clarksburg firm. Working together, Shay, Anderson and Moorman went before Judge Robert Maxwell in United States District Court. Anderson recalled the most telling evidence given to Maxwell were photographs taken by Conservancy member Sayre Rodman, scouting Otter Creek in response to King's earlier request for monitors. One story went that the judge asked Rodman if these photos showed the worst of the operations, and he said, no, they showed some of the best.

The story continued in the August 1970 *Voice*, credited to McGinnis and the Elkins *Inter-Mountain:*

[Judge Maxwell] has granted the Conservancy a preliminary injunction banning road building and timber sales in the 18,000 acre Otter Creek basin. The injunction was directed against Island Creek Coal Company, owner of most of the mineral rights in the basin, and the U.S. Forest Service. The judge had previously issued three 10-day restraining orders on June 2, June 15, and June 24.

Island Creek had nearly completed the first of five planned temporary roads to take core samples in the basin — a mile-long road between the two main forks of Moore Run beginning at the McGowan Mountain Road — when it was stopped by the court.

Island Creek has appealed the preliminary injunction and has asked for a trial, which will probably be held in August. It is expected that there will be an eight-month delay before the coal company can resume operations even if the final decision is in the favor of the company.

"The problems of law here are immense," the district judge commented. "The questions of law that must be passed upon are significant. I would be inclined to think in my particulars, they are novel"
"The continuation of the road building process would effectively ...destroy the opportunity for judicial review...and would in a very real way defile and upset and perhaps destroy the delicate fragile evidences of nature that are sought to be preserved and upgraded and

perpetuated…If the plaintiffs have a right to prevail in the final analysis, if the Environmental Policy Act was Congressional expression that is valid and applicable to the title of this property, if the Multiple Use Act is applicable and viable in the application of this property, then…we must be sure that the stay earlier imposed by the temporary restraining order is continued on through the final development of the intricate and highly complex problems of law.

"In other words, we must perpetuate the stay of the temporary order so as to prevent the area from becoming blighted by use, much as we are now in the process of preventing or reclaiming blighted area in strip-mined fields, in the areas of urban renewal projects to clear up living areas that have become blighted.

"Here we are working towards the end of preventing a blight if that is preventable under law."

Within a few years, Anderson and Moorman dropped out of Conservancy activity, but both enjoyed distinguished careers in environmental law. Anderson was the first president of the Environmental Law Institute in Washington, D.C., taught in Utah, and returned to Washington in 1985 as Dean of the American University Law School. Over his career he has consulted and published, and become an authority on the National Environmental Policy Act and other environmental legislation. He joked in a 2006 interview of meeting in Arkansas with a Mr. Webster Hubbell at the Rose Law Firm (later made famous by President Clinton's Whitewater scandal). From 1993—2003 Anderson was a partner of Moorman's at a large Washington firm.

Moorman stayed active in the Conservancy briefly enough to play an early but important role in the Davis Power Project (see Chapter 5). At a Conservancy meeting, Moorman agreed to file a "petition to intervene" with the Federal Power Commission on the Conservancy's behalf. Within a few years, however, he had moved to San Francisco as President of the Sierra Club Legal Defense Fund and oversaw the Sierra Club's involvement in the hearings and court proceedings of the Davis project, through Washington attorney Ron Wilson. During the Carter administration, Moorman served as an Assistant Attorney General. He then entered private practice with a Washington firm, and was re-united with Anderson. In 2007 Moorman was president of Taxpayers Against Fraud, a not-for-profit public interest group.

Although both these well-known environmental lawyers were raised a few hundred yards apart in Rutherton, North Carolina, a town of 3,000, Anderson said, "We really didn't get to know each other until years later."

In the September 1970 *Highlands Voice*, King used his "President's Comments" to review the Otter Creek battle so far. A year earlier, at the October Fall Review the Conservancy had proposed Otter Creek as wilderness, but the Forest Service thought it unqualified. At the Mid-Winter Workshop, Dorrell, Monongahela National Forest Supervisor, had presented his alternative, a multiple use plan for Otter Creek, that he said was non-negotiable. Although Island Creek's Mr. MacDonald had said that his company had no plans for the underlying coal, two weeks later they had announced plans for twenty-eight miles of roads and core drilling.

After hosting two public meetings to advise local residents, in Parsons and Elkins, on April 30 the Conservancy filed an appeal with the Forest Service, requesting a stay of further activity within the area until the appeal could be heard. "This appeal," said King, "was drawn up by Fred Anderson in only one week." On May 7, Congressman Hechler introduced his bill for Dolly Sods, Otter Creek, and Cranberry. By mid-May the coal company was cutting their first road. On May 31, Rodman and King took extensive photographs of the operation. On June 2, Shay filed for the injunction. After hearings in June and July, a preliminary injunction was issued. Meanwhile on June 9, Senator Randolph introduced his wilderness bill. In late July, the coal company appealed Judge Maxwell's ruling to the Fourth Circuit Court of Appeals in Richmond. On July 27 the Conservancy finally received a reply to its appeal to the Forest Service from April. "And that is Otter Creek to date," concluded King.

Later in the same issue:

> On August 22, 1970, Senator Jennings Randolph at the request of Marvin Watson, President of Occidental Petroleum, called a meeting at Blackwater Falls to bring officials of Mr. Watson's company and its subsidiary Island Creek Coal together with conservation representatives and mayors of nearby towns…Mr. Watson explained…that they were going to assess the quality and quantity of coal in Otter Creek. If they can't, then they felt the government must. He stated that Otter Creek cannot become a wilderness area until this is done.

Mentioning the three possibilities of poor coal and no mining, good coal and mining, or good coal and sell to the government, the president of Island Creek reiterated that no one actually knew how much coal underlay Otter Creek. He thought the Forest Service's estimate was eighty-five million tons.

In January 1971, King had stepped down as president, replaced by Burrell, and Anderson was elected to the Conservancy Board of Directors. At the 1971 Mid-Winter Workshop, King reported on Otter Creek that Judge Maxwell had refused a request by the Forest Service and Island Creek Coal Company to dismiss the injunction he had issued in August. The injunction was appealed to the U.S. Fourth Circuit Court of Appeals in Richmond and Moorman, Anderson, and Shay had filed a 55-page brief on behalf of the Conservancy.

In April it was reported:

> The U.S. Fourth Circuit Court in Richmond has denied the Forest Service appeal of the preliminary injunction issued by the Northern Federal District of West Virginia. The preliminary injunction prohibits activities that would be detrimental to the Otter Creek area that has been proposed for wilderness designation. The case will now go back to the Northern Federal Court District for trial at some time in the future.

A year later, in April 1972, the *Voice* included Anderson's Otter Creek report:

> The Federal District Court recently gave the Island Creek Coal Company limited permission to drill 5 of the 25 planned test holes in the Otter Creek drainage. The prospecting will be done by packing equipment in on mule back. The Conservancy was expressly permitted to inspect the drilling sites at any time and the court ordered Island Creek to report back to it in May 1972, on progress with the drilling. All rights which the Conservancy has have been expressly preserved.

According to Anderson, during the hearing the judge called a conference. Instead of a helicopter, someone, he doesn't remember who, half-heartedly recommended taking the drilling equipment into Otter Creek by mule, thus saving the need for building roads. The Conservancy readily agreed, if the company would try it.

In July 1972, McGinnis added several details in an article titled "Otter Creek Core Drilling." After preliminary background, she wrote:

> Judge Maxwell ordered lawyers representing the Conservancy and the coal company to get together to agree on a method of sampling

[the coal] that didn't require roads. Pack horses and helicopters were two alternatives for getting the heavy core drill rigs to five sites within the basin. In December 1971, Island Creek announced that horses were the choice. Work began almost immediately in early January. An old road starting at the Showalter Farm just northeast of the basin was reopened to the boundary of national forest land, and the drill rigs brought there by truck. Here they were taken apart and loaded onto a specially designed litter-shaped platform suspended between two draft horses. Mules perhaps would have been preferable, but they have all but vanished from this part of the country. A commercial riding stable at Deep Creek Lake is renting Island Creek riding horses and several teams of draft horses.

A team can carry 800 pounds at a time on the platform, and it takes nine trips to transport an entire rig. Once at the drilling site, it must be reassembled. The work is hard on the horses, and they must have a day or more of rest after completing a round trip. When I first met the crew in April, the team was standing almost knee-deep in mud. The ground is frequently rocky, and the horses are constantly loosing shoes.

The Highlands Conservancy owes a debt of gratitude to the lawyers — Jim Moorman, Fred Anderson, Willis Shay, and their assistants — and to the others who have managed to keep the Otter Creek wilderness intact — for the time being.

On August 23, 1972, Skip Johnson, highly-respected writer for *The Charleston Gazette*, announced the decision, in an article titled, "Otter Creek Prospecting Put on Shelf":

> Island Creek Coal Co., which spent $100,000 on a unique horse-back core-drilling operation in the Otter Creek area of the Monongahela National Forest, has at least temporarily abandoned plans for further coal exploration there. F.A. MacDonald, an attorney for the Huntington-based firm, confirmed Tuesday that Island Creek has decided that "for the present time and for the foreseeable future" it will do no more prospecting in Otter Creek.
>
> The horseback core drilling operation — unique in the nation — came about after the West Virginia Highlands Conservancy objected to Island Creek's plans to bulldoze roads into Otter Creek. The conservation group went to court and obtained an injunction that prohibited the company from building roads to transport drilling equipment. In proceedings before Judge Robert Maxwell of the U.S. District Court of Northern West Virginia at Elkins, the coal firm and the conservancy agreed upon the horseback method. The laborious operation started

last January and was completed in June. A total of five holes were drilled.

The coal firm and the Highlands Conservancy took different viewpoints on whether Island Creek's decision to shelve plans for further coal exploration in Otter Creek means it didn't find sufficient coal there. Conservancy lawyer Shay said analysis of all five drilled holes, taken together, indicated the coal there is "of questionable value." He said that one 30-inch seam — which he described as "marginally operable" — was found at 667 feet below the surface, and that other seams were smaller.

MacDonald, the coal firm's lawyer, said, "it's a matter of who evaluates it. We found Sewell coal in varying thicknesses, so we know it's there." Asked if Island Creek considers the coal under Otter Creek economically feasible to mine, he commented that "everybody can draw their own conclusions. We're satisfied for the present."

The Otter Creek victory has since been called the Conservancy's finest hour. Burrell remembered it as such in 2006, as he did at the time. Burrell, Conservancy President, published in the September *Voice* a letter to Willis Shay, expressing the Conservancy's appreciation:

Dear Willis:

It is a rare day when the West Virginia Highlands Conservancy can claim an almost complete victory. Our lot seems to be one of constant reversals and disappointments, but the recent decision regarding the final findings on the Otter Creek core samples was a pleasant shot in the arm to remind us all to keep our noses at the grindstone, as you have so ably shown us. The decision by Island Creek Coal Co. to pull out of Otter Creek for good was very good news to these tired ears.

The West Virginia Highlands Conservancy desperately needs other attorneys living in West Virginia to become concerned with such problems and help us out. You have been a pioneer and have blazed a well-marked trail that I hope others will soon follow.

In July 1972, Dorrell, the controversial Supervisor of the Monongahela National Forest, left his post for Washington, D.C., to become Assistant Director of the Division of Fire Control at the U.S. Forest Service. Ernie Nester, the new *Voice* Editor, added his analysis:

Many people who love the West Virginia Highlands do not feel that Dorrell did a good job as Forest Supervisor and are not unhappy to see him move to Washington. A few of the policies and actions of the Forest Service during Dorrell's reign that raised the ire of conservationists were: extensive clear-cutting; opposition to the establishment of wilderness areas; construction of open roads through wild areas; inadequate concern over effects of coal mining; insufficient concern over the effects of logging operations and roads on trout streams and wildlife; the lack of meaningful communication between Dorrell and the public; and the absence of any real cooperation with the Department of Natural Resources.

In many respects the past three years have been a disaster for the Monongahela National Forest. I sincerely hope that Mr. Troutt [his successor] will provide the leadership and direction that is needed for the protection and wise use of our National Forest.

Otter Creek was now saved from mining and road building and the Forest Service was enjoined by court action to retain its wilderness character, pending congressional action. During the Otter Creek legal battle, what had been happening with Dolly Sods and Cranberry and what was going on in Washington in the debate over "Eastern Wilderness and the Purity Theory"?

Dolly Sods

At this point Dolly Sods had been designated a Scenic Area by the Forest Service, was the subject of McGinnis's *Hiking Guide*, used as a model for Otter Creek and Cranberry, and would later be included by Rep. Hechler and Senator Randolph in their respective wilderness bills. While Otter Creek was in the news statewide and the subject of a two-year court battle, Dolly Sods maintained a lower profile. Like Otter Creek, the mineral rights were privately owned, but no one expected any coal exploration to come to Dolly Sods.

In August 1970, McGinnis reported:

On July 18-19 Russell Cahill, a staff member of the President's Environmental [Quality] Council, and Tita Thompson, a staff member of NBC television, visited the proposed Otter Creek and Dolly Sods Wilderness Areas. Miss Thompson is doing research on eastern wilderness as part of a planned NBC special on American wilderness that will probably be shown next January.

Over the next year, Otter Creek would dominate wilderness news, the proposed Davis Power Project was threatening the Canaan Valley, the issue of clearcutting was emerging, and Shavers Fork was threatened by mining. If that wasn't enough, the abolition of strip mining was actively being promoted statewide and some in the Conservancy wanted to become more actively involved in that issue. Things were busy. About the only mention of Dolly Sods in *The Highlands Voice* during this period were reminders of the availability of the *Hiking Guide*.

One reason little was happening at the congressional level was the Forest Service's continued resistance to wilderness designations in the East. Some believed the Forest Service designed timber sales to gut potential wilderness areas of interest to local conservationists. The Conservancy had certainly faced this on both Otter Creek and the Cranberry Back Country.

The logjam seemed to break in mid-1972. Supervisor Dorrell had invited Conservancy wilderness activists to a meeting to discuss new ways to preserve wilderness. President Nixon had recently directed the Secretary of Agriculture, through the Forest Service, to identify eastern wilderness candidates, which was a welcomed reversal of Forest Service policy. Conservancy leaders were understandably cautious.

In July another breakthrough was reported: The House Appropriations Committee approved funds to enable the Forest Service to begin acquisition of the privately held mineral rights under Dolly Sods. Surprisingly the announcement came from Rep. John Slack, of Charleston, not known for his pro-environment positions. The article also reported that the Nature Conservancy had recently purchased an option for mineral rights under 15,617 acres for $600,000. The appropriation would cover at least half this amount beginning the next fiscal year. Slack was quoted:

> This is a very gratifying development. It gives me about as much personal satisfaction as anything I have done during my years in Congress. I think it points us in the right direction and sets us on a promising course. The only way we can be certain that outstanding areas like Dolly Sods will remain protected is through Federal ownership of the mineral rights privately held.

By September 1972, Otter Creek's coal prospecting was shelved, the divisive Dorrell had left the Monongahela National Forest, and Dolly Sods' mineral rights were moving toward federal ownership. In the October *Voice*, McGinnis' update included more on the mineral rights buy-out. She reported that the appropriation had been defeated in the House, but restored by Senator Byrd in the Senate. She also reported that the Potomac Appalachian Trail Club had signed an agreement to be responsible for trail maintenance on Dolly Sods.

But McGinnis still worried about Dolly Sods. One alternative routing of Appalachian Corridor H highway (see Chapter 4) would go along
its western flank. Another problem was that half of the Red Creek watershed, adjacent to the scenic area, was owned by private industry, most by
the Western Maryland Railway Company. "There is no guarantee that
this land will not be strip mined or built up with vacation homes eventually. Ideally, it should be purchased by the U.S. government...but there
has been little progress in this direction," warned McGinnis. Finally she
worried that the Davis Power Project, proposed for nearby Canaan Valley,
would increase the attractiveness for Dolly Sods as a vacation subdivision.

Cranberry Back Country

Although discussed separately in this volume, the struggle to save all
three wilderness areas was going on simultaneously. As noted previously,
the Cranberry was threatened by a large deep mining proposal by Princess Coal Company, whose President, David Francis, would also meet the
Conservancy on Shavers Fork (see Chapter 3). A hiking guide was out for
distribution, and the Cranberry area was included in Hechler's and
Randolph's wilderness legislation. A small but active group of Conservancy members were working on the Cranberry issue.

In June 1970, most of *The Highlands Voice* was devoted to the Cranberry and its threats. Ernie Nester, who later succeeded Burrell as *Voice*
editor, presented a thorough analysis of the coal-mining issue in the
Cranberry Back Country. Tracing the chain of mineral ownership, the
companies and their subsidiaries, the need for railroad extensions and
processing plants, he concluded that unfortunately the Forest Service
would not have much control over the proposed mining operations in
the Cranberry area.

Nester reprinted an editorial from the *Charleston Daily Mail* of May
5, 1970:

> Coal of low sulfur content is needed to meet federal anti-pollution
> regulations, and it isn't found just everywhere. One of the places it is
> found in large and mineable quantities is under the great Monongahela
> National Forest which occupies more than 800,000 acres in West
> Virginia.
>
> These owners [the private sector mineral owners] have a right to
> their property and it is not difficult to anticipate that they will assert
> those rights as the market for low-sulfur coal expands. It is just as easy
> to predict widespread mining, both underground and surface, could

ruin much of the most valuable scenic and recreation areas of the forest.

...there is not any good reason the federal government should not subject the subsurface acreage to the same fine control which has made the surface acreage what it is today. One without the other is pointless.

It will require some congressional action, particularly some congressional money action, to get these minerals which are valuable. Whatever it takes, and we hope it isn't too long, we believe it will be worth it to the people of the nation generally and West Virginians particularly.

Ron Hardway, a new writer, who would follow Nester as a *Voice* editor, wrote his first article for the *Voice* in October 1970, titled "A Special Report: Present Status of the Cranberry Back Country." Hardway reported that a small coal company had already opened one mine and signed a lease with Princess Coal for the entire watershed. Like the proposals in Otter Creek, the company promised hardly any surface disturbance, although road construction, power lines, and ventilation shafts were a certainty, Hardway wrote. Even worse, the coal tipple and sludge ponds were planned at the entrance to the wilderness area. He continued, "Coal mining is not compatible with wilderness and [the company's] claims to the contrary demonstrate the contempt with which coal operators and big business in general regard the national interest, popular opinion, and public intelligence."

Hardway also raised the threat of logging. "The Forest Service has become a Frankenstein that has turned on its creator, the forest," wrote Hardway. The Forest Service seemed determined to increase logging, even with clearcutting, destroying any potential for wilderness and by so doing, ruin the best black bear habitat in West Virginia. A local Izaak Walton League chapter [Richwood] was very upset by the clearcutting and had called for a moratorium on logging in potential wilderness areas. (They led the crusade against clearcutting discussed in Chapter 6.) Hardway called for prompt congressional protection for the three wilderness areas, since time would only give the mining companies further opportunities to destroy the forest.

By December 1970 things were moving quickly. A gas-drilling rig, set up just outside the Cranberry Back Country, struck gas. Mines were located or planned just outside other sections of the boundary. To make things confusing, the exact boundary was in dispute. Conservancy Wilderness Committee Chairman George Langford reported his committee's recommendations. Of the 53,000 acres of the Cranberry

Back Country, the committee decided to exclude areas recently timbered or containing access roads. Their recommendation for a wilderness study area was 37,000 acres. On the issue of mineral ownership, Langford added, "it may be prohibitively expensive for Congress to condemn the minerals underlying recreational-use areas in the National Forest."

The February 1971 *Voice* reported on the recent Mid-Winter Workshop. The Wilderness Committee's recommendations were accepted, that only 36,000 acres of the 53,000 acre Back Country be proposed as wilderness. A fifty-page report from the committee gave the boundaries and other specifics. A resolution was passed calling on the Forest Service to manage these acres to ensure their wilderness character until congressional action was taken. To the Conservancy, this was beginning to sound familiar. With the recent decision of the appeals court forcing Otter Creek to be preserved as wilderness, the Forest Service placed a "temporary hold status" on new timber sales in the Cranberry area.

Ernie Nester became *Voice* editor in February and was following the Cranberry issue. In June, he reported mining was underway again as well as planning for additional openings by Francis and Princess Coal Company, this time actually within the Back Country. Meanwhile the Forest Service was completing a management plan for the Cranberry. Langford's report encouraged members to write congressmen supporting de facto wilderness protection. The Nixon administration was said to be supportive.

In 1972 the Nixon administration was directing the Forest Service to study and protect wilderness areas in the East. To implement this in West Virginia, Supervisor Dorrell convened a meeting in April with wilderness advocates from the Conservancy and other groups. But the citizens were cautious. There was too much at stake in too many places on the Monongahela National Forest, and the Forest Service had been anti-wilderness for too long.

Otter Creek now had judicial protection, thanks to the Conservancy's trio of lawyers. Dolly Sods' mineral rights were under option, with a likelihood of federal purchase. But the Cranberry wilderness area, as large as the other two combined, was still subject to active mining, gas wells, and other threats. When Dorrell departed for a new job in July, all bets were off. While wilderness advocates waited for Washington to decide the "eastern wilderness purity" issue, the Conservancy continued to distribute its hiking guides and make public presentations, but time was running out.

In the years of 1973 and 1974 many of these battles continued. A few of the highlights worth noting include:

- A proposal for a 11,656-acre wilderness for Laurel Fork, on the Virginia-West Virginia border, and a part of the George Washington National Forest, as advocated by the Virginia Wilderness Committee
- Many Conservancy leaders presented testimony at House and Senate wilderness hearings in Washington. An additional field hearing in Roanoke was chaired by Sen. Floyd Haskell, whose legislative aide reportedly enjoyed a hike in Otter Creek
- Congressional repudiation of the Forest Service's overly-strict interpretation of wilderness to exclude any eastern forest timbered in the past
- After having Otter Creek reduced from "instant Wilderness" with Dolly Sods, to "Wilderness study area" with the Cranberry, the Conservancy mounted a successful lobbying campaign in the Senate to restore Otter Creek to "instant" status
- Congressman Harley O. Staggers, whose district included all four wilderness areas, conducted a voters' poll, and to his surprise, 75% favored all four wilderness areas.

Eastern Wilderness Areas Act

Finally, Conservancy members celebrated the passage of the Eastern Wilderness Areas Act of 1974 on December 18, 1974. "Wilderness Bill Passes," screamed the headline in the January 1975 *Highlands Voice*. Three large photos, one each of Dolly Sods, Otter Creek, and Cranberry Back Country accompanied the article:

> After more than five years of frustrating postponement, compromise and revision, the Conservancy's efforts on behalf of eastern wilderness bore fruit on December 18 with Congressional passage of S. 3433, the Eastern Wilderness Areas Act. The Act created sixteen "instant" wilderness areas, two of which were Dolly Sods and Otter Creek.
>
> The third area which the Conservancy had proposed for wilderness designation, the controversial Cranberry Back Country, was included in the bill as one of seventeen Wilderness Study Areas. A fourth area in which the Conservancy had an interest, the Laurel Fork unit of the George Washington National Forest, was not included in the bill.
>
> One important management provision of the act will make future protection for Study Areas much easier. The Study Areas are to be managed during their study period "so as to maintain their presently existing wilderness character and potential for inclusion in the Na-

tional Wilderness Preservation System until Congress has determined otherwise."

Passage of the Eastern Areas Wilderness Act has also removed a persistent obstacle to eastern wilderness – the "pristine pure" concept of wilderness envisioned by the U.S. Forest Service. The language of S. 3433 unconditionally rejects the Forest Service definition of wilderness.

Editor Ron Hardway provided additional perspective, under "Two wins, one loss, one tie":

The creation of the Dolly Sods National Wilderness Area and the Otter Creek National Wilderness Area brings to a close one of the most entertaining chapters in Conservancy history. For over five years the Conservancy has cussed and discussed, been cussed and discussed, investigated and been investigated, sued and not yet been sued, earned respect and enmity, finally emerging with a record of two wins, one loss and one tie.

We won, of course, Dolly Sods and Otter Creek, overcoming strong objections from the Forest Service, the timbering industry, the road builders, and the ORV freaks. We lost Laurel Fork (for the time being), largely to the Forest Service and the loggers. We have tied the coal industry for Cranberry. The Back Country is in limbo for the present. It is not a wilderness area, but it will be managed as one just the same while it is being studied for possible inclusion in the Wilderness Preservation System. We may yet lose it, or win not enough of it to have made the effort worthwhile.

The Conservancy has gained many things from this bitter wilderness fight besides two wilderness areas. We have come of age as an organization, leaving behind us the days of a handful of letter writers and an occasional group picnic or hike.

We are now recognized as the leading environmental organization in West Virginia by every major environmental group beyond our crabby borders. Within the state government agencies and politicians with whom we must deal now realize that the Conservancy is not an idle group of do-gooders, but an organization of active, intelligent and informed environmentalists.

We are not unrecognized by the people of West Virginia either. The last of *the Highlands Voice* mailed in 1972 went out to less than 400 members. The last issue of the *Voice* in 1974 went to more than 800 members.

Clearly this still-young organization could be proud of its accomplishments. Other issues stood before it: dams on several major rivers, mining threats on Shavers Fork, strip mining statewide, power plants, clearcutting across the national forest, and more. But in less than ten years from its first event, it had established itself. It published a monthly periodical, *The Highlands Voice*, and three hiking guides for the three wilderness areas, and had just published its first edition of the *Hiking Guide to the Monongahela National Forest*.

The Cranberry Battle Continues

As 1975 progressed, Hardway and others kept a watchful eye on the Cranberry Back Country. The Forest Service received an appropriation to assess the coal under the wilderness study area. Mid-Allegheny Corporation, the mineral owner, insisted on core drilling addition holes to reach their own conclusion. Trails became muddy haul roads and the public objected. The Conservancy revised and re-issued the Cranberry Guide, quietly allowing the Dolly Sods and Otter Creek guides to go out of print. As discussed in Chapter 6, the origin of a larger *Hiking Guide to the Monongahela National Forest* was partly intended to draw attention away from the wilderness areas. So much public awareness had been necessary to mobilize the lobbying efforts to protect them, that to West Virginians they were practically household place names. As a result all three were experiencing rapid increases in visitation. To protect their fragile wilderness character, the Conservancy wanted to reduce their publicity.

The Fall Weekend Review of 1975, ten years after the first one on Spruce Knob, focused on the Cranberry Back Country. Both Charlie Carlson, now the fifth Conservancy president, and Ron Hardway, *Voice* editor, were well versed and passionate about the Cranberry.

In October 1976, the *Voice* carried an article advising that a new coal company, Powellton Coal Company, had leased Mid-Allegheny's mineral rights, applied for state water discharge permits, and planned to open two deep mines. The Conservancy had retained the services of Charleston attorney Ray Ratliff, who had been researching the issues. (This was not Ratliff's only project with the Conservancy. Ratliff had a major role in the Davis Power Project, which is discussed in Chapter 5.)

In the February 1977 *Highlands Voice,* Larry George reported that the Conservancy, together with the Izaak Walton League, had sued both the coal company and the Forest Service, claiming that the Cranberry Study Area must be managed to protect it from any activity that would detract from its wilderness character. (The Wilderness Society later joined the suit.) It was Otter Creek all over again!!

Interestingly the same issue included another article by George titled "Chessie System Behind the Cranberry Mines." He revealed that Mid-Allegheny Corporation was a wholly owned subsidiary of the Chessie System. George reported a meeting with the Chessie Vice President for Coal Development, who told George their primary reason for developing coal mines was to increase coal traffic on their railroad. The Cranberry mines specifically could generate $60-65 million in revenues for the railroad, plus royalties. George speculated that Chessie was both testing the Wilderness Act provisions and hoping to increase the mineral value, should the Forest Service decide to buy them out.

Burrell, in a 2006 interview, expressed his belief that the proposed mining on Otter Creek, Dolly Sods, Cranberry, and Shavers Fork (see Chapter 3) were all ploys by the various mineral owners to jack up the price they could get from a federal buyout. At the time of each threat, the Conservancy had to consider each proposal as legitimate, but in hindsight, Burrell questioned whether these were just ways the mining industry was extorting the taxpayer.

> **Larry George** first became involved in the Highlands Conservancy during the battle to save the Cranberry Back Country. A lifelong resident of Huntington, he brought an interesting combination of expertise to his environmental activism. Beginning his college education at Marshall with an engineering major, he transferred to Virginia Tech, concentrating on water resources, geological engineering, and regional planning. While at Tech, he spent six months of the academic year at the Huntington District of the Army Corps of Engineers, reviewing hydropower projects and representing them on strip mine issues. He simultaneously served as a volunteer coordinator in Rep. Hechler's unsuccessful gubernatorial campaign.
>
> In his statement of candidacy for a seat on the Conservancy's board printed in the February 1977 *Voice*, George described his personal activities over the previous eight years, as a backpacker, whitewater paddler, photographer, and trout fisherman, primarily in the highlands region. Active both as a youth and an adult leader in the Boy Scouts, he was proud to be both an Eagle Scout and a recipient of West Virginia's Golden Horseshoe Award.

George became very active in mobilizing an entirely new generation of West Virginians to protect the state's special places. Working with many college groups, especially at Marshall University, he led a major political lobbying effort on behalf of Cranberry.

In 1983 George became the President of the Conservancy. Along the way, he obtained a law degree from West Virginia University, was appointed by Governor Rockefeller in 1978 to serve on the state Water Resources Board, later became the Deputy Director of the Department of Natural Resources, and, briefly, Director of the Department of Energy, in the Gaston Caperton administration. His tenure with the Conservancy was somewhat controversial, and his conservation record contributed to his having a rough time in state government. In 2007 he was practicing law in Charleston.

Since the Forest Service was not aggressively regulating the coal companies developing mines within the Cranberry Study Area, some thought the state's required mining permits might be used as leverage. With a new Governor, Jay Rockefeller, the pro-mining bias of his predecessor, Arch Moore, had ended. Accordingly, a group of West Virginia University students found a Morgantown legislator, House of Delegates member Clyde Richey, who agreed to introduce legislation to force a moratorium on mining during the period that Cranberry was under study for wilderness potential.

These and other details were reported in the March *Voice* by WVU grad student Keith Kirk. He wrote that the West Virginia Student Public Interest Research Group (WVSPIRG), an affiliate of Ralph Nader, conducted a 350-person demonstration at the Morgantown Chessie office. Other groups became involved, including Save Our Mountains, increasing public awareness and publicity statewide. Behind the scenes the Cranberry Technical Committee, replacing the now inactive Wilderness Committee, was researching mining proposals and providing its expertise to all who were interested.

April 1977's *Voice* announced several Cranberry developments. The Forest Service had told the federal District Court that Powellton and Mid-Allegheny must get federal approvals after all, and the case was continued another month. Other articles discussed the just-completed legislative session. New Conservancy President Linda Cooper Elkinton reported that the campaign to create a moratorium on Cranberry mining brought more public response than any other issue of the legislative session. Because of phone trouble, calls to state senators were routed through the Governor's office and averaged an impressive fifty a day. Richey's moratorium bill passed the House of Delegates 95-6, but was ultimately killed in a Senate committee. Morgantown's Earth House raised more than $500 for Cranberry litigation through sale on the WVU campus of "Save the Cranberry" t-shirts made by Conservancy members Lois and George Rosier.

In June, an article reiterated that the Forest Service had begun to restrict mining in Cranberry and planned to accelerate the Wilderness Study, to be completed July 1978, two years early. The U.S. Environmental Protection Agency had not yet issued its permits. The coal company was fighting a deposition request in the court case. Although U.S. District Judge Dennis Knapp wouldn't hold his hearings until July, the author (probably Editor Hardway) wrote:

> Regardless of the decisions Judge Knapp makes in regard to these preliminary matters or the suit on July 7, the Conservancy, the Wilderness Society, the Izaak Walton League and Charles Carlson, as plaintiffs have already seen a great deal achieved in this suit...protection of the Cranberry Wilderness Study Area, until Congressional Action is taken, looks 100 percent better now than it did in February when the suit was filed.
>
> The battle is far from over, however, Congress must decide whether Cranberry is ultimately protected. And that's going to take a lot of work.

A small box announced the new, fifth edition of the *Cranberry Backcountry Trail Guide and Wilderness Proposal*. Obviously all the publicity and citizen interest in the Cranberry had made the first four editions sell.

Marking the Conservancy's tenth anniversary in September 1977, under its sixth president and third *Voice* editor, provided an opportunity to assess its successes and challenges. That month's *Voice* noted:

> Wilderness preservation has been the major point of emphasis for Conservancy action down through the years. In fact it was a threat of a road being built across Dolly Sods, which sparked the informal organization of the Conservancy back in 1965. The people who attended that first gathering on Spruce Knob in 1965 could not foresee that it would take exactly ten years to remove the Dolly Sods forever from the threats of road builders.

49

The signing two years earlier by President Gerald Ford of the Eastern Wilderness Areas Act had immediately protected Otter Creek and Dolly Sods, but had left the Cranberry Back Country open to coal mining exploitation with a passive Forest Service looking on. While the Conservancy activists were deeply engaged in a host of other issues that year, everyone waited for Judge Knapp's decision.

With several major legal and public awareness campaigns underway, the Conservancy had been trying to raise money for each project on a pay-as-you-go basis. In December 1977's *Voice*, George, Conservancy Cranberry Fund Chairman, announced that the goal of $10,000 had been reached. He stated that most of the money came in the form of contributions from individuals averaging $10. This set a new high-water mark in Conservancy project fundraising.

In the March 1978 *Voice*, a front-page story by Linda Elkinton and Kirk reported that the West Virginia Legislature had become involved again. Two delegates, Jim McNeely and Jerry Tighe, had introduced a bill to prohibit mining in the Cranberry Wilderness Study Area until the Forest Service completed its study and Congress acted. At joint House-Senate hearings Senator Carl Gainer, of Richwood, a pro-timber, pro-mining advocate, personally attacked Tighe. After much citizen lobbying, the House passed the bill 85-10. To bypass Gainer's Natural Resources Committee, which had killed the 1977 bill, a campaign was mounted to get a different committee referral. The "Save the Cranberry Coalition" was formed, composed of twelve other groups, totaling 14,000 members, the largest of which was the West Virginia Wildlife Federation, conservative, but politically influential. The effort was successful, although Gainer tried to sabotage the bill with crippling amendments. Some last minute maneuvering by Cranberry supporters brought the Senate vote of 27–7. The authors concluded:

> A victory? Yes. But, the fight is not over. The coal company will no doubt challenge the constitutionality of this bill, and Congress still must act to fully protect Cranberry. We still need Senator Randolph's very powerful support to achieve this Congressional action.
>
> Still, let it be known by all those who will take note that passage of H.B. 950 reflects this unwavering citizen mandate: We want the Cranberry area protected. We want Cranberry added to the National Wilderness Preservation System.

The following month a photo appeared in the *Voice* showing Gov. Rockefeller signing the Cranberry bill. In the photo, in addition to various politicians, were Conservancy President Elkinton, members Sally Hunter and Larry George, and Wanda Hauser of the Izaak Walton League. It was indeed a victory.

RARE II

While West Virginians were working on the specific, Cranberry, Washington was dealing with the general, something called RARE II, an initiative under President Jimmy Carter. In *The Enduring Wilderness,* Doug Scott described RARE II. As a result of widespread discontent in Congress with the unwillingness of the Forest Service to look at potential wilderness area candidates, Carter's Assistant Secretary of Agriculture (whose jurisdiction included the Forest Service), Conservancy co-founder and former Wilderness Society Assistant Director Rupert Cutler, organized the Roadless Area Review and Evaluation program, based on a flawed 1971 Forest Service effort (RARE I). Scott wrote:

> The goal was to better inventory and study national forest de facto wilderness...This time, with the purity theory officially abandoned, it included roadless areas on national forests in the eastern half of the country. Nearly 3,000 roadless areas were identified and mapped, totaling 62 million acres.

In West Virginia, nineteen areas were included in RARE II, including several areas adjacent to the three already included in the Eastern Wilderness Areas Act. The Forest Service spent much of 1977–78 evaluating each area for its report. Using a list of variables, applied to each area, numerical scores were derived. Jeanette Fitzwilliams, a government researcher in Washington and the Conservancy Board representative of the Potomac Appalachian Trail Club, gave readers a thorough analysis in a three-part series for the *Voice*.

Among Fitzwilliams' conclusions were that Seneca Creek and the Dolly Sods Addition (Roaring Plains) had the highest scenic ratings, while Cranberry received a high rating because of its unusual glades.

Near the end of her extensive analysis, Fitzwilliams wrote:

> I spent Memorial Day Weekend trail clearing in the Dolly Sods Wilderness. I spoke to nearly 100 backpackers. Of that number, only one had heard of RARE II. Many of them did not know what a wilderness was and thought it was any forest. Many thought wilderness

just happened. If we want wilderness or a particular wilderness then we have got to show we care. That means writing our comments to the Forest Service.

It is important not only for the cause of wilderness or dispersed recreation or a combination of the two (if that is what you want) or even if you are opposed to some candidate because it is important to show the Forest Service, local, state, and federal government that the people of West Virginia do care what happens not only in their state but in the country…Right now governments everywhere are making an effort…to involve the public in the decision making process. If we do not respond, they are going to stop. If Conservancy members respond on Wilderness, then it becomes that much easier when the WVHC wants to take a position on some other issue.

Cranberry Re-Emerges

Under an August 1978 *Voice* headline, "Wilderness Status for Cranberry," it was reported that, although the RARE II study remained ongoing, the Forest Service had recommended that the Cranberry become a congressionally designated wilderness area. A modest adjustment from 36,300 acres in the Study Area, to 35,500 acres in the recommended wilderness, was primarily to exclude the Cranberry Glades, which would continue to be protected as a Biological Area. The Forest Service had filed its proposal with the EPA.

Referring to the RARE II study, the article reported that the Wilderness Attribute Rating System showed Cranberry's composite score topped by only one of the fifty-five areas in the Northern Appalachian and New England states. Widespread public support also favored Cranberry's wilderness status. Three evenings of public hearings would allow public comment. Following the close of the comment period, the official recommendation would be transmitted to Congress in early 1979.

All the effort to convince the Forest Service to support Cranberry as a congressionally designated wilderness area had paid off. The fight was not over, but a major hurdle had been crossed.

In November, the Conservancy announced its recommendations from the RARE II study. In addition to Cranberry, the group strongly recommended Cheat Mountain, Seneca Creek, North Mountain-Hopewell, and SW Dolly Sods-Roaring Plains for wilderness protection. Laurel Fork North and South were just below, with remaining areas needing further data or evaluation.

Over the next five years, until January 1983, the *Voice* would report the slow progress of congressional wilderness legislation. What had seemed the toughest part, getting the Forest Service to support wilderness, had been only a warm-up. Now it took sustained lobbying, countering timber- and mining-industry opposition, and building massive public support. A few highlights:

- The Carter Administration's Forest Service recommended Laurel Fork North and South and Seneca Creek, in addition to Cranberry, for a total of 68,370 acres of new wilderness. Cheat Mountain was recommended for further study.
- After a Conservancy delegation's visit, Congressman Harley O. Staggers agreed to introduce legislation supporting Cranberry, which he finally did in September 1979. Senators Byrd and Randolph were less willing to commit to wilderness proposals.
- As the state mining moratorium in Cranberry expired in December 1979, there was worry mining might re-start unless the legislation was expedited.
- In the spring of 1980, Rep. Staggers proposed to cut the Cranberry Wilderness to one-third its original size, leaving the balance for mining and timbering. The Conservancy was outraged!
- House committee hearings on all four West Virginia areas were held, with Past President Linda Elkinton and Cranberry Committee Chairman Larry George presenting testimony, along with eight other Conservancy members, including Pocahontas County residents Bill McNeel and Leslee McCarty.
- The bill passed the House November 28, but died in committee in the Senate. Senators Byrd and Randolph cited a complex land swap between Chessie and the federal government, gaining Cranberry's mineral rights, as the cause. Because of a new Congress in January, the legislation had to start over again. Rep. Staggers was replaced by Republican Cleve Benedict. Benedict had committed during his campaign to the Cranberry Wilderness, but it was too early to tell what to expect from the Reagan administration.
- Rep. Benedict worked out a compromise and introduced a bill for Cranberry, Laurel Fork, North and South, but not Seneca Creek. Cranberry's mineral rights would be bought over a three-year period. He also wanted "release language," allowing non-wilderness management of all other RARE II areas. This fit the Reagan Administration's

pro-timber, pro-mining policy initiatives. No formal action however was taken in 1981 by either house.

- George testified in early 1982 in support of Rep. Benedict's bill, now opposed by Reagan's Forest Service, but supported by CSX (formerly Chessie) President John Snow. The Conservancy hired McCarty as a short-term Cranberry Coordinator. She reported that Senator Byrd promised a fair hearing if and when the bill reached the Senate.
- The August 1982 *Voice* contained a special supplement on the Cranberry Wilderness. The House had passed Rep. Benedict's bill and pressure was needed on Senators Byrd and Randolph. The anti-wilderness forces, urged on by the Reagan Administration, were pushing "hard release," or pro-development language, of non-wilderness areas. National conservation groups were opposed.
- The Senate failed to act before adjournment, but a "lame duck" session held hope.

Finally, at 2 AM on December 21, 1982, as the Congress was rushing to adjournment, the Cranberry Wilderness Bill passed the Senate and went to President Reagan. The bill established the Cranberry Wilderness Area of 36,000 acres, the largest in the eastern United States, and the Laurel Fork Wilderness Area of 12,000 acres.

According to an article in the January 1983 *Highlands Voice*, passage of the bill in the Senate was the result of careful work by Senators Byrd and Randolph, who crafted a provision to provide $2.2 million to Pocahontas and Webster counties to offset the coal severance tax revenue they would have received if the Cranberry area had been mined. Under the legislation, CSX would receive vouchers for purchase of federally owned mineral rights elsewhere. (McGinnis remembered seeing a letter from the conference committee referring to the high cost of purchasing the mineral rights to Cranberry, saying that it should never happen again.)

Committee Chairman George praised those who helped, "Senator Byrd personally saved this bill so many times, I lost track." CSX was also credited for its assistance. As 1983 began, the successful campaign for the protection of the Cranberry Wilderness Area, and the addition of Laurel Fork, gave the Conservancy a reason to celebrate. Also in January, George was elected as the new Conservancy president.

On January 13, 1983, President Reagan signed the Cranberry-Laurel Fork bill.

In February the *Voice's* front page was headlined, "After 12 years Cranberry Becomes Wilderness Area." An accompanying photo showed George receiving a framed front-page story from *The Charleston Gazette*, announcing the Cranberry victory.

Although President Reagan was in the White House as the Cranberry bill passed Congress, there was no doubt that this wilderness, and many others, were the result of the Carter administration's RARE II data collection and advocacy. Conservancy co-founder Cutler's work had been instrumental in establishing many wilderness areas across the country, including the Cranberry.

The *Voice* article continued:

> When the battle began to save these West Virginia wonders, few believed the effort to save the land would take so long. "Back in 1977," said WVHC President Larry George, "I figured this would be all over in two years."
>
> "The popular press and the people never gave it [the Cranberry bill] much of a chance," George said. "When you see the hoops it had to jump through you can see why."
>
> The hoops were often shrouded in political subterfuge. Congressional representatives, who privately supported the bill, refused to lobby for its passage on the floor of the House; underhanded tricks – using slight-of-hand to substitute the original bill with crippling amendments – threatened its failure and finally, over a decade's worth of work hung in the balance as House Bill 5161 lay on the desk of a President renowned for his stands against wilderness.

The article reviewed the Conservancy's long history with Cranberry. It began with the initial proposal in the Eastern Wilderness Areas Act, followed by publishing the hiking guide, the mining threats from Mid-Allegheny and Powellton and the Forest Service's failure to regulate these developments, and finally the court injunction won by the Conservancy. But then the West Virginia Legislature had injected itself into the fray. After the record-breaking outpouring of support for a mining moratorium, which included college students, especially from WVU and Marshall, both houses had passed the Cranberry bill by overwhelming votes. But Congress was less enthusiastic. Representative Staggers was lukewarm. Senators Byrd and Randolph deferred to Staggers. Then Snow of CSX indicated he supported the bill, which provided a handsome buyout of their mineral rights. Things began to move.

The year when Reagan was elected, Cleve Benedict also became the Congressman representing Second District, including the Cranberry area. Luckily, he had pledged during his campaign to support Cranberry, which Staggers had not. As Benedict fought off a threatened veto from Reagan, Byrd and Randolph worked on compensation for the counties for lost coal tax revenue. This would be the first time anywhere a wilderness bill would compensate an area for lost tax revenue. Conservancy members Jim McNeely and Perry Bryant solicited the support of the AFL-CIO and the United Mine Workers, which helped encourage Byrd's support. After holding off a last-minute "poison pill" amendment, Byrd obtained passage, the last bill of the 97th Congress to pass. According to George, Senator Byrd even had to personally lobby President Reagan to sign the bill.

In George's first "From the President" column in the February *Voice*, he reflected on the Conservancy's progress to date, much of it with wilderness:

> During the past decade the Conservancy has either provided the leadership or significantly contributed to the accomplishment of several important conservation goals:
> • Designation of the Otter Creek and Dolly Sods Wilderness Areas in 1975;
> • The Federal Surface Mining Reclamation Act of 1977;
> • The final defeat of the proposed U.S. Army Corps of Engineers reservoirs on the Cheat and the Cacapon rivers in the late 1970s;
> • And, only weeks ago, the Conservancy received one of its most gratifying victories in recent years with Congressional passage and President Reagan's approval of the Cranberry Wilderness bill.
>
> These accomplishments, more by accident than design, have propelled the Conservancy forward to its present role as one of the State's leading conservation groups. As a result, West Virginians in general, and conservation leaders in particular, have come to develop high expectations for the Conservancy's ability to accomplish its goals and its willingness to become engaged in new projects and issues.
>
> With the successes of recent years, both elected and appointed government officials have come to rely upon the Conservancy in an ever increasing degree for input in natural resources decision making.
>
> The bottom line is that there exist high expectations for the Conservancy's standard of conduct in public forums and for its ability to competently advocate its positions on natural resource issues in the technical, legal, and public policy aspects. With the great diversity of

issues with which the Conservancy is involved today, it is only prudent that we carefully select the difficult issues that we often tackle in order to avoid overtaxing the limited resources of a basically volunteer lay conservation group.

From his Cranberry experience, George proposed more reliance on committees within the Conservancy, with the board serving as a final policy and oversight function. It was also clear that he felt the Conservancy, just over fifteen years old, was a major conservation player in West Virginia. He would not be the first, or the last, Conservancy president, to try to reorganize it.

(In a footnote added in 2007, Conservancy board member Bill McNeel noted that of the $2.2 million paid to Pocahontas and Webster counties, the former received two million. "The Pocahontas County Commission," McNeel wrote, "instead of rushing out and spending the money as soon as it was received, sensibly put it in the bank. After the 1985 flood this money was used as part of the funding for the construction of a new Pocahontas Memorial Hospital, located well out of the flood plain [which the old hospital was not]. The new facility was dedicated in October 1995 — in January 1996, Marlinton was under water again — talk about perfect timing!")

1983–2000: The Quiet Period

If one of the major issues absorbing the West Virginia Highlands Conservancy from its organization in 1967 to 1983 was wilderness protection for qualifying areas within the Monongahela National Forest, the next eighteen years was the opposite. The Conservancy was deeply involved in various other important issues, discussed in virtually all the chapters in this volume, but wilderness was seldom the subject of *Highlands Voice* articles. When it was mentioned, it was the result of yet another threat to the integrity of the wilderness character of the now five protected areas (Dolly Sods, Otter Creek, Cranberry, and Laurel Fork North and South). One measure of this reduction could be seen by the index of articles related to wilderness. In the fourteen years from 1969 (first issue) to February 1983 (Cranberry victory), there were 171 articles and some of that time the *Voice* was a bi-monthly. By contrast, in the eighteen years from February 1983 to March 2001, there were only fifty-three articles and some years no more than one or two.

If there were any themes to those few *Voice* articles, they were watching the Monongahela National Forest's management of the wilderness areas to be sure that prohibited or discouraged activities were treated as such; the transfer of mineral rights from private ownership to the Forest Service; and an increasing interest in expanding Dolly Sods, both north and south (Roaring Plains).

A major reason for the silence on new wilderness proposals was "release language" in the Cranberry-Laurel Fork bill that precluded additional wilderness proposals during the implementation of the next Monongahela Forest plan, adopted in 1985. It would be nearly twenty years before this moratorium would be lifted. (See Chapter 6).

Wilderness in the New Millennium

Growing up on a farm in upstate New York, **Dave Saville** was an active boy scout, and especially enjoyed camping. With his family, he helped make Christmas wreaths from balsam fir. These and other farm products were sold at local farm markets. During these years, he also raced snowmobiles and worked with farm machinery.

When Saville eventually found himself in West Virginia, these three threads of experience came together again. Fairly quickly he began to race motorcycles, especially in the Blackwater 100, a muddy race through the northern end of Canaan Valley. After a couple of years, he became increasingly bothered by the race's impact on the local environment. He became active in the Canaan Valley Task Force, looking for common ground among the users of the valley. He also rediscovered the balsam fir, learning that Canaan's were the furthest south in the country. He soon realized that the mature trees were dying from an unusual disease and organized a seed-banking and reforestation program that became a model of citizen reforestation, involving hundreds of people planting tens of thousands of seedlings.

After graduating from West Virginia University with a master's degree in Forestry, Saville started work as a part-time staffer for the Conservancy, primarily managing membership renewals and orders for the *Monongahela Hiking Guide*. Eight years later, he became the Conservancy's first full-time employee and was a prime mover in growing the Conservancy from four hundred members in 1998 to over two thousand in 2006. He still managed those first two functions, but his scope had expanded to include the balsam project, networking with organizations and members over a wide array of issues, and helping lead the West Virginia Wilderness Coalition's effort to increase wilderness on the Monongahela National Forest.

Saville's interest in wilderness in the late 1990s, when very little was happening because of a prevailing anti-wilderness climate in Washington, sparked first a few others and then many more to share his vision of more West Virginia wilderness. With key support of the Wilderness Society and others, the West Virginia Wilderness Coalition was launched. Their unprecedented success placed West Virginia once again at the center of the wilderness movement.

On March 30, 2005, Saville received the Mother Jones Award, presented by the West Virginia Environmental Council (WVEC), an umbrella group of many state environmental organizations. The Mother Jones award was symbolic of one who fights the good fight, day in and day out, as did its namesake, Mother Mary Jones. Frank Young, Past President of the Conservancy and Treasurer of the E-Council, had the honor of presenting the award to his good friend.

During 2006, Saville advocated, and the board approved, the establishment of the "Friends of the Mon" as a section of *The Highlands Voice*, focusing on the many points of interaction between the Conservancy and the Monongahela National Forest. Areas of cooperation included the development of the *Hiking Guide*, the scheduling of extensive outings, and the balsam fir reforestation project. Other areas where there was a difference of opinion included the need for additional wilderness areas. But as Saville said in a 2006 interview, "There is no other organization that has been an advocate and a supporter of the Monongahela National Forest, over more issues, than the Conservancy." (See Chapter 5 for more on the balsam fir project, and Chapter 6 for more on the Friends of the Mon.)

In April 2007, however, Saville resigned as the Conservancy's Administrative Assistant, to devote full time to the Wilderness Campaign.

If Howard Zahniser can be considered the "father of the Wilderness Act of 1964," then in a strange way, his son Ed Zahniser, might be considered at least a catalyst, if not the father, of West Virginia wilderness in the new century. When the Highlands Conservancy met for its Spring Review in 2001, the theme was "Celebrating West Virginia's Wilderness" and Ed Zahniser was the evening speaker.

As noted above, Saville had already identified wilderness as poten-tially the next campaign for the Conservancy. He produced a 28-page tabloid that chronicled the Conservancy's wilderness battles, giving background on what was wilderness, summarized wilderness in bordering states, and looked at potential areas in West Virginia.

A resident of Shepherdstown, West Virginia, and a National Park Service writer and editor, Ed Zahniser reflected on wilderness and wild-ness in West Virginia. His talk was reprinted in the June 2001 *Highlands Voice.* As a lifelong wilderness activist, he reviewed the "wilderness move-ment" and reminded the audience, many of which had joined the Con-servancy after the early 1980s, that the West Virginia Highlands Conser-vancy had a storied part in that movement. Zahniser vividly described his father, Howard, an evangelist of wilderness, for an audience who had never met him, and most had never heard of him. Then he said:

> I know you have a lot on your agenda, with the Blackwater Canyon, mountaintop removal, and other important issues. "How can we work on wilderness and all this other stuff?" you may ask. Well, I believe that work for wilderness — working for eternity in the now — will inspire people. There are places on your forest that, except for mechanized travel, are already managed as wilderness. They need to be protected as wilderness.
>
> As Brian O'Donnell [of the Wilderness Support Center] says, Virginia has just succeeded with a great wilderness campaign in hard political times, and Pennsylvania is gearing up. Let's not let West Virginia be the missing link in what should be a regional drive for more wilderness designations.
>
> Ours is an errand into the West Virginia wilderness that none of us here tonight will see completed. Because we are working for eternity. Ally yourself with hope. Remember Ron Hardway writing in 1975 of your historic wilderness campaigns, "We have come of age as an organization." Yes, we have a wilderness genealogy. We are working for eternity – and the Wilderness Act campaign took only nine years. This is like a relay race, isn't it? Bob Marshall, Aldo Leopold, Olaus Murie, and Howard Zahniser did not live to see the Congress pass and the President sign the Wilderness Act. In fact, my father once said that creating a National Wilderness Preservation System was not even as important in itself as the fact that so many of us would one day take that step together. That step is now a 37-year journey – and the West Virginia Highlands Conservancy was in the thick of it by 1967.

So I challenge us, wilderness is our roots. Wilderness is our genealogy. Who else but the West Virginia Highlands Conservancy can and will do it here in West Virginia? We have wilderness in the blood. Let's go and re-imagine more designated wilderness on the land.

Several other factors would combine to fire up a new wilderness campaign, but Ed Zahniser certainly sounded the call.

One factor was a new generation of wilderness advocates, most of whom had not been involved in the earlier round of effort. Second, the national organizations, notably the Wilderness Society, through their Wilderness Support Center, the Sierra Club, and later the Campaign for America's Wilderness, obtained increased funding and made a renewed commitment to provide technical support to the grassroots citizen wilderness groups. And finally, in West Virginia the Monongahela National Forest was coming to the end of its 1985 Forest Plan and the window would open on consideration of potential wilderness areas once again as the release language expired.

In April 2002 the Highlands Conservancy joined the Friends of Allegheny Wilderness and the Wilderness Society to sponsor the West Virginia-Pennsylvania Wilderness and National Forest Planning Training and Volunteer Workshop. By the end of that weekend, a core group of Conservancy members had decided that the time was right for another West Virginia wilderness movement. They included veterans Helen McGinnis, recently returned to West Virginia after a twenty-five-year absence, Mary Wimmer, representing the West Virginia Chapter of the Sierra Club, Saville, representing the Conservancy, and Sierra Club member Beth Little, of Pocahontas County. Later Saville recruited additional workers, younger and less experienced, but committed wilderness advocates, primarily from West Virginia University and Shepherd University. (For a profile of Wimmer, see Chapter 6.)

In the August 2002 *Highlands Voice*, McGinnis reported on the April workshop. She explained that within the Monongahela, at least thirty areas needed to be evaluated. Some were leftovers from RARE II, some adjacent to already-designated areas, and still others were new candidates. Volunteers were needed to visit these areas and bring back their impressions. Saville wrote, "Wilderness Areas – What's It All About?" After reminding readers that true wilderness required congressional action, he explained that the Monongahela National Forest Plan revision process offered a perfect opportunity to become active. A broad coalition would be necessary, Saville said, if widespread public support, and therefore political support, were to be achieved.

That October Saville explained that the Forest Service had begun the plan revision process by issuing a call for comments on May 3, 2002. After the 90-day "scoping" period closed, 688 comments were tallied. Saville reported 630 were consistent with Conservancy positions, including "well over 500" specifically favoring increased wilderness designation. Now the forest planners would begin their research. And the Conservancy was cranking up its wilderness campaign.

Wimmer described the formation of the West Virginia Wilderness Coalition. The three founding organizations, the West Virginia Chapter of the Sierra Club, the Wilderness Society, and the Conservancy each appointed two representatives who became a working group. Each of the three groups would fund the Coalition equally, at approximately $20,000/each per year, and the Conservancy would serve as fiscal agent. The funds would support a staff coordinator, travel and office expenses. It was a big step for all three groups.

In November, a job announcement appeared for the position of "Wilderness Campaign Coordinator." The Conservancy, the West Virginia Chapter of the Sierra Club, and the Wilderness Society were listed "seeking a person with energy and organizational skills to work with volunteers, agencies, the public and other conservation staff to move our wilderness efforts forward." This was clearly an indication of major resources and a major organizational campaign for wilderness in West Virginia.

In *The Highlands Voice* of February 2003, Saville announced the hiring of Matt Keller as Wilderness Campaign Coordinator. He also reported on the formation of the Wilderness Coalition, consisting of the three organizations listed above. A steering committee was composed of the Sierra Club's Wimmer (the Chair) and Beth Little, the Wilderness Society's Fran Hunt and Brian O'Donnell, and the Conservancy's Saville and Bob Marshall.

Saville introduced Keller, who had won the position after a nation-wide search. He lived in Morgantown, with family across the state. A graduate of Ohio University, he held a master's degree in Geography, focused on wilderness. An avid outdoorsman, Sierra Club volunteer, and GIS technician, he seemed a perfect fit. As events unfolded, Keller would prove extremely significant to the wilderness campaign's efforts.

In contrast to previous wilderness campaigns in West Virginia, young paid professionals, not just volunteers, would staff this one.

In a 2006 interview, Wimmer said the hiring of Keller "was the best thing we ever did." The committee members had lots of experience in public advocacy, but Keller had talents they needed: an organizing ability and expertise in GIS and mapping. He shared their commitment to wilderness preservation.*

Beginning the following month, Keller provided a monthly "Wilderness Campaign Update" to *Voice* readers. According to his updates, Coalition volunteers were busy visiting potential areas, gathering data, meeting with state and federal officials, generating maps, and making presentations. Clearly their goal was to have wilderness areas researched and ready by the time the Forest Service's planning process opened for public input.

In her 2006 interview, Wimmer discussed the differences between this Mon Plan revision process and the one in which she had been so involved in 1985. This time, instead of being welcomed into the Forest Service offices in Elkins and mentored as earlier MNF planners had done, she found meetings very tough. In this round the Forest Planner seemed not really interested in public involvement, saw little justification for wilderness, and she said, "made us feel like we were doing something bad." By contrast to the 1985 MNF leaders, she said, "If Gil Churchill [Forest Planner] and Ralph Mumme [Forest Supervisor] had been there, they would have been so proud of what we were doing. [This round] whenever we went in, current Supervisor Clyde Thompson would play Devil's advocate –every single time."

Back in 1985, Mumme had told someone that the conservation comments were "the quality of a dissertation," a high compliment to Dr. Wimmer. She said they made her and others feel valuable to the process. This time it was different. Now it was more like the national wilderness people said she should expect. By her own admission, she had been "spoiled" in the first round. Now it was less collaborative, less respectful, and more confrontational.

Beginning in 2000, the Highlands Conservancy had pointedly upgraded its outings program. As discussed in Chapter 6, this effort came

---

*Since Chapter 6 focuses on the Monongahela National Forest, for all things except wilderness, the revision of the plan might logically fit there. However, most of the Conservancy's interests in this round of planning concentrated on wilderness, hence the discussion remains in this chapter, whose focus is wilderness.

to be called "West Virginia Mountain Odyssey: Outings, Education, and Beyond." The program had an obvious two-fold purpose: To attract new members through providing organized hiking, canoeing, and other expeditions, primarily into the Monongahela National Forest, and secondly, to take people into threatened or areas of special significance. The potential additions to the wilderness system fell into this latter category and beginning in 2002, the listing of outings clearly gave preference to these areas. As a follow-up, trip reports appeared regularly in *The Highlands Voice,* often accompanied with beautiful photographs. Together these reports and their photographs increased awareness and interest in many potential wilderness areas.

As the Forest Service conducted its studies for the revised forest plan, the Wilderness Coalition continued to research areas and build public support. In July 2004 the *Voice* reprinted a *Charleston Gazette* article by Rick Steelhammer. According to his sources, the Forest Service planners had identified fourteen areas, encompassing 138,500 acres, qualifying for further wilderness study. Another sixteen were rejected as not meeting the qualifications. Some names harked back to the RARE II process twenty years earlier. In the qualifying group were Big Draft, Canaan Loop, Cheat Mountain, Cranberry Expansion, Dolly Sods Expansion, Middle Mountain, Roaring Plains, Seneca Creek, and Upper Shavers Fork.

To reinforce the need for patience and remembering how long congressionally-protected wilderness areas often took to achieve that protection, the September 2004 *Voice* headlined, "Wilderness Act Turns Forty." Commemorating the September 3, 1964, signing by President Johnson of the Wilderness Act, the article brought the system up to date, with 105 million acres designated nationally and more pending. Readers were reminded of West Virginia Senator Laird's role as a co-sponsor, of Congressman Hechler's sponsorship of the Eastern Wilderness Areas Act in 1975, and of Senator Byrd's critically important maneuvering to save the Cranberry bill in 1983.

A month later, the first ever, full-color front page of *The Highlands Voice,* featured a photograph of a backpacker on a rocky outcrop (the same as on the cover of this volume). Articles on recent outings to Seneca Creek, Dolly Sods, Otter Creek, and Roaring Plains appeared. A supplement to this issue was a tabloid produced by the Wilderness Coalition that celebrated the fortieth anniversary of the Wilderness Act. It included a report on the Wilderness Advocacy Week, held in Washington, D.C., September 17-22 and attended by several Conservancy members. During the event five national awards for wilderness leadership were made and two went to West Virginians, Senator Robert C. Byrd and Mary Wimmer.

Almost buried in all the color photography was the Wilderness Coalition's list of recommended wilderness areas. First starting with thirty roadless areas, the list had been reduced to eighteen for further study. After eliminating several for various reasons, the remaining fifteen, called "A Vision for a Wild Mon," recommended areas, encompassing 143,000 acres that sounded familiar. They included expansions to Dolly Sods and Cranberry, Roaring Plains, North Fork Mountain, Cheat Mountain, Seneca Creek, East Fork of the Greenbrier, Upper Shavers Fork, Middle Mountain, Spice Run, Big Draft, Turkey Mountain, Little Allegheny Mountain and two different Laurels, one a Fork and one a Run. Now came the public education and advocacy stage to get them into the pending Monongahela National Forest Plan.

In December, Keller reported that fifty businesses and twenty organizations had endorsed the Coalition's proposals. There had been regular meetings with the congressional delegation to keep them informed. The state DNR had also been consulted extensively. While the near-goal was to have these areas included in the Forest Plan, the ultimate decision on wilderness designation remained with the Congress, so the plan's recommendations would only be an intermediate step.

Sometime in the late 1980s the Highlands Conservancy put up its first web site. Now the web was a major outreach and communication tool. The Wilderness Coalition, having been born in the new century, immediately went online. Thanks to the inspired photography of Jonathan Jessup, both sites shared his photographic images with the world. If a picture was really worth a thousand words, a book this size was saved by his highly praised photography.

As 2005 began another anniversary was noted, the thirtieth anniversary of the January 3, 1975, signing of the Eastern Wilderness Areas Act, which established West Virginia's first two wilderness areas. In January's *Voice*, McGinnis and Sundquist recounted some of their early experiences.

By June 2005 the grassroots organizing was in full gear. The Wilderness Coalition sponsored a weekend workshop that month on Spruce Knob to educate and train more people in the skills needed for public advocacy.

In August's *Voice* it was announced, "Draft Plan for Monongahela National Forest Hits the Streets." The subtitle was equally important:

"This month is the launch of one of the biggest conservation efforts in the history of West Virginia to help protect the Monongahela National Forest and we need your help." Anticipating far fewer recommended wilderness areas than the Coalition proposed, the *Voice* was filled with photos and reports of the best candidates. A new staffer, Harrison Case, had been hired as Outreach Coordinator, supplementing Keller's efforts. The full-court press was on!

Case was already in print by August. He reported a new DVD was available, hosting a "house party" was a recommended tactic, and naturally letters to the Forest Service and the congressional delegation were critical.

By October 2005's *Highlands Voice*, a full-page poster was included titled, "The Future of the Monongahela National Forest is in Your Hands!" The text stated that the Draft Forest Plan had recommended "Alternative 2," which promoted logging and road building in protected areas. Most wilderness areas proposed by the Coalition were excluded. The Coalition recommended people support "Alternative 3," which it described as "a balanced proposal that would permanently protect the Mon's wildest places." The Coalition actually recommended more than "Alternative 3," namely adding an expansion of Dolly Sods, and new areas of North Fork Mountain, Lower Laurel Fork, Roaring Plains, Little Allegheny Mountain, Upper Shavers Fork and Laurel Run. Other recommended citizen comments dealt with no increases (as Forest Service wanted) of logging and clearcutting, and primitive management of water and backcountry areas. Public comments were to be accepted until November 14, 2005.

In the same issue, Case reported on a major lobbying trip to Washington in September:

> At this critical time for the future of the Monongahela National Forest, a diverse group of West Virginians trekked to our nation's capital to express the broad support for protecting the Mountain State's special places.
>
> Volunteers from each of West Virginia's Congressional districts visited the offices of Representatives Shelley Moore Capito, Alan Mollohan and Nick Rahall and Senators Robert Byrd and Jay Rockefeller during the West Virginia Wilderness Coalition's inaugural West Virginia Wilderness Week in Washington, September 26–28.
>
> "We stressed the importance of a good Forest Plan and eventually a Wilderness bill," said Brent Rowley of Shepherdstown. "But more

importantly, we shared our personal reasons for wanting more wild areas permanently protected on the Mon: our passions for hiking, photography and cross-country skiing; our desire to keep the watersheds clean; our belief that West Virginia can build an economy based on appreciation and use of our natural resources, not destruction of them."

On Tuesday evening, the West Virginia Wilderness Coalition presented the Washington premiere of *A Vision for a Wild Mon*, featuring Jonathan Jessup's photography, the music of Wolf Creek Sessions and narration by Larry Groce. The video, which is also being shown at dozens of Wild Mon House Parties across the state, drew a large crowd of Congressional staffers, national conservation group professionals and friends of the Mon from across the DC area. Congressmen Mollohan and Rahall also attended the reception at the Capitol, and spoke to the crowd about their past, present and future efforts to protect West Virginia's forests. Morgantown musicians Chris Haddox, Jim Truman and Corey Bonasso provided old-time music for the celebration.

Participants came from across the state and from a wide variety of backgrounds. Students from Shepherd University, Fairmont State University and West Virginia University joined representatives from Christians for the Mountains, West Virginia Chapter of the Sierra Club, Greenbrier River Watershed Association and the West Virginia Highlands Conservancy.

"It was great to see so many people coming together to celebrate West Virginia's best-loved areas," said Dee Quaranto, who made the trip from her home in Monongalia County. "I met rock climbers from South Carolina who use the National Forest every year and folks from as far away as California who recently discovered the unique areas on the Mon. I think a lot of people who have worked on Wilderness issues elsewhere were surprised to hear that we have had such success working with both the Forest Service and our Congressional delegation."

Wilderness Coalition campaign coordinator Matt Keller explained that the week was the result of cooperation by a number of groups and individuals.

"Because of the success of the Wilderness campaign so far and the prospects for protecting some of the East's last remaining wild areas, we were able to secure funding from a national organization, the American Wilderness Coalition, for this lobby week," Keller said. "The Wilderness Society, Campaign for America's Wilderness and all of our state-level organizations came together to make this effort a success. But most important of all it was our volunteers, who set up the meetings, brought the message to their representatives and showed Washington what makes West Virginia so special."

From this article, a few important differences were evident that contrast with the Conservancy's past wilderness campaigns. For one, a true coalition had been formed. It wasn't the Conservancy, with added support from other groups. It was a new group with shared governance. Second, outside funding had been received. The Conservancy had obtained grant funds and the two other partners had invested funds of their own. Third, college students were widely involved, although this had been true of the Cranberry battle. Fourth, a paid project staff of two was coordinating the grassroots effort. For better or worse, the level of effort needed to be greater than volunteers alone could provide. And perhaps most important, virtually all of the congressional delegation were either actively supporting, or at least not opposing, this new wilderness campaign. The concept of wilderness was now respectable.

Another full page of the October *Voice* was a reproduction of a proclamation by Governor Joe Manchin III, signed on September 29, 2005, declaring September as Wilderness Month in West Virginia. The presentation ceremony in the State Capitol was filled with Conservancy, Sierra Club, Council of Churches, and Citizen Action Group members.

By the time of the 2005 Fall Review, the Wilderness Coalition was ready for a two-day strategizing session. Next steps were carefully discussed. Staff members of the Wilderness Society, the Campaign for America's Wilderness, and veteran volunteers from across West Virginia discussed a phone-bank blitz, securing business and state legislators' endorsements, writing op ed pieces for influential newspapers, and many other ideas. Everything was intended to flood the Forest Service planners with pro-wilderness comments before November 14, and, longer-term, build strong support with the congressional delegation for the needed legislation regardless of the Forest Plan's recommendation.

In December's and January's *Voice* issues, Keller reported more than 15,000 comments were received by the Forest Service, 90% favoring Alternative 3 or other wilderness. While a complete analysis had not yet been completed, Keller said the new emphasis would focus on the congressional delegation.

Ironically, while waiting for the Forest Service to tabulate, and more important, consider the impact of, these 15,000 comments, the West Virginia Highlands Conservancy announced a new initiative with the

Monongahela National Forest. Declaring itself, "We're Friends of the Mon," Saville led a new cooperative emphasis, bringing under one umbrella the many ways the Conservancy and the Forest Service had worked together, and at other times, been in conflict. (See Chapter 6.)

As 2006 progressed, *The Highlands Voice* continued to list schedules of outings into many proposed wilderness areas and print post-trip reports, often illustrated by Jonathan Jessup's photography. Another Wilderness Workshop was scheduled for June.

In the September/October 2006 *Voice*, Bob Handley reported that Congressman Nick Joe Rahall II joined a group of wilderness activists for a first-hand hike in the Big Draft area near Lewisburg. He continued:

> Our trek started "off trail" following a vague path up through the woods on top of Gunpowder Ridge. There was a short, very steep section that led up to a flat ridge top with large oaks and hickory trees and many wild flowers. There was one place where a black bear had recently ripped an old log apart looking for beetles and grubs. There were also signs of white tailed deer all along our path, but no snakes.
>
> This part of our trek being "off trail" had no markers or beaten path. We just followed the narrow ridge top scrambling at times over fallen logs and occasional rock outcrops. After a little over a mile, the ridge abruptly ended and we made our way down a long, steep slope through open woods to an established trail along Anthony Creek. Nick turned out to be an accomplished hiker. He's quite a guy — smart, easygoing, adaptable, not complaining, an all round neat hiking companion.
>
> When hiking "off trail" the chances of meeting other people is slight, but we were on a marked trail now and headed for the Blue Hole, a beautiful swimming hole on lower Anthony Creek. There were a few people already there, either in the water or on the sandy beach. Three of our party enjoyed a dip, but Nick had unfortunately left his swimsuit in his van so could only watch and talk to the other people (who were surprised to meet a US Congressman in the Wilderness). Soon we headed back down the trail toward the grove of large old growth hemlocks and white pine near the Greenbrier River. Then we followed the trail up the river and across the bridge to our cars. Thus our hike ended – a very enjoyable afternoon in a very small part of WVWC's proposed Big Draft Wilderness area.
>
> The proposed Big Draft area is small at 5,300 acres, but encompasses eight miles of Anthony Creek with its great fishing and some very rugged terrain. One has no difficulty finding quiet solitude or

miles of hiking trails all within five miles of White Sulphur Springs. Big Draft is one of the proposed wilderness areas located in the Greenbrier Valley. The others are Spice Run and Middle Mountain on the Greenbrier/Pocahontas County line, the East Fork of the Greenbrier north of Thornwood in Pocahontas County, and Laurel Run and Little Allegheny Mountain east of Neola in Greenbrier County. At this time there is no wilderness in the Greenbrier Valley part of the Mon (more than a quarter of the total National Forest area.). WV Wilderness Coalition has proposed nine other areas in the Mon that are mostly in the northern highlands.

The Southern Group of WVWC is working to get more recognition of the six Greenbrier Valley areas. This hike with Congressman Rahall gave him a chance to get out into one of our proposed Wilderness areas; to see and experience first hand some of the wilds the WVWC and our Congressional Delegation has been working to preserve for future generations. Wilderness also, if allowed to grow undisturbed, reduces flood crests, enhances the quality of our drinking water, improves our air by removing carbon (as carbon dioxide) and releasing oxygen, provides better hunting and fishing, hiking, camping, swimming, white water paddling, horse back riding, photography, and nature study of all sorts. ("Each forested acre takes up roughly 4.5 tons of carbon a year.") In general wilderness is good for tourism, which is the lifeblood of many towns in our beautiful valley.

Congressman Rahall indicated that next year he will work to introduce and help pass legislation that will very likely include more proposed areas than the new (soon to be released) Monongahela Forest Management Plan recommends. This has been the case for wilderness legislation in many other states in the last few years. President Bush has signed all of the Wilderness bills presented to him.

The proposed wilderness areas involve only public (Mon Forest) land and when declared wilderness (by Congress) does not affect any private land (other than to make it more valuable).

Finally, nearly a year after the comment period opened, the Forest Service released the Final Monongahela National Forest Management Plan. The October 2006 *Highlands Voice* ran this headline, "Forest Service ignores 13,000 public comments in its final Management Plan. Contact West Virginia's Congressional Delegation and ask them to support wilderness legislation!" The article reported:

> The Final Monongahela National Forest Management Plan released
> on September 18th, the U.S. Forest Service has ignored ...the record

number of nearly 13,000 individuals who commented on the draft plan, and over 90% firmly rejected the Forest Service's 'preferred' Alternative 2 which recommends only a small amount of wilderness designations to Congress and opens up several of our backcountry areas that qualify for this designation to logging and road building. The public almost unanimously favored Alternative 3 and/or the West Virginia Wilderness Coalition's Citizens' Wilderness Proposal, both of which recommend much more wilderness designation to Congress and protect the most important wild areas on the Mon.

Fortunately, the decision to protect wilderness, which only happens through federal legislation, is in the hands of West Virginia's Congressional Delegation. They need to hear from you that the public's voice is not being heard by the Forest Service and that you want them to introduce legislation that goes above and beyond the insufficient recommendations in the MNF's final plan. Please write a letter to both Senators Byrd and Rockefeller as well as to your Representative who will be key in protecting areas that the Forest Service is ignoring. Be sure to mention areas like Seneca Creek, East Fork of Greenbrier, Spice Run, Big Draft, and the Dolly Sods Expansion, all left out of the Final Plan's wilderness recommendations.

Here are some talking points you could include:

• The U.S. Forest Service has ignored the overwhelming will of the public in its final management plan, and West Virginia needs you to fix this situation by sponsoring legislation that will protect all deserving areas as designated wilderness.
• It is critical that we protect not only the areas recommended by the Forest Service, but also areas that the citizens' groups and the public at large have identified as important and in need of protection. Key areas like Seneca Creek, East Fork of Greenbrier, the Dolly Sods Expansion, Spice Run and Big Draft have been ignored by the Forest Service, but must be protected permanently.
• The Forest Service plan does not recommend any wilderness in the Greenbrier watershed, which currently has no designated wilderness and is a source of drinking water for many West Virginians. The 24,000-acre Seneca Creek Area would protect the entire headwaters of one of the best trout streams in the East. And the Dolly Sods Expansion would protect Red Creek's headwaters as well as reduce user pressure on the popular existing Dolly Sods Wilderness.
• Protected public land like wilderness helps diversify and stabilize economies by attracting and retaining new businesses, residents, and a

local workforce, in addition to generating travel and tourism, one of the fastest growing sectors of West Virginia's economy.
• Wilderness provides unparalleled primitive and traditional outdoor recreation opportunities, such as hunting, fishing, hiking, camping, horseback riding, bird watching, whitewater rafting, kayaking, skiing, snowshoeing, and much more. Be sure to mention what activities, if any, you participate in on the Mon.

Readers were encouraged to send a letter or email to their congressional decision-makers, even if they had written to them about wilderness in the past. One letter copied to the senators, your representative and the governor would be very powerful, the article concluded.

The Fall Review in 2006 was back at the Cheat Mountain Club on the banks of Shavers Fork. And again that year, the Wilderness Campaign was at full throttle. On Saturday, in the place of the traditional set of hikes, tours, and other outdoor activities into threatened areas, the program dealt with grassroots organizing for Wilderness. Doug Scott, Policy Director of the Campaign for America's Wilderness and a frequent visitor to West Virginia, was the guest of honor.

Scott began the morning session by reviewing the history of "the wilderness movement." He felt it was now stronger, broader, and more energetic than he had seen in his forty years of wilderness work. He reminded those in attendance that from the first introduction of the Wilderness Act to the present, that West Virginia had always been a critical player. West Virginia brought three essential elements, Scott continued, the Monongahela National Forest with its history of stopping clearcutting and two of the first eastern Wilderness areas; a "dream" congressional delegation, with seniority, committee chairmanships, and bipartisanship, with a track record of Wilderness support; and a group of practical and dedicated activists. Scott praised the West Virginia group by saying "you are happy warriors," referring to Senator Humphrey's famous epithet.

The Saturday evening forum, also a Fall Review tradition, had two parts. To begin, Forest Supervisor Clyde Thompson and his staff presented the recently released Final Forest Plan, explaining the rationale for each major recommendation, including a minimum of wilderness protection. The usual interaction, polite disagreement, and technical dialogue followed.

Then it was Scott's turn again, this time a presentation, called "Practical Idealism in Building our National Wilderness Preservation System."

With Thompson in the front row, Scott reviewed the history of wilderness preservation, emphasizing its origin within the Forest Service, beginning in 1924. Scott stressed the bipartisan nature of wilderness legislation, from the initial congressional sponsorship of Rep. Saylor on through the current Bush administration. He discussed the shifts in Forest Service policy on eastern areas and noted it was the Staggers-Hechler bill in 1970 that produced the "purity" argument that Congress repudiated with passage of the Eastern Wilderness Areas Act of 1975.

Reflecting on his forty years of experience fighting for wilderness legislation, Scott concluded with several lessons:

1) Organize – where the wilderness is
2) Learn about rural concerns — by listening to rural citizens
3) Align wilderness with rural aspirations, like the economy and quality of life values
4) Build broad coalitions
5) Accommodate and compromise – where possible

He didn't take time to apply these to the current campaign, but if he had, they would have fit well. The West Virginia Wilderness Coalition had organized throughout the counties included within the Monongahela, had reached out to those rural residents and connected with their interests, had built an extremely broad coalition, and had compromised in boundary recommendations to accommodate other user groups.

While the final conclusion to this campaign was yet to be determined in 2007, the West Virginia Wilderness Coalition, strongly supported and co-managed by activists within the Highlands Conservancy, would remain politically active and the outcome was likely to be additional congressionally-designated wilderness areas in the Monongahela National Forest. Certainly the Democratic take-over of Congress in the November 2006 mid-term elections was certain to help. Senator Byrd assumed the Chairmanship of the Senate Appropriations Committee and Rep. Rahall became Chairman the House Natural Resources Committee. Within a day of the election, Rahall announced his intention to support "more pristine lands in West Virginia."

Sources:

Anderson, Fred, interview, November 7, 2005
Burrell, Bob, interview, June 21, 2006, and correspondence
Charleston Daily Mail, May 5, 1970

Cutler, Rupert, correspondence

Elkinton, Dave, personal observations at Fall Review, October 21, 2006, at Cheat Mountain Club, Cheat Bridge, W. Va., and at Wilderness Coalition meeting, October 24, 2005, at Cheat Mountain Club, Cheat Bridge, W.Va.

Frome, Michael, *Battle for the Wilderness*4 (New York: Praeger Publishers, Inc., 1974)

The Highlands Voice, articles by Stark Biddle, Bob Burrell, Harrison Case, Dave Elkinton, Linda Cooper Elkinton, Jeanette Fitzwilliams, Larry George, Bob Handley, Tom King, Keith Kirk, Matt Keller, George Langford, Leslee McCarty, Helen McGinnis, Ernie Nester, Dave Saville, Bruce Sundquist, Mary Wimmer, Frank Young, Ed Zahniser, and Nick Zvegintzov, among others.

Johnson, Skip, "Otter Creek Prospec ting Put on Shelf," *The Charleston Gazette*, August 23, 1972

King, Tom, interview, March 30, 2006

McGinnis, Helen, interview, July 7, 2006, and correspondence

McGinnis, Helen, article in Elkins *Inter-Mountain*, reprinted in *The Highland Voice*, August 1970

McNeel, Bill, correspondence

Saville, Dave, ed., *Celebrating West Virginia's Wilderness*, supplement to *The Highlands Voice*, issued in advance of the Spring Review 2001

Saville, Dave, interviews, June 21 and November 8, 2006, and correspondence

Searls, Tom, article in *The Charleston Gazette*

Scott, Doug, *The Enduring Wilderness: Protecting Our Natural Heritage Through the Wilderness Act* (Golden, Colorado: Fulcrum Publishing, 2004)

Smith, Robert Leo, article in Morgantown *Dominion Post*, May 17, 1970 (reprinted in *The Highland Voice*)

Steelhammer, Rick, article in *The Charleston Gazette*

Sundquist, Bruce, interview,, June 22, 2006

Wimmer, Mary, interview, November 8, 2006

Chapter Three
Free-flowing and Clean Rivers:
Fighting dams at Royal Glen, Rowlesburg, Swiss, Stonewall Jackson, and the New, and preserving Shavers Fork

Even before the official organization of the West Virginia Highlands Conservancy, conservationists from several states had strongly opposed the proposal by the United States Army Corps of Engineers for the Royal Glen Dam on the South Branch of the Potomac River near Petersburg. Forty miles to the west, the Rowlesburg Dam was proposed for the Cheat River. Both would eliminate the free-flowing, recreational rivers loved by canoeists. Both were classic struggles between downstream (out-of-state) interests needing either water or flood relief or both and upstream farmers and other landholders who did not share these problems. The conservationists quickly lent their expertise as lawyers, researchers and politically savvy organizers to the upstream interests and formed a common bond.

Within the next five years, the Conservancy would fight to preserve many of the state's most scenic rivers. These included the West Fork River from the Stonewall Jackson Dam (which was ultimately built), the Gauley River from the Swiss Dam, and the Greenbrier River from a series of dams above Marlinton. The Conservancy spearheaded West Virginia's part of the national movement to bring an end to the high-rise dams of the Corps of Engineers.

Within one year of its official birth in January 1967, the Conservancy had established a Scenic Rivers Committee, co-chaired by Lovell (Lou) Greathouse and Mrs. John (Carolyn) Killoran. Other members included Bob Dennis, Executive Director of the Potomac Basin Center, Jean

Rodman, of the Pittsburgh Climbers, George Blackburn, Mrs. John P. Jones, Randall Atkins, Steve Moler, from the West Virginia Department of Natural Resources, Bob Harrigan, Conservancy co-founder and representative of the Canoe Cruisers Association in DC, Mrs. Kyle (Eleanor) Bush, of Philippi, and Robert Burrell, of Morgantown.

At the January 1968 Mid-Winter Workshop, the committee's report set the tone for future river conservation work by recommending that:

1.) Letters from <u>individuals</u> be sent to State Legislators in Charleston urging their acceptance of the concurrent resolution concerning scenic rivers.

2.) The West Virginia Highlands Conservancy pass the resolution in favor of the concurrent resolution on scenic rivers and forward it to members of the State Legislature.

3.) Support and work for strengthening amendments to the Federal Wild and Scenic Rivers Bill soon to be considered by the House of Representatives.

4.) There be future appointment of local committees to carry forward with the inventory and promotion of scenic rivers in West Virginia. In this connection the Subgroup on Scenic Rivers took the following action:

  a. The appointment of Bob Harrigan and Creed Sions to develop, particularly in the Grant County area, public understanding and support of scenic rivers status for [the] Smoke Hole segment of the South Branch of the Potomac River.

  b. The appointment of Mrs. John Killoran, Mrs. John Paul Jones, and Mrs. Kyle Bush as a committee nucleus to enlist their support for the preservation of scenic rivers, with particular reference to the South Branch of the Potomac, Smoke Hole section.

5.) The West Virginia Highlands Conservancy firmly opposes the construction of any dam which would back water into the Smoke Hole or Hopewell Canyons. The Conservancy should further urge the exploration of alternative possibilities for recreational development and flood control at other nearby and existing impoundments.

Following the January 1968 Workshop, the Scenic Rivers Sub-Committee published a series of purple ditto newsletters, beginning with Volume 1, Number 1, dated March 1968. [This was exactly one year before the initial issue of *The Highlands Voice* would appear.] The Editor/

writer was Bob Burrell, who later would become the *Voice's* first Editor. The opening paragraph read: "This little blurb will inaugurate an attempt to keep us all informed and in contact between meeting dates so that we may continue our work begun at the Mid-Winter Workshop."

Burrell then announced the departure of co-chair Lou Greathouse, Recreation Planner for the State of West Virginia, who had accepted a similar position in Georgia. President Tom King had apparently asked Burrell to assume Greathouse's duties as Rivers leader.

Not being a founding member of the Conservancy and perhaps not widely known even to members of the rivers committee, Burrell introduced himself:

> I am Bob Burrell, an adopted West Virginian, living in Morgantown. I am active in the Izaak Walton League and the West Virginia Wildwater Association. I am also a member of the Canoe Cruisers Association and I spend most of my free time camping or canoeing, which might explain why I am interested in this committee.

The remaining paragraphs of this two-page newsletter discussed the status of both federal and state legislation pertaining to rivers. Burrell concluded by inviting participation in the annual Petersburg White Water Festival in April. In an interesting signal of future Conservancy interest, he invited those not involved in the Petersburg slalom races on Sunday to join him on a section of Shavers Fork. [Although Shaver's was more commonly spelled with an apostrophe in the early years, the more modern Shavers (without apostrophe) became common after 1980.] "We have selected Shavers Fork since it is: 1) one of the rivers on the West Virginia Scenic Rivers Resolution, 2) suitable for beginners, yet very attractive for the more experienced, and 3) very near the hub of activities at the North Fork.

By the second issue in April, Burrell announced the Second Annual Tygart's Valley River Tour in early May. This trip focused on the Middle Fork of the Tygart, which Burrell called "my favorite West Virginia river" including Valley Falls and the "Arden run." He concluded the issue by describing how a group from Uniontown, Pennsylvania enlisted residents along the Cheat River to help plan a "huge recreational complex." Burrell wrote, "Are there lessons to be learned here? Can we find something here that we can use? Might not this be a way to avoid some of the problems we are facing? Are West Virginians amenable to such a plan?"

By the seventh issue of the newsletter in December 1968 Burrell was ready for a year-end review. First the bad news: Hominy Falls and Farmington mining disasters, Barron administration scandals, and an allegation of gubernatorial candidate James Sprouse making a killing in land speculation near Seneca Rocks. Then the good news: in West Virginia new advances in public awareness of air and water pollution, strip mine laws appeared to be working, the biggest yet Petersburg White Water Weekend was held, plus a strong Tygart River Tour, the Royal Glen Dam was still not a reality (neither is the approved Rowlesburg Dam on the Cheat), Shavers Fork remained the most scenic river in the state, and the Coal and Kanawha were actually being cleaned up and improved.

Then the meat of the issue followed: Burrell described mining threats to the Cranberry and Williams Rivers, a proposed dam at Swiss, and a West Virginia Department of Natural Resources (DNR) proposal on scenic rivers in the state that was woefully inadequate. He concluded by inviting attendance at the Conservancy's Mid-Winter Workshop February 1-2, 1969, at Blackwater Falls State Park.

With these seven issues of a rivers committee newsletter over a nine-month span, it was not surprising that Conservancy President Tom King wanted Burrell to inaugurate the first issue of *The Highlands Voice,* which came out in March 1969. He would serve as editor for two years, then continue writing a column "Overlook" until 1978.

Shavers Fork – The Early Years

For a variety of reasons including location, wild character, multiplicity of challenges, ownership patterns, and others, the Shavers Fork of the Cheat River has remained a constant issue over the forty-year history of the Conservancy. It was selected for recreational outings, offering a wide variety of levels of boating experience. As discussed in Chapter 4, the construction of the Corridor H bridge over Shavers Fork became the end point to the route east from Elkins, eventually forcing a retrenchment to a northern route for the highway. The presence of the Bowden National Fish Hatchery on the banks of Shavers Fork, which depended on the cold, pure water of two nearby springs, became a critical tipping point in the Corridor H struggle.

For background, Shavers Fork begins near the present site of the Snowshoe Mountain ski resort complex in Pocahontas County and flows north through the Monongahela National Forest, crossing private land near Bowden, then re-entering the Forest, until it meets the Black Fork to form the Cheat River at Parsons. During most of its length it flows across public land and has therefore been afforded a measure of protection that other rivers have not. However, the "upper Shavers Fork," the first seventeen miles, were owned until 1988 by the Mower Lumber Company and managed for resource extraction, both timber and coal. The struggle between environmentalists, led by the Conservancy, and the extractive industry, Mower and its sub-contractors, would consume many years.

The third issue of the new *Highlands Voice* in June 1969 included an article aptly titled, "Can Shavers Fork Be Saved?" Because no author credit is given, it can be assumed that Burrell wrote it. The article reviewed the fragile ecology of Shavers Fork, including its shallow soils and naturally low ph levels. Because of Mower Lumber Company's ownership of 60,000 acres of surface and mineral rights in the headwaters and its past and future plans for logging and mining, there had been major acid and siltation problems that the state DNR had been ineffective in controlling. The article stated that, "the installation of a coal washer, if allowed, would be the final blow." It concluded:

> Bald Knob above Cass and the headwaters of Shavers Fork not too long ago was considered a wilderness. The only people that could get into this area were backpackers and anglers willing to walk several miles. Native brook trout abounded in the pools only last summer. Now you can drive all the way up on Lumber Company roads for 25 cents a car. On Memorial Day pleasure automobiles and Hondas were all over the place. Anybody want to take bets on whether there will be any native brook trout by the end of the summer?
>
> We pour money into state and federal governments who in turn pour trout in at one end while powerful, private interests pour mud and acid in from the other. Just who is in charge here anyway? Shavers Fork? Oh, it's a nice stream to canoe, but I wouldn't want to fall in it.

By the time the next *Voice* article appeared about Shavers Fork eighteen months later, in December 1970, the Conservancy's plate of issues was overflowing. During these months, the Conservancy had been active in proposing Dolly Sods and Otter Creek for Wilderness, even obtaining a court order to stop mine prospecting in Otter Creek (see Chapter 2), testifying at hearings on the Blue Ridge hydro project proposed on the New River, monitoring the proposal for a dam on the Gauley at Swiss, and most recently, responding to the Davis Power Project proposal for

Canaan Valley (See Chapter 5.) Despite all these issues requiring the organization's attention, Burrell would not forget Shavers Fork.

Burrell put his "An Open Letter to David Francis" on the first page of the December 1970 *Voice*. (Francis was the outspoken president of the Linan Smokeless Coal Company and the Princess Coal Company.) Burrell reviewed Francis' company's proposals to mine on the upper Shavers Fork and in the Cranberry Back Country. He rebutted Francis' public statements casting political motivations on the DNR mining regulatory staff that had denied his mining permit applications. Then Burrell expressed the now-classic approach the Conservancy members would take in developing their policy positions and ultimately a public awareness campaign:

> Neither I nor the West Virginia Highlands Conservancy can at this time reject or endorse your proposal. We cannot evaluate the technical aspects of your proposal only on the basis of your press releases, and many similar demands on our environment have prevented our personal inspection thus far. All we know is what we read in the newspapers, and the Highlands Conservancy doesn't formulate positions on that basis. We will be observing you objectively in the months to come. We will form a field study team to look into the matter, deeply. Sportsmen familiar with the area have already contacted us. This winter our hikers and backpackers will familiarize themselves intimately with the area. This spring when the water is high and beautiful, expert whitewater boaters will be in the area. We will be consulting civil engineers, water treatment experts, wildlife biologists, and others with expertise on the matter. If things are as you say, you have nothing to worry about. If your plans are compatible with other things of equal or greater value in the area, we will publicly say so. After gathering as much information as possible, we will attempt to present what we believe would be the public's view of your project, for we do not believe the public's view should be molded and shaped by a one-sided public relations campaign.

On January 30, 1971, Burrell was elected the second president of the West Virginia Highlands Conservancy. Shavers Fork was still very prominent in the news and the Conservancy's new leader was one of its strongest public advocates.

Another was Conservancy member and Baltimore fisherman **Bill Bristor**. In correspondence in 2006, Burrell remembered Bristor:

Good Lord, what a character! WWII bombardier, shot down over Germany, spent rest of war as a P.O.W. Worked as personnel chief for Ma Bell in Baltimore. I guess he called me about Shavers Fork after having seen something in the *Voice.* Since he got free phoning privileges with the phone company, I heard from him several times a week. He and wife Alice were consummate fly fisherfolk. Somehow he discovered the "Fish for Fun" section of Shavers Fork and thought he had stumbled on to the lost graveyard of the elephants! He traveled to SF many times a year always staying at Dabney Kisner's restaurant and motel nearby. We eventually met and were drawn to each other by a mutual sense of rowdy humor. Later I would travel to Baltimore to visit them and we would get up early to drive to the Blackwater NWR on the eastern shore to bird watch and eat crabs. Bill would invite big city sports page editors, outdoor writers, and even book authors (Lefty Crays comes to mind) to see the wonderful asset of Shavers Fork and its attributes as well as those of WV appeared in many an eastern newspaper as a result. Bill never killed a fish and returned many HUGE rainbows and goldens to the river that other fishermen would kill for.

His home was the same way. He refused to kill spiders that set up shop in his home. When he encountered a turtle trying to cross a highway, he always stopped, holding up traffic if necessary, and shepherded the creature safely to the side. Every time he and Alice made some guacamole, they would try to germinate the seed. If it did, they planted it. Each seedling was lovingly cared for and each grew and grew, some 6, 7, 8' or more high. Fall and spring were big deals in their households. It was a labor of love to carry all of these potted trees from their back yard to their basement in the fall and vice versa in the spring (complete with spider webs)! They called it the Bristor National Forest and clear-cutting was forbidden! As you approached their house driving down the street, it was easy to pick out their house. It was the one in which the unpruned shrubbery hung over onto the sidewalk, forcing pedestrians to take to the street for a detour. Their living room was exciting. No flat surface was empty, each being covered with stacks of magazines, newspapers, letters, photo albums, etc. The walls were covered with photos of exotic memorabilia such as photos of well-known people holding up great fish before returning to the river, Bill's WW II silk scarf, a piece of fuselage with bullet holes in it, and various other equally conversation-generating esoterica. Once, Alice was taking groceries into the house from her car and noticed some things moved around and even missing, so she called the police. When the cop came he said, "They sure made a mess, didn't they?" Alice did not want to tell him that this was the way the place looked like ALL the time. Bill had some health problems even as early as the late 80s. I lost track of him when I moved to NC and I googled him last summer to discover we had lost him a few years ago. I don't know where Alice is. [In 2006, she was still a Conservancy member.]

Burrell added, "Bill died December 7, 1999 (I think he would have liked the coincidence) and is buried in the Baltimore National Cemetery."

Bristor was quoted in the *Voice* in the April 1971 issue in a verbatim dialogue of his testimony in support of the denial of a permit for a controversial deep mine on Shavers Fork. He recounted reading about Shavers Fork in *Life* magazine in 1967 and his visit from Baltimore in 1968. "It was unbelievable. I had been looking for something like this for 25 years. I found a true wilderness area, good fishing, along the fish-for-fun line, super-good fishing, a balanced wildlife, wild flowers, birds, everything you look for if you are a wilderness lover and a fisherman... I think it is unique. I have been places where the fishing was as good and I have been places that are almost as beautiful, but I have never in the east found a place that combined the wilderness beauty with excellent fishing."

In June 1973 both Burrell and Bristor joined Congressman Ken Hechler in presenting testimony to the U.S. House of Representatives supporting inclusion of Shavers Fork in the National Wild and Scenic River System. They were three of the Conservancy's most vocal, active and persistent advocates for the protection of Shavers Fork.

Conservationists were unanimously opposed to Linan's underground mining permit along Shavers Fork as a threat to the fragile water quality. In October 1970 Ed Henry, Chief of the Water Resources Division of the state DNR, denied the permit application. The state Water Resources Board considered the company's appeal during extensive hearings in December and January. Bristor traveled from Baltimore to present his testimony. Subsequently the Board overruled Henry and issued permits for three mines on Shavers Fork.

The August/September 1971 *Voice* carried a four-page article by Burrell titled, "Shavers Fork: Its status and its future." After reviewing his early impressions and paddling adventures on the lower sections, Burrell said, "But of the upper river, I waited too long. Like so many things, I put off visiting the headwaters when I should have gone, thinking that such a large piece of land would be around for awhile." The history of small strip mines was presented, with a warning of future acid mine drainage problems. Then he turned to Linan. He predicted that Linan would re-open its deep mine at Yokum Run, followed by perhaps three more. Burrell concluded:

> The pressure on the public is enormous. It is being made to choose between an environment and jobs and in doing so will fail to realize that it is an extremely unfair choice. Why can't the public have both? Each move towards the opening of the mines is accompanied by much publicity in the newspapers. The big questions are: Will these activities be compatible with water resource, wildlife, watershed, and recreation uses? Will wilderness knowledgeable people be content to fish under a coal tipple? Can the water quality of Shavers Fork be maintained in the face of all of these planned activities? If not, who will be the loser and who will make it right?

In February 1972, Craig Moore announced in the *Voice* the creation of a Shavers Fork Task Force. It would be composed initially of Burrell, Craig Moore, Bristor, Carolyn Brady Wilson, Bill McNeel, Bill Brundage, Don Gasper, and Roger Peterson. Each had agreed to research and/or monitor one or two aspects of Shavers Fork's challenges. This was the first, but certainly not the last, Shavers Fork Task Force.

The following June, Moore had good and bad news. The good: despite a major effort to obtain valid permits to mine, Linan had lost interest. Now the bad: at the same time the Mower Lumber Company, which owned the mineral rights under Forest Service land along Shavers Fork, had applied for two more mine permits. According to Moore, the language in the deeds of the Forest Service land conveyed the surface rights to the government, but reserving the mineral rights, stated the mineral rights would revert to the government after forty years, unless mines were operated "to commercial advantage" for an average of at least fifty days per year during the last five years. That deadline would be August 16, 1975. If the fifty-day rule was met, the deeds were extended another five years, under the same qualifications. In short, the proposed mining was primarily an effort to protect Mower's ownership of the mineral rights after 1975. To make matters worse, Forest Service counsel had apparently ruled that extensions would be issued if timely and reasonable efforts at mining occurred. In other words, permit appeals were as good as mining to hold on to the title.

Moore concluded that Mower was positioning itself to hold the mineral rights until 1980 in the hope the Forest Service obtained funding to buy them out.

> People who are in the coal business and know this area tell me that the commercial value of deep mining this coal is non-existent or very minimal. But we will very likely be forced to buy it with tax money in order to keep Shavers Fork from being prospected to death (in order to assure extensions and continued ownership by the private mineral owner). Those ethicalists [*sic*] among us will say this is blackmail and those businessmen among us will say its shrewd management duly expected by stockholders. Somewhere in the middle is the public interest.

The Conservancy continued to publicize threats to Shavers Fork, gather background information, and follow permit applications for mining activities. Periodically the *Voice* mentioned trout stocking changes forced by high siltation levels and a loss of 700 pounds of trout at the Bowden hatchery due to siltation plugging pump intakes. At the Mid-Winter Workshop in January 1973, half of the afternoon symposium was reports on Shavers Fork.

Based on Moore's analysis, it was hardly surprising when the April 1973 *Voice* announced an agreement between Mower and the Forest Service, suspending all Mower mining, including Linan, under the Monongahela National Forest, until September 3, 1978, while the Forest Service performed a land-use and mineral evaluation study. The purpose of the study "is to determine whether or not the Forest Service should seek funds from Congress to purchase Mower's mineral holdings under the Monongahela National Forest." The Forest Service would also agree to extend Mower's forty-year mining reservation until August 15, 1982. Conservationists greeted this announcement as a plus for the environment. It had not ended the mining, but had at least suspended it.

In June 1973, Burrell and Bristor went to Washington to testify in support of Rep. Hechler's bill to add Shavers Fork to the National Wild and Scenic River System. All three made the point that the excellent trout fishing was in jeopardy from mining interests and that the management by the Forest Service was ineffective in assuring sufficient protection.

Burrell provided an update in the October 1973 *Voice*. After reviewing the moratorium on mining within the Monongahela National Forest and the pending Hechler bill, he listed the still-existent threats: Corridor H construction at Bowden, strip mining on private land at Bemis, Highland Scenic Highway funding in the headwaters, and then he wrote:

> Last, but not least, is Operation Snowshoe, a multi-million dollar private recreation complex consisting of ski slopes, condominiums, golf courses, and private clubs slated to go in on the very headwaters of Shavers Fork (on land purchased from Mower). They also plan to impound Shavers Fork to make a lake.

Noting that it would require tertiary sewage treatment, when most West Virginia municipalities didn't even have secondary, Burrell concluded:

> Thus the outlook for this once magnificent treasure is very bleak. No place in West Virginia seems to be a greater victim of exploitation due to the absence of land use controls than does Shavers Fork. The Forest Service has announced Unit Plan Hearings for the river, but they will only be considering a part of the river which won't help if problems in the headwaters are not carefully dealt with. Such a study currently has a hollow ring to it anyway because it is doubtful if any positive recommendations could be funded due to administration cuts in Forest Service budget for anything but timber management and the edict to markedly increase annual timber cut on public lands.
>
> The next report on Shavers Fork, due in 1975, may well be its epitaph.

In the September *Voice* it was reported that the upcoming Fall Review would focus on Shavers Fork. Field trips would include Corridor H at Bowden and Snowshoe, both posing serious threats to Shavers Fork. The Saturday evening forum would be moderated by now-past president Burrell and include Dr. Thomas Brigham, President of Snowshoe. The following month it was reported that Brigham was kept another hour after his presentation, as some of the hundred members present engaged him in an animated discussion.

The December 1973 *Voice* reprinted an article by Paul Frank, the Editor of the *Allegheny Journal*. [He would become the *Voice* Editor a decade later]. In "Snowshoe Assessed" Frank reviewed the particulars of the Snowshoe proposal and detailed the virtual lack of land use controls that existed in West Virginia. What few regulatory hurdles did exist, primarily environmental regulations, were waived by Governor Arch Moore, who was personally steamrolling the proposal. At one point Frank contrasted the Snowshoe proposal with the now-shuttered Linan mine. It had been scrutinized for every possible detail, yet Frank wrote, "a $90 million project gets nothing but a peremptory 'ya-hoo' from the state's chief executive."

The Snowshoe development would pose both the most extensive threat to the Shavers Fork headwaters, and yet offer the citizens of Pocahontas County a tax-producing machine to fulfill their wildest dreams. Ski enthusiasts could look forward to the challenges on Snowshoe's slopes, while environmentalists would watch closely as the development came on line. Snowshoe would therefore become a classic example of the transition to a tourism-based economy that many counties in the highlands would experience in coming years. The Highlands Conservancy would not run short of proposals to follow.

Over the next few years, Shavers Fork remained in the news, albeit at a lower profile. Snowshoe suffered financially, flirting with bankruptcy and a lack of snow, for which there was little relief. Downstream strip mines were proposed and opposed by the Conservancy. The state DNR even denied permits, but was overridden by the state Reclamation Board of Review.

Then the proposal by New Era Resources for a coal washing plant on Shavers Fork, near Cheat Bridge, hit a nerve. A public hearing in Elkins drew forty-two speakers, thirty-one opposed, including Burrell on behalf of the Conservancy. His complete testimony was printed in the *Voice* in February 1976. Of his many paragraphs of articulate writing, those directly attacking Mower Lumber Company and its owner J. Peter Grace, were the sharpest:

> Until such time as the landlord of the upper Cheat watershed exercising some public conscience and sees to it that his managers and tenants behave in environmentally and legally acceptable manners, we refuse to agree to anything. Until such time as companies, especially from out-of-state, can set up an operation working with professional biologists and technicians this state employs and not against them, when these companies can exert reasonable care for what they are doing (and it is possible), and until it is realized that it is in everybody's interest to do a job carefully, then the W. Va. Highlands Conservancy

cannot be expected to look with favor on projects such as this. We find little in the company's plans or activities to date to commend it.

It may be J. Peter Grace's coal and property, but fellow Mountaineers, it is our river. We join with many other groups, with government agencies, and with hundreds if not thousands of Randolph County citizens in requesting that the permit be denied without delay or provision.*

The New Era proposal brought a new dimension: for the first time the West Virginia Wildlife Federation, the state's largest but most conservative conservation organization, threatened a court fight if the permit was issued. Behind them would also be the resources of the National Wildlife Federation. Judy Frank, wife of Paul Frank, and herself a future *Voice* editor, writing in the Elkins *Inter-Mountain*, quoted David Brantner of the WVWF, "We have never gotten into any controversy with the state government in the past over strip mining operations, but we felt the time had come. We felt it was necessary to take safeguards to protect Shavers Fork."

Perhaps the years of public advocacy for Shavers Fork's protection by Burrell, Bristor, Hechler, and others was beginning to reap the benefits of attracting help from the general public, the press, and other organizations. It was none too soon.

Within a few months, the state Water Resources Division denied New Era's permit, but the Water Resources Board, at that time always a friend of the coal industry, overruled that denial, and gave New Era the go-ahead to operate.

A nice accolade for hard work came in a front page story in the June 1976 *Highlands Voice*, where it was reported that Bristor's river conservation efforts had earned him one of the ten American Motors Conservation Awards for 1976. Tom Cofield, a well-known outdoor editor of the *Baltimore News-American*, made the primary nomination, stating:

> Without reservation or exception, [he] has demonstrated a totally selfless disregard for his own time, money, and often his best interests in his objective and highly effective efforts, and Bill's approach to each problem that arose, coupled with his bulldog refusal to give up, has been the key factor in the success he has achieved and the high regard he has earned from state sand federal authorities involved.

* Ironically, this statement appeared opposite the first *Voice* article on windpower. Thirty years later the twin issues of coal mining and windpower would still dominate the Conservancy's agenda.

The *Voice* article continued:

> Perhaps the extremely high regard for Bristor shown by a man of Cofield's stature is best exemplified by Cofield's opinion that Bill's work constitutes the most significant conservation progress seen in the writer's 35-year experience!

In his regular *Voice* column "Overlook," in November 1976, Burrell reviewed the eight-years of Governor Arch Moore. These, plus one, were the first nine years of the West Virginia Highlands Conservancy. Among issues such as Corridor H, Canaan Valley's Davis Power Project, and the Rowlesburg and Royal Glen dams, Burrell focused on several issues on Shavers Fork. The Linan mine, proposed by David Francis of Huntington, was subjected to such rigorous regulation that Francis claimed he was being politically persecuted. Then followed the Snowshoe proposal, which seemed to have well-greased skids in the Governor's office before it was even announced to the public, and finally the New Era coal washing plant. Wrote Burrell:

> Well, New Era has won and won grandly. Not only does the presence of their washer signal the ultimate doom for Shavers Fork (because such a large operation will require an enormous amount of coal to be extracted nearby, hence more strip mines on Shavers), but their method has shown quite convincingly how to win at the game. This then is the legacy left by the Moore administration: Moore-picked-men on the Water Resources and Reclamation Boards of Review who in effect can and do routinely overturn every conscientious permit denial of the DNR professionals.
>
> West Virginia could not afford another term with Arch Moore as governor. All eyes are focused on how his successor will approach similar problems.

In another article in the same issue *Voice* editor Ron Hardway reported that S. Franklin "Frank" Burford, former coal operator, had leased Snowshoe for the coming season, providing a third major infusion of capital to Snowshoe President Brigham's development, which had been plagued by undercapitalization and construction delays. Hardway wrote:

> Most of all, let's wish Snowshoe well because, after all, when the fine trappings are shorn away, Snowshoe is what it's all about – an alternate land use for the West Virginia Highlands, something other than strip mining, timbering, and scenic highways. However much one might regret the urbanization of such a remote area as Cheat Mountain

on Shavers Fork, we must keep in mind the alternatives – logging, slap happy road building, possibly another extension of the Jennings Randolph Memorial Highway, eventually strip mining. Snowshoe is not the best thing that could have happened to the upper Shavers Fork, but it is far from the worst.

Hardway thus captured a basic contradiction that had, and would continue to face the Conservancy and other environmentalists: how to support better, less-extractive and harmful proposals for economic development in the highlands, without giving a green light to a new generation of exploiters in the name of tourism, replacing the older generation of timber and coal barons. There would be no easy answer, as development proposals and threats to the highlands continued steadily onward. This theme would continue over the years as the Conservancy addressed proposed highways, power plants, other ski developments and even wind farms.

Meanwhile, Shavers Fork would recede into the background over the next three years as the Conservancy became actively involved in protecting other rivers and their communities. Snowshoe Resort would eventually develop into a multi-season resort complex, complete with massive real estate holdings and attracting skiers and other visitors from many states. It would become the major tax revenue generator for Pocahontas County.

Swiss

By way of introduction, the 104-mile Gauley River begins high on Gauley Mountain; passes Camden on the Gauley, near the border of Nicholas and Webster counties; travels along the border of the Monongahela National Forest; into the Summersville Lake, through its dam; down a rapid descent to Swiss; and then on to Gauley Bridge, where it meets the New River to form the Kanawha River.

Burrell and Paul Davidson, in their 1972 book *Wild Water West Virginia*, described the section just below Summersville as follows:

> Pull out all stops on the superlatives to describe this unique wildwater river. It is the absolute swirling, pounding, crashing end. In 1965 it was rafted. The reports were frightening. It was 1968 before it was paddled in white water boats by a group of the world's most expert paddlers. The word spread and the number of paddlers has increased each subsequent year. The Gauley has become the East's qualifying

cruise for the title of expert paddler. It is big, it is long, it is inaccessible, it is tough, it is dangerous, it is intoxicating.

The first mention of a proposed dam at Swiss on the Gauley River appeared in the newsletter of the Scenic Rivers Subcommittee of the Highlands Conservancy, dated December 1968. Burrell, newsletter editor, called it "another challenge so fantastic that I refused to believe it at first." It was a proposal both from the U.S. Army Corps of Engineers and the Southeastern Power Administration. Burrell believed the Corps was proposing it as an alternative "to offset increasing resistance to plans for damming (damning) the Greenbrier." As proposed, the Swiss dam would be 800 foot tall (the tallest Corps dam in the U.S.), have hydroelectric facilities (of interest to the Southeastern Power Administration), and create an impoundment back to the brand new Summersville Lake. He warned against the false dichotomy facing conservationists, namely which of these two rivers are you willing to sacrifice?

By issue number 1 of *The Highlands Voice* only four months later, in March 1969, Burrell, now its editor, repeated the specifications, and pondered again if it was a phony alternative to dams on the Greenbrier. The people along the Greenbrier were known to fight to protect that river. Noting that the Gauley passed primarily through wilderness-like area with little population, he asked, "Who will fiercely protect the Gauley?"

But there were more pressing threats to other important rivers. The Royal Glen Dam on the South Branch of the Potomac, the Rowlesburg Dam on the Cheat, the Blue Ridge private pumped-storage power project on the New, and all of the various threats to Shavers Fork were plenty enough to occupy the attention of the Conservancy's river warriors.

In the August 1967 *Voice* there were more details on the Swiss dam. Now rising to 875 feet, it was planned for 1985, would erase twenty miles of free-flowing river, and be only one of fourteen planned on the Kanawha Basin by the Corps. In a *Charleston Daily Mail* article on July 9, 1969, quoted by Burrell, Pete Samsell, Director of the state DNR, was said to favor Swiss over a dam on the Greenbrier, because more people would see the scenic beauty of the latter. Burrell added, "The Gauley's beauty is remote and seldom seen by human eyes. There are probably not more than a dozen canoeists in the eastern U.S. who are capable <u>and</u> willing to run twenty-six miles of continuous Class 4-5 water in a roadless, peopleless wilderness."

Questioning the entire basis for such a project, namely helping supply additional water quantity to the downstream industrial areas of Charleston, Burrell wrote:

> Conservationists should demand reasoning and accounting for the Swiss dam as well as any others. People are tired of being told – "This is good for you. You need it. We, the Big Government, will give it to you and you will pay for it cheerfully."

It remained until January 1975 before the *Voice* announced "Swiss Project Nears Decision." Apparently, the Corps had been quietly conducting research on technical aspects and expected to release its recommendation in March. Public hearings were conducted in January and Paul Davidson, Conservancy member and Burrell's co-author of the popular white water book, presented his testimony, published in February's *Voice*. Davidson reviewed the truly rugged wilderness characteristics of the Gauley canyon and presented data on the rising popularity of rafting on the Gauley. In both 1973 and 1974, the Gauley Downriver Races attracted over a hundred paddlers. In a truly prophetic statement, Davidson added:

> The potential of the whitewater paddling sport as a recreational industry has not yet been scratched. It has the appeal, the challenge, and the excitement of skiing without the overwhelming problems of crowded, expensive facilities and undependable weather conditions in the mild winters of West Virginia. The season for paddling at the elevation of the Gauley is virtually year round…There is a unique recreational future for West Virginia in the sport of whitewater boating both in commercial rafts and with individual whitewater canoes and kayaks.

There were no further references to the Swiss dam in the *Voice* archives. According to Burrell in 2006 correspondence, when the new 7.5 minute USGS topographic maps replaced the older 15.0 minute maps (from circa 1910), the Corps of Engineers found that a dam high enough to retain the impoundment they desired, would be higher than surrounding land. At that point, said Burrell, "They threw in the towel."

But there were plenty of other rivers in danger. In 1975, articles were appearing monthly on the proposed Rowlesburg, Stonewall Jackson, and Blue Ridge projects, all of which had more powerful governmental backers. In fact, the fate of the Gauley would later become intertwined with that of the New River.

Rowlesburg

Rowlesburg is a small town in Preston County, south of Kingwood, located on the Cheat River. It is a choke point on the river, and therefore had been identified as an ideal site for a dam. Over many years, the downstream barge interests on the lower Monongahela River, approaching Pittsburgh, had yearned for more water. The series of Corps of Engineers dams on the Monongahela main stem, from Fairmont north, had partially solved this problem, but a dam at Rowlesburg continued to be discussed. Any year that the Cheat flooded, downstream of Rowlesburg, the discussion would restart.

As is often the case, the land to be lost to an impoundment behind a high dam is worth saving and the farmland south of Rowlesburg fit that description. Along the Cheat lay open, productive farmland, mostly in Tucker County, and it constituted most of the county's prime acreage. Citizens of Parsons and their neighbors to the north became the local opposition to the Rowlesburg dam.

The Rowlesburg dam, like the Stonewall Jackson dam, discussed below, was an idea going back decades before the Highlands Conservancy was formed. Some trace its origin to a particularly severe flood in Pittsburgh in 1936. From time to time senators and congressmen would see that the Corps had funding to conduct feasibility studies. By the late 1960s, as the Conservancy was being organized, Rowlesburg was thought by many to be a done deal. It was "authorized," meaning it would be built as soon as construction funding became available. The public hearing process had already been completed. Of the many issues facing the new Conservancy, such as wilderness preservation, highway opposition, Shavers Fork preservation, and Monongahela National Forest land acquisition for the Spruce Knob- Seneca Rocks National Recreation Area, the Rowlesburg dam was not one. Not yet.

It remained until the February 1970 issue of the *Voice* before the Rowlesburg dam was given space. Two items appeared in that issue. One was a short story, reprinted from *The Parsons Advocate*, Tucker County's weekly paper, and a vocal opponent of the Rowlesburg dam. The story, credited to Clish McCleaver, a pseudonym used by Editor Bob Burrell, was a humorous discussion at the Corps office of what to name the impoundment behind the Rowlesburg dam. "Byrd's Paradise," was the punch line. The other item was an upcoming float trip in May described as follows:

A funeral for St. George. Herb Eckert has suggested a float trip from Parsons to Rowlesburg as a last tribute to this beautiful river valley and the historic St. George, Tucker County's oldest village. You see, our legislators and the army have decided to place a pork barrel here and Herb would like Conservancy members to see the beauty before it is gone. A splendid canoe trip for young and old.

The idea to bring public awareness to endangered areas was not new. Across the country famous people like Supreme Court Justice William O. Douglas often led hikes into threatened areas. In West Virginia the Conservancy had been involved in the Petersburg White Water Weekends, hikes to proposed wilderness areas, and other trips which gave participants first-hand experience that would motivate their political involvement. Frankly, that was what the Fall Highlands Weekend Review was all about. So the idea to canoe the endangered Cheat, threatened by the Rowlesburg dam, was almost predictable.

Clish McCleaver made another appearance in the following month's *Voice*, this time as author of the "Ballad of St. George," reprinted from the Morgantown *Dominion Post*. Then in May, Burrell wrote a very thoughtful article titled "Land of 10,000 lakes – Minnesota or West Virginia?" He began with Royal Glen, taking apart all the arguments put forward by the dam's proponents, and then turned to Rowlesburg:

This will undoubtedly become the biggest pork barrel in the state. Again, hearings were held, many arguments were given against the dam, few were for it. Yet it has been decreed, "It shall be!" The people in Rowlesburg have been sold on the story that there will be no more floods, that everyone will have jobs, and all kinds of tourist money will come their way. They fail to realize that U.S. 50 will become obsolete when the new Appalachian corridors are built, none of which will come near Rowlesburg… Senator Byrd has been an extremely vocal proponent of the dam, demanding that funds be freed for its construction. He has been joined recently (don't politics make strange bedfellows?) by Governor Moore, something his conservation-minded predecessor Hulett Smith would never have done.

Burrell continued:

If there were no reasons given for the Rowlesburg Dam, then why is it being built?..The answer is Pittsburgh and environs….Now let's get to the real reason. River traffic. If the Monongahela carried more water in the summer months, greater tonnages could be shipped on barges what with all the new locks being built to accommodate larger barges (another Corps project). Justifications for the Rowlesburg Dam include the little publicized benefit that the Monongahela will be provided with an additional 6" of water in the summer months. You can float an awful lot of coal out of West Virginia (the principal transported commodity) with 6" more water…But who pays for the dams, the increased flow rates, the new locks, the use of the locks? The Corps and you and me. But the barge operator (usually a subsidiary of a big coal company), NOT A DAMNED DIME!

There followed a report on Eckert's float trip to St. George, which would be covered by ninety feet of water, according to Don Good, identified as one who "has spent a great deal of time fighting this dam." The float trip participants toured the St. George historic cemetery containing burials back to the late 1700s. Concluded Burrell:

> The only people interested in seeing these hand carved monuments in the future will be SCUBA divers. It was a sad tour, followed by a sad canoe trip. Oh the sun was out, the water was clear, and the birds were singing, but the thought of so much beauty to be put on the block in order to get more coal out of state faster was very sad indeed.

Note several points: for one, the assumption of Eckert's float trip and Burrell's essay was that the Rowlesburg would be built. Secondly, Senator Byrd was identified as the lead advocate and source of funding. Third, out-of-state interests favored a project that local West Virginians opposed.

In August the *Voice* announced the formation of the Cheat River Conservancy, whose purpose was to oppose the Rowlesburg Dam. It was reported that they had legal assistance, and "seem prepared to go all the way towards obtaining an injunction against Federal action." Added Burrell:

> The new organization has an important mission, one that we in the Conservancy should support vigorously. It will be a tough battle. Senator Byrd has viewed this as a pet project of his for some time and has been exceedingly vocal in his support. Governor Moore is in favor of it and has released $900,000 to get the project rolling…We ask that all Conservancy members in the area attend [the next meeting] to see how they can help these sincerely-motivated people.

At this point, mid-1970, the four-year-old West Virginia Highlands Conservancy had become the leading activist organization in the highlands. Much in the news, the Conservancy's members were at work saving rivers, wilderness areas, stopping highways, and generally protecting the environment. Single-issue groups, like the Cheat River Conservancy, were cast in the same mold and often came to the meetings of the Highlands Conservancy to share their concerns and even ask for financial backing.

In December's *Voice*, Burrell devoted a full page to the Cheat River Conservancy's progress. He reported that in a short six months, they had signed up 400 members, visited Governor Moore several times, and generated considerable publicity — in short, become very effective. But since Tucker County was so small in population and therefore not politically significant, the Cheat River Conservancy had chosen to go to court. The Appalachian Research and Defense Fund, based in Charleston, as well as local attorneys, would handle their case, but it would cost money. Burrell requested financial and technical expertise be donated to this effort.

In June 1971, the *Voice* reported:

> The Corps has frozen funds for land acquisition and construction. It has contracted a private firm to evaluate an environmental impact statement which it must file. Unless the firm digs into the matter itself and secures their own information, the "evaluation" will be meaningless and will not be what the Governor requested. Probably [there] will be no other further developments until November. Meanwhile opponents are gathering their own data for their own environmental impact statement.

The Governor had requested an independent environmental impact statement, under the still-relatively new National Environmental Policy Act of 1970 and the Corps had complied. (Ironically, this same EIS requirement was actually being used as an effective weapon against Governor Moore's Corridor H planning. See Chapter 4.)

The June 1972 *Voice* reported on yet another St. George canoe trip. Twenty canoes and kayaks made the trip. The article concluded, "the canoeing conditions were spectacular, the beauty of the terrain was unsurpassed, and new discoveries and historic events were momentous. St. George and the upper Cheat Valley must remain forever."

The next month, the *Voice* carried a back page article titled, "Hechler Raps Rowlesburg Dam:"

> Rep. Ken Hechler, D-W. Va., went on record Monday as opposing construction of the Rowlesburg Dam on the Cheat River saying the project is unsafe to area residents. "This project threatens to flood a

large, productive section of Tucker County and ruin the beautiful Cheat River – one of the few remaining wild rivers in the eastern United States," Hechler said. Hechler, a staunch advocate of conservation and environmental protection, said the dam "would destroy the small communities of St. George and Holly Meadows, erode the tax base of Tucker County, create unsightly mud flats and damage one of the most scenic areas in West Virginia. The West Virginia Democrat told the House appropriations subcommittee on public works a good way to save $143 million would be to eliminate the project. The dam already has taken $2.54 million by the U.S. Army Corps of Engineers in design and planning, he said. Hechler's remark came when $200,000 was sought for additional studies on the proposed dam.

Over the next two years, the momentum clearly shifted. From a sad float trip and a perceived inevitable dam, there was now optimism that between EIS requirements and lack of funding, the dam actually might be stopped. A special edition of *The Highlands Voice*, distributed at the Highlands Weekend Review in October 1972, summarized all current issues the Conservancy was involved in. Eckert, by now a Conservancy vice president and Cheat River leader, reported the status of the Rowlesburg Dam:

> The construction of a massive, high-level dam at Rowlesburg by the U.S. Army Corps of Engineers became more of a reality around 1969 when land acquisition activities and appropriations ear-marked for dam construction were announced. Residents doomed to have been flooded out and other interested citizenry quickly organized to form the Cheat Valley Conservancy. Along with expertise offered by the West Virginia Highlands Conservancy, facts concerning the detrimental and utility values of such an impoundment were gathered, weighed, and disseminated.
>
> With the assistance of the Highlands Conservancy, the true issues were expressed in public forum and in small meetings. Conservancy leaders traveled to Washington, D.C., to Charleston, the capitol, and to Pittsburgh, Pennsylvania, the regional location of the Corps of Engineers. Despite repeated attempts to arrange open forums in various locations proximal to the Upper Cheat Valley, only a few culminated in sessions attended by elected officials, governmental appointees (the Corps), and proponents for and against impoundment creation. The Highlands Conservancy was well represented. Although many features were appraised, the issue of environmental deterioration

associated with the impoundment, presented by a Conservancy expert, appeared striking.

The Corps of Engineers, desirous for its own environmental impact study, contracted with an outside firm. The results of the contract study, from present day information, seemed unacceptable to the Corps.

A springtime weekend canoe trip in the scenic Upper Cheat Valley was held for the past 3 years expressly to offer the chance for anyone to behold the virtues beyond expression…Next spring, please try it — you'll see for yourself…Let's hope it won't be the last chance.

It was clear from Eckert's article that the Highlands Conservancy had been deeply involved in the efforts of the Cheat Valley Conservancy. Eckert, Burrell and others provided their knowledge and experience, gained in simultaneous battles for other issues, some even in Tucker County, like Otter Creek and the Davis Power Project. Taking on the Corps of Engineers, the congressional delegation, even the powerful Senator Byrd, was not dissimilar to Conservancy conflicts with the US Forest Service, the Federal Power Commission, or the state Highway Department. Finding sympathetic elected leaders, like Hechler, and good legal help, like Appalachian Research and Defense Fund, would become hallmarks of the Highlands Conservancy.

There were brief mentions of the Rowlesburg dam in the *Voice* over the next year or so, but most were just promoting the annual float trip. Each year there were more canoes, and more people were "introduced to the folly of the Rowlesburg dam," as reported in the May 1975 *Voice*.

In December 1975, the *Voice* carried an article titled, "Rowlesburg Dam demanded by Pittsburgh group." It quoted the president of the Waterways Association of Pittsburgh as urging the Office of Management and Budget to approve funding for the Rowlesburg Dam. Clearly the justification was a greater water flow that would facilitate Pittsburgh steel companies to move coal by barge from West Virginia. The same group urged quick action on the Stonewall Jackson Dam for similar reasons. The article concluded by saying that two weeks earlier West Virginia's United States Senators Randolph and Byrd had announced the appropriations subcommittee had recommended $100,000 for "advanced engineering studies." The Rowlesburg Dam was still alive!

In February 1977, the *Voice* reprinted an article from *The Charleston Gazette*. Under the headline, "Will Cheat Project Die?" the article recounted how Congress had authorized the Rowlesburg dam in 1965, but subsequent studies had seriously questioned underlying assumptions. For example "pollution dilution," or water quantity augmentation, was advocated by the state of Pennsylvania, but opposed by West Virginia. The article implied that West Virginia state leaders were having second thoughts, especially since virtually all the benefits would go to Pennsylvania. The author finished, "Perhaps the re-evaluation of the Rowlesburg project by the Corps of Engineers will reach the conclusion that the water resources division reached – that it isn't environmentally or economically feasible, and should not be built."

In November 1977, Burrell's "Overlook" column brought the good news:

> In mid-November, conservationists learned of some good news for a change; Governor Rockefeller has asked the Corps of Engineers to stop all planning on the Rowlesburg reservoir and place it on "inactive" status. For those long opposed to this classical pork barrel, both environmentally and economically unsound, this comes as most jubilant news.

Burrell devoted many paragraphs to the history of the Rowlesburg proposal and the fierce resistance from Tucker County residents. Along the way DNR wildlife biologists had produced helpful research findings that cast doubt on the wildlife benefits claimed by the Corps. In recent years, the Corps itself had dropped unsound and/or controversial projects, preferring to build those with widespread public support. That helped too. He drew the lessons:

> From the Overlook we can see a warning and also make some suggestions. First, let us not be too jubilant or relax our vigil until Congress and the Corps de-authorize Rowlesburg entirely. Should a new governor replace Rockefeller next term, he could easily reactivate Rowlesburg.... Incorporated into Rowlesburg design was a huge water storage area. One reason for the large size was to catch the tremendous amount of silt coming down from the upper watershed and it is no secret that by far the most siltation comes from the upper Shavers Fork....The imminent threat of the Rowlesburg Reservoir was a limp excuse offered by highway planners for not wanting Corridor H to take the Parsons–Coffindaffer alternative routing. Since this is no longer a threat, we make renewed appeal to the Department of Highways to take note.
>
> Well, we lose a few and win fewer. I think the losses are ahead, but we must publicly thank Governor Rockefeller for at least making a decision where before nothing but a vacuum existed. We wish that

Stonewall Jackson could have gone the other way [see below], but are glad that Rowlesburg didn't go the same route.

Burrell thus tied the Rowlesburg project to Corridor H and the Stonewall Jackson dam. In fact, despite treating them separately in this volume, there was and is an interconnection between and among the various projects proposed in the highlands. None exist in isolation.

The West Virginia Highlands Conservancy could now end its first official decade with a sense of success, yet there was little time to savor the victory over the Rowlesburg project. The Stonewall Jackson Dam had been lost, the Davis Power Project was still very active, mining issues were increasingly a concern, and many other issues required their attention.

With the exception of a brief re-examination following the devastating flood of 1985, which especially hit hard in Rowlesburg, Albright, and downstream Cheat communities, the Rowlesburg Dam proposal has remained dormant.

Stonewall Jackson

In many ways, the Rowlesburg and Stonewall Jackson dams were a matched-set. Like the Rowlesburg Dam, which dated back to 1936, the Stonewall Jackson Dam had been proposed for the West Fork River, upstream of Weston, for many years. Both were rationalized as providing flood protection to the upper reaches of major tributaries of the Monongahela River system. And like Rowlesburg, Stonewall Jackson's impoundment area would flood out many family-owned small farms and thereby displace many residents. Both came to be opposed by the combination of local citizen resistance together with those who favored other flood control strategies over high-rise dams for environmental and/or economic reasons. As referenced above, the political decision to proceed with both dams fell to Governor John D. (Jay) Rockefeller in 1977, after Governor Moore had successfully stalled both decisions for eight years.

There were several differences between the two dams, however. One was the nature of the river to be impounded. While the Cheat from Parsons to Rowlesburg was a beautiful scenic watershed that lent itself to float trips, which thus became an annual "show-me" tour starting in 1970, the upper West Fork was much smaller and each of the fingers of the proposed lake were small creeks that drew little attention. The strategy used to draw public attention instead became an annual Skin Creek Festival, in which the local residents featured handmade and farm-raised products.

Additionally, inside state government, the fisheries biologists of the DNR's Wildlife Resources Division, while not finding great benefit from Rowlesburg's impoundment, believed the Stonewall Jackson Lake would be a fisherman's paradise.

And there was another crucial difference: the Rowlesburg dam would have been located in Preston County, but would have flooded farms were in Tucker County. Tucker would not receive the presumed downstream benefits, but only the resulting loss in tax base. For a county already predominantly owned by federal government (the Monongahela National Forest), this was a major issue. By contrast, the Stonewall Jackson dam was in Lewis County and the major benefits would include water availability, flood protection for the county seat of Weston, and the creation of a major resort state park. All of the benefits would accrue within the same county as the property and tax losses. The political support of local elected officials made Stonewall Jackson a stronger project to federal and state leaders.

There had been more than seventy-five articles in *The Highlands Voice* on river threats, proposed dams, and related subjects before the first mention of the Stonewall Jackson dam in February 1975. Thomas Bond, a Lewis County resident, summarized the status at that point:

> The Corps of Engineers had been working on its $106 million proposal that would buy out and flood about one-twelfth of the county's surface area. The political and economic leaders of Lewis County, along with local media, had become active advocates.
>
> An alternative costing much less, was proposed by the Upper West Fork Watershed Association, and would consist of a series of small watershed dams to be built by the US Soil Conservation Service, displacing few residents, and keeping the land on the tax rolls. The same benefits, flood control, water supply, and recreation would be achieved without massive disruption of the rural communities.
>
> Opponents took exception to the cost-benefit calculations for Stonewall Jackson, citing numerous outdated figures and questionable assumptions. One major issue was the State of West Virginia's cost sharing, and two successive governors, Smith and Moore, had refused to sign the necessary agreement. Without the state's commitment, the project would be stalled.

January 1977 marked several anniversaries and changes. John D. "Jay" Rockefeller IV became West Virginia's Governor. Linda Cooper

Elkinton became the sixth president of the Highlands Conservancy, which itself was celebrating its tenth anniversary of incorporation.

The March 1977 *Highlands Voice* carried an article by Conservancy Washington Vice President Nicholas Zvegintzov, bringing readers up to date on the Stonewall Jackson Dam. The Corps' 1971 environmental impact statement had ignored the alternatives of smaller watershed dams. In 1974 the newly formed Upper West Fork Watershed Association sued in Federal Court, citing this omission. In 1976 Judge Robert Maxwell ruled for the Corps. The article indicated that federal guidelines were tightening and the judge supported "pollution dilution" as a justification, although the federal law had eliminated it. The state's United States senators had also given the Stonewall Jackson project a special exemption to certain federal regulations to facilitate state funding for recreation. Zvegintzov concluded:

> But why would the government go to such humiliating lengths to avoid an alternative proposal that on its face appears to satisfy some-what all the announced goals of the project, and in addition to leave the people in possession of their homes, churches and way of life? Presumably for the mundane reason familiar in all conflicts with the Corps from the top of Spruce Knob to the tip of the Mississippi delta — that the Corps' oldest mandate is to promote free and unimpeded navigation and that all these lakes are desired in the hills of West Virginia in order to float those new and bigger barges up to Pittsburgh in a dry year.
>
> It is for this reason that (as the Corps frankly says in its Environ-mental Impact Statement) "small rural communities and scattered farms will give way to a large transient population looking for recre-ation and relaxation."
>
> There is an irony to this alternative. The people of the Watershed Association are alive and well among the rolling hills of Lewis County, going to church, enjoying music festivals and ramp feeds, and generally minding their own business. Such tranquility is the scarcest resource in our society. Its opposite, the apathy, anomie, and anger that go with displaced populations are our society's greatest burden.

The same *Voice* also carried a reprint of *Charleston Gazette* columnist Skip Johnson's article "Abandon the Boondoggle." Johnson cited Presi-dent Carter's cut of nineteen water development projects, which could not be justified under current guidelines. He pled with Rockefeller to do likewise and stop the Stonewall Jackson Dam. Although authorized since

1966, the lack of the governor's signature on cost sharing would doom the project, Johnson wrote. He further cited various DNR divisions that preferred the small watershed alternative. "Whatever the cost, it would not be worth the dubious benefits when weighed against the environmental and social costs of taking 21,000 acres of private land and uprooting hundreds of people [actually 1800] from their homes and ancestral land," concluded Johnson.

But a little box, beginning with the ominous words, "as this issue of the *Voice* went to press," indicated that Governor Rockefeller had just signed the cost-sharing agreement, pledging $10 million for a recreation complex that would become the Stonewall Jackson State Park, allowing the Corps to proceed. Apparently despite the publicity of a large coalition of groups endorsing the watershed alternative, including the Highlands Conservancy, the support of influential media outlets like the *Gazette*, and widespread public opposition across the state, the Stonewall Jackson Dam would be built. It was a defeat that was not expected and certainly marked a dark day for the West Virginia environmental community.

As discussed above, later that same year, Rockefeller requested deauthorization of the Rowlesburg dam. It would be rumored that Governor Rockefeller agreed to Stonewall Jackson, while stopping the Rowlesburg dam, believing that one but not two could be justified. So 1977 was the year of dam decisions.

There remained several efforts to stop the Stonewall Jackson dam, including political candidates running in 1978 on both sides, including the election of Bob Wise as congressman in 1980 and his heroic efforts to rescind the Corps authorization through legislation. But in the end the Stonewall Jackson Lake and Dam were subsequently constructed. The state's third and fanciest resort state park, also named Stonewall Jackson, was opened under a unique public-private management arrangement. Financial difficulties have plagued the project from its onset and, as late as 2006, bond payments were still being missed with the possibility of financial re-organization under bankruptcy protection appearing in the media.

New/Gauley

Although the Gauley River was threatened by a proposed Corps dam at Swiss upstream of its confluence with the New, the New River itself had been the target of controversy. An upstream pumped-storage hydroelectric project in Virginia, the Blue Ridge Power Project, had been formally proposed in 1962. It would generate abundant tax revenue and electricity for Virginia, but in West Virginia it would only produce "pollution dilution," or "low-flow augmentation," as it was technically called, downstream through the New River Gorge and into the Kanawha River valley.

Although not a leading participant, the Highlands Conservancy had closely followed the Blue Ridge Project as early as 1970. There had been a widespread understanding, at least among Conservancy board members, that the definition of "the highlands" certainly didn't stretch to include southern West Virginia.

In *The Highlands Voice* of May 1970, Editor Burrell devoted a full page to an update on Blue Ridge. According to Burrell, the Appalachian Power Company's original proposal was for a "modest sized" dam, but the US Department of Interior requested a larger one, thus producing a larger impoundment. In that way, additional water flow would be guaranteed down the Kanawha. Studies by the state DNR found such increases would scour the river and cause fast currents, both having a negative impact on fishing.

The following month, Burrell reported on a two-day Federal Power Commission hearing on the Blue Ridge project. The Conservancy was asked to file testimony in support of conservation intervenors, the West Virginia Division of the Izaak Walton League and the West Virginia Natural Resources Council. Burrell presented a ten-page statement. Burrell praised state Attorney General Chauncey Browning for "his sharp cross-examination of the spoilers." (Little did they know, that Browning, the Izaak Walton League and the Conservancy would soon meet again before the FPC, this time debating the Davis Power Project.)

Burrell reported:

> The Conservancy was represented in Beckley on July 21 for hearings before the Federal Power Commission concerning the Blue Ridge Project on the New River. It was an interesting session. The Conservancy's statement was the sixteenth one in the morning session, and with one exception none of the sixteen supported the project…It was interesting to see how many good reasons there were against it.
>
> People and organizations from North Carolina, Virginia, and West Virginia do not want the project, only Kanawha Valley industries. If the FPC approves the project it will be a case of ignoring the wishes of a vast majority of the people affected in favor of satisfying private interests. The public is being asked to sacrifice a tremendous public

resource for the private gain of a very few privileged people. This is America?

The Conservancy is indebted to Mr. Shirley Love of WOAY radio and TV in Oak Hill who put us on his radio interview and his 6:00 p.m. TV newscast to explain our position to the entire southern West Virginia listening audience. We couldn't have bought such a magnificent opportunity.

The Conservancy was becoming very well informed about pumped storage power projects. While the FPC considered the Blue Ridge case, the Monongahela Power Company proposed the Davis Power Project, a pumped storage proposal for Canaan Valley, in June 1970. (See Chapter 5.)

A year later in August 1971, the *Voice* reprinted an article from the *Mid-Appalachian Environmental Newsletter*, under the title, "Blue Ridge Hydroelectric Project Receives Tentative Approval." It reported that the FPC had issued a modified license to the Appalachian Power Company, limiting the low flow water discharges, and appearing to support the conservation intervenors and the State of West Virginia. The newsletter added: "The victory may be more apparent than real."

The national and congressional willingness to use "pollution dilution" as a substitute for point-source pollution control was changing. In February 1972, the *Voice* reprinted an article from *The Roanoke Times*. It reported that the Environmental Protection Agency had requested from the FPC an opportunity to evaluate the volume of impounded water at Blue Ridge, and recommend the appropriate size that will minimize or eliminate pollution dilution. State Attorney General Browning and the three conservation intervenors supported the EPA request.

After a series of additional modifications to placate the West Virginia DNR and the EPA, according to an article in the September 1974 *Voice* titled "New River Battle Nearing a Climax," a new monkey wrench was thrown into the works. First in late May the US Senate passed a bill to place a seventy-mile stretch of the river in North Carolina and Virginia in the study category for the Wild and Scenic Rivers Act. Then in mid-June, the FPC finally issued the Blue Ridge license, which would destroy forty-four of those very miles. But the FPC suspended the license until January, to allow for House consideration. A major inter-state, inter-house battle in the House of Representatives was underway. Conservationists were urged to communicate with their elected representatives.

In December 1974, the *Voice* reported that the House Rules Committee tabled the New River bill, despite strong support from Rep. Ken

Hechler and Rep. Harley O. Staggers. They requested the Speaker to suspend the rules and allow floor action in the remaining few days left in the session. The decision to table appeared to be heavily influenced by a letter in support of Blue Ridge written by Governor Moore. Already local groups were planning a memorial service for the New River.

In an effort to both focus on the effects of the Blue Ridge project, if built, and understand alternatives, including a proposed New River Gorge National Park, the Conservancy scheduled its Mid-Winter Workshop at Hawks Nest State Park for January 1975. Representatives of government environmental agencies and local citizens were invited to make presentations.

In June 1975, *Voice* readers learned that the FPC license, effective January 1, 1975, had been suspended again by the Court of Appeals in Washington, pending a fuller review. Meanwhile, the state of North Carolina (upstream of the dam, which was in Virginia) requested a Wild and Scenic River study from the federal government for the North Carolina stretch. Rep. Hechler's House bill had passed very late in December by a vote of 196-181, but failed on a technicality. An update in October indicated several other court challenges and strong North Carolina opposition to Blue Ridge. The license remained suspended.

In the September 1976 *Voice,* under a banner reading, "The New River...Like it is!" author Zvegintzov, calling himself "White House Correspondent for *The Highlands Voice,*" reported that on September 11, "President Gerald Ford signed into law a bill giving Wild and Scenic River status to 26.5 miles of the New River in North Carolina, effectively nullifying the FPC license to the Appalachian Power Company to build the Blue Ridge Project." It was President Ford who coined the phrase "The New River...Like it is!" and applause ensued. Attending were North Carolina Governor Holshouser and Rep. Hechler, both of whom had opposed the Blue Ridge project. Zvegintzov devoted the balance of the article to options and opinions of how West Virginia should best protect its share of the New River. The clear impression was that federal protection by the National Park Service, possibly as a National River, might be effective.

But just as conservationists began to celebrate, Burrell's "Overlook" column in October was headlined "The New River Saved?" He raised the question that the need to publicize the New River, the explosion of rafting companies, and the talk of national park status, might add the New River to a doomed list. Wrote Burrell, "We have already loved too damned many of West Virginia's natural wonders to death." He seemed to be more cautiously optimistic by his January column. Speaking of the law protecting the North Carolina portion and stopping the Blue Ridge project, Burrell wrote:

> This was a remarkable environmental achievement because of the immense power of the lobbies that supported the pumped storage project. Thanks to many untiring citizens and a few courageous Congressmen, the protection finally came about. For those who worked so hard on the bill, the final success was a very heady experience. But it was easy! Now I know that statement will cause offense to many, but I am speaking in comparative terms. No environmental effort is easy, but it much easier to stop a project, in this case the Blue Ridge project, than it is to do something constructive, e.g. achieve wilderness protection for the Cranberry backcountry.

There followed a clarification of what was and was not saved. West Virginia's New River was not. And what the protection options might be: full national park status, which Burrell thought unlikely, or some lesser, but protective status, as proposed by various federal agencies. One option, a national recreational area, brought back bad memories for Conservancy members who saw the Forest Service expand the idea of saving Spruce Knob and Seneca Rocks into an eminent domain-driven property dislocation in the Conservancy's earliest years. (See Chapter 6.)

Then Burrell shared his experience and wisdom:

> Now for those getting ready to embark on one of these plans, please heed some advice the Conservancy has learned over the years: 1) where possible try to come up with a plan favored by those living and working in the area; 2) after such heady success defeating Appalachian Power, avoid the temptation to be conceited and think you can do anything. This time it will be you who wants to do something constructive and it will be very simple for the againsters to prevent you from doing it; 3) legislation is a slow route – eight years for Dolly Sods and Otter Creek. Don't be so naïve to think you are going to accomplish something in one year. Our Senators and Congressmen are not noted for enthusiastic and aggressive activity in this sphere of activity (Cong. Hechler excepted, but he can't help you now) [He was no longer in Congress]. Two congressional districts are involved for this river and you will need the approval of both. That of the Chairman of the Second [Harley O. Staggers] will be difficult to come by; 4) above all avoid the idea that you can manipulate a legislator to come around

to your view. This is a fatal mistake. Try to work with them and play their rules; otherwise you won't get anywhere.

In March 1978, the *Voice* ran an unsigned article which opened with the following:

> The major interest groups, who have fought for the last 10 years, often acrimoniously, over a formula for protecting the New River Gorge area, have come to an agreement, and there is an excellent chance that enabling legislation can pass Congress this year. The formula calls for the creation of a New River Gorge National River, with land to be acquired by the U.S. and administered by the National Park Service, with some innovative and humanized provisions for avoiding condemnation.

The remainder of the article reviewed the history of the river and especially the various confrontations and alternative approaches to protection that had been actively promoted. Credit for building a consensus among these interests was given to Destry Jarvis, identified as "lobbyist for the National Parks and Conservation Association, one of Washington's most careful and knowledgeable lobbyists for conservation and a long-time fan of the New River.

The draft plan tentatively received the support of the two West Virginia Senators, plus Congressmen Rahall and Staggers, whose districts were separated by the New River. A "National River" designation, a name deliberately chosen to avoid the restrictions of the Wild and Scenic River status, enabled Congress to tailor the form of acquisition and protection to local conditions including the continued use of the railroad along the river. Condemnation would only occur when property was found to have a new or substantially altered use that was incompatible with the management of the area. (This would avoid massive land condemnations such as those in the Spruce Knob – Seneca Rocks NRA.) Additional provisions included no mining if the surface was disturbed, no FPC or other government water projects if they would cause negative impacts, and a positive support for Amtrak's continued usage. Letters of support to the Carter administration were urged.

In the December 1978 *Voice*, Zvegintzov, the Conservancy's Washington Vice President, opened his article "New River Now National," with these words: "On the evening of November 10th, without ceremony, President Carter put his signature to the National Parks and Recreation

Act of 1978…[whose] title IX designates the New River Gorge National River."

Zvegintzov continued by describing the conditions of the legislation, including a "landmark" provision allowing federal purchase through condemnation only when current uses were discontinued. Finally, almost as an afterthought, he mentioned that tributaries of the New, the Bluestone, the Gauley, and the Greenbrier, were designated for study under the Wild and Scenic system.

In January 1980, the *Voice* announced "W. Va. Rivers Coalition Formed." This short article would prove significant beyond its size. The Coalition would include the Audubon Society, Sierra Club, and local groups Braxton Environmental Action Program, Upper West Fork River Watershed Association, Tug Valley Recovery Center, Save the New River, and Friends of the Little Kanawha. It was modeled after the Kentucky Rivers Coalition, with its purpose being the development of a rational and comprehensive statewide water policy, including the preservation of free-flowing streams and rivers. Interim Coordinator would be Sharon Rogers of Lewis County, a veteran of the Stonewall Jackson battle.

As the new decade opened, the Rivers Coalition would assume the primary responsibility for river protection, allowing the Highlands Conservancy to concentrate on rivers it had already been working on — Shavers Fork, the Potomac branches, and the Cheat's tributaries.

That spring, Zvegintzov, one of the most active Conservancy members on coal mining issues (see Chapter 7), *Voice* writers, and an active Washington Vice President, resigned and moved to New York City. In one of his last articles, he profiled someone special, an original incorporator of the Conservancy in 1967.

The March *Voice* article, "Run the New River with Sara, May 18," was illustrated with a photo of **Sara Corrie** holding the handlebar of a wheelchair. He wrote:

This is Sara Corrie at the Mid-Winter Workshop in January, demonstrating the proper use of a wheelchair, namely to wheel it in front of yourself in case the person you're talking to would like to sit down. The sight of Sara walking and talking up her usual storm was a special joy to those of us who heard last year that she was lying crippled in a paraplegic rehabilitation hospital.

Sara's special love is whitewater boating…and free drop rappelling (*i.e.,* going down or up a free hanging rope in the open air or in a cave.) She was coached in rope techniques by Bill Cuddington, a caver who originated many of them. This was in 1959, when Sara was, let's say, in her 40s. Bill recalls that people figured caving was a sport for the young, and she would have "a couple of years" to enjoy it.

Well. In 1966 she was on the first team to make a 1000' descent on a rope. She was one of the first women to make the deepest free drop in a cave — nearly 1100' in Sotano de las Golondrinas in Mexico. She is known to have been on the first team to rappel off a certain man-made landmark in West Virginia which shall remain nameless. (Hint: take the river trip described below.) She has been active in the planning and training for a possible rappel off the incredible Angel Falls in Peru.

In 1978 she was testing rappel equipment in Ohio when a device failed. She dropped vertically onto her left leg, breaking bones in the foot, ankle, leg, pelvis and spine. She doesn't remember the fall. "It's nature's way so I don't lose my nerve," she says with a grin.

After recovering from the concussion she was put in a paraplegic rehabilitation hospital. Most of the other patients were young people injured in automobile accidents. There were various stories of her confounding the doctors who told her she was paralyzed — by sitting up from the waist, by wiggling her toes. "I've always been a wiggler," she says.

There were black times, which Sara speaks thoughtfully of, despite her bantering tone. People tell her she might be able to help others recover because she's been through it. "I'd like to," she says, "but, you know, it doesn't work that way. You just feel so jealous and hopeless. When I couldn't get out of bed, I saw a woman drag herself across the room and pour a cup of coffee. I thought, "I'll never be able to do that."

"Of course there's always a challenge," she adds. "Two years ago I wanted to rappel off Angel Falls. A year ago I'd be thankful just to sit up. The main thing for me," (she roasts her listener with a feisty smile), "is to play to win."

When her doctors told her she could drive again, she drove her van to (yes) Colorado to help with a rappelling exercise off the Grand Canyon. In Silver Plume, Colorado, former Conservancy board member Keith Kirk was riding with some other mine inspectors when he saw Sara on crutches by the side of the road. He told his companions, "Wait – there's a caving buddy of mine – and she's hitch-hiking!" (She wasn't actually hitch-hiking, but waiting for her van to be tuned up.) Sara reports that Keith was looking happier and more relaxed than ever.

Last year, also, Sara attended the annual meeting of the National Speleological Society and accepted their Certificate of Merit to a standing ovation. [She had represented the NSS on the board of the Highlands Conservancy for many years.]

This brings Sara's story up to date, and now's the time for the commercial. Every year Sara books a whitewater raft trip down the New River — this year it's on May 18, on the wilder, lower half from Thurmond to Fayette Station. Her idea is to meet old friends, make new friends, and introduce you to the New River if you don't know it.

Would you like to meet the rambunctious New River and the rambunctious Sara Corrie? She'd like to meet you.

There would be a major decline in Highlands Conservancy activity and *Voice* articles on the New and Gauley after 1980. Occasionally an update would announce additional National Park Service activity or new acquisition of property. More often the reports would discuss the increasing rafting activity and even the need for state regulation.

But the pendulum would swing back. The Conservancy's spring meeting in 1983 was held at Camp George Washington Carver and focused on the New River. Trips to various sites were scheduled and Park Superintendent Jim Carrico was the evening speaker. A full page of photos by Frank Pelurie appeared in the June *Voice*. Pelurie reported on the status of various studies of potential Wild and Scenic River candidates. He concluded:

> The crown jewel of river studies completed to date is on the Gauley River between Summersville Dam and the community of Swiss.
> Of all the rivers ever studied in West Virginia, including the New River, this section of the Gauley is the state's only river of national significance.
> "The Gauley is the premier whitewater river east of the Mississippi. In a remote, wilderness canyon, it provides unmatched whitewater recreations as well as fishing, hiking, hunting and other outdoor recreation opportunities. As far as we're concerned, there is no river

east of Colorado as deserving of inclusion in the national system," Brown said. [Chris Brown was Conservation Director of the American Rivers Conservation Council.]

Yet the threats to this river are the greatest.

This statement certainly echoed those of Burrell and Davidson a decade earlier quoted before in the hearings on the proposed dam at Swiss. And the Highlands Conservancy was certainly not forgetting its historic role as river protection leader.

The January/February 1984 *Highlands Voice* headlined "Conservancy to Focus on Rivers." The article reported that, following a presentation by Glen Eugster, Chief of Natural Resource Planning for the National Park Service, the Conservancy Board authorized its officers, led by President Larry George, to apply for a planning grant from the state to coordinate planning on the Gauley, Greenbrier and Bluestone rivers.

Reports from the Mid-Winter Workshop were also in that issue and focused on presentations by the Corps of Engineers representative, advocating a hydropower facility on the Gauley; by Chris Brown, of the American Rivers Conservation Council, continuing to describe the Gauley as in a class by itself of eastern rivers; and by David Brown, a leader in Citizens for Gauley River. The sum total of coverage indicated that the Conservancy was deeply involved in the Gauley and nearby rivers.

The May 1984 *Voice* again was all about river protection. One article and two photos featured Congressman Bob Wise receiving the 1984 Distinguished River Conservationist Award at the Ninth Annual National Conference on Rivers in Washington, D.C. He was chosen for his efforts to stop the Stonewall Jackson Dam and his opposition to the hydro project proposed for the Gauley. Conservancy Washington Vice President Linda Winter, Rivers Committee Chair Ray Ratliff (see Chapter 3), and his wife, new *Voice* Editor Mary Ratliff, attended the conference on behalf of the Highlands Conservancy.

The Gauley River and four other West Virginia rivers continued to receive protection from various proposals while they were in the three-year Wild and Scenic River study period. Then in April 1985, the National Park Service recommended the Gauley not be included in the system, due to the high cost of land acquisition. The protection then ended and the Corps' hydro project, or any other proposal, could now be considered. There was a new urgency to save the Gauley.

The February 1986 *Voice* reported:

> The West Virginia Highlands Conservancy has recommended that the Gauley River Canyon and the lower Meadow River be designated by Congress as a National Recreation Area to be managed by the U.S. National Park Service.
>
> This action was taken in response to a request by U.S. Rep. Nick Rahall (D-WV) for a Conservancy recommendation for protection and management of the Gauley River Canyon. The WVHC also requested that Rahall join other members of the West Virginia Congressional delegation to sponsor legislation designating a Gauley River NRA.

According to the May *Voice*, Congressman Rahall came to the Conservancy's Spring Review and announced plans to protect several rivers, including the Gauley and the New. The article continued:

> The bill, to be called the "West Virginia National Interest River Conservation Act," will be introduced next year during the first session of the 100th Congress if Rahall's negotiations with interested parties are successful.
>
> As proposed by Rahall, the bill would contain three major components. These include provisions for Wild and Scenic River designation for the Bluestone, National Recreation Area status for the Gauley River Gorge, and boundary modifications to the New River Gorge National River.
>
> "Protection of recreational opportunities on the Gauley and conservation of its outstanding scenic values should have more permanency so that the splendor of the gorge will be preserved — as we have done on the New River — for the enjoyment of future generations," Rahall said.

Rahall shared his views on other conservation issues of interest to the Conservancy and asked for their active support of this legislation. For the first time, the protection of the Gauley, often called a crown jewel of eastern rivers, seemed within reach. The battle was not over, but at least one important congressional leader was not only supporting the Conservancy's idea, he was leading them and fashioning better proposals. Rahall and the Conservancy would be working together for many years, and many issues, to come.

When he finally introduced the bill on January 29, 1987, he not only had the other three West Virginia representatives, Wise, Staggers, and Mollohan, as co-sponsors, but also Morris Udall, Chairman of the House Interior and Insular Affairs Committee, where the bill would be considered.

The April 1987 *Voice* featured a centerfold on the Gauley River. One article by Allen Haden presented the Gauley from the perspective of a whitewater raft guide. Haden eloquently described the isolated beauty and rugged terrain that had helped protect the Gauley Canyon from development, even from whitewater enthusiasts. He credited John Sweet as the first to run the Gauley in 1961, but there certainly was more to the story, as related below. By 1986, only twenty-five years later, Haden reported that 28,000 people ran the river during the short twenty-day drawdown season, referring to releases from the Summersville Dam. The one-day peak was 2,700 people.

But of equal or perhaps greater interest to Conservancy readers, was the companion article by long-time Board member Sayre Rodman, entitled "The First Run," reprinted here in its entirety:

> People seem mildly intrigued by the idea of the first run, ever, on the whitewater section of the Gauley River. Nobody had the faintest idea what was down there, even around the next corner. Jean and I and a few friends seem to have lucked into the experience. What was it like?
>
> Compared to the way people think about white water today, any trip in those days was in another world. If you write about a present-day trip with intent to impress people, plenty of potential readers will know what you're talking about. Hundreds will think that they could have run it better. Most of them could. And hundreds of thousands, or maybe millions, have been bounced or splashed on commercial raft trips. They know what Class IV or V water looks and feels like from river level. Serious white water means something to lots of people.
>
> Twenty-five or thirty years ago, talk of 500,000 people who've felt big water would have sounded like weekends on Mars. Only the idea of a useful computer for a few hundred bucks would have seemed sillier. [Remember that this was written in 1987!] If you were on or near nice rapids then, you were very alone. Well, almost alone.
>
> One warm summer morning in 1956, a young couple was skinny-dipping along the Ohiopyle Loop of the Youghiogheny up in Pennsylvania, confident of privacy. On a day like that today, a few thousand people go by. But in 1956, apparently no boats had ever run that river, until Jean and I sloshed into sight, spooking the couple out of the water into the bushes. Sorry about that, you two. Wish we'd told people our names along the river. Don't you think "Naked Lady Rapids" is more easily remembered than "Cucumber Rapids"? But I digress.

Jean and I didn't write much about being probably first down the Yough and the Gauley because, over a few shared six-packs, we did tell almost everyone in the Middle Atlantic States who knew what we were talking about. We and a few friends went down anything we could find within a weekend radius from Pittsburgh, rowing Air Force surplus rafts. Rigid boaters? Berry and Harrigan and Sullivan in Washington and Bickman and Sweet at Penn State were acquiring their impressive skills, swapping river descriptions with us. In 1961, if everyone who'd run West Virginia Class V water in anything that floats came to a Highlands Conservancy Review, we still wouldn't have broken even.

Why do we think we were the first to boat the hard part of the Gauley River for fun? Hard to be sure. Oldtimers at Swiss told me that kids had gone down in dead low summer water a long time ago, walking parts and floating pools on air mattresses or something. But they were certain that no one was idiot enough to have done it in even moderate water before we did.

Real credit for finding the Gauley, and inventing ways to run it, goes to Ray Moore of Alexandria, Virginia. He was an innovator, who loved to try his own methods of getting where no one else had been, on rocks, in caves, or on rivers. His early tries at Cass Cave would give the NSS apoplexy. In the '50s, he discovered Air Force surplus rafts and West Virginia white water. He was not a slow learner. A February Class IV run in the rain in blue jeans, without life jackets, had seemed reasonable but turned out to be totally unsatisfactory. Don't do it again. He learned efficient ways to row a 6-man raft, solo, with big oars, Western-style. He taught Jean and me what he knew about rafts, short-fused dynamite sticks, and other subjects where one should pay close attention. There was no authority to guide people. If trying freaky ideas disturbed you, you stayed off the rivers.

Our first run at the Gauley was a fiasco. Early in 1959, Ray and a few friends from Washington, plus two of us from Pittsburgh, met at Summersville, far beyond our familiar Potomac headwaters. (Jean opted out; our first kid was still sort of new.) Only Ray knew where he meant to run, and we didn't exactly get there.

We put in at Route 39 east of Summersville. We hit the first interesting water (now under the lake) at the old Route 19 crossing. The river was sort of high, out of its banks. We soon were in the woods, lining around rapids, laboriously roping from tree to tree in water over our heads. Rafts may be better than kayaks for this. The owner of a house along the river took pity on the sodden group, and sheltered us for the night. He talked bitterly about the proposed dam, which would one day drown all his land.

We made a few more miles the next day, but it wasn't much fun. One shaken man said that his big raft did an ender cleanly over his head. Fortunately, Ray's guys were good at reentering their rafts via the bailing-bucket roper. Totally exhausted, we camped just above the dam site. Ray wanted to continue but was too tired to argue, except lying down.

Next day, I kicked rhododendron out to the now-vanished community called Sparks, hitched a ride to the proposed takeout, and returned with a car. I'd already learned that, on Ray's exploratory runs, you bring topo maps and pack frames. With enough psychological drive, you can hump out two deflated rafts per trip. Ah youth. Gauley 1, boaters 0.

I thought of that stream often in the next two years, as our friends developed a more practiced and conservative approach to raftime. Row precisely, wear good life jackets, scout big rapids. Details like that. Then in late May in 1961, six people from Pittsburgh tried again, with much better results. The river was probably below 1500 CFS, a bit low, no complaints. Jean and I have had worthwhile outings in nice places. Consider first seeing the tip of Mount Everest by moonlight on New Year's Eve from Tyangboche Monastary. The first Gauley run was about that good.

On day One, we sat out a snow squall under the old Route 19 bridge, ran superb water the rest of the day, and camped precisely under the present dam. Not many people have run that part. Take the best of the rapids on the Cheat run below Albright; add many more; pack them into shorter distance. A few gentlemen's Class V's; nothing really hairy. I remember it as much better than the part below Sweet Falls. My old slides show a dark foggy day. We enjoyed it, immensely.

You will never see that run, nor will your children. When next you feel grateful for a scheduled release from the Summersville dam, think of the once free-flowing riverbed, down in the mud under the lake. We delighted in running it, a quarter of a century ago. The dam builders took something very special from you.

Then, on a bright day, six people, more privileged than we knew, were the first semi-competent modern boaters to find and scout and run the rapids that define the Gauley for thousands today. The run to the Meadow River was just fun. We'd earlier scouted a big one below Carnifax Ferry, big waves but no problem. Below the Meadow, we quickly saw things were getting more interesting. The first serious rapids ate one of my oars. Was it Sweet's "Broken Paddle"?

I think the rapids that nearly killed one of us is now called Iron Ring. Several rafts ran it, impressing the operators but doing nothing unpredictable. Then Kay's boat stalled upstream, and vanished, like a fly taken by a trout, in mid-river. A remarkable lady, she dove, making the snap decision that going thru a hole ahead of a big raft is better than the alternative. We, including her husband, watched the downstream, as did her 6 by 12 foot raft with oars still in tact in the oarlocks. Twice she had come up in the dark, and grabbed a breath. Behind the long slab leaning on the bank, river right, flows a lot of water. In hindsight we might have read the surface currents better.

We were then in no mood to see if we could manage Sweet Falls. We saw it as a sure-fire slicer of raft bottoms, at that water level. Carrying around was easy. While we did so, Kay's lost bailing bucket caught up with us.

We found a campsite on a sandbar, built a huge fire, and enjoyed our second night on this lovely river.

The last day was brilliant and clear, and the purple rhododendron was in bloom along the canyon walls. For a while, we had good fast water to enjoy, with nothing to worry Kay, who felt a tad cautious now. When we hit the quieter water above Swiss, we knew we'd had three memorable days.

Now twenty-six years after that memorable trip, the United States Congress was considering permanent protection for that same river. Once again, the victory came to the patient.

The House passed the bill, but it was stalled in the Senate. Finally a year later, in April 1988, the Senate Committee held hearings, reported in the May 1988 *Highlands Voice*.

It was ironic that that same issue reported the death of Sara Corrie, who died March 15, 1988, at the age of 73. She had been an incorporator, and had served on the Board of the Conservancy until January 1987. Among her distinctions was that, after having been paralyzed three years earlier, Corrie set the world record in her age group for the women's 100-foot-mechanical climb in a competition at the National Speleological Society's Annual Rope Climbing contest at Western Kentucky University. Most tributes to her emphasized her zest for living life to the fullest and willingness to push herself to new challenges. At the same time, she was deeply interested in people and enjoyed nothing more than sharing stories around a campfire, even when she was the oldest member of the circle.

The November *Voice* brought the news that the Rivers bill had passed and been signed by President Reagan on October 26, 1988. The Gauley, Meadow and Bluestone rivers were now protected and minor changes to the New River Gorge National River were included as well. All four congressmen from West Virginia were supportive and both senators had put their weight behind the final effort to gain passage. Past President John Purbaugh's personal letters of appreciation to Congressman Rahall and Senator Rockefeller were reprinted as well.

Three years after Rep. Rahall addressed the Conservancy, proposing a National Recreation Area for the Gauley, it was accomplished. It had taken longer to permanently protect the New River, but that too was certain. River conservation was a long-haul job and victories were not common.

Shavers Fork — The Middle Years

The Early Years of Shavers Fork discussion earlier in this chapter ended as 1977 began. As related, 1977 was a decisive year for both Rowlesburg and Stonewall Jackson, as Governor Rockefeller faced a series of difficult decisions relating to environmental issues. In this climate, Shavers Fork remained in the background.

It would be another two years before a *Voice* article would focus on Shavers Fork. In the January 1979 issue, Editor Tom Dunham's headline "Assault on Shavers Fork," alerted readers of trouble ahead. As discussed in the earlier section, Mower Lumber Company, owner of mineral rights under Monongahela Forest surface between Bemis and Cheat Bridge, proposed to open deep mines and recover the coal. Dunham wrote, "Mower estimates that there are 70 million tons of medium volatile metallurgical coal, all economically recoverable from minimum 28 inch seams." With additional coal south of Cheat Bridge and elsewhere nearby, Mower expected 40-45 years of mining. A moratorium agreed to between Mower and the Forest Service had recently expired and had been a chance for the government to assess and consider the purchase of these mineral rights. Now Mower was moving ahead with their planning and attendant public relations campaign emphasizing job creation.

The Forest Service had issued a draft Sub-Unit Management Plan and Environmental Impact Statement for Shavers Fork the previous summer and received public comments. A revised plan would be issued, according to Dunham, if the Forest Service could identify a water quality standard that would preserve the trout habitat. Many commenters believed the mines would discharge iron and trace metals, which would be toxic to Shavers Fork's already fragile water quality. Other issues concerned environmentalists as well, including a large proposed timber cut over the coming ten years.

A year later, in the January 1980 *Voice*, Dunham updated readers. The Forest Service EIS was still not out, but not expected to deter Mower's mining plans. Over the intervening months, the state DNR had agreed to Mower's plans, with a limitation of no more than six mines at one time and appropriate haul road restrictions. The federal Office of Surface Mining was waiting until its regulations were established, before it became involved. Dunham wrote:

> For those concerned with the environment of the Shavers Fork, the Environmental Protection Agency appears the best and last hope. EPA must issue a water quality permit, known as an NPDES permit. However, what is needed even prior to the consideration of a permit is a thorough environmental impact statement. The Sierra Club has written EPA asking that an EIS be completed. But more public input is needed.

Once again, the Environmental Impact Statement process, established under the National Environmental Policy Act of 1970, might buy the time needed to protect a pristine West Virginia natural resource permanently.

Meanwhile Mower was going ahead with plans to open the first two mines, leased to a contractor, Enviro Energy. The State DNR had received the necessary permit applications and a public hearing was scheduled in Elkins on May 13, 1980. In the May *Voice*, Dunham's headline was "D-Day For Shavers Fork." He wrote:

> Sadly and disgustingly none of the governmental agencies charged with protection of the natural environment appear the least bit interested in halting the latest assault on Shavers Fork. – Not the Monongahela National Forest that owns the surface rights over the proposed mine sites...From its hands-off attitude position, the Forest Service has stated that it sees no threat to the water quality of Shavers Fork.
>
> Not the Environmental Protection Agency which is attempting to take the easy way out by considering the proposed mines as existing sources and not new sources of water discharge. By classifying Mower's application as existing sources, EPA can legally consider water quality problems only. New source mines must meet far tougher standards and indeed a full environmental impact statement considering much more than water quality must be written. Some ten years ago, the area over

one of the proposed mine sites was "faced-up" in preparation for mining, but the job was abandoned. Yet this "face-up" has provided EPA with a reason for considering the proposed mines as existing sources....But as Conservancy Board members heard from EPA, Region III, EIS Chief Steven Torok at the April 21 Board meeting, EPA considers mining permits a "zero priority," meaning little attention will be given to them.

Dunham then sharply criticized state DNR Director David Callaghan for approving a Mower mining plan without public involvement. After a public outcry, the DNR scheduled a hearing on May 1, two weeks before EPA's scheduled hearing on May 13. Concluded Dunham, "the first step in getting the agencies to work for the public instead of for Mower is to attend the EPA hearing on May 13 and speak up for Shavers Fork."

Most of the balance of this *Highlands Voice* was devoted to Shavers Fork. Rivers Committee Chairman Perry Bryant reviewed the details of the two mining sites. Ironically, the one "faced up" was a Linan site, in other words, excavated and otherwise prepared for the extraction of coal.

Another long article reprinted a petition filed for the Conservancy by Charleston attorney and Conservancy Mining Committee Chairman David Wooley, under Section 522 of the Federal Surface Mine Act of 1977. That section provided for designation of certain areas as "unsuitable for strip mining," and gave the Office of Surface Mining the power to permanently prohibit mining in those areas. The petition argued that the Highlands Conservancy believed that the federal lands in the Shavers Fork basin should be so classified. The 522 Petition would become an important weapon in protecting Shavers Fork.

The November 1980 *Voice* updated Mower mine activity on Shavers Fork. An unsigned article reported that the EPA NPDES permits had been issued in September and resulted in a request for an evidentiary hearing by the Conservancy. Meanwhile, the petition to OSM for a designation of unsuitability had been met by OSM claiming Mower had "valid existing rights," a determination that was also appealed by the Conservancy. In the mean time, Mower and Enviro Energy began building haul roads. When the Conservancy's Fall Review was held in nearby Huttonsville, a group made a field visit. The article ended reporting that further appeals by the Conservancy were a viable possibility.

The following month's *Voice* indicated that the Conservancy and Mower's lawyers had filed briefs and presented oral arguments before the

U.S. Office of Surface Mining's Board of Review. The issue was "valid existing rights," which if denied, would stop mining. OSM had ruled the VER existed, notwithstanding the ongoing appeal that the entire area was unsuitable for mining under Section 522.

By February 1981's *Voice*, it was announced that Mower and Enviro Energy were actively mining at the first site and preparation for five more mines was underway. The state DNR agreement to a limit of six active mines at one time was in place, but negotiations with the Forest Service for additional sites were already starting. In addition, upstream New Era Resources proposed a 354-acre strip mine on Mower land.

Several additional paragraphs outlined the costs and benefits of litigation:

> W.Va. University law professor Pat McGinley (he was recently made a lifetime member of the Conservancy for the legal aid he proffered not only in connection with the Fork but also on other environmental issues) said this week that he and the Conservancy are seriously considering seeking another federal court injunction. That injunction would halt the work until U. S. Office of Surface Mining's board of appeals issued a final ruling on a Conservancy appeal of an earlier OSM ruling that granted Mower "valid existing rights" to mine its minerals, rights which would vest in Mower regardless of any decision to declare the watershed off-limits to mining.

> McGinley asserted that the prior denial of the Conservancy's injunction request by U. S. District Judge Robert E. Maxwell in Elkins – which incidentally, is itself being appealed – rested largely on the contention that the Conservancy had failed to give adequate notice to the United States Secretary of Interior, the individual at whom the injunction was aimed.

> The entire rear-guard action has so miffed Mower Lumber Company that the firm finally decided to sue the Conservancy for nearly $8,000 in attorney fees and other court costs, contending that the court action was "clearly intended merely to harass Mower and Enviro in order to delay their exploitation of Mower's coal resources."

> That suit was also filed before Judge Maxwell in Elkins who has declined to issue a decision until such time as the Conservancy's appeals processes are exhausted. McGinley openly scoffed at the suit, calling it "absurd," while another spokesman for the environmental group called it a "transparent attempt to intimidate" the Conservancy's membership as well as other environmental groups in the state.

In April, an unsigned front-page *Voice* photo and article were likely the work of new *Voice* Editor Judy Frank, also a reporter for the *Elkins Inter-Mountain*. OSM had held public hearings in Elkins to gather information before issuing its decision on the Conservancy's unsuitability for mining petition for Shavers Fork. In the photo were Michael Kline, who had raised eyebrows as he sang "They Can't Put It Back," the anti-strip mining anthem; Bard Montgomery, the Conservancy's Shavers Fork Chairman; and Billy Jack Gregg, OSM attorney. The caption continued that Secretary of Interior James G. Watt, whose department included OSM, would make the final decision. The decision was expected, according to the article, by April 25, 1981.

Montgomery had seen a draft of OSM's report and led off the hearing with a detailed critique of its deficiencies. Mower's lawyer naturally criticized it as not including supportive information they had provided. A sidebar quoted Montgomery as saying, "This decision will be the first of its kind in the East, and the first rendered by the new [Reagan] administration."

The OSM decision was actually issued by Regional Director Patrick Boggs in Charleston, after consultation with Interior Secretary Watt. It denied the Conservancy's claim that Shavers Fork qualified for "unsuitability" designation, according to a page one *Voice* article in June. Nonetheless, the decision was laced with statements and data supporting the fragile conditions of Shavers Fork, outlining longstanding recreational use of the area, and urged state and federal mining regulators to work on a case-by-case basis to protect Shavers Fork. Both the Conservancy and Mower announced appeals.

In September, Mower's suit to recover the $8,000 in attorney fees was rejected by Judge Maxwell. WVU Law School professor McGinley was pursuing a variety of OSM appeals, one of Boggs' decision and one of the appeal board's VER issue. Meanwhile the state DNR had obtained warrants for Enviro Energy for water discharge violations.

As the new year began, the January *Voice* revealed more permit applications to OSM for individual mines and requests from the Conservancy for opportunity to comment. Equally ominous was an article outlining a proposal by a drilling company to explore for natural gas under Forest Service land on Shavers Fork. In March, the Conservancy notified Enviro Energy that it intended to sue over a pattern of pollution violations that neither the Forest Service nor OSM seemed able to control.

By June/July's *Voice*, the suit had been filed in U.S. District Court in Clarksburg, charging OSM had suppressed a critical report on one of the mines, giving it to the company, but withholding it from the public. The suit sought to enjoin further mining until OSM issued all pending decisions.

Three articles by Montgomery, Shavers Fork Committee Chairman, in the February 1983 *Voice* brought readers up to date. OSM was still considering the applications, filed two years earlier, for six deep mines of Enviro Energy. Montgomery testified at an OSM public meeting that the Conservancy favored a full environmental impact statement on mining on Shavers Fork. The Conservancy's suit was still pending, with no date for a decision. In a second article, Montgomery reported that the decision of the OSM appeals board had "overturned the 1981 order by the Office of Surface Mining (OSM) which would have placed restrictive conditions on mining in the petition area." Both of McGinley's appeals had lost. The appeals board had taken the position, not supported by either side, that OSM didn't have jurisdiction, since the Forest Service already was responsible to protect the land. A proposed refuse pile at the Cheat Bridge coal washing plant, now run by Ingram Coal, formerly known as New Era Resources, that the Conservancy previously opposed, was given a state permit. On Shavers Fork things were not going well.

A year later, the March 1984 *Voice* reported the logjam had broken. Montgomery wrote:

> Six mine permits in the Shavers Fork watershed of the Monongahela National Forest have been approved by the U.S. Office of Surface Mining Director James R. Harris. Four of the mines of Enviro Energy, Inc. are already operating to extract coal belonging to Mower Lumber Co. that underlies national forest land.
>
> Shortly after the last of the permits were being approved by Harris, a long stalled court case was resolved in favor of the West Virginia Highlands Conservancy, casting doubt on Enviro's right to mine in the area. The Conservancy had appealed OSM's 1980 decision that Enviro had "valid existing rights" to mine coal when the 1977 Surface Mining and Control Act went into effect. The Interior Department's Board of Surface Mining Appeals refused to hear the Conservancy's appeal. U.S. District Judge William Kidd on February 1 ordered the appeals board to hear arguments from the Conservancy. Therefore the board will have to decide the issue of Enviro's "valid existing rights."

As the Conservancy moved into river protection as a major priority beginning in January 1984, *The Highlands Voice* carried articles on many river threats, but little on Shavers Fork. Enviro Energy was mining a limited number of mines, overseen by the Forest Service and the state DNR and the Conservancy had been increasingly frustrated to stop them. Many members, especially Shavers Fork chairmen, had worked hard to find ways to protect Shavers Fork, but in the end, between Snowshoe's development in the headwaters and the Monongahela National Forest's stewardship between Cheat Bridge (Rt. 250) and Bemis, there were few real ways a comprehensive protection plan could be fashioned. Activists found more satisfaction protecting the Gauley, the New, and becoming engaged in other issues facing the Highlands. It would be a quiet decade and a half.

The August 1986 *Highlands Voice* announced an effort by the Trust for Public Land to acquire 40,000 acres on Cheat Mountain at the headwaters of Shavers Fork. It had reportedly negotiated an option with Mower Limited Partnership. A five-year purchase was envisioned, beginning with a $14 million deal. The Congress was considering an appropriation of the first $6 million. The article stated that this might be the final opportunity for public ownership, since Snowshoe and nearby Silver Creek (another ski resort) made private recreational development more attractive than ever.

According to George Deike's article for the Spring Review 2000 tabloid, Mower Lumber sold their remaining acreage to the federal government in 1988, when it became a part of the Monongahela National Forest.

Shavers Fork — The Recent Years

Ruth Blackwell Rogers, with her husband Hugh, moved to Elkins and settled into a loose network of young families that enjoyed the rural ambiance of Randolph County, its thriving arts and music scene, and seemed content to improve their small farm along Leading Creek. Soon after they settled there, the Rogers began to attend Highlands Conservancy meetings. When serious planning began for Corridor H going up Leading Creek north of Elkins, the Rogers became key leaders in the Corridor H controversy. Hugh moved through several Conservancy officer positions and became President in 2005.

Ruth Blackwell Rogers was trained as and has been a successfully practicing multi-media artist. She has painted small pieces, and installed large exhibits, even a small forest, large enough to walk through. She has presented her art overseas, including Seoul, Korea, where she and Hugh served with the Peace Corps.

After twin floods hit the area in 1996, a Davis and Elkins College student named Zach Henderson organized a multi-disciplinary and interagency task force to address a variety of issues related to Shavers Fork. She was impressed by the leadership and initiative of this college student and began to attend meetings. Her quiet yet systematic style became important in brokering among the many interests represented. Blackwell Rogers served first as Secretary, and then when Henderson went to graduate school, she became the President, convener and leader of the Shavers Fork Coalition.

According to an article Blackwell Rogers wrote for the Spring Review in 2000 on Shavers Fork:

> The Shavers Fork Coalition had its beginnings in a senior thesis written by Zachary Henderson in 1996. While attending Davis and Elkins College, Zach had fallen in love with the Shavers Fork River and watershed. He had a scientific interest in the river's physical dynamics and water quality, and a personal interest in the outstanding recreational opportunities and aesthetic beauty of the area. That summer, Zach wrote and received a West Virginia Stream Partners grant. He organized public meetings that brought together watershed residents, businesses, recreational users, agencies, farmers, and private and government landowners.

Over time, the coalition began a host of projects. These included clean-up projects, tours with foresters, sponsoring internships in 1998 and 1999, publishing research findings, ongoing water quality monitoring, and general public awareness efforts. Blackwell Rogers reported that in 2000 the concentration was on the headwaters, where sedimentation and red spruce research were underway.

The June 2000 issue of *The Highlands Voice* announced, "West Virginia Highlands Conservancy Joins Historic Commitment to Shavers Fork." Written by Dave Saville, the article reported that twenty-five public, private, and non-profit organizations had joined with local landowners and others concerned with the future of the upper Shavers

Fork River. Henderson, of the Shavers Fork Coalition, had coordinated a two-day conference at Snowshoe called the "Healing the Headwaters Summit." Additional sponsoring groups included the Canaan Valley Institute, Trout Unlimited, Friends of the Cheat, the Highlands Conservancy, and the WVU Division of Forestry.

Said Henderson, "We wanted to highlight the wide variety of conservation initiatives that we have already begun here, and to create a renewed interest in watershed stewardship." The Healing the Headwaters manifesto both gave a short history of Shavers Fork, and also nine action items to which members of the group committed themselves. It was a new generation and they had new energy.

Blackwell Rogers later provided a summary of various projects. There was the first planting of red spruce seedlings at the old town site of Spruce, by some boy scouts and Trout Unlimited. The Conservancy collaborated on one or more of these tree-planting excursions. During the Conservancy's 2000 Spring Review, tree planting was one of the outings offered and the organization continued to co-sponsor plantings in October and April 2000.

A year or so later, the *Voice* published an article about conflicting interests on upper Shavers Fork. An excursion train that transported about twenty tree planters upstream also carried a group of tree cutters who jumped out periodically with clippers and saws to cut down trees and saplings which obscured the view of the train from rail fan photographers!

In 2003, the Coalition received a challenge grant from the Columbia Natural Resources Company to help "restore the native Red Spruce ecosystem of Upper Shavers Fork watershed and its associated aquatic resources to historic levels of structure, function, and productivity." Under the grant, tributaries impeded by railroad culverts or other man-made structures where they enter Shavers Fork would be identified and mitigation measures suggested.

At the Shavers Fork Coalition meeting in 2005, the day before the Conservancy's Fall Review, both at the Cheat Mountain Club, along the upper Shavers Fork at Cheat Bridge, the format was a roundtable discussion, more like an academic conference than anything else. The session was billed as a "sharing and brainstorming day," focused on identifying recommendations for the final report to complete the grant. To get started, Dr. Todd Petty, a fish researcher from WVU Wildlife Division, and Zack Liller, his graduate assistant, presented their latest research findings. Dr. Jim Van Gundy, Professor Emeritus of Biology at Davis and Elkins College and the incoming President of the Shavers Fork Coalition, summarized temperature and flow research data.

The audience included biologists from the DNR and Forest Service as well as representatives of the Nature Conservancy, Friends of the Cheat, Trout Unlimited, and eight members of the Highlands Conservancy. The atmosphere had changed from the old days. Gone was the dark shadow of private economic interests out to ruin a precious ecosystem. Instead, in public National Forest ownership, Shavers Fork was discussed as a mammoth outdoor laboratory that contained uncounted research opportunities. Somehow, despite all the mining and development threats, Shavers Fork had continued on, year after year, presenting itself to a new generation, whose mission would be to pass it on again for the next generation to enjoy.

Sources:

Burrell, Bob, interview, June 21, 2006, and correspondence

Burrell, Bob, newsletter dated March 1968 (later *The Highland Voice*)

Burrell, Bob, and Paul Davidson, *Wild Water West Virginia: A Paddler's Guide to the White Water Rivers of the Mountain State* (Parsons, W.Va.: McClain Printing Company, 1972)

Elkinton, Dave, author's notes from Shavers Fork Coalition meeting, October 11, 2005

Frank, Judy, article on Shavers Fork in Elkins *Inter-Mountain* (1976)

The Highlands Voice, articles by Thomas Bond, Perry Bryant, Bob Burrell, Tom cofield, Paul Davidson, Tom Dunham, Herb Eckert, Allen Haden, Bruce Jarvis, Tom King, Craig Moore, Dave Elkinton, Ron Hardway, Clish McCleaver, Bard Montgomery, Frank Pelurie, Mary Ratliff, Sayre Rodman, Dave Saville, Linda Winter, Nick Zvegintzov, and others

Johnson, Skip, article in *The Charleston Gazette*

Rodman, Buff, interview, June 22, 2006

Rodman, Jean, interview, June 22, 2006

Rogers, Hugh, interview, June 20, 2006

Rogers, Ruth Blackwell, interview, June 20, 2006

Scenic Rivers Subcommittee newsletters

Schoenbaum, Thomas J., *The New River Controversy* (Winston-Salem, N.C.: John F. Blair)

Spring Review 2000, published by WVHC, tabloid prepared for that event, with articles by Ruth Blackwell Rogers, George Deike, Zach Henderson, Bryan Moore, and others.

Chapter Four
The Billion-Dollar Boondoggle:
Appalachian Corridor H

The Original Idea

One of the organizing principles for the Conservancy, opposition to highway construction through pristine areas, foreshadowed several highway battles to come. The first proposal, the Allegheny Parkway (patterned by its boosters after the Blue Ridge Parkway), was to follow the highest peaks and connect Spruce Knob, Dolly Sods, and other peaks. (See Chapter 1.) The second idea was the Highland Scenic Highway, a portion of which was actually built in Pocahontas County between the Cranberry Visitor Center and US Route 219 north of Edray. The third scheme, the infamous Appalachian Corridor H, was designed to link I-79 at Weston with I-66 in Virginia. All three have had their boosters, attracted massive opposition, and ultimately were scaled back or even stopped before the first spade of dirt was turned. But by far the longest struggle and the proposal that has changed the most often was Appalachian Corridor H.

An east-west four-lane highway across north central West Virginia had been a dream of developers for all the years the Highlands Conservancy had been in existence and earlier. Yet the basic fact remained that it was impossible to select a route for a major highway that would not endanger numerous pristine trout streams, interfere with the wilderness experience of areas already protected by Congress, or cut through historical battlefields. Nonetheless, there were waves of activity by federal and state government highway planners, with corresponding mobilization by opposing agencies and citizens.

The first article in *The Highlands Voice* focusing on Corridor H appeared in the June 1972 issue. Bob Burrell reported on a briefing by Governor Arch Moore's Administrative Assistant Bill Loy, who stated that

Corridor H would go east from Elkins at least to the community of Alpena, a distance of thirteen miles. "Mr. Loy was vague as to how it would then go north, presumably up over Middle Mountain. He did say it would not go through Dolly Sods, but the Dolly Sods boundaries mean different things to different people." It seemed to Burrell that the Conservancy was worried about Dolly Sods, but not Corridor H itself. However, within a short two years, the Conservancy would become a major player in the Corridor H issue, in which it would remain involved for the next thirty.

By 1972, there had already been signs of trouble. In the August-September 1971 *Voice*, Burrell had written a lengthy status report on the Shavers Fork, hinting at trouble at the Bowden National Fish Hatchery. He reported a warning from the U.S. Bureau of Sport Fisheries and Wildlife that "any further deterioration of water quality in the Shavers Fork would not only seriously endanger hatchery fish populations, but may also reduce or eliminate desirable species of fish from the river," since the natural buffering capacity of Shavers Fork had been reached. In other words, for Bowden to continue as a major hatchery, the water quality of Shavers Fork could not deteriorate.

At that time, the development of Corridor H was both a low visibility proposal, promoted by various chambers of commerce, and an idea generally seen as such an expensive undertaking that it was unlikely to ever be built. Also, the Conservancy in the early 1970s was very busy with wilderness proposals, dam opposition, and other real concerns in need of immediate attention.

East from Elkins

In 1974, Corridor H came to the center stage. While construction had already begun from Elkins east to Bowden, there was a raging discussion over its routing from there further east. At the Mid-Winter Workshop, held in Elkins in January that year, the major discussion according to a *Voice* article, was a panel centering on highway development in the scenic highlands region. Among the panelists was John McBee, representing the Federal Highway Administration. Conservancy members learned that a draft environmental impact statement (EIS) for Corridor H, from Wymer (east of Bowden) to Strasburg, Virginia, would be completed by September 1974 and that full public hearings would follow. McBee noted that no definite route for Corridor H had been determined beyond Wymer. This was the first, but certainly not the last, EIS deadline that would prove overly optimistic. (The first leg, already under construction, either was exempt from the EIS requirement or it had been issued without public controversy.)

A story in the June-July 1974 *Highlands Voice*, "Corridor H: The Conservancy's Position Paper," contained a detailed statement and two-page map, outlining nine alternative routes and their impacts. The position paper was written by Conservancy President Dave Elkinton and submitted within the comment period that followed. It was based on reports from Conservancy members in attendance at three nights of hearings held in Davis, Petersburg, and Romney in May. An accompanying article by Lowell Markey reported all three hearings were well attended and strong opposition to all routes had been expressed.

In essence, the Conservancy questioned the basic need for a controlled-access four-lane highway, preferring instead an upgrade of existing U.S. Route 33, U.S. Route 50, and other feeder routes. In addition to specific concerns of the several proposed routings, the Conservancy also proposed an examination of two other alternatives: the "original" routing via Mouth of Seneca and a northern route from Elkins toward Parsons. Neither was included in the environmental impact planning.

Of the routes included in the EIS, the Conservancy had major issues with those through or near Canaan Valley, Laurel Fork, Gladys Fork, Dry Fork, Red Creek, Dolly Sods, Greenland Gap, and the Trough, among other places. The Conservancy position stated:

> Each of these is an area of truly unique environmental importance. First the several lines that either cross or proceed along the free-flowing rivers in the area will cause irreparable harm to these rivers. [These] are all unspoiled, magnificent mountain streams known widely for fishing and the rapidly growing sport of whitewater canoeing...In fact this combination of rivers is perhaps one of the best networks of rivers in such a small geographical area in West Virginia, or perhaps in the nearby states, for offering more miles of unequalled whitewater canoeing...Highway construction would create environmental degradation that would never be overcome, and these rivers would lose forever their unspoiled natural beauty and character.

Markey addressed the timetable for completion of this extremely expensive highway. An eight- to ten-year construction schedule was predicted, subject to available federal funding and unforeseen delays. (Thirty years later, however, Corridor H was still under construction.)

While the controversy centered on the routing from Wymer to the Virginia state line, construction was already underway on the portion of Corridor H from Elkins to Wymer, including a bridge over Shavers Fork at Bowden. The August 1974 *Voice* featured a photo and short article on the Bowden Fish Hatchery, titled "Corridor H Finally Does It." Echoing Burrell's article in 1971, it continued:

> Disaster has stricken the Federal fish hatchery at Bowden on Shavers Fork despite months of warning from environmentalists. Sometime in June construction activities on Appalachian Corridor H directly opposite the hatchery trespassed on the South Springs, one of two coldwater springs that feeds the hatchery in the summer. The ensuing mudflow into the hatchery waters choked to death 150,000 four-inch trout scheduled for stocking next year in West Virginia streams.

Because the Bowden Fish Hatchery produced the majority of trout stocked in the state, Corridor H had suddenly become a major statewide environmental issue, not just one of interest to those in the highlands. Influential *Charleston Gazette* outdoor columnist Skip Johnson wrote a column titled, "Corridor H: In the Wrong Place:"

> If the State Department of Highways, Federal Highway Administration and Governor Moore want to do the right thing about Corridor H construction, they should admit they made a mistake and stop the highway where it is now.
>
> They should then backtrack to Elkins and build the road north to Parsons, thus sparing further danger to the $4 million Bowden Federal Fish Hatchery, to probably a dozen quality trout streams, and to a wilderness area west of Canaan Valley [Otter Creek].
>
> There seems to be an obsession in West Virginia for building roads through wild places, as opposed to following perfectly good existing roads. Corridor H and the Highland Scenic Highway are classic examples.

Johnson continued by analyzing the northern route from Elkins to Parsons, which was originally favored by the state Department of Natural Resources, until Governor Moore forced the agency to support his preferred routing east from Elkins. Johnson cited several court decisions that provided precedent for changing directions after environmental impacts are found to block original routings. He quoted United States Supreme Court Justice Hugo Black, "It is hereby declared to be national policy that special effort should be made to preserve the natural beauty of the countryside and public park and recreation lands." Concluded Johnson, "Any route Corridor H takes north of Wymer will violate this declaration."

The issues were thus defined: there were no feasible alternatives east from Elkins that would minimize impacts on numerous trout streams, scenic areas and wilderness areas. Already the cold water supplies for the Bowden Hatchery were in danger. A growing chorus insisted that the routing north from Elkins, through Parsons, and climbing Backbone Mountain would be preferable, and the cost of the leg from Elkins to Bowden would have to be written off as a mistake. Although this would eventually become the preferred route, it would take another twenty years to concede the mistake and ten additional years to begin to build it.

In March 1975, Burrell reported in his *Voice* column on a Conservancy delegation's trip to Washington, D.C. Joining Burrell were Conservancy members Geoff Green, a professional civil engineer, and Markey, recently elected Conservancy Highlands vice president and a community development planner from Potomac State College. Burrell recounted a briefing with aides to Senator Jennings Randolph, Chairman of the Senate Public Works and Environment Committee, who was widely considered the "father of Corridor H":

> What really impressed all present was the brilliant presentation and study prepared by Geoff and Lowell. Dave Elkinton some time ago had encouraged these fellows to make a social and economic impact study of Corridor H and compare it with a similar study of the alternate proposal (north via Parsons). Although these fellows had almost finished their study when notified of the meeting, they had not collated the material, analyzed it completely, nor even had it typed out and collated. But then they did it essentially [in] a weekend! And it was not a superficial, sloppy job by any means. When they received a sharp question from the lawyers, our gang had the answers and one could see that the questioner was greatly impressed.

According to Burrell, the Washington aides were upset that the construction of Corridor H near Bowden was causing significant environmental problems and that many more could be predicted as the highway pushed east. There was serious discussion of stopping at Bowden and reconsidering a northern route towards Parsons. Burrell continued:

When we suggested that the highway be stopped and pulled out a rerouting north to Parsons, nobody batted an eye at this or threw up their hands as I had expected. On the contrary, they talked about this as a viable alternative. They were impressed that state and federal officials from other agencies were talking this way on their own.

Burrell concluded with high praise for the efforts of Markey and Green:

We did not go there with a negative view, but rather suggestions for a sound positive alternative and this alternative was well documented. There was no emotion (if any was expressed, it was on the part of the Public Works Councilors) and we dealt rationally with the facts and the data. Outstanding credit must go to Lowell and Geoff for their exceptional efforts. We in the Highlands Conservancy have many excellent human resources, but none of us have ever performed as well on a critical issue as this. We are growing and we are maturing. Each presentation we make is better than the last.

Burrell, whose opinion was highly respected both within the Conservancy and by observers outside, declared that Markey and Green had performed in the highest Conservancy tradition. They had studied the issue, found a feasible alternative to the one with severe environmental impacts, prepared a report and presented their alternative to policy decision-makers. Over and over this would be a hallmark of how the West Virginia Highlands Conservancy approached environmental issues.

In the July *Voice*, Burrell reported on a major meeting held in Charleston attended by federal and state agencies and environmentalists. By this point, the Conservancy, Trout Unlimited and others had pressured the United States Fish and Wildlife Service (formerly the Bureau of Sports Fisheries), who owned the Bowden Hatchery, to confront the state Department of Highways over the loss of Bowden's cold spring water, essential for trout production. USFWS leaders were insisting on a comprehensive environmental impact statement from Bowden to the Virginia line, but DOH insisted on a segmented EIS. Conservancy representatives wanted the Parsons routing included as well in any comprehensive EIS. Another alternative, of course, was no road at all. Burrell concluded:

We stated that we were in favor of the highway, but not at the expense of the 16 rivers and streams yet to be muddied, the inviolate mountains and wildlife habitat yet to be invaded, and the scenic vistas yet to be destroyed. Once again we pointed out the results of the Markey-Green report and requested that if amateurs such as ourselves could turn up such important reasons for building the highway along the northern route, why couldn't the professionals follow up on them.

Burrell recounted all the meetings with various federal and state officials over many months in an effort to avoid litigation over Corridor H. He concluded, "once again, the Conservancy finds itself reluctantly being forced to the Courts." Clearly the DOH, with the backing of the state's two senators, the Appalachian Regional Commission and the Federal Highway Administration, was full-speed ahead on a route east of Bowden. On the other side were the U.S. Fish and Wildlife Service, the U.S. Forest Service, and the environmental community.

By September, Burrell had become more optimistic. He opened his "Overlook" column with a major understatement:

> It does appear that the Corridor H controversy has been resolved. The highways people have finally agreed to do an environmental impact statement (EIS) on the entire alignment, including the alternatives such as the Parsons route. They had no choice. They simply had to obey the law and take recognizance of the weight of the opposition from Federal agencies. The Conservancy's efforts to keep Corridor H in the limelight resulted in more people and organizations becoming actively involved in seeing that these laws were obeyed.
>
> Now of course, don't start applauding yourself yet. The EIS could possibly conclude that the way Corridor H is now going is the best way and the cheapest (thanks to an already wasted $20 million). So what would have been accomplished besides delaying the project a few years and making it more expensive? The worst part of this is that it would tend to prove Highway Commissioner [William] Ritchie correct, who stated earlier this summer that this is all an EIS accomplishes anyway. The Conservancy has always tried to bet with some excellent cards in the hole and we are currently working quietly on two in case the EIS opener gets trumped.

His column, "Corridor H Not the Only Threat to Shavers Fork," made the case that Corridor H was a controversy involving many public agencies, all of which ultimately depended on public and political support. He contrasted that with the upper Shavers Fork watershed where the land was owned by a private company, Mower Lumber Company, owned by J. Peter Grace, thus its ability to collaborate with logging and mining interests and destroy the river forever. This was an example of the merging of two issues within the Conservancy, highway development and river conservation.

In early 1976, there was a spirited five-way race for the Democratic nominee for governor of West Virginia. The candidates were Jay Rockefeller (who had lost once before, campaigning on an anti-strip mining platform), Congressman Ken Hechler (long an ally of the Conservancy and speaker at its 1976 Mid-Winter Workshop), Charleston Mayor John Hutchinson, H. John Rogers (a perennial gadfly), and James Sprouse (past candidate and party favorite). The Conservancy sent each candidate a questionnaire to discover their views on significant environmental issues and then published the results in the *Voice*.

Surprisingly, when asked about Corridor H, Rockefeller responded:

> I favor no further construction of Corridor H in the vicinity of Bowden Fish Hatchery until a full evaluation of all alternative routes can be completed. Before construction can proceed, we must make sure that there will be no further adverse effects on the water supply in that area and that the environment as a whole will be adequately protected. [In the next question, he also announced that he was opposed to the Davis Power Project, which was triumphantly received by Conservancy members.]

This became significant when Rockefeller won the primary election and eventually was elected governor. (Rockefeller's answer to the question on the Davis Power Project would also prove important. See Chapter 5.)

In July 1976, Markey updated readers of the *Voice* on the status of Corridor H. Markey reported that federal and state agencies were considering only two alternative routes of Corridor H; Bowden north through Canaan Valley, to Romney, connecting with US Route 50 at Winchester, Virginia, and Bowden to Seneca Rocks, to Moorefield, connecting with I-66 at Strasburg, Virginia. Despite the Conservancy's research and public awareness campaign, the Elkins to Parsons route would not be considered.

A second round of hearings was held in Moorefield, Romney, Keyser and Davis. Using a new format, tabletop discussions with brainstorming and prioritizing techniques, the DOH still found widespread opposition in all four towns and no alternative emerged with significant support. A side benefit, according to Markey, was that the local opposition groups began to get acquainted and coordinate their testimony. (Hugh Rogers pointed out that the same thing happened again sixteen years later, leading to the formation of Corridor H Alternatives, described later in this chapter.) The Parsons alternative was still not on the table and various comments indicated that court action might ultimately be used to force its consideration.

After the election, Burrell reviewed the eight-year environmental record of outgoing Governor Moore. He remembered that Moore's Director of Federal-State Relations, Dr. Billy Coffindaffer, had written Moore back on May 28, 1969, enclosing a study on the basic alternatives for Corridor H. The Elkins to Parsons route, it said, would be cheaper, avoid the environmental challenges and still meet the highway's purposes. Because of Moore's stubbornness in choosing the route east to Bowden, Burrell said, "this decision has cost West Virginia taxpayers hundreds of thousands of dollars and will go on costing them much more." After eight years, all the taxpayers had was a four-lane to Bowden and some right-of-way on east to Wymer (which was never to be used). This was hardly the legacy of a governor who said he wanted to be remembered as the one who brought roads to West Virginia.

At the Conservancy's board meeting in October, Markey proposed a change in its policy position on Corridor H, namely that the Conservancy support the "no-build" alternative and also support the upgrading of the existing highways in the proposed route areas. The motion passed.

Because the Rockefeller administration faced many urgent environmental and fiscal issues when it assumed office in early 1977, it would be nearly another year before Corridor H was worth a *Voice* headline.

In November 1977, Markey reported on yet another DOH survey of residents of a six-county area in eastern West Virginia. As governor, Rockefeller had in fact added two new routes to the consideration; one Elkins-Parsons-Greenland Gap-Moorefield, the other Elkins-Parsons-New Creek-Romney. Both were variations of recommendations in the March 1975 Markey-Green report and the 1969 Coffindaffer recommendation to Governor Moore. It had taken numerous meetings, public hearings, eight years and a change of governors just to begin the analysis of a logical alternative. Because of the added alternatives, a DOH spokesman advised that the Elkins to Virginia EIS would be delayed from September 1977 to mid-year 1978.

But it would be late November 1979 before Markey reported the pending release of the draft environmental impact statement that included the Parsons routings. Following a full round of public meetings, a final routing would be chosen. The Parsons-Thomas-Moorefield route was cheapest ($300 million), followed by the Parsons-Romney route

($312 million). All routes east of Elkins through Bowden were more expensive. But more waiting was to come.

Eighteen months later, in May 1981, the *Voice* reported the release of the EIS, the scheduling of public meetings, and later, public hearings. It was clear that the Rockefeller administration had made a new commitment to moving ahead with construction of Corridor H. Although Markey was no longer active with the Conservancy, his former co-author Green was on the Conservancy Board and agreed to quarterback the Conservancy's participation. In June the *Voice* reported widespread support in Elkins for the Parsons route, as Green began preparing for the public hearings. The Department of Natural Resources announced its support for the "no-build" alternative in a July letter to the DOH, but said that if a highway was to be built, it should be north via Parsons.

"Ding, Dong, the Wicked Road is Dead" blared from a *Voice* headline in February 1982. The Rockefeller administration and the Appalachian Regional Commission, bowing to the Reagan administration's wish to cut economic development projects, had agreed to shelve Corridor H. The article left the door open, should federal funding become available at a later time. As Conservancy activists had learned, however, some projects had nine lives.

Within the year, the December 1982 *Voice* had two related stories under the banner "Corridor H Makes a Comeback." One, from *The Charleston Gazette's* Skip Johnson, announced that the DOH had tentatively chosen the southern route for Corridor H. "But whether the highway actually will be built is still a question mark," wrote Johnson. This routing would proceed east from Bowden, pass near Seneca Rocks, on through Petersburg and Moorefield to intersect I-81 at Strasburg, Virginia. (Ironically, this was the original Corridor H route proposed back in the 1960s.) A DOH spokesman was quoted as saying a final EIS would take another one and one-half years to complete. Johnson quoted Ralph Mumme, Supervisor of the Monongahela National Forest, which opposed that route, as saying "The DOH hasn't shown conclusively that this is the only prudent alternative."

The second article, "Resource Agencies Oppose Route" quoted the state DNR's Don Phares saying the route chosen is the "most damaging to the environment of all the alternatives considered." In addition to the DNR, the United States Fish and Wildlife Service also opposed the southern route, because it was fearful the highway would destroy the springs upon which the Bowden National Fish Hatchery relied. The

USFWS's Chris Clower informed the state that his agency would request a seldom-used full review by the President's Council on Environmental Quality if the southern route was chosen. The DOH said a final EIS would not be published until early 1984. Clearly, Corridor H was not dead.

In 1984, the election of Moore for an unprecedented third term, following Rockefeller's eight years, would return the "highway-building governor" to office. The election signaled that Corridor H, which had spent Rockefeller's eight years in the study category, might be back in business. However, the lack of federal funding and the lack of support for any alternative had kept construction to a minimum. The Moore administration used what funds they had to plan the less-controversial sections between Buckhannon and Elkins.

It would be September 1990, under yet another governor, Gaston Caperton, before Corridor H would re-emerge. (Looking back in a 2006 interview, Hugh Rogers also credited the elevation of Senator Robert Byrd to Chairman of the Senate Appropriations Committee as a pivotal event.) In June 1990 the state initiated a procedure to reevaluate the draft EIS of 1981. This was a federal requirement since more than three years had expired since the last draft EIS and no final EIS had ever been published under the Rockefeller or Moore administrations. Public comments needed to be weighed, updated agency input sought, and cost analyses made current. A "Supplementary Draft EIS" was therefore required. DOH officials insisted that the route east to Seneca Rocks was no more preferred than any other. The SDEIS would be a new, standalone document scheduled for review in early 1992. Another full set of public hearings would be scheduled.

Once again, the Conservancy began to mobilize its resources. President Cindy Rank fired off a letter to Highway Commissioner Fred Van Kirk reiterating the Conservancy's long-standing involvement in Corridor H routing. She summarized the Conservancy's position: 1) questioning the need for the highway, 2) continuing to urge upgrading of existing highways in the region, 3) considering the Parsons-Thomas alternative if the "no-build" alternative fails, 4) no alternative through Canaan Valley was acceptable, 5) advocating a careful consideration of impacts on the Bowden Fish Hatchery, Seneca Rocks, Lost and Cacapon rivers, other trout streams, and threatened and endangered species, along with several miscellaneous additional considerations.

By this time, the battle over the most controversial highway proposal in West Virginia history had already lasted twenty-five years. After four governors, numerous DNR and DOH staffers, eleven Conservancy presidents, and meetings and public hearings too numerous to count, the bridge over Shavers Fork at Bowden still marked the eastern endpoint of Corridor H. Persistence had kept the Conservancy in the game, outlasting almost all the other players, with the exception of one United States senator. With the SDEIS process, a new phase was opening that could potentially shift to a route north, not east, from Elkins.

North from Elkins

Hugh Rogers and Ruth Blackwell (see preceding chapter) came from very different backgrounds. Hugh's family had followed the textile industry south from New England to North Carolina. Ruth was a full-fledged southerner, born in Winston Salem, North Carolina. Both attended graduate school at the University of North Carolina, Hugh in law school and Ruth studying art. As they began to date, they talked about working in different cultures and communities. In 1968, shortly after they married, they joined the Peace Corps and went to Korea.

When they returned to the United States, it took a few moves before they settled with Peace Corps friends near Elkins. They soon became part of a thriving network of young couples that were attracted to that part of the state by its combination of livable small town qualities, Monongahela National Forest recreational opportunities, and arts flavor. Around 1977 Fred and Karen Bird, already active in the Conservancy, invited Hugh and Ruth to their first Conservancy event, but it would be several more years before they became actively involved.

Ruth Blackwell Rogers, in addition to her involvement with Corridor H, became a second, or third wave, leader in the preservation of Shavers Fork. Her role in that issue is discussed in the preceding chapter.

In 2006, Hugh remembered the origin of their involvement: "By 1992, we were no longer living on shared property; the two other couples we had lived with had moved away. It was Terry Miller, who lived a few miles away in Montrose, who invited us to a community meeting about Corridor H, and Marion Harless, our neighbor, who first showed us maps of the proposed alternatives

— one of which would come up the Leading Creek Valley toward Parsons and change our pastoral community forever. Shortly after, we began meeting with Chuck Merritt and Pam Moe; together with Terry, this became our core group. At the outset, we called ourselves 'Down the Road — Highway Alternatives'."

As had happened back in 1976, opponents found each other at DOH-sponsored public hearings and looked for ways to merge their efforts. Bonni McKeown, of Capon Bridge, in Hampshire County, had organized a group in Hampshire and Hardy counties called simply "H-No!" Charlie Winfree, in New Creek, Mineral County, was the lead activist in "Citizens Against Scheme E," named for the proposed alternative that would connect to US 50. And Tony Coogan, of Lebanon Church, in Shenandoah County, Virginia, was whipping up opposition along VA 55 between the WV border and I-81. These four groups joined to form Corridor H Alternatives, which would lead the fight until it finally, perhaps inevitably, reached the federal courts.

As their involvement progressed, Hugh Rogers, a lawyer, would shepherd the Conservancy and Corridor H Alternatives into a lengthy court battle, then a protracted mediation, a first for the Conservancy. Ultimately he would watch as Corridor H became a reality, yet significantly modified as a result of these efforts. Along the way, Rogers became a board member, chair of the Highways Committee, secretary, and eventually Conservancy president.

As the 1990s began, Corridor H had a new lease on life. The 1991 Spring Review met in the Seneca Rocks area and focused on Corridor H. It was evident that the Conservancy was still worried that the original routing (Elkins-Bowden-Seneca-Petersburg) was very much in play and the Conservancy wanted to be active as the state prepared its supplementary draft EIS. At that Review, Sierra Club leader Mary Wimmer made a strong case against the southern route and in favor of the northern route via Parsons. A DOH representative reviewed the upcoming process and a leader from the Martinsburg area spoke in favor of a northern route. The Conservancy reaffirmed its preference for the "no-build" alternative, but if built, preferred the northern route.

Throughout 1991 and early 1992, *The Highlands Voice* ran letters to the editor and short notices urging members to express their opposition to the southern route.

Although a *Voice* article by Wimmer in March 1992 warned that a decision by the state and release of the SDEIS was imminent, still a year later the *Voice* headlined "Decision Soon on Corridor H Route." That article added that over the previous months a new organization had formed, called the Corridor H Alliance, a coalition of business, taxpayer, and sportsmen groups that favored the northern route. The article also stated that the major advocate for construction was Senator Byrd. By then, he had stepped down as Majority Leader to become Chairman of the Appropriations Committee, with the avowed purpose of bringing federal funds to West Virginia. Corridor H was on Byrd's list of projects to fund.

Finally, the April 1993 *Voice* announced "WVDOH Picks Scheme D5 for Corridor H." A companion article by Conservancy member Chuck Merritt, also a leader in Down the Road/Highway Alternatives, analyzed the likely damage from Scheme D5, a compromise northern route. Proceeding up Leading Creek toward Parsons, it veered east over Cheat Mountain and across Shavers Fork, up Backbone Mountain, splitting Davis and Thomas, then off the Allegheny Front near Scherr, and on east toward Petersburg and Moorefield. The only bow to environmental concerns was a proposed sub-scheme to avoid Greenland Gap.

Now all parties knew the state's preferred route. It had taken twenty years, since Burrell first read Conservancy comments at a public hearing in 1973, to stop one destructive route and substitute another. Many people wondered how long it would take to fund this unbelievably expensive project, if it ever was going to be built.

As the summer of 1973 progressed, the rationale for Scheme D5 became more questionable. In the *Voice*, a lengthy unsigned article (written by Charlie Winfree, said Rogers in 2006), "The Michael Baker Two Step," exposed how the state's consultant had distorted letters opposing other schemes as favoring D5. Finally, as 1993 ended, the *Voice* featured Rogers' carefully footnoted analysis and historical review, "A Billion Dollar Exit Ramp." Thousands of more words from Rogers would appear in the *Voice* over the next dozen years.

Rogers was elected to the Conservancy board at the October 1994 Fall Review. More surprisingly, the United States Environmental Protection Agency Regional Director, Peter Kostmayer, dropped in for a comprehensive discussion on a variety of environmental issues. It was unusual for the Philadelphia-based Regional Director to be in West Virginia and even more unusual for him to initiate a meeting with citizens. Conservancy members discussed Corridor H, the inadequacy of the draft supplemental EIS and how the EPA might help facilitate a more environmentally compatible routing. Kostmayer got the message.

Merritt reported on an October ribbon-cutting at the Corridor H bridge over the Tygart Valley River, just west of Elkins. Although the bridge was only partially completed, it was, after all, a week before the election and Senator Byrd again was on the ballot. But he was in for a surprise! As the high school bands played and the politicians arrived, banners unfurled saying "H-NO Stop Corridor H Now!" A small plane even circled low overhead, towing the same message. It was clear the continued route east was going to run into trouble.

Merritt reported that after Byrd reviewed the history and need for Corridor H:

> The Senator called the opponents of Corridor H a "bunch of classic negative thinkers." Then he really threw the book at us, which was, the Bible! He quoted scripture (Isaiah Chapter 40 verse 4 to be exact) and said, "that the mountains shall be laid low and the valleys exalted." He concluded, "that God has ordained that these highways shall be built." At this point a Christian 'road warrior' could no longer contain himself at this out of context and inappropriate use of the Bible and said clearly and succinctly, "God doesn't drive no bulldozer!"

Merritt concluded philosophically:

> I found myself wondering at how backwards and upside down it had all become. The road proponents were all for spending huge sums of money (10 to 18 million per mile) while creating more high walls with water quality problems and a host of other environmental ills to go with them. The permanent jobs that would possibly be created will, in the large part, be minimum wage jobs or trucking related, as a conduit for West Virginia raw materials (timber and chicken parts) is created to the east. What will be imported besides trucks and more congestion can't be foretold, but all that comes will not be positive, of that I am sure!
>
> How backwards and upside down to label the opponents of Corridor H "negative thinkers." Please save me from blind "positive thinkers" that rush to destroy and forever alter what is so preciously found these days. And that is – a livable, beautiful and bountiful piece of this planet – a home, my home, your home! Not just a place to live, but a home to be happy with and excited about. One that is not just like

every other place. A home can possibly mean many things but to those who have one in their heart, they will know what I mean.

Merritt announced that the final Alignment Selection Supplemental Draft Environmental Impact Statement for Corridor H would be released December 2, 1994, with public comments due by January 23, 1995. Public hearings were set for January 3, 4, and 5 in Elkins, Canaan Valley, and Moorefield respectively. Virginia would hold associated hearings January 11 and 12 near Strasburg. It would be a busy Christmas season as the environmentalists prepared!

April's *Voice* brought readers up to date. Rogers, who by now was chair of the Conservancy's Highway Committee, abridged his comments submitted by the Conservancy. (The Conservancy's credo: if you want the Conservancy to address an issue, you have to stay to do the work). Another article, from *The Charleston Gazette*, detailed the court challenge Rogers and Corridor H Alternatives waged, represented by lawyer and Conservancy Secretary Jackie Hallinan, to force the DOH to open to opponents the thousands of letters received during the public comment period. A preliminary count reported 88% supported the "no-build" alternative. It wasn't surprising then why the DOH wanted to prevent access.

In May the *Voice's* front page was all Corridor H. Ken Ward, of *The Charleston Gazette*, reported on a Freedom of Information Act suit that brought release of EPA Region III's position on Corridor H. Its conclusion was that "Corridor H from Elkins to Virginia should not be built." The staff scientists at Region III had found Corridor H to be "environmentally unsatisfactory" – the lowest grade possible. Ward continued:

> After complaints from West Virginia Sens. Robert C. Byrd and Jay Rockefeller and Gov. Gaston Caperton, EPA Administrator Carol Browner overruled the Region III findings.
>
> Regional Administrator Peter Kostmayer refused to sign a watered-down rating of Corridor H and was later told he would be replaced by June 1.

Ward wrote that Governor Caperton had written to Browner, saying that "Regional Administrator Kostmayer is trying to stop progress in West Virginia."

Elsewhere in the *Voice*, the Editor reported he had received more clippings on Kostmayer's firing than he had on any issue since he assumed the editorship. Reprinted articles from *The Philadelphia Inquirer* and *The Charleston Gazette* indicated that Kostmayer was "flabbergasted" that carrying out his duties was wrong, that Rep. Mollohan called him "full of integrity," and that environmentalists were using Kostmayer's firing to question the environmental commitment of the Clinton administration. Finally, there was a copy of a letter from Cindy Rank, Conservancy past president, to Browner praising Kostmayer and expressing deep regret at his firing. It had been a short six months since Kostmayer had dropped in at the Conservancy's 1994 Fall Review in Canaan Valley.

As the Conservancy planned its annual Fall Review for 1995, once again Corridor H was front-and-center. In a change of format and time, the Review was scheduled for mid-September in Canaan Valley, on the weekend just before the state legislature's interim meetings at Canaan Valley State Park. It was hoped candidates for office might attend the Conservancy's event. Kostmayer, the fired EPA Regional Director, returned to participate in a panel on Corridor H, along with a legislative leader, John Doyle, and the Conservancy's Rogers. The biggest hit of the evening, however, was a song by Kate Long that encapsulated thirty years of Corridor H argument in three motivational verses. Conservancy President John McFerrin wrote in his *Voice* column afterwards:

> I want to thank Kate for her songs. They were great. I also want to thank her for the lesson in the power of music to move people. It is as true today as it was in the 1950's and will be forever: music has the power to touch people. If Corridor H is stopped it will be in no small part because of those who, like Kate, were able to touch people with their songs. [McFerrin was referring to a song, "Federal Money," included in a cassette titled, *Down the Road*, produced to raise awareness about Corridor H.]

In March 1994, as planning for Corridor H north of Elkins proceeded ever-so-slowly, a new place name was introduced in the headline of Rogers' *Voice* update: "Impasse at Corricks Ford." This inconspicuous crossing of Shavers Fork, south of Parsons, had been a significant Civil War site. At the Battle of Corricks Ford, Confederate forces retreating from the Battle of Rich Mountain had been defeated, thus ensuring western Virginia remained in the Union for the remainder of the war. The state had argued that its plans to cross the river ninety-two feet above the battlefield on a 1700-foot long bridge would have no significant impact.

Rogers reported:

> In late December, the Keeper of the National Register of Historic
> Places determined that the site was eligible for protection and its
> boundaries were larger than Baker [the state's consultant] had
> contended…The long bridge at Kalar's Ford, where the troops first
> clashed, would have to go. Streamside construction was out. This part
> of West Virginia remained unspoiled, for the time being.

Rogers then discussed how the state DOH simply rerouted the
highway around the impasse. The fact that its own EIS published only
months before had argued why such rerouting was impossible was ignored. Rogers concluded by soliciting contributions to the "Corridor H
Legal Fund," implying that the DOH's behavior would bring a legal
challenge from the Conservancy.

On August 2, 1996, two years behind schedule and still incomplete,
the Federal Highway Administration's Record of Decision (ROD) was
issued for Corridor H. The ROD allowed construction to begin unless a
lawsuit stopped it.

Rogers enumerated several key omissions in the ROD, including a
failure to respond to a ten-page analysis submitted months before by the
Conservancy and concluded, "Lawyers for Corridor H Alternatives and
the Conservancy are studying these and other points to include in a
lawsuit."

In October 1996, a *Voice* article entitled, "Corridor H Tagged As $1
Billion Boondoggle in Road to Ruin Report," reported that Corridor H
had been named one of twenty-two highways "that waste money, ruin
our communities, and harm the environment" by the national Taxpayers
for Common Sense. Corridor H had gained a national reputation as a
notorious pork barrel project.

As the Conservancy had so often discovered, working alone or with
only a few other groups, it could not raise the funding and public awareness to be truly effective. Instead, from its very beginning, the Conservancy had itself been a coalition of, or had sought to form coalitions
with, many other groups. When necessary, it had reached through them
to mobilize additional resources for major campaigns. Corridor H was
becoming such an effort.

By November 1996, Rogers was reporting success on several fronts.
The pending lawsuit would now include nine additional West Virginia
organizations as co-plaintiffs and several national environmental groups

were expected to present *amicus curiae*, or "friend of the court," briefs as well. The West Virginia groups listed were Corridor H Alternatives, West Virginia Environmental Council, Ohio Valley Environmental Coalition, West Virginia Citizens Action Group, Harrison County Environmental Citizens Organization, Resource Alliance, Concerned Citizens Coalition, Downstream Alliance, and Student Environmental Network. Heartwood, a regional group, had also joined, and the Sierra Club was considering joining with their own counsel.

In another development, the anti-pork barrel mood of Congress had stopped Senator Byrd from funneling construction money into Corridor H for the third straight year. Wrote Rogers, the "Road to Ruin designation gave Corridor H the right kind of notoriety just in time for the annual fund-fight."

Ken Ward, of *The Charleston Gazette,* announced the filing of the suit to stop Corridor H:

> The organizations, led by Corridor H Alternatives, say the 100-mile road would destroy forests and rivers without providing promised benefits…the groups charge that highway planners failed to consider – as required by law – alternatives that might provide greater benefits and not do as much damage…The suit alleges that the impact on two Civil war battlefields and the Fernow Experimental Forest will not be addressed until too late in the construction process.

The thirty-page lawsuit was filed in United States District Court in Washington, D.C., by Washington lawyer Andrea Ferster and Clarksburg attorney (and Conservancy Treasurer) Tom Michael. According to a 2006 interview with Rogers, the choice of whether to file suit in D.C. or West Virginia was Ferster's and her belief was that, if it had to be appealed, plaintiffs would have a better chance in the D.C. Circuit than in the Fourth Circuit in Richmond. (Other Conservancy suits have since proven that true.)

Ward quoted the plaintiffs as alleging that "Highway planners never, through a series of studies conducted since 1990, considered whether alternatives to a four-lane road would improve transportation and economic development without harming the environment."

After several delays and some concessions by defendants, federal and state agencies, the Corridor H case was heard September 10, 1997 by District Judge Thomas Hogan in Washington, D.C. Rogers dutifully reported his impressions in the October *Voice.* Several of the judge's questions and the inadequate answers by the state DOH and federal Department of Transportation indicated skepticism on the judge's part. Rogers had heard WVDOT Secretary Richard Jemiola tell a reporter that "It didn't matter what the judge decided, they would build the road anyway." His attitude was quite familiar to Conservancy members. "That's why," Rogers added, "we expect to win the case."

The judge's skepticism did not predict his ruling, however. Rogers wrote in the January 1998 *Voice*, "Judge Hogan bowed to the political decision to build Corridor H." Basically he adopted a conservative judicial philosophy that supported the federal and state highway agencies. "The Court does not substitute its own judgment for that of the agency; instead the Court is directed to give deference to agency decisions that are not arbitrary or capricious," the judge wrote.

The Conservancy and the other fourteen plaintiffs planned to appeal. Wrote Rogers, "If the decision stands, parks, wildlife preserves, and battlefields anywhere in the country are threatened. For that reason, our appeal is beginning to attract several more *amici curiae* who will join us in arguing that the decision must be reversed."

A year later, Rogers reported that an injunction was issued by the D.C. Court of Appeals. All construction activity had to stop until a decision on the full Corridor H suit was rendered. "This was one of the high points," he said later, "that got everybody's attention." The state immediately blamed the environmentalists for the layoffs from construction jobs just before Christmas. Ferster, plaintiffs' attorney, said the WVDOT was trying to portray the Court as "The Grinch Who Stole Christmas." Rogers pointed out that the state had assured the court that no construction was imminent during the appeal's duration, yet had simultaneously advertised for bids. Said Rogers, "It seemed the agency was trying to bulldoze the court."

In the February 1999 issue of the *Voice*, Conservancy President Frank Young eloquently summarized the Corridor H struggle after thirty years. Under the headline, "Still an Unwise Boondoggle," he wrote:

> For more than 30 years, politicians with money to burn have tried to sell West Virginians a billion dollar white elephant. Corridor H is a proposed four-lane highway through a few rural, remote eastern panhandle communities that want mostly to be left alone.
>
> Three decades of starting and stopping, assessing and reassessing, locating and relocating, and litigating and relitigating have not taught

the West Virginia Department of Highways anything. It still spends millions of dollars a year trying to promote its largest and most unwanted project.

Some of the debate is about local disturbances to the ecological, historical and existing populations of the region. These are all important human concerns. But there's more to Corridor H than building a road and preserving the directly adjacent physical environment, even if that were possible.

The Potomac Highlands of West Virginia is one of the remaining great greenscapes of the central Appalachian region. Only in this area of the region can one travel all day, through county after county, while enjoying hundreds of exhilarating, yet relaxing, mountain majesties and valley views. Only in this region can one enjoy the tranquility one finds at places like Seneca Rocks, Canaan Valley, Dolly Sods, "The Trough," Smoke Hole and, of course, Blackwater Canyon. Residents and tourists there can still enjoy peaceful, unbustled communities like Harman, Davis, Thomas, Wardensville, Capon Bridge and Romney.

But Governor Underwood and the West Virginia Department of Highways would have us believe that this area, too, must have 65 or 70 mile per hour highways, accompanied by billboards bigger than houses, fast food restaurants at every intersection and 40 ton trucks speeding through the hills and valleys. Have they no shame!!?? When will enough concrete and blacktop be enough? Is there no end to how much we will pave, just because an out of control, spendaholic Congress lets money flow like water from Washington? Is there to be nowhere left where significant natural areas can be enjoyed in their uncluttered greatness?

Corridor H is about interrupting, degrading and destroying the natural and human environment of the southern and western portions of the eastern panhandle. Opposition to Corridor H is about conserving the remaining peaceful and uncomplicated greenscapes remaining in the region.

For more than 30 years the West Virginia Highlands Conservancy has said that we need natural areas and greenspace for the enjoyment of this and future generations. But Governor Underwood and the West Virginia Department of Highways don't even want to talk about it. They go on wasting millions of dollars a year to oppose leaving even this one remaining significant natural area alone. Their ecological judgements, their social judgements and their financial judgements are all faulty. That's three strikes against them. Under the rules, they should be out.

In March, Rogers updated *Voice* readers on the federal appeal:

> On February 9, the United States Court of Appeals declared that West Virginia's highway department could not split the 100-mile Corridor H into smaller segments and build some while studying others. Section 4(f) of the federal transportation law protects historical, recreational, and other sites from adverse impacts by federally funded highways. The Court ordered WVDOT "to complete the section 4(f) process before proceeding further with the Corridor H project."

While this case had been pending, all construction plans had stopped, except for one non-controversial segment, the bypass, north of Elkins. Rogers continued by stating that the parties had agreed that very limited construction would continue while they enter into mediation on possible changes in the project. The purpose of the mediation was to find alternatives that could avoid or reduce impacts to historic sites and areas.

After thirty years, the highway planners had finally agreed to mediation. This would also mark the first use of mediation in the numerous cases brought by the Conservancy.

Rogers discussed the mediation on Corridor H in a 2006 interview. There were times, he said, when a further appeal might risk the progress made so far. Mediation could be the most useful if both sides shared that fear. In the Corridor H case, the appeals court already had a mediation system established and recommended it to both sides. There were three mediators, one appointed by each side, and one by the court. Unlike lawsuits where both sides prepare their filings, maybe prepare for oral argument, then meet in court once or twice, the climate of mediation was more intense and unrelenting. Rogers spoke of going to Washington once a month for grueling day-long meetings, during which they would sometimes caucus separately and try to work out their internal differences. Between those trips, the parties had to confer a lot and write position papers, always feeling the pressure to compromise. The Rogers, Chuck and Pam Merritt, Bonni McKeown, and their attorney, Ferster, represented the plaintiffs. Rogers said their side of the table usually numbered about five. The defendant agencies were all represented by counsel and their side of the table often numbered from fifteen to twenty. "It was a David and Goliath situation," Rogers said. For a lawyer used to filing appeals after careful wordsmithing, this was a different type of experience indeed.

Ultimately mediation resulted in 40% of the corridor mileage being changed to some extent, mostly between Kerens and Parsons and at the head of Blackwater Canyon near Thomas. The parties agreed to avoid many of the critically significant historical and environmental areas.

Whether mediation as a process for conflict resolution would be more beneficial than traditional court litigation, in terms of time, cost and energy remained an open question to the Conservancy and the broader environmental community. At the beginning of the mediation process, with which none of the parties were particularly familiar, there were many questions and some misinformation.

In the April 1999 *Voice*, Rogers laid out some of the details. The parties agreed to a bypass, under construction, north of Elkins to U.S. Route 219. There were no issues on this limited segment. More significantly, he wrote:

> The parties agreed to use mediation to explore changes in the project that could avoid, reduce, or mitigate impacts to Section 4(f) [historical] properties...Mediation is different from binding arbitration. The parties did not agree to accept whatever the mediator suggested, and the mediator has no authority to enforce a compromise. If we can reach agreement on any part of our dispute, the Court will approve it. The parties will meet face-to-face to seek solutions with the mediator's help.

During mediation, no right-of-way acquisition would occur and only preliminary design work if it supported mediation efforts. Finally the WVDOT agreed to involve the plaintiffs in 4(f) studies as they occurred, rather than give them a brief comment period after the research was completed. It was the beginning of a new technique.

After six years of near-monthly updates in *The Highlands Voice* from Rogers, there was a seven-month blackout during the period of intensive mediation. Then the front-page story in the February 2000 issue:

> Corridor H Lawsuit Settled! *Highway Broken up*
>
> Corridor H Alternatives, the West Virginia Highlands Conservancy, and our thirteen co-plaintiffs have reached a settlement agreement in federal court with state and federal agencies. The proposed highway will be broken into nine separate projects—some could be built soon, others won't see the bulldozers for years to come and not at all if resistance is successful. The state does not have the money to build even a third of the total now. The battle will continue over each

project's funding and environmental impacts. As a single $1.5 billion project, Corridor H is dead. Here are the important details:

(1) From Kerens to Davis, through the Monongahela National Forest, the highway department (WVDOT) must start all over. It has agreed to study new alignments to avoid Corricks Ford Battlefield, in the valley of the Shavers Fork, and the Blackwater Canyon from Hendricks to Thomas. The environmental impact studies (EIS) will take two years or more.

(2) From just west of Wardensville to the Virginia line, there will be no construction for twenty years, unless Virginia reverses its decision not to build Corridor H to I-81, or traffic increases dramatically on WV 55. The latter exception must meet specific standards. Wardensville will receive $1 million over five years to help it prepare for the transition.

(3) There could be another realignment around Greenland Gap, whose eligibility for increased protection will be decided by the Keeper of the National Register of Historic Places. That process will require further delay.

Altogether, the delays affect close to 40% of the Corridor.

(4) North of Elkins, construction will resume immediately as far as Kerens. Elsewhere, historic-site studies are continuing, but new construction is likely soon from Moorefield over South Branch Mountain to Baker. Those projects can't be challenged on the issues already decided in court. However, if new issues come up involving other environmental laws or future actions by the highway department, they may be litigated.

(5) This year, WVDOT will study the necessary improvements on US 50 from the Keyser area east, and will publicize its findings and plans. That highway carries much more traffic than the roads to be replaced by Corridor H. It is an obvious rival for the "matching" money the state plans to spend.

(6) Other points covered in the agreement: complete avoidance of Big Run Bog's watershed; release at last of funds for the rail-trail through Randolph, Tucker, and Grant counties; better enforcement of truck weight limits on US 219 – traffic has increased as truckers avoided the better-policed routes; removal of the "Build-It" signs from highway right-of-way; redesign of an unsafe Corridor H intersection at Kerens; and publication of projected schedules and other information.

From the beginning of this controversy, WVDOT has had a single-minded idea on how to improve transportation in the Highlands region: Just build Corridor H. Our opposing view has recognized many factors, including environmental, historic, economic, and broader transportation issues. In the same way, while they have one view of the settlement, we know it is a complex document.

They say the agreement is all about removing obstacles to construction. However, we settled only the pending litigation. We got as much as we could reasonably expect from our 4(f) lawsuits: protection for the Shavers Fork and Blackwater Canyon areas, further study of Greenland Gap, and breathing space for Wardensville. We held on to the right to sue if necessary over the Kerens-to-Davis environmental impact statements, the outcome at Greenland Gap, the Wardensville delay, and other commitments in the agreement. Issues that come up in the future may be brought to court as well. We specifically reserved the right to sue under the Endangered Species Act.

Delay is built into the agreement, from the EIS preparations in the west to the moratorium in the east. Delay is important to us because it allows time for more reasonable decisions on how to spend our limited tax dollars. Polls we have seen over the past two years show support for our position increasing. The agreement should launch us into new efforts to protect the Highlands.

Henceforth, there would be only very occasional articles as Rogers and the Conservancy monitored the progress of Corridor H. And yes, there would be "shenanigans" by WVDOT and yes, it still remained to be seen whether the nationally protected Greenland Gap would be severely impacted or just grazed. But overall the Conservancy, Hugh and Ruth Blackwell Rogers, and Corridor H Alternatives could begin to devote their collective energies to other activities.

For the Conservancy, this meant devoting its attention and resources to current issues such as fighting mountaintop removal mining, advocating for additional wilderness preservation as the Monongahela National Forest revised its management plan and defining its policy on wind farm proposals in the highlands, just to name a few. The struggle was taken over thirty years to stop a boondoggle that threatened so many of the Highlands' special places. Ironically, the volunteers of the Conservancy had outlasted most of the professional engineers, planners, and lawyers on the other side. Only a few DNR biologists and local activists had been involved from the beginning. The senior senator from West Virginia, Robert C. Byrd, had reached the chairmanship of the Appropriations Committee during that time, which had prolonged the struggle.

Once again, strong volunteer-produced research, coalition-building among state and national environmental groups, and savvy environmental lawyers had produced a result that preserved special places in the highlands, and forced the governmental agencies, funded by Congress, personified by Senator Byrd, to follow the law as they carried forth their pet projects.

For the Rogers family, it meant Ruth could continue to provide leadership to the Shavers Fork Coalition (See Chapter 3), and for Hugh, it meant first assuming the duties of Conservancy secretary, then in 2004 becoming the president of the West Virginia Highlands Conservancy. It had been a long road since they first went to a meeting on Corridor H in 1992. What had happened to their plan to live peacefully in the country north of Elkins, raise their family and enjoy their beautiful view?

Sources:

Byers, Robert, article in *The Charleston Gazette*

Corridor H Alternatives, archives at Hugh & Ruth Blackwell Rogers' home

Down the Road, cassette recording of various artists, produced by Corridor H Alternatives, PO Box 11, Kerens, WV 26276, 1993

The Highlands Voice, articles by Bob Burrell, Dave Elkinton, Geoff Green, Bonni McKeown, Lowell Markey, Chuck Merritt, Cindy Rank, Hugh Rogers, Ken Ward, Frank Young, and others

Johnson, Skip, article in *The Charleston Gazette*

Rockefeller, John D. "Jay", statement during governor's race, 1976

Rogers, Hugh, and Ruth Blackwell, interview, June 20, 2006, and subsequent correspondence

Ward, Ken, article in *The Charleston Gazette*, November 1996

Chapter Five
Saving the Promised Land:
The Davis Power Project and the Canaan Valley National Wildlife Refuge

Author's note and disclaimer: This is one of two chapters that could have easily become a self-contained book. (The other is Chapter 7.) The complexity of both the Davis Power Project and the Canaan Valley Wildlife Refuge, with their associated political, legal and legislative battles, deserve to be fully chronicled. Unfortunately that is beyond the scope of this volume. Instead the discussion will focus on the role of the West Virginia Highlands Conservancy and its leaders, rather than documenting the more complete saga.

Now the disclaimer: Of all the issues discussed in this volume, I personally was most deeply involved in the subject of this chapter. I was married to Linda Cooper Elkinton from 1968–1990, including all the years she was the major force leading the Conservancy's involvement in protecting Canaan Valley. In my own right, I participated significantly in the organizational efforts and was a named plaintiff and defendant on several of the legal challenges later in the struggle. From 1971–1972 I left the work force to devote my time to research and preparing for the upcoming hearings before the Federal Power Commission and attended much of the ten weeks of hearings in Washington. In short, I offer close, first-hand observations and knowledge, but the reader is on notice that my best efforts at objectivity may be inadequate.

Linda Cooper Elkinton had no idea when she and her husband moved back to her native state in 1970 that her life was about to change forever. The third of seven children born to a fourth-generation farming couple in Canaan Valley, as she grew up in the

50s her family struggled to grow crops in the harsh, cool climate of the 3200-foot elevation valley. During this time, cauliflower and broccoli became the valley's most successful agricultural products and her father often trucked his and his neighbors' produce to out-of-state markets.

There had been a few signs that Canaan Valley might draw tourists, but as Linda was growing up development was never a threat. The Washington, D.C. Ski Club leased a nearby farm, and installed a primitive rope tow for their weekend use. Linda picked up a few bucks working there during high school. Another neighbor gave several thousand acres to the state for a future state park, but no progress to develop it occurred until the early 1960s, when federal grants were obtained. Throughout the 1960s, additional property was purchased, some by eminent domain, to supplement the original gift of land.

In 1964, Linda left for Berea College in Kentucky. Under Berea's unique program, no tuition was charged, but each student worked ten hours a week for the college. One of Linda's was with the Council of Southern Mountains, headquartered in Berea, where she helped form its Youth Commission, and later its Appalachian Volunteers program. Over the next few years she became a leader in the movement of college-age students that fanned out throughout the southern Appalachian mountains to work with local communities to fight poverty, oppose strip mining, start health clinics, improve literacy, or address whatever other issues seemed critical. At its peak, the Appalachian Volunteers sponsored as many as 500 volunteers. In addition, other people, like volunteers with faith-based organizations (including her future husband) and federally funded VISTA workers, joined together to form one of the largest waves of "missionaries" the mountains had ever absorbed.

Within three short months of their return to West Virginia in 1970, Linda and her husband opened a copy of the *Parsons Advocate*, Tucker County's weekly newspaper, to find that the Monongahela Power Company and two sister companies had announced plans to build something called the "Davis Power Project." As described, this proposed hydroelectric facility would flood 7,200 acres of Canaan Valley's floor and 550 acres on Cabin Mountain. To generate 750 MW [later raised to 1,000 MW] of power the water from the upper reservoir would be drained into the lower. Cooper Elkinton immediately knew her beloved home of Canaan Valley would never be the same again.

As the fight to preserve Canaan Valley became her major avocation, Cooper Elkinton became active within the Highlands Conservancy, ultimately becoming its first woman president in 1977. She undertook the role as if it were her job, and devoted nearly full-time to reorganizing virtually all aspects of the Conservancy. Because of her leadership on the Canaan Valley issue, she was offered a paid position as Assistant Regional Director of the National Audubon Society in 1979, where one of her primary tasks was to work on Canaan Valley preservation.

In the mid '70s Cooper Elkinton earned a Master's in Social Work degree from West Virginia University, with a concentration in community organization and development.

Since 1997, she has worked in wellness programming, at the West Virginia University Health Sciences Center, in the Department of Community Medicine. She helped create and lead the West Virginia Land Trust and Friends of Blackwater, and currently serves as President of Citizens for Responsible Wind Power.

As the following chapter unfolds, it will become clear that the community organizing skills Cooper Elkinton learned in Kentucky, and refined at WVU, her dedication to her native valley, and her sheer hard work would serve to ultimately defeat the Davis Power Project and establish, literally in its place, the Canaan Valley National Wildlife Refuge.

From Announcement to Hearings

When the Monongahela Power Company, one of West Virginia's largest corporations, announced its proposal in June 1970 to flood the Canaan Valley with a 7,200-acre lake, neither power company planners and executives nor citizen conservationists could have guessed how tortuous the course would be before the ultimate outcome of the proposal was known. It would only come after thirty years, hundreds of thousands of dollars in legal fees (primarily those of the power company), the attention of four presidents, three West Virginia governors, and ultimately a decision of the United States Supreme Court. This is the story of the West Virginia Highlands Conservancy and its efforts to protect Canaan Valley.

155

There had been rumors for decades that the northern end of Canaan Valley might be used for a power project. In fact the West Penn Power Company, an affiliate of Monongahela Power, had owned approximately 20,000 acres of the valley as long as anyone could remember. Back in the 1930s the Monongahela Power Company had purchased the nearby Blackwater Canyon with the intention of building a series of hydroelectric dams to utilize the canyon's sharp descent. The people of West Virginia had recoiled at that proposal and the state legislature passed legislation to prohibit such a development. Later, the power company donated the property that became Blackwater Falls State Park, but retained much of the canyon ownership. (This would be very significant in the fight to protect Blackwater Canyon in the 1990s.)*

As she read the front-page story in the *Parsons Advocate*, in June 1970, Cooper Elkinton was stunned. Immediately, she knew she would devote her energy to opposing the project and began to organize allies. Ultimately these would comprise two separate groups: the locally-based opposition, made up primarily of the Elkintons and the Roscoe Beall family and their circle of friends, and the conservationists, led by the Highlands Conservancy and eventually including a very wide coalition of state, regional and national groups.

The first step Cooper Elkinton took was to contact an acquaintance from her Kentucky community organizing days, West Virginia State Senator Paul Kaufman. A respected lawyer from Charleston, Kaufman had just formed the Appalachian Research and Defense Fund. Nicknamed "APPALRED," it was a public interest law firm whose mission was to challenge the social and environmental issues facing Appalachia, including strip-mining, corporate land-ownership, political corruption, among others.

With Kaufman's encouragement and guidance, the Elkintons filed a simple letter as a "Petition to Intervene" with the Federal Power Commission. (Many years later a U.S. Senate committee report on public participation cited the Elkintons' petition as the first from individual citizens accepted by the Federal Power Commission.) APPALRED also filed its own petition and assigned the case to J. Davitt McAteer, a young associate.

---

* The relationships among the companies: the Monongahela Power, West Penn Power, and Potomac Edison Power companies, together comprised the Allegheny Power System, a name they increasingly used.

Recognizing that help would been needed if they were to have any success, the Elkintons assembled information on state conservation groups, and learned of the Conservancy, which was receiving coverage in the news because of the Otter Creek and Dolly Sods wilderness proposals. The Elkintons contacted the board members of the Highlands Conservancy, and many members encouraged the Elkintons to attend the Conservancy's Fall Weekend Review in October 1970, scheduled in Richwood, and present their concerns to the full board of directors.

Meanwhile, a Canaan Valley neighbor, Roscoe Beall III, whose family's farm lay at the southern end of the proposed lower reservoir, was consulting his long-time friend, attorney Ronald Brown in Kingwood, artist Bill Gerhold, and other friends and they formed the Canaan Valley Association and filed their own Petition to Intervene. Through one of these friends, Frank Potter, the Environmental Defense Fund in Washington also became an intervenor.

The Highlands Voice of August 1970 devoted five articles to the proposed Davis Power Project. After outlining the workings of a pumped storage power plant, Editor Bob Burrell described extensive recreational facilities the company planned at the southern end of the lower reservoir, based on a study by their consultant, Scruggs and Hammond.

Other articles outlined the wildlife impacts expected from the project and one even raised the specter of a coal-fired plant on the lower reservoir. Burrell tried to present a variety of facts that would guide the Conservancy's board at its October meeting.

The Elkintons attended their first Highlands Conservancy event in October 1970, spending much of Saturday's field trips discussing the Davis Power Project with fellow hikers. By the opening of the Sunday morning board meeting, it was clear to them that a sizable number of board members held serious misgivings about the proposal. Power company representatives had met individually with several Conservancy officers and had presented the proposal as a non-polluting, economically beneficial, positive asset to Tucker County.

After extensive discussion, the Conservancy adopted a carefully worded resolution to neither support nor oppose the Davis Power Project but to intervene in the FPC proceedings (with the aid of Conservancy member, attorney Jim Moorman.) The Conservancy position recognized that the plan provided tax benefits for Tucker County but that many adverse features must be considered before any license could be granted.

For example, it urged that consideration be given to the relocation of the 500-acre upper reservoir outside the Red Creek drainage. It also noted that although the company owned much of the land involved, that fact did not necessarily carry with it the right to modify the environment as a whole.

The resolution then listed nine "additional considerations." These included a concern that additional coal-burning would be necessary to power this project, thus causing additional air pollution; that no consideration to conservation measures had been explored; that uncontrolled recreational development would destroy additional land; that the company's public relations brochures were overly optimistic, if not actually misleading, including the unfounded prediction of a freshwater tidal ecological community; and "most importantly" that the state must not consider this proposal independently of similar proposals from competing companies before the FPC.

A committee was formed to undertake a comprehensive fact-finding effort and a full report to be made at the Mid-Winter Workshop in late January.

Under Moorman's leadership, the Davis Power Project Committee recruited members and distributed work assignments. Both Elkintons signed on to help prepare for the January presentation. Helen McGinnis, the leading advocate for Dolly Sods, joined especially to evaluate the impact of the upper reservoir. Bruce Godwin, of Pittsburgh, also became a member. There were several meetings at the Roaring Creek Cultural Center nearby, just as there had been when wilderness research was underway. (See Chapter 2.)

In the December 1970 *Voice*, Cooper Elkinton wrote the first of her many signed articles. Titled "The Davis Power Project As Seen by a Canaan Valley Native," she wrote:

> There are many reasons why I am opposed to the construction of the proposed Davis Power Project by the Allegheny Power System. These range from sentimental attachment to the injustices that have been and will be rendered to the people of the immediate area if the project is carried out as proposed. Having grown up there, I have through the years despairingly watched it be consumed by gas wells, pipelines, power lines, road ways, ski ways and a golf course. Some of the scenic landscape and magnificent wildlife still remain in the Valley, but what will be left after it is further consumed by W. Va.'s largest lake?

While it is true that the present power interests own or have options to buy all but less than a half dozen small tracts of land necessary for the construction of the lake and power plant in Canaan, and therefore, as most people would say, should be allowed to do with it as they please, I think it is very important to be aware of how they came about acquiring some of this land and what their plans are for the Valley and the surrounding area.

This is a history that extends over almost half a century connected with the purchase of land for the proposed project. About every 10 years or so the rumors would spread that a lake was going to be built and the land would be condemned, or if you want to stay out of court and get a good price for what you own, you'd better sell now. Few people ever really knew the purpose of the lake, its size, etc., but they always knew there was a willing buyer in the power companies if for some reason, money was needed.

The people desired to stay out of court, which would have involved high costs they could not afford and embarrassment and ridicule from supposed friends. Relentless pressure was ever present, from every conceivable angle, on these residents who continued to resist. This type of duress has kept these residents from improving their property or even planning ahead more than one year at a time. In addition, if an accident [occurred] or an improvement was contemplated, a power company representative always seemed to be nearby. Close friends, employers, creditors, and lending agencies have also been tools in the process. One resident remarked: "I thought a corporation was the same as an individual under the law. However, I see this one difference – a corporation has no <u>heart</u>, <u>soul</u>, or <u>conscience</u>." Land buyers from huge lucrative interests, whether a power company or the U.S. Government never seem to understand that no amount of condemnation money can pay for a life time of joys, hard work, and troubles invested in the land one owns.

Cooper Elkinton concluded by acknowledging the financial benefits to Tucker County. Indeed she was a product of its school system herself. Yet she believed there were alternatives including publicly owned utility development, like those in the Pacific Northwest. Considering all the wildlife and social impacts, she felt the project was of "questionable" value to Tucker County and West Virginia.

Conservancy members reading this article might well have thought they were back in the meetings a few years earlier, hearing from landowners complaining about the Forest Service's plans at Seneca Rocks. (See Chapter 6.)

At the 1971 Mid-Winter Workshop, held in Blackwater Falls, Burrell was elected to succeed Tom King as President. Burrell had expressed significantly more opposition than King to the Davis Power Project. The new committee presented a comprehensive report on the Davis Power Project. Each member took a different aspect: McGinnis, the geology, flora, and fauna; Bob Broughton, the physical aspects of two reservoirs and the economics of pumped storage; Fred Anderson, the recreational and environmental impacts; Godwin, possible alternatives; and Dave Elkinton, the future impacts on the Canaan Valley. The committee would continue to study problems and report at future board meetings.

In 1971 the Fall Highlands Review focused on Canaan Valley. Field trips on Saturday included a walking tour of northern Canaan Valley, led by McGinnis and Cooper Elkinton; an auto tour of the Canaan Valley State Park, led by John Killoran; and a "rugged" hike down the Blackwater Canyon.

As the trip participants returned full of stories of their day's activities and gathered for the catered evening meal at the Davis High School, the town's fire siren sounded. It would be another hour, and well past dark, before the Blackwater Canyon hikers arrived back, having been rescued by the fire department. The local view of the Highlands Conservancy's members was not reported in the *Voice*.

The now-traditional Saturday evening panel presentation was well attended, with many local residents adding to the Conservancy members. Entitled "The Future of Canaan Valley," the panelists were Luther Singley, Executive Vice President of the Monongahela Power Company, Ira "Sandy" Latimer, Director of the state Department of Natural Resources, and Robert Leo Smith, professor of Wildlife Management at West Virginia University. A lengthy discussion ensued.

Singley mentioned that the power company had submitted its "Initial Statement of Environmental Factors" to the FPC the previous June. (The conservation intervenors believed the power company's environmental assessment would not satisfy the FPC's responsibility to produce an environmental impact statement, under the National Environmental Policy Act of 1970, and they would be proven correct.)

Latimer delivered the DNR's position paper on Canaan Valley, weaving together the differing positions of his wildlife managers and the state park operators, yet still remaining consistent with Governor Arch Moore's pro-project position. He emphasized the unique ecosystem and plentiful wildlife. If the project was licensed, Latimer hoped restrictions would limit development to the far western edge and that facilities would be limited. His statement, "We feel that a land use plan or county-wide zoning commission should be adopted for wise planning and management of the entire region – especially Canaan Valley," seemed naïve to anyone familiar with Tucker County. But his recommendation that any potential for a coal-fired additional power plant be prohibited in the license received local support. The DNR was experiencing a raging internal debate, since its constituent divisions had conflicting positions on the power proposal. Latimer's presentation was a delicate compromise position and would re-emerge in the FPC hearings at a later time.

Dr. Smith, WVU wildlife professor and Sunday columnist in the Morgantown *Dominion Post*, was unalterably opposed to the Davis Project and spoke eloquently for the preservation of Canaan Valley, as he had written in a series of articles.

The Federal Power Commission was delayed in scheduling hearing dates on the Davis Power Project application. The reason was a court decision in Greene County, New York, that ruled the FPC was required to write its own environmental impact statements, rather than rely on an applicant's submission. The FPC staff would need additional time to prepare this document before hearings could be scheduled.

In a special edition of *The Highlands Voice*, timed to be available for the Fall Review of 1972, David and Linda Cooper Elkinton reported on Canaan Valley. The FPC hearings were still unscheduled. After meeting overwhelming opposition to the large-scale recreational development proposal, the power company had reduced its proposal to day-use only and arranged to have the DNR manage the wildlife habitat on the lower reservoir's eastern shore. In an echo of another Conservancy issue, they wrote:

> One new development has been the oft-repeated rumor, now confirmed, that the DNR is proposing to the Federal Power Commission that the entire Canaan Valley be included within the project boundary. Whether this would mean that the power companies would buy out all private landowners immediately, or that the DNR would gain only "wildlife management" rights to this area is yet to be determined. Naturally this development has deeply concerned local citizens, many of whom have ardently supported the project, but are now having second thoughts.

The specter of the elastic project boundary brought back memories of the Spruce Knob – Seneca Rocks National Recreational Area to Conservancy members. (See Chapter 6).

At the annual membership meeting held in January 1973, Dave Elkinton was elected the third president of the West Virginia Highlands Conservancy. (Outgoing President Burrell, would continue his monthly column in *The Highlands Voice*, under the title "Overlook." Newly appointed *Voice* Editor Ron Hardway began his tenure by publishing the *Voice* as a tabloid, with more news in less space, and it has remained so since.)

McAteer went to work for Ralph Nader, and APPALRED eventually assigned the Canaan Valley case to Ray Ratliff. The national Sierra Club became involved and its sister organization, the Sierra Club Legal Defense Fund hired Washington lawyer Ron Wilson, who had been involved with the controversial Storm King case on New York's Hudson River. The environmentalists formed a team, dividing the legal work between Ratliff and Wilson. Barbara Bramble, Wilson's young associate, also became an important member of the team.

Cooper Elkinton focused on publicizing what was happening in Canaan Valley. Over a period of several years, she gave presentations to many groups, including conservation organizations, local sportsmen's clubs, and as often as possible, state and national organizations, such as the Sierra Club.

The Federal Power Commission hearings were now scheduled for January 1974. Because of the Greene County case, the power company's environmental assessment had not been used, and the FPC had been forced to prepare its own Environmental Impact Statement. The intervenors took advantage of their opportunity to submit comments. The Conservancy noted Canaan Valley and adjacent Dolly Sods were unique areas and were enjoying the growth in interest that they deserved. The Elkintons felt the presence of the Conservancy and other intervenors had forced compliance with the National Environmental Policy Act.

The Federal Power Commission Hearings

Dave Elkinton reported on the long-delayed FPC hearings. On March 26 an FPC Administrative Law Judge, Jair Kaplan, had taken testimony from Tucker County residents, most of whom were favorable to the project. The few environmentalists present were booed and subjected to unfriendly remarks, Elkinton reported, leading the judge to comment that the hearing was not a "political convention." Cooper Elkinton spoke in opposition, focusing on lack of planning, unaddressed geological and wildlife mitigation issues, and the need to study alternatives. Other Conservancy members, Lowell Markey, Steve Richards, Helen McGinnis and Joel Shifman, added testimony in opposition. One Conservancy member, Parsons resident Don Good, spoke for the Izaak Walton League but in support of the power project.

The hearings adjourned to Washington and reconvened April 2 to take power company and intervenor testimony. Elkinton reported the first week was devoted to cross-examination by intervenors and the FPC staff of applicants' witnesses. The Conservancy was represented by attorney Ratliff and the Elkintons. During the first week of testimony it was disclosed that testimony of the wildlife biologists of the West Virginia Department of Natural Resources was being suppressed. Five professional wildlife experts, including Conservancy member (and future President) Joe Rieffenberger, had prepared testimony to be submitted by the Attorney General of West Virginia, also an intervenor. Apparently these five were clearly opposed to the construction of the Davis Project, but if it would be licensed, they favored the Glade Run alternative, also in the Valley, but with a much-reduced lower reservoir. Their testimony was not cleared by the Director of DNR, Ira Latimer, although among the five were the Chief and Assistant Chief of the DNR's Wildlife Resources Division. The Federal Power Commission staff requested the judge to issue a subpoena for these five, which he agreed to do if Latimer would not agree to allow them to testify voluntarily.

The "DNR Five," as they became known, made big news in West Virginia. Skip Johnson, the respected outdoor columnist of *The Charleston Gazette*, broke the story within hours of receiving a tip that the FPC was about to issue a subpoena. Johnson, who loved the Canaan Valley and was close to many DNR wildlife biologists, embarrassed the Moore administration for suppressing important expert testimony because of the Governor's desire to license the Davis project.

To many people, **Joe Rieffenberger** would be forever associated with bears. Partly it might be because he was a large, imposing, bearded man who struck first-time acquaintances as a little gruff, until revealing a soft heart underneath. But primarily it would be because his professional life as a wildlife biologist included nearly thirty years as West Virginia's first expert on black bears.

During his tenure researching, tagging, and tracking bears for the West Virginia Department of Natural Resources, the bear population increased from a low of approximately 500 in 1972, to an estimated 10,000 in 2000. By 2007 the official DNR estimate had grown to 12,000, although Joe thought it might be several thousand higher.

In 2003 in honor of his "outstanding lifetime contributions in the field of wildlife education, management or research," Rieffenberger was awarded the first Mountaineer Award from the West Virginia Chapter of The Wildlife Society.

"Joe Rieffenberger's contributions to the sportsmen and citizens of West Virginia have spanned a lifetime," said Paul Johansen, Assistant Chief in Charge of Game Management for the Wildlife Resources Section of the Division of Natural Resources. "In particular, Rieffenberger was one of the first wildlife biologists in West Virginia and helped to further the research and restoration of the State's natural resources. The citizens of West Virginia will be benefiting from his work for generations to come."

What many Highlands Conservancy members wouldn't remember was that Rieffenberger held several Conservancy distinctions as well. He was the only person to have served as Conservancy president two different times, completing the author's term in 1974-5 and serving a full term 1979-81. (He remembered that *Voice* Editor Ron Hardway called him the "Grover Cleveland" president.)

Even less well known was that he was present before and at the founding (see Chapter 1) in his role as a DNR staffer who assisted Lou Greathouse in organizing the first several Fall Highlands Review events. Beginning in 1965, Rieffenberger had worked with Greathouse in Charleston promoting the idea of a multi-disciplinary umbrella organization of users of the highlands region. Even after Greathouse moved to Georgia, Rieffenberger would remain a primary link between the DNR and the Conservancy over several decades.

In an interview in 2007, Rieffenberger remembered meeting Greathouse when Greathouse was superintendent of Holly River State Park in 1954. Rieffenberger was fresh out of the University of Illinois with a master's degree in Ecology, and had just started what would be a forty-six year career with the DNR.

After returning to Elkins from Greathouse's planning team in Charleston in 1966, Rieffenberger played a very significant role in the late 1960s in researching the wildlife characteristics of the Canaan Valley. It was Rieffenberger's "cover map" that formed the basis for his testimony, and the DNR's wildlife management recommendations, to the Federal Power Commission. Thirty years later, he remembered going to Washington under subpoena for a week of FPC hearings.

But Rieffenberger was always more at home in the wildest parts of the Mountain State than indoors. Even in retirement, a *Charleston Gazette* feature story in February 2007, written by the retired Skip Johnson, showed Rieffenberger tromping through snow with his DNR successors, checking a tag Rieffenberger had placed in a bear twenty-seven years earlier.

Rieffenberger attended scores of Conservancy board meetings over the decades, especially after his wife, Mary Moore Rieffen-berger became the official representative from the Brooks Bird Club.

In 2007, at age eighty, Rieffenberger was serving as president-elect of the Brooks Bird Club. He and Mary Moore continued to live a quiet retirement at their beautifully landscaped home near Elkins.

But meanwhile back in 1974, the FPC staff had conducted its own independent investigation of this project and raised numerous questions as to its advisability. The staff had not taken a firm position in opposition or favoring the issuance of the license, but in their Environmental Impact Statement they supported many of the questions raised by intervenors, including the Highlands Conservancy. Their interest in hearing the state's wildlife experts indicated their concern with the wildlife losses that would be caused by the project.

Elkinton reported that the required wildlife mitigation plan prepared by the DNR and the Federal Bureau of Sports Fisheries and Wildlife (later the Fish and Wildlife Service) called for the entire valley to be included in the project boundary and all lands not flooded to be managed for wildlife. In addition the power company would be required to provide several thousand acres outside the valley for the same purpose. Clearly the wildlife issues could significantly increase the cost of the project, cause its cost-benefit analysis to change, and eliminate the potential for recreation and second home development in the southern end of the valley. These were major developments indeed. He concluded with this opinion:

It is quite encouraging to see a regulatory agency, like the FPC, actually looking at environmental questions. They even hired Conservancy member and expert witness, Dr. Charles Baer of WVU as a consultant. It was the feeling of environmental intervenors that the FPC staff was beginning to assume the role that groups like the Conservancy have had to assume in the past. They have paid professional staff and budget, which we do not, and rightfully should do such a good environmental job, our efforts would not be needed. However, our presence in this matter may have stimulated their interest, and our continued interest and activity may be needed to sustain theirs.

Dr. Baer, a founding member of the West Virginia Chapter of the Nature Conservancy and an Ecology professor at West Virginia University, had been involved with Canaan Valley for many years. One of his doctoral students, Ron Fortney, had researched the flora of Canaan. Fortney would later manage the state park system and completed his career teaching at several West Virginia colleges and universities. Another graduate student of Dr. Baer was Eddie Crouse, who became a key environmental staffer at the FPC, and was largely responsible for the FPC's Environmental Impact Statement being supportive of preserving Canaan Valley.

In a 2006 conversation, Cooper (dropping the name Elkinton in her 1990 divorce) remembered Administrative Law Judge Kaplan. She described him as a 50-ish, formal, seemingly conservative governmental lawyer, giving the impression that he was definitely not an outdoors person. She remembered one occasion when he wanted to see the Canaan Valley for himself and the State DNR had offered to transport him in their helicopter. As he landed in the floor of the Valley, having circled Dolly Sods and the site of the upper reservoir, he was overcome with excitement as he deplaned. To the gathered party on the ground, he shouted, "We saw an eagle, we saw an eagle!" The conservationists in the group believed thereafter that Kaplan was more inclined to preservation than they had thought.

Dave Elkinton wrote in the May 1974 *Highlands Voice:*

> After only a day or two, it became clear that the FPC staff was highly critical of the proposal that would flood 7,000 acres of Canaan Valley and 500 acres atop Cabin Mountain adjacent to Dolly Sods. Repeated cross-examination by staff attorneys has produced numerous admissions that the power companies have underplayed the environ-

mental, geological and economic effects. In addition, the Administrative Law Judge, Jair Kaplan, asked many witnesses his own questions. He has paid particular attention to the Glade Run alternative, also in the Canaan Valley, but flooding only a small portion of the 7,000 acres needed for the larger reservoir proposal. The Glade Run alternative has been favored if a project is built by the so-called "Renegade Five" of the Department of Natural Resources.

Appearing under subpoena, a rarity in FPC proceedings, but made necessary because Ira Latimer, DNR Director, refused to allow them to appear voluntarily, these five wildlife professionals testified in opposition to the proposed project. The five included Division Chief Dan Cantner, Assistant Chief Pete Zurbach, Assistant Chief James Ruckel, William Santonas, Supervisor of Planning, and Conservancy member Joe Rieffenberger, Wildlife Biologist. Their testimony was lengthy due to attempts by the power company attorneys to discredit their position. The judge seemed impressed, and indeed, these five represented the most damaging threat to the project yet for their expertise is unmatched both for the depth of their analysis and their professionalism.

After 24 full days of cross-examination with more to follow, the consensus seems to be that the project may be in danger. In any event, the three quick weeks of testimony that were expected have been nearly tripled primarily due to the cross examination of the power company witnesses by intervenors, including the Conservancy and the Sierra Club, and by the active role of the FPC staff in both cross examining applicants and in the presentation of their own witnesses. If the project license is denied either because of insufficient evidence or because the judge feels the Glade Run alternative is preferable, the power companies will have to reapply or decide to abandon the entire project. In either case the disposition of lands in Canaan Valley owned by the power companies will be extremely important to the preservation of this unique area. Efforts are already underway to explore the possibility of permanent preservation in such an event through acquisition by private conservation groups.

But a blockbuster was about to occur. In June a front-page article by Cooper Elkinton caught *Voice* readers' attention. The U.S. Department of Interior had finally made known its position on the Davis Power Project. Assistant Secretary of Interior Royston C. Hughes wrote that Interior recommended, "that issuance of the license under consideration be denied and an alternative project to produce power outside Canaan Valley be developed." The letter cited a report prepared by the Bureau of Sports Fisheries and Wildlife in cooperation with the Division of Wildlife

Resources of the West Virginia Department of Natural Resources which advised that no development should be placed in the Canaan Valley "on grounds that it would not be in the in the best interest of the State of West Virginia or the United States." This was a victory for the environmentalists!

Cooper Elkinton quoted Secretary Hughes' letter:

> Of equal importance however is "the Valley's tremendous potential for non-consumptive recreation and educational uses, particularly as an adjunct to the nearby Blackwater Falls and Canaan Valley State Parks." The letter goes on to state that "Canaan Valley with its impressive size (over 25 square miles in the Valley floor) and the highly unusual ecological characteristics and associations, offers tremendous opportunity for both the people of West Virginia and the eastern United States to enjoy a semi-wilderness experience.
>
> Thus it should be kept in its present condition and managed only in the interest of preserving those values, which made the area unique.

This was Interior's third and strongest position. Their previous comments to the FPC had included the need for mitigation of wildlife losses to be included in the final EIS and as a license condition. Because of the failure to get adequate response in the EIS, they now opposed the issuance of a license for the project altogether. The so-called "Missouri Plan," for mitigation, proposed by both Interior and DNR's Wildlife Division, would set aside all remaining valley land not flooded and an additional 4,250 acres outside Canaan Valley.

After eight weeks of hearings at the Federal Power Commission in Washington, three primary factors had emerged that threatened issuance of a license for the Davis Power Project: mitigation of wildlife and fisheries losses, leakage problems in both reservoirs, and consideration of the Glade Run alternative. All would be subject of further consideration when the hearings reconvened.

A staff geologist for the FPC had raised serious question about the porous nature of the valley floor and therefore its ability to hold water. Judge Kaplan's continued interest in the Glade Run alternative indicated he might license it instead. Elkinton commented that the company stuck to their commitment of recreational facilities in the unflooded areas, minimal wildlife mitigation, and refused to exclude the possibility of a coal-fired second plant. Finally an Interior witness had again indicated that if the project was not built, "there are private organizations interested in preserving the Valley for the people of the United States."

In the March 1975 another surprise: The *Voice* headlined, "FPC staff vetoes Davis Power Project." The FPC staff had recommended to Administrative Law Judge Kaplan that he deny the project license. In the Staff Counsel's brief filed February 28, they concluded, "the losses of the natural resources...outweigh the resulting benefits." The FPC staff argued that while the proposed project might serve the narrow economic and recreational interests of the immediate area, the FPC was required by law to regard the overall public interest and the uniqueness of Canaan Valley in a regional or even a national perspective required its preservation.

It was indeed unusual for an agency staff to recommend to an agency law judge that he veto a project. The conservation groups had seen a gradual change within the staff, starting with the EIS, then the subpoena for the DNR biologists, and finally this formal position. But Judge Kaplan was under no obligation to accept the FPC staff recommendation nor was the full Federal Power Commission obligated to ratify whatever Kaplan eventually decided.

The Conservancy, represented by Ratliff, argued that other alternatives existed, both within and outside Canaan Valley. Being careful to avoid supporting the Glade Run alternative, Ratliff nonetheless asserted that it was a preferred alternative, both less expensive and less destructive environmentally. Elkinton praised the Sierra Club's Wilson and Bramble. He wrote:

> The burden of establishing the uniqueness and importance ecologically of the Canaan Valley has been consistently shared between the Conservancy and the Sierra Club in this proceeding. Working with a larger budget, the Sierra Club attorneys were able to document the natural features of the Canaan Valley, and show the destructive impact the proposed project would have. The Conservancy's brief incorporated by reference the brief of the Sierra Club since both groups shared this position and were in basic agreement.

After Judge Kaplan made his ruling, the members of the Federal Power Commission would then make the final decision.

Meanwhile back in West Virginia, as the 1976 primary election approached, there was a wide-open Democratic race for Governor. After the eight years of Arch Moore's anti-environment record, promoting Corridor H, the Davis Power Project, pro-mining and anti-wilderness, the environmental community was ready for a change. Ken Hechler left a Congressional seat to run but was woefully underfinanced. Jay

Rockefeller, who had run four years earlier, had modified his anti-strip mining position and was expected to do well. James Sprouse, a long-time Democratic Party leader, John Hutchinson, Mayor of Charleston, and H. John Rogers, a Wetzel County lawyer, completed the field.

For the first time, the Highlands Conservancy sent out a voters' survey with questions about environmental issues. The candidates' answers appeared in the *Voice*. The April issue included a real surprise. In answer to the question on the Davis Power Project, Rockefeller said:

> I am firmly opposed to the construction of the dam in Canaan Valley. In 1975 the staff counsel of the Federal Power Commission recommended against construction of the Davis project in order to preserve the unique ecological system of the Canaan Valley. In 1974, the U.S. Dept. of Interior made a similar recommendation against the dam. Clearly, there is no convincing case for the FPC to award a license for the dam, especially since there are alternative sites that are more suitable.

Rockefeller won the primary, then the general election in November. Later, Conservancy activists would remind Governor Rockefeller of this paragraph.

In June 1976 Judge Kaplan ruled, licensing the Glade Run alternative to the Davis Power Project. Instead of flooding 7200 acres of Canaan Valley, only 785 acres would be sacrificed. Essentially the upper and lower reservoirs would exchange water during peak demand periods, thus reducing the impact on the larger Canaan Valley. A spokesman for Monongahela Power Company was quoted saying the company might not accept a license for Glade Run, since it was not contained in the original application.

It had been six years since the project was first announced and there still remained additional hurdles to cross before construction could begin. The Conservancy had led a coalition of state and national groups, working with a parallel group of state and federal environmental agencies, gaining the surprising assistance of the FPC's own staff. Together all agreed Canaan Valley was a national asset, a unique ecological wetlands system with plentiful wildlife that deserved preservation.

The following month, Dave Elkinton provided his perspective to *Voice* readers. Judge Kaplan's opinion had supported many of the environmental arguments of the Conservancy, the Sierra Club and other environmentalists. "For the past year and a half, no one on either side has felt confident of the outcome," wrote Elkinton. When Kaplan's ruling finally came, there was something for everyone. The Conservancy's arguments on the uniqueness of the Valley were supported. The power company's argument for additional capacity was also accepted. Only by licensing Glade Run, Kaplan wrote, could the uniqueness of Canaan Valley be preserved.

In his response, the Conservancy's Ratliff both supported Kaplan's decision and pointed out that all the arguments against the larger project could be made against the smaller alternatives. In any event the record was far from complete on Glade Run and additional studies would be necessary.

In speculating on the eventual decision of the full Commission, Elkinton said, "Environmentalists in the Conservancy and elsewhere can take comfort from the fact that it would be rare, though by no means impossible, for the FPC to rule in favor of a project, such as the original proposal, that both the FPC staff and FPC administrative law judge had opposed on environmental grounds."

In January 1977, Cooper Elkinton announced in a *Voice* article that the Nature Conservancy was interested in Canaan Valley. The "private conservation groups" referred to by the DNR and Interior Assistant Secretary Hughes had now been identified as the Nature Conservancy. The Nature Conservancy had recently petitioned the FPC indicating its interest in negotiating with the Allegheny Power System affiliates to preserve, through purchase, their holdings in Canaan Valley. The Sierra Club and the Conservancy asked the FPC to reopen the case to admit this new evidence.

As Jimmy Carter became President in 1977, his energy platform pledged to disband the FPC. For its part, the Nature Conservancy had just completed a statewide inventory under the Heritage Trust Program, listing Canaan Valley as a top priority for preservation. West Virginia's Heritage Trust Program, led by Canaan expert Fortney, was based on Governor Jimmy Carter's program in Georgia. Remembering Rockefeller's opposition to a dam in Canaan, Cooper Elkinton wrote, "Perhaps post-inaugural reminders are in order at this time. A strong stand by the governor would make a big difference in these proceedings, and perhaps also in the Nature Conservancy's negotiation offer."

At the 1977 Mid-Winter Workshop, Cooper Elkinton was elected Conservancy president. As president she would continue to keep the Conservancy in a leadership position in the struggle to save the Canaan Valley.

In her first "From the President" column, appearing in the February 1977 *Voice*, she wrote:

> Rumors are very strong that the Federal Power Commission now plans to license the original Davis Power Project that would flood 7200 acres of the Canaan Valley and open the way for massive recreational and industrial development of the area. This is the first word we have received about the full Commission's decision and every effort is being made to keep it from happening.

She urged readers to write Governor Rockefeller in support of the Nature Conservancy's efforts to acquire the area. "Don't let Canaan become our first 1977 'energy crisis' casualty," she pleaded.

On March 17, President Cooper Elkinton, with Conservancy members Keith Kirk and Ellen Snyder, attended a roundtable discussion on energy with President Carter, Interior Secretary Cecil Andrus, Energy Secretary James Schlesinger, and EPA Administrator Douglas Costle. Governor Rockefeller was working closely with federal government leaders to promote West Virginia as a source of coal. On a panel discussion addressing environmental issues, Ed Light, of the West Virginia Citizens Action Group, and Judy Stephenson, Executive Director of Save Our Mountains, specifically mentioned the Davis Power Project and Cranberry Wilderness Area mining threats as examples of significant concerns.

Meanwhile, as the four FPC Commissioners were considering the Davis project for the first time, the day before President Carter came to Charleston, State Attorney General Chauncey Browning flew to Washington and personally petitioned the FPC to re-open the record to permit Governor Rockefeller to change the state's official position. Former Governor Moore had prohibited the DNR biologists from testifying against the proposal. Browning had been attorney general throughout the entire process, but now he had a new governor as a client and the state's position had switched. Rockefeller wanted to file a statement opposing both the original Davis proposal and the Glade Run alternative. The FPC issued a two-week postponement.

Rockefeller's switch came after an intensive effort by representatives of the West Virginia Highlands Conservancy, the Sierra Club and others. Cooper Elkinton, Conservancy Vice President Lowell Markey, and Conservancy attorney Ratliff had met in February with members of the Governor's staff, and had been assured the Governor's position "as stated in *The Highlands Voice* of April 1976" was unchanged. This was the pre-primary candidate response discussed earlier.

But there was more. The petition filed by Attorney General Browning not only opposed the power project, it suggested Canaan Valley be included in the National Wildlife Refuge System as recommended by the U.S. Fish and Wildlife Service instead of being destroyed by a power project. This brought the state into agreement with the legal positions of the Conservancy and the Sierra Club.

Although Rockefeller's position might appear to be a victory for environmentalists, commented Cooper Elkinton, it was apparent at the FPC hearing when Browning had flown to Washington, that the commissioners planned to issue a license for the original project, perhaps within a month. The commissioners conducted the hearing in a very informal manner, frequently asking opinions of various FPC staff members in attendance.

Cooper Elkinton reported that the decision to license the original project was vigorously supported by Commissioner James Watt, formerly Director of the U.S. Bureau of Outdoor Recreation under President Nixon. He downplayed the unique ecological character of the Canaan Valley and argued that the project would "improve" recreation opportunities. This was an apparent reference to the substitution of man-made flat-water lake recreation for natural stream and wilderness experiences.

This was the same James Watt, who later as Secretary of Interior under President Reagan, would become the lightning rod for environmental activism. It was unclear if this was the first time the Sierra Club encountered James Watt. It certainly would not be the last!

The FPC Decision, New Refuge Proposal, and 404 Permit

[Because these three developments are so intertwined, it is impossible to discuss one independent of the other two.]

On March 31, 1977, the Federal Power Commission issued a license for the Davis Power Project to the three companies of the Allegheny Power System. A front-page story by Cooper Elkinton appeared in the April 1977 *Highlands Voice*. She also reported that the U.S. Fish and Wildlife Service had prepared a report recommending that Canaan Valley be made a National Wildlife Refuge.

Judy Frank, a reporter for the Elkins *Inter-Mountain* (and later a *Highlands Voice* editor), had obtained the wildlife refuge report, Cooper

Elkinton stated. It contemplated a 27,764-acre refuge, with $286,000 in annual payments coming to Tucker County. This contrasted with $35,000 in annual tax receipts presently produced from the same land. The power project had projected as much as $2 million when completed. Cooper Elkinton urged all readers to write to the Congressional delegation in support of the refuge proposal.

Cooper Elkinton reported the vote on the Commission as 3-1, but a formal order had not yet been entered. Already the Sierra Club and the State of West Virginia indicated their intention to petition for a re-hearing and, failing that, were considering an appeal to federal court.

The summary so far: The FPC had issued a license that was opposed by the administrative law judge after hearing eight weeks of testimony, by many of its own staff, by several federal agencies, by the governor, and by major environmental organizations. The case was destined to land in court and now the U.S. Fish and Wildlife Service was proposing a competing use for the same real estate. There was a new administration in Washington, headed by Jimmy Carter, whose environmental record had been excellent in Georgia. No one could predict the ultimate outcome. There had been several surprises already and there would be more to come.

In May, Interior Secretary Andrus joined Governor Rockefeller and the environmental groups in petitioning for a rehearing to consider the plan for the wildlife refuge. At a meeting in June, the FPC allowed Interior to become an intervenor, but announced denial of all petitions for rehearing. An appeal in federal court was actively being considered by the Conservancy to force the FPC to consider all alternatives, especially the refuge proposal. Because President Carter had proposed the replacement of the FPC in legislation currently before Congress, any rehearing might well be assigned to a newly- created body. The speed and unwillingness to reconsider shown by the FPC might be attributed to their desire to act while they remained in authority.

In August 1977 government and environmental groups filed a suit against the Federal Power Commission to prevent construction of the Davis Power Project. Plaintiffs including the State of West Virginia, the U.S. Department of Interior, the Sierra Club, the Highlands Conservancy, and the Appalachian Research and Defense Fund. Plaintiffs asked that the D.C. Circuit Court of Appeals declare the FPC license illegal and invalid. Meanwhile, the Fish and Wildlife Service planned to complete their study of the valley for inclusion in the National Wildlife Refuge System in the near future.

As the Conservancy awaited the next developments in the Canaan Valley struggle, it took stock of its first decade. It really was amazing that in such a few short years, not only was the Canaan Valley still not flooded, but nearby Otter Creek and Dolly Sods had been protected as Wilderness areas, Cranberry was a Wilderness Study Area, Corridor H had been stopped, the Rowlesburg and Royal Glen dams stopped, clearcutting abolished, and strip-mining more strictly controlled. There had been losses too, including battling unsuccessfully the many threats to Shavers Fork. As President Cooper Elkinton wrote in her "From the President" column in the September 1977 *Voice*:

> As a result of the hard work of many faithful and dedicated members and in light of our many successes, we have earned the right to blow our own horn every now and then. We need to do it more. There are many people who, if they knew more about the Conservancy, would want to join... Blow our horn whenever you get a chance and keep helping the Conservancy protect our beautiful West Virginia highlands!

By November the West Virginia Legislature had formed an ad hoc committee to promote the Davis Power Project and convince Governor Rockefeller to reverse course yet again. Composed of ten members, it included Guy Smith, a Tucker County delegate, Senator C. N. "Bud" Harman, a Canaan native, as well as eight other pro-industry legislators. Holding a public meeting at Blackwater Falls State Park, they had heard only power company supporters, refusing to hear opponents who were present. Not surprisingly, they unanimously voted to support the Davis project and oppose the Canaan Valley refuge.

President Cooper Elkinton wrote:

> Time is running out for Canaan Valley. Pressure on state and federal officials will mount over the next few months as the Allegheny Power System unleashes its big guns to push through the Davis Power Project. Governor Rockefeller, Attorney General Browning and Interior Secretary Cecil Andrus, all of whom oppose the DPP, need letters immediately to encourage them to continue their opposition.
>
> The Canaan Valley is a unique natural area, and its preservation should be of primary concern to every West Virginian. When ill-conceived supporters of the DPP castigate Canaan as a "worthless swamp," picture instead a power plant, an industrial pond unable to

support life, and mud flats. Compare that image with the existing spruce and firs, the meandering Blackwater River, the deer browsing and woodcock starting up from a thicket, and reflect on the definition of "worthless."

There was an obvious desperation among the Conservancy leaders who had spent seven years fighting to preserve the Canaan Valley. The optimism they had felt when first the FPC staff, then the administrative law judge, then Governor Rockefeller, and finally the Interior Department had opposed the power project, had given way to a new pessimism. The outgoing FPC commissioners, led by Watt, and now West Virginia legislators, were part of a well-heeled movement to resurrect the original proposal. It would be a tough winter.

As 1978 began, the Conservancy's federal appeal was in preparation. The Federal Energy Regulatory Commission had succeeded the FPC under President Carter's re-organization legislation. The Conservancy argued that the wildlife refuge plan of the Interior Department should have been reviewed before the FPC issued the license because it was indeed an alternative use of the Canaan Valley. Conservancy lawyers quoted Judge Kaplan's description of Canaan Valley as "a rare ecological phenomenon of extraordinary educational and scientific, aesthetical and recreational value."

In February, the *Voice* reported that the draft Environmental Impact Statement for the proposed Canaan Valley National Wildlife Refuge would be released shortly. Hearings would be held in Parsons, Morgantown, and Charleston, and members were implored to attend and testify. The backers of the Davis Power Project were expected in large numbers. In recognition that the Canaan Valley was of interest to a widening constituency, two of the three hearings were scheduled outside of the local area.

"During the first few days of May the fate of the Canaan Valley may well be decided," began an April *Voice* article announcing the dates of public hearings on the draft EIS for the Canaan Valley National Wildlife Refuge. Describing the refuge proposal as the most significant alternative to the power project, the author stated, "The success of this proposal will determine whether Canaan Valley is preserved or flooded." It was that simple: power plant or refuge. Three successive nights, May 8, 9, and 10, in Morgantown, Charleston and Parsons respectively, would determine Canaan Valley's fate.

"In an effort which may serve to divert attention away from the Refuge proposal," the article continued by announcing another wrinkle that would be of major significance:

> The power companies have filed an application for a Section 404 permit from the U.S. Army Corps of Engineers. Consequently the Corps has scheduled a public hearing at the Tucker County Courthouse in Parsons on May 3, only five days before the Refuge hearings! Section 404 is that part of the Clean Water Act designed to protect the nation's wetlands from development. Without question, the power project would destroy West Virginia's most significant wetland resource.
>
> The Governor, through the State Department of Natural Resources, is expected to recommend that the Corps deny the 404 permit, as is the U.S. Fish and Wildlife Service. It is considered rare indeed that the Corps will act against the wishes of a Governor and the Fish and Wildlife Service. However, environmentalists need to attend the May hearing.

Meanwhile, the Canaan Valley Refuge proposal, first considered as early as 1961, had not been actively pursued until recently because the federal emphasis had been on high-density recreational development. After the federal and state wildlife agencies had seemingly lost their wildlife mitigation proposal of a 20,000 acre set-aside in the FPC decision, Lynn Greenwalt, Fish and Wildlife Director, had given the go-ahead for development of a full-blown refuge proposal.

The EIS for the wildlife refuge recommended acquiring "a major portion of the approximately 28,000 acres of mixed wetlands, upland and farmland habitat" for preservation and maintenance the unique ecosystem. Property acquisition would be a mix of outright purchase, easements, or agreements with agricultural practices that were compatible with the management objectives. It was pointedly stated that congressional action was not required. Finally an addendum stated that Senators Byrd and Randolph had been consulted on potential sites for refuges in West Virginia, but the implication was that Canaan Valley was not their preferred choice. Letters to the senators and Congressman Staggers were urged.

Cooper Elkinton's President's column added her perspective, calling the refuge a concrete plan for Canaan Valley's protection. She continued:

It is not just a "pie in the sky" idea any longer, it is a well-documented, competently-formulated alternative that is well within the realm of possibility and one that we have waited a very long time to see.

The challenge that conservationists and all interested persons face in protecting the Canaan Valley as a National Wildlife Refuge is formidable. No significant action by our Federal government, such as this one, that would alter the land use of a 28,000 tract owned by a powerful utility company and a variety of land speculators backed by local bankers, county and state chambers of commerce, a variety of enterprising real estate agencies, local labor unions, regional travel promoters, and miscellaneous other wheeler-dealers cannot escape the notice of both the powerful and the opportunistic. The conflict that exists between the two views of the "highest and best possible use" (the Davis Power Project and the National Wildlife Refuge) of the geographic area in question – the Canaan Valley – will rage in the weeks to come.

For the Conservancy, the battleground is different but the forces are quite similar. We've faced similar obstacles before and we are familiar with the accusations that have and will again be made about economic peril that support for this alternative will bring to local communities, as if there were only one good answer to all such questions – the sacrifice of a high-quality natural area to the forces of high-intensity industrial and highly speculative recreational development.

In all our actions we seek positive alternatives that will both benefit a West Virginia local economy and preserve what is unique about our precious West Virginia way of life. Now such an alternative exists. We can be "for" a viable alternative and nor merely "against" an ill-conceived, wasteful and environmentally unsound proposal. We can favor a plan which will promote our State's valuable resources and exercise that broadened vision that recognizes the intrinsic value of more than just one force that makes our State attractive to the varied interests of both those who live here and those who choose to visit.

The Canaan Valley eminently qualifies for protection. And, to our knowledge, no better method for such protection exists than through the establishment of the Valley as a National Wildlife Refuge. However, to see the idea through to fruition will take the help of many people. Already our Congressional leaders, recognizing the implications of this action for their political futures, are making sure they do not commit themselves too early to the "wrong side." Senator Randolph continues to promote the preposterous notion that both a Wildlife Refuge **and** [emphasis in the original] a power plant are feasible side-by-side in the Canaan Valley, and Senator Byrd wants people to know that he favors the establishment of a Wildlife Refuge somewhere in the state but not necessarily in the Canaan Valley where the best possible place for it would be.

It's inevitable that political forces are brought to bear in such battles. We are seeking a change in thinking, in priority setting, in physical planning and in economic development in our State – changes that have the potential for affecting many people's lives both those who depend on the Valley for high-quality recreational and aesthetic benefit and those who seek to cash in on the acclaimed economic boom that they are told would accompany the power plant development – the town houses, condominia, the shopping centers, the fast food chains: all the features we may welcome in our small towns and large cities but which have no place in such a fragile and unique biological "treasure house" like Canaan Valley.

Having laid out the issue at hand, Cooper Elkinton urged everyone to communicate with the congressional delegation. She pointed out letters, phone calls and spreading the word had made the difference in protecting Dolly Sods, Otter Creek, and Cranberry, among other issues, and they would be what would make the difference this time.

Canaan Valley dominated the May 1978 *Highlands Voice*. First a report on the recent public hearings, held in five locations: three by the Fish and Wildlife Service on the refuge proposal and two by the Corps of Engineers on the 404 permit needed by the power project. Not surprisingly, the refuge hearings restricted testimony to the refuge proposal, while the Corps solicited testimony on the power project.

In an unsigned article, one author reported that while conservationists and power company spokesmen generally stayed close to the relevant topic, the Tucker countians did not. Clearly they were of one mind, and the hearings brought out that the county was nearly united in favor of the power project. The glue holding the county together was money.

Attracted by the estimated $2 million to be generated by the power plant, Tucker County Chamber of Commerce representatives saw the salvation for a "destitute" school system. In head-on conflicting testimony, the proponents and opponents each chose their most sympathetic venues. The article continued:

At Parsons, Monongahela Power's Executive Vice President Don Hollen [who had succeeded Singley], argued that the project will have benign environmental effects: "The Davis Project will not inhibit use of any of the recreational facilities which currently exist in the Canaan Valley and the project will not mar the wilderness character of the

Dolly Sods scenic area." Conservancy President Elkinton countered at Morgantown, maintaining that "The Davis Power Project offers Canaan Valley noisy pumping turbines and visually assaulting high-tension power lines, power house and generators; weekly water fluctuations that would expose hundreds of acres of barren mud flats and not a 'fresh water tidal zone,' as the power company continues to allege; a sterile high mountain 7,000 acre 'industrial pond' that would provide very attractive spawning ground, not for the vast variety of fish and aquatic life that thrive in the Valley's wetlands now, but for further power generation facilities – coal fired or nuclear powered…"

More than forty individuals spoke at each hearing. Many valley owners expressed fear of being removed from their homes if the refuge becomes a reality. Howard Larsen, Regional Director of the Fish and Wildlife Service, countered that contrary to a local newspaper report of 169 families being evicted, very few if any would be removed. The Service expected to make its decision in October 1978.

The *Voice* reprinted the full text of Conservancy President Cooper Elkinton's statement and the Sierra Club's, as well as lengthy excerpts from the power company and the Izaak Walton League, West Virginia Division. The Morgantown hearing had pitted the Conservancy's Cooper Elkinton against Mon Power's Hollen. According to Tom Dunham, now editor of *The Highlands Voice*, "lining up with the Conservancy and the Sierra Club were the West Virginia League of Women Voters, the Nature Conservancy, the Grouse Society, the National Spelunker [*sic*] Society, and an array of private citizens." Backing the power company were among others, chambers of commerce and local legislators.

When the same hearing moved to Parsons, two nights later, Dunham described a different atmosphere indeed. "The yahoos were out in full force in Tucker County recently — all ready to sell themselves to the highest bidder." No pro-refuge speakers appeared, but the Fish and Wildlife officials were treated to four hours of non-stop local 'tongue lashings" from the opposition, a long parade of local elected public officials, business owners, and private citizens. Dunham's description continued:

> The county is dazzled and gripped by the prospect of a power plant. It is seen as the savior and cornucopia of the county. If anything dominated the remarks of the residents, it was their 30 pieces of silver. The issue is clear to them. The power plant will bring $2,000,000 per year in taxes to the county while the Fish and Wildlife Service will pay

the county just $300,000 per year if the refuge is established. That figure in itself is eight to ten times higher than what the county now gets from the land that would make up the refuge. But what's $300,000 compared to $2,000,000?

To provincial Tucker County the state interest accounts for nothing, and the national interest means less than nothing. At the Morgantown hearing, the President of the Tucker County Board of Education wondered why hearings were even being held outside Tucker County, for obviously only Tucker County residents should have a voice in the issue. Tucker County could make its $2,000,000 and run and the hell with everyone else.

In her "From the President" column, Cooper Elkinton presented a status report in the *Voice* of June 1978. She asked:

> Industrial pond or wildlife refuge? Will the U.S. Army Corps of Engineers issue the 404 Permit that will move the Allegheny Power System one step closer to the destruction of the Canaan Valley? Will the U.S. Fish and Wildlife Service protect the Canaan Valley by designating it a National Wildlife Refuge? Will Canaan's wetlands, wildlife and scenic beauty continue to exist or be excavated and mutilated?

She explained that the Corps was expected to make its decision very soon. The Fish and Wildlife Service would make their decision by October. Senators Randolph and Byrd and Congressman Staggers were still uncommitted. The Department of Interior, Governor Rockefeller and the DNR remained firm in their support of the refuge. However, the legislative subcommittee, which had held the one-sided hearing in 1977, had now invited the DNR to justify its position. She added:

> There's much to take heart from. The uncertainty, while burdensome, is neither unendurable nor particularly discouraging. No Davis Power Project has been built. Canaan Valley remains beautiful, wild and wonderful. And, a Canaan Valley National Wildlife refuge remains a very definite possibility. Its realization continues to rest on the support that can be rallied. Much has already been received. The following is not an exhaustive list of organizations who have and continue to provide support (testimony at hearings, much needed financial contributions, letters, information to their members) but it is an impressive one: On the national level the Sierra Club, the National Audubon Society, the Nature Conservancy, Friends of the Earth, the Defenders of Wildlife, Audubon Naturalists Society, American Youth

Hostels, Inc, International Backpackers Association, the Wilson
Ornithological Society and the Ruffed Grouse Society; on the more
regional or state level, the West Virginia Wildlife Federation, the
League of Women Voters of West Virginia Inc, the Brooks Bird Club,
National Speleological Society (Mid-Atlantic Region), Trout Unlim-
ited, Sutton Audubon Society, West Virginia Citizens Action Group,
Citizens for Environmental Protection, Mountain Community Union
and Wildwater Expeditions Unlimited Inc; and up in Michigan, the
Walter Hastings Audubon Club, Inc.

This was the first glimpse that *Voice* readers had seen of the results of
several years of organizing by Cooper Elkinton. They had heard various
media reports on Canaan Valley, seen articles in the newsletters of other
organizations to which they belonged, but until now, there had not been
a recitation of the anti-power plant, pro-refuge team members. It was an
impressive list. No wonder she was not discouraged.

On July 14, 1978, Col. Max Janairo, Jr., District Engineer in the
Corps of Engineers, Pittsburgh District, denied the 404 permit to the
Davis Power Project, marking a real environmental victory in the
Conservancy's eight-year battle for the preservation of the Canaan Valley.
The decision to deny the permit was the final act of Col. Janairo, who
retired from the Army the following day. Janairo was quoted as saying, he
had expected his job as District Engineer to have some controversial
issues, "but I had not expected anything like the Davis Power Project."

Not only had Governor Rockefeller's position, favoring the refuge
over the power plant, been critical, but also the Corps relied on a special
study it commissioned by a national expert on fresh water wetland areas.
This expert had agreed with the Department of Natural Resources,
Conservancy, Sierra Club and Audubon experts who had presented
evidence throughout the course of the battle to preserve this national
area.

The power company reacted to the 404 permit denial by predicting
blackouts and brownouts during the early 1980s and announced it would
appeal Col. Janairo's decision. Conservancy President Cooper Elkinton
called the threats "scare tactics" and called on Allegheny to re-examine
alternative sites and energy conservation measures.

Senator Randolph, in a serious re-election challenge from former
Governor Moore, maintained his combination power project and refuge
stance, although the Fish and Wildlife Service considered them mutually
exclusive. Recently Randolph had convened a meeting of all governmen-

tal parties (but not including conservationists) to broker a compromise solution. Janairo's decision had killed the power plant half of Randolph's position.

The momentum had turned. Cooper Elkinton reported, "Conservationists now feel more confident in their struggle since the Corps of Engineers, not traditionally known as a protector of environmental values, has officially recognized Canaan Valley's unique natural qualities."

In a 2006 interview, Cooper discussed receiving the news of the Corps 404 denial:

> I remember exactly where I was. I was in Canaan riding on a tractor, raking hay on the farm. I got a message that Skip Johnson [of *The Charleston Gazette*] called and said that the Corps had denied the 404 permit. I took my radio to the field and listened to the news on the tractor.

At the October 1978 Fall Review, one trip visited portions of the proposed Canaan Valley Wildlife Refuge, led by Cooper Elkinton and Dave Harris. Harris was the staff biologist for the Fish and Wildlife Service who had worked carefully over the past several years as the primary researcher and author of the EIS for the proposed refuge. During that time, he had not been a welcomed visitor in Parsons or in or near Canaan Valley, yet he had worked methodically to prepare the scientific background needed to justify the refuge. He had provided background support to sympathetic citizen-activists like Cooper Elkinton, since as a federal employee he could not lobby.

The U.S. Circuit Court of Appeals in Washington heard arguments in the appeal of the FPC, now FERC, license to build the Davis project on October 15, 1978. Plaintiffs, including the State of West Virginia, the U.S. Department of Interior, the Sierra Club, and the Conservancy, argued that the license would illegally destroy a unique natural area, deserving of preservation through establishment of the refuge. Lacking a required wildlife mitigation plan and study of alternatives, the plaintiffs argued that the resulting costs of the project could not be determined and therefore its cost-benefit ratio could not be known.

Meanwhile Allegheny Power filed its appeal of the 404 permit denial in U.S. District Court in Washington, D.C. The Davis case would be the first instance where a 404 permit denial would kill a FERC license. The power company hired Clark Clifford and his prestigious Washington law firm, while the U.S. Department of Justice would defend the Corps of

Engineers. Joining the Corps would be the Sierra Club, the National Audubon Society, the Environmental Defense Fund, the National Wildlife Federation, and the Highlands Conservancy. All parties recognized the stakes involved in this inter-agency conflict over whose license or permit would prevail.

Senator Randolph, ever closer to election day, requested a meeting with Secretary of the Army Clifford Alexander, and asked for his personal review and reversal of the District Engineer's decision to deny the 404 permit. Secretary Alexander agreed to a procedural review only, explaining that any further involvement was precluded by the pending court action. Cooper Elkinton reported that Randolph had personally lobbied President Carter on behalf of the Davis project as well.

The Canaan Valley Alliance and Task Force

By March 1979, the Canaan Valley Alliance had formed, to coordinate and publicize information on the proposed Canaan Valley Wildlife Refuge. It would become a broad coalition that would develop the political support for the refuge. Here was a chance for conservationists to support a positive project, in contrast to the all-too-frequent fighting against destructive developments. Cooper Elkinton, on behalf of the Conservancy, and Frank Dunstan, of the National Audubon Society's Mid-Atlantic office, organized the Alliance. Other Conservancy members included Board member Steve Bradley, his wife Pat, and Keith Kirk, a Board member representing National Speleological Society.

A sharply worded article in the March 1979 *Voice*:

> The West Virginia Highlands Conservancy today expressed its strong disapproval to the recent political intervention by West Virginia Senators Byrd and Randolph and Congressman Harley Staggers in the proposed pumped storage power plant in the Canaan Valley, Tucker County.
>
> The three legislators met with President Carter on February 20 in an attempt to secure an executive review of the Corps of Engineers denial of Allegheny Power Company's [*sic*] application to construct a power plant in the Valley.
>
> The Corps, according to Highlands Conservancy spokesman, Linda Elkinton, "rightly denied the permit under Section 404 of the federal Clean Water Act." This section mandates the Corps of Engineers to protect the nation's wetlands, such as the Canaan Valley. Elkinton said, "We deplore the attempted circumvention by Senators Byrd and

Randolph of what the Corps of Engineers was by federal law required to do."

The article continued by requesting Conservancy members to keep communicating with the congressional delegation to counter the one-sided lobbying that the Davis project's backers were obviously undertaking.

By April construction by the power company of three major roads, including one to the Dobbin Slashings area of Dolly Sods, was destroying the integrity of the potential wildlife refuge. Cooper Elkinton reported that the Interior Department, Sierra Club, and Conservancy had filed a motion with FERC to prohibit further construction activities by the power company.

Meanwhile, on March 28, Governor Rockefeller had announced the reversal of his position on the Davis project. Because of a decrease in Iranian oil imports, Rockefeller had stated that he would now support the pumped storage power plant for the Canaan Valley. The reaction to the governor's reversal was swift. At a press conference in Charleston, March 30, a coalition of citizen groups, including the Conservancy, denounced the governor's turnabout. A few days later, *The Charleston Gazette* editorialized against the governor's new position and called for energy conservation, not the Davis plant. The West Virginia Sierra Club fired off a letter accusing him of undercutting the work of the Department of Natural Resources on endangered species for the valley.

In a statement that would echo years later, Cooper Elkinton wrote:

> It is time West Virginia stopped sacrificing its environmental quality for the benefit of wasteful energy policies of utility systems located hundreds of miles away. Pumped storage projects rob miners of markets for their coal because the Davis Project will supplant coal generated electricity and help spread nuclear energy.

Meanwhile Steve Bradley, Conservancy Board member and assistant coordinator of the Canaan Valley Alliance, reported a threatening phone call from Pat Nichols, Prosecuting Attorney for Tucker County. Known as an ardent supporter of the Davis Project, Nichols represented Tucker County and the county Chamber of Commerce in the FERC license appeal. Bradley called this threat "highly questionable behavior from a member of the Bar and certainly not the epitome of professional legal and ethical behavior."

Rockefeller justified his switch to promote increased American power production and thereby reduce dependence on Iranian oil production.

He announced withdrawal of the state's opposition to the Davis Power Project and support of a 404 permit by the Corps.

A *Voice* article reported a public controversy had formed over the Scruggs and Hammond Report, a ten-year old study of potential nuclear facilities on the project's lower reservoir. First denying it, the power company later corrected itself, but dismissed the `study as unrealistic. But clearly in a state dominated by coal, the prospect of a nuclear facility was anathema, and provided fuel for the Davis project opponents in winning the war of public opinion.

In a special insert to the May 1979 *Highlands Voice*, Editor Dunham headlined, "Move 'Em Out or (Development in Canaan): The Scruggs and Hammond Report." The first few paragraphs set the tone:

> An industrial, commercial, and recreational development of gigantic proportions that would nearly obliterate the Canaan Valley, as we know it is planned by Allegheny Power System. This information is contained in an internal Monongahela Power Company (a subsidiary of Allegheny) document extraordinary for its heretofore secrecy.
>
> For at least 10 years, the Allegheny Power System through Monongahela Power has been telling the people of Tucker County that it wanted to build a pumped storage power plant – **and nothing else**. Such a project the company said would provide jobs and revenue to the county government. [emphasis in original]
>
> Now we have learned that all along the power plant was merely the tip of the iceberg. Surfacing once the plant was safely under construction would be land moguls from sophisticated New York and East Coast development corporations. Gone would be the hunting and trapping areas, the fishing holes, and the wildlife. In their place would be resort homes for the rich, second homes for the near rich, hotels and motels, new roads, an airport, and even chemical plants on the Blackwater River.

The article quoted extensively from the Scruggs and Hammond Report, outlining its concept of maximum development around Davis' lower reservoir. Even the Conservancy's most seasoned Canaan Valley preservationists found this frightening reading. Throughout the entire licensing proceedings, refuge hearings, and now court reviews, the Scruggs and Hammond Report had been underplayed, but Dunham had blown it wide open. *The Charleston Gazette* was running similar articles, including a quote from the FERC, "Any pumped storage project is just tailor-made for a nuclear plant."

Clearly the level of public debate had heated up. The power company and its backers were pulling out all stops, especially political intervention from the congressional delegation, to influence the Carter administration to back the power plant. It didn't help that OPEC oil prices were rising rapidly and that Carter was feeling an energy crisis at hand. The conservation community was simultaneously fighting the Davis project, trying to promote the refuge as an alternative, advocating conservation measures that the public could employ to actually reduce their energy demand, and deal with political leaders who changed positions. The nuclear option in Canaan Valley added an entirely new dimension to the battle.

On May 30, 1979, the U.S. Fish and Wildlife Service released its Final Environmental Impact Statement and plan for the Canaan Valley Wildlife Refuge. In her analysis, Cooper Elkinton reported the plan would acquire 28,000 acres of "unimproved wet areas and uplands in Canaan Valley." The purpose of the refuge would be to protect the ecological integrity of Canaan Valley and insure that its wetland, plant, and wildlife resources remained available to the citizens of the United States. The 500-page EIS would form the basis for a final decision by the USFWS Director on or after July 3.

Canaan Valley Alliance representatives had recently met with both Senators Randolph and Byrd. Both favored the power project, but were trying to accommodate a refuge as well, according to a *Voice* article. The power company had indicated no interest in a smaller power project, like the Glade Run alternative, because they wanted the 7,000-acre "industrial pond for 'other purposes.'"

Cooper Elkinton asked, "Who will make the final decision on the Canaan Valley refuge?" Referring to the Director's upcoming July 3 decision, she underlined the involvement and influence of a host of government officials and agencies. From the congressional delegation, to the FERC and Corps of Engineers, to the governor and the DNR, was it realistic that the refuge could be established without additional funding? The USFWS claimed they already had initial funding on hand. But congressional appropriations would be needed if significant land acquisition were to be initiated. Again, she urged Conservancy members to write to Senators Byrd and Randolph, Governor Rockefeller, and Interior Secretary Andrus.

In the August *Voice,* Conservancy member Perry Bryant wrote an article showing a weakening demand for peak power, thereby undercutting the rationale for the Davis project. Using the power company's projections from 1972, he showed the effects of conservation, resulting in far lower growth than predicted. "Conservation has reduced the need for Davis by 81% according to the power company's own inflated figures," concluded Bryant. Using FERC's data from the license, an 88% reduction had been achieved.

In late June 1979, President Carter, under pressure from all sides, had requested the new Department of Energy to conduct a study of alternatives to the Davis Power Project. Under Carter's instructions, "alternatives to the Davis project" would be considered, giving the clear implication that the Corps 404 permit denial had rendered Davis dead. To study these alternatives, the Energy Department would form a task force, including FERC, Interior, EPA, and the Corps and report regularly to the President's Council on Environmental Quality. The public would be kept informed throughout the study and have the opportunity to provide comments when a draft was released. The Fish and Wildlife Service suspended their decision on the refuge until the task force report was completed.

Meanwhile, the Canaan Valley Alliance, under its President and Conservancy Board member Steve Bradley, had become deeply engaged in a public advocacy campaign promoting the Canaan Valley Wildlife Refuge. Using a slide show, members fanned out across West Virginia and surrounding states to urge support for the Refuge. In addition to support from the Conservancy, National Audubon Society, Sierra Club, National Wildlife Federation, and Environmental Defense Fund were specifically mentioned as part of the Alliance. Cooper Elkinton once again urged Conservancy members and its constituent members to write to the congressional delegation in support of preserving the Canaan Valley.

One significant event hosted by the Canaan Valley Alliance was a wine and cheese reception at the National Wildlife Federation building in Washington, D.C. in June of 1979. Eighty guests attended, including Congressional staffers and Washington conservationists. After a showing of the Canaan Alliance slide show and comments from Cooper Elkinton and Audubon's Frank Dunstan, Associate Director of the U.S. Fish and Wildlife Service Jim Pulliam and Vice President Thomas Kimball, of the National Wildlife Federation, spoke to the gathering. This was the largest and most influential national event in the long battle to preserve Canaan Valley.

By September 1979, the National Audubon Society had opened a West Virginia field office and hired Cooper Elkinton to staff it. As a Past

President of the Highlands Conservancy and Coordinator of the Canaan Valley Alliance, she was obviously already a leader in the Canaan efforts. Working under Dunstan, she would primarily focus public awareness and advocacy of the preservation of Canaan Valley, as well as provide assistance to Audubon's West Virginia chapters and membership.

In December, Cooper Elkinton reported on the Canaan Valley Task Force in a *Highlands Voice* article. Before the Task Force had even issued its report, Tucker County politicians, especially state Senators "Bud" Harman and J.D. Hinkle, were already discrediting it. They called the Task Force a "massive rip-off of the general public" and one that made "a mockery of the nation's so-called energy crisis." Cooper Elkinton found it ironic that many of the local politicians had been the very ones who intervened with the congressional delegation to get President Carter involved in promoting the power project. Now his administration was studying alternatives.

To conduct the necessary study, two consulting firms had been hired to prepare a draft report by December, with a final report scheduled for February 1980. Major attention would be devoted to determining the demand for, and alternative means of producing, peaking power within the Allegheny System's service area. Answering the question, "What does all this mean for the Refuge?" Cooper Elkinton summarized:

> It is of utmost importance that the work of the Task Force be kept in perspective. At worst, a recommendation for both a power project and a wildlife preserve of some type surrounding it could emerge from the study, in which case two lawsuits remain pending and, if it's the Glade Run alternative, it's back to the hearing room all over again. At best, their report could do something like confirm the Corps' previous decision, recommend logical and feasible alternatives for power production (not the least of which are conservation, time-of-use or other rate structures and use of existing hydroelectric facilities scattered across their service area), rule out other possible power plant sites in the valley and cool the controversy. But the Task Force report will **not** under any circumstances in itself protect Canaan Valley. The only agency that can do this is the U.S. Fish and Wildlife Service with their Refuge proposal. And the only way the USFWS can move is with the concurrence of your favorite fiddle player and mine, Senator Robert C. Byrd. [emphasis in original]
>
> Powerful Senator Byrd, who serves at the will of his West Virginia constituents and represents the entire nation in his official capacity as Senate Majority Leader, is the one most important person to the

Valley's protection as a National Wildlife Refuge. In his position as Majority Leader he sits on the Senate Appropriations Committee that must act on Refuge appropriations. And despite the fact that it was he, Senator Byrd, who first asked for the study of potential Refuge sites in the state, it is also he who must now be convinced that the USFWS's prime nomination is indeed most worthy of distinction.

So, while the Task Force can play an important role in seeing the Valley protected, make no mistake about it: Nothing short of constituent pressure is going to move Senator Byrd, our other Congressional delegation members, Secretary of Interior Andrus and Governor Rockefeller to take action to see Canaan Valley protected now.

The message was clear, and it had not changed: Conservancy members, indeed anyone interested in protecting Canaan Valley, needed to contact Senator Byrd, and the other political leaders without delay.

But as the Task Force report was delayed, an intriguing alternative had emerged, a power-sharing arrangement with Virginia Electric and Power Company (VEPCO)'s Bath County, Virginia, pumped storage plant, which had excess capacity. Meanwhile, to prevent a potential buyout of all remaining landowners in Canaan Valley, should a massive wildlife mitigation plan be adopted, local residents were considering incorporation as a small town. Ironically this concept had first been proposed by the Scruggs and Hammond report a decade earlier. Local developers continued to scare residents that the refuge would condemn all local land ownership, although that was clearly incorrect. Cooper Elkinton, working with the Conservancy, the Audubon Society and the Canaan Valley Alliance, was organizing a massive letter-writing campaign to Senator Byrd and Interior Secretary Andrus.

Despite repeated delays in releasing the Task Force report, Editor Dunham reprinted preliminary studies by one of the consultants in the June 1980 *Voice*. He worried in an introductory note that the final report might never be issued. Apparently the power company had strenuously objected to very early draft sections and been successful in forcing additional delays. Dunham castigated Governor Rockefeller for a "disastrous environmental record," citing the Governor's support of the Stonewall Jackson Dam, switch in position on Canaan Valley, and lax enforcement of strip mining laws and regulations.

As the 1980 November elections approached, all pending issues became subject to surprises. Cooper Elkinton, the Conservancy's Canaan Valley Committee Chair and Audubon staffer, wrote that time was rapidly running out for refuge backers. Ronald Reagan was seriously challenging Jimmy Carter and there was a fear that a Reagan administration would reverse course. USFWS Director Greenwalt had patiently waited over a year for the still-pending Department of Energy Task Force report before proceeding with the decision on the Canaan Valley Refuge. Just recently, the Monongahela Power Company had announced it was joining VEPCO in building the Bath County pumped storage facility, yet stressed the continued need for the Davis project. Cooper Elkinton stressed the need to end the decade of uncertainty that had left local landowners, county officials, and wildlife agencies in limbo, not knowing which, if either, proposal would win out.

Although Cooper Elkinton called Interior Secretary Andrus "an ally to the Refuge," he had already announced his departure, regardless of the election's outcome. She wrote that whether the refuge decision was a "yes" or "no" now depended on public support, the support of those who knew and loved Canaan Valley in its present condition or who recognized and appreciated the existence of species diversity, majestic scenic beauty, the joys of observing abundant and unusual plants and animals in a quiet and unspoiled natural setting in the few desirable places where it remained. She continued:

> There is absolutely no other time for which it is more important that a letter expressing your interest in the Valley's protection be written than right now. Government officials will only act positively on the Canaan Refuge if we insist they do, many of us, all of us together. Now.

In the 1980 election, Reagan defeated Carter, ushering in the repeal of many progressive, pro-environmental laws and regulations. While it would be some time while until it became clear exactly how this affected Canaan Valley, it was the former FPC Commissioner, James Watt, who became the most controversial Secretary of Interior in decades and the reason for a surge in the membership of environmental organizations.

The Task Force report was finally completed in late December 1980. Alternatives had been identified that would meet the company's peak power demand, including several other locations in West Virginia. But the first alternative identified by the DOE study was "the aggressive pursuit of conservation and load management [as] an important component of any alternative strategy since, if implementation is successful, economic benefits outweigh costs by a significant margin."

Because Allegheny had already agreed to buy into the Bath County project, the DOE study stated that additional capacity could be postponed until the 1990s. Power company reaction was predictably cool, but environmentalists hailed the report as confirming their long-held beliefs. Cooper Elkinton said she was glad the report stressed conservation and load management, coupled with reduced demand.

Just as the Task Force report was completed, Washington, D.C., District Court Judge John Lewis Smith ruled that the U.S. Army Corps of Engineers did not have the right to grant or deny a permit for the Davis Power Project. Ruling shortly before Christmas, the judge addressed his decision to just one of almost a dozen points in a civil suit filed by Allegheny Power System lawyers, headed by former Secretary of Defense Clark Clifford.

The Conservancy and its associated environmental groups had already announced plans to appeal, citing another case that held the opposite. Meanwhile the FERC had issued a stay to its license to the power company and all work was suspended. The USFWS had been awaiting the final Task Force report before deciding on the refuge's future.

Two months later, FERC asked the U.S. Court of Appeals in Washington to return the project license for reconsideration by FERC. The West Virginia Attorney General stated that, if successful, this might delay the project another ten years, since a second EIS might be required.

At the April Conservancy Board meeting, Cooper Elkinton reported she felt the prospects for a Canaan Valley Wildlife Refuge were poor. Since the election, new Interior Secretary Watt favored a freeze on additional refuges and newly elected Republican Congressman Cleve Benedict favored the Davis Power Project. The court cases continued to move slowly in Washington.

In September, Cooper Elkinton and Jenni Vincent, new President of the Canaan Valley Alliance, reported that Congressman Benedict had personally met with Secretary Watt to move the Davis project ahead. Watt, credited with having written the FPC license decision when a commissioner, now overseeing the USFWS, could kill the refuge proposal. Meanwhile the final DOE Task Force report might never be issued, since it would not be supported by the Reagan administration. (As a formality, one copy of the consultant's report would go into the DOE file, but it was never officially published.) Finally, the Corps of Engineers appealed the District Court's decision denying the Corps jurisdiction for a 404 permit on a FERC project. Now both the FERC and 404 cases were before the same Circuit Court in Washington.

In October's *Voice*, under a headline "Reagan v. Canaan," readers learned that Democratic senators would hold a retreat at Canaan Valley State Park in early October. The National Audubon Society organized a mini-bus tour and press conference to address the Reagan Administration's threat to Canaan Valley and other significant natural areas. Conservancy co-founder, M. Rupert Cutler, a former Assistant Secretary of Agriculture in the Carter Administration, now a Senior Vice President of Audubon, and Cooper Elkinton, Audubon Regional Representative, wanted to throw a national media spotlight on Canaan Valley by taking advantage of the press covering the Democrats' retreat.

Development Continues

Over the next year, occasional articles reported the fast pace of real estate development in Canaan Valley. Over the decade of the 1970s the population had increased eighty-six percent, the number of housing units was up by four hundred and everything continued to accelerate. Trout Unlimited and the Conservancy contested the sewage treatment permit of Land of Canaan, a condominium complex, in an effort to force adoption of non-chlorine technology. Trout often were killed by over-use of chlorine. A negotiated settlement led to the change. A plan for spot zoning to control development was under discussion, but awaited official county adoption.

During 1983 Canaan Valley residents worked on land use controls for the valley's southern end. Because of lack of support at the county level, they sought state legislation. In the March 1984 *Highlands Voice*, Cooper Elkinton described the conflict caused in Charleston:

> The Canaan Valley Authority Act, Senate Bill 415, was introduced by Senator John "Si" Boettner on February 3, 1984. He has had little peace about it since. Senate President Warren McGraw promptly assigned the bill to the Senate Judiciary Committee chaired by Senator Boettner rather than to the Natural Resources Committee where WVHC officials had been told it would suffer a quick death.
>
> But this is exactly what Senators Bud Harman and Ash, who represent Tucker County, have assured will happen to the bill in Senate Judiciary. Harman, long a champion of development interests in Canaan, visited Boettner in his office just before the bill was introduced. Reports say Harman came across Boettner's desk shaking his

finger in Boettner's face and saying he would do all he could to hurt Boettner politically if he introduced the bill. (Boettner is an announced candidate for Attorney General.) Senator Harman's rampage continued on the floor of the Senate after the bill was introduced and apparently even before he had read the bill.

Later in the week, Senator Gino Colombo of Harrison County claimed the bill would hurt an investment he made five years ago when he purchased 34 acres in Canaan. He referred to his "Deerfield Village" complex in Canaan, a development of 160 one, two, and three bedroom condominiums with private swimming pool, tennis courts, fitness center and jogging, walking, and cross-country ski trails. Colombo ignored his conflict of interest problems in his remarks.

The bill provided for a nine-member authority composed of six Canaan Valley landowners and three state and local officials. The authority would develop a comprehensive land use plan for the valley by January 1, 1985, including enforcement provisions. Those opposing it claimed it would halt private development, cost many jobs and ensure condemnation for expansion of the Canaan Valley State Park.

A group of forty local landowners had approached Boettner for sponsorship, after Harman and Ash refused. Since the first discussion of the Davis Power Project back in 1970, the Conservancy had consistently supported land use planning in the highlands and was therefore supporting the Boettner bill. (Boettner was no stranger to environmental efforts. He had been an original partner at the Appalachian Research and Defense Fund, with Paul Kaufman and Ray Ratliff, back when the Conservancy had sought their help in 1970.)

In reporting on the Canaan bill and its conflict, Skip Johnson of the *Charleston Gazette* wrote:

> The Boettner bill is not a no-growth bill. It simply allows for orderly development. What is so terrible about that? Well, a lot, according to Sen. Bud Harman, R-Taylor. Harman jumped on Boettner with both feet – how dare a senator from Kanawha County meddle in the private affairs of Canaan Valley? He has scheduled a meeting in the valley this weekend to map plans for stopping this nefarious scheme.
>
> Obviously it did take political courage for a senator from Kanawha County to introduce a bill involving Canaan Valley, even if the valley is a state treasure. But Boettner has shown that kind of courage in the Legislature.

Johnson gave the bill odds of 100–1, which he called "about the same odds that the chipping away at the valley will not continue."

The newly appointed state DNR Director, Willis Hertig, was asked about Canaan Valley. "I guess what I am concerned about," he said, "is that with extensive development in the valley, we're going to end up destroying the very thing that makes the valley attractive for development. It's kind of like a case of cutting off your nose to spite your face or killing the goose that laid the golden egg." His term would come to an end in December, when Governor Rockefeller ended his second term as Governor.

After the legislative session, Cooper Elkinton reflected on the legislative effort in an article for the April *Voice*. The Canaan land use bill had indeed never left Boettner's committee, but its publicity had succeeded in focusing local and statewide attention. A new group, the Canaan Valley Land Planning Association, had formed to develop a land use and management plan for the valley. Elkinton reflected that for the first time in the Conservancy's history in Canaan protection issues, local people worked for protection. The forty CLPA members had signed petitions, made calls to legislators, and otherwise lobbied for the bill. Instead of always opposing projects, as conservationists were often accused of, she wrote, here was a chance to be for something.

Rapid private development in the southern end of Canaan Valley continued, with an occasional opportunity for the Conservancy's Cooper Elkinton to file comments on a sewage discharge permit. But because no other building codes or zoning permits were required, the only other impediment to development seemed to be an occasional lack of adequate capital. Meanwhile, Arch Moore returned to the Governor's office in 1985 and the power project and refuge plan remained before the Circuit Court of Appeals in Washington, D.C.

The state Water Resources Board designated streams in Canaan Valley as "national resource waters." Said Cooper Elkinton, "It is not only the first time the Board and the Department of Natural Resources have recognized the existence of such waters in the state, but it is also the first time a state agency dealing with water resources has given formal recognition to the importance of natural resources in Canaan Valley."

The action resulted from a consent order by the Board, following the Conservancy's protest of yet another water discharge permit by a developer. Other pending permits, also under protest, would now be released. Under the new classification, the Chief of Water Resources was required to identify trout streams in the Canaan Valley area and develop and require sewage discharge restrictions that would protect these streams. Several major lagoons had exhibited algae blooms that year as the private developers continued the housing boom. A recent sale of one-third interest in a mountainside tract of two-hundred acres had brought $1.6 million. Groundwater and stream quality were at risk as never before.

Governor Moore's Surprise

Suddenly after months of relative quiet, Canaan Valley was in the news. Governor Moore had informed U.S. Interior Secretary Donald Hodel, who followed Watt, that West Virginia was withdrawing from the suit challenging the 1977 FERC license. In an enigmatic statement, Moore was quoted saying that Monongahela Power was willing to turn over to the state land now owned privately for building the Davis Power Project. The plant would combine pump storage with one million tons of coal per year to generate its power and would produce $2 million in tax revenues for Tucker County. In addition Moore pointed out that the 7,000-acre lake that the project would create would provide ideal development sites for second homes and vacation residences.

This was every conservationist's worse nightmare! Moore had been promoting state-owned energy generating plants, had cut a deal to take over the Davis Project, but provide virtually no wildlife mitigation, and add a coal-fired plant on the lower reservoir. Now he wanted FERC to waive jurisdiction. *The Charleston Gazette* quoted a power company attorney saying that, if all state and federal agencies withdrew, the environmentalists would stop their legal actions.

In December 1986 Conservancy President John Purbaugh stated that any power plant in Canaan Valley was destructive to the unique habitat, no matter who the owner. He also announced that the Conservancy and Cooper Elkinton had been sued for $25,000 by Canaan Village for "abuse of process," for exercising their legal rights to protest a sewage discharge permit for that developer's motel and restaurant project. He concluded, "Neither of these recent developments should divert our attention and efforts from the real issue at Canaan: the valley is worth saving."

Morgantown attorney Allan Karlin, and WVU Law School professor Charles DeSalvo, took the defense of the Conservancy and Cooper Elkinton pro bono [free], and successfully argued that citizens' rights to comment on permit actions were protected as free speech. (Ironically, their defense was based on Webb v. Fury, Rick Webb's libel case discussed in Chapter 8.) The case was dismissed.

The Final Court Decision

Finally, the dam burst when the U.S. Court of Appeals ruled that the Davis Power Project needed a Corps 404 permit. Cooper Elkinton was delighted and called on the Allegheny Power System to make their Canaan Valley land available for a wildlife refuge. The National Wildlife Federation, working with their West Virginia affiliate, had become increasingly active in recent months. Jacki Bonomo, the Federation's Mid-Atlantic Regional Executive, said, "The best way to move ahead is to let the U.S. Fish and Wildlife Service complete plans for a national wildlife refuge." Other pro-refuge comments came from the League of Women Voters, National Audubon Society, and Sierra Club.

It had been a decade since the FPC license had been issued and the first appeal filed. During that time, power project proponents had tried several end-runs. Several serious efforts to control development had resulted in water pollution controls, but development continued nonetheless. Now the momentum had turned again. The coming 1987 Spring Review in April would focus on "Making Canaan Valley a National Wildlife Refuge." Speakers from USFWS would answer the questions "What will it take? When will it happen? What will it mean?"

After the Court of Appeals rejected Monongahela Power's request for a rehearing, the power company filed an appeal on April 13 with the U.S. Supreme Court.

As the Conservancy prepared to celebrate its 20th anniversary at its 1987 Fall Review at the old logging town of Cass, the September *Highlands Voice* announced that the Conservancy, along with four national conservation groups, had filed a brief with the U.S. Supreme Court. The Conservancy opposed the power company's request for reversal of the 404 permit ruling. "As far as can be determined, this is the first time in WVHC's twenty-year history that the group has been involved in a case before the nation's highest court," the article stated.

The next month, the U.S. Supreme Court effectively pulled the plug on the Davis Power Project, declining to review the Appeals Court decision. "I think this is the end of the Davis Power Project as we know it," said Purbaugh. The Supreme Court's decision not to review the matter "answers the question for all time about whether the power company needs a 404 permit to build their plant. The highest court in the nation says they need one, and they don't have one." Sierra Club's Ron Wilson added, "We're all growing old together," speaking of the assortment of conservationists, lake proponents, and power company advocates who had taken part in the campaign. Yet, the Sierra Club lawyer stopped short of saying the battle was won.

What would happen next was anyone's guess. The power company re-evaluated their options, but it would still be many years before the power company land would be permanently protected.

Over the next few years, there was only a very occasional mention of Canaan in *The Highlands Voice*, usually another plea for letters to decision makers to establish the refuge. Gradually the other threats to the valley, like second home developers or the annual Blackwater 100 motorcycle race through the wetlands, began to form background noise, but nothing big happened. The Conservancy still maintained a Canaan Valley Committee and Cooper Elkinton was still its chair.

In 1990 a new Canaan Valley Task Force was organized by Congressman Alan Mollohan and convened by the Environmental Protection Agency. Mollohan had reached a position on the Appropriations Committee where he could influence EPA's budget and provide funds for the new Task Force. The purpose of Task Force was to protect the unique ecosystem and natural resources of Canaan Valley while also considering community needs. It was comprised of representatives of federal, state, and local government, conservation organizations, and residents of Tucker County, including local officials, businesses, land, and homeowners. Meeting monthly, the open dialogue led to positive communications and began to ease the hostility built up over decades of entrenched positions. Various investigations of specific problems like water quality led to professional information that local community groups could use. Fact sheets were prepared that highlighted development trends and related land use issues. As time went by, the leadership gravitated to USFWS's Chris Clower. By the summer of 1992 the task force had won a Certificate of Environmental Achievement from Renew America as a model for community decision-making.

Dave Saville was working for the promoter of the Blackwater 100 and began to attend the meetings of the Task Force. As a trained forester, Saville began to have serious misgivings about the motorcycle race and its destruction of Canaan Valley's wetlands. Eventually he left the race. By 1994 the Blackwater 100 had caused such destruction to the wetlands that the state Water Resources Division was requiring pollution controls. Ultimately the race, which by then attracted 40,000 annually to Davis for Father's Day Weekend, was moved entirely out of Canaan Valley to protect the wetland areas.

In the May/June 1994 *Highlands Voice*, an article by Rick Steelhammer was reprinted from *The Charleston Gazette,* with a headnote saying, "The good news is that the Blackwater 100 race has been cancelled, the bad news is that the progress towards a refuge is now temporarily blocked."

Steelhammer wrote that the Monongahela Power Company had denied the race permission to use power company land in the lower valley wetlands. After years of nearly unlimited access to their land, the company was now responding to a study that thirty percent of the northern end of the valley had been damaged by all terrain vehicle and off road vehicle use. Mountain bikers, who also used the area, were banned as well.

Meanwhile, a group of Tucker County residents and businesses filed suit against the Fish and Wildlife Service alleging that the Service had no authority to condemn land for the refuge, and that the 1979 refuge environmental assessment failed to consider the alternative of "no action." After granting a temporary injunction, U.S. District Judge Robert Maxwell, citing a conflict of interest, transferred the case to Judge Frederick Stamp in Wheeling.

Finally, the Refuge

The September 1994 *Highlands Voice* ended many months of quiet about Canaan Valley in its pages, with a banner headline: !!!!CANAAN VALLEY!!!! The article certainly justified that exclamation. The headnote and article read:

> A lawsuit blocking the purchase of land for the Canaan Valley National Wildlife Refuge was dismissed Thursday, August 4, 1994 in U.S. District Court in Clarksburg…The first property was purchased Thursday, August 11th…WVHC is delighted to reprint, with the gracious permission of *Parsons Advocate* Editor Mariwyn McClain Smith, her front page coverage of the momentous event as it appeared in the Tucker County newspaper August 17, 1994 – Cindy [Rank]

Tucker County to be home of the 500th National Wildlife Refuge

After 33 years of planning, West Virginia's first refuge entirely within state borders has seen its first land purchase. And, that land is in Tucker County.

The US Fish and Wildlife Service purchased nearly 86 acres of critical wildlife habitat Aug. 11, recording that deed in Tucker County Courthouse on Thursday afternoon, establishing Canaan Valley Wildlife Refuge as the 500th national wildlife refuge.

The article quoted Karen Bonner, president of the Tucker County Planning Commission and Canaan Valley Task Force member, as saying, "I'm very pleased that it's finally come to fruition." The first tract was identified as the Raymond Harr farm, on Freeland road, across from the White Grass Ski Center.

According to the article, the total refuge would eventually encompass 24,000 acres, but that land purchase would not involve condemnation. The Canaan Valley Refuge would be only the state's second, but the first entirely within the state. Two years earlier, the Ohio River Islands National Wildlife Refuge, encompassing thirty-eight islands along a 362-mile stretch of the Ohio River, was dedicated. Much of it was also in West Virginia.

To help celebrate, the Conservancy planned its Fall Review the next month in Canaan Valley and, after the years of controversy, it would be a real celebration.

Conservancy President Cindy Rank's editorial was titled "Canaan: The Fantastic 500th":

> Rarely do groups like the Highlands Conservancy have as much reason to be proud as we do after August 11th when the U.S. Fish and Wildlife Service recorded in the Tucker County Courthouse the first deed to the first piece of property purchased as part of the Canaan Valley National Wildlife Refuge!!
>
> Granted, there have been several governmental agencies, dozens of organizations and hundreds of individuals who have worked untold numbers of hours over the past three decades to make the Refuge a reality, but for WVHC, names like Linda Cooper, Dave Elkinton, and Jenni Vincent will remain emblazoned in our minds as some of the diehard individuals who had a dream and believed in that dream so much that they rebounded time and time again after any number of defeats and setbacks.

Rank remembered Cooper Elkinton's remark at the previous summer Board meeting about attending her forty-fourth public hearing on the refuge, and also her answering machine message left August 12th that she felt "really good, really rich" that day. Rank compared "this all abiding spirit that sometimes won't let a person quit" to the dreams of Cranberry, Otter Creek, and Dolly Sods wilderness areas, the New River National Recreation Area, and others.

Board member Carroll Jett called the refuge establishment "probably the biggest triumph for environmental preservation and protection in the history of West Virginia."

Rank described the October 22, 1994, dedication of the Canaan Valley Wildlife Refuge. Several hundred people gathered on a beautiful sunny day to dedicate the 500th refuge. She noted the absence of representatives of the Monongahela Power Company, but lots of environmental activists and wildlife agency folks were on hand. She counted five past Conservancy presidents among them. The U.S. Director of the Fish and Wildlife Service, Molly Beattie, the Assistant Secretary of the Interior, George Frampton, and Congressman Alan Mollohan had all come from Washington. But the keynote speaker was Senator Robert C. Byrd, who had been absolutely pivotal in recent years in establishing the Refuge. USFWS Elkins office head, Chris Clower, who with earlier staffer Dave Harris had often been the object of local opposition, was presented a service award by Senator Byrd. Clower's leadership with the Canaan Valley Task Force received repeated praise from various speakers, calling it a '90s way to achieve success when parties were seemingly far apart.

How had the establishment of the Canaan Valley Wildlife Refuge finally been achieved? Some might say that the stars were finally aligned. In 1994 Bill Clinton, a Democratic president, was in office and therefore his appointees as Interior and USFWS heads were more preservationist, Robert C. Byrd had become Chairman of the Senate Appropriations Committee, Alan Mollohan was a high-ranking member of the House Appropriation Committee and Gaston Caperton was governor of West Virginia. This comprised a formidable political pro-refuge team.

Certainly these leaders had heard the continuing crescendo of public support for the refuge, orchestrated by the Conservancy and literally dozens of other supportive groups, by the media and by national environmental organizations that had found out about Canaan Valley. Even the local residents, comprised of more and more recent arrivals to Canaan

Valley, had turned the local political tide from opposition to support. It had been a long twenty-four years for the Conservancy, but it was a sweet victory.

In what one letter writer called "the thud of a wet blanket dropping," the Monongahela Power Company, by far the largest Canaan Valley landowner with more than 24,000 acres, announced plans to cut its timber. Letter writer Mike Smith quoted an unconfirmed report that one parcel alone would yield fourteen million board feet. There never would be an end to Canaan Valley's surprises.

As time went by, the refuge continued to expand. By 2002 it contained 3,200 acres, but still the power company land was not included. Then in February 2002, Monongahela agreed to sell 12,000 acres of prime wetlands to the USFWS for Refuge acreage. With the help of Senator Byrd and Congressman Mollohan, a deal had been struck.

As yet another Fall Review was scheduled at Canaan Valley in 2002, Cooper wrote perhaps her last Canaan Valley article, titled "Canaan Valley – A History of Activism." She published a chronology from 1970 to 2002, showing the circuitous route to preservation. Also she noted where the literally dozens of file drawers of records had been deposited for historical access. The Highlands Conservancy, the Canaan Valley Alliance, and her personal records would reside at the WVU Library Regional History Collection. The Walter Gumbel papers, including early power company records, were housed at Fairmont State University.

By then Cooper had found other battles, including saving the Blackwater Canyon and stopping massive wind farms that were proposed for the highlands. (See Chapter 8)

The Balsam Fir Project

After twenty-four years of articles on Canaan Valley, *The Highlands Voice* went the five years of 1995-2000 without a single article. When there finally was one, it was on a completely new subject. Dave Saville, by then the Conservancy's Administrative Assistant and previously a member of the Canaan Valley Task Force, wrote for the July 2000 *Voice* that the Conservancy was undertaking an urgent project to preserve a rare subspecies of balsam fir found only in West Virginia. "Most stands found scattered around the highlands have exhibited 80 percent or higher mortality in the last five years," he wrote. According to Saville, the few remaining pockets in West Virginia primarily consisted of mature trees only. The natural re-seeding process was being stopped because the abundant populations of white tail deer consumed the seedlings. Starting first with the owners of Blister Swamp in Pocahontas County, Saville and representatives of several state and federal agencies and conservation organizations fenced off an area to permit seedlings to mature. Now with a bumper crop of cones on the mature trees, he organized cone collections. These would be incubated and the seedlings replanted in selected areas of the Mountain State. Since Canaan Valley was known for having the largest such stand of balsam in West Virginia, this project might help preserve its heritage.

The next month, Saville reported twenty volunteers had collected several bushels of cones from over one hundred trees in Canaan Valley State Park, in the Canaan Valley Wildlife Refuge, and on private land. Each stand's cones were tagged and kept separate, and would now be sent off for germination. In addition to the deer-browsing problem, a second issue, an insect called the woolly adelgid, was so destructive that the balsam preservationists were seriously considering how to address that threat as well.

In February 2006, Saville reported completion of the first phase of the Balsam Fir Restoration Project in Canaan Valley. With financial support from the Environmental Challenge Fund of NiSource (Columbia Gas Transmission), the project included seed banking, construction of numerous fenced deer "exclosures," and replanting of seedlings. Over the past five years, Saville reported, many volunteer partners not previously involved with the Conservancy had invested hundreds of volunteer hours. The 2003 adelgid treatments were expected to be repeated in late 2006. Saville reported widespread positive publicity for this project, both in local newspapers in Elkins and Parsons, and in conservation newsletters across the region. In addition relationships had been strengthened with the state DNR, the Wildlife Refuge, and the Forest Service, as well as with numerous conservation organizations. The project was expected to remain active indefinitely.

Sources:

Cooper, Linda, interview, November 9, 2006, and correspondence
Cooper, Linda, papers, in West Virginia Regional History Collection at West
    Virginia University Library
DiSalvo, Charles, correspondence
Gumbel, Walter, papers at Fairmont State University Library

The Highlands Voice articles by Perry Bryant, Bob Burrell, Tom Dunham, Dave Elkinton, Linda Cooper Elkinton, Helen McGinnis, Charles Morrison, Dave Saville, and Jenni Vincent

Hughes, Royston C., U.S. Asst. Sec'y of the Interior, letter quoted in *The Highland Voice*, 1974

Johnson, Skip, article in *The Charleston Gazette*, 1970

Karlin, Allan, correspondence

Rieffenberger, Joe, interview, March 28, 2007

Rockefeller, Jay, statement on Davis Power Project, reported in *The Highland Voice*, 1976

Saville, Dave, interview, June 21, 2006, and correspondence

Steelhammer, Rick, article in *The Charleston Gazette*

Chapter Six
Friends of the Mon:
The Monongahela National Forest

This chapter will discuss all areas of the relationship between the Conservancy and the Monongahela National Forest, except wilderness preservation, discussed extensively in Chapter 2.

Spruce Knob-Seneca Rocks National Recreation Area

The origins of the West Virginia Highlands Conservancy are traced from the first mass meeting under a revivalist's tent on top of Spruce Knob (See Chapter 1). Preservation of portions of the Monongahela National Forest, often shortened to "the Mon," were the reason people had gathered. Some were motivated to protect rivers from government dams, others to protect scenic areas from proposed highway construction, and still others just to preserve special places.

Very early the protection and ultimate management of what became the Spruce Knob-Seneca Rocks National Recreation Area (NRA) was the subject of heated Conservancy meetings. Many citizens, mostly from outside the immediate area, urged the establishment by Congress of the NRA within the Monongahela National Forest, as a means of protecting the NRA land from timber and other potential development threats. No one, least of all the members of the fledgling Conservancy, understood that the establishment of the NRA would lead to massive property acquisition by eminent domain. Local farmers, especially near Seneca Rocks, the nearby Germany Valley, and all along the North Branch and main stem of the South Branch of the Potomac, were faced with government condemnation in the name of protecting these natural areas.

At the third Highlands Review Weekend in October 1967, held at Mouth of Seneca, the Saturday evening program was "A Plan for the Highlands." Forest Supervisor Ephe Olliver would discuss the Forest

Service's Management Plan for the two-year old Spruce Knob-Seneca Rocks NRA. Responding to Olliver, Phil McGance, legislative assistant to U.S. Senator Jennings Randolph, state Senator J. Kenton Lambert, and outdoors author Mike Frome would follow.

Setting the tenor for a contentious evening, Supervisor Olliver made only general comments on the Plan; it was not yet ready for release. According to a letter by Bob Broughton to other Conservancy leaders, written in December 1967, the Forest Service relied on totally inflated visitation estimates of 5 million visitor-days/year by 2000 (still 35 years in the future). Using these projections, the planners were justifying a high level of development and, therefore, large property acquisition. Broughton's words spoke for themselves:

> That figure [5 million visitor days/year], which was used to justify overdevelopment, is logically dependent upon the overdevelopment it is used to justify. (In the growing field of techniques for lying with statistics, this one is known as the "Planner's Special" – mostly used by highway and recreation planners.) Unless and until the Forest Service can show that the kind of overdevelopment they propose is desirable in and for itself in the areas where they plan to put such development, we should continue to challenge them. [Emphasis in the original].

Broughton wrote that the Forest Service seemed totally unaware that its plans affected "real people, people with emotions and aspirations just like any of the rest of us living in West Virginia. They are not, emphatically, 'hillbillies.' " Joe Harper, who owned both Seneca Rocks itself and a well-known local general store, had apparently explained that those in West Virginia now, were the ones who had chosen to stay, rather than move to America's big cities to seek employment after World War II. This attitude affected Broughton. He wrote:

> Maybe they made the wrong decision economically — maybe they would be richer if they had moved out to the cities. Alternatively, maybe they would be living in rat-infested slums, gradually losing their ability to breathe because of smog-caused emphysema. If the Forest Service proposes to say to them, "Because you made the wrong decision 20 years ago, you now have a farm which is worth $5000 or $2000 or $1000, and we are going to force you off your land and into cities now, after you're too old to get a job," then it seems to me that the Conservancy has a responsibility to oppose the Management Plan that goes far beyond the aesthetic preferences of hikers and climbers and canoeists and the rest of us.

Two observations, from the advantage of post-2000: First, using overblown projections of high-density recreation activity would become a recurrent issue with other proposed developments over the next decades. The Conservancy would specifically meet this in relation to the Davis Power Project, Corridor H, Snowshoe Ski Resort, and several ski areas that thankfully died before construction could even begin. Second, repeatedly there would be developments that undervalued local residents' love for their land, some of which had been in families for many genera-tions. People did not want to be forced to move by big government. The Conservancy would need to remember that many of the earliest settlers to present-day West Virginia had originally come to escape the tyranny of centralized governments, especially as expressed through taxes and prop-erty seizure.

By March 14, 1968, Conservancy President Tom King issued a message to Conservancy members and members of affiliated groups. Headlined "Emergency-Emergency-Emergency," the bulletin stated, "A grave crisis has arisen" and described a local landowner revolt to repeal the NRA legislation, or at least removal of the power of eminent domain. King continued, "If either of these two goals are achieved, West Virginia's brand new National Recreation Area is finished."

It should be noted that until the NRA legislation, the Monongahela National Forest had not been authorized to use eminent domain to acquire property, but rather relied on willing seller-willing buyer negoti-ated sales. Granted it took longer to acquire desirable inholdings, but local opposition was minimized.

King continued:

> The power of eminent domain was written into our law by men who understood that occasions arise when the public good must be considered before the rights of the private individual – I believe this is one of those times.
>
> West Virginia needs the NRA, the economy of the South Branch valley needs the NRA, and the people of the United States need it. In view of this need, private land must be purchased to form the facility just as private land was bought to form the Great Smokey Mountain National Park, or the Shenandoah National Park, or the new State Park in Canaan Valley. No public facility of this nature can be formed in this crowded day without the purchase of some private land. Still we must recognize the right of the individual to fair treatment.

The landholders are protected in two ways: Their land is appraised by private land experts who have no connection with the government whatsoever. If the price thus arrived at is not satisfactory they may appeal it to a claims court where it will be reviewed and adjusted as necessary.

King concluded in all capital letters:

THE FUTURE OF THE SPRUCE KNOB-SENECA ROCKS NATIONAL RECREATION AREA STANDS IN JEOPARDY AS OF THIS DATE AND ONLY YOU CAN HELP! DO YOU WANT TO FISH OR CUT BAIT? HERE'S HOW YOU CAN HELP!

Following these words, were instructions on writing to the congressional delegation. For members or representatives of the affiliated organizations, there were requests for resolutions in support of "the NRA as it is presently constituted." Others were asked to write letters to the editor, lobby and otherwise publicize the need for NRA support.

In a Conservancy newsletter dated November 15, 1968 (before the advent of *The Highlands Voice*), King wrote a recap of the recent Highlands Weekend Review at Seneca Rocks Grade School. Apparently the controversy from the previous year had not subsided. Four hundred people attended the evening meeting. He wrote:

Following our program...the Conservancy made the podium available to some of the local landowners who pointed out several hours before the meeting that they had never been given an opportunity to present their views on the National Recreation Area to the conservationists. Their presentation was brief, and effectively pointed out their opposition to present land acquisition methods and their understandable reluctance to give up their homes.

Shortly thereafter, in the December 1968 issue of the Newsletter of the Scenic Rivers Committee, Bob Burrell reflected on the past year. He wrote:

It was a year of more black eyes for West Virginia...There was the allegation that recent Democratic governor candidate Jim Sprouse was involved in an illegal land dealing company that bought up much of the land in the proposed Spruce Knob-Seneca Rocks area and then made a killing in profits reselling the land to the Forest Service, speculators, and in at least one instance, a conservation organization. Whether these allegations are true or false remains to be determined in court, but regardless of the final decision, the publicity could well be the final death knell of the Spruce Knob-Seneca Rocks NRA plans.

It would be the August 1969 *Highlands Voice*, before there was further mention of the NRA land acquisition controversy. Burrell reported that the Forest Service had made payment for nine tracts containing 755 acres and 445 acres in mineral rights, since the inception of the NRA. Additionally sixteen willing sellers were under option, adding another 2,778 acres. A court-determined price would be established in 1969. The Forest Service lamented that shabby real estate developers were subdividing remaining tracts, knowing this would increase their value and cause the government more hassle in purchasing. One sentence read, "Fiscal year 1969 funds could not be used for condemnation," perhaps implying that Congress had sent a message to the Forest Service to deal more equitably with the landowners.

In the October issue, an article titled "Highlands Review '69" stated:

> The most interesting event of the weekend occurred when Mr. George Ours of Petersburg and Mr. George Trumbo from Onego presented the landowners' side of the NRA land acquisition methods for the Spruce Knob-Seneca Rocks area. In particularly eloquent statements, these men recounted the bumbling inefficiency with which the Forest Service began its land acquisition in 1965. In unemotional arguments, these men presented their predicaments and pointed out how conservationists unwittingly have created further problems for them. The next speaker was Tony Dorrell, Superintendent [*sic*] of the Monongahela National Forest. Stepping right into the middle of this controversy early last spring, the new superintendent found himself in a tough spot. Following the statements of Messrs. Ours and Trumbo, Mr. Dorrell could only be diplomatic and perhaps to some, unsatisfactory. As one charged with carrying out government plans, he is obliged to execute them as messed up as they have already been made. Dorrell pointed out that by far most of the landowners had settled amicably and the audience was left with the impression that Dorrell would have liked to have been able to say to Seneca Rocks owner Mr. Buck [Joe] Harper and others who have been treated unfairly, "Let's forget all that has happened and start over," but his hands are tied. In earlier action at the Board meeting, Duquesne law professor Bob Broughton was designated to testify in behalf of Mr. Harper later this fall during condemnation proceedings in Elkins. During the lengthy discussion which followed, Vic Schmidt summed up the general conclusion that

our present condemnation procedures are obsolete and fail to take into account the special qualities of lands like Seneca Rocks.

In the following months, the *Voice* kept readers updated on the land acquisition. In the October 1970 issue, after articles about the front-burner issues of clearcutting, the new Davis Power Project, Cranberry Back Country, Otter Creek, strip mining abolition, and Rowlesburg dam, Burrell wrote, "How Are Things at Spruce Knob –Seneca Creek?" He reported continued sub-division by private interests and criticism of the conservation community from at least one pro-environmental group. Burrell reminded readers that part of the blame resulted because the initial governmental contact had not treated local landowners fairly. He reminded readers of a lesson from the 1969 Fall Review, namely the inadequacy of the compensation laws and procedures.

This would be the last reference to land acquisition in the NRA. Clearly the still-new Highlands Conservancy had learned a couple of lessons. One, good ideas for preservation were easier if the land was in public ownership, like proposed wilderness areas on the National Forest. Second, sensitivity to implementation details of seemingly good ideas was critical. Who had expected protection of Spruce Knob and Seneca Rocks to include condemning working farms in Germany Valley? Third, when government officials and local interests were at loggerheads, there was a place for opening communication, like offering the podium at a meeting when requested. All of these lessons and the associated scar tissue would be important in the wilderness, river, and other battles discussed in previous and succeeding chapters.

Clearcutting

In the late 1960s, timber-harvesting practices, especially clearcutting, were receiving widespread public criticism. One reason was increased mechanization that permitted larger timber operations, more land scarred, and more runoff into nearby streams. As West Virginians were out in the woods hunting, fishing, or hiking, these denuded areas were very noticeable.

In the inaugural issue of *The Highlands Voice*, March 1969, Editor Burrell mentioned clearcutting for the first time among the Highlands Conservancy members:

> Foresters in recent years have changed their thinking on timber management methods. Many feel that the practice of clear cutting (as

opposed to selective cutting) is in certain instances a valuable tool in forest management. The West Virginia Division of the Izaak Walton League of America has been on record as favoring the use of even-aged management as a tool. The controversy [with residents of Richwood and Nicholas County] has arisen in that many feel that the Forest Service has adopted the practice without regards to esthetic, watershed, or wildlife values. Although the practice does look like hell for a while, the Forest Service has definitely taken watershed and wildlife management into consideration. Many misunderstand the Forest Service's intentions and believe large (100-300 acre) tracts will be clear cut when in fact such tracts will be limited to widely separated smaller tracts of about 25 acres each…the whole situation might be resolved if both [sides] could continue their productive hearings and discussions on the matter. The new Monongahela Forest Supervisor, Tony Dorrell of Elkins, or the Forester in charge of timber tract sales for the Gauley District, Norm Arsenault at Richwood, should be able to provide Conservancy members with more information on this matter. It is of course hard to re-educate the public to new practices when they have been taught for so many years that there was one right way to do things (selective cutting), but the fact that so many ordinary citizens are so concerned and well informed about such vital matters is an extremely healthy sign for conservationists.

In a "Special Supplement to *The Highlands Voice*," at the request of George Langford, chairman of the Conservancy's Wilderness Committee, three multi-page letters were included. The first was a detailed policy statement from Supervisor Dorrell, issued in April 1969, announcing a basic change in Forest Service policy and its rationale. The second was a letter from the Richwood Chamber of Commerce president, L.W. Dietz, dated June 11, outlining some of the fears and sentiments of residents. The third was Dorrell's answer. It is oversimplifying nine pages of dialogue to say that the Chamber favored small clear cuts and leaned on the Forest Service's multiple use mandate to promote tourism and conservation within the Forest. Dorrell's answer further justified his decision, citing widespread support from the congressional delegation, the Regional Forester, and the general public.

"Clearcutting and the Gauley District or Let's Not Widen our Credibility Gap," appeared in the October 1969 *Voice*. Apparently written by Burrell, the article described his conclusions after some personal research. To promote the variety of species in the forest, most of which were shade-intolerant, clearcutting was necessary, and was based on scientific observation, not on making it easier to harvest timber. Using figures from the now infamous Gauley District, he demonstrated that clearcuts average less than 1% of total acreage per year, and were limited district-wide to 1200 total acres, and no single clearcut over a hundred acres. Most averaged thirty-five acres. He gave another example that was selective cut, rather than clearcut, because of proximity to a tourist area.

He concluded, "I cannot find any evidence to substantiate the claims that the Forest Service is lousing up our timber, that clearcutting is a bad practice, or even that it should not be used as the major system of timber management in the Gauley District." On management of the Cranberry Back Country, Burrell did see a difference of opinion, however. Conservationists favored wilderness management; the Forest Service favored management for timber production.

Burrell continued by suggesting the Forest Service undercounted conservationists who hiked, paddled, and otherwise used the remote Forest areas. On the other hand conservationists needed to seek out the facts from the myths. "Hopefully," he said, "we can resolve this issue and make it more clearcut (ouch!)."

At the 1970 Mid-Winter Workshop, Conservancy members heard reports on Otter Creek from Art Wright, of the Wilderness Society, Tony Dorrell of the Forest Service, and several of its own members. Against this background, the proposed National Timber Supply Act, which would increase the Forest Service's commitment to timber harvesting, was moving through Congress quickly. Accordingly, the membership passed a resolution calling for a three-year moratorium on all clearcuts exceeding thirty acres, during which research on the impacts of clearcutting on wildlife, water resources, and recreation would be studied.

In late February, the House of Representatives killed further consideration of the National Timber Supply Act, in the face of unanimous opposition from national conservation and sportsmen groups.

In the June 1971 *Highlands Voice*, Langford reported on the Senate hearings in April, chaired by Senator Frank Church. Responding to widespread criticism of clearcutting, Church looked at national forest management practices. According to Langford, the testimony constituted indictments of (1) clearcutting as a practice and (2) the Forest Service as an administrative body. The Multiple Use – Sustained Yield concept had been surrendered to the timber industry. Wrote Langford, "Clearly the Forest Service is now dominated by the timber industry – timber production is paramount, nearly everything else (including the environment) is second, and public uses of the forest are last."

The clearcutting controversy, fueled by the perception that the Forest Service was increasingly controlled by the timber industry, continued to boil. The Conservancy, meanwhile, was busy trying to protect specific areas. Dolly Sods and Otter Creek were in the news (see Chapter 2) as proposed wilderness areas. Beginning in 1970, the Conservancy was in court to stop mine prospecting. Surprisingly to all concerned, Judge Robert Maxwell ruled for the Conservancy.

The West Virginia Izaak Walton League, driven by their Richwood chapter, had asked the Conservancy to be a co-plaintiff in a lawsuit to control clearcutting. The Conservancy had agreed. In the August 1973 *Voice*, an article entitled "Clearcutting Gets Final Test," stated:

> Arguments began Friday August 17 in U.S. District Court in Elkins which will decide the fate of clearcutting on the national forest. [A] suit had been brought against the U.S. Forest Service for violation of the Organic Act of 1897 by the Sierra Club, the National Resource Defense Council [*sic*], the West Virginia Division, Izaak Walton League and the West Virginia Highlands Conservancy.
>
> The Organic Act of 1897 stipulates that only dead, mature, or large trees may be sold, that trees to be sold must be marked or otherwise specified, and that all cut timber must be removed from the logged area after cutting. The conservationists' suit contends that the Forest Service violates these provisions on national forests through clear-cutting, a timber management practice [in which smaller trees] are left to rot on the site after higher quality trees have been removed.
>
> Conservationists and government arguments have been presented to Federal Judge Robert E. Maxwell for an initial decision. Both sides have already expressed their intentions of appealing the case to the U.S. Supreme Court if Maxwell's decision goes against them.

It had been the Izaak Walton League chapter in Richwood that had kept the pressure on. They were aware that the Conservancy had prevailed in the Otter Creek case. They had watched as their nemesis Tony Dorrell moved on, replaced by the more publicly savvy Al Troutt as Forest Supervisor. But the national picture was still one of timber industry domination of the Forest Service. Finally, after exhausting all other avenues, they had put together a case against clearcutting.

On November 8, 1973, according to a December *Highlands Voice* article, Judge Maxwell issued his second unexpected pro-conservation decision, banning clearcutting on the Monongahela National Forest. He affirmed the conservationists' argument that the Organic Act had been violated and further concluded that clearcutting was an "unwarranted intrusion into the exclusive area of congressional province." Troutt issued a statement implying an appeal was likely. This case was to become known as "the Monongahela Decision."

The Forest Service appealed the decision to the Fourth Circuit Court in Richmond. In December 1974 a brief notice appeared that the Court's decision would be delayed. The Fourth Circuit later affirmed Judge Maxwell, although details were not carried in the *Voice*. Within the year, however, the December 1974 *Voice* announced that the U.S. Department of Justice, representing the Forest Service, had decided not to appeal to the U. S. Supreme Court. Forest Service Chief John McGuire was quoted as saying that no further clearcutting would occur in West Virginia, Virginia, North Carolina and South Carolina. The clearcutting ban was permanent.

There was speculation that the Forest Service did not take the case to the Supreme Court because, had the government lost at that level, the decision would have been applied nationwide and the Forest Service didn't want to take that chance. A less conspiratorial rationale was that the Forest Service hoped the new Congressional authorization would restore their ability to use clearcutting as a management tool.

It didn't take long to hear from Congress. According to a *Highlands Voice* article by Gordon Hamrick in March 1976, Senator Jennings Randolph, of West Virginia, introduced S. 2926, National Forest Timber Management Reform Act of 1976 on February 4, 1976. Hamrick provided a thorough analysis. At many opportunities, Randolph's bill supported the Organic Act of 1897 and the Multiple Use – Sustained Yield Act of 1960. Clearcutting got short shrift, with selective cutting the preferred technique. Clearcutting would be permitted in very restricted situations only, such as salvage or fire, and then only twenty-five acres or less.

But far more significant than its restrictions on clearcutting, Randolph's bill established a comprehensive forest planning system. Each national forest would be required to use a multi-disciplinary team to plan for all multiple uses, with timber sales projected for five years. All elements of the plans would be subject of public hearings. A timetable was set, determining how many new plans would be developed each year until all forests were in compliance.

Another bill, sponsored by Senator Hubert Humphrey, of Minnesota, S. 3091, was described as "a timber industry bill," and simply sought to nullify the Monongahela Decision. Hearings were scheduled in Washington and Conservancy members were urged to send letters favoring Randolph's bill.

The August 1976 *Voice* contained an article by Tom Barlow and Brock Evans, apparently reprinted from another, but unidentified, environmental publication. It stated that in the rush for a September adjournment, there was fear that a poor timber bill would get through Congress. Randolph would be offering strengthening amendments to Humphrey's bill, and public support was urgently needed. The House seemed likely to pass an even more pro-timber bill. A "Coalition to Save Our National Forests" was formed and was coordinating political advocacy.

Unfortunately, later issues of the *Voice* do not reveal the outcome.

Forest Planning — Round One

Raised on a dairy farm in upstate New York, young **Mary Wimmer** loved sports and the outdoors. But she liked to read too. As she moved through the local school system, it became clear that she was headed for college and might not remain on the farm with her brothers. At the State University of New York at Albany, Wimmer worked toward a degree in chemistry, while also playing two sports and becoming the president of the Women's Athletic Association.

At the University of North Carolina at Chapel Hill she worked on a PhD in biochemistry, yet found time to referee intramural sports, ultimately becoming Head Referee.

After three years in Philadelphia in a post-doc cancer research position, she accepted an offer from West Virginia University in 1979, and joined the faculty in the Microbiology Department of the Health Sciences Center. It did not take her long to begin to explore West Virginia, and by 1984 she had become the first co-chair of Conservation Committee of the brand-new West Virginia Chapter of the Sierra Club.

It so happened that 1984 was the beginning of the planning cycle for the first major Monongahela Forest Plan. Since virtually all important conservation issues important to the Sierra Club were involved in the Mon's planning, it was inevitable that Wimmer would become involved. Over the next few pages, that involvement will be discussed.

Following completion of the Plan, and its implementation, Wimmer remained active in the Sierra Club, serving as a chapter representative on the regional Appalachian Conservation Committee, among other duties. She also was the leader of a major trail restoration project on the Mon, following the horrendous flood of 1985. That project involved numerous trips, and lasted over a ten-year period. During all this time on the Mon, her knowledge of the forest was continually increasing.

In 2001, Dave Saville was organizing for another wave of wilderness preservation, including providing input into a revision of the Monongahela Forest Plan, and recruited Wimmer's involvement. Before long, the West Virginia Wilderness Coalition had been formed (described in Chapter 2), and Wimmer, along with Beth Little, became the Sierra Club's representatives on its steering committee. Her leadership, and her storehouse of knowledge back into the early 1980s, became invaluable, both to the plan revision process and to the wilderness campaign.

Wimmer has been a Highlands Conservancy member since 1986, although most of her work has been through the Sierra Club. It should be stated that this profile might easily have been included in the discussion of Wilderness in Chapter 2, but for the legacy of "Mary's Woods."

In a lengthy article in the March 1977 *Voice*, the Draft Environmental Statement and Land Management Plan for the Monongahela National Forest was analyzed. Released February 2, this plan contained 340 pages and addressed major issues facing the Forest, including timber, wilderness, Shavers Fork, mining, trails, off-road vehicles, highways, and more. Various Conservancy members with special interest in each of these issues provided comments. Four years in preparation, the plan was the first time under new federal forest planning law that citizens had been asked for their involvement. Since the Conservancy's major committees each dealt with aspects of the Forest, this opportunity for citizen comments was not to be missed.

In March 1981, *The Highlands Voice* published the first article in a series leading up to another forest plan. According to Forest Planner Gil Churchill, a series of small local public meetings had been scheduled across the Monongahela to elicit comments on issues the new plan should address during its three-year preparation period. Forest Supervisor Ralph Mumme, who had replaced Al Troutt, expected the plan to set the direction of the Mon for as long as the next forty years. To facilitate communication with the public, the Forest Service published a tabloid outlining the planning process and soliciting public participation. They pledged a new effort to keep the public informed throughout the process.

The following month, the *Voice* provided a list of many of the initial comments that came by mail or through the public meetings. Some were very specific, such as closing a particular gate to facilitate cross-country skiing. Others were more general such as encouraging more softwoods.

There were periodic reports on the planning process, but more often reports on the specific areas of interest to the Conservancy, such as proposed wilderness areas, mining permits, or endangered species, but it would be January 1985 before the *Voice* returned to the Forest Plan. That month it reported release of a ten-year plan, for which comments would be received for ninety days. Five basic alternative scenarios were outlined, each emphasizing a different mix of forest practices.

According to a detailed article in the February *Voice*, the Forest Service analysis of the five proposed management alternatives would require up to three "major prescriptions" for implementation. The Conservancy was reported to be preparing extensive comments for submission.

Due to public interest and the sheer volume of material to digest, the Forest Service extended the comment period, as requested by many environmentalists. The decision was announced by Senator Byrd's office. Reports of local meetings indicated the plan was generating considerable controversy.

In the April/May 1985 *Voice*, a front-page note stated that the Conservancy had requested that the Forest Service "withdraw the forest's Draft Management Plan and prepare a new one for public comment." President Larry George cited the need for "fundamental and comprehensive revisions to the plan and numerous adverse impacts on the forest resulting from its implementation." The announcement revealed that Sayre Rodman, Chairman of the Conservancy's Public Lands Management Committee, had filed a document of comments and a petition to withdraw and revise with Supervisor Ralph Mumme's office in Elkins.

Rodman's analysis concluded that the Draft plan would accelerate timber sales at the expense of all other uses. Thousands of miles of new roads were proposed, opening up virtually all roadless areas, many of which were potential wilderness areas. Mining was promoted. Returning to the clearcutting controversy, Rodman felt clearcutting was overemphasized in the draft. In an echo of past debate on the NRA, the Conservancy Board withheld its endorsement of Forest Service plans in the NRA until local landowners were heard from.

Over the next six months, the Forest Service was kept busy digesting all the public feedback they had welcomed. Conservancy members were kept informed.

- The response of 3,600 comments, Churchill said, "is more than any other forest in the nation has received." The previous plan in 1978 generated only 250 comments.
- The Forest Service identified seven major concerns from the comments and prepared a response to each. These were 1) Special Place management, 2) timber harvesting, 3) coal mining, 4) remote habitat, 5) roads, 6) conifer succession, and 7) range of alternatives. The Forest Service circulated a newsletter discussing these concerns and their proposed responses. Public meetings were also scheduled.
- After the meetings and public comment, the Forest Service officials made changes in the remote habitat prescription (6.1) and developed prescription 6.2, which set aside 120,000 acres for non-motorized, dispersed recreation. Twelve other specific changes were announced to provide for increases in remote habitat on the Forest.

As things eventually emerged, it was Wimmer of the Sierra Club who was given credit for developing "prescription 6.2," basically a *de-facto* wilderness management practice. One Forest Service official good-naturedly joked that the 125,000 acres preserved under 6.2, should be called "Mary's Woods." This prescription would hold these acres in their present condition and set the stage for the wilderness campaign associated with the next forest planning cycle in 2005 (See Chapter 2).

In a 2006 interview, Wimmer described the warm, respect-filled relationship she and other Sierra Club representatives developed with Mumme, Churchill, and their staff members. During the comment period, she took five weeks of her vacation and traveled the state making presentations. The Forest Service provided her with slides, but did not try to control her comments. At one point, seeing her spending many hours working in Churchill's office, Mumme good-naturedly asked if he should get her an office of her own. Wimmer said, "Gil and Ralph both appreciated the fact that we wanted to learn about forest planning and they bent over backwards to help us."

Because of the release language in the Cranberry-Laurel Fork Wilderness bill, this forest plan could not recommend additional Wilderness areas, yet many comments favored protection of *de-facto* Wilderness areas. Wimmer said, "We needed to find a way to protect back-country areas. Writing that prescription was very important. Finally, after I kept objecting to their drafts, they gave it to me and said, 'just write it." That became Prescription 6.2, covering fifteen percent of the Forest, a total of 125,000 acres. "They listened! And for over twenty years there were zero controversies over 6.2 areas," she added.

In April, the *Voice* announced the departure of Forest Supervisor Ralph Mumme, after twelve years overseeing the Monongahela. Mumme was moving to a position responsible for timber programs in thirteen southern states. At the Spring Review, Mumme was presented a framed print in appreciation of his cooperation with the Conservancy during his tenure. James F. Page arrived in July as the new Supervisor.

August's *Voice* announced, "Final MNF plan released, looks good." It was described as 1500 pages, weighing fifteen pounds, and would become effective following a thirty-day comment period. In November, Sayre Rodman was quoted, "If you compare the final plan to the draft plan of a year ago, it's easy to see that the Forest Service clearly listened to the comments of the Conservancy and many other organizations and individuals. We won — it would appear."

The planning process was complete, at least for the next decade or so. During that period, the Conservancy would follow implementation of the plan, monitor unanticipated issues, such as low-flying military jet training exercises, and otherwise enjoy the Monongahela as a place to hike, camp, fish, and enjoy. Along the way, the Conservancy sued the Forest Service over a major timber sale on East Gauley Mountain, forcing — through settlement — many modifications. Other issues also arose, dialogue usually followed, and ultimately both sides compromised.

Forest Planning — Round Two

As discussed in Chapter 2, the late 1980s and all the '90s were a quiet period on the Monongahela National Forest. As the fifteen-year planning period was coming to an end, the forest planners and the public would reopen the old debates as a new plan was developed. For the Conservancy this was a new opportunity to promote wilderness areas and identify issues that had escaped attention in the last round.

An article by Frank Slider in *The Highlands Voice* of May 2002 opened the discussion. A series of public meetings in late June were planned by the Forest Service to begin the public participation planning process.

In June 2002, Dave Saville, writing in the *Voice*, provided a brief history of the Mon and discussed the Forest Plan revision. His commentary on the significance of this process was memorable:

> If you care one iota about the Monongahela National Forest it's time to speak up. You know, that place that is home to such spectacular and favorite locales as Dolly Sods Wilderness, Seneca Rocks, Spruce Knob, Cranberry Wilderness, Otter Creek, Seneca Creek, Shavers Fork, the Blackwater, Cheat, Williams, Greenbrier, Elk, Tygart, Cherry, and Gauley Rivers; the place with excellent hunting and fishing, boating, hiking, climbing, camping, touring, mountain biking. Yeah, that's the place, the one that provides us, and millions of others, recreational opportunities, clean waters and free flowing rivers, with scenic wonder, protected watersheds, with Wilderness and wildlife habitat. You bet! ... But there's a dark side... The Mon also has valuable resources that profiteers want to get their hands on. And they often do. Logging, coal, oil and gas interests, as well as commercial recreation, motorized off-road vehicles, and cattle and sheep grazing all want a piece of this public-lands pie. Who gets how much is determined in the Planning process.
>
> The Management Plan for the Monongahela National Forest is being revised.
>
> The current management plan is outdated. This is the first time since 1985 that we have had a chance to significantly change how the Forest will be managed. The West Virginia Rivers Coalition describes the process as determining "if the Forest's one million acres of public land will be an all-you-can-eat buffet for the logging industry, or managed with conservation in mind." This is well stated and true. This Plan revision will determine how the Mon will be managed for the next 10–15 years. The Mon truly needs your help! **NOW!!**
>
> The Forest Service published its "Notice of Intent" to begin the plan revision process on May 3, 2002. This started a 90-day clock. The public now has until August 1st to offer comments suggesting how the current plan needs to be changed. This is the first, very important, step in a long process.

Without going into too much detail and using too many technical terms or Agency lingo, I will attempt to explain how the current plan is organized and implemented. Then, I will describe the process currently underway to revise this, now 17-year old, plan. It is important to understand the current Plan, because the revision process is just that. What the Forest Service is now doing is revising the current Plan, not starting over and developing a new plan. The "no action" alternative identified in the Environmental Impact Statement will be to stick with the current Plan.

Saville listed each management prescription, its acreage and characteristics, followed by the particulars on the six public "scoping" meetings.

Finally, the report from the recent Spring Review at the DNR's Handley Wildlife Cabin: Focusing on the Mon. Trips included the upper Williams River, a hike into the Cranberry Wilderness, a car trip on the Highland Scenic Highway, including the Cranberry Visitor Center, the Cranberry Glades, and the Falls of Hills Creek. The Saturday evening program centered on the Forest Plan revision, and key staffers were present to explain the process and urge involvement.

In February 2004 the Plan revision was still a work-in-progress. The Forest Service scheduled six open houses across the region to discuss elements of the revision. Using technology not available to prior planners, the Forest Service posted drafts as they were completed on a publicized web site for public review and comment.

In a summary, written by Don Gasper, of current Supervisor Clyde Thompson's comments to the Conservancy's Fall Review in October 2003, Gasper wrote that Thompson "seems to be a reasonable, competent man and a good listener — almost in spite of his rapid schedule of plan completion.....The connections the Highlands Conservancy has made between wilderness and recovery is generally thought to be valid, and he thought we were going about our Wilderness Campaign in the right way."

The Draft Management Plan was finally released in August 2005. (For a fuller discussion, see Chapter 2). By 2005, the West Virginia Wilderness Campaign, heavily supported by the Conservancy, had become the major, but not exclusive, input from the Conservancy. After a record-breaking deluge of public comments, the Final Plan and EIS were released in August 2006.

Whereas Sayre Rodman had commented in 1985 how responsive to new data and public comment the Forest Service had been and modified the plan accordingly then, no such comments were made this time. Instead, Saville wrote in the October 2006 *Voice*:

> The just-completed Forest Service planning process was an opportunity for the public to weigh in about our desires for the future of the National Forest. Some 13,000 people submitted comments. Sadly, the agency ended up making mostly cosmetic changes to its draft plan, sending what amounts to a "we knew best all along" message. Worse, in explaining his decision the regional forester in Milwaukee, Wisconsin, flatly misrepresented what the public said.
>
> To "explain" why they added not a single acre to their initial wilderness recommendations, the Regional Forester wrote that "Wilderness is a polarizing issue for the public." Repeatedly insinuating that public opinion was sharply divided, he noted that "Many people wrote in, describing their favorite potential wilderness areas, and I know they will be disappointed not to find these areas... recommended. Other people will be disappointed that any areas are being recommended at all." And, again, "many people were concerned about how wilderness would affect access to public lands. Some felt that it would further restrict their access, while others wanted to see areas better protected from motorized access."
>
> This clever wording suggests public opinion on protecting more wilderness in West Virginia was all over the map. What he carefully does not report is that, in fact, over 90 percent of the 13,000 public comments wanted more wilderness preserved than the agency draft proposed. Ninety percent is a landslide in anyone's book!
>
> Fortunately, deciding what West Virginia lands will be preserved as wilderness is not up to a Forest Service official in Wisconsin to decide. Instead, the historic Wilderness Act of 1964 provides that our elected representatives in Congress will make this decision. The Forest Service has made its recommendation — but so can every one of us. As it did in protecting our beloved Otter Creek, Dolly Sods, and Cranberry Wilderness areas, it seems Congress will have to once again step in and protect the areas that the Forest Service has failed to. Wild wonderlands like Seneca Creek, Spice Run, and expansion of the Dolly Sods Wilderness will be preserved — if we all call and write our U.S. senators and representatives.
>
> In voting for the 1964 Wilderness Act, Senator Robert C. Byrd, Jr. observed that opponents of wilderness preservation "seem to consider the chances of exploitation or further development of remaining areas of wilderness better under administrative determination." This new, deeply flawed and unresponsive Monongahela plan proves Senator

Byrd's wisdom in insisting that wilderness will be more surely preserved through legislation.

When Supervisor Thompson and his planners attended the Fall Review in 2006, the discussion was pointed and heated, although never openly hostile. Some observers thought privately that the Bush administration's pro-timber, anti-wilderness policies had forced the Monongahela to toe the line. Others, including Wilderness guru Doug Scott, who followed Thompson's presentation with one of his own, reported the Bush administration had remained open to wilderness, signing a California wilderness bill just the previous week.

But clearly, there was tension between the Monongahela National Forest leadership and staff and the West Virginia Highlands Conservancy as their fortieth year of engagement approached.

The Hiking Guide to the Monongahela National Forest

Bruce Sundquist, a native of Minnesota, had moved to Pittsburgh to work in US Steel's research lab, after getting his Ph.D. in Metallurgy. As a white-water paddler and hiker, it was only natural he would discover West Virginia. After arriving in Pittsburgh, Sundquist became active on outings sponsored by the Pittsburgh chapters of the American Youth Hostels (AYH) and the Sierra Club. (See a brief profile at the beginning of Chapter 2.)

Before long, he became the editor and printer for the AYH, producing a canoe and hiking guide for western Pennsylvania areas. When he met a group working on West Virginia issues, it was logical that he would end up collaborating with Helen McGinnis on a Dolly Sods Hiking Guide and Wilderness Proposal. Shortly thereafter, he worked with fellow Pittsburgh residents Sayre Rodman and Vic Schmidt, helping produce a similar guide for Otter Creek. Still later, he assisted George Langford and others to develop a third one, for the proposed Cranberry Wilderness.

As these booklets were being composed, edited and printed, AYH and Sierra Club projects were also in production. The basement of Sundquist's house must have been very busy. Along the way, distribution systems were needed: how to meet the demand for individual copies as well as bulk shipping to wholesalers such as outdoor shops.

It had been critical to raise public awareness in support of the three West Virginia areas proposed for Congressional action as permanent additions to the wilderness system. Now there was a concern that additional publicity would cause overuse. The Highlands Conservancy consciously decided to draw attention to the vast system of hiking trails throughout the Monongahela National Forest, outside the wilderness areas, in an effort to disburse the hiking pressure.

Sundquist became the first editor of the *Hiking Guide to the Monongahela National Forest*. The first edition, in 1973, was a corner-stapled, 8½ x 11, ninety-page booklet. As time went by, editions sold out, updated editions were written, and a smaller book-like format was used. By the third edition, the guides were sent camera-ready to a printer, although Bruce continued to handle all bulk sales and shipping. Later Allen deHart, an author of other hiking guides, became a co-editor. In January 2003 the Conservancy Board of Directors awarded both Sundquist and deHart life memberships in recognition of their dedicated service to the Conservancy through the decades of hiking guide editorships. In November 2006, the 8th edition was released with a color cover, 368 pages; it sold for $17.95.

The first mention of a hiking guide for areas outside Dolly Sods, Otter Creek, and Cranberry Back Country, appeared in *The Highlands Voice* in August 1971, when the Highlands Conservancy was a young four-years old:

> A hiking guide to the Monongahela National Forest is being planned — to be published and sold by the W.V.H.C. The job is partly done already: the U.S.F.S. has "trail logs" of many of its trails; we already have guides to Cranberry Backcountry, Otter Creek, and Dolly Sods, and Pittsburgh A.Y.H.'s "Hiking Guide to Western Pa. And Northern W.Va." already has write-ups on several M.N.F. trails. Much work needs to be done, however — much more than could readily be accomplished by a few people. Volunteers are needed to "adopt" various sections of the forest (or just one trail) and to prepare trail write-ups.
>
> Those interested in helping…should contact Bruce Sundquist…who will coordinate the various efforts, prepare the final draft, handle printing, etc.

In the world of prophetic statements, this one certainly ranks high. By 2007, as this volume was being written thirty-five years later,

Sundquist was already working on the 9th edition, and one wonders what was contained by the "etc." in his announcement.

A year and a half later, a short article titled, "MNF Hiking Guide Nearly Ready," appeared in the April 1973 *Voice*:

> In 1972 a committee of about thirty people in the WVHC spent a few thousand man-hours exploring many of the hiking trails on or near the Monongahela National Forest. Their scouting reports, along with a lot of material and advice from the U.S. Forest Service, were compiled and printed as a ninety-page hiking guide. These the Conservancy will sell to promote an appreciation of the MNF as an outstanding source of dispersed recreation opportunities in the heart of the densely populated northeastern U.S. We also hope to make some money. To get your copy send $1.50 to Mary Moore Rieffenberger [address given].
>
> Despite its large size, this new hiking guide does not cover Dolly Sods, Otter Creek, or the Cranberry Back Country. Guides to these three areas are also available…at the following rates: Cranberry, $.80, Dolly Sods, $1.10, Otter Creek, $.50.
>
> It is hoped that the new guide will help to take some of the pressure off the proposed Wilderness areas which are starting to receive very heavy use.

Note the prices of all the guides: less than we would pay today for their postage. And note too, the purpose of the MNF Guide was to help disperse the hikers across the entire Forest, and away from the proposed wilderness areas. And finally, the Conservancy also hoped to make a profit to support its conservation efforts.

In 1974, a second edition, consisting of 151 pages was printed, and sold for $3.25. By May 1976, three years later, Sundquist supplied the following to the *Voice*:

> If the trend continues, we will be sold out of the 5,000 copies of our *Hiking Guide to the Monongahela National Forest and Vicinity* by this fall. It is time now to think about what additions and improvements to make before we get another 5000 copies printed late this coming summer.

Once again Sundquist asked for trip reports, then added, "Contributors to the guide receive a free copy as soon as the new guide comes off the press."

In November 1977, *Voice* readers found, "New Mon Forest guide available":

The third edition of our "Hiking Guide to the Monongahela National Forest and Vicinity" is now available. It has been enlarged by 20 percent, from 160 pages to 192 pages. Only 46 pages of the old edition survived unchanged. The two most important changes in Ed. III are the inclusion of the 10 trails of the Flatrock Plains – Roaring Plains Area and the inclusion of a new set of topographic maps of the Cranberry Back Country area.

Looking ahead to Ed. IV, don't think that Ed. III is complete – or that the best time to write up your scouting report is the week before the deadline. We could use a lot more scouting work, especially in the southeastern parts of the MNF (White Sulphur Springs and eastern Marlinton ranger Districts). Photographs (B&W) from that area are also needed.

Interestingly the price remained at $3.25 plus postage.

The *Voice* announced in April 1983, "The Conservancy's new and improved Monongahela National Forest Guide has been completed and is now on sale. This updated version includes 50 pages of trail updates and new information on Otter Creek, Dolly Sods, and Cranberry Backcountry. The guide costs $7.00 (postage paid.)"

Within two years the Mon opened itself to public comment on its draft management plan, and one wonders how many of the guide owners that have driven it into now four editions, sent in comments on the Forest's management.

Five years from publication of Edition IV, the *Voice* announced Edition 5, in May 1988:

Edition 5 of the WVHC **Monongahela National Forest Hiking Guide** is now available. This edition is bigger and better than ever, with 320 pages, 60 maps, 39 photographs, descriptions of 164 trails totaling 780 miles, a new section on ski touring, and a full-color cover. The authors are Allen deHart and Bruce Sundquist. Allen hiked all the trails of the Monongahela N.F. over the past few years. Bruce edited Editions 1-4. The hiking community provided the authors with trail reports and photographs.

The fifth edition sold for $9.95 plus tax and postage. Although the prices were continually rising, the guides remained competitively priced and were consistent good sellers throughout the region. Profits continued to support the Conservancy's increasingly active conservation activities.

Somehow the sixth edition was little noticed in the pages of the *Voice*, but apparently it was successful, because in June 1998, Sundquist reported the sixth edition was sold out, and a seventh would go to press later that summer.

After many years of behind-the-scenes work, publishing what became a major source of revenue to the Conservancy, Sundquist finally received some well-deserved recognition. In the July 1999 *Highlands Voice*, Tom Rodd put the Guide into the larger Conservancy picture:

> Reminiscences — A Hiking Guide Makes Me Cry: *The Judge Said To Use Mules!*
>
> Part I of the Review of the New Hiking Guide by Tom Rodd, Co-Chair, WVHC Publications and Outreach Committee
>
> *"If something is threatened, and then the drawing you make of it is still crisp and sure and tender, it shows that people's affections can be stronger than those forces that might tear the world to pieces."*
> — Tony Hiss, The View From Alger's Window, 1999.
>
> I have a romantic, inspirational theme for this (two-part) book review of the new, hot-off-the-presses, Seventh Edition of the *Hiking Guide to the Monongahela National Forest*, published by the West Virginia Highlands Conservancy, and edited by Allen deHart and Bruce Sundquist. (At press time, I hadn't had a chance to interview co-editor DeHart, so that will come in part two, in the next issue of the *Voice*.)
>
> Here's my theme: like the West Virginia Highlands Conservancy itself, this remarkable Guidebook is a product of the human spirit — honoring and protecting the creation — in celebration and in struggle! Am I being too romantic? I don't think so. I cried several times last week after I left Bruce Sundquist's house in Pittsburgh, Pennsylvania, where I was part of a "work party" helping put business reply cards in the new Guidebooks, so buyers can send in and get a six-month free trial Conservancy membership. I cried thinking about the touching and inspirational stories that Bruce — and Sue Broughton, another Conservancy member — told me about the early days of the Conservancy and the origins of the Guidebook. (Art and Betty Evans, Marc Levine, Jean Rodman, WVHC Administrative Assistant Dave Saville, and Gail Gregory were at the work party, too.)
>
> I may have gotten some of this information wrong, but I'll give my best recollection. Bruce got into outdoor guidebook writing in the 1960s, with American Youth Hostels. Trip leaders would write trip accounts, and they were collected for others to use — and these evolved into hiking guides. (Bruce has also been an author of other guidebooks: the *Hiker's Guide to the Laurel Highlands Trail*; the *Allegheny National Forest Hiking Guide*; the *Hiker's Guide to Western Pennsyl-*

vania; the *Canoeing Guide to Western Pennsylvania and Northern West Virginia;* and *Ski Touring Western Pennsylvania.*)

Bruce joined the Highlands Conservancy in 1969, and worked on writing the first wilderness proposals for the Cranberry Backcountry and Dolly Sods. Bruce remembered Helen McGinnis, the "Mother of Dolly Sods" — who worked as a paleontologist at the Carnegie Museum, and who convinced the Wilderness Society to push for wilderness status for Otter Creek and Dolly Sods in the Eastern Wilderness Act of 1975.

The Conservancy's *Hiking Guide to the Monongahela National Forest* evolved out of the recreational trail sections in these wilderness proposals. Like the recent *Resource Assessment of the Blackwater Canyon* (available from the Conservancy for $9.50), the *Mon Forest Hiking Guide* was created as a tool — one could even say a weapon — in the struggle to protect the land and landscape of West Virginia. (I would say the Guidebook is still such a tool and weapon.)

Many of those who were involved in organizing the Conservancy and leading the efforts to promote wilderness and protect outdoor recreation areas in West Virginia were from out of state — including a number of Pittsburghers. One of these people is Sue Broughton, who arrived at Bruce Sundquist's house after we had put all of the business reply cards in the new edition of the *Guidebook* — we really worked fast! Sue was willing to tell me a couple of stories from those days.

One story was about Judge Robert Maxwell, a federal judge in Elkins — who coincidentally has been assigned to hear the Conservancy's pending Blackwater Canyon endangered species lawsuit against Allegheny Wood Products — where our lawyer is Jason Huber. (Go, Jason!).

In 1975, Island Creek Coal owned the mineral rights under the Otter Creek area. Island Creek saw that the Eastern Wilderness Act was coming, but they hadn't done "core drilling," to establish what value their minerals might have. So they made plans to build roads and haul in drill rigs, and to drill down to see what coal was there.

This threatened road building (not the drilling) could have ruined the area's chances for wilderness designation. Jim Moorman, who became a leader of the Sierra Club Legal Defense Fund, held a heated "rump session" at a Conservancy Review — in Jim's room at Blackwater Falls State Park Lodge. People were spilling out into the hall, the room was so packed. "It's now or never," Moorman said. "We've got to sue the coal company." (Have I heard these words other times?) The Board voted to file suit.

At the time, Sue told me, it was a very "far-out," frightening thing for this small group of hikers and climbers to do — to take on a giant coal company in court.

But they did — and they won!

Judge Maxwell ordered the coal company not to build roads. He said that if the company wanted to core-drill, they would have to haul in their drill rigs with mules and horses!

So they hauled in the drill rigs in pieces, with teams and wagons and sleds, over existing trails. And when they drilled, thankfully they found that there was no valuable coal.

(Now let's hope that Judge Maxwell is as creative and courageous in our endangered species suit! By the way, some time later, a couple of Conservancy members met a couple of coal company engineers at a local tavern. The engineers admitted that the coal company had saved tens of thousands of dollars, by using mules and horses!)

There are plenty of stories like this, for each of the Conservancy's campaigns — over thirty years — to protect West Virginia's natural environment. I get a little teary, thinking of those people at Blackwater Falls Lodge, daring to challenge the coal industry, and fighting for something more important than profits.

For over twenty of those years, the Mon Forest Guidebook has been a unique weapon in that struggle, and a great tool for experiencing the Mountain State, in a human way, at a human pace. Order your copy now! And in the next issue of the *Voice*, I'll continue this review, with a closer look at the book itself — and maybe another story.

In November, Part II appeared, titled, "An Interview with Co-Editor **Allen deHart**":

Q: Allen, how did you first become involved with the *Mon Forest Guidebook?*

I became involved with the MNF Guidebook about 25 years ago. I had hiked the Appalachian Trail and became interested in trails that adjoined the AT. The result was an effort to search for guidebooks in the 14 states through which the AT passes. West Virginia did not have a guidebook on all the state's trails, but the 2nd edition of the Conservancy's *MNF Hiking Guide* had been published in 1974.

Already an avid hiker in West Virginia (where I lived during part of my childhood), I used the early Conservancy MNF guide-book for trails near the Virginia border. I accepted a request from the Appalachian Mountain Club Press in Boston to research and write guidebooks on the North Carolina and West Virginia state trails. For *West Virginia Hiking Trails; Hiking the Mountain State*, I gave as much attention to all the trails outside the MNF as to the inside of MNF. It was after this research I alerted the WVHC to misinformation in the *Guidebook*. In attendance at some of the WVHC board meetings the questions began to focus on my possible assistance with Bruce to make major changes in the *Guidebook*. The rest is history.

Q: How did you become interested in hiking and outdoor recreation?

My brother Moir (12 years my senior) first took me hiking in West Virginia before I was 5 years old. We lived near Beckley. Those hikes and others when we moved back to Virginia left an indelible image. My mother has said that I had to be watched when still crawling because I headed for the forest instead of the street. In Virginia my family lived at the base of the Blue Ridge Mountains where the Blue Ridge Parkway was being constructed. A CCC Camp was only four miles away, and one of my uncles was its supervisor. My cousin and I spent many hours there; we watched the CCC men build trails near Rocky Knob. Soon, as early teenagers, we were taking our younger brothers on hikes — we even constructed a shorter route with a trail through the forest to reach our public school. At that time the Appalachian Trail was nearby. I dreamed of eventually hiking it all the way, continuously. (It happened 40 years later.)

Q: What are the notable changes in the 7th edition of the *Guidebook*?

Bruce Sundquist and I planned to have the 7th edition ready for purchase about four months after the 6th edition was completely sold. But our ambitions to make changes took longer than expected. One change was to use an entirely different computer lettering type — less of a typewriter style. We also desired it be proofed carefully for grammar and spelling. There were trails to be deleted and new ones to add. For the first time we sent old copy and our changed copy of manuscripts to each district ranger and to headquarters staff. In one district we almost changed the entire chapter.

The introduction was highly modified, some from requests by readers. We left in the same message of the book's purpose, but stream-lined the process. We omitted or redesigned some maps and charts that had become obsolete. We would have taken even longer had we not received the assistance of Joe Robles, forest recreation specialist in Public Service of the MNF.

Q: Please tell me something about your relationship with the people who run the Mon Forest.

I would consider it close and open. I try to be understanding about the lack of adequate staff in the MNF, and the bureaucracy under which they function. I have never been denied information for maps and trail files. I show respect for their continuous efforts to serve the public inquiries. I have observed the public expecting more than the staff can provide. There has been a decline in funding, particularly for trails. And sadly, very few Conservancy members and other organizations have adopted trails to consistently maintain or rebuild after floods and natural disasters. Only once have I been lectured for my support of the Conservancy. It happened about three years ago when a new staff member had been assigned and he knew very little about the MNF or those of us who have been both devoted to the MNF trails and what the Conservancy has done to promote and support the MNF. Jo Robles and Linda White have been prime examples of staff with strong efforts for sharing and cooperating with Bruce and me.

Q: What has been your career, outside of Guidebook writing?

American History and Psychology Professor for nearly 20 years. I have an M.A. degree and Ph.D. courses from the University of Virginia, and with Duke University and Florida State University. I have taught hiking and backpacking, canoeing, and mountain climbing for more than 20 years at Louisburg College. My 12th book is *North Carolina's Mountains to Sea Trail* to be published by the University of North Carolina Press next spring. I am a graduate of the Adjutant General's School in the U.S. Army and served six years overseas. I have lived in 20 different states, three foreign countries, and hiked trails in all but four of the states in the U.S. My wife, Flora, and I have dedicated 88 acres of land for the DeHart Botanical Gardens. Both will forever be preserved.

All my life I have been a writer. As a child I wrote the poems and drew the illustrations for family greeting cards. At the age of 16 I was writing articles for publication in the city of Danville's *The*

Danville Register. I was also a reporter for the U.S. Army *Stars and Stripes.* My articles have been in national magazines and many newspapers throughout the Southeastern United States. It was a natural for trail guidebooks. I wrote *Hiking and Backpacking Basics;* among books such history books on colonial Virginia, trail guide-books on Virginia, three on North Carolina (one of which has sold more than 100,000 copies), one on South Carolina, and one for the Sierra Club called *Adventuring in Florida and the Georgia Sea Islands.*

Q: Do you have any thoughts about the future of the Mon National Forest?

Yes. It is priceless and loved by millions of visitors throughout its history. Like all national forests it has had it public demands for it to be many values for a variety of public groups. It will survive all the natural disasters and its critics, right or left. I foresee it chang-ing to more recreational in services and, much like the Pisgah and Nantahala National Forests in North Carolina, less timber cutting. I hope it can receive additional funding to advance its acreage.

In the March 2003 *Highlands Voice*, both Sundquist and deHart were made life members by the Highlands Conservancy. Editor John McFerrin wrote the opening:

The Board of the West Virginia Highlands Conservancy has voted to recognize the decades-long contributions of Allen deHart and Bruce Sundquist by making them lifetime members. This is a rare step for the Board, one it had taken only three times before in our thirty-five year history. In taking this step, the Board recognized that neither canoniza-tion nor awarding the Nobel Peace Prize was within its authority, but it did what it could.

Mr. deHart and Mr. Sundquist's most visible contribution to the well being of the Conservancy has been through their efforts on the *Monongahela National Forest Hiking Guide.* They were both there, more or less, when it began and have regularly updated it for new editions. Bruce has always assumed an enormous responsibility in its distribu-tion. The Hiking Guide has, in turn, been of enormous value both as a steady fundraiser and in making the Monongahela National Forest, that has always been so precious to the Conservancy, more easily accessible to the public. Through the Guide, we were able to publicize the Conservancy as a group with a longstanding interest in the Forest. It was in appreciation for these invaluable contributions to the Conservancy that the Board voted to recognize Mr. deHart and Mr. Sundquist as lifetime members.

There followed photos of both men, and lengthy profiles by Helen McGinnis, long-overdue recognition.

A new wrinkle came in March 2005 when a compact disc version of the 7th edition was offered for sale. Jim Solley, a retired but active Conservancy member, converted the *Hiking Guide* to a pdf format, adding color maps, available only in black and white in the print edition. The electronic edition was priced at $20.00.

There was considerable Board discussion before this was released; no one wanted to hurt the sales of the Conservancy's bestseller. Solley and others argued that an electronic edition would allow downloading and printing of a single trail, avoiding taking the entire Guide every time a hiker went into the woods. Also as maps were improved, trails moved or closed, corrections could be made between editions.

As 2006 drew to a close, the 7th edition had sold out at $14.95 plus $3.00 shipping. The 8th edition was released in November 2006. The CD version of the 7th had sold modestly enough that the 8th edition would be available in that format as well.

Mon-Athon 2000 and the Mountain Odyssey

Over its entire lifetime, the Highlands Conservancy had sponsored outings, usually field trips into places threatened by mining, logging, dam building, highway construction, or some other development needing public awareness. Certainly the battle to preserve West Virginia's first three Wilderness areas had been greatly enhanced by the publication of combination hiking guides and wilderness proposals that received wide distribution (see Chapter 2).

And then there were the annual Fall Reviews, and the newer Spring Reviews, which always included a series of excursions to places of interest to Conservancy members. But the Conservancy left it to the Sierra Club and other affiliated groups to organize and implement a formal outings program. In fact, in the early years, the Conservancy publicized its affiliates' outings, in the place of running a formal program of its own.

All that changed in 1999. In an article titled, " Look! Outings Program," by Peter Shoenfeld in the September 1999 *Highlands Voice*, he announced the new program:

> At the Conservancy summer board meeting we discussed the possibility of a regular Conservancy outings program and decided there should be one. A committee was appointed — Dave Saville and myself are the initial members. We were charged with initiating the program and seeking more members for the committee. Anyone with ideas for outings or wishing to participate in other ways should contact Dave or myself.
>
> Actually, there has long been an excellent and extensive Conservancy outings program, led recently by Dave. However, since most of the outings take place on the same two days, at the semi-annual reviews, it's been hard to pack them all in. We'd like to fix that and offer similar opportunities on many of the year's remaining fifty weekends.

That article described the inaugural outing to Dolly Sods North, scheduled for October 1999. As would be true of virtually all of the subsequent trips, this one was focused on an area in the Monongahela National Forest, which explains why the Conservancy's re-energized outings program is discussed in this chapter.

Within a couple of months, the outings program had a new cheerleader. The Conservancy's Outreach Co-Chair, Tom Rodd, announced in February 2000 the "Mon-Athon 2000" program, and provided *Voice* readers with its rationale:

> "Mon-Athon 2000" is a corny name for a new West Virginia Highlands Conservancy (WVHC) project. The purpose of Mon-Athon 2000 is to: a) celebrate and enjoy our Monongahela National Forest (affectionately known as "The Mon") in the year 2000, and b) to stimulate, coordinate, and celebrate outdoor recreation in The Mon.
>
> Mon-Athon 2000 is a good project for the WVHC, for several reasons: (1) we publish the esteemed *Hiking Guide to the Monongahela National Forest* (deHart and Sundquist, editors); (2) our organization has its deepest roots in the fight to protect The Mon; (3) The Mon is one of the great public resources of our State and Nation; — and (4), IT'S A WAY TO HAVE FUN!
>
> In Mon-Athon 2000, WVHC members and friends — and other outdoor groups and individuals — will make a special effort, in the year 2000, to get out and hike, bike, bird, botanize, camp, paddle, ski, and otherwise enjoy the Mon. There will be a number of outings that are especially organized for Mon-Athon 2000. And we want to include and promote outings organized by other groups, besides the WVHC.

Additionally, anyone who does any sort of outdoor recreational activity in the Mon can report it, and have it included as part of Mon-Athon 2000. All Mon-Athon 2000 activity participants will be entered in drawings for cool prizes like outdoor gear, meals and tours in the Mon, and more. T-Shirts with the Mon-Athon 2000 outdoor recreation silhouette logo … will be distributed to Mon-Athon 2000 participants.

Mon-Athon 2000 participants will be asked to report on trail and other Forest conditions, and otherwise on their experiences (especially the funny parts!), and to submit photos of their activity. There's a good chance that reports and photos will be excerpted in the Highlands Voice. And again, they may be a resource for updating the WVHC's Hiking Guide!

Tom Rodd is currently acting as overall coordinator for Mon-Athon 2000 — and many others have agreed to help out. Look for more information on Mon-Athon 2000 as it progresses in each subsequent issue of the Highlands Voice. See You in the Mon!

And Rodd concluded:

We want to develop this project in all possible ways. We want to get materials about Mon-Athon 2000 in the hands of outdoor recreational and related businesses around the Mon. We want to network with other groups – scouts, camps, schools, outdoor recreation businesses, advocacy and other groups, who might be interested in having their activity be included as a part of Mon-Athon 2000. What are your ideas, suggestions, offer, ideas, and other notions?

By all accounts, including many trip reports that were printed over the next nine months, the Mon-Athon 2000 program was highly successful. But what would follow in 2001? In *The Highlands Voice* in January 2001, the successor was announced:

Come one, come all, and join in a festival of heady highlands journeys designed to excite and delight the eyes, exult the arms and legs, and enrapture the soul – Mountain Odyssey 2001!

This is the Conservancy's sequel to the lively trail blazed by Tom Rodd last year in his brainchild, Mon-athon 2000 – and, keeping alive the energy that Tom generated with this project – the Outings Committee has been hard at work insuring that Mountain Odyssey 2001 will turn out to be an equally worthy effort. We are planning on a long list of outings, increasing the diversity of offerings, and hoping to reach out to many more folks this year. And with your help and participation, we'll have one of the best outings programs in these parts!

This year, we are offering three different kinds of outings: Recreational Outings, Educational Outings, and Volunteer Outings

Recreational Outings will include day hikes (with a repeat performance of Hugh and Ruth Blackwell Rogers' Peak Experience!), backpacks (with a three day Dolly Sods "Stem to Stern" ramble), canoe trips, caving trips, bicycle trips, and, hopefully, some cross country ski excursions, and others. Something for every palette.

Educational Outings will include a unique outdoor experience called an "EarthWalk," natural history excursions, culturally and historically oriented activities, and trips designed to better familiarize the public with locations that are the focus of Conservancy projects and concerns. The EarthWalk program provides a thrilling hands on experience in the wild that integrates activities in sciences and humanities into a seamless whole with the aim of connecting people more deeply and delightfully to the natural world – **and** to their concomitant role in protecting the earth. Thus far, two trips are in the making. One of these will be an exciting experience featuring Ruth Blackwell Rogers' "Four Worlds So Far" scroll painting of the Hopi creation story. These journeys are especially geared to young people. Teachers will also find these outings of interest we think. In addition to EarthWalk, the Outings Committee is also soliciting folks to lead natural history oriented trips – wild flowers, birding, wetlands, botanizing, unique environments in West Virginia, etc.; and also historical and cultural explorations, and experiences aimed at educating people about sites that are the target of advocacy activities of the Conservancy.

Volunteer Outings will be a new and wonderful part of MOUNTAIN ODYSSEY 2001. Participants will contribute their time and energy to conservation, reclamation, and development and maintenance projects in the Monongahela National Forest. We should not only enjoy the forest, but should also contribute to sustaining its viability as one of the Eastern gems of the National Forest System. Dave Saville and Ruth Blackwell Rogers and others are working on developing a continuing volunteer program there. Also, another Tree Planting is being planned on the Upper Shavers Fork for April 21st - as part of the effort to restore the Red Spruce Ecosystem there. More to come!

How Can I Get Involved in All This Mountain Madness?

Participate in an Outing. In fact, participate in many outings! Coming on an outing is a great opportunity to really get to know other Conservancy kindred spirits. We work to protect WV, but we also need to enjoy it. Look over the current Outings List at the end of this article or, alternatively, find the listings posted on the Conservancy webpage, www.wvhighlands.org, and choose what journeys pique your interests. Be sure to contact the leader immediately as space may be limited! The trip leader will explain the details of the trip to you. Remember, outings are being added all the time, so if you don't find anything that appeals to you, keep checking the website and the *Voice* for something to turn up.

Volunteer to Lead a Trip. The Outings Committee is actively soliciting volunteers to lead trips. We are encouraging folks to share what they love and cherish about the highlands with others. Don't keep it a secret! If you would like to lead a trip, contact Jack Slocomb or Peter Shoenfeld. We will discuss your proposed outing with you and provide you with a Trip Information Form to complete. The outing will then be listed on our website and in the *Voice*. As soon as you sign up to be a leader, you will receive a Leader's Information Form which explains the protocol for leading Conservancy outings and everything else you need to know. We would like volunteers to lead or help lead any kind of outing — Recreational, Educational, or Volunteer. We especially welcome people who are interested in sharing their knowledge of West Virginia history and culture. If you would like to share a place you love with others, but you feel uncomfortable leading the trip by yourself, not to worry. We will try to find an experienced leader to assist you.

Join the Outings Committee: We need your help! Especially in advertising Mountain Odyssey 2001. Our outings program is a major outreach tool for the Conservancy! Therefore, the more people we can entice to participate, the more possible new members we can recruit to keep our ranks filled and support our great conservation initiatives in WV. Although current outings will be published in the *Voice* and posted on the website, we could reach many, many more folks if this information appeared regularly in some major local newspapers. So if there is anyone out there who could help us with this, you would most certainly make an invaluable contribution to this project. It would also be very helpful if people could list outings in organizational newsletters. We really need to get the word out if Mountain Odyssey 2001 is to be a success. If you'd like to join the committee, contact Jack Slocomb, Outings Chair.

The Outings Committee is looking forward to a wonderful season of outdoor adventure and fellowship

And this is just the beginning, folks. You ain't seen nuthin' yet!

WE WANT YOU TO JOIN US IN THE FUN!

This message brought to you by your Way Out Outings Committee: Jack Slocomb, Dave Saville, Ruth Blackwell Rogers, Peter Shoenfeld, and Bob Marshall.

Clearly the Highlands Conservancy had added a new dimension, a well-organized outings program. It had leaders, it had places to go, it had a year of experience, and it was on a roll. There was a new generation of recreational users of the Monongahela National Forest and its ultimate preservation might well depend on motivating these users to join the fight.

Over the next five years, each issue of *The Highlands Voice* listed details of upcoming outings, and frequently included trip reports of recent excursions. By reviewing these over even this short a period, readers could keep abreast of changes in special areas, or learn about new areas with which they were previously unfamiliar.

We're Friends of the Mon

It should be abundantly clear from this chapter and even more so when combined with Chapter 2, tracing the wilderness movement in West Virginia, that the Monongahela National Forest and the West Virginia Highlands Conservancy have been inter-twined together since the founding of the Conservancy. Over these forty years, the relationship has been tumultuous: sometimes very contentious, sometimes cordial, survived several major lawsuits, given each other awards and occasionally been in nearly open warfare at times. Amazingly, there remained a strong bond between the two groups.

Within this context, Saville conceived the idea of gathering all the different and sometimes divergent ways the Mon and the Conservancy inter-related, and publish in *The Highlands Voice* a section dubbed "We're Friends of the Mon." In fact the Conservancy could make a strong case that it had been the Mon's best friend, willing to criticize or praise the Forest Service, as only a true friend would do.

Accordingly, *The Highlands Voice* of March 2006 announced "Highlands Conservancy Kicks Off Initiative on Monongahela National Forest." Saville wrote:

> Within this issue of the *Highlands Voice*, we are kicking off a new Highlands Conservancy program called *We're Friends of the Mon!* This program will coordinate our current efforts on behalf of the

Monongahela National Forest and gradually expand our work to include more service projects like trail maintenance, stream and forest protection and restoration efforts, and a more concerted effort to educate our membership and encourage their engagement in projects and special uses of the Mon Forest.

These are things we've always done; we're just working to better coordinate these efforts and increase our effectiveness. For over 40 years the West Virginia Highlands Conservancy has been working to protect and restore, and to help people enjoy and appreciate the Monongahela National Forest. Beginning in the mid-1960s, the group was founded, in large part, to address direct threats to our Wild Mountain Treasure, the Mon. Highways, dams, massive clear cutting of the forests, pipelines, power transmission lines, misguided management, car races, ATVs, reckless district rangers, gas exploration, and now an outright "For Sale" sign on 4,836 acres of the Mon. All these issues, and more, have kept us busy fighting, struggling, working hard, and forever vigilant, to protect the Mon.

It was the Highlands Conservancy in the 1960s that led the campaign to protect Dolly Sods and Otter Creek as Wilderness. We filed a successful lawsuit in the mid 1970s against large-scale clear cutting. This famous legal victory called "The Monongahela Decision" ultimately catalyzed legislation, sponsored by the West Virginia delegation, called the National Forest Management Act (NFMA). This law changed how all National Forests would be managed to this day. It limits the size of clear cuts and requires each National Forest to have a Management Plan specific to that Forest.

In 1983 a 12-year Highlands Conservancy campaign came to a successful conclusion with designation of the Cranberry and Laurel Fork Wilderness Areas.

Partnering with the Forest Service we have sponsored trail maintenance work crews and volunteer outings working on forest restoration and stream protection projects. Our *Monongahela National Forest Hiking Guide* is now in its 7th edition (8th edition coming later this year) and has been used by thousands of hikers to explore the Mon and learn of its wonders.

More recently we have continued this proud tradition as a founding member of the West Virginia Wilderness Coalition. In this Coalition we are working cooperatively with the West Virginia Sierra Club, The Wilderness Society and many other groups and individuals to permanently protect additional roadless areas of the Mon as designated Wilderness. Our epic campaign to engage the public in the Mon's

Management Plan revision, currently underway, has been successful far beyond anyone's expectations.

In keeping with this proud tradition, we are currently expanding and formalizing our programmatic efforts regarding advocacy for the Mon. Our new program, *We're Friends of the Mon*, is a continuation of our successful *Mountain Odyssey* outings program, a re-invigorated effort to work with the Forest Service on service projects to protect and restore the Mon, and to better coordinate forest watch activities to keep a watchful eye on Projects (like logging) and Special Uses of the Mon.

To achieve these ambitious ends we have retained Dee Quaranto to coordinate the *We're Friends of the Mon!* program. Dee is a resident of Fairmont, West Virginia and is passionate about the Mon. She has been an active volunteer with our Wilderness Campaign and frequent participant in the Mountain Odyssey program. Dee will be working part-time to organize volunteers, oversee the Mountain Odyssey outings schedule, and to wrap up all our Mon related activities in one special place in our Monthly Newsletter, *The Highlands Voice*. In coming weeks, the Highlands Conservancy's web page will be updated with a special new and easy to use section for *We're Friends of the Mon!* Check out what our new website guru, Jim Solley, has updated so far on our home page! www.wvhighlands.org

He's the same Jim Solley who developed our new map-rich *Monongahela National Forest Hiking Guide* on CD. The same Jim Solley that created all the beautiful functional maps for our Wilderness Campaign and mountain top removal displays. Just as Jim taught himself how to manage hordes of digital data and create maps like a wizard, he has now learned the finer details of web design. So check out our new site and come back and visit often as many changes are in store!

Even as we are just getting this special program underway, the objective is clear. We are confident that through a more organized effort, the effectiveness of our work will be strengthened. As Dee identifies and engages more and more people interested in what we are doing, this program will grow and we will become more effective in our efforts.

So, please look inside this edition of the *Voice* for our new *We're Friends of Mon!* pages, and learn how you can become more engaged and how you can help us protect and better enjoy our wonder-full Monongahela National Forest!

Clearly these two organizations were related like members of a family! Their destinies likely would be dependent on each other for the foreseeable future.

Sources:

Broughton, Bob, correspondence to other Conservancy leaders, December 20, 1967.

Dietz, L. W., Richwood Chamber of Commerce, policy statement, June 11, 1969

Dorrell, Forest Supervisor, policy statement, April 1969

Fritz, Edward C., *Sterile Forest: The Case Against Clearcutting* (Austin, Texas: Eakin Press, 1983)

The Highlands Voice articles by Tom Barlow, Bob Burrell, Brock Evans, Don Gasper, Gordon Hamrick, Ron Hardway, Tom King, George Langford, John McFerrin, Tom Rodd, Dave Saville, Peter Shoenfeld, Frank Slider, Bruce Sundquist, among others

Saville, Dave, interview, June 21, 2006

Sundquist, Bruce, interview, June 23, 2006

Sundquist, Bruce, and Allen deHart, *Monongahela National Forest Hiking Guide*, all editions, published by the West Virginia Highlands Conservancy.

Wimmer, Mary, interview, November 8, 2006

Chapter Seven
Coal Mining's Curse:
Abolition, Control, and Mountaintop Removal

The history of coal mining in West Virginia certainly deserves a book-length treatment, which this volume cannot provide. Other sources are available, or will be soon, that tell the story of coal and its impact on the people and the environment in West Virginia. The discussion in this chapter will focus primarily on mining issues as experienced through the activities of members and leaders of the West Virginia Highlands Conservancy. For convenience only, an arbitrary division has been made between the first twenty-five years of the Conservancy's history and the next fifteen years, i.e. 1967–1992 and 1993–2007. Naturally many issues spanned both periods.

Part One — The First Twenty-five Years

The history of West Virginia is the history of coal. While an oversimplification, it is true that the presence of coal deposits in fifty-three of its fifty-five counties has been a determinant of much of the economic and social history of the State of West Virginia. Unfortunately, coal mining has frequently victimized the people and natural environment. Early mining techniques, primarily underground mining, left less surface effects, but did, and still do, produce tremendous amounts of polluted water that eventually comes to the surface. Beginning in the 1960s, and then at an accelerating pace thereafter, surface mining expanded across the coal regions, offering an alternative to some of the dangers of underground mining methods. Using less manpower and employing mammoth-size earth-moving equipment, surface mining lent itself to coal seams that were relatively near the surface or were too thin to mine by traditional underground tunneling techniques.

Surface mining has often been called strip mining, a term that originally described the horizontal terracing around mountains that characterized much of the 1960s era. In more recent years, "area mining" might have been a better term, as entire mountain tops have been removed to expose the coal seam, which, when removed, has led to the process being repeated as if a layer cake was devoured top to bottom.

As the West Virginia Highlands Conservancy was forming, with its focus in the northern Highlands region, coal was primarily a secondary issue. However, very soon, as the wilderness campaigns developed (see Chapter 2), Otter Creek, and later Cranberry, were both nearly lost as potential wilderness areas because they were underlain by coal which had remained in private ownership when the Monongahela National Forest was established. Later, Dolly Sods was similarly threatened.

Major rivers of interest to Conservancy members were likewise repeatedly threatened by coal mining. The Conservancy's struggle to preserve Shavers Fork in particular was replete with proposed deep mines, strip mines, coal preparation plants, and road construction. Until the upper headwaters became a part of the Monongahela National Forest in 1988, the Conservancy battled against owners of both the surface and mineral rights. (See Chapter 3. West Virginia, like other Appalachian states, has had a long history of unsuspecting surface owners, a century ago, selling their mineral rights with no way of knowing what future mining would entail. See books by Harry Caudill and Denise Giardina.)

The West Virginia Highlands Conservancy has maintained a two-pronged approach to mining issues over its existence. One prong has been the fight against mining threats to specific areas that needed protection, such as wilderness areas, on a case-by-case basis. The second prong has seen the Conservancy involved at the policy and regulatory level, repeatedly advocating for strict regulation of the industry, hoping to minimize negative impacts on each individual location. Occasionally, policy or regulatory reform occurred from a protest of an individual site permit. As the years progressed, and this chapter explains, the Conservancy's mining activists became almost entirely policy advocates.

In one of the earliest references to mining issues, Conservancy President Tom King discussed some of the current development threats to the Highlands in his invitation to the 1967 Highlands Review Weekend. King wrote:

Strip mining has been extremely destructive of natural values and continues to be a serious problem even on lands within the boundaries of the [Monongahela] National Forest and the National Recreation Area. Although the surface of the land is owned and managed by the Forest Service, the right to strip away the covering vegetation and soil and extract the underlying coal is owned, in some portions of the Forest, by private mining interests. The problem is closely related to road development, for as public roads open new regions, it becomes economically profitable for mining companies to begin operation. Roaring Plains, which lies along the proposed route of the Highland Scenic Highway/Allegheny Parkway, is one example of an area threatened with the possibility of being "stripped" if made easily accessible.

In December 1968, Bob Burrell, editor of the newsletter of the Scenic Rivers Subcommittee, reviewed the year from a conservation perspective. On the positive side, he wrote that the "strip mine laws have been in use, and on the whole, appear to be working well and acceptable to both conservation and industry." But on the negative, he cited coal-mining threats to both the Williams and the Cranberry Rivers, where Princess Coal Company, the mineral owner, had announced mining plans. He specifically worried that haul roads would ruin the primitive nature of the Cranberry Back Country. Burrell continued:

> For those who have never seen a coal company haul road, just picture how the land is torn up when a new interstate is put in and at first used by the giant earthmovers. Such roads are incompatible with the delicate natural beauty of one of the East's few remaining semi-wilderness areas. To say that such practices will not result in serious soil erosion or water pollution is chicanery of the first magnitude. The company has been informed that they can expect a vigorous reaction from conservation. Let's not disappoint the company.

It would be the third issue of *The Highlands Voice*, in June 1969, also edited by Burrell, before a significant story on mining appeared. Discussing threats to Shavers Fork, he reported that the Mower Lumber Company, owner of more than 60,000 acres at the headwaters, "plans to reactivate strip mining in this area, as well as even deep-mining activity on these holdings. Haul trucks have been seen right in the stream gouging out the banks, and dredging for gravel has even occurred. The installation of a coal washer, if allowed, would be the final blow."

Burrell stated that the Department of Natural Resources (DNR) could control some aspects of the mining operations, e.g. strip miners must be able to show and carry out reclamation procedures and possess a discharge permit after July 1 for any new deep mine.

In the August 1969 *Voice*, Zip Little, a leader of the Izaak Walton League, reported on a recent hearing under West Virginia's then two-year-old strip-mining law. The Royal Sparks Mining Company had proposed to mine across from Grandview State Park's namesake overlook and had fought the provision that protected aesthetics. This was the first example of the Conservancy's interest in the policy and regulatory aspects of the mining laws.

The battle to protect Otter Creek from mining in 1970 was the first intense mining confrontation of the Highlands Conservancy. Discussed extensively in Chapter 2, the Conservancy forced the Island Creek Coal Company to conduct its core drilling by transporting all the equipment by horse back, thereby minimizing the impact on Otter Creek's wilderness character. The same year, the Linan Coal Company's plans for Shavers Fork, and Princess Mining/Mid Allegheny Corporation's proposal for the Cranberry area, forced the Conservancy to confront coal-mining threats as never before.

By the end of the year, *Voice* Editor Burrell advocated a closer look at the broader picture. There had been an increase of thirty-three percent in strip-mine permit applications and a sixty percent increase in acreage during the past year, and there was no end in sight. The coal rush was on and every one was after it, particularly in the Monongahela National Forest. Citing Princess and Linan for a particularly vigorous public relations campaign concerning their twice-denied Shavers Fork mine, he claimed they had undermined faith in the DNR and created the impression with the public that their permit denials were politically motivated. He continued:

> Meanwhile a backlash has developed against strip-mining in general. One organization has been formed whose sole purpose is to outlaw strip mining. The Highlands Conservancy Board of Directors rejected this approach inasmuch as there are many areas within the state that are amenable to strip mining and the operators of these areas have done a good job on the whole in holding up their end of the bargain. The complete outlawing of strip mining seems reactionary and doesn't face a more serious problem, that of any kind of coal mining in the National Forest. Congressman Ken Hechler has called for a state-wide, non-partisan drive to protect the entire Monongahela National Forest from coal mining of any kind. Although the Conservancy has

not dealt with the problem in this light, this editor supports Mr. Hechler's plea to the fullest. It is my feeling that coal mining is incompatible with the multiple use concept. You can't have mining <u>and</u> any other currently recognized legitimate forest use.

Burrell reported a second group, Concerned West Virginians, Inc, had formed to deal with strip mining in what he called "a more realistic way." More a reform group, concentrating on slope restrictions, water pollution and enforcement, it contended that the necessary changes could be made by the Reclamation Commission itself without need for additional legislation.

At the Mid-Winter Workshop in January 1971, when Burrell was elected Conservancy president, a resolution on mining in the Monongahela National Forest was passed. Citing "the rapacious, plundering destruction so evident across the face of West Virginia," the Conservancy called on federal and state government agencies "to control this destruction, preferably by the elimination of coal mining in the Monongahela National Forest, or at least by stricter control." The resolution continued by urging purchase of mineral rights under public land and/or mining be done as a model for the rest of the state.

Abolition

But control was not enough. The 1971 Legislature was totally preoccupied with the abolition of strip mining. Bills favoring abolition were introduced in both houses. Secretary of State Jay Rockefeller, widely expected to face Governor Arch Moore in 1972, threw his full support behind the abolition movement. Joint committee hearings were held to an overflow attendance. Rockefeller was the first to testify. Bill Riley spoke for the Highlands Conservancy:

> The Conservancy is not unaware of the economic significance of strip mining in our state or of the high demand for our coal. And yet, in times past and present we have seen our forests up-rooted, our mountains ravaged, and our streams silted and polluted by poor mining practices. We, as taxpayers, have paid and will continue to pay an astronomical price to support an industry that should have never been allowed a foothold in our state. It is our position that to let the short-term economic gain outweigh the high cost to West Virginia of attempting to correct the devastation wrought by strip mining and the loss of industry and tourism that will not come to a ravaged state is a very short-sighted view indeed.

247

In the April 1971 *Voice* several articles recounted the legislative battle. Norman Williams, Deputy Director of the DNR, had testified favoring abolition, directly counter to Director Ira Latimer. Because of Williams' high state position, excerpts of his testimony appeared in *The Charleston Gazette* and were reprinted in the *Voice*. In summary, he had asserted that the industry "outclassed" the state, forcing a weak regulatory effort. He criticized both former Governor Hulett Smith and current Governor Moore for giving in to the industry's "unrelenting pressure." He continued:

> The Governor has seen fit, for reasons best known to himself, to withhold the revised rules and regulations. He has seen fit to maintain the status quo, to prevent the [Reclamation] Commission from discharging its legal responsibility, and to keep totally silent on the matter of where he stands on this vital issue, the abolition of strip mining in West Virginia.
>
> If the Governor of the State of West Virginia is afraid to speak out or to release the new rules and regulations on strip mining, what are we to expect of the reclamation inspector who earns $500-$600 per month and whose decisions every day affect millions of dollars worth of coal?
>
> Until such time as my question is answered, I shall continue in my stated belief that the inheritance of our children and of their children, the environment of this magnificent state of West Virginia, stands in serious jeopardy from further strip mining; and that we must turn our energies to the many and complex environmental problems which lie neglected on every side; and that West Virginia, for reasons I have presented to you today, can no longer afford the terrible price of strip mining.

No one in West Virginia was shocked to hear that Williams resigned soon thereafter. He became the first director of the Mid-Appalachian Environmental Services Center in Charleston, funded by the Conservation Foundation and designed to provide objective information on environmental issues throughout the Appalachian region. (The Conservancy's Sayre Rodman served on their board of advisors.) A few years later, Williams moved to Washington and joined the staff of the House Interior Committee, where he played a pivotal role in writing the federal Surface Mine Control and Reclamation Act of 1977.

In the end both houses of the state Legislature passed differing bills and compromised on a two-year moratorium on strip mining in twenty-two of the fifty-five counties. Before the session adjourned, Governor

Moore gave "outsiders" hell for stirring up the Legislature and singled out Rockefeller for a special attack.

On almost the same day as the Charleston hearing, Rep. Ken Hechler introduced HR 4556, a bill that would ban all strip mining for six months and prohibit all coal mining in wilderness areas. By March 22 he had sixty co-sponsors from twenty-two states.

At the Conservancy's 1972 Mid-Winter Workshop, Rev. Richard Austin, former coordinator of Citizens to Abolish Strip Mining, and Williams updated Conservancy members on current activities. In an article in February's *Voice*, John Parks reported on an abolition rally in Charleston. Eleven legislators were present, and were supporting Sen. Si Galperin's abolition bill again. Rep. Hechler and Rockefeller spoke as well.

On March 3, 1972, Conservancy President Burrell wrote Ben Greene, Chief of Reclamation, to protest a permit issued to Greer Steel Company to strip mine on Shavers Fork. Wrote Burrell:

> We protest this permit as we protest all Shavers Fork permits because of the already incredible damage this fine stream has suffered, its already low pH, its already outrageous silt burden, and its serious threat to the water quality of the Bowden National Fish Hatchery located immediately downstream from the proposed site. Finally, we protest this particular site because it will be in view of the heavily used tourist highway of U.S. 33. Is this what we want to lure tourists to the state to see?

In summary, the Conservancy was active on a statewide basis trying to abolish or at least sharply regulate strip mining and was keeping abreast of federal legislation sponsored by Congressman Hechler. Meanwhile, on a local level it monitored Shavers Fork mining permit applications, was in court over Otter Creek mining, and was watching carefully the threat of mining to the Cranberry Back Country.

At the Mid-Winter Workshop in January 1973, the Conservancy elected Dave Elkinton the new president, succeeding Burrell. Assuming the gavel immediately upon his election, he was abruptly caught in a crisis. As he wrote in the February 1973 *Highlands Voice*:

> Those of you who hung on until near the end of the Board Meeting, will recall perhaps one of the thorniest parliamentary problems that ever faced the Conservancy, let alone a brand-spankin' new president, in my first attempt to weld a group of rugged individualists into an organized group. The business at hand was one of the most

concise resolutions on a complicated subject ever introduced: "The West Virginia Highlands Conservancy urges the prohibition of all strip mining for coal throughout the State as doing permanent and irreparable harm to the soil, water, and human resources of the state out of all proportion to the value of the mineral extracted." Regardless of how one might feel about this issue, it must be one of the clearest statements of the abolition position that has been made.

The discussion that preceded the vote was cloudy to say the least. Well-known abolitionists were speaking in opposition to the resolution, claiming the Conservancy was already clearly an abolition organization. Other abolitionists felt this a better statement than past resolutions. The author of this resolution, a new member, was under the mistaken impression that the Conservancy had never taken a position on strip mining. And there were those who did not favor abolition anyway.

When the vote was taken by a show of hands, the resolution barely passed. Here is where I should have quietly rejoiced that a resolution basically in line with my beliefs had passed and kept my mouth shut, but I didn't.

Instead, observing that many had voted, on both sides, who were not Board members, I pointed out that, since this was a Board meeting, if anyone wished a re-vote, with only Board members voting, it would be granted. Of course it was requested. A re-vote was taken. The vote was tied.

I have seldom been in such an awkward position. After some thought, I voted against the resolution. Instead of a brief explanation at the time, I decided to explain it in the *Voice*, but the story only got more complicated.

By an honest mistake, our hard-working Publicity chairperson, Bobbi Nagy, thinking the resolution had actually passed, sent copies to two newspapers. Their articles were subsequently picked up by at least one wire service and we all read and heard the press tell us that the Conservancy had passed the resolution in question. Then came the problem of explaining to Board members who had voted against the resolution why the press had reported this.

Finally, we were faced with trying to explain to the press why they were incorrect, yet trying not to appear to be pro-stripping.

Elkinton would never forget that meeting. It was his first encounter with new member Nick Zvegintzov.

For the April 1973 *Voice* Zvegintzov wrote the first of some seventy articles that would appear over the next seven years. His style was always lively, his opinions stated with flair, and there were no sacred cows. During the mid to late 1970s *Highlands Voice* readers counted on Burrell, Hardway, and Zvegintzov to provide the spice in the environmental reporting from West Virginia.

From his home in Washington, D.C., Nick Z, as he came to be known, wrote on federal hearings, policy debates, as well as the battle to keep the small community of Duo alive.

His April 1973 article reported on United States Senate hearings on two strip-mining bills. The Nixon Administration bill, Zvegintzov wrote:

> …was a sort of thalidomide baby, i.e. without limbs or guts. Actually I never heard it mentioned at all. I believe it was an embarrassment in the context of the hearings which were conducted at a high level of technical and rational argument.
>
> I was impressed by the hearings as a vehicle for debate and education. As to what they indicate in terms of impending bills, I cannot feign to tell you. I learned one other thing in Washington: Washington environmentalists are as inscrutable as a mole in a laurel patch.

The following October, Zvegintzov wrote "Perspective on Stripping":

> First, the bad news. 1) One-fifth of West Virginia is now strip-mined. 2) Strip mining is cheaper than deep mining. 3) It destroys that natural ability of the hillsides to hold water and soil, causing sterility on the ridges and landslides and floods in the valleys. 4) West Virginia leads the nation in acreage reclaimed is a sweet-talking way to say West Virginia leads the nation in acreage stripped. 5) The West Virginia law appears to regulate the industry, but it has been a constant battle to get the Governor to administer even the letter of it, to say nothing of the spirit.
>
> Now, the good news. The realities of the time are against the strippers. 1) No more free lunch. The city voter who is being made to pay for polluting the air with his auto and power plant, and the water with his sewage, is not going to let the West Virginia stripping company profit from a free license to scarify the land. 2) No more ignorance. We can now measure with computers the employment loss caused by the rise of stripping in Appalachia. We can map from satellites the declined fertility. For $9 you can get from the U.S. Geological survey a satellite picture of your own home, and a map of every clearcut, road, and mine for 100 miles. 3) No more sugartit. The consumer has learned that no energy source is a free gift. He is ready to count the cost of agricultural land destroyed, deep mining jobs fore-

gone, and the loss of a strategic stockpile of energy that should be kept for a real emergency.

These trends are just the front of a creative change that is coming to America, a true reclamation. The Conservancy is part of this change. Our scattered membership, our volunteer action, our freedom in individual projects, our elusive leadership — these are lessons in how to sustain the wide branches of interdependent society without losing the deep roots of a community. The wanton waste of land in strip mining (and of men in deep mining) will both be gone when the American puts into practice the lessons we have learned from the mountains and the mountaineers:

The earth is a mother and not a whore. Life is for living, not spending. Living things are not a means to be exploited, but ends in themselves.

This relatively short piece captured both Zvegintzov's style and a widely held perspective in the mid-1970s. Re-reading it thirty years later, when the ravages of mountaintop-removal mining remain essentially unchecked, one begins to understand how naïve an opinion this was.

While there was interest in specific sites where mining was threatening, such as upper Shavers Fork, the Conservancy kept its eye on the national and state regulation of strip mining. In March 1974, Bob Handley (see Chapter 2), a leader in the Citizens to Abolish Strip Mining, provided a front-page *Voice* article. He reported that coal companies were stripping at increasing rates, but that in West Virginia citizen protests had resulted in stricter enforcement of the law. He articulated the West Virginia mining paradox:

Historically, West Virginia politicians have favored the coal industry and out-of-state interests in general. If not this, then why do the people who live here in the middle of fantastically abundant natural resources suffer from the lack of adequate health facilities, poor schools, poor roads, and sub-standard communities. Strip mining has added insult to injury, in that in many instances it has taken from the already underprivileged a place to live. Their homes have been repeatedly flooded and their roads, their streams, and their hills have been virtually destroyed.

Handley wondered why Governor Moore didn't promote low-sulphur coal, plentiful in southern West Virginia, instead of fighting for relaxed air pollution regulations to allow for higher-sulphur strip coal to be burned in the nation's power plants? Meanwhile, he urged *Voice* readers to contact congressional leaders who were considering comprehensive regulation. Although short of abolition, Handley wrote that such legislation would apply an even standard across the region and lead to tougher enforcement in West Virginia.

The Federal Law

Zvegintzov added an article on the details of the pending federal strip law. House committee chairs Morris Udall, D-AZ, and Patsy Mink, D-HI, had visited the coalfields and "viewed some of our finest devastations." Elements of their bill included returning land to its approximate original contour, a stronger bond and permit procedure, and public advertising and comment opportunities. Rep. John Seiberling, D-OH, had added a $2.50 per ton fee that would go to abandoned waste clean up or health and safety compensation. On the other hand, the Nixon Administration was proposing weakening amendments.

This law, said Zvegintzov, had little to do with West Virginia's coal and much to do with coal in the western states. He wrote:

> The energy industry shows every sign of wanting to move out of the Appalachians and into Montana, Colorado, Utah, and Arizona. These states cannot control this mining even to the extent that West Virginia does, because much of the coal is federally owned and the states have no jurisdiction. So there is going to be a federal law — but it is up to you and me to see that it isn't a law that says you can cut up West Virginia as long as you put a band-aid on Montana.

By October 1974, the Conservancy was managing multiple issues as usual. The Eastern Wilderness Areas Act was finally moving through the House of Representatives and West Virginia Rep. Harley O. Staggers's voters poll indicated 75% favorable for wilderness. The New River's inclusion within the Wild and Scenic Rivers protection bill had passed the Senate and was awaiting House action. Corridor H construction had recently polluted a key water source for the Bowden Fish Hatchery. The U.S. Department of Interior had come out against the Davis Power Project. Conservancy members were seen in that month's *Voice* viewing the site of Snowshoe Ski Resort.

Against this noisy backdrop, Zvegintzov authored three articles in one issue of the *Voice*. Both the House and Senate had passed different strip-mine bills; thus a conference committee would hold the fate of the bill. Two issues, wrote Zvegintzov, were critical. One, the "Mansfield amendment," would prohibit surface mining of federal coal under private surface ownership (common in the West), and the second would prohibit mountaintop mining, although both houses had voted to permit "head-of-the hollow and valley-fill methods of dumping soil on the downslope which are among the most destructive stripping methods in Appalachia."

Over the next few months, Conservancy members were urged to write Congress urging a strong bill, but the new Gerald Ford Administration and the industry were busy weakening any stringent regulations. Ultimately, a compromise bill passed both houses, but was vetoed by President Ford.

As the West Virginia Highlands Conservancy met in January 1975, Zvegintzov was elected the new Washington, D.C., vice president. He had already shown himself as the federal legislation reporter, and the election simply formalized that relationship. In related business, the Conservancy Board voted to join a lawsuit against EPA, appealing the blanket waiver of pollution permits for strip-mining companies. Zvegintzov reported on the congressional passage of strip-mining legislation and its veto by President Ford.

While federal legislation remained in limbo, Zvegintzov and the Conservancy focused on West Virginia. The *Voice* had begun in 1974 carrying monthly lists of pending strip mine permits and encouraging members to file letters of protest. Editor Ron Hardway reprinted his correspondence with Monongahela National Forest Supervisor Ralph Mumme, debating whether the Forest Service could protect the Cranberry from mining threats. Zvegintzov wrote an article, "Strips, Floods and Politics," beginning his campaign to raise public concern about flooding caused by mining. He began:

> Does strip mining increase flooding in this state? If so, why? And is there any remedy?
>
> These are grave questions in a state where strip mining is a major industry and where people live in narrow valleys which they share with tempestuous mountain creeks. The answers to these questions are:
> • Strip mining does increase flooding.
> • Because it drains the hills and silts the valleys.
> • We have to assess the costs and charge them to those who cause them.

His article quoted research studies that compared flooding in two watersheds, one of which had been stripped. Ultimately, if the U.S. Army

Corps of Engineers was charged with the control of flooding, it should have upstream, watershed control, but in the case of mining, it did not. Zvegintzov philosophized:

> In the Conservancy we have the great privilege of searching for the truth without much more self-interest than our love of the mountains. But with this privilege comes an unpleasant burden — that of bearing and exposing unpleasant truths like "strip mining in this state causes floods" against the natural opposition of all unpleasant truths. We have to endure until the truth becomes so obvious to the community at large that community agencies such as the Corps or the Department of Natural Resources are free to act on it as solidly and righteously as if they had admitted it all along.

He wrote these words in 1975 and it would be another decade before the Conservancy would learn how prophetic they were.

In June 1975, after another veto by President Ford of another strip-mine bill, the House failed by a slim three votes to override his veto. Zvegintzov's article indicated uncertainty among the Washington environmental lobbyists on next steps.

Meanwhile, *Voice* Editor Hardway wrote a commentary, reflecting on how strip mining had changed in the past decade:

> Before the days of the Abolish Strip Mining movement, coal counties suffered greatly from what we came to call "fly-by-night" operators. These birds were very small companies, often family affairs, who got permits for 20 or less acres, stripped it, then fled in the dark of night, leaving behind broken-down equipment, 100 feet highwalls, 200 feet spoilbanks, and substantial tax bills owed to county governments. The companies would then go "out-of-business," usually declare bankruptcy, then reorganize under another name and repeat the process in a different county. The county sheriff would always impound the abandoned equipment and try to sell it at public auction. But no one ever bought the junk, and everyone's time was wasted while the county went begging.
>
> Then came the great national effort to abolish the industry. Politicians, well aware that environmentalists give neither a dime nor a darn for politicians, "compromised" with the abolitionists and passed some "tough new laws." To their surprise, and the fly-by-nighters chagrin, the laws turned out to be tougher than was intended, especially when environmentalists began monitoring strip jobs to make sure the laws were enforced.

By late 1973 practically all the fly-by-night coal operators were forced out of business because they could not meet the incredible costs of reclamation. No longer did the streets of Webster Springs and similarly situated towns vibrate at 3 a.m. from muffled passage of heavy machinery on its way to asylum in a foreign country.

With the landscape left to the big companies, Hardway wrote, strip-mine permit applications declined in number, but increased in acreage. When the energy crisis of fall 1974 arrived, the big companies were in control. Small coal contracting operators, bankrolled by the few large players, appeared to be local, but the profits accrued primarily to the major firms. The industry had consolidated.

Sugar Lane

In the July 1975 *Voice*, in a two-page centerfold with accompanying photos, Zvegintzov introduced readers to Sugar Lane in Marion County. Located between Fairmont and Morgantown, the rural community of a dozen families, only wanted DNR enforcement of a local strip mine. They had formed an association, raised the money, and paved their one road into the community, only to see it destroyed by a strip mine operator. The operator was a partnership of two men, both of whom had records of violations precluding their ability to gain new permits. Despite a variety of alleged problems and forty-three petitioners opposing the permit, the DNR had issued it. As soon as operations began, seven women from Sugar Lane were arrested as they blocked the coal trucks on their road.

The residents appealed the permit to the State Reclamation Board of Review. Under West Virginia law, the qualifications of members of this board practically guaranteed that they would have an industry bias. Two issues emerged: one, did the unincorporated community association have "standing" and two, was the operator "under the control of" an individual prohibited from obtaining a permit? Zvegintzov said the state opposed the standing issue, not wanting to open the door to informal local groups who might protest strip mine permits elsewhere. The Sugar Lane group pointedly had neither offered the name of a token resident as a plaintiff, nor taken the opportunity to incorporate their group.

On April 29, 1975 the Board rejected Sugar Lane Improvement Association's standing, because it was unincorporated and ruled that the company employed, but was not managed by, a prohibited operator. The Sugar Lane group filed an appeal to Marion Circuit Court. Zvegintzov wrote, "They are the first group in the State to get this far in the judicial process using the State's surface-mining law."

While Marion County was definitely outside the highlands region, the Conservancy had followed this case carefully, mindful to the precedent implications. Standing was important to community groups statewide. Prohibition of past violators would keep the worst coal abuses out of the system.

As the Conservancy assembled for its Mid-Winter Workshop in January 1976, Zvegintzov assembled a panel presentation featuring four anti-strip-mining groups. They represented Morgantown, Elkins, Lincoln County, and Fairmont. All saw their local mining protests as part of a statewide community-based, anti-strip mining movement. The Lincoln County group was called Save Our Mountains and would later develop into a state leader in the fight against strip mining.

Duo

In February 1976, Zvegintzov introduced *Voice* readers to a second small community, Duo. A former coal camp in western Greenbrier County, which had been home to both deep mines in the 1930s and strip mines in the 1940s, the company town had been sold to its residents. Zvegintzov had apparently found the pace of this very ordinary community to his liking and had rented a house. Now a legal advertisement for a pending strip mine might mean destruction to a frail community water system and to a one-lane road, and basements vulnerable to flooding. Having fought strip mining in the abstract, Zvegintzov was faced with it first hand.

At its April meeting, the Board of Directors approved Zvegintzov's request for Conservancy support and funding to mount a legal challenge to the Duo strip-mine permit application. The basis of the protest would be incomplete information in the file at the time of the public advertisement.

Frequently, Zvegintzov wrote articles describing the struggles of various coalfield communities trying to either prevent, or modify, planned strip mining near them. Statewide, groups such as Save Our Mountains and at least four countywide organizations tried to alert citizens to strip mining's destruction and regulatory issues. At the same time, the Conservancy was carefully monitoring mining threats to Shavers Fork, Cranberry, and other high-interest areas. Strip-mining issues were covered regularly in the mass media and *The Highlands Voice*.

On February 23 the state Reclamation Board of Review heard the Duo appeal. It had been nearly three years since the Conservancy had seen the same board in action in the Sugar Lane case. With several Conservancy board members and the press in attendance, the Conservancy argued that the application must be complete before the public can be expected to comment meaningfully. In its decision a month later, the board agreed that the current procedures allowed public notice before applications were complete, but that the DNR Director did not act "unreasonably or illegally." They expressed the opinion that future applicants be required to submit complete applications before public notice was published.

The Conservancy, Save Our Mountains, and Zvegintzov appealed to the Greenbrier County Circuit Court to vacate the Reclamation Board's decision and halt all further permits until the procedure was corrected.

With the arrival of a new Congress and a new president, Jimmy Carter, in January 1977, the COALition Against Strip Mining met in Washington, D.C., with Zvegintzov and two other Conservancy members present. Forging a bond between the Appalachian region and the western states, the COALition focused on strengthening the federal legislation pending in Congress. Rep. Morris Udall, D-AZ, was assuming the Chair of the House Interior Committee, and West Virginia's newly elected Nick Rahall was a committee member. A *Voice* article by Larry George concluded:

> The next five months will probably see the closing chapters of Federal strip mining legislation. Both President Carter and the Congress are making this legislation a priority item. Rep. Udall has said he hopes to see passage of a bill by next June. ...The type of bill that is finally adopted may rest largely upon the input of people in the areas actually affected by stripping, and the efforts of groups such as the Conservancy.

In July 1977 Congress again passed a compromise federal strip mine reclamation bill. Environmentalists were disappointed in its requirements, but tougher bills had been vetoed twice before by President Ford. This bill required restoration of mined land to approximate original contour and imposed a tax to pay for reclaiming former strip mine abuses. Despite calls for his veto by several anti-stripping groups, President Carter signed it on August 3, 1977. Zvegintzov wrote that according to Congressman Hechler, "the best thing that can be said about this [signing] ceremony, is that the President said he was not satisfied with the bill and would prefer it stricter and that this statement got tumultuous applause that visibly surprised him." Zvegintzov characterized the federal bill as "little more effective than the West Virginia bill."

Opposite the article in the *Voice* on the federal bill was a photo and review of Bob Gates and his film "In Memory of the Land and People." A Conservancy member and Save Our Mountains leader, Gates had left Union Carbide as an engineer for the life of a photographer and film-maker. Said one writer:

> What is truly unique about Memory is that it is almost completely a one-man show. Gates not only conceived the film but was also its editor, artist, and producer. But what is perhaps most impressive is that the film is so effective as both a documentary and an artistic statement. Sure, there is no narrator nor acting, no script nor story line, but there is undeniable drama and pathos here; there are good guys and most definitely there are villains.
>
> The heart (and guts) of the film focuses on those gigantic strip mining machines with sadistic names like "The Mountaineer" and "The Gem of Egypt" (named for Ohio's once-fertile Egypt Valley, the entirety of which it has nearly devoured in the name of electric power.)

Gates would continue to use his filmmaking skill for conservation over the next thirty years, along the way becoming a Highlands Conservancy Board member.

In November 1977 Zvegintzov wrote "Fools Against Stripping." Summarizing his motivation for the six years of meetings, trips, hearings, lawsuits, and articles, he shared these thoughts with *Voice* readers:

> It seems to me that only a fool would fight strip mining. A wise person would not pick a course where there is nothing to look forward to for years but defeat after defeat after defeat. Yet stripping is such an ecological horror, orders of magnitude worse than clearcutting or dam building or ski resorts, that anybody with an ecological conscience should be a fool and get ready for as many demoralizing miserable defeats as it takes to win a victory.
>
> A problem of this fight is that the sensitivity to nature and human-ity that pushes a person into it will drain a person's energy and will. I used to wonder why anti-stripping people never answer their mail or their telephone messages, why anti-stripping groups spring up with the flamboyance of maple leaves in spring and then are gone like those leaves at Christmas, and why differences of opinion on anti-stripping

tactics can cause such bitterness among those who ought to be allies. It has to do with need and hope and failure. It's hard to answer letters if all one can say is "We probably can't help." It's hard to keep a group together when there's never anything to celebrate. It's hard to have amiable debate on tactics when all the tactics seem to fail.

Our best tactic as individuals is not to throw ourselves into the struggle with the passion that it seems to deserve, but with the caution of marathon runners who start the first mile at a pace they can hold in the twentieth. The best tactic for County and State groups may be to take on some mixture of "respectable" projects like nature hikes and scenic areas just to have some accomplishments at the end of one year to carry on to another.

Six years of fighting stripping have convinced me that only a fool would get into it. But…there's worse than a fool. There's the dullard who cannot see the evil. There's the cold heart who ignores it. There's the Judas who condones it for gain.

Zvegintzov might well have applied these observations to the Conservancy more generally, as it celebrated its tenth year. How many members had experienced the frustrations of defeat after defeat: Shavers Fork, Canaan Valley, Stonewall Jackson Dam, Corridor H, Cranberry, to name a few? The victories were fewer: Otter Creek, Dolly Sods, Royal Glen. What kept the Conservancy's activists going? Was the best tactic indeed to take on a mixture of projects? In fact, would only a fool get into it?

As 1977 ended, Zvegintzov reviewed a variety of mining issues for *Voice* readers. That year there had been three major floods in the Big Sandy watershed on the southwestern border of West Virginia. Immediately, many voices had blamed strip mining for aggravating the flooding. Various federal agencies and environmental groups pressed for a federally funded study.

One was the voice of Jack Spadaro, an outspoken DNR dam engineer and Conservancy member. He told a United States House committee in November that provisions of the new federal Strip Mining Control Act did not adequately control flooding due to strip mining. "The probability of dam failures will be increased many times with the construction of numerous sediment control dams in areas that are heavily populated downstream." In answer to a question about "areas unsuitable for strip mining," he added:

> Any areas which have been subjected to severe flooding should be eligible for deletion of strip mining in the watershed…Designation of

areas unsuitable for strip mining should be mandatory in all flood prone watersheds and areas which are landslide susceptible...Citizen petitions for designations of areas unsuitable for strip mining should be given the highest priority. In West Virginia such citizen petitions have been completely ignored in the past.

In June 1978 Conservancy Board member Keith Kirk, in an analysis of the federal Surface Mine Act, focused on the concept of "primacy." Under the law, if and when a state could prove that its enforcement would meet all the federal standards and regulations, it could take over primary enforcement. Significant federal grants would support such a transfer. Wrote Kirk, in words that would echo for decades into the future:

> Primacy has ominous implications in West Virginia because, once this state is so designated, the Federal Office of Surface Mining may literally rubber stamp state actions pertaining to strip mining. Right now, from what we have been able to determine, there might as well be no Federal Surface Mining Act if West Virginia receives primacy with its present unworkable surface-mining enforcement program.
>
> The Highlands Conservancy has been dissatisfied, to say the least, with West Virginia's enforcement of its regulations for controlling surface mining...For this reason, the Conservancy's Strip Mining Committee may actively oppose the state receiving primacy until many changes are made in the existing state regulations and until the present enforcement program is totally revamped.

Kirk continued by enumerating a litany of changes needed in the state system to meet the federal standards. Among them were the public-notice regulations and the still-inadequate permit application, the subject of the Duo lawsuit. Clearly having won the victory of a federal strip-mining law, enforcement was only as strong as a weak West Virginia political system.

In the *Voice* of August 1978, the headline, "Victory at Duo," indicated one of those rare accomplishments in the battle against strip mining. Zvegintzov wrote that an out-of-court settlement with the state had given the Conservancy all it wanted. Henceforth, all applications would be required to contain "a complete reclamation and mining plan for land to be disturbed... prior to publication of the Class III legal advertisement." Now when citizens examined the DNR files and considered whether they should file a protest letter, all of the pertinent details would be available to them. It had been twenty-nine months since the original incomplete application had been filed and twelve months after the stripping had been completed.

Zvegintzov wrote:

> This case leaves a bitter taste in this writer's mouth. It is unpleasant to think that the State would force the people to spend around $1200 in legal and stenographic fees, plus countless hours of volunteer labor, to force them to administer the law as plainly written. It is this sort of stupidity and bad faith on the part of Charleston (and of many other State governments) that brought the passage of the Federal surface-mining law. If Charleston now complains of the heavy hand of Washington, they have only themselves to thank.

The Highlands Conservancy joined three other groups in serving notice of their intention to sue both the federal and state strip-mining regulatory agencies for failing to enforce new federal regulations on mountaintop-removal strip mining. Their complaint cited twenty-seven sites in West Virginia that should have been closed. "The groups anticipate that mountain-top removal may never be feasible at a number of these sites if the law is strictly enforced." Thirty years later, the Conservancy would still be actively working for control of many mountaintop removal sites in southern West Virginia.

Braxton Environmental Action Program

In November 1978 a small announcement in *The Highlands Voice* would open a major chapter in the Conservancy's battles to control mining. A new environmental group had been organized in central West Virginia, called Braxton Environmental Action Program (BEAP). Rick Webb, a native of Virginia who had come to Braxton County four years earlier and bought a hundred acres, was listed as co-organizer. Webb would distinguish himself in his conservation activities within and outside the Conservancy in the months to come.

BEAP had begun by circulating a petition asking the DNR to withhold issuing further permits on the Laurel Creek watershed in Webster and Braxton counties. Already one permit had been issued for a preparation plant at Erbacon and one was pending for Centralia, both on Laurel Creek, a tributary of Sutton Lake. Since the primary coal seam to be mined was the Kittanning, known for its acid content, local streams would experience toxic pollution.

Opposite a second article explaining why Webb and BEAP had been denied their request to the state Water Resources Board to suspend the already-issued permit on a technicality, was a notice that Conservancy activist Larry George had been appointed to that same board. Maybe next time they would get a more favorable hearing.

In January 1979 Zvegintzov reported that the threat of a suit to halt mountaintop-removal mining had been enough to end its "indiscriminant use." Of the twenty-seven sites mentioned in the lawsuit notice, two had been shut down by the DNR, two more probably would be, eight had converted to "approximate original contour," nine were justified or negotiating, and six had not started operations. Although the threat of the suit did lead to revisions in the mining plans, Zvegintzov felt its greatest success was proving "the Federal law can compel State action much more effectively than the State law ever could."

As the West Virginia Legislature met in early 1979, the state law and regulations needed to be updated to allow for the transfer of primacy from the federal Office of Surface Mining (OSM). Here was an opportunity for environmentalists to lobby for stringent rules in a state noted for lax regulation of mining. The carrot was the flow of funding to clean up abandoned mining scars. Both the industry and the environmentalists wanted the state to achieve primacy; the industry because they already had a relationship with the regulators and the citizens because OSM had been extremely under-staffed and unable to conduct effective enforcement over the previous eighteen months. The balance between state and federal law and the threat to withhold (or later, take back) primacy would be a recurring theme far into the future.

In April's *Voice*, Webb and BEAP were back in the news. At issue were permits requested by a subsidiary of Monongahela Power Company for strip mines within a 2,000-acre tract near Cowen. Conservancy member and DNR fish biologist Don Gasper had determined that this mine would jeopardize fish in Birch River and its tributaries. Past mining nearby had left acid seeps, although there were no notes in the permit file to so indicate. Webb and BEAP requested a geologic study to determine compliance with the new federal law.

Meanwhile representatives of six environmental groups, including the Conservancy and BEAP, working with three DNR water officials, had developed a volunteer water quality surveillance program, called Mountain Stream Monitors. The project had grown out of a regional EPA conference and would be funded by a $6,650 EPA grant. West Virginia

Citizen Action Group (WV-CAG) would administer the grant. Webb would become the project's coordinator.

On the legislative front, the industry had forced passage of a bill giving the DNR nearly another year to comply with federal mandates. OSM wanted stronger enforcement, the industry weaker. The DNR would try to please both if it could. Conservancy member and lawyer David Wooley was leading the effort to mobilize citizen involvement supporting stronger enforcement.

Other articles that month included a challenge to the Board of Reclamation, whose members allegedly violated conflict-of-interest provisions of the federal strip mine law, an announcement that final strip mine regulations were issued by OSM, and a status report on a Lincoln County lawsuit to restrict mining. Lincoln County resident Julian Martin, a member of Save Our Mountains, wrote the first of his many articles for the Highlands Conservancy.

The Rockefeller Amendment

In November 1979 the "Rockefeller Amendment" to the federal Surface Mine Control Act was a hot topic. Conservancy Board member Ed Light described the Rockefeller Amendment as "an underhanded attempt to relax key environmental protection provisions of that law." In essence it would allow states to substitute their own standards for the OSM standards to implement the federal law. West Virginia and its Governor Rockefeller were leading the charge in Washington. Light continued:

> Passage of the Rockefeller Amendment will not increase coal production, but will represent a major step backwards in the effort to modernize our coal industry and make it responsive to the needs of coal fields residents. Those who will suffer should the Amendment pass include coal-field residents who will be forced to live in hazardous areas subject to landslides and floods, with their water supplies polluted and their fishing streams ruined.

Light pointed to the lax effort by the West Virginia DNR, after the federal law's enactment, to promulgate effective regulations. Rather than use it to strengthen the regulations, Light said the DNR had actually taken the position of defending coal operators who had continued to cause environmental damage in violation of the federal law. He continued:

The most blatant example of DNR's basic opposition to provisions of the Federal Act was its refusal to even begin to enforce the prohibition on mountain-top removal where a higher land lawsuit was filed by citizen groups in 1978. Even now, a number of mountain-top removal operations are being permitted to continue in violation of this Federal statute.

Before he completed his critique, Light had taken the state to task for its absence of concern for groundwater protection, secrecy instead of public participation, opposition to topsoil and sediment control pond regulations, and promotion of valley fills (placing excess soil into stream beds). Light saw the Rockefeller Amendment as nullifying all of the OSM protections and accused Rockefeller himself of "becoming the coal industry's leading advocate of their protection." This certainly was a 180-degree turnaround from the Rockefeller who had originally supported the abolition of strip mining!

Zvegintzov reported that the amendment passed the Senate, along with other weakening amendments, 69–22, and was currently in the House. West Virginia Congressman Rahall was attempting to maneuver around the opposition of Interior Committee Chairman and bill author, Rep. Udall.

The following month, Rep. Udall wrote an op ed piece, "Rockefeller Amendment Would Gut Good Law," published in *The Charleston Gazette*. After reviewing the sham justification of states rights vs. federal control and his disappointment over the gutting of a bill that had taken six years and had overcome two presidential vetoes to survive, Udall made several observations on the future:

> Without the new law, these challenges [to each state's regulations], would be – in fact are now – before a single judge. With the new law, these challenges would go to district courts in each state. For years to come, we will then have innumerable judges making decisions on highly technical coal-mining issues on which they have little or no expertise, and without the aid of regulations that interpret the law.
>
> Sometime in the late 1980s all this confusion and conflict will have settled out and the coal industry will have a clear idea of just what are the rules of the game. But because judges from Virginia to Montana will have written differing reclamation plans, states that have upgraded their standards, like West Virginia, will be at a competitive disadvantage to other states that are less interested in good reclamation.

Udall's comments seem ironic, even optimistic, today, considering how many countless hours and thousands of dollars were ultimately spent in West Virginia over the next twenty-five years in an attempt to restore provisions of the federal Surface Mining Act that were gutted by the state. Much of the remainder of this chapter tells that story.

That same *Voice* issue, December 1979, announced one of the first massive mountaintop-removal projects in southern West Virginia. Covering parts of Logan and Mingo Counties, Paul Sheridan described the shear immensity of the Island Creek Coal Company project. Already four permits were issued totaling 2,423 acres, an additional 1,612 acres were pending, and ultimately 68,000 acres would be stripped over a twenty-five to thirty year period. Without any announcement to the residents who lived on or near these mines, the planning by the operators had involved large-scale purchases and staging of massive pieces of equipment. As plans became public, local citizens groups expressed worry about their water supplies, flood threats, and other impacts. Sheridan and fellow staff members at the Tug Valley Recovery Center in Williamson were attempting to coordinate among the citizens groups.

That month Zvegintzov announced his departure after five years as Washington Vice President for the Highlands Conservancy. In that time he had written more words for *The Highlands Voice* than anyone but the editor, had served as Conservancy Mining Committee Chairman, and had become one of the state's leading critics of strip mining on both the national and local levels.

In a February 1980 *Voice* tribute, titled "Farewell to Zvegintzov," Editor Dunham wrote:

> **Nicholas Zvegintzov** has resigned as the Conservancy's Washington Vice President and will relocate in New York City. His departure from the Board and from active participation in Conservancy affairs will leave the organization without one of its strongest voices for protection of West Virginia's natural environment. Nicholas served on the Board of Directors for eight years, and for most of that time, held the mining chairmanship. No one who attends Board meetings could mistake his presence and influence on the Board. I have known him for only three years, but while observing Board meetings and later while serving on the Board, I have always been amazed at how one who lives in Washington, D.C., can know so much about West Virginia's environmental problems.

Nicholas consistently came to Board meetings well prepared and delivered an excellent statement capped by a motion that he always seemed to get. His example is testimony to the adage that one who is prepared and handles himself well gets what he wants.

Nicholas took his vice-presidency duties seriously. Because of his efforts, the Conservancy was never in the dark regarding what an agency of the federal government was doing with an issue that affected West Virginia. From his Washington base, he put in countless hours lobbying for Conservancy interests. The past year he, along with Larry George, secured commitment from West Virginia Congressman Nick Joe Rahall that he would work for a Corps of Engineers study of the Big Sandy watershed in Mingo County. This study would determine future effects of mining, other land uses, and precipitation on the watershed.

Members will also recall Nicholas's hard work and eventual victory in the Duo case. Before Duo and before Zvegintzov, strip miners could deposit the barest details with the Department of Natural Resources when a permit application was filed. During the ensuing 30-day public comment period, a citizen could not see the complete mining and reclamation plan and was, therefore, prevented from making informed protest. As a test case, Nicholas chose a small strip mine near Duo in Greenbrier County. After shepherding the lawsuit for over two and one-half years, he was rewarded with a victory in July 1978 when the DNR Director agreed in writing to require that complete mining plans be filed prior to the public comment period.

Seeing it as a means of credibility, Nicholas also took the Conservancy's publication, the *Voice*, seriously. Past presidents may disagree when I say that no member has appreciated his help more than I as *Voice* Editor. When I assumed the editorship two years ago this past January, I expressed some apprehension to outgoing editor, Ron Hardway, over the matter of securing enough copy for each issue. Hardway assured me that Nicholas would come through each month with a sizable share. As *Voice* readers know, Hardway's confidence proved well founded. Each month Nicholas's copy arrived, the articles well researched, well written, and even well typed with layout suggestions. It is writers like Nicholas who make editors superfluous.

It can be said for all those who worked with him that Nicholas carried out his duties with tenacity, intelligence, and political skill and, in the process, winning many friends and earning a lot of respect. The Conservancy wishes him all the luck in the Big Apple.

With Zvegintzov's resignation, many Conservancy members certainly wondered who would fill his roles as Washington representative and mining activist?

The answers would come soon. Stark Biddle volunteered to accept Zvegintzov's vice presidency. An avid canoeist and hiker, he had tramped much of the highlands, and would provide continuity in Washington. Zvegintzov's particular interest in mining issues would find another successor or two.

Friends of the Little Kanawha

In the January 1980 *Voice*, Editor Tom Dunham wrote about strip mining in Upshur County, specifically on the Little Kanawha River watershed. The Holly Grove Coal Company, of Clarksburg, had planned to mine 184 acres near the community of Rock Cave. In response, a group of local residents formed the Friends of the Little Kanawha (FOLK). Because of their protest and the history of mining-caused acid pollution in that region, DNR Director David Callaghan then denied Holly Grove's permit. The company appealed to the now-familiar Reclamation Board of Review, which set a hearing in October 1979. With Charleston attorney Jim Humphreys, FOLK filed a petition to formally intervene. Three days before the hearing the company withdrew its appeal, but FOLK members expected a stronger permit application would be re-submitted in the future.

Dunham continued by quoting FOLK members Jim Weist and Paul Rank that the Little Kanawha was "lightly buffered" and acid seeps could permanently damage the river. The entire area was characterized by acid soils overlying the coal seams. Dunham continued:

> FOLK is a small local organization not opposed to strip mining in general, but to it when a community's water, transportation, recreation, peace and quiet, and health is threatened. Weist reports that in FOLK's talks with people up and down the watershed, it has become clear that the owner of Holly Grove, James LaRosa, along with his son, own the surface rights to over 50% of Upshur County. One wonders what a strip miner wants with all this land. Moreover, a special surface-mine task force made up of industry, DNR officials, and West Virginia

University personnel has been formed in an attempt to develop mining methods that can handle acid-producing overburden. In its nine months of existence, FOLK feels that it has come to know and fear that plans are being made for the extensive strip mining of central West Virginia.

That same month Rick Webb and the Braxton Environmental Action Program conducted a workshop on citizen involvement in water resources protection. An article discussing the workshop was the first of what would be hundreds, by Cindy Rank, identified as a member of FOLK.

Webb provided two articles for the March 1980 *Highlands Voice*. In the first he recounted the negotiations between the Braxton Environmental Action Program and the Brooks Run Coal Company, which controlled 23,000 acres in Braxton, Nicholas, and Webster counties. Beginning with a complex of six deep mines, the company expected to develop a large surface mine complex as well. BEAP had determined that construction of a preparation plant near Erbacon violated the Clean Water Act and filed notice to sue with EPA. Surprisingly, Brooks Run wanted to negotiate an agreement with BEAP.

Webb relied on a year of water-quality data collected by volunteers of Mountain Stream Monitors and projected that any acid would cause serious problems due to minimal alkalinity in the receiving streams. To address sediment control during pre- construction timbering and later activities, he reported Brooks Run was willing to hold its contractors to a stringent standard. EPA had become involved, and Webb was guardedly optimistic of a positive outcome.

In his second article, Webb criticized EPA for proposing an oversimplified method of issuing NPDES point-source permits for West Virginia coal mines. Unable to adequately process the two hundred permit applications per year, EPA had produced river basin maps with color-coded areas indicating the degree of potential pollution from new mines. Already the Monongahela and Gauley basin maps had been issued. The Highlands Conservancy and at least four other groups had testified to the inadequacy of the maps.

Webb believed that under the National Environmental Policy Act, EPA must assess the cumulative impacts of mining, not just issue permits for the period of active mining operations. The history of West Virginia, where acid mine drainage was the state's number one water pollution problem, showed that post-mining drainage was often worse. Any methods for water treatment were often abandoned when the company ceased mining, causing a permanent degradation of stream quality. Webb concluded:

> While EPA may be justified in attempting to speed-up its permit process, EPA is not justified in making permit decisions on the basis of inadequate or inaccurate information. The national emphasis on coal does not authorize EPA to abdicate its responsibilities under the National Environmental Policy Act and the Clean Water Act.

On March 25, 1980, Governor Rockefeller signed the new state surface mine law. Because the state law was demonstrably weaker than its federal counterpart, the Conservancy and other environmental groups announced plans to seek federal takeover (primacy) unless the state law was strengthened.

At a hearing in United States District Court in April, Friends of the Little Kanawha won a sixty-day stoppage against the Holly Grove Coal Company, to give EPA a chance to assess the need for a full-scale EIS on the headwaters of the Little Kanawha. The Court accepted FOLK's claim that the watershed's inability to absorb even minimal acid discharges without total destruction of water quality justified EPA's review. A plea for financial support of FOLK was signed by Cindy Rank, FOLK Secretary.

The Libel Suit

At the July 1980 Conservancy Board meeting, mining issues dominated the agenda. Mining Chairman David Wooley reported on the inadequacies of the state's regulations and outlined OSM's process for review, including a period for the state to meet any deficiencies. The Conservancy had joined a coalition in petitioning OSM to declare Shavers Fork "unsuitable" for mining under Section 522 (see Chapter 3). Webb gave an update on BEAP and Mountain Stream Monitors. While MSM awaited word on an extension of their EPA grant, the Board voted to lend them funds to continue operations for a month.

Almost as an aside, Webb reported one mining company had filed a libel suit against him and the two organizations. And finally, the Conservancy had recently appealed to the Reclamation Board the issuance of a permit just north of Bear Rocks and Dolly Sods. Among other arguments was that a proposed haul road in northern Canaan Valley would potentially jeopardize land for the proposed national wildlife refuge. It certainly seemed that mining issues were becoming more dominant.

In the August *Voice*, a short article reported on a FOLK victory:

> The Environmental Protection Agency has decided to prepare an Environmental Impact Statement on the proposed coal mining operations on the Little Kanawha River. This decision was made after Friends of Little Kanawha (FOLK) and other environmental groups sued EPA in U.S. District Court for failing to carry out their legal obligations under the Clean Water Act. This EIS marks the first time that EPA has agreed to write an EIS on an entire watershed in which several coal mines are proposed. An initial meeting was held July 24 in Buckhannon to discuss the EIS and solicit public comments. Approximately 200 persons attended and testimony was evenly divided between those favoring the EIS and those opposed.

While EPA was preparing the EIS, expected to take eighteen months, FOLK was gathering baseline data at twenty-four sites. One tributary, Fallen Timber Run, suffered from strip mining in the 1970s and required further reclamation. In an ominous statement, the unnamed author (probably Webb) wrote, "Fallen Timber Run seems to require perpetual treatment to maintain acceptable water quality. Such treatment is a costly and totally undesirable way to achieve the water quality goals of the Clean Water Act." Environmental activists, indeed state officials, would come to understand more about "perpetual treatment" as the nation maximized its dependence on coal as an energy source.

An article in September 1980 gave more details on the libel suit as reported to the Conservancy Board:

> A law suit, filed by DLM Coal Corporation in Upshur County, alleges that Rick Webb, Mountain Stream Monitors (a project of WV-CAG), and Braxton Environmental Action Program, engaged in libelous and defamatory actions in publishing a newsletter that stated that seven miles of the Buckhannon River had been destroyed by strip mining activities. In addition, the suit charges the groups provided federal regulatory authorities with false and defamatory information which damaged the corporation. The company seeks $100,000 in compensatory damages and $100,000 in punitive damages.

Webb's defense was simple: the information provided was true. "There's no question that this company has polluted trout streams in that area of the Buckhannon River," he commented. "We plan to fight this suit to prove to the West Virginia public that the problem does exist, and to protect the public's right to speak out," he added.

There was a tremendous appeal to the idea that local residents could get training, could borrow equipment and test their own watershed for pollutants. That such activity, funded by the federal government, might subject the citizens to a lawsuit seemed outrageous. Could presentation of testimony, or even just attendance at one of the numerous public hearings, make a citizen liable for damages to coal companies? It would not take long to find out.

The West Virginia Supreme Court ruled 5-0 to bar additional action in Upshur Circuit Court against Webb, Braxton Environmental Action Programs, and Mountain Stream Monitors, whom DLM Coal Co. named in the libel suit. Defense attorney Gene R. Nichols said his clients had an absolute right to communicate privately with any federal agency and that the written work is assured by the right of free speech. The lawyer alluded to the libel suit as a "smokescreen" and said it was used by DLM to get all sources of data that Webb had and all names of persons in concert with him.

Attorney David Grubb told the Supreme Court that Webb's communications with federal agencies were deemed "absolute privilege" under the First Amendment. "This is an infringement on the right to petition government," Grubb said. "These things are covered by the First Amendment," he stated, and added, "The purpose of absolute privilege is to prevent lawsuits like this."

Upshur County Judge Fury had denied a motion for change of venue, prompting the appeal to the Supreme Court. The case would be known as Webb v. Fury.

The DLM libel suit continued to make the news. The West Virginia Wildlife Federation, together with its parent body, the National Wildlife Federation, filed a "friend of the court" brief in support of Webb and the two organizations. Already, the American Civil Liberties Union, the Natural Resources Defense Council, and the Center for the Law and Social Policy had offered help. The West Virginia Supreme Court hearing was set for January 13.

Grubb expressed confidence following the hearing. Also representing Webb's First Amendment rights was the prestigious Washington, D.C. law firm of Wilmer and Pickering, as well as the U.S. Department of Justice. *The New York Times* reporter Ben Franklin had called the issues "far-reaching." DLM was now blaming Webb's communications with EPA for the required EIS on mining in the Buckhannon River watershed.

"The Problems of Coal, the Supreme Court and Environmentalism," in the August 2001 *Highlands Voice*, told Webb's story. Called "West Virginia's premier environmental activist," he had simply, maybe naively, believed that "the laws ought to apply to the coal companies, too." Because of the DLM libel suit against him, the nation's attention had converged on the modern-day problems of Appalachian coal mining. Because of sympathetic coverage in *The New York Times*, on Charles Kuralt's "CBS Sunday Morning," and ABC's "Nightline," the coal companies were shown in a negative light. And although the publicity helped alert the nation to these issues, Webb felt that the purpose of the suit, to have a "chilling effect" on the exercise of his rights, was partially achieved because of the massive time required to prepare for his court case. He believed many others were similarly silenced.

Ultimately, the West Virginia Supreme Court upheld his First Amendment rights, but at what price? "It can pretty well wipe you out if you have to go to court," Webb explained, adding, especially if the person sued has to pay his own legal costs. Luckily he had received offers of legal assistance from the nation's topmost attorneys. The article continued:

> The tenor of submerged rage that infuses Webb's flurries of information — that welter of facts and figures that have become his trademark as in federal and state regulatory circles — that tenor still comes through when people ask him how he feels about "winning" the libel suit. As he told Robin Toner, a reporter for the *Charleston Daily Mail* who was writing a piece on Webb for the Sunday edition of *The New York Times*: "What I tell people when they ask that, is that nothing has changed." That, if anything, is the "message" Webb has: Strip mining of the Buckhannon River's watershed — once one of the purest and most pristine in the state and the East — is still continuing in violation of federal and state laws.

DLM was also extending its operations, as well as Brooks Run Coal Company, who would be mining directly under Webb's mountain. Webb reflected on his struggle:

> He says he saw it coming a long time ago, and, in fact, his prescience was the reason for becoming involved in the first place.
> We came back here to find a farm I could afford, to find a lifestyle that wasn't such a struggle with the rest of humanity." He speaks fondly

of his grapes, his blueberries and raspberries, all sending their roots into the deep, loamy soil of his mountaintop. "The place has a lot of potential…It's my lifetime's investment," he remarks. When he observed the operations in neighboring Upshur County, atop the same seam that underlies his own farm, he decided that "if the law is not applied here, it won't be applied anywhere."

The problem, he says, is that "nothing ever happens unless somebody sticks his neck out." DLM's hatchet-like libel suit forced a lot of people who might have stuck their neck out in protest to pull it back again. For those who did protest, "it did no good…Legal action," he says, "is the only thing that works."

"They don't deny permits," he explains. "We've got a coal economy, and trying to regulate the industry — well, they've got more power than you realize."

Webb credited DNR fish biologist and long-time Conservancy member Don Gasper with providing much of the water quality data that DLM and others found so threatening. At one point Brooks Run even flew Webb to Roanoke in their corporate jet for a forty-five-minute meeting. Despite many attempts to gather data and work with mining companies and state officials, Webb said his victory was in establishing a citizen's right to participate in the "free exchange of ideas," in other words "to stick his neck out."

The State Supreme Court's thirty-three-page opinion, written by Justice Darrell McGraw, had put it differently:

> We shudder to think of the chill our ruling would have on the exercise of First Amendment rights were we to allow this lawsuit to proceed. The cost to society in terms (of the) threat to our liberty and freedom is beyond calculation. This cost would be especially high were we to prohibit the free exchange of ideas on such pressing social matters as surface mining. Surface mining, and energy development generally, are matters of great public concern. Competing social and economic interests are at stake. To prohibit robust debate on these questions would deprive society of the benefit of its collective thinking and, in the process, destroy the free exchange of ideas which is the adhesive of our democracy. Our democratic system is designed to do the will of the people, and when the people cannot express their will, the system fails. It is exactly this type of debate which the First Amendment protects; debate intended to increase our knowledge, to illustrate our differences and to harmonize those differences in order to form a more perfect union.

Webb had surely won a victory for all environmentalists, but he had also paid a dear price. He was tired.

As 1981 began, the new Reagan Administration clearly differed from the Carter Administration in its view of the environment. James Watt was Secretary of Interior, to which the Office of Surface Mining reported, and OSM was considering the Conservancy's petition to set aside Shavers Fork as a land "unsuitable for mining." Watt was well known to the Conservancy for his role in licensing the Davis Power Project. *The Wall Street Journal* was reporting that the administration was relaxing requirements on mineral leasing in wilderness or potential wilderness areas, a serious concern in West Virginia. And the Monongahela National Forest had just opened another planning process. (See Chapters 3, 5, & 6.) To say that the environmental community was worried on many fronts would be an understatement.

Back in October 1980 Scottie Roberts Weist, of Rock Cave, had reviewed the EPA process developed for the EIS on the Little Kanawha. EPA had assembled a carefully balanced advisory committee, including members of FOLK, but also politicians and coal company representatives, to represent the community. Publications of the West Virginia Surface Mining Association were presenting the issue as state authority vs. federal intervention.

Because it was October in an election year, Weist wrote, "Whoever is in power will be making, re-making, or un-making laws which give the environment a chance. It is an important year to study the issues, the men running, and get out to vote!"

Cindy Rank, of FOLK, wrote that the draft of the first phase of the Little Kanawha EIS would be delayed another sixty days. "EPA is unable to make a decision at this time 'due to the national issues involved and the changing administration.'" Although the technical data appeared complete, Rank and other FOLK members were obviously nervous. They were "fearful that a decision will be based on these pressures rather than the scientific assessment of the area's potential to produce toxic acid mine drainage." It brought to mind Weist's comment the previous fall about those in power.

An ominous front-page *Voice* photo in May 1981 showed Charles Miller, head of the Holly Grove Coal Company, pointing out "experimental mining techniques" to Governor Rockefeller and DNR Director Callaghan. The caption continued: "The trio are viewing one of the first demonstrations of a new strip mining technique in which hazardous [acidic] overburden is packed between layers of alkaline material and the whole 'sandwich' suspended several feet off the floor of the strip pit before it is backfilled."

After several months of delay, during which Holly Grove was presumably preparing its rebuttal to a critical EIS written by EPA, a long *Voice* article in July 1981 indicated the high level of frustration of the Citizens Advisory Committee. Originally appointed by EPA and chaired by Kathy Gregg, a Sierra Club leader, the committee said it was "confused, frustrated, and angered by the prolonged delay in the decision…and the committee hopes for action and decisions that will restore its waning confidence in the federal EPA." Gregg told a reporter EPA had denied the Committee consultant reports and draft decision documents.

Meanwhile, Secretary Watt was bent on weakening the 1977 Surface Mine Act. The U.S. Supreme Court had only recently upheld the constitutionality of the Act, but Watt and the Reagan Administration wanted to delegate significantly more power to the individual states. As states proposed weakening regulations, Watt was approving them. The DNR's Callaghan was quoted as saying, "I think it will, in the long run, be an advantage to West Virginia's industry." In line with Reagan's anti-regulatory philosophy, the single national approach to strip mine regulation that environmentalists had fought for during the 1970s was being dismantled and returned to the states where industry money had undue influence.

By August new developments were emerging. Island Creek's expanding complex in Upshur County, labeled the largest strip mine east of the Mississippi, was in trouble. DNR Director Callaghan had informed the company that no further permits would be forthcoming "until effective methods of reclamation are developed." Continued Callaghan: "It's not a discretionary matter. If it can't be reclaimed, it can't be mined." Past mining had led to long-term water degradation, he said. He also discouraged other companies interested in the same region of Lower Kittanning coal, including DLM and Holly Grove. Island Creek had already made significant investment in their mining complex, including a massive preparation plant and seven miles of railroad to Buckhannon. Island Creek had 40,000 acres under lease, employed three hundred and was stripping about twenty acres a month. Most of the coal was shipped to Romania. Because of continued acid discharges, even where the reclamation was well done, it was now called "the Lower Kittanning anomaly."

In September the *Voice* reported on the EIS for the upper Little Kanawha. EPA, recognizing the potential for acid discharge, nonetheless issued a permit to Holly Grove Coal Company to mine 251 acres. In light of the expected pollution, EPA recommended the company pay fifteen to fifty cents a ton to treat the expected acid-mine drainage. A public hearing on the full draft EIS was scheduled in Buckhannon in October. Even under the very latest and best available techniques, EPA determined that acid mine drainage would result from mining in the Lower Kittanning coal seam.

In October the West Virginia Rivers Coalition tried a different approach. It filed a petition to declare all of the Buckhannon and Middle Fork watersheds in Upshur and Randolph counties as "areas unsuitable for mining." Similar to the unsuccessful attempt by the Conservancy on Shavers Fork, the Coalition petition would be adjacent to, but exclude the Little Kanawha watershed. Rather than petitioning the ever-weakening federal Office of Surface Mining, the Coalition relied on current, but unused, state law. The Reclamation Commission would have ten months to evaluate the petition, during which no new permits could be issued. The Coalition recognized that Callaghan had already promised Island Creek no new permits until adequate reclamation was completed. Ironically, the spokesman for the Coalition was Rick Webb.

More than three hundred people packed the West Virginia Wesleyan College student union in mid-October to comment on the Holly Grove EIS. At the hearing it was confirmed that the 251-acre application was but the first in a massive development in concert with the Consolidation Coal Company. CONSOL saw this area as "one of the last, untapped, strippable coal lodes in West Virginia." The pro-mining attendees, many wearing hard hats, cheered their spokesmen and heckled the citizen-environmentalists.

The response to EPA's recommendation of a bond to treat potential acid mine drainage was "universally negative." The coal companies believed EPA's assessment was based on incorrect data and mining history. The environmentalists wanted the permit denied. The chair of the Public Participation Committee, Kathy Gregg, reported that the committee unanimously agreed that EPA's conclusions "must have been based on information which has not been made public." Recalling that EPA established the committee to "foster a spirit of openness and mutual trust among the EPA and the public," the committee said it was precisely what

EPA had failed to do. With no appeals, mining could begin in late spring 1982. With appeals, it was anyone's guess.

In a footnote to the Webb saga, the *Voice* reported that the state Water Resources Board had heard his appeal of a water discharge permit from Brooks Run Coal Company. In an effort to satisfy him, Brooks Run's attorney said the mining plans had been altered specifically to avoid mining under his farm.

In December a front-page photo in the *Voice* showed DLM covering fifty-five acres with a heavy plastic to prevent rainwater from infiltrating the soil and adding to the acid drainage. Clearly hoping to avoid a DNR ruling sustaining the Rivers Coalition petition, DLM, CONSOL and other companies were definitely taking the petition seriously. The hard-hat wearing, foot-stomping, anti-environmentalists were being organized for the upcoming public hearing later in December. The article said, "Miners have threatened to line up enough speakers to see that the hearing will last at least three days, and to loudly jeer anyone who op-poses their position."

Citing almost entirely conclusions previously drawn by the Reclama-tion Board of Review, before which the petition was to be heard, the Coalition cited the now-widely quoted letter from Callaghan to Island Creek denying additional permits until reclamation was shown to be effective. Webb had been quietly, but methodically, collecting evidence, had assembled it in a new package and submitted it in the name of the Rivers Coalition.

It was an interesting Mid-Winter Workshop in mid-January 1982. Callaghan had accepted the Conservancy's invitation to address a variety of issues. No fewer than four different articles in the February *Voice* discussed Callaghan's visit at the Conservancy meeting or outlined issues between the Conservancy and Callaghan's department. Starting with the broad opinion that the "state's natural resources have never been managed better," he addressed specific issues of concern to Conservancy members. On mining, he asserted that West Virginia's regulatory program was the best in its history, but acknowledged additional improvements could be made. He contrasted the last ten years of regulation with the previous century. Now, lingering past problems like acid-mine drainage from abandoned mines, burning gob piles, and other problems would benefit from at least $40 million that state had committed. New environmental lawyers, increases in budgets and staff positions would make regulatory enforcement even stronger, Callaghan claimed.

A United Press International story reported the fate of the Rivers Coalition petition. Callaghan, the Reclamation Commission chair, and the other members had ruled that mining could continue, but recommended that the DNR carefully review new permits, monitor closely any operations allowed, and that "coal development not be accelerated" because of the acid-drainage potential. An additional permit of 150 acres was issued to Island Creek Coal Company, using new technology to prevent acid drainage. Callaghan said a declaration of "unsuitability for mining" might have been open to reversal because of a federal exemption if substantial legal and financial commitments had been made prior to 1977, the year of the federal law. On the positive side, Callaghan said, "We profited enormously from the exercise," adding that a wealth of information had been gathered that would be useful in the future. "It has caused us to look at the cumulative impact of mining," he added.

Callaghan announced the current permit for the Holly Grove Coal Company-proposed mine on the Little Kanawha was no longer valid and mining could not begin, even if EPA granted its permit. "Major changes and revisions" would be necessary, he said. He acknowledged published reports, still unconfirmed, that Holly Grove had been sold to CONSOL. When Holly Grove began its mining operation, FOLK had sued and the EPA had stopped all mining until its EIS was completed. That process had frozen most mining operations in several counties in central West Virginia.

Just as OSM offered "primacy," or state take-over, of strip mining regulations to the DNR's Reclamation Division, EPA offered primacy in water enforcement to its Water Resources Division. Cindy Rank wrote an analysis in a *Voice* article in March 1982.

Under the federal Clean Water Act, Rank wrote, states could assume EPA's water permit role, if the state program met federal requirements. In this way, permits could be coordinated within state government and the federal role would revert to one of oversight only. Naturally the industries that required National Pollution Discharge Elimination System (NPDES) permits favored state primacy, as the mining industry did with OSM. Under the state's proposal, the NPDES-delegated water permits for mining operations would be coordinated through the powerful Reclamation Division. Rank worried that permit review and enforcement would suffer under this arrangement. EPA would still retain its right to comment on individual permits if it wished and would review the delegation and coordination arrangements annually. Because no "federal action" occurred with a permit issuance, no EIS or other compliance with the National Environmental Policy Act would apply. The Conservancy had used these provisions on a variety of occasions and was troubled to lose their applicability. Asked Rank, "Are we about to do away with duplication of effort — or are we about to do away with an ailing-but-necessary system of checks and balances?"

Meanwhile, Rank presented her comments at the public hearing on the NPDES take-over. The memorandum of agreement between EPA and West Virginia was overly simple and she worried about the lack of detailed implementation plans. Referring to ongoing and long-standing conflict between the Reclamation and Water Resources divisions of the DNR, partially the result of unequal pay scales and differing levels of commitment to environmental protection, she stated, "EPA cannot afford to entrust NPDES to an agency unable to work out its internal differences. Nor can the residents of West Virginia afford such animosity in the regulatory agencies."

Webb wrote that Mountain Stream Monitors was urgently in need of $25,000 to continue training citizens across the state to test their local streams in at least fifteen communities. Only a month later, the *Voice* reported that Gulf Oil Company had chosen Webb as one of America's top twenty-one environmentalists of 1982. The honor, presented at a Washington, D.C. dinner, included a plaque and $500 honorarium. Gulf called the winners, "symbolic of the very best in our society, the unsung conservation heroes and heroines who set an example for all of us in their battle for a better and more livable environment." Gulf had assumed sponsorship the previous year from American Motors, which had started the program in 1953. (In 1976 Conservancy member Bill Bristor was also honored for his work on Shavers Fork. See Chapter 3.)

The West Virginia coal industry's newsletter, "Coal Bell," roundly criticized Gulf for its award to Webb. In a counter-measure, Conservancy Board member Bard Montgomery, announced a "Thanks Gulf Oil" campaign, requesting that conservationists write thank you notes to Gulf Oil headquarters, and personally praise Gulf's award to Webb when filling up at their local gas pump.

While watching local problems, the Conservancy continued to monitor the bigger picture as well. The September *Voice* reported on proposed changes in the regulations of the federal Office of Surface Mining. Under Interior Secretary Watt and the Reagan Administration, these changes were called "a calculated attempt to override our basic environmental policy and disregard long-term values in favor of short-term economic gain," by Webb.

John Purbaugh, Conservancy Mining Committee chairman, and later president, called the changes a "disaster" and filed comments on the Conservancy's behalf, focusing on the "unsuitable for mining" section of the law. OSM had prepared a draft environmental impact statement that Purbaugh called inadequate, noting that in West Virginia for example, 270,000 acres of mineral rights, including those under the Monongahela National Forest, were not even discussed in the EIS. To make matters worse, petitions for unsuitability, such as the Conservancy had filed for Shavers Fork, would now be limited to property owners and companies could modify permits after the close of the public comment period. Had someone in Washington been studying what the Conservancy had been doing for the past decade?

In October 1982 Rank wrote about the Little Kanawha, FOLK, and new threats. It had been a long process so far. First, in 1979 Holly Grove Coal had applied for a permit, been denied, appealed, withdrew, then reapplied in 1980. FOLK had sued EPA, OSM, and DNR, winning a settlement in which EPA would prepare an EIS before issuing a NPDES permit. Suddenly, in April 1982 Holly Grove withdrew both their NPDES and state permit applications. EPA responded by ruling that no further EIS work was necessary and, according to Rank, "put an end to Phase B and the original intent of the full EIS, which was to evaluate the cumulative impacts of mining in the Little Kanawha headwaters area as far as the Burnsville dam." In mid-1981 the LaRosa family sold their mineral rights to CONSOL, but retained the gas rights.

Now in 1982 gas drilling was going full-speed ahead along the Little Kanawha. Wide rough roads, timbering, and general construction were discharging sediment loads never permitted by mining companies. In addition deep mines were being proposed. Rank noted the irony that, of all the research and study for the EIS, no one expected deep mining to occur. The basic question addressed for Holly Grove, namely the impact of mining on water quality, was unanswered for deep mining. The history of mining in West Virginia was a legacy of often permanent acid mine drainage. And now the NPDES permit responsibility lay with the state and no longer the federal EPA. Rank concluded:

At stake in all this is the Little Kanawha, the surface and the groundwater reserves that feed it year-round and make it the high-quality stream that it is, and the lives of people who depend on these waters as an integral part of their existence.

As 1983 began, the Conservancy made several leadership changes. Larry George was elected president, Brian Farkas replaced Paul and Judy Frank as *Voice* editors, and Stark Biddle, Zvegintzov's successor as Washington Vice President, was replaced by Linda Winter a few months later.

The September 1983 *Voice* reported that Webb had moved to the University of Virginia to pursue graduate studies in environmental science, and Mining Chairman Purbaugh gave an update on DLM. DLM had made Webb and itself famous by threatening his First Amendment rights, but meanwhile had quietly been mining on the Buckhannon River. Now mostly reclaimed, Purbaugh reported twenty active water-treatment ponds had been built. Against the feared perpetual acid mine drainage treatment, the state held only $200,000 in bond money to cover it. Not far away, Island Creek was at work on a 35,000-acre surface mining complex, trying to learn any lessons from DLM. Various "experimental" techniques were being tried but final results could not be accurately predicted. Purbaugh continued:

> DNR's reputation is now on the line: If the combination of experimental techniques underway at Tenmile do not work better than the previous disaster at DLM, the mineability of billions of tons of Kittanning series coal in the Buckhannon and Middle Fork River watersheds will be jeopardized. DNR Director Callaghan expects results, of whatever kind, within a year to 18 months.

In April 1984 Purbaugh reviewed the permit consolidation that had occurred when the state had achieved primacy in both mining and water permits from the federal government. Now after a year in operation, the Conservancy's concerns seemed to have been well founded. The still-intense rivalry between the Reclamation and Water Resources divisions caught mining operators between conflicting requirements, field inspections and staff specialties. Both OSM and EPA were exercising their oversight function, and both had made substantial negative comments.

Omega Mining

Omega Mining Company had received a permit to open a drift mine in southern Monongalia County in the acid-producing Upper Freeport coal seam. A group of local citizens had filed an appeal to the state Water Resources Board. John McFerrin, a lawyer with the Appalachian Research and Defense Fund (APPALRED) in Charleston and later a Conservancy president and *Voice* editor, represented the citizens. Richard "Chico" diPretoro, a geology graduate student and future Conservancy Administrative Assistant, provided technical advice. The Reclamation Division had issued the mine permit, ignoring the likelihood of perpetual acid mine drainage. When the Water Resources staff had caught the oversight, they requested a higher bond to protect the state from future costs. The Governor's office had overridden their objection. Joan Sims, of the 4-H Road Community Association, was spokesperson for the group appealing the permit. The Conservancy's Board voted in May to contribute $350 to the legal costs, if the 4-H Road group raised another $1,000. Sims would also become a future Conservancy Board member.

The July 1984 *Highlands Voice* included several updates. Rank was appointed to a vacant Conservancy board seat (and remained in it in 2007). President Larry George wrote of Rank:

> Cindy has been a leader in Mountain Stream Monitors for many years and has specialized in surface mining and water quality issues, particularly acid mine drainage, as they affect central and northern West Virginia. Cindy has been a familiar face at the Legislature and at state and federal hearings on environmental regulations since 1977 when she began her work in this area. Some of Cindy's best work has included the 200-page report prepared by her on behalf of Trout Unlimited concerning sediment pollution problems at Snowshoe Ski resort in Pocahontas County. This report resulted in extensive news coverage of Snowshoe's disregard for any attempt to control construction-related soil erosion on its property and resulted in the appointment of a Special Prosecutor by Circuit Judge Lobban to prosecute Snowshoe officials for willful and wanton stream pollution.

Milton Zelermyer, the representative of Mountain Stream Monitors on the Conservancy's Board, reviewed MSM's history. From its start as an outgrowth of Braxton Environmental Action Program, MSM had received several grants, including from the Conservancy, and spread its water-sampling techniques into seven counties, including helping establish a pilot program in the Randolph County schools. Its early leader Rick Webb had moved away, but the group now boasted seventy members and had formally become incorporated in 1982. Its office was now in Morgantown.

In a July hearing before Circuit Judge Larry Starcher in Morgantown, the 4-H Road Community Association sought a temporary injunction against Omega to stop the construction of the up-dip mine. All parties wrestled with the changing regulations, first prohibiting up-dip and then exempting irregularly dipping. Omega might be either and no one would know until it was opened. OSM and DNR knew they wanted to prevent acid water discharges, but were inconsistent in their regulations. Meanwhile the community members were contesting a DNR Water Resources permit in a Charleston court.

At the October 1984 Fall Review, McFerrin was elected to a seat on the Board (still occupied in 2007), and became Mining Committee chairman as well. Tom Michael was re-elected Senior Vice President, and Larry George re-elected President. Along with Board members Ray Ratliff, Purbaugh, and Zelermyer, all six were lawyers, and most had or currently were representing the Highlands Conservancy.

Over the next several years, the Highlands Conservancy continued to maintain its two-pronged approach to mining issues. At the local level, it followed individual mining permit controversies, sometimes siding with local residents against abusive coal companies, at other times publicizing emerging issues that state and federal regulatory officials needed to address.

At the same time, the national and state policies on both deep and strip mining continued to evolve. Now that West Virginia had obtained primacy in mining and water regulation, the federal oversight agencies would only become involved in unusual circumstances. Several times a year Conservancy representatives would appear in Charleston, or even Washington, D.C., to present the Conservancy's testimony on the policies under review.

The DOE and Kenneth Faerber

With the return of Republican Arch Moore for his third term as governor in 1985, the West Virginia Legislature considered a massive re-organization of state government. The 702-page bill created a new Department of Energy, which would assume all mining-related duties of the DNR, the old Department of Mines, and Oil and Gas Division. The Water Resources Board and the Reclamation Board would be abolished, with their authority to set water quality standards transferred to the new Commissioner of Energy. Among many other details, civil service protection would be removed for surface and water resources inspectors and higher level officials. With so many controversial issues in play simultaneously, it was anyone's guess what the eventual outcome might be.

The House passed Moore's bill by a wide margin, but only after making significant changes. The Senate passed the Governor's original bill. When they went to a conference committee, the Senate strong-armed its bill through. In his President's column in April 1985 Conservancy President George wrote:

> I have little doubt that Thursday, April 11, 1985 will be remembered as the day West Virginia conservationists received their worst defeat in a decade — the day Gov. Moore's Energy bill passed the Legislature… This day will also be remembered for the consummation of a new progressive coalition between the United Mine Workers of America, West Virginia Citizens Action Group, House Speaker Joe Albright and his leadership team, and the Conservancy.

George expressed his hope that by the next year, the Conservancy, working with its new progressive partners, would succeed in modifying the new legislation. Other alternative strategies included court action and appeals to federal agencies to rescind primacy. The Conservancy had weathered eight years of the earlier Moore administration and was preparing for another siege of anti-environmental legislation.

At its May Board meeting, the Conservancy decided to challenge the Department of Energy bill. Joined by the West Virginia Citizens Action Group (WV-CAG) and Trout Unlimited, the Conservancy filed a formal request with the federal Office of Surface Mining, requesting review of the new legislation and until remedies were adopted, take-over strip mining enforcement itself. If the request was not addressed, the Conservancy indicated it would sue in federal court. Said Perry Bryant, the Conservancy's Vice President for State Affairs, "The DOE bill was so sloppily and hastily put together that we are likely to end up with no state surface mine program at all after July 11," referring to the repeal date of the old law. At risk from a fiscal viewpoint was $2 million annually in federal funding of the state's program. Ironically, Democratic Speaker of the House Joe Albright addressed the Conservancy's board meeting a day earlier, and called for cooperation with Republican Governor Moore. The energy bill conflict, which Albright called "an exercise in raw, naked power," was the exception. Both houses of the legislature, he hoped, would continue to work with Governor Moore.

Born in Atlanta, Georgia, **John McFerrin** actually grew up in Barbourville, Kentucky. His father was a librarian at Union College and his mother taught kindergarten. Although Barbourville was not in the center of the coalfields, it was still in eastern Kentucky, and it was obvious to John that coal dominated the regional economy. Coal trucks rumbled through town, and it was only a short drive away to strip mines in Kentucky, Virginia, and Tennessee.

McFerrin attended the University of Kentucky, majoring in English, and graduated in 1973. Duke Law School followed. John returned to Barbourville in 1976 to work with the Appalachian Research and Defense Fund of Kentucky, APPALRED of Kentucky, concentrating on a legal aid practice. In 1982 he switched to APPALRED of West Virginia, based in Charleston, where he became the in-house environmental attorney. From these two positions, it was already clear that McFerrin was not only interested in environmental protection, but in how environmental threats impacted individuals and small communities.

A fellow public interest lawyer, John Purbaugh, invited McFerrin to attend a Conservancy meeting. McFerrin had become aware of the Highlands Conservancy, and soon found it compatible with his values and interests. Within the Conservancy, McFerrin became Chair of the Mining Committee and was elected to the Board in 1984. He later served as Senior Vice President, before becoming President in 1994, serving two terms.

Having married in 1990, McFerrin moved to Beckley, where his wife, Karen, was a public defender. Thus McFerrin held the distinction of being the only Conservancy president from southern West Virginia.

Following Frank Young's election as President in 1998, McFerrin remained an influential Board member, serving as past president during Young's six years as president. When Hugh Rogers followed Young in 2004, McFerrin was elected secretary. Shortly thereafter he also became the editor of *The Highlands Voice*, the first editor to have come to that position as a past officer.

McFerrin was a representative of the Highlands Conservancy on many occasions over these years. He was a frequent guest columnist for *The Charleston Gazette*. But a significant opportunity occurred when Governor Cecil Underwood appointed McFerrin to his Mountaintop Mining Task Force. McFerrin knew he was the token environmentalist, but used the opportunity as a way of learning about the industry from the inside. Ultimately his Minority Report probably received more publicity than did the report of the Task Force itself.

McFerrin took leave in 2006 to deal with a serious health problem and he was able to return in 2007 to both his roles as secretary and *Voice* editor. As a writer, both positions seemed well suited for McFerrin, a thoughtful, compassionate, but quiet wordsmith whose contributions to West Virginia remained understated, but always effective.

The lead article in the August 1985 issue of *The Highlands Voice* was titled, "Secretary of Interior supercedes part of Energy bill." In July U.S. Secretary of Interior Donald Hodel issued his decision on the legislation creating the West Virginia Department of Energy and took the unusual action of superceding several provisions of the new law. The Secretary took this action after the Conservancy and other environmental groups filed a Notice of Intent to Sue in May calling upon the U.S. Office of Surface Mining to reject many of the changes in the existing state law imposed by the DOE bill.

Hodel had imposed special bonding and reclamation on the two-acre exemptions in the new law, asserted that OSM regulations on conflicts of interest applied to the commissioner and virtually all employees of the DOE, strengthened the restrictions against permits to persons with a previous record of violations, and voided some of the Commissioner's critical discretionary powers.

At its July Board meeting, Bryant called Hodel's ruling a victory for the Conservancy, but he urged continued opposition to Governor Moore's nomination of coal operator Kenneth Faerber as DOE Commissioner. Earlier that month, the Conservancy, WV-CAG and the League of Women Voters had filed for a court injunction to stop issuance of two-acre permits. Both the threat of severe environmental damage and procedural issues were cited in the court filing.

In October Conservancy members learned that the temporary injunction won by the Conservancy, prohibiting the two-acre exemption, was not being contested by the state. At least for 1985 the Conservancy could enjoy this small victory.

In an echo from the past, the October *Voice* reported the state would assume treatment of acid mine drainage on the DLM site in Upshur County. Governor Moore had announced in August that DLM would transfer more than $850,000 in assets to the state, in exchange for release of its environmental liability. As Webb had predicted, despite being sued for libel in saying so, DLM had found no permanent solutions to acid mine drainage. After several years of mining, DLM was reportedly spending $300,000 per year on treatment with no end in sight. Because this was not technically a bond forfeiture, DLM escaped the prohibition that would have followed and could apply for new permits elsewhere. The article expressed the environmentalists' concern that by allowing DLM to shed its liability, a dangerous precedent had been set. Another nearby company, Enoxy, with an even larger operation, might ask for similar accommodations.

The Floods of 1985

November 1985 would be remembered forever in West Virginia for its extensive flooding that killed more than fifty people and caused unprecedented havoc throughout the highlands. Massive damage to rivers, adjacent farmland, and communities characterized the branches of the Potomac, the Cheat, and the Greenbrier. (According to the December issue of *The Highlands Voice*, it also washed away the November issue somewhere between the printer in Glenville and the post office.)

OSM notified Department of Energy Acting Director Faerber on October 25 that he had ninety days to sell his ownership in companies that OSM determined constituted conflicts of interest. His major holding was the Green Mountain Company, a reclamation company that contracted with both private mining firms and the state. This conflict of interest had been widely publicized and was the subject of a Conservancy appeal to OSM and threatened lawsuit.

As the 1986 legislative session began, the Conservancy's agenda focused on the needed strengthening of the energy bill passed the year before. The Legislature would be considering the issues of conflicts of interest, political appointments, and the two-acre restrictions. George replaced Bryant as the Conservancy's Charleston lobbyist.

As Faerber began selling his interests in mining to comply with OSM requirements, he learned that he was in a second conflict. Under EPA rules, he would be ineligible to issue NPDES permits to mines for another two years and therefore could not assume that function from the DNR in the energy reorganization.

In March George reported "modest gains" at the Legislature. The pending Senate confirmation of Faerber was "receiving the most public attention in the conservation field this year." To avoid EPA's requirement that NPDES permit-issuing officials have no financial interest in a regulated industry within the previous two years, the DNR, not the DOE, was continuing to manage those permits. George had testified against Faerber before the Senate Confirmations Committee, the first ever opposition by the Conservancy to a gubernatorial appointment.

But the greatest surprise of the session was the refusal of the Moore administration to propose a package of energy bill corrections to satisfy OSM's criticisms. Although leaders of both houses and the press had called the 1985 act a debacle or worse, there was no explanation for Gov. Moore's inaction. DOE Commissioner Faerber was not confirmed until the last day of the session.

In May 1986 Judge Margaret Workman of the Kanawha County Circuit Court ruled that the two-acre exemption in the 1985 law was illegal. The Conservancy had challenged the exemption and obtained an injunction preventing implementation of the regulations until a decision on its merits. George hailed the decision as an important victory.

Enoxy

In August Purbaugh reported on the Enoxy Coal Company permits. Earlier applications to mine seven hundred acres in acid-prone Kittanning coal in the headwaters of the Buckhannon River had been protested by the Conservancy. EPA had agreed with the Conservancy and required in-stream treatment be relocated and acid treatment be further explained. Recently the DNR had re-issued its permits with new require-ments. A major acid release into a trout stream in July gave conservation-ists reason to worry.

In December 1986 the *Voice* reported that EPA had overruled the DNR's second attempt to issue a permit to Enoxy Coal. Meanwhile the West Virginia Supreme Court had overturned the DOE permit at the same site, in a case brought by a landowner. The Conservancy had opposed both DNR permits based on the failure of nearby mines, includ-ing DLM, to control acid mine drainage. After two tries by the state, EPA had assumed exclusive authority to issue any further permits. In an echo of the Conservancy's Duo case, the Supreme Court had invalidated the Enoxy DOE permit because it had been significantly revised after the close of the public comment period.

In the February 1987 *Voice*, Richard diPretoro discussed two proposals by Enoxy. "The future of the mining operation on one hand, and of the receiving rivers on the other hand, hangs in the balance," he said. One proposal was a 500-acre extension of mining on Right Fork of Tenmile Creek, toward the DLM site, and the other a centralized acid mine drainage treatment impoundment. Both would mine the infamous Kittanning coal seam. The new mining would affect the last unaffected tributary of Right Fork. Said diPretoro, "Every previously healthy tributary mined so far by Enoxy or DLM has had its ability to support native brook trout reproduction destroyed and there is no reason to suppose that the latest proposed operation would be any different."

The instream impoundment was the result of a negotiated consent order between DNR and Enoxy over Enoxy's repeated treatment failures. Unfortunately, such structures were prohibited by law, diPretoro asserted. The acidic pollution from Tenmile eventually would affect the Buckhannon River, ultimately Tygart Lake and on downstream toward Pennsylvania. "So the question of allowing more acid sources to be created on a remote tributary of the Buckhannon River in Upshur County has regional significance and economic implications far beyond the maintenance of a single mine for a few more years," diPretoro concluded.

The following month, diPretoro announced the formation of the Buckhannon-Tygart River Coalition to inform the public about the values of, and threats to, the Buckhannon-Tygart River system. Continued mining of Kittanning coal in Upshur County posed the major threat and had motivated at least six organizations to form the coalition. They included the Highlands Conservancy, the West Virginia Wildlife Federation, Mountain Stream Monitors, Sierra Club, Friends of the Little Kanawha, and Trout Unlimited. The new application from Enoxy for five hundred acres was of immediate concern. Already the coalition had presented testimony to the DOE in opposition to Enoxy's proposal, citing previous statements of the DOE and EPA. Now that EPA had retained permit authority, the coalition wanted a full environmental impact statement addressing the cumulative impacts of mining.

If the reader is getting weary, imagine how the local residents and, even the mining companies, felt. The regulatory process was time-consuming at the least, especially when proposals involved fragile ecosystems where only a small acid discharge would kill a stream's living creatures.

In May the *Voice* updated mining issues. First, the West Virginia Supreme Court had ruled against the 4-H Road Community Association. Omega Mining was not required to post an unusually high bond to cover post-mining discharges. That would be considered only after mining was completed. The Conservancy and 4-H Road group had suggested the best time was before mining began. Second, the Buckhannon-Tygart Coalition filed an appeal with the Reclamation Board of Review appealing the permit for Enoxy's in-stream treatment facility.

In October 1987, the Conservancy celebrated its twentieth anniversary at the Cass Scenic Railroad State Park. That same year was the tenth anniversary of the federal Surface Mining Control Act of 1977. Conservancy President Purbaugh prepared testimony for the House Interior Committee, reflecting on how the act had impacted West Virginia. Purbaugh focused on acid mine drainage and central West Virginia. From Holly Grove, DLM, Island Creek, and now Enoxy, the Conservancy's volunteers had seen and heard it all. Along the way numerous administrative and judicial appeals to DNR, DOE, EPA, OSM had consumed incredible hours of time and considerable cost. In the end, perpetual treatment by the state seemed to be the result with bonds that were too insufficient to cover treatment costs. The West Virginia taxpayer ended up paying the bill. Purbaugh urged the committee to consider this issue in its legislative revisions.

As if to punctuate his comments, a massive fish kill occurred on the Tygart River. Acid mine drainage was the suspected cause.

The Laurita Case

The criticism of the federal surface mine regulators had reached a new level. According to a *Charleston Gazette* article of February 27, 1988, both Rep. Udall and Rep. Rahall were highly critical of OSM under the Reagan administration. Udall complained that alert citizens and Congress, not OSM or state inspectors, had discovered most of the problems. He singled out misspending of Abandoned Mine Lands (AML) funds for inappropriate and wasteful items, not for cleaning up lands scarred by mining.

Conservancy member Sims complained to Rahall that a prominent strip mining company in the Morgantown area had been issued a permit despite outstanding violations in Pennsylvania. The Conservancy had agreed to help Sims appeal that permit because of its policy implications.

The 4-H Road Community Association and the Conservancy had filed suit in U.S. District Court in Clarksburg against the state DOE and OSM, seeking to have the permit issued to Mepco Mining Company revoked. Morgantown attorney Tom Rodd represented the plaintiffs. James Laurita, Sr., had first applied under the name Stone King Mining, but failed to list 290 violations his three companies had received in Pennsylvania. Under threat of a lawsuit, he withdrew his application and his son, James Laurita, Jr., filed under his corporate name, Mepco. A recent OSM investigation showed that both Lauritas worked together, hence neither were eligible for a permit until all violations were resolved.

Sims commented on the significance of this case:

> The federal court case will address the serious and widespread coal-mining problems that result when a permit-blocked coal mining operator has a friend or relative apply for a permit for him that he himself is unable to obtain. This situation certainly undermines the intent of the Federal Surface Mining Act.

Sims told Rahall, "We have to spend our time and our money to protect our community because DOE won't do its job."

Conservancy President Purbaugh reviewed the now-lengthy history of the Highlands Conservancy, both addressing policy issues and attempting to respond to communities searching for help. He particularly emphasized how a relatively strong state program had been replaced by a federally driven one and then weakened by the creation of the state Department of Energy, whose stated mission was to promote the coal industry, not regulate it. Inspections were reduced, fines often minimized, and permits issued without adequate review.

Sims reported that James Laurita, Jr., had withdrawn the Mepco permit application that her group and the Conservancy sought to have revoked. The July court case against state and federal agencies would continue to resolve related issues. In another court case, Kanawha County Circuit Judge Andrew McQueen had approved a consent order settling the Conservancy's suit against the state for failing to issue itself a permit when it took over the DLM treatment system three years earlier. Conservancy Board member Rank commented, "Hopefully this gives us some reassurance that these agencies will be there treating acid mine drainage for as long as necessary." The order required that DNR and

DOE "operate a treatment works for all wastes discharged or emanating from the former DLM property...for so long as such wastes cause or might cause or contribute to pollution." Purbaugh said he'd be surprised if treatment could be ended in his lifetime.

In July *The Charleston Gazette* updated the DLM perpetual acid treatment story. Soon the DOE would have spent more than $1 million in the three years since the state assumed DLM's responsibilities. Using funding from the state Special Reclamation Fund, most of the money went to purchase chemicals to neutralize the water.

On September 16, 1988, eight state and national organizations notified the West Virginia DOE and the federal OSM of their intention to sue over DOE's failure to perform mandatory duties in virtually all aspects of its programs. Purbaugh said that this was the "inevitable next step" in the Conservancy's four-year battle to force adequate strip mine enforcement. A long list of failures were cited, including lack of inspectors, low fines for violations, and inadequate checking of past violations of applicants, among others. A spokesman for Washington's Environmental Policy Institute said, "We believe West Virginia is now running the worst regulatory program in the nation." Under federal law, citizens could petition OSM to conduct a formal review of West Virginia's program and the Conservancy and its partners demanded just that.

New Leadership

As 1989 began, change was in the air. The Conservancy had a new president, Cindy Rank, the state had a new governor, Gaston Caperton, and the country a new president, George H.W. Bush. More changes were inevitable and there would also be some surprises.

In her first column, "From the Heart of the Mountains," in the January 1989 *Highlands Voice* Rank introduced herself:

> My husband, Paul, and I moved here [southern Upshur County] from Pittsburgh in the early '70s...We bought property in December 1971 and, with the help of several equally inexperienced friends, built the first part of our present home, and moved to the hills in May of 1973.
>
> We left behind a life of chaos and convenience to explore a world we hoped would be more simple, though a bit more rugged, one that might keep us in touch with some of the more essential values of our own lives and the life of the earth and those around us.

The relatively rugged and labor intensive aspects of our chosen lifestyle remain, and do tend to keep us centered on some of our basic loves and joys, but the chaos has returned with a vengeance.

The chaos in part comes from the stark realization that the demands and challenges of society are no less imposing in the hills than they were in the city. They're just different. The thoughtlessness and the greed that threaten to destroy human dignity and the earth we live in are not the private property of the concrete portions of our society.

This realization began only a few short years after we arrived in Canaan …feeling our house shake as core drilling trucks rumbled by and as seismographic survey trucks set off charges in search of coal, oil, and gas reserves; hearing the thunder of a power company helicopter as it invaded our air space totally unannounced to spray noxious-smelling chemicals on our newly cut power line; watching local gas drilling companies tear apart our roads in the winter and poorly construct access roads and pits which spill mud and other wastes onto our roads and streams each time it rains; tasting the awful salt- and metal-laden water at a neighbor's home which is located below a Department of Highways garage and salt-storage pile, have made us painfully aware that in order to enjoy the life and land we love (and certainly in order to preserve it for future generations) we must also be actively involved in watchdogging the activities which directly affect our own property and the world around us. To believe otherwise is folly.

Rank's story sounded strangely familiar. In earlier chapters, similar stories of Hugh and Ruth Blackwell Rogers, fighting against Corridor H; or Dave and Linda Cooper Elkinton, struggling to save Canaan Valley; and, in this chapter, Rick Webb and Joan Sims and their tenacious efforts to force government to protect their communities. All these personal experiences illustrated the threats, often surprising local residents, that faced literally thousands of West Virginians. The Conservancy had frequently come to the aid of such people and often found its future leaders among those it helped.

The first surprise was when Governor Caperton appointed Conservancy Past President Larry George as Deputy Director of the state Department of Natural Resources. In his new position, George would be responsible for policy development and state and federal legislation in environmental and resource conservation programs.

He was well qualified as both a conservationist and as a former state official. George had served as Conservancy President 1983–1986, represented the Conservancy before congressional and legislative committees, and been particularly active in support of the Cranberry Wilderness bill in 1982 and the federal West Virginia Rivers Act in 1988. Governor Rockefeller had appointed him to the state Water Resources Board, where he served from 1978–1982. He was both a civil engineer and a lawyer. Purbaugh, himself a lawyer and the immediate past president of the Conservancy, appreciated these twin qualifications, and stated, "Larry's background as both engineer and lawyer serve as good preparation for his new job. Too often, agency administrators are fluent in either the science or the law and politics of the field, but are unable to combine the two into coherent policy, as Larry can."

Within a month of taking office, the new Caperton Administration had shown things really were different. K&B Coal Company applied for a permit to mine the Kittanning and Stockton coal seams in the trout-supporting headwaters of the Holly River and Rank had represented the Conservancy at the public hearing. When the new DOE Director subsequently issued the permit, it prohibited mining of Kittanning coal, "due to the potential acid mine drainage problems associated with mining in this location."

Rank was cautiously optimistic. "It's a step in the right direction," she said, "a first step toward official recognition of the acid problem associated with mining the Kittanning coals in the north-central part of the State, a problem which has plagued the Buckhannon River for the past 10 years." She called the commissioner's decision "courageous."

Maybe all the years of work by Rank, Webb, diPretoro, and others had finally been appreciated. Or maybe the state was just afraid of another million-dollar treatment bill.

Yet, if progress was coming in West Virginia, the tide was going the other way in Washington. OSM was holding a series of regional hearings on a list of weakening amendments to the Surface Mine Control and Reclamation Act. Its proposal, written in the final days of Secretary of Interior Watt, would permit mining in parks, wilderness areas, wildlife refuges and near residential neighborhoods — all banned under the 1977 Act. At the nearest hearing to West Virginia, held in Knoxville, Tennessee, more than three hundred citizens attended. McFerrin, Chairman of the Conservancy's Mining Committee, wrote:

> In West Virginia such an action would be more than just illegal. It would be a disaster. Much of the coal was severed from the surface estate in the early part of the twentieth century. Since then, owners of

the surface have used that surface to build houses, schools, parks, etc. Under proposed Option 1, owners of the coal could mine right up to houses, schools, cemeteries, etc. Allowing that to happen is a long step backward toward the old days when mining companies could trample on people with impunity.

Later when Skip Deegans, Conservancy Vice President for Federal Affairs, reported that the Department of Interior had withdrawn the proposed rule, he said more than 4,700 individual public comments — a record — had been received before new Interior Secretary Manuel Lujan withdrew the plan. It was estimated that more than fifty million acres were at risk in the proposal. "All citizens involved in protecting these critical areas can claim a well-earned victory," said Deegans, a Mining Specialist with the National Wildlife Federation.

In July a new pro-active program called "Living Streams" was announced to address the problem of acid mine drainage in north central and central West Virginia. According to Jenni Vincent and Linda Cooper Elkinton, both Conservancy board members, Living Streams was developed by Mountain Stream Monitors and would empower local groups through provision of technical expertise and legal support. Citing the many examples of communities that had already sought help from the Conservancy, Trout Unlimited, or Mountain Stream Monitors, they hoped Living Streams would meet this growing need. Tom Rodd and diPretoro, both Conservancy veterans, were prime movers of this new effort.

Rodd explained:

More and more individuals and small community groups are being forced to take action to protect the streams that traverse their property or community. The technical and legal issues involved in each individual case are nearly always identical, and these ad-hoc stream fights are very important. But one stream at a time is a difficult way to deal with this problem, and not the most effective way. A broader-based approach is needed.

diPretoro added:

With pre-mining analysis of rocks above and below the coal seams and other tests, we can now, with very high levels of confidence, predict which sites will be acid-producing, and we must, most aggressively, apply this knowledge to prevent the damage acid-mine drainage is causing.

At its summer meeting, the Conservancy Board discussed details of a pending settlement with the state DOE and the federal OSM in the Conservancy's suit. Termed "months of grueling negotiations," the slow pace over weeks and months "did not represent steady and developing understanding and agreements but a frenetic series of changes by the hour." President Rank cautioned against interpreting it as a victory.

On July 17, 1989, an agreement was signed resolving issues brought by the Conservancy and the now-fourteen other groups in December, charging the DOE with failing to perform its duties, resulting in a breakdown of strip mine enforcement. Most of the issues had been settled and those still in dispute were subject of a timetable for their resolution. Rank specifically thanked Tom Galloway, Jim Lyon, and Josh Barrett, all lawyers who had invested huge amounts of their time over the past eight months. She added that ultimately "changes on the ground" would prove the effectiveness of the settlement.

In a *Charleston Gazette* article of March 30, 1990, Paul Nyden wrote that twenty Monongalia County residents had sued Omega Mining Company and the state Division of Energy, alleging stream pollution from Omega's underground mine. Morgantown lawyer Rodd wanted Omega to post a $1 million bond to guarantee treatment of acid discharges for the next hundred years and $10 million in punitive damages. He cited the fact that Sims and the 4-H Road Community Association had protested the mine seven years earlier, but Omega had promised no long-term pollution. In 1989 even OSM had issued a cessation order to Omega and criticized DOE inspectors for lax enforcement. Remembering the DLM transfer of liability to the state, and the excessive costs for treatment, the suit sought damages from Omega. Rodd called the suit a first of its kind, and added, "We're not seeking damages for past pollution. We want companies to set aside enough money for future treatment when they mine acid seams of coal…We're trying to save the taxpayers the millions of dollars it will cost to treat this problem." It had been a long seven years, but now the post-mining costs, disallowed in the original permit appeal, were front-and-center.

Meanwhile on June 7, Governor Caperton appointed Larry George to be Commissioner of the Department of Energy. He had served eighteen months as Deputy Director of the Department of Natural Resources. George would replace George Dials, whose tenure had been widely criticized.

Meanwhile Rodd and others had organized a rally at the State Capitol to pressure the special legislative session into further reforms, especially addressing permits in acid-prone areas. Both Sims and McFerrin were present and discussed their experiences with small communities fighting mining pollution. In a nod to a long-standing complaint, the Legislature had finally separated the DOE's twin missions of promoting and regulating coal, giving the former to another agency.

McFerrin wrote, "The real work of the Department of Energy involves taking seriously the concerns of people affected by mining." He feared, however, that the Department's history of alliance with mining companies would remain. He continued:

> If there is no enforcement of the law at the new Department of Energy, then removal of the promotion duty from the statute is no more than a cruel joke. If the new Department of Energy continues the old promotion-by-no-enforcement then Governor Caperton has gained an opportunity for some posturing about how interested he is in the environmental protection while we have gained nothing.

In September the *Voice* printed an interview with Commissioner George. Among improvements he hoped to make were employing more inspectors, upgrading health and safety regulations, and addressing acid mine drainage. He also discussed a proposal to merge all state environmental agencies.

In November, George was fired. Apparently differences between George and Bolts Willis, a well-connected former UMW official, had arisen, and the governor had asked for his resignation. The Conservancy Board, meeting at the Fall Review, sent a strong letter to Governor Caperton. Rank wrote:

> We are deeply concerned about the changes in personnel at the Division of Energy and about the events surrounding these changes.
> For many of us the credibility of your commitment to sound environmental protections was solidified by two actions in particular:
> 1) By your appointment of individuals to head the Division of Energy and the Division of Natural Resources who were to emphasize enforcement and environmental protection as the primary goal of these agencies;
> 2) By your initiating legislative action in the June '90 special session that removed the promotion of coal from the statutory directives of the

Division of Energy, thus strengthening the regulatory and enforcement powers of the Agency.

Events of the past weeks have seriously diminished the credibility of your office on both counts.

President Rank complimented George for bringing a fresh approach to DOE, in stark contrast to its culture before. He had focused on pressing issues such as of bond requirements and acid drainage. She concluded her letter by seriously questioning the administration's underlying commitment to environmental protection.

In Governor Caperton's reply, while praising George as "a very talented and capable lawyer for whom I have great respect," he nonetheless felt George was not the best person to direct DOE. Addressing her broader concerns, the Governor wrote:

> Please know that despite the current transition at the DOE, my administration remains committed to environmental issues. We need to work together in this endeavor. As the 1991 legislative session approaches, I hope that you will work with my administration and the West Virginia Legislature to formulate the best possible environmental program.

E.W. "Woody" Wayland was eventually appointed. Wayland had been plant manager at South Charleston's FMC plant. Paul Nyden quoted Rank, in *The Charleston Gazette*:

> We need someone with substantial knowledge and understanding of both the law and the problems of the agency. I am deeply concerned. Mr. Wayland may be just great. But I have not heard anything yet that would convince me of that.

In December Sims reported that the Living Streams program was alive and well. It had received $11,000 in grant funding after the initial $500 from the Conservancy. diPretoro analyzed every mine permit application for its acid potential. If problems were found, he and Rodd filed comments with the state. A photo showed diPretoro with his small private plane and announced that he had been chosen to study long-wall mining in Europe later that spring.

Frank Young, a future Conservancy President, ended 1990 by noting with sadness the death of Harry Caudill, author of the influential book, *Night Comes to the Cumberlands*. From it, Young had learned about the heritage of Appalachian residents being swindled out of their land, and especially their mineral rights, by smooth-talking land agents. Caudill had detailed company towns, company stores, and the companies' desecration of the environment. Caudill had influenced the War on Poverty under President Johnson and later Young's own "appetite for social concern." Young finished his tribute this way: "Slowly, slowly, but ever so slowly, Appalachia may become a better place because of Harry Caudill. We owe him our best."

A front-page photo of Rank with a big grin greeted *Highlands Voice* readers in January 1991. Rank had just been chosen to receive the second annual Mother Jones Award by the West Virginia Environmental Council. The award was named for the famous Mother Jones, an ardent supporter of West Virginia coal miners, known for her signature "Mourn the dead and fight like hell for the living."

Two months later, Rank used her *Voice* column, "From the Heart of the Mountains," to advocate the return of primacy to OSM. In 1988 the Conservancy and fourteen other organizations had sued the West Virginia Department of Energy, claiming the state had failed to perform statutory duties under the federal law. There had been a truce as Governor Caperton's team took over in early 1989. A settlement agreement had been signed in July 1989.

But now after the third legislative session since the suit was filed, she wrote, she finally must agree with those who, back in 1988, argued against the lawsuit and in favor of OSM taking back the enforcement itself. She cited the just-completed 1991 session of the Legislature, in which the coal industry had fought real reform, and therefore only cosmetic changes had been made. "A reluctant but firmly convinced convert, I fully support whatever actions are necessary to bring on OSM," she stated.

In a statement that echoed from other commentators cited earlier, she concluded:

> But the historic and deeply rooted influence of an industry accustomed only to the red carpet treatment by its minions in government and regulatory agencies continues to thwart even the loftiest of good intentions. OSM must be involved in all areas of the program.
>
> Such a program will allow the coal industry to continue but will also provide greater guarantees that today's profits are not garnered out of the pockets of tomorrow's citizens.
>
> A coal industry, that is an equal partner with the long-term sustainable future of the State, its economy, people, and environment, is long overdue.

Rank wrote of the just completed legislative session. She compared the session to the Land of Oz, where things were not always as they seemed. The DOE had insisted it needed $3 million in additional funding to cure the deficiencies listed in the settlement agreement and had tried to forge a coalition of interests to support its proposal, to assess a couple of cents per ton on every ton of coal produced. The industry first agreed, but then gradually questioned the need, the solution, and finally the funding mechanism. Now with less than $300,000, and the endless excuses from DOE leaders that lack of staff prevented full implementation of the agreement, she wrote, "Although visions of working with the Federal bureaucracy are not all pleasant or comforting, involvement of OSM at this point may well be a refreshing change and may, over the long term, create some of the reform and direction so badly needed in the state surface-mine program."

In a *Charleston Gazette* article on April 19, 1991, writer Paul Nyden quoted Harry M. Snyder, director of OSM, writing to the state: "We are unable at this time to conclude from your response that resources will be available to remedy deficiencies with respect to staffing and technical resources." Caperton promised Snyder he would seek additional funding from the Legislature "to the extent that additional funding is needed." Snyder cited critically lax inspection frequency, caseloads double those in surrounding states, lack of technical experts on staff, and deficits in the Reclamation Fund. It seemed OSM was prepared to reclaim its enforcement obligations in West Virginia. Maybe "primacy" would prove real.

In July Board member Carroll Jett wrote a strong letter to the editor of *The Highlands Voice*. In perhaps the perfect summary title for this chapter, he said, "I believe the coal industry has too much political and economic clout to ever be effectively regulated by state government." Jett carefully cited the history of the domination of West Virginia politics by the coal industry, drawing upon Corbin's book *Life Work and Rebellion in the Coal Fields*, bringing it up to date with the imprisonment of former Governor Arch A. Moore for accepting "sleaze money" from a coal operator. Continued Jett:

> The federal government has now served notice that it intends to take over enforcement of several aspects of our mine regulatory program, due to consistent refusal by the state to enforce its own laws.
>
> The point is that the political influence of the coal industry is pervasive in both major parties — always has been.

In short, a federal takeover of the regulatory process is the only apparent source of protection we have from the coal mining industry, short of insurrection — and that has already been tried.

Insurance Pays

In an update on the Omega mining issue, where the 4-H Road Community Association had sued over post-mining acid discharges, on May 21, 1991, the 4-H Road group received a $1.2 million settlement. But there was an important new twist, according to Conservancy member Rodd, who had represented the group.

State law required all coal companies to carry liability insurance for damages caused by pollution. Rodd argued that this liability insurance covered the cost of abating the pollution. The insurance companies apparently thought the claim was strong enough. They settled out-of-court for $1.2 million. Most of the settlement money, $1.1 million, would go into a trust fund to construct a centralized water treatment facility.

The case was unprecedented in West Virginia. It could be the largest settlement ever obtained by an environmental citizen action group. The outcome of the case would send a message to both the insurance and coal industries that the creation of environmental disasters was not something West Virginians would allow them to walk away from.

Sims, president of the 4-H Road Community Association, added:

> The bottom line is that coal should never have been mined. The state's own experts told them this, but the company and the state DNR leadership refused to listen.
>
> The DOE must stop issuing permits in these highly acid-producing coal seams. If the DOE will not do this, the Federal OSM must take over the permitting program to stop these disasters from being created.

Meanwhile Rank wrote about a renewed effort between the staff of OSM and the DOE to identify the deficiencies and the costs to address them. She wrote that a seventy-five-page report had recently been released urging 242 new staff positions at a cost of $4.8 million in state funds, matched by a like amount from OSM. A special legislative session in September would address these recommendations.

The Department of Environmental Protection

The story continued. In the October/November 1991 *Highlands Voice*, Rank wrote:

In answer to the question "How can we improve the Division of Energy (DOE) and get OSM off our backs?" the legislature passed House Bill 217 during the special session that took place the first three weeks of October.

In a nutshell, H.B. 217 abolished the DOE, authorized the executive branch (subject to legislative oversight) to reorganize all state environmental regulatory programs currently under the authority of the super secretary for commerce, labor, and environmental resources (including those from the DOE) into a new DEP (Department of Environmental Protection). H.B. 217 also required the coal industry to provide more money for the surface-mining regulatory program by assessing $.02 on every ton of clean coal produced to go to the program, and authorized promulgation of a limited site-specific bonding provision to apply to future mining permits.

Rank explained that the governor could choose to move other regulatory programs from the DNR until June 1992. The Legislature would act on the bill in its 1993 session. Governor Caperton appointed David Callaghan, DNR Director under Governor Rockefeller 1977–1983, as the first DEP Director. While the Conservancy had worked with Callaghan, the continual rearranging of state agencies and responsibilities consumed much Conservancy and legislative energy, without necessarily changing the policy and enforcement philosophy.

In December 1991, Rank paused to look ahead to the Conservancy's twenty-fifth anniversary year, about to begin. She wrote eloquently of the origins of the Conservancy, its early battles, and the proliferation of issues. Wrote Rank:

> Our attention seems to have been divided between two different sets of concerns, i.e. to these "special places" and to this "specialness of place." However, it becomes clear after tens of dozens of issues of newsprint that the Conservancy has always recognized the interconnectedness of the two and that it is perhaps more accurate to think of the differences in terms of viewpoints rather than actual difference in content.

She recited how she became involved in the Highlands Conservancy. As a leader of FOLK, she had asked for, and received financial and technical help from the Conservancy. All it had asked of FOLK was involvement. "I had some spare time and was the logical person to uphold our end of the bargain," she added.

I was still reluctant, and more than a bit apprehensive, because I felt my own concerns to be far more limited than the grander goals of the WVHC. Where I wanted to protect the specialness of place in my community and the head waters of the Little Kanawha River from the ravages of acid-mine drainage, the Conservancy had its sights set on those special places like Canaan, Cranberry, etc. that were state and national treasures.

First as a FOLK board representative, then as a director at large, she eventually was asked to stand as a candidate for president.

By then I had come to recognize the interconnectedness of what I perceived to be my concerns and those of the Conservancy. Those special places and that specialness of place are but different points in the web of life where what we do at one particular instance can be felt at every other point to some greater or lesser degree. The policies and laws and attitudes that determine how we treat the small headwater stream on my property are the same attitudes that guide our actions on the rivers in the Mon Forest or in the New River Gorge. If there is little respect on the one level, there can be little on the other.

My backyard is but a small piece of the bigger backyards of the WVHC, the State of W.Va., the nation, and the world. Our level of commitment to protecting, preserving, and conserving the natural resources in any one of those yards is indicative of how willing we are to protect others. I've arrived at that perspective from trying to protect a specialness of place; WVHC seems to have started from a desire to protect special places.

How well we do at any of this, how much we can do, and what we focus on at any particular time depends upon the determination, talents and energies of everyone who has been willing and able to work together over the years.

These words, integrating both the focus on places with easily recognized names, and the passion borne from defending one's own "backyard," aptly described the West Virginia Highlands Conservancy as it began its twenty-fifth anniversary year celebration. It might also have summarized the twin threads of mining issues Rank and others had followed through such meanderings of law and regulations. The threads had included small communities such as Sugar Lane, Duo, Owl Creek, and antagonists such as the Lauritas, Island Creek, and Omega. But they had also included the threads known by their initials: OSM, DNR, DOE and now DEP.

Part Two — The Next Fifteen Years

During the first twenty-five years of the Highlands Conservancy, its focus had been primarily on a well-agreed region known as the highlands. Its issues had been wilderness preservation, river conservation, the saving of Canaan Valley, and a variety of issues that affected the Monongahela National Forest. It had become involved in mining threats to proposed wilderness areas or on Shavers Fork and gradually become a self-appointed protector of small rural communities where coal mining made victims of their residents. The Conservancy had offered legal and financial support in these cases, often becoming involved in precedent-setting administrative and legal rulings.

The Highlands Conservancy had also been a major player in the setting of federal and state policy on mining, particularly strip-mining. Its officers had presented testimony, researched issues, become key sources to sympathetic media, and raised public awareness of mining abuses. The Conservancy had developed a group of young public-interest attorneys who had won key victories in a variety of court actions.

But just as the first twenty-five years had focused often on the areas where coal would likely produce acid mine drainage, namely northern West Virginia, the next fifteen years would be dominated with the issue of mountaintop-removal mining, primarily in southern West Virginia. As this section will show, the total destruction of the southern coal counties would become the issue of the new millennium, and it would remain an open question whether the political and economic juggernaut of the mining industry in West Virginia could ever be effectively controlled.

Under the 1991 state law creating a new Department of Environmental Protection, its director was authorized to develop certain regulations. By the summer of 1992 Rank was concerned Director Callaghan had gone overboard. It had been the bill's intention that the regulations address the site-specific bonding issue, but instead, he had issued eighty-five pages of regulations, covering the entire surface-mining program, and hoped to get legislative approval of the package in its entirety.

Rank specifically questioned the regulations covering permits in acid-prone coal seams, the uses of the bankrupt Special Reclamation Fund and the exemption for state-operated water treatment plants, among others. "These changes so increase the discretionary authority of the Director," she wrote, "that they subvert both federal and state law. The law must clearly define requirements that will adequately direct whoever is head of the regulatory agency, be that Ken Faerber, George Dials, Larry George, Woody Wayland, Dave Callaghan, or ?" Except for one section, she proclaimed the rest illegal if enacted.

The Charleston Gazette of August 15, 1992, reported that the proposed DEP regulatory package was under attack from all sides. Even House Speaker Chuck Chambers had written Callaghan that the package was far too broad. Small coal companies expected that the higher bonding levels would put them out of business. The coal association agreed that the proposals exceeded the legislative intent. Rank reiterated the Conservancy's position that reclamation included water quality and opposed mining in acid-prone seams. Rodd, representing Mountain Stream Monitors, worried that these regulations were "a blueprint for more permitting of mines in acid-producing seams, because it removes limits and the requirements set by law and leaves it to the discretion of one individual — the director." At the hearing, Rodd brought along bottles of polluted water he dubbed "Chateau Callaghan," taken from streams allegedly polluted under permits issued by Callaghan.

The Associated Press reported, "The Middle Fork River, once one of West Virginia's premier trout fisheries but now a dead stream, presents state mining regulators with a simple, if thorny, choice." A joint state-federal task force estimated cleanup costs to be $1.2 million to install, and $818,000 annually to operate, water-treatment facilities. The article noted the 1981 citizen petition to declare the watershed unsuitable for mining.

A *Gazette* article by Eric Niiler, dated July 18, 1992, added that the headwaters of the Middle Fork were where James LaRosa had mined in the 1970s and 1980s. When he stopped mining in 1983, the state accepted an $115,000 settlement and released him from further liability.

The Record Delta of Buckhannon outlined problems on the Left Fork of the Buckhannon River. An excellent fishery had been lost due to "overtreatment" of mine wastewater. Don Garvin, Secretary of the Mountaineer Chapter of Trout Unlimited, was quoted. "What happened up there is a sin against all residents of Upshur County," he stated. "This is one of the few remaining pristine and beautiful areas in Upshur County." Garvin would later become a leader in the West Virginia Environmental Council and member of the Conservancy's Board.

In response, Governor Caperton announced in August that at least $14 million would be dedicated statewide to treating acid-mine drainage from coal mining over the next four years, under the new Stream Restoration Program. Caperton said that more than 1,900 miles of West Virginia streams and rivers were affected by acid-mine drainage. Three likely choices for treatment were the Blackwater River (above Davis), the Middle Fork of the Buckhannon, and the North Branch of the Potomac. Some of the clean-up funding would come from the Abandoned Mine Lands Fund of the federal Surface Mining Act.

As if to ignore the increasing concerns outlined in these articles, Island Creek Coal Company sought permission to discharge more chemicals than permitted by the state into Ten Mile Creek, a tributary of the Buckhannon River. The Water Resources Board heard Island Creek's appeal of its state permit on the same operation Rank and FOLK had been protesting for years. The City of Buckhannon would incur additional drinking water filtration costs if the request was granted. Rank remembered several summers before when city water plant operators struggled with water so hard that "soap would not lather and non-dairy creamer 'curdled' when poured into coffee." She criticized Island Creek's continued efforts to shift to others the costs of degrading the county's resources.

In March 1993, Rank wrote:

> In mining policy we are fighting a back-sliding of monumental proportions that will not only leave untreated hundreds of miles of acid-mine drainage-damaged streams, but also create more sources of acid under the preposterous assumption that guaranteed limited-perpetual treatment is possible and acceptable.
>
> As the state cleans up its image by closing the book on the infamous DOE (Division of Energy) brainchild of Arch Moore, the newly created DEP (Division of Environmental Protection) is taking on the look of the good old wolf in sheep's clothing. Where aggressive across the board environmental PROTECTION is needed, the defining legislation is enshrining an insidious and pervasive emphasis on a BALANCE of the kind that invites political power and influence — a scenario all too familiar in W.Va., but hardly a posture that will see her kindly into the next decade.

In May's *Voice*, Rodd discussed how the Omega case, and other cases, had been based on emerging legal precedents from bankruptcy, superfund legislation, and asbestos litigation. Companies would no longer be able to evade post-mining acid treatment through bankruptcy, as they often had. Rodd thought when the huge payouts caused the coal companies to be unable to gain insurance, they would be forced to move to less perilous areas to mine. Meanwhile provisions of the Clean Air Act would make northern West Virginia coal less desirable anyway. While still no substitute for no mining in the first place, Rodd certainly seemed proud of hitting the insurance industry as the financier for "perpetual treatment" costs. At least it wasn't the taxpayer again.

Conservancy Board member Sims also discussed the Omega saga. Although the 4-H Road Community Association received a $400,000 payment from Omega's insurance company, they were still in need of a disposal site. After ten years, the acid had filled the mine, and was choking Owl Creek and Booth Creek on their way to the Monongahela River. Whatever disposal plan would eventually be used, she predicted:

> In two years, when the $400,000 insurance is gone, this mining mess will probably end up back in the lap of David Callaghan, who issued this permit against the advice of his own technical staff. What goes around comes around. Mr. Callaghan recently admitted to me that the issuance of this permit was a mistake. Will they ever learn? Maybe.

[Fifteen years later, in 2007, Rank reported that Omega's sludge was being trucked and disposed of in Preston County.]

In June, Rank reported that Rodd, who had been a stalwart environmental lawyer in Morgantown, had joined the office of Darrell McGraw, the state Attorney General. One of his duties would be to close down what she called "scofflaw coal companies who owe the state millions of dollars in reclamation and bond monies." Rank reflected on the age-old question of whether it was most effective to work for change inside or outside the system. She wrote:

> After all is said and done, I suppose what gives me pause is when, or if, we will ever see enough people (on all levels — professional or nonprofessional, in all areas of concern, both inside and out) working together to make a dent in the same old – same old business-as-usual.

Rank sounded discouraged. She had fought for protection of her community, of northern West Virginia, and ultimately for the entire state against now several governors, repeated reorganizations, a parade of state officials, and myriad regulatory changes. How long could one person sustain that commitment?

In July, Rank was still reflective, if not cynical:

I no longer fantasize about that dream of youth and promise of democracy that assume responsible people can reason together to arrive at reasonable solutions to common problems. In fact I rarely accept anything at face value anymore, but rather find myself searching for the hidden agenda or underlying meaning, as though by instinct I realize that what goes on in the unseen subterranean maze of motives (usually power, money, or politics) has more to do with the outcome of a particular endeavor than whatever other more visible elements of reason or principle can be brought to bear.

What was the source of such cynicism? She explained that in dissecting Governor Caperton's much-publicized Stream Restoration Program, it had become clear that the problem was 50% larger than first believed (3,000 miles, not 1,900) and that much of the $14 million in state and federal funding was already obligated. Using funds generated where streams were "sold," by which she meant totally buried under valley fills and thus lost through mining, and for which the state received "mitigation," and bond forfeitures, much of these funds would be focused where the greatest public impact might be shown. Therefore watersheds like Middle Fork, Blackwater, North Branch of the Potomac, Upper Tygart, and Meadow Creek on the New River would be improved at the cost of unnamed watersheds in Mingo and McDowell counties.

Rank also questioned the use of these funds to relieve coal companies from their legal obligations. For example, Middle Fork was polluted from two main sources, and one was the subject of a citizen complaint filed by the Highlands Conservancy in 1991, and currently on appeal within the Department of Interior. This was the LaRosa mine, where the Conservancy contested its release from liability in 1983 in exchange for $115,000. The company was still in business and should be held accountable, she wrote. To use the Stream Restoration Program to bail out LaRosa, or any other operating company, was wrong. She concluded:

> Maybe these things will fix part of the Middle Fork; and they should definitely help fix the image of the state regulatory agency that has come to be identified with dead fish floating in bottles of orange metal-laden water. And surely, industry should be happy for the opportunity to whitewash some of their less-than-admirable screwups without digging deeper into their pockets to come up with additional money to do more. And some state politicians might breathe a sigh of relief to know that a few of the hundred or so post-act Kittle Flats type sites that haunt them occasionally can be fixed a little without their

309

political careers suffering a lot from the political heat, which would result from extracting more money from industry to truly **fix** [*her emphasis*] the Special Reclamation Fund.

So why is it that this cynical adult has the creepy feeling that the fix is in?

Luckily the members of the Conservancy that month could get engaged in other issues. The Kumbrabow State Forest was slated to be timbered, a plan that had been kept secret until approved. Understandably there was widespread public outrage now. There was Corridor H and the "Michael Baker Two Step," (see Chapter 3), in which letters favoring the no-build alternative were counted by the Department of Highways consultant as favoring construction. The fairly new *Voice* Editor Bill Ragettè ran a sandwich-size sketch of the "Extinct Species of the Month" in each issue. To be a conservationist in mid-1993 was not all fun and games.

Then, the other shoe dropped. In the August 1993 *Highlands Voice* an extensive article on mining in southern West Virginia by Gordon Billheimer, identified as a Montgomery lawyer and former strip-mine firm official, discussed what would come to be called "Mountain Top Removal Mining." His article focused on Amax Mining Company, working in the Upper Kanawha Valley watershed, and described the total destruction as multiple seams of coal were mined, leaving little that resembled the original landscape. Mountaintop-removal mining had first appeared in *The Highlands Voice* fourteen years earlier, in an article by Paul Sheridan. It would come to dominate the Conservancy, its Mining Committee, and Rank's life for the next decade and longer.

In February 1994 an administrative law judge, buried within the U.S. Department of Interior, ruled for the Conservancy. Rank reported the welcome news under the headline, "Judge Rules LaRosa Must Treat Water at Kittle Flats." She outlined the history of the case and its decision. The Conservancy had filed a citizen complaint with OSM earlier, complaining that LaRosa was not treating acid discharges from his dormant mine. In December 1991 OSM agreed with the Conservancy and issued a notice to the state to take action. Because the state had settled in 1984 with LaRosa for a sum of $115,000, state officials were now in charge. After the state refused to take action, OSM subsequently issued LaRosa a cessation order in April 1992 ordering him to install, operate, and maintain acid-treatment facilities. It was LaRosa's appeal of that order that led to the current decision.

The significance of this particular site was that it produced ninety percent of the acid drainage to the Middle Fork, which flowed north through Buckhannon, then Audra State Park, and eventually into Tygart Lake. A dead zone of forty miles downstream from this site was all that remained of a once fine trout fishery.

The OSM administrative law judge ruled the state erred in settling with LaRosa and, in any event, OSM did not release LaRosa's liability, but maintained its oversight function throughout. OSM's cessation order was legal and sustained. According to the article, if LaRosa complied with the ruling, bonding would be required to guarantee treatment if LaRosa failed to do so. If LaRosa refused to comply at all, he would forfeit current bonds and be blocked from further mining anywhere.

Rank stated that the implications of this decision reached far beyond the site-specific impacts. She wrote that "In the ongoing state and federal level debates and discussions about regulation and policy governing mining in acid-prone areas, …there is a painfully long and ever growing list of enforcement failures…Kittle Flats now becomes one more of those glaring and depressing examples."

She added the projected $325,000/year at Kittle Flats to the $500,000/year at DLM, $1 million-plus/year at the Enoxy-Consol Tenmile complex, and the $480,000/year at Sandy Creek, all before the Tygart River reached the Tygart Lake at Grafton. The Conservancy had fought for the end of mining in these areas, and now the cost of perpetual treatment was $2.3 million each and every year, even if no further permits were issued!

She continued:

> Coal states, especially West Virginia, often argue that OSM has no right "interfering" in any state action if that state has received primacy (OSM approval) for its regulatory program. In this decision, Judge Torbett refers to the issue by citing a 1991 decision…and affirms that "OSM is required to insure compliance with the law regardless of the actions or inactions of the state regulatory authority."
>
> The Torbett decision is one of the bright lights in an oftentimes bleak landscape. WVHC should be proud to have played a role in the proceeding so far.

The next step was up to LaRosa, and it remained to be seen how the story would end. At least Rank's often-stated cynicism had taken a deserved break to enjoy a victory.

In an ironic combination of two companies the Conservancy had met before, Sims reported that Mepco Mining Co., one of the Laurita companies, had filed for a permit to fill the Omega mine with fly ash from nearby power plants. Because fly ash was alkaline, it theoretically would neutralize the acidic discharges. The 4-H Camp Road group was carefully negotiating permit conditions, but they were wary of the DEP's enthusiasm for what it called "revolutionary, new technology."

Then, in an eloquent statement that spoke for many other families faced with similar threats, Sims wrote:

> One lesson we have learned is that as long as there is coal to be mined in our watershed, someone will keep trying to mine it. We could give up and leave our community for a suburban neighborhood, where rules and regulations carefully spell out what can and cannot be done. But this is where we want to live. We have raised our children and planted trees here. We like to be able to have music parties that last all night, and build an unusual-looking greenhouse without complaints from neighbors.
>
> So we will stay, and continue to work and persevere for what we believe in. Probably, Mepco will receive their permit, and the State will take steps to treat whatever polluted water still flows from the Omega Mine after it has been filled with fly ash…And someday, we will be called "that eccentric old couple who live by Booth's Creek," which is fine with us. Even if fish don't begin to live in our creek again, at least we will be able to ski beside it and know that it is still clear and pretty because of our work. And maybe fish will live in it someday.

Was this a sentiment shared by Rank and countless environmental activists who fought for their home communities? Was this what kept them going?

In April the Conservancy — along with the West Virginia Wildlife Federation, Trout Unlimited, and West Virginia Citizen Action Group — asked the state Supreme Court "to order state environmental officials to reclaim all abandoned coal mines and to treat all streams polluted by acid mine water." These tasks were estimated to cost a minimum of $50 million, according to state and federal officials. The state's Special Reclamation Fund had only $8.6 million. Without court intervention, West Virginia taxpayers would absorb the rest.

In early June, newly appointed OSM Director Robert Uram fulfilled his promise to come to West Virginia and meet with citizens. According to Rank, Uram spent a day and a half looking at acid-mine drainage sites in northern West Virginia. Visiting nearly every site mentioned in this chapter, he gathered more information personally than all his predecessors combined. She summarized his visit, filtered through her experience:

> Though he offered a sympathetic eye and ear, spoke strongly of enforcing the law, and appeared willing to do the right thing, ...Director Uram has yet to face down the pressures from industry and lackluster state-agency attitudes. The final chapter is yet to be written and the details are always the most difficult.

Mountaintop Removal

Rank discussed her recent visit to southern West Virginia in the July 1994 *Voice*. Mountaintop-removal mining was getting going in full swing, and she said nothing had prepared her for its destruction. And this was someone well versed in mining devastation! Here's a sample:

> Let me tell you how amazed ...appalled ...overwhelmed ...repulsed ... humbled ...bewildered ...perplexed ...confused ...sickened ... angered ... horrified ...dismayed I was by the spectre of the massive mining operations now being conducted in southern West Virginia.
>
> Nothing could have prepared me for the sights and sounds of the recent DEP Office of Mines and Minerals tour through some of our southern counties — not articles by Paul Nyden in the *Gazette*, not pictures of the giant draglines out West, not even Bob Gates' film "In Memory of the Land and People."
>
> I venture to say that as recently as ten years ago no one could have imagined, or would even have suggested, the enormity of the mines we visited in Nicholas, Fayette, Kanawha, Boone, and Logan [counties.]
>
> Standing on the edge of a Grand Canyon-like landscape with 18 splits [seams] of coal exposed along a 600-foot wall that extended from high above to far below our level on the canyon ridge, I couldn't help but wonder how these sites comply with the intent or letter of either the Clean Water Act or any Surface Mine laws.
>
> Surely these vast projects are engineering feats to rival the seven wonders of the world, but the significant alteration of the earth mass is experimental at best. And this experimentation is not just on one or two sites, but seems to be the wave of the future in southern West Virginia. (All of course moving full speed ahead before the results of the initial experiments are known.)

With most of the Conservancy's membership living in or north of Charleston, the Conservancy had missed the biggest change in mining in decades. The Rockefeller Amendment (discussed earlier) had been the open door that permitted states to impose alternative regulations to the federal mining regulations, and many thought mountaintop removal mining was the result.

By 2007, more than a dozen years after Rank's comments just cited, the situation would be greatly expanded. The balance of this chapter will discuss several individual local battles, describe the resolution of battles already outlined, and explain how the ravages of mountaintop removal mining came to dominate the Conservancy's mining agenda.

"This is a complete victory for our clients. This opinion could not have been any stronger." These were the words of Conservancy lawyer Phil Scott, who with Pat McGinley, was quoted on the front page of the August 1994 *Highlands Voice*. The state Supreme Court had ruled unanimously that the DEP had a mandatory, non-discretionary obligation to spend at least twenty-five percent of the funds in the Special Reclamation Fund to treat acid-mine drainage. In response Director Callaghan had said he doubted the opinion would change what his department was already doing. Currently the DEP was spending a million dollars a year, mostly in Upshur and Preston counties. The Court ruling would double that amount. Rank had criticized Callaghan for telling the Legislature the previous year that DEP was not required to treat acid-water problems. "This decision means he can't lie to the Legislature or auditors anymore. He has a mandatory duty to treat water. We also continue to believe that the state remains liable for water treatment at all forfeited sites," she told the *Gazette's* Paul Nyden.

In 1994, Rank completed her third two-year term as Conservancy President, having served longer than any previous incumbent. In her final "From the Heart of the Mountains," monthly column in October's *Voice*, Rank reflected on her tenure and the Conservancy's issues. She wrote:

> I had thought about dramatizing our accomplishments of these past few years — outlining what we had planned and how we fared, but chose not to since a fair overview would have to include so many ups and downs of so many phases of each issue that it would be a repetition of all the *Voices*. Truly one of the more frustrating aspects of working with groups like the WVHC is that there are rarely any clear beginnings or endings: Old issues seem to go on forever, and new ones just

keep barging in screaming for their share of attention as well. And time? Well, time just keeps marching on.

Surely it wime is slipping quickly through our fingers, let us not linger too long, for there is ever so much more to do...

In many ways, Conservancy members could relate to the frustration of the "ups and downs" of so many issues, to the lack of definite beginnings and endings, and to the new issues "barging in screaming" for attention. Yet the basic assumptions of its history remained: volunteers would determine issues receiving energy, the Highlands would be the focus, and the Conservancy would continually shift its role with its "companion" groups. (Readers of this volume may well relate to this description, too.)

As Rank turned the gavel over to McFerrin, the major issues of the Conservancy were quietly shifting too. McFerrin lived in Beckley and was the first Conservancy president from south of Charleston. Forestry controversies, epitomized by the timbering of the Kumbrabow State Forest, wind-energy farms proposed for the highlands, which dominated the October 1994 *Voice* front page, and the less optimistic mood among voters at both the state and federal levels, these forces would challenge the Conservancy almost thirty years from the initial organizing discussions in 1965.

In December, Rank assumed the position as Conservancy Mining Committee chair, just vacated by McFerrin. She would continue to provide news and analysis on issues related to mining in West Virginia. She reviewed the ten years since the state had been awarded "primacy" by OSM. She wrote:

> Anyone who has followed this saga over the last decade knows how convoluted the process has become and how the tug-of-war continues. OSM holds the line on one end and industry pulls on the other with the states standing somewhere in the middle, but often much closer to industry's position.
>
> From the effects of mining proposals along Shavers Fork, to minimizing developments in individual communities across the state, WVHC has commented on individual permit applications and on proposed regulatory changes, utilized the citizen complaint provisions of the Act, and at times pursued court actions when necessary to address problems at specific sites or programmatic deficiencies in the state program and regulatory agency itself.

Many of the issues under consideration in this most recently proposed WV program amendment were the focus of the 1988 law suit by WVHC and 15 other local, state, and national groups,…which held that the state of West Virginia was not meeting its mandatory duties under both the Federal and State Surface Mining laws. Unfortunately, since several of those substantive deficiencies continue to be ignored or denied by the state regulatory agency, WVHC took to the courts again in 1994 (the WV Supreme Court this time) …challenging the state's refusal to treat mine drainage at forfeited sites.

Now, she continued, it had become clear from correspondence between DEP and OSM that basic philosophical differences existed between them. The Conservancy would, therefore, submit its comments to OSM as it reviewed the state program. Rank described the issues with the clarity readers had come to expect. But her cautionary final comments were equally typical:

WVHC has consistently relied on the sound judgment of the OSM engineers and again must defer to those more knowledgeable about the rapidly evolving engineering technologies that are part of this debate. WVHC offers only the cautionary note that, when choosing the course for the future at the giant fills now being permitted statewide, but especially in Southern West Virginia, great care must be taken to choose the most cautious route. To err on the side of expediency at the expense of long-term durability and stability will visit dire consequences on future generations as well as major portions of West Virginia.

January 1995 began with Rank writing about the Middle Fork, whose history of acid mine drainage was familiar to many. Under Governor Caperton's Stream Restoration Program three years earlier, Middle Fork had been selected as one of the pilot streams. Another pilot was Blackwater River, where the past September a six-drum limestone treatment system had been installed. Of interest to Conservancy members, similar units were first used on Otter Creek and the Cranberry River.

The Conservancy had only recently reiterated its disapproval of instream systems, in favor of on-site abatement or treatment alternatives. Conservancy complaints and court suits back to 1991 had attempted to establish the responsibility of mining operators on their permit areas, rather than shifting responsibility to the state or downstream facilities. OSM Law Judge Torbett had even sided with the Conservancy in 1993, voiding reliance on the 1984 release by the state of LaRosa from liability. "The Conservancy cannot accept damming the Middle Fork as an acceptable abatement alternative," she wrote.

Rank continued, "The [Stream Restoration] committee is now viewing a selection of different shades of makeup to cover a jaundiced body [she wrote in bold and underlined]. The more appropriate action would be to treat the cause and not the symptoms."

This was the Conservancy's position: operators and/or landowners should follow the laws. If they did not, the bonds, fines, and other remedies imposed by government should protect citizens. The government should not accept the responsibility that rightfully belonged to the owners. That principle was at the heart of nearly all of the Conservancy's issues in mining, and other matters as well.

On January 31, 1995, attorneys Tom Galloway and Walt Morris filed several extensive citizen complaints with OSM on behalf of the Conservancy and National Wildlife Federation. Plaintiffs asked OSM to address the now-familiar issues of bonding, treatment of forfeited sites, and avoidance of permit blocking, among others. OSM Director Uram, the one to whom Conservancy activists had given a personal tour, had ordered his staff to investigate these complaints. The disappointing DNR response was to question the legal qualifications of the attorneys to represent these clients. Rank wrote:

> Beginning with some of the first issues in the mid '60s, the *Voice* has been filled with articles and discussions of mining and WVHC efforts as part of the responsible, informed citizen input envisioned by SMCRA [the federal law] to be an essential element in the effective regulation of coal mining. From the move to abolish strip mining, to the development and passage of SMCRA, to the proposed mining on Shavers Fork, to the debacles of DLM and F&M, to the Island Creek Tenmile fiasco on the Buckhannon, to the near fiasco on the Little Kanawha, to the 1988 and 1994 court actions, to the LaRosa-Kittle Flats and Middle Fork saga, to the dozens of recent citizen complaints — all are stories of the roller coaster ride that seems to accompany any challenge to the mining program in West Virginia.
>
> This recent effort promises to be no less exciting. At stake with these complaints are some fundamental policy decisions that will directly affect the waters of West Virginia that WVHC members depend on whether they live in state or visit the mountains to paddle, hike, bike, fish, hunt, study, breathe, or just relax.

In May OSM issued a "status report" that praised the state for addressing the deficiencies and admitted that the Conservancy's allegations were significant. Then in a slick bureaucratic turn, OSM said "until OSM, in conjunction with other interested parties, has clarified the appropriate standard against which to measure the state's actions, it is premature for the agency to evaluate the performance of WV or any other state regulatory authority with respect to enforcement of the CWA [Clean Water Act] requirement."

Rank felt that, although the Charleston OSM field staff generally supported the Conservancy's concern about bonding, forfeiture, reclamation funds, etc., the long delay and projected further delays were ominous.

OSM Director Uram returned to West Virginia to solicit comments on cleaner water regulations. Don Garvin, Conservancy Board member and Trout Unlimited leader, praised Uram for "preparing to go ahead with this, given the national political climate."

Predictably DEP Director Callaghan and coal industry leaders called OSM's proposed requirements "extremely expensive and difficult." Callaghan also asserted that OSM did not have the authority to require the states to treat pollution or acid-mine drainage from abandoned mines. To this Uram had said, "Land cannot return to productive use if there is acid-mine drainage in the streams. Congress obviously intended to have streams protected after mining."

Coincidentally, Callaghan retired that day as Director of the state Department of Environmental Protection.

McFerrin used his "From the Heart of the Plateau" column in August 1995 to review some history and sound an alarm. He wrote:

> For as long as I can remember, politicians have promised to cut out waste, fraud, and inefficiency in government. Every President at least as far back as Jimmy Carter has announced an intention to make government more efficient.
>
> Now West Virginia, its people, and such of its fish who manage to survive are about to feel the effect of the drive for "efficiency." The Congressional knives are sharpened to cut out the enforcement of coal-mining regulations by the federal Office of Surface Mining.

He explained that there had been a two-tiered system since 1977 when OSM was created. Mostly, environmentalists had favored this system, because even if a state received primacy, the federal officials retained oversight and could intervene. Indeed the Conservancy had repeatedly used the OSM citizen-complaint process and even filed suit asking that OSM revoke primacy because West Virginia's own program was so much weaker. Now congressional budget-cutters proposed to wipe out OSM's role. One could only guess how much weaker the West Virginia program would then become. Said McFerrin, "I shudder to think what positions the state would be taking if the Office of Surface Mining were not there." OSM's enforcement powers are not a duplication, he continued, "That enforcement power is what keeps West Virginia's mine regulatory program from taking a long step on the road to ruin."

Rank noted that she was experiencing "a growing inability to capture any meaningful snapshots of the moving targets of our appeals, lawsuits, state program amendment comments, etc.; as they are batted about by the inevitable barrage of political waffling." She continued:

> Unfortunately, my level of fatigue and waning enthusiasm is only exacerbated by the antics of this current self-proclaimed 'pro-citizen' Congress that is about to tear apart the very fabric of the laws that protect us and the agencies charged with enforcing those laws. It's a scenario that causes a friend familiar with the internal workings of the James Watt regime to mutter quietly "WORSE THAN WATT."
>
> I happen to believe that good laws are often all that stands between preservation of our homes and lives and the destructive tendencies of greed and profiteering. And good lawyers are a must to counter those lawyers who do the bidding of the special interests who stand to profit from stretching the law for their own economic benefit.

The main reason good environmental laws have often not worked, she continued, was because they haven't been enforced well enough. Industry had developed a fierce resistance and outspent citizen groups in marshalling the media, working the judicial system, and, one might add, funding campaign coffers. Then she wrote:

> Coal industry profiteers must be laughing on their way to the bank secure in the knowledge that Congress is about to do for them what they have been unable to do for themselves in other forums, lawsuits, challenges, and delays of the past two decades.
>
> It is particularly disappointing to know that official voices of the state of West Virginia are supporting these actions against SMCRA and OSM.

> The funding cuts proposed by Congress for OSM…will emaciate the agency. The resulting toothless, clawless, starving tiger of an agency (OSM) is hardly the protector of citizens and coalfield communities envisioned by the Congress nearly 20 years ago when SMCRA was made into law.
>
> From the commentaries by Nicholas Z in the 60s [*actually the 70s*] to more recent stories and commentaries by the George's, Purbaugh's, Sims', Rodd's, and McFerrin's of the WVHC, *Voice* readers have heard the message over and over again. From the 1988 lawsuit with 15 other WV groups vs. the State of West Virginia for failure to meet the mandatory duties of the SMCRA (i.e., not doing its job) to the more recent rash of citizen complaints…piece by piece WVHC has worked to make the law work as it was meant to work, i.e., protecting citizens and the environment in the coalfields.

Rank had lost faith in the state, but hoped that the federal government's regulatory system would stay funded well enough to exercise its oversight and stronger enforcement regulations. But she too was worried. To whom then were citizens and communities to turn to get relief from the abuses of mining?

During 1996, with Rank as Mining chair and diPretoro as Conservancy administrative assistant, *Voice* readers were given at least an article a month on mining issues. Various legal challenges were moving slowly ahead. OSM was trying to do more to oversee a recalcitrant state system and avoid budget cuts from Congress. The more things changed, the more they remained the same.

But in December 1996 a barely noticeable shift began again. Rank's article was titled, "Mitigation…and more — the Leveling of Southern West Virginia." Mitigation, she explained, was the fee paid to the state by a mining company for the right to totally destroy and/or bury a stream with a valley fill. To illustrate the massive extent of this practice, an integral part of mountaintop-removal mining, she included a map of the Hobet Mining Company permit for 2,073 acres in Boone and Lincoln counties. It was estimated that already 148 stream miles statewide had been buried in the past four years. In a few short years, mountaintop removal had gone from a possible mode of operation to the routine in the multi-seam counties of southern West Virginia. International conglomerates, with massive budgets and equipment to match, had gotten a good start and things were only likely to get worse.

The state was reviewing a proposal by A.T. Massey Coal Company in Raleigh and Boone counties for a 1,200-acre valley fill/MTR project. Hobet had won approval for 2,000 acres, in addition to the 8,000 already stripped. These numbers were, and are, impossible to imagine without a first-hand view.

A pleasant, if ironic, surprise was contained in the August 1997 *Voice*. Commemorating its twentieth anniversary, the federal Office of Surface Mining had announced an award to the West Virginia Highlands Conservancy because it "epitomizes the very nature of citizen action in preserving and protecting the natural heritage of West Virginia." The article explained that OSM valued citizen participation in permit decisions, inspections, rulemaking petitions, commenting on proposed rules, participation at hearings, state program evaluations, court cases, reclamation plans, emergency projects, and protection of sensitive resources by petitioning to have fragile lands declared unsuitable for surface mining. The irony was that the Conservancy's participation for twenty years had often been to no avail and that OSM itself had often opposed the Conservancy positions.

President McFerrin wrote Kathy Karpen, OSM's new director, a letter of cool acceptance. After thanking OSM for the recognition, and noting that many others deserved to share in it, McFerrin wrote:

> We regret that the Office of Surface Mining is not doing more to enforce the Act. Awards are nice; enforcement is better. Given the choice, we prefer enforcement.
>
> Mines are still burying streams at an increasingly alarmingly rate. They still fill valleys. They still create those awful fills with little more than a hope and prayer that the material is durable and the fills stable. Mines still create acid-mine drainage. We still have a special reclamation fund that is sorely under-funded. We still have a post-mining land-use program that is a cruel joke. Instead of useful land, we have land that is left useless for generations.

As the Conservancy began its fourth decade, non-mining issues dominated its agenda. The "garbage wars" raged on (how much out-of-state garbage should West Virginia accept?), Blackwater Canyon was threatened by John Crites and his Allegheny Wood Products Company, Corridor H had just lost a round in U.S. District Court, and timbering was unregulated and threatening several areas, including the Blackwater Canyon.

In mining issues, it had been a decade of battles with state and federal regulators, weathering political changes in Charleston and Washington, and perpetual treatment acid-mine drainage in areas where mining never should have been permitted. In the coming decade, mountaintop removal would be the dominating theme in mining.

But the entire nation learned about mountaintop mining in West Virginia in August 1997. New *Highlands Voice* Editor Bill Reed, who lived in southern West Virginia, wrote in December 1997:

> When Penny Loeb opened my eyes with her article in the *US News and World Report*, I had been shocked, and I felt like I'd been duped into some degree of complacency. I was still further shocked at the sight I saw below me on the airplane. Huge sprawls like massive crab-like aliens blotted the land surface in tans and blacks.
>
> The thought provoking question keeps coming back to me over and over, "How did this outrage ever come about, and why do the citizens of West Virginia allow this to happen?"*

In May 1998 President McFerrin described a recent tour of the massive Hobet 21 Mine, operated by Arch Coal. OSM Director Kathy Karpan had been the guest of honor and OSM had asked that environmental representatives, including McFerrin and Rank, be included for balance. McFerrin wrote:

> The mine is an awesome thing. They have been at it on that site since the early 1980s. By now, the mine covers about 10,000 acres. They have a map which shows the whole mine.
>
> During the tour, we moved from the part that had been mined and "reclaimed" in the early 1980s to the part that Arch is ripping up at this very moment. We know it is being ripped up at this very moment because the big machines run twenty four hours a day, seven days a week. There is no moment when the land is not being ripped up. It is safe to assume that it did not shut down to celebrate Earth Day.
>
> In the oldest part, the part where the mining and "reclamation" was finished fourteen years ago, they have established a "forest." By now the trees tower up to seven feet, their two-inch trunks standing firm against any wind that roars across the plains that have been newly created nearby.
>
> As the tour bus rumbled across the landscape, we saw nothing but grass and occasional "wildlife plantings." These are clumps of bushes

---

*Author's note: I recommend to everyone flying over southern West Virginia. There is no better way to see it.

where the wildlife are supposed to seek food and shelter. We occasionally passed ponds where, we were told, the water quality is "excellent."

Finally we reached the active mining. There was a crew drilling holes to prepare for the next blasting. There were the gargantuan trucks moving coal around.

And there was the dragline. Calling it a shovel is like calling King Kong a monkey. It scoops up loads of earth the size of houses, swings around, and deposits them a hundred yards away. It moves dirt on a scale that, unless you have seen it, is hard to imagine.

The Arch Coal officials who led the tour seemed proud of it. If one accepts their assumptions as valid, they should be. The mine does what Arch Coal wants. It gets a lot of coal out of the ground quickly and, from their perspective, efficiently. It makes money.

The difficulty is that their assumptions are not valid.

The maps that show the different parts of the operation are blown up versions of maps originally published by the United States Geological Survey. If one looks closely, one can still see the little squares. Those are where houses used to be. If one had a full-color version of the map, one could see the blue lines. Those are where streams used to be. Arch Coal can only be proud of its operation because it assumes that it is acceptable to destroy streams and communities. So long as the coal comes out quickly and efficiently, they can be proud. The streams and the communities are what the generals call an "acceptable level of casualties" in a war.

McFerrin continued that despite the presence of "wildlife plantings," all he saw that day were two buzzards and one duck. The post-mining land-uses envisioned in the 1977 federal surface mining law did not include sizable, topsoil-barren tabletops, totally cut off from road access or utilities and miles from the nearest resident. West Virginia did need flat land for commercial development, but not in places like that. Commented McFerrin, "The entire 10,000 acres are in violation of federal law. Arch Coal may be proud of its 'award winning' mine, but the law is the law and they're not even close to compliance with the requirements on post-mining land use." And after remembering that federal law prohibited degradation of streams, he wondered how Arch Coal could explain filling several miles of streams without any degradation of those streams?

With Karpan's tour as a backdrop, it was not surprising to learn that the Conservancy, along with ten citizens, had filed a formal notice to sue the state Division of Environmental Protection over the agency's enforcement of surface mining laws. The suit would aim to "rein in the strip-mining practice, known as mountaintop removal, in which whole tops of mountains are taken off to uncover the coal reserves."

Specific allegations, which would later become key areas of litigation, included the following:

> Strip mine waste piles called valley fills are illegal, because the U.S. Army Corps of Engineers is not allowed to issue "dredge and fill" permits under the Clean Water Act for dumping waste materials in streams.
>
> Valley fills violate federal rules that prohibit strip mining within 100 feet of a stream. This "buffer zone" requirement may only be waived after regulators make a series of specific findings that allowing the mining will not violate state or federal water pollution limits.
>
> The DEP has established a pattern and practice of issuing strip-mine permits without requiring companies to thoroughly study the impacts of their mines on water quality, and without requiring complete plans for how companies will minimize those impacts.

The citizens who were co-plaintiffs included three couples from Blair, two from Uneeda, one from Madison, and one from Delbarton.

Joe Lovett, a Charleston attorney with the nonprofit firm Mountain State Justice, Inc., Patrick C. McGinley, a West Virginia University law professor and veteran litigant for the Conservancy, Suzanne M. Weise, a Morgantown attorney, and James Hecker, of the Washington group Trial Lawyers for Public Justice, comprised the legal team.

However, despite the pending suit, the state made no effort to correct deficiencies, so on July 16, 1998, the Conservancy and the coalfield residents formally filed the lawsuit in the United States District Court for Southern West Virginia challenging mountaintop-removal mining. The 48-page complaint charged state DEP officials with numerous violations of the 1977 Surface Mining Control and Reclamation Act and the Clean Water Act, including blasting, water pollution, dust, and flooding violations. The defendants were DEP Director Miano, EPA, and three officials of the Army Corps of Engineers, the agency required to approve "dredge and fill" permits. Col. Dana Robertson was the highest Corps official named and plaintiff Patricia Bragg came first alphabetically, hence the suit was styled Bragg v. Robertson.

In July President McFerrin announced that Governor Cecil Underwood had recently appointed him to a task force on mountaintop removal. Knowing that he was the token environmentalist, appointed to "give a whiff of balance," McFerrin still was "determined to resist the destructive force of cynicism." He added a seldom-mentioned belief:

> In this world of contentiousness, there is one abiding principle that we must all cling to. We must never forget the inherent goodness of our opponents. We must never forget that they, too, are human beings who struggle as we all do [to do] what is right. Even those who have spent a lifetime apologizing for the coal industry have it within themselves to reach wise conclusions, to help Governor Underwood to a sound public policy.

McFerrin would discover that his appointment provided a bully pulpit.

Although the Conservancy was challenging the state and federal officials on mountaintop mining issues, *Highlands Voice* readers were reading about another issue in 1998: the saving of the Blackwater Canyon. A series of front-page stories, field trips, and major fund-raising campaigns were underway to stop a logging company from destroying the canyon. Until the campaign spun off under a new organization, the Friends of the Blackwater, a few years later, the Conservancy led these efforts. It was in this effort that a new name began to appear in the *Voice*. That name was Julian Martin and he would become extremely active in the campaign against mountaintop-removal mining also.

> **Julian Martin** was born on West Virginia's Coal River, across from Gripp and up the river from Emmons, later made famous as the place Jay Rockefeller worked in the 1960s. After his dad lost his eye in a coal mine accident, the family moved to St. Albans. Martin is proud that his grandfather was a miner and fought for the union at the Battle of Blair Mountain. Martin said that the family move to St. Albans probably saved him from the coal mines. After graduating from St. Albans High School in 1954, Martin went north to West Virginia University, received his degree in chemical engineering and, upon graduation, became a chemical engineer with American Cyanamid at Willow Island.
>
> In 1961 he became the first West Virginian to enter the brand-new Peace Corps and served two years in Eastern Nigeria. When he returned, his international experience led to a position as foreign student advisor at West Virginia University from 1964–1968. He was on campus during some of the turbulent student demonstrations and political action of the mid-1960s. The period 1968–1971 Martin spent in San Francisco, during what he later called the "hippy wars."

Among other things, Martin was active in the presidential campaign of Robert F. Kennedy and with the Committee of Returned Volunteers, a group dedicated to ending the Vietnam War.

When he returned to West Virginia he moved to Lincoln County and for twenty-two years taught physical science, physics, and chemistry at Duval High School, until he retired in 1998. During the decades of the 1970s through the 1990s, Martin was extremely active in the anti-school consolidation movement in Lincoln County, which became a bellwether for the rest of the state. He was also involved in a group that prevented two strip mines in Lincoln County during the 1980s.

After retirement Martin became active in the Save the Blackwater Canyon campaign and, a little later, the anti-mountaintop-removal mining efforts. In February 1999 the West Virginia Environmental Council recognized Julian as "Organizer of the Year" at its annual awards ceremony at the State Capitol. Linda Mallet wrote in the March 1999 *Highlands Voice*:

In the past year he and his partner Mae Ellen Wildt have injected more energy into the Blackwater and mountaintop campaigns than anyone can believe. Countless trips across the state, thousands of signatures on petitions, and more meetings than either one of them care to remember are just some of the things Julian and Mae Ellen have accomplished. And they did it as volunteers.

Because Julian had a lot of time on his hands, he also became an important member of our lobbying team this year. .You're likely to run into him anywhere people are gathered together. Julian is a marvel and a joy. He is one of the major reasons that our movement is stronger and more powerful today than it was a year ago.

During the last few years of the 1990s, and the first decade of the new century, Martin continued to volunteer as a campaigner for both causes, serving on the Highlands Conservancy Board and later becoming Vice President for State Affairs, walking across the state to raise public awareness of mountaintop removal and writing numerous letters to politicians and newspapers. But perhaps his most significant contribution was as outreach chair for the Conservancy, where his "I (heart) Mountains" bumper stickers, ball caps, shirts, and other merchandise were taken and sold to members and non-members alike. Over fifty thousand of these now-famous bumper stickers could be seen across the state, and indeed beyond its borders, as a symbol of opposition to the abuses of mining.

On his blog, Martin summed up his environmental credo simply: "I love our mountains and hate strip mining and mountaintop-removal coal mining in West Virginia."

Several articles on mountaintop removal (MTR) mining appeared in the July 1998 *Voice*. Interestingly, one by the editorial page editor of *The Charleston Gazette*, Dan Radmacher, described his experience on yet another three-day surface-mine tour. Another by state senator Jon Hunter, D-Monongalia County, detailed corruption at the highest level of the state DEP. Hunter also mentioned recent MTR exposes by *The New York Times, U.S. News and World Report,* and ABC's "Nightline." The West Virginia Conference of the United Methodist Church, the denomination of Governor Underwood, even passed a resolution calling for an immediate halt to MTR until a scientific study of its impacts could be completed. This was the origin of the task force to which McFerrin had been appointed. According to Hunter, Underwood "weighted it heavily with coal officials, regulators, and consultants."

The third article was by West Virginia native Charles Peters, founder of *The Washington Monthly* magazine. His opening paragraph read:

> Growing up in West Virginia was a continuing lesson in the evils of the coal companies. Mostly controlled by out-of-staters, they avoided paying anything like their fair share of taxes and their contempt for workers and the environment was seldom concealed. Have they changed? Not a bit.

Peters reminded his readers that Underwood was himself a former coal company executive and that coal industry people had contributed over a half million dollars to his campaign and inauguration funds. It was no wonder there were seventy-five MTR projects underway and that Underwood was trying to encourage more.

Four environmental groups filed a suit to remove Mike Miano, Underwood's DEP Director and a long-time coal industry executive. In a conflict-of-interest, reminiscent of Ken Faerber thirteen years earlier, these groups cited Clean Water Act provisions requiring a permit-issuing official to have been out of a regulated industry for at least two years. Miano did not meet this requirement.

Meanwhile McFerrin kept Conservancy members updated on the workings of the Governor's Mountaintop Removal Task Force. He reported that a DEP official had hoped the task force would determine what the long-term effects of valley fills were. McFerrin wondered why this had never been addressed before. Certainly state officials must have calculated the environmental impacts prior to issuing the first MTR permit. He compared the rush to permit MTR with the nation's rush to build nuclear power plants, only belatedly realizing the environmental costs that had been ignored.

Martin took issue with the comments of Task Force Chairman, Dr. Wade Gilley, president of Marshall University. In a *Gazette* commentary, Gilley had referred to "professional testifiers," those who were "proudly pointing to their past appearances before various public groups on this and other topics." He excluded coal industry spokesmen, state regulators, and was clearly dismissive of citizen-environmentalists. Martin wrote:

> How can he prejudge people who are concerned about things in their communities and who speak out about their concerns? Why does he find it odd that people are proud of the stands they have taken for things they care about? What in the world is wrong with being active in your community and being proud of it? Gilley makes it sound like a crime or deviant behavior.
>
> Name-calling is a time-honored method of discrediting opponents. I guess we are just lucky he didn't call us communists. He has already made clear that if people are not in one of his approved four groups that they are just wasting his time, they will not be listened to! What kind of chairman is it that writes off speakers at public hearings? How can he be fair? Is it thoughtful when he publicly calls people names who have spoken to the task force on mountaintop removal?
>
> I proudly count myself in the group he wants to degrade with name-calling. I am not a coal company executive or lobbyist, nor a paid environmentalist, nor a miner, and I don't live right on the edge of a mountaintop removal project. But I know that the coal companies will take tops off every mountain that has coal in it, anywhere they can. They will not stop with what they have removed so far — they will destroy every coal-bearing mountain in sight if they own it. Nothing is holy to them but money.

It was classic Martin and he would be heard from many times over the next decade. The following month he was elected to the Conservancy Board and was still serving in 2007.

It was ironic that it had been exactly twenty years earlier that the Highlands Conservancy had threatened to sue OSM and the state for failing to enforce federal regulations restricting mountaintop removal mining. The details were a little different, but it had been twenty years of frustration trying to apply the 1977 law. The massive economic jugger-naut of the mining-regulatory complex in West Virginia had been a Goliath to the Conservancy's David.

If the twenty pages of the monthly *Highlands Voice* were any indica-tion of the Conservancy's priorities, clearly mining issues were now at or near the top. In most issues, there appeared three or four mining articles, a couple more on the fight to save the Blackwater Canyon, and several more philosophical pieces, which Editor Reed hoped would stretch readers' thinking.

That year's Fall Review in October would be a little different. First it was to be held at Camp Virgil Tate in Sissonville (north of Charleston), the furthest west it had ever been. Second, it would be co-sponsored with the Ohio Valley Environmental Coalition, an increasingly important leader in state issues. Its theme would be mountaintop-removal mining, and former Conservancy administrative assistant and geologist, diPretoro, a pilot, was offering fly-overs. Field trips on the ground were scheduled to Kayford Mountain and Blair, and a canoe trip was offered on the Coal River. It would be memorable.

Frank Young, elected to succeed McFerrin as Conservancy president, appealed to members for financial support. While the cost of litigation to save Blackwater Canyon had generated new contributions and recruited new members, the MTR lawsuits had not and were eating away at the Conservancy budget.

Young wrote his first *Voice* column as president, calling it "From the Western Slope of the Mountains," reflecting his residency in Ripley. He had served as senior vice president and been active in a variety of issues. (A more complete profile is found in Chapter 8.) Now he would lead the Conservancy through three of its most active issues: Blackwater Canyon, mountaintop removal, and wind energy.

Governor Underwood received both "majority" and "minority" reports from his Task Force. On the "majority" report, the *Gazette's* Ken Ward reported Task Force Chairman Gilley, turned over a long list of recommendations to Governor Underwood, commenting that the governor and the Legislature together would need to implement those changes. Focusing on the legislative branch, where inherently political decisions such as this issue were vested, the report recommended further study on the long-term environmental impacts, the creation of a new office in the DEP to address the human and community impacts, the repeal of the "mitigation" bill setting the fees for burying streams and an increase in water quality emphasis in all mining regulations. McFerrin was the only member who voted against the report.

McFerrin had labored as a "minority of one" on Governor Underwood's coal industry-dominated MTR Task Force. The Conservancy board had supported his involvement, and *Voice* readers had received periodic updates. On January 2, 1999, McFerrin issued a "minority report" to the Governor. He wrote:

> After considering all the testimony at public hearings, my own study, and various documents, it is my belief that mountaintop removal mining should be banned. To the extent that any of the committee reports allow for its continued existence then I disagree with them.
>
> My conclusion comes from many sources. First, it is not economically useful. Coal mining is at best a temporary benefit to our state's economy. The historical record is overwhelming that the presence of coal mining does not contribute to the long-term economic health of West Virginia. In counties where it is found, it is the dominant economic activity. Yet the non-coal economy does not thrive. If coal does anything for an economy, it is that it creates a prosperous economy for coal companies and temporary employment for some (although the number is declining) workers. It does nothing for the economy as a whole. If this were not true, the coal counties would not be the poorest in a poor state.
>
> Second, it is environmentally damaging. This should be an uncontroversial conclusion. The process takes millions of tons of dirt and rock and dumps it into valleys. It fills streams. It replaces living, growing forests with grass and (on rare occasions) struggling seedlings. Nature has awesome recuperative powers. Several centuries hence it will have corrected this damage. To say that the mining is not environmentally damaging is ludicrous.
>
> That the mining is environmentally damaging does not, of course, fully answer the question of whether we allow it to continue or not. Most things we do are environmentally damaging. Were there economic or social benefits that outweigh the environmental damage, then continuation of mountaintop-removal mining would be a reasonable option.
>
> Mountaintop-removal mining is the most intrusive, most hideous, most environmentally destructive practice one can imagine. The very name says it all. Were it producing the best schools, the best roads, the

healthiest people, and the most prosperous economy, then one could consider tolerating this practice. Since it is not, the environmental damage is not tolerable.

McFerrin continued. Third, the people opposed it. Fourth, it was illegal under the Clean Water Act. Fifth, it was immoral, and he cited five major religious denominations that opposed it. Sixth, and most persuasive to him, the industry had corrupted state government, and would continue to put its interests ahead of the public interest.

He discussed the assumption that coal mining was good for the economy. Then he turned to the novel idea, supported by the Task Force, that DEP should establish a Bureau of Community Impact to address individual and community needs. McFerrin found no reason to expect that the DEP would become committed to community protection, since they had not yet proven their commitment to the environment. He called the idea "charming," but no substitute for already-established citizen rights under prevailing law. Any such bureau would only have a chance if it were outside DEP and had the power to make binding permit recommendations, which was highly unlikely.

Finally the environmental considerations: Two incorrect assumptions had been made. One was that headwater streams had no environmental value and the other was that "approximate" in "approximate original contour" was too vague to define. Both, McFerrin argued, were totally wrong and to base further recommendations on these assumptions doomed them from the start.

His minority report, comprehensive, logical, and well presented, appeared in *The Charleston Gazette*, which gave it a wide audience. There is no record that it was even read by the governor, however.

Meanwhile, by the time of its final release in December, OSM's "months-long delayed" report on West Virginia's regulation of mountaintop-removal mining had been watered down. Although a strong draft had appeared in August, tough criticisms had been modified. On the important issue, the definition of "approximate original contour," OSM was still thinking about leaving it up to individual state discretion. Both Senator Byrd and Congressman Rahall had expressed their disappointments as well. A *Gazette* editorial concluded, "OSM has miserably failed in its duty to oversee West Virginia's regulators. This report was a belated attempt to rectify the situation. Sadly, it simply compounds past failures and resolves no major issues."

In another landmark legal agreement, the Conservancy and its co-plaintiffs agreed to a partial settlement in their federal court suit, intended to place new limits on mountaintop-removal permits. Michael McCabe, EPA Regional Administrator, said, "This will change the way mountaintop mining is conducted in West Virginia and every other Appalachian state." Rank said, "It's time now for major reforms at DEP."

McCabe indicated EPA had agreed to perform a comprehensive environmental assessment over the next two years about the impact of mountaintop mining and valley fills, although stricter standards would likely apply to only new permits, not existing operations. Rank objected that the state's largest mountaintop-removal operation, Arch Coal's Spruce Fork mine, would therefore be exempt. Local activists were upset. James Weekley, one of the plaintiffs said, "The new policy is likely to help in the future. But it doesn't protect Pigeonroost Hollow, where my family has lived for over 200 years."

This Environmental Impact Statement on mountaintop removal mining would become a major political football.

However, the settlement resolved only three claims from the Conservancy's suit, and the other twelve remained before U.S. District Judge Charles Haden.

On January 30, 1999, a Rally for the Mountains attracted more than five hundred people to Charleston expressing their opposition to mountaintop removal mining. Organized by the Ohio Valley Environmental Coalition, speakers included Secretary of State Ken Hechler, author Denise Giardina, Kayford Mountain resident Larry Gibson, and the Conservancy's Rank and Young.

A little over a month later, on March 3, 1999, Judge Haden granted a preliminary injunction to the Conservancy and its co-plaintiffs in their 1998 suit. Although three issues had been resolved earlier, Judge Haden issued a forty-seven page order requiring the state and federal regulators to withhold permits for the 3,100-acre Arch Coal Hobet mine in Logan County.

Judge Haden's order chronicled a fly-over that, even with light snow, had shown previously mined areas as devoid of tree growth. He wrote that the Conservancy and co-plaintiffs had "raised substantial, serious questions" that the DEP Director Miano had abused his discretionary powers.

A hearing was scheduled for the following September.

To understand the reaction to Judge Haden's decision, it is necessary first to understand Judge Haden. In an excellent profile written by Rudy Abramson for the *APF Reporter*, Haden was described as a 61-year-old West Virginia Republican. He had served in the legislature, been Governor Moore's Tax Commissioner, served on the West Virginia Supreme Court, and never lived outside West Virginia. When he was sworn in as U.S. District Judge in 1975, he was the youngest member of the federal judiciary. Now, Abramson wrote, "After more than two decades on the federal bench, he was thought of as a 'strict constructionist,' and coal industry executives and lobbyists, some of whom referred to him as 'Chuck,' found his assignment to the case reassuring."

In his March *Voice* column Young wrote that, "For the first time in many years, some of us have hope that some of the most blatant violations of SMCRA [the federal law], caused by official negligence (partially admitted by OSM, and denied by WVDEP) might get a fair, official review."

McFerrin wrote a thoughtful analysis in the same issue explaining how the issues had come to the point where now coal miners were being laid off, mining operations shut down and environmentalists scapegoated. Had the laws been enforced in the first place, such personal disruptions could have been avoided, he noted. Referring to his task-force minority report, he reiterated that mountaintop-removal mining by definition would not leave the land at the required "approximate original contour" and the massive amounts of soil and rock had no place to go but into the valleys, thus violating the Clean Water Act's prohibition on stream destruction. On two counts, this type of mining was illegal. He continued:

> At first glance, the judge's decision appears bold and dramatic. It is telling a big coal company that it cannot do exactly what it wants to do. For West Virginia, that's dramatic.
>
> As bold and dramatic as it seems, it is really no more than a victory for the rule of law. We have laws regulating strip mining and controlling water pollution. They have to mean something. We can't just have an industry and a state agency who ignore the ones which are inconvenient.
>
> It is unfortunate that the industry and the agency did not follow the law all along. Had they not wandered so far beyond what the law allows then being forced to follow the law would not seem like such a dramatic step.

Another rally against mountaintop removal was scheduled for April 24, 1999. Giardina, a well-known passionate speaker, and sometime candidate for governor on the Mountain Party ticket, would be the keynote speaker. The Highlands Conservancy was listed among eight organizational co-sponsors.

Feelings were running high, to say the least. Between the injunction issued by Judge Haden and the scheduled hearing in September, rallies on both sides were held. Letters to the editor were filling local and metro newspapers. The *Voice* reprinted an exchange between Conservancy Board member Martin and two other Lincoln County residents. One had personally attacked Martin for pointing out a series of euphemisms and how the coal industry was marshalling public opinion against the "environmentalist." The other defended Martin and criticized the personal nature of the coal supporters' attacks. Responding to the charge of being an "out-of-state extremist," Martin wrote:

> My family has been in this state since the early 1800s when Isaac Barker settled at White Oak Creek on Big Coal River. My dad, a UMW miner, lost an eye in the mines, my grandfather fought on the side of the union at Blair Mountain. My uncles, brother-in-law, son, friends and former students have been miners. I am not from out-of-state, and being for the mountains as they are seems far less extreme than destroying the mountains. Absentee-controlled coal companies like Arch Coal of St. Louis and Massey of California are the "out-of-state extremists."
>
> Trying to make your opponents look like evil people is a way to divert attention from the real issue. The real issue is that the mountains of West Virginia are being destroyed, forever. Those destroyed mountains will provide no jobs in the future. On the 300,000 acres that have been strip-mined in West Virginia, 180 million board feet of hardwood lumber could have been cut every year, forever. Hardwoods don't grow on so-called "reclaimed" strip-mine sites, the ground is as hard as concrete.

The "environmental extremists" of the Conservancy appreciated Martin; the July 1999 *Highlands Voice* had a close-up of Martin and Mae Ellen on its cover. Inside readers learned of a planned 490-mile "Walk for the Mountains," scheduled to begin July 7, 1999, in Harpers Ferry and proceed west across the state, taking the opportunity to discuss mountaintop-removal mining along the way. Organized by the Ohio Valley Environmental Coalition, three of the walkers would be Larry

Gibson, of Kayford Mountain, Mitchell Stanley, and the Conservancy's Martin. To kick it off, a rally on July 3 on Kayford Mountain would include Hechler, among others. The walk was scheduled to conclude August 21. The Highlands Conservancy was listed among the supporting groups.

President Young announced a series of rapid developments in the August *Highlands Voice.* He outlined a proposed settlement in the big mountaintop-removal federal lawsuit. Most, but not all, of the issues in the suit had been agreed upon by July 26, 1999. Young wrote that it was hard to believe the state DEP Director Miano really intended to redefine "approximate original contour," change the bonding procedures and requirements, redefine post-mining land uses, and accept oversight of technical issues by an independent technical advisory committee. This was the same department that had insisted they were in compliance with the law the old way.

It soon became apparent how change might occur. Miano was resigning. Then the second shock: Judge Haden would withhold his approval until after a period for public comment. Young felt encouraged, but admitted that any settlement, even a court order, depended on compliance of all parties. Miano's departure, Young wrote, was a positive signal.

McFerrin pointed out that the fundamental question of the legality of filling valleys with soil and rock was still in dispute. The other issues included an engineering definition of "approximate original contour," and stricter application of post-mining land uses. No longer, for example, would scattered grass qualify as "wildlife habitat." The unsettled issue would await Judge Haden's decision.

Meantime, since Judge Haden had requested public comment, Conservancy members were encouraged to provide letters addressing the major issues.

Martin wrote about the "Walk for the Mountains" in the August *Voice.* The journey had been mostly hot and dry, and they were averaging about fifteen miles per day. One highlight was an interview by Jim Hightower, populist politician from Texas, for his national radio program. Martin reported many signs of support and hospitality. Giardina had joined them on occasion. In southern West Virginia, local supporters had organized rallies. They expected to arrive at the Capitol on August 21.

Unfortunately not all who walked the roadways that summer met with such support. In August a memorial march on Blair Mountain, organized to commemorate traditional miners, past and present, had ended in a rowdy skirmish. Among the marchers was 84-year old Secretary of State Hechler, who was shoved, kicked, and tripped before the police arrived. Rank was present, but not involved in the skirmish.

Judge Haden's Decision and Its Aftermath

On October 20, 1999, U.S. District Court Judge Charles Haden II issued his long-awaited decision. To virtually everyone's surprise he prohibited the West Virginia Department of Environmental Protection from granting further mining permits for mountaintop mines. He declared valley fills, a necessary component of mountaintop removal, to be illegal. Although the Conservancy and other co-plaintiffs had agreed to compromise a number of permit details earlier in the year, the judge's decision was more than they had expected! Among the environmental community, it was a happy day indeed!

On the other side, the coal industry, working together with the former coal executive, now governor, Cecil Underwood, opened a full campaign to reverse Haden's ruling. First, emergency appeals to the Fourth Circuit would be made. The Governor had already begun the misinformation campaign by declaring this the end to all surface mining in West Virginia. His tax commissioner was predicting a state financial crisis. Within two days the Governor ordered a state hiring and spending freeze. Conservancy President Young wrote, "Exaggeration designed to create an artificial public frenzy has taken on record levels of official endorsement recently in West Virginia."

After nine days of watching this frenzied over-reaction, Judge Haden issued a stay, pending appeal, not because the defendants' motions for the stay were convincing, he said. Rather, the Judge said, because he wanted to diffuse irrational fears generated by political exaggeration and hyperbole. Judge Haden explained:

> A firestorm of reaction has come forth from Defendants and state government officials, predicting that the court's injunction will cause unprecedented economic and social dislocation throughout West Virginia. In short, the Court believes it preferable to attempt to defuse invective and diminish irrational fears so that reasoned decisions can be made with all deliberate speed, but with distractions minimized.

In his ruling, Judge Haden had simply affirmed, based on the Surface Mining Act, that fills could not be dumped into streams that flow year-round or part of the year. The following day, OSM Director Karpan threatened to revoke its "stream buffer rule" which was designed to achieve the same purpose.

All five members of the West Virginia congressional delegation issued a joint press release stating that Haden's ruling did not represent congressional intent and stated they would consider legislation to overturn his decision.

Rank, the Conservancy Mining Chair, said she had expected politicians to try to overturn the ruling if the Conservancy won. "I certainly hope they don't change the law. The law was put there so mining could occur and the environment could be protected. There can still be mining. It just can't be as big," she said.

Abramson would later write, "Not since the late U.S. District Judge Frank Johnson desegregated Alabama buses and schools and opened state voting booths to African Americans in the 1950s and '60s has a federal judge confronted the political and economic powers of his native state more conspicuously."

As the Congressional effort to overturn the ruling began to gain momentum, national environmental groups became more vocal.

Even the powerful Senator Robert C. Byrd was unable to attach a pro-coal rider to a piece of legislation to circumvent the Surface Mine Act and the Clean Water Act. Amazingly, twenty Republican members of Congress who opposed Byrd's rider had written President Clinton, "The adoption of a rider to block this decision would be a particularly egregious abuse of the legislative process."

As the new millennium began and the American public worried about Y2K, West Virginians also discussed the status of mountaintop removal mining. The Fourth Circuit Court in Richmond had inherited the hot potato of Judge Haden's ruling.

To begin the year 2000, President Young commented upon a recent statement by Governor Underwood. Speaking at a coal industry event, Underwood had said of environmentalists and their lawsuits, "This is not an economic issue for them; it's a sociological and political issue." Young used that statement as his text to begin his analysis. He wrote:

> That statement by our governor tells us so much we wish we didn't have to know about his value system. Apparently, his only measure of the value of resources is in terms of economics. How many dollars will the extraction of this resource generate? How many dollars will it cost to avoid unnecessary environmental destruction?

I believe that most folks consider many of nature's gifts to be priceless. Priceless does not mean worthless. Priceless means having value beyond finite measure. Some things are worth so much that we would put no price on them. Our children. Our parents. Our other loved ones.

Likewise, the gifts of nature that enable this and future generations to live are priceless, although some segments of society place artificial values on these resources for purposes of commerce.

How much is clean water worth? Clean air? Clean soil upon which mankind may live, work and grow food? Again, except for the artificial economy, these resources are priceless. To put a price on the elements of our life support system, the environment, is to put a price on life itself. That's because when the environment is debased and depleted, regardless of the "economic" value received, life itself will become worthless because it will cease to exist. Wasting and destroying a part of the environment is wasting and destroying a part of life.

At the risk of having this column labeled as "anti-corporate," I respectfully submit that it is the corporate mentality that all values are measured in terms of dollars, or other units easily converted to dollar values, that has created more human-generated environmental destruction by pollution and depletion in the past century and a half than in all of the previous history of mankind's habitation of earth.

Is it just a coincidence of time that the corporate economy, an artificial economy created by artificial institutions, has prospered most in parallel time with the most environmental mayhem? The answer is no, it is not a coincidence. To generate a "profit" in an artificial, corporate economy, the human and natural systems must be exploited of the immeasurable "value" of labor and the priceless "value" of the environmental reserves on which life depends. In other words, corporate profit is the dividend corporations reap from the labors of real people and the pollution, waste, and depletion of real, natural goods.

I think it should be the obligation and duty of government to regulate the artificial economies of mankind in such a manor as to minimize "profits" and maximize natural resource protection. But that doesn't happen when the profit from exploitation is used to elect or otherwise instill government that unabashedly encourages wasteful natural resource consumption, at artificially low prices in the artificial, corporate economy.

Governor Underwood's simple remark that "This is not an economic issue for them..." tells it all. It is perhaps the best explanation of what the battles over coal and other exploitation is really about. The battle is about the corporate drive to "profit" in the artificial economy, regardless of the actual costs to priceless resources.

… Underwood's assessment goes a long way in defining and underlining the problems.

Perhaps this commentary by a seasoned Conservancy leader really did identify the basic clash between the environmental community and its corporate opponents. McFerrin too was a leader who was drawn to the individual and rural communities that were impacted by mining. The past two *Voice* editors, Bill Ragettè and Bill Reed, both lived well out in the country, as did Rank. And although the Conservancy included many members from Charleston, Morgantown, and indeed urban centers outside West Virginia, part of its vision of itself was as a protector of those impacted by mining, and that mining, especially mountaintop-removal mining, inevitably occurred in isolated rural areas. Yes, as Underwood said, it was really a sociological and political battle.

A letter to the Conservancy and its co-plaintiffs from Carolyn Johnson, of the Citizen's Coal Council, began by praising the courage and persistence of those involved in the MTR case. But then she wrote:

> I want to tell you what will likely happen in the coming months.
> As everyone surely knows by now, citizens won a great victory on November 18 and defeated Senator Byrd's effort to weaken the clean water and coal mining regulations for all coal mines everywhere.
> Hundreds of groups and tens of thousands of people joined in to stop the Byrd rider because protecting our streams is so important. All the national environmental groups worked hard on this, and the issue got a lot of television and newspaper publicity.
> We expect Senator Byrd to try again next year. I can't promise that we will win again, but I think we have a very good chance. Certainly the chances look better to me than they did at the end of October before Byrd's first attempt.

It didn't take long before Johnson's predictions began to come true. In February 2000, the Clinton Administration was already considering both legislative and regulatory positions that would undermine (pardon the pun) Judge Haden's ruling. The U.S. Justice Department had also filed an appeal. The Administration was proposing to redefine "fill" in the Corps' "dredge and fill" permit to exclude mine waste. By so doing, dumping mine waste in streams would become legal.

To add insult to injury, the Justice Department's Notice of Appeal also indicated that it would appeal citizens' rights to sue state officials in federal court for their failure to enforce federal environmental and other laws. A Justice Department argument that the Eleventh Amendment barred such citizen suits even when they were explicitly authorized by Congress went beyond even what the most conservative members of the Supreme Court had so far been willing to do. If such an argument were to prevail, citizens would lose one of their most important means of assuring that federal environmental laws were enforced by the states.

Should this provision become law, the Conservancy's last thirty years of efforts to bring reasonable regulation of mining and protection to individuals and small communities would end, for it was that very ability to sue in federal court that had led to some dozen legal actions. The most recent, visible, and politically volatile had resulted in Judge Haden's decision.

Vivian Stockman, who had worked on the Conservancy's Blackwater Canyon Campaign and was now with the Ohio Valley Environmental Coalition, noted the thirtieth anniversary of Earth Day on April 22, 2000. "The state of our environment does not look good," she wrote, and then continued:

> In West Virginia, the evidence that corporations control our government is most horribly visible in the massacre of our mountains by the coal industry. Our last three heads of the West Virginia Department of Environmental Protection (DEP) have been coal industry executives, who profess that no environmental harm comes from blasting hundreds of feet off mountain after forested mountain, and burying mile after mile of headwater streams. The DEP spends loads of taxpayer money defending the way it has issued mountaintop-removal permits, even though the permits clearly violate sections of the Clean Water Act and federal surface-mine law.
>
> Collusion between government and industry is evident on all political levels. The nation's top mining regulator, that was Kathy Karpan of the Office of Surface Mining, is promoted instead of fired when she seeks employment as the nation's top mining lobbyist. The agencies that are supposed to regulate mining are instead promoting whatever the industry wants. Our Senators and Representatives and the Clinton/Gore Administration rush to weaken decades-old environmental laws so that coal companies will be now LEGALLY able to continue mountaintop removal — dewatering, deforesting, despoiling and destroying the life support system of Southern West Virginia.

Those who gain from mountaintop massacre — the CEOs of out-of-state corporations and their well-greased politicians — insist that this assault on our future must continue. They would have us believe their self-serving myth that the way things are is the way things have to be. What else can we have in the coalfields, but the coal industry they ask? This question plays upon people's fear of change and utterly discounts the power, ingenuity and creativity of community-minded people who work together.

We cannot allow King Coal and his politicians to continue mountaintop massacre with its increasingly unbearable toll on our state, enriching the few at great cost and peril to us all, including unborn generations. We cannot leave the future this legacy from blind, insatiable greed. The brutalized landscape that mountaintop removal leaves is like a scream from the Earth, telling us we must change, we must stop this assault.

The Highlands Conservancy was just three years old when *Voice* Editor Bob Burrell had reported on the first Earth Day in 1970. Since then, there had been a long, but small parade of citizen-activists within the Highlands Conservancy who had fought for balanced mining and environmental protection. Through numerous governors and their agency directors, White House occupants and their OSM directors, now a dozen lawsuits, the struggle continued, but had progress really been made? Without all the citizen efforts, by the Conservancy's members and increasingly by its allies, the environmental consequences would no doubt have been much worse. But a serious question was apparent: How long would citizens be able to sustain the battle in the face of an ever-more-savvy governmental-mining industry complex?

The Conservancy was deeply involved with saving the Blackwater Canyon, Shavers Fork (again), the threatened Balsam Fir, monitoring the construction of Corridor H and the very newest threat to the highlands, wind energy. The Conservancy was well along with a rejuvenated outings program, Mon 2000, its *Hiking Guide* was in its sixth edition, the twenty-page *Highlands Voice* appeared monthly and, perhaps most important, the membership had doubled in the past two years, reaching an all-time high. But amazingly, during the year following Judge Haden's decision, there were fewer *Voice* articles about mining than in almost any year since the early 1970s. Could the mining activists be exhausted?

Young's October 2000 *Voice* column revealed there had been activity quietly going on all along. He compared Conservancy Board member

Carroll Jett's 1991 letter to *The Charleston Gazette* with the reality nine years later. Young wrote:

> Almost nothing has changed — not even the rhetoric — in the past decade. The West Virginia Department of Environmental Protection (WVDEP) staffing, considered unacceptably low by the United States Office of Surface Mining (OSM) a decade ago, has decreased, not increased, over the ensuing years. And the insolvency of the bond pool for post-1977 forfeited surface-mined sites has ballooned beyond WVDEP's ability to calculate.
>
> Now, nearly 10 years later, the United States Office of Surface Mining (OSM) is still serving notices of intent to take over the state's surface-mining regulatory program from WVDEP.
>
> And if anything puts fear into the minds of the governor and the coal industry, it is the serious prospect that someone other than a state agency would actually be operating the surface-mining program.
>
> In July 2000 the Conservancy filed a Notice of Intent (N.O.I.) to sue OSM, asking the court to order OSM to take over the surface-mining permitting and enforcement program from WVDEP because of its failure to implement the program at even a minimally acceptable level. In informal response to that Notice, OSM only continues to ask the WVDEP for evaluations of its own delinquencies and gets virtually nothing in meaningful response.
>
> WVHC Past President and mining committee activist John McFerrin, in a paraphrase, says that OSM's response to our N.O.I. is: "DEP has been a mess for at least ten years. In another ten we may have the problem figured out and be ready to start thinking about a possible solution. We'll get back to you."
>
> Carroll's 1991 article continued, "The political influence of the coal industry is pervasive in both major political parties — always has been. We don't have the privilege of voter initiative and referendum. In short, a federal takeover of the regulatory process is the only apparent source of protection we have from the coal-mining industry, short of armed insurrection."
>
> But John McFerrin said recently that since the courts frown on the use of guns, the only resort is to sue.
>
> I agree, then, with Carroll Jett who concluded, in the 1991 article, "If we buy into some sort of compromise (cop-out, in other words) we will probably get a brief respite of six months or a year, during which the industry will make a half-hearted attempt to play by the rules. But it will soon return to its destructive orgy, running roughshod over the land and people. The pattern of "progress" is predictable. Depleting the

resources of one area, operators move on to the next hollow, where the process begins anew under a different corporate name — leaving behind a legacy of broken hearts, environmental nightmares, and unpaid bills."

Last month the WVHC's Executive Committee authorized the Conservancy's attorney to file suit in federal court to require that surface mining permitting and enforcement in West Virginia become a federal government (OSM) responsibility.

OSM obviously doesn't want to actually have the responsibility of running the program. But federal law requires that when the state agency does not operate the surface-mining regulatory program in compliance with federal laws, that OSM shall run the program itself.

OSM may or may not perform its obligations to our full satisfaction. But certainly it could do no worse than WVDEP.

Considering that the local good ol' boy political network is easier to keep greased on a local (state) level than on a federal level, OSM could probably do noticeably better.

The more some things change the more they stay the same. There is no MORE room for compromise.

Young, Jett and McFerrin had reached a similar, and cynical, conclusion. Others might say, realistic. As West Virginians entered the new millennium, with the ever-growing appetite for energy, would there ever be enough energy of citizen-activists to control West Virginia?

Meanwhile the Conservancy's efforts were receiving much-deserved recognition. On September 11, 2000, the West Virginia Highlands Conservancy was awarded a major honor by Friends of the Earth - International, meeting in Berkeley Springs. On the Conservancy's behalf, Wayne C. Spiggle accepted the prestigious award that recognized a community or organization demonstrating outstanding leadership on behalf of the environment.

In his October *Voice* article reporting on the award, he related that the Friends of the Earth said:

> The West Virginia Highlands Conservancy has fought against powerful corporate and political interests on behalf of the environment. The Conservancy stood up for coalfield citizens and the environment when the state of West Virginia refused to. They have partnered with Friends of the Earth to fight the destructive practice in which mining companies blast the tops off mountains to reach coal underneath and then dump waste into nearby streams and valleys.

Friends of the Earth has networked with the Highlands Conservancy and others in combating the U.S. Environmental Protection Agency's and the U.S. Army Corps of Engineers' proposed change to a critically important Clean Water Act rule issued for public comment in April, to allow wastes to be dumped into rivers, streams, and wetlands across the United States" — effectively overturning Judge Haden's ruling on mountaintop mining. Friends of the Earth was particularly helpful to the brave band of Conservancy members who went to Washington last November to defeat a legislative rider by Senator Byrd which would have overturned Judge Haden's decision.

Spiggle commented that he was the one who was honored, by being asked by Cindy Rank to represent the Conservancy at the award ceremony. He added, "I have long admired the responsible stewardship and the potent advocacy of the Highlands Conservancy. The roster of officers, board members, and committee chairs listed each month in the *Highlands Voice* is truly a list of my heroes."

As if to remind *Voice* readers of the enormity of mountaintop-removal mining, continuing unabated while Judge Haden's decision awaited the Fourth Circuit's decision, Stockman shared her recent experiences. She wrote:

> The loss of life to mountaintop removal is staggering and Judge Haden's ruling won't stop it. So much death so we can have plenty of cheap energy. So we can keep on using more, more, more. That's why members of the Ohio Valley Environmental Coalition, the Coal River Mountain Watch, the West Virginia Highlands Conservancy, and other environmental groups are holding a Funeral for the Mountains on October 28. We will join together to express our grief over this needless slaughter. We will send a unified a message to legislators and regulators that this is enough death. We will renew our commitment to fight like hell to save what remains of southern West Virginia's mountains.
>
> We will mourn the dead and renew our commitment to the living mountains.
>
> From the ground it's difficult to grasp the incredible scale of mountaintop removal. If you travel the turnpike, the deceptive "beauty strip" is pretty well preserved. Only here and there can you get a glimpse of what one national publication called "strip mining on steroids." If you go up Kayford Mountain, a green island in a desert of active MTR sites, you begin to understand the scale of mountaintop removal, though you really can't believe it.

I sure can't believe that the Army Corps of Engineers actually calls this "no significant environmental impact." It's incredulous that King Coal and its minions in government create and allow this. It's flabbergasting that some of the news media condone this. It's audacious that King Coal and other fossil fuel giants have so much political power (campaign cash!) that they squash federal initiatives for research and development on energy conservation and efficiency and renewable energies. It's incredible that we who live in America can be so energy hungry that we rationalize and justify this annihilation, this civil war on our ecosystem.

From about 1,500 feet up in the air, the scale of mountaintop removal is still difficult to grasp. My mind can't wrap around the immensity of the sites. Big John and its cousin, 20-story tall draglines that can take about a gargantuan bite — about 200 cubic yards — out of a mountain with each bucketful, were dwarfed by the naked scars of blasted, scalped and mined land. Huge dump trucks, that send a mountain of dust into the air each time they dump their 150-200 ton loads of former mountains into former valleys, looked like Tonka toy trucks. Slurry ponds, a convenient way for coal companies to avoid the formalities of valley fills, looked like lake-size abscesses of black pus. Sickening indeed.

There is site after site like this. No one seems to know how much mountaintop removal there is. We have probably lost at least 1,000 miles of streams and at least 300,000 acres of hardwood forest and the habitat it provided for mammals, birds, wildflowers, and trees. Southern WV towns like Blair, Kayford, and a host of others are dying or dead because of mountaintop removal. Scores of water wells and homes have been lost to mountaintop removal. [Carol] Jackson's mock MTR graveyard includes 1,000 mock tombstones, each representing a stream, mountain or community lost to King Coal's greed.

Here was a relatively young environmental leader, now active with a multi-state coalition organization, with which the Highlands Conservancy often cooperated. Maybe, indeed, there was a new generation coming on.

In January 2001, newly elected Governor Bob Wise represented a younger generation, a different political party, and generally was viewed as a progressive. His legislative career and his service in Congress, while not always satisfying the Highlands Conservancy, did more often than not. Certainly there was an expectation as he assembled his cabinet that the change of administration might lead to implementation of some of

Haden's reforms. Martin wrote that Governor Wise believed in "responsible mountaintop mining," Martin noting the absence of the term "removal." The Governor had also given a high state position to one of the men who had incited the mob that attacked Hechler, eighteen months earlier.

Young was more optimistic. "I am pleased to hear Governor Wise," Young wrote, "in last month's State of the State message, say that the state will enforce environmental laws. I hope that he and various state agencies follow through with that commitment."

Fourth Circuit Appeal

On December 7 and 8, 2000, a three-judge panel of the Fourth Circuit Court of Appeals based in Richmond, Virginia, heard oral arguments in the challenge to Judge Haden's mining decision. Judges assigned to this case were some of the court's most conservative, namely judges Paul V. Niemeyer, J. Michael Luttig, and Karen Williams — the first appointed by President Reagan and the latter two by President Bush.

Because much of the case revolved around inadequate regulations that the state established under OSM's grant of "primacy," there was considerable debate whether this case should be in state court, rather than federal court. Before a crowd of approximately one hundred interested people representing all sides, Joe Lovett and Jim Hecker argued for the plaintiffs. Another attorney represented both the coal industry and the United Mine Workers of America, prompting one judge to comment that he had never seen such a relationship before. A ruling was not expected until the following spring.

In early April 2001 Judge Haden issued a second decision. Ruling on a separate case filed by the Conservancy, this one against the DEP and OSM, it challenged the amount of bond required so that enough funds were available to cover abandoned mine sites. Haden ruled that since OSM had declared West Virginia's bonding program insufficient, henceforth the state would be "superceded" by the federal level. Haden distinctly insulated this case from the Bragg case, already on appeal. Under this ruling, the state could, at least temporarily, be blocked from issuing any permits.

Rank said, "Unless the coal industry is made to pay for these liabilities and clean up all these problems, the rest of us are going to get stuck with this." She continued, "Given all the flak and criticism that Judge Haden has received in the past over his rulings on the surface mining act, you have to applaud him for taking what is a very brave step, but on this issue is exactly what the law requires."

OSM had annually reviewed the state's reclamation program, the judge wrote, and consistently said the bonding was insufficient. Yet OSM had actually done nothing. Haden continued, "Because the West Virginia alternative bonding system has been found inconsistent with and less rigorous than the minimum federal standards, the State DEP Director has a non-discretionary duty to comply with minimum federal standards for bonding."

Earlier in February, Martin had written a piece for the *Gazette*. Remembering his childhood and Peace Corps service, he wrote:

> I rode through the Big Coal River Valley the other day, the valley of my birth, where I learned to swim, where my dad, grandpa, uncles, brother-in-law, and son worked in the underground coal mines. Random memories floated through my mind of the one-room school, taking cows up the hollow, the barn full of wonders, tossing "Frisbees" of flat, dry, disc-shaped cow piles, watering the horses at the river ford, sleigh riding in the snow and the earnest prayers in the little church across the river. But no matter how many times I pass through that valley, I am stunned out of my reverie by the dreary, desolate abandonment that envelops it, as does the black coal dust.
>
> Before the robber barons, before the virgin forests were cut, before coal mines, Coal River Valley must have been gorgeous. It would be interesting to know what the Indians thought of it and what they named it. If you want to see the local benefits of the coal industry, take a drive on Route 3 up Big Coal River. The roads, dirt, mud, and trees along the edges are black with coal dust, every other mountain has been gouged and altered. Huge piles of "spoil" and "overburden" have been pushed into the hollows and tower menacingly. Those valley fills look like some huge, black glacier getting ready to ooze out into the roadway.
>
> Stop at the Coal River Mountain Watch office in Whitesville and look at the maps that show mountaintop-removal mines under consideration. The blast zones overlap at Marsh Fork High School.
>
> Drive on up the road and see for yourself the gigantic sludge dam hovering over a grade school, which is also within the blast zones of the two newly proposed mines. It might forewarn of the tragedy in Wales when a mountain of coal refuse broke loose and covered a grade school, crushing and smothering all the children inside. There is a sludge dam expansion that will be nearly as high as the New River Gorge Bridge.

Whitesville was once a thriving community with an active, exciting downtown, where thousands of miners came and spent their money. Many of the storefronts are now abandoned. Whitesville is a dilapidated, decayed, dirty skeleton of its past. There are at least 11 coal mines in the area, and they have produced the very opposite of prosperity.

The view along the road between Whitesville and Marsh Fork looks as bad as anything I saw in the so-called Third World in the early '60s. The rural areas of Nigeria actually looked much better. In Nigeria, people lived off farming of the land and there was little environmental damage. They worked hard to bring enough to eat out of poor, sandy soil. But their environment was intact and there was a joyful celebration of life. There was nothing in that rural area of Nigeria as bleak, joyless, and depressing as the Whitesville and Marsh Fork environs.

I feel certain that the people who run the coal industry will not hesitate to take the top off every coal-bearing mountain in West Virginia. As the demand and price for coal goes up, there will be excuse to mine the high-sulfur seams in northern West Virginia, those mountaintops might will be leveled.

And if you think that some places will be too pristine to be stripped, too beautiful, too much in public view, take a look at the strip mine and the quarry at Snowshoe, the quarry in Germany Valley, and stand on a ridge above Webster Springs and look out at the beautiful ridges and see that one in the middle distance has been stripped. "Alarmist!" you may accuse. But if someone had said 50 years ago that the mountaintops of West Virginia would be removed, he too would have been called an alarmist. How could the tops of the mountains be removed in the Mountain State? This is severe, extreme environmentalism. For the most part it is out-of-state extreme environmentalism. Arch Coal got its name from the arch near their headquarters in St. Louis. Massey is a part of an international conglomerate. The Addington brothers are from Kentucky.

Coal River Valley suffered a greater defeat than Jay Rockefeller when he lost in his first bid for governor. Rockefeller got his political start at my birthplace of Emmons on Big Coal River. He was then in favor of the abolition of strip mining. I believed him and put his bumper sticker on my truck. How I wish he had spent enough money to get elected that time. How I wish the money he sent to Democratic bosses in Southern West Virginia had not ended up being used to support Arch Moore.

Rockefeller said in December 1970, "I will fight for the abolition of strip mining completely and forever." He must have been kidding, for just seven years later, as governor, Rockefeller testified to a U.S. Senate subcommittee considering the new strip mine law, "mountaintop removal should certainly be encouraged, if not specifically dictated."

If you have the stomach for the devastation, drive to the Stanley Family graveyard on Kayford Mountain just above Whitesville. There you can look down at what remains of mountains that used to cast shadows on the cemetery; see the earth turned upside down, a treeless wasteland, forever useless; see the future for the Mountain State if this beast isn't stopped.

Almost Heaven, West Virginia, has become, in the Coal River Valley and other little valleys and hollows, an Almost Hell, West Virginia.

Martin, a son of the coalfields of southern West Virginia and now a Conservancy Board member, had become for the Conservancy and many other people a real "conscience of the mountains." His writings, travels, and activities would carry on the tradition of Conservancy activists. Some were younger but no one had seen more or was more articulate.

On April 24, 2001, the Fourth Circuit Court issued its decision, overturning Judge Haden's decision on procedural grounds. Judge Neimeyer, writing for the court, cited the Eleventh Amendment of the Constitution and claimed the state could not be sued in federal court. Ken Ward wrote, "The main issue — whether Haden was correct to use a stream buffer zone to limit the size of mountaintop removal's valley fills — was not resolved. The 4th Circuit sent the case back to Haden, and instructed him to dismiss it so it could be filed in state court instead."

The jubilant celebration of eighteen months earlier had been replaced again by cynicism and worry that West Virginia would never get control over its mining industry. Martin wrote:

> More than one friend has asked me if I think we can win these environmental battles. They point out the incredible odds, the mountains of cash put into destroying our mountains, buying our politicians and the false twists and spins that industry executives and public relations companies put on the facts.
>
> My answer to the question can we win in the struggle to save our environment is that I don't know if we can win or not. I know that I am going to die but I don't quit living. I also know that we could lose out on some of our efforts to preserve nature (ourselves included) but that doesn't mean we should stop trying. We have to speak the truth whether it prevails or not. It would be bad enough to lose but still worse to lose without speaking the truth.

The national publication *In These Times* cited the West Virginia Highlands Conservancy as a "Green Hero" in its April 30 issue. The citation noted the Conservancy's dedication to trying to preserve southern West Virginia's mountains from mountaintop-removal mining. Of the nine awardees as "green heroes," three were from the United States, two from Latin America, and one each from Russia, India, and Kenya.

Meanwhile, the results of the studies by four federal agencies on the environmental impact of mountaintop-removal mining, originally promised in 1998 by EPA as part of the settlement with the Conservancy, were finally released in May 2001, but only after a Freedom of Information Act request. Described by Ken Ward of the *Gazette* as eight boxes, containing 40,000 pages of documents, these studies indicated that the Appalachian area might not recover from damage from mountaintop-removal mining for centuries. The controversial study had predictably been caught in political turmoil. In October 2000 EPA had delayed release at the request of West Virginia legislative leaders. Then, just before George W. Bush took office in January 2001, another try was made, but Governor Wise objected. In May a final report had yet to be completed.

The Floods of 2001

It didn't take long for the abuses of mountaintop removal mining to re-appear in the news. In the spring and early summer of 2001 there were four federally declared disasters as major floods plagued southern West Virginia. By July the Highlands Conservancy and other groups called for stronger enforcement of mining and timbering regulations, and the Conservancy announced a flood relief fund for southern West Virginia. In the first five days the Conservancy raised $4200.

Stockman, of the Ohio Valley Environmental Coalition, wrote: "The apologists for Big Coal and Big Timber are falling over themselves to blame this latest disaster solely on God or natural causes. Granted, there was a lot of rain in a short time. But why are we seeing so-called 100-year floods every few months? Scientists say it's because of human-induced global climate change, caused in large part by the burning of fossil fuels like coal."

Nathan Fetty, of the West Virginia Rivers Coalition, pointed out that DEP inspectors and local residents had seen more flooding problems in areas downstream of large strip mines. "Given that DEP has issued over a dozen cessation orders to mine operators because of flooding from this past weekend, it's even harder to imagine that valley fills and sediment ponds are designed with the public's safety in mind," Fetty said.

Fetty continued, "DEP inspectors readily acknowledge that mountaintop removal has contributed to flooding. Local residents directly downstream of the mines have had some of the biggest flooding headaches. We're long overdue in reigning in these extractive industries. Individual residents and community safety should be the primary concerns when mountaintop removal operations are given permits."

Charleston veterinarian and Conservancy Board member, Bob Marshall, reported on the delivery of relief supplies on July 17, 2001:

> The first delivery of supplies to Coal River Mountain Watch (CRMW) in Whitesville, Boone County, was made by myself and a group of our members on Sunday afternoon. A trailer load of cleaning supplies, shovels, bedding, and food was handed out to flood victims within minutes of its arrival at CRMW headquarters. All the recipients were extremely appreciative of the help, as were the CRMW staff, led by Judy Bonds.
>
> Afterward, we were able to tour some of the nearby sites of flooding with the help of one of the local residents. The level of destruction, and amount of damage was overwhelming. Most folks lost everything they had, and few had any flood insurance. The force of the waters destroyed most bridges, undercut roadways, and washed houses off their foundations. It really reminded me of a war zone, with the National Guard everywhere, manning checkpoints at each intersection, and army bulldozers and trucks clearing and hauling away debris!
>
> I came away with a feeling that although the devastation was massive, these determined folks will do whatever it takes to restore their communities.
>
> Obviously, much remains to be done… We are planning more deliveries this week, and next. The support from our members so far has been tremendous.
>
> August 6, 2001. As our relief effort developed in the following weeks, thousands of dollars of donations have been given to WVHC, for CORL [Coalition for Responsible Logging] to distribute to the needy. We had a follow-up delivery by Dave Saville, with help from Frank Slider and Doug Miley, a paddler from Ohio, about a week from the first trip to Boone County. The supplies were immediately snatched up by folks who truly appreciated the help, and often were falling thru the cracks of the systems in place in the flood areas.
>
> Most recently, we have elected to work through two local groups, Plateau Action Network (PAN) in Fayette County, and the Southern

Appalachian Labor School (SALS). Both groups received $1,000 from the WVHC the first week of August, to be used in the long-term recovery process, such as to help rebuild homes and repair salvageable buildings. We felt that people who already had a presence in the flood area could better utilize and distribute the funds, and I feel that both PAN and SALS are kindred groups to WVHC, as we share many of the same views and goals.

I cannot personally thank enough all those who responded to our call to action for the flood victims (who truly are victims of the greed of the extractive timber and coal industries in southern WV). We can all be proud to be a part of an organization that doesn't just talk, but backs it up with action. I have learned that our love of this state really shines when the chips are down. Let's not forget all the victims of this tragedy, but rather resolve to continue to extend a helping hand whenever and wherever we can. Let's also not relent in our efforts to change the system of abuse and environmental destruction in WV, for that is the only way we will ever truly help those living in harm's way to recover their quality of life and peace of mind.

It was a new project for the Conservancy to become a relief agency for the victims of flooding, caused by mountaintop removal mining and massive logging, but it was not inconsistent with the Conservancy's long record of support for those in rural communities whose lives were at risk from under-regulated extractive industries.

Following the flooding, Governor Wise appointed another task force to investigate the relationship between mining and timbering and the recent flooding. It was already under attack. It was to be headed by DEP Director Mike Callaghan and included Rank, representing the Conservancy. Already Callaghan had told the press that mining's effect was "insignificant."

Conservancy President Young, in his column in the September 2001 *Highlands Voice*, wrote:

> It is human nature for people to want to defend their previous public statements. And both Wise and Callaghan are on record as defending the coal and timber industry against charges of having contributed to the severity of flooding. How can the "task force" they appoint and head up do other than conclude that their previous statements on flooding are anything other than correct?
>
> The coal industry is quick to point out that it flooded because it rained — an "Act of God" the industry calls it. This simplistic explanation is about like saying that an automobile became wrecked because

the vehicle "left the highway." That the vehicle may have had bad brakes, bad tires, bad steering, an unfit driver, etc, is not reflected in simply saying that it "left the highway." If we leave it at that we can call the wreck an "Act of God." The result is no accountability for those who may be responsible, no matter how tragic the wreck was.

Simply saying that it flooded because it rained says nothing about surface mines that scalp the landscape of trees and other vegetation that would absorb and slow water runoff from rainwater. It says nothing about topsoil being ripped loose, buried in valleys, and only rock and compacted barren soil surfaces that cannot absorb rainfall remaining. And it says nothing about these practices usually being performed in areas prone to fast runoff because of steep mountain slopes.

Some places, like the steep mountains of southern West Virginia, are simply not suitable for surface mining as it is practiced there.

As a practical matter, the West Virginia DEP and the state Division of Forestry are clones of and for the mining and timber industries. The evidence of this is in recent public statements by the DEP that the coal industry had "agreed to" a watered down regulatory scheme for reclamation bonding of surface-mining sites. The state was obviously not going to implement any regulatory plan not totally agreeable to the mining industry.

We can expect that any "task force" report developing from these agencies will largely exonerate these industries — as the governor and the DEP agency head already have. The industry will be exonerated, but not because of the lack of culpability. It is because of the prevailing attitude of state government that the coal and timber industries can do no wrong. With that mindset, anything can be justified.

In contrast to the political leaders seeking to inoculate regulators and the regulated industries from blame, the *Voice* printed a first-person story of the flood of July 8, 2001. The author, Doug Hurst, recounted his family's experience and their appreciation for the Conservancy's relief efforts. He wrote:

> Outdoor travelers are at the mercy of the weather. It is often noted that nothing makes one feel smaller than nature's awesome power. I have known this for many years. On the morning of July 8th at our home on Laurel Creek in Beckwith, WV (Fayette County) my wife, two children, mother-in-law, and myself learned a lot more about nature's power and feeling small.
>
> I remember reading in an ecology textbook in 1988 that any stream of water over three meters wide is technically a river. Judging from the normal appearance of Laurel Creek, a quaint trout stream in the New

River Gorge, I was surprised to be informed that I was living on a river. Over the years I forgot that fact. On July 8th, 2001, I was reminded. On that day, my family and I witnessed a river in our back yard.

At 7:00 a.m. we awoke to a rainy Sunday morning. Ah, a day of rest and reading. I knew it had been raining since about 4:00 a.m. The creek looked just a little high; not out of its banks, not threatening. Soon we noticed how fast it was rising. A rising that was new, different. Coupled with the sudden realization that this loud, heavy, unceasing rain meant business, we found ourselves facing the possibility of a flood. Yet even then we had no idea what the next 5 hours was to bring.

In the next 50 minutes we saved from the rising and ever more powerful water, in no particular order, the following belongings: canoe, artwork, homemade things, computer, creek-side water pump (for watering the gardens), propane tank, assorted boxes, documents, and furniture. Confusion and disbelief increased with the water. My wife's mother, living next door, was the first to receive our attention since her house is (was) closest to the creek (river). About twenty minutes there and another thirty at our house was all the time we had. This was not enough. We grabbed what we could, retreated to higher ground, surrendered to the river, and watched. For about four hours all we could do was watch. Most of what we saw seemed surreal. A sixty-foot walnut tree seemed to melt silently into the river and disappear. I estimate there was about 20 times more water in the creek than we had ever seen. The force of the water, though, was hundreds of times magnified.

Suffice it to say life may never be quite the same again. About half the homes on Laurel Creek were totally destroyed. Almost all suffered significant damage. Fortunately, there were no injuries or lost lives in our community. My heart and prayers go out to those less fortunate. In the ten or so days after the flood we were most blessed with an enormous outpouring of volunteer help. Family, friends, friends of friends, church groups, and strangers appeared at our home in Beckwith, willingly working in flood mud up to their elbows and doing whatever else was necessary. They seemed to be drawn by some primal urge to repair the emotional damages to their fellow human beings, to return humanity to the delusive position of strength in the face of nature's omnipotence. Hope and home were restored by these very actions. Thank you all.

Yet, laborers, shovels, saws, and levels can't completely right the damage from this flood. Enormous erosion is best repaired with big machinery; vegetation by time. It is now August 13th, and people and nature have barely begun to heal the big scars from the flood. Recovery is just beginning. The numbers of phone calls, forms, and visits by officials that we have dealt with has been numbing. Except for FEMA, the big governmental agencies, like oversized B-52's, are just getting airborne from the point of view of the average family. There is waiting and uncertainty. Plans are on hold. Second to nature's power, being on the huge waiting lists make us feel small, too. Yet I am thankful for the government waiting lists. As one of my friends said upon a visit to Beckwith, "this looks like Honduras after Hurricane Mitch except they had to recover with only one one-hundredth of the resources." The works of many people in the Fayette County Emergency Services, Red Cross, State Road, National Guard, Natural Resource Conservation Service, Fire Marshal's office, FEMA, Small Business Administration, law enforcement, etc., have led to a solid foundation for eventual recovery. Thanks to everyone who has given of their blood, sweat, and tears to this effort. If the commitment continues and southern West Virginia is not forgotten, short-changed, or dismissed as a lower caste of useless hillbillies, then full recovery is possible, and deserved. After all, West Virginia is America, not a third-world country.

Grassroots organizations and just plain folk are generally able to respond more quickly, even if more modestly. West Virginia Highlands Conservancy has raised around eight thousand dollars from a single e-mail notice for supplies and donations to West Virginia flood victims. Bernie Sharp of The Store in Beckwith organized a fund-raiser for Laurel Creek victims and over four thousand dollars have been raised so far. Plateau Action Network (PAN) donated five hundred dollars to Mr. Sharp's fund raiser and another five hundred dollars to needy families in Oak Hill. PAN members and hundreds of others also volunteered their time and energy to help victims clean up and get back on their feet.

The real job of planning the future is now at hand. The basically opposite goals of quick relief and long-term improvements makes this a time for careful, smart decisions. This is not the time for egos and politics. This will be either opportunity seized or squandered. Haste and poor planning may leave us vulnerable to more of the same in the future. Obvious issues which the flood exposed are our region's inadequate sewer treatment and the terror of heavy rains on the exposed lands of surface mining, timbering, haul roads, and pavement on the steep terrain of Appalachia. Flooding will increase if more land surface is exposed. I really fear for our future when I think that things could get worse because of current political trends toward mining more coal, cutting more trees, and paving more lots. There is a call from the people for legislation to allow for regulating the quantity of water a watershed can carry as well as its quality. I know we can't control the rainfall, but that's all the more reason to take steps to control what we can. Can't there be a law that allows only a certain percentage of a watershed's surface area be un-vegetated at one time, with a consideration of the steepness of the land figured in? And can't that law err on the side of protecting people's life and property instead of erring on the side of short-term corporate profits? A drive through or flight over southern West Virginia easily reveals we have erred on the side of profits far too long. Isn't it the people's turn to get a fair shake? The profiteers will keep calling for more "scientific proof" of environmental damage until the last mountain is pushed into the last valley. Is it asking too much to expect adequate sewage treatment so our waters that we play in and obtain water supplies from are not a health hazard? Wouldn't such policies save money and boost the economy in the long run? How long should West Virginians accept the substandard conditions of the past when technologies and lessons of the present are with us?

We will stay on Laurel Creek and enjoy the sweet side of nature — great blue herons, king-fishers, raccoons, mink, trout, the gift of flowing water. We will do all we can to make the post-flood life better than before. We will continue the fight to save the mountains and rivers, for proper living conditions, for economic justice, for respect, and a future for those who love it. In the mountains we are tall, deep, and proud.

In January 2002 the Conservancy was back in court, in the seemingly endless battle to try and force the federal overseers in turn to force the state regulators to fix more than two-dozen deficiencies in the state program. Again the judge was Judge Haden, and the Conservancy lawyers indicated some of these issues had been discussed for over a decade. John W. Barrett, a lawyer for the Appalachian Center for the Economy and the Environment, representing the Conservancy, reminded Haden how lax OSM was in forcing the state to correct program deficiencies. Haden himself had ruled in a related case about reclamation bonds that DEP and OSM inaction had created "a climate of lawlessness, which creates a pervasive impression that continued disregard for federal law and statutory requirements goes unpunished, or possibly unnoticed. Agency warnings have no more effect than a wink and a nod, a deadline is just an arbitrary date on the calendar and, once passed, not to be mentioned again."

The floods of 2001 were not forgotten. Dave Saville reported that the Conservancy had collected close to $10,000 in flood relief donations, spent the money to support volunteers, buy supplies, and for several "mini-grants" dispersed to Highlands Conservancy member organizations who were doing flood relief work in affected areas and to other organizations who were getting the needed help to people and places that were falling through the cracks of the traditional flood relief mechanisms.

He noted the funds went to the Fayette Recovery Team, the Southern Appalachian Labor School, Plateau Action Network, Coal River Mountain Watch, the Organizing Project, and the Big Creek People in Action. He thanked everyone who had helped make this effort a success, especially the West Virginia Rivers Coalition and the Ohio Valley Environmental Coalition.

Young summarized his personal views, but perhaps also those of the Highlands Conservancy, in an article titled "An Atmosphere of Lawlessness and Corruption," in the March 2002 *Voice*. He wrote:

> Coal. The black rock that burns. Coal is West Virginia, some say. When the coal is gone, there will be nothing left, some say.
>
> Politically, coal means the coal industry. The coal industry includes coal-mining companies, railroad and trucking companies, and loading docks and transport barges, banks and insurance companies that finance and insure coal operations, law firms that work feverishly to fend off pesky government regulations and civil actions against coal, and a host of "supporting" services from fuel suppliers to manufacturers, sellers and servicers of giant dozers, trucks, loaders and draglines. And, of course, the coal industry includes the people who work at jobs all these components of the industry employ.
>
> Coal controls the West Virginia statehouse, some say. It's hard for an observer who has spent much time observing the legislature to argue with that one. Coal rules at the legislature. What coal wants, it usually gets. If coal doesn't get exactly what it wants, it takes it anyway.
>
> Witness coal trucking. 80,000 pounds is the maximum legal weight for motor vehicles on any public highway in West Virginia, less than that on most roads. Trucks hauling coal routinely haul twice that much. Yet coal truck owners and operators are indignant about criticism for lawbreaking, yelling, "We're not outlaws!"
>
> I write this at the end of a week which saw citizen outrage at and toward the legislature like we haven't seen since the "garbage wars" of the early 1990s. The outrage is expressed most by coal miners and their

neighbors, friends, and relatives who are tired of seeing other friends, relatives, and neighbors killed by outlaw coal truck owners and operators.

The current outrage over coal-truck outlaws is but another layer in the atmosphere of lawlessness in the coal industry.

"Atmosphere of lawlessness? Who says so?" one might ask. A federal judge says so. In ruling on lawsuits filed by the West Virginia Highlands Conservancy and others, Federal District Court Judge Charles Haden has said that the issuance of coal-mining permits and the mining of coal in West Virginia has been taking place in "an atmosphere of lawlessness".

Time after time the courts have ruled that state permits are issued contrary to established law, that state regulators operate a wholly inadequate and therefore illegal coal-mining reclamation bonding system, and that hundreds or thousands of miles of streams are illegally filled with debris. And the records rooms of regulatory agencies are awash in file after file of citation after citation of charges relating to water quality violations, illegal impoundments, and dozens of other kinds of illegal coal operations activities.

Yet, aside from the writing of numerous "Notice of Violations" forms, many to the same operating companies and for the same violations, nothing changes. Citations are rarely prosecuted to the point of assessing meaningful penalties. Those that are prosecuted are challenged in an almost endless legal maze of appeals. Even then, they are usually whittled down to petty fines that are not a significant deterrent to further lawbreaking. Repeat violators are almost never punished by "cease and desist" type actions, and I don't know that there ever was a real person criminally prosecuted for breaking any laws related to mining of coal under any permit ever issued.

In short, then, it is evident that coal does virtually whatever it wants to do, unimpeded by either respect for the laws, by regulatory agencies or, up until now at least, by even the courts. I submit that the network of private companies and public agencies that conspire to virtually exempt coal from the law is nothing short of a criminal enterprise and constitutes public and private corruption.

From the issuance of bogus permits, to illegally mining the coal, to the failure to provide for bonding for reclamation of lands debauched by coal operations, to illegally transporting the coal to loading docks and other facilities, coal is indeed mined and marketed in an atmosphere of lawlessness and associated violence to affected communities and public highway users both near to and far from the actual natural placement of coal deposits.

Indeed, Coal is King. Through political manipulations Coal virtually makes its own laws. Then it violates and disregards the laws it doesn't like, and conducts its operations in a violent and threatening manner in what is nothing short of a condition of terror — a reign of terror.

I saw and heard the terror this week in the eyes and the voices of coalfield residents begging for relief from the siege of outlaw coal trucks and their operators who are killing and injuring their families and their neighbors. I see and feel the terror every time I drive on a highway in the southern coalfields and strive to steer my vehicle clear of the nearly 100-ton trucks barreling down on me on a two-lane road designed for Model Ts and which is so "grooved" by heavy trucks that my vehicle follows the "groove" instead of in the direction of steer. I hear the threats from Coal Association spokesperson Bill Raney and coal-trucking company owners who say that coal trucks "must" haul grossly overweight, regardless of the law. I see the violence in the pictures of passenger cars flattened by overweight trucks that could not be stopped in time. I see violence in the devastation caused by floodwaters that poured off barren, unreclaimed mine sites that are unable to hold back, absorb. and release in a natural, restrained flow even the normal rains of mining regions.

West Virginia state government has spent millions of dollars to fight "terrorism" and to provide for "security" from unknown, imagined somethings or somebodys, somewhere. But what about homegrown terrorism? What about coal? We know where it is. We know who it is. We spend so much in providing "security" from phantom "terrorists". But what about security against the acts of the coal terrorists? The breach in security in the coalfields of West Virginia is a gaping breach, begging to be secured. Yet we ignore — NO, WAIT, we don't ignore — we nourish the coal terrorists right here among us.

Coal. If coal turns the lights on, why are our leaders at the statehouse all in the dark? Someone needs to turn their lights on. Our leaders need to stop the lawlessness, the violence ,and the reign of terror resulting from the reign of King Coal.

The Bush Administration End Run

In the May *Voice* there were reports on two efforts by the Bush Administration to change the regulations relating to mountaintop-removal mining. First, in yet another attempt to circumvent the Clean Water Act and its application to mining, the Bush Administration wanted to change the law to legalize large valley fills from mountaintop-removal mining operations. To do mountaintop-removal mining, the coal industry had to dispose of the dirt and rock that once was the top of the mountain. The current practice was to dump it in a nearby valley, a valley which in most if not all cases contained a stream. While there were upper reaches of valleys which had no streams, or at most, "ephemeral streams," also called "wet weather streams," the lower parts of valleys routinely had streams.

Under current law, the fill material (the dirt and rock) was considered a waste product. As a waste product, it could not be dumped into streams. To allow this fill to be dumped into streams would be contrary to the longstanding Clean Water Act policy of not using streams for waste disposal.

The fact that the practice was illegal had not, of course, prevented it from going on. The Army Corps of Engineers had allowed the filling of one thousand miles of streams in West Virginia alone. Now the Corps wanted to legalize its past practice. It wanted to change the definition of fill material so that it could permit the filling of West Virginia streams. It wanted to change the definition so that the material was no longer considered waste and could be disposed of in streams. A permit from the Corps of Engineers would still be required.

The Clinton Administration had made a similar proposal in 2000, but after 17,000 public comments were registered protesting the rule changes, decided not to finalize the proposal. The Bush Administration was poised to reverse that decision and make the rule final. Worse, the Bush Administration was planning to finalize the rule without any public notice that this rule change was under consideration or any additional opportunity for comment.

The lead article in the April 2002 *Voice* was a disappointment indeed in the Conservancy's long struggle to make "federal oversight" a meaningful concept. Titled "Federal Judge Lets OSM Slide," the unidentified author wrote:

> Federal judge Charles Haden II has declined a West Virginia Highlands Conservancy request for an injunction requiring the federal Office of Surface Mining to immediately assume control of West Virginia's coal-mining regulatory program. In doing so, he has given the federal Office of Surface Mining more time to force the West Virginia Department of Environmental Protection to correct problems in its surface-mine regulatory program.

Most prominent among the weaknesses is the deficiency in the bonding program. Other weaknesses concern flood control, blasting limitations, replacement of residential water supplies damaged by mining, and post-mining land uses.

In November 2000, the West Virginia Highlands Conservancy filed suit, seeking to force the Office of Surface Mining to assume control of the regulation of mining in West Virginia. In August 2001, Judge Haden ruled that the Office of Surface Mining had "unreasonably delayed" action to take over the West Virginia program. At that time, the Judge did not require the Office of Surface Mining to take over the West Virginia program because the Office of Surface mining and the West Virginia Department of Environmental Protection promised to move promptly to correct the deficiencies.

Based upon what appeared to be progress, the court declined to order that the Office of Surface Mining take over the West Virginia program immediately. In doing so, the Court said, "For more than a decade, OSM was derelict and dilatory in the extreme, but recently, and clearly in response to this litigation, stepped up agency action promises a state surface-mine regulatory program that conforms to [federal] requirements."

The Office of Surface Mining has promised to make a final decision on the West Virginia Department of Environmental Protection's proposals for correcting the deficiencies in the bonding and Special Reclamation programs by May 28. It has promised to approve or reject West Virginia's proposals in other areas by May 1.

In making his ruling, the Judge praised the Highlands Conservancy for its "heavy lifting...producing figures and proposing answers to the question, what will constitute sufficient...funds." He praised the Conservancy's "well-placed pressure and persistence" in pursuing this issue.

The effect of the litigation, once again, had been to motivate the reluctant state authorities to improve the state program so that it would meet federal requirements. Calling OSM's record "derelict and dilatory in the extreme," Judge Haden set specific dates for compliance, hoping this was not just another exercise in delay.

A second Bush Administration proposal to avoid Judge Haden's decision was to exempt mountaintop-removal coal-mining operations from a decades-old stream "buffer zone" provision of the nation's surface-mining laws, which banned coal strip-mining within 100 feet of streams.

Among the many uniformly negative reactions from environmentalists opposed to changing the buffer-zone rule, was that of Fetty, issues coordinator of the West Virginia Rivers Coalition:

The buffer zone rule is a key legal protection that coalfield citizens fought for years and years to pass into law. Now President Bush would snuff out this protection, appeasing his friends in the coal industry and continuing an open-ended assault on our mountain streams. King Coal refuses to do business according to the rules, so the president wants to change the rules yet again. Could there be a more arrogant and crooked way for the coal industry to make a fast buck?

Janet Fout, co-director of the Ohio Valley Environmental Coalition (OVEC) put it a little differently:

> In a way, these absurd proposals are a bittersweet victory for us. Obviously, the lawsuits have shown that we are right — the way the coal industry is blowing up mountains and burying streams in southern West Virginia is illegal. Now, we see a dangerous precedent set by Bush and his appointees, many of whom came from the industry they are supposedly regulating. They obviously have taken a cue from the West Virginia Coal Association: If you don't like the law, break it. If someone challenges you in court, get the politicians you fund to change the law in your favor.

Joe Lovett, the Conservancy lawyer before Judge Haden, and Robert F. Kennedy, Jr., President of the Water Keeper Alliance, worried about the nationwide implications:

> The Bush administration rule change will create a loophole in Clean Water Act regulations big enough to drive a coal truck through. Other industries, including hard-rock-mineral mining operations, demolition companies, waste-disposal operations — all will be able to take advantage of this loophole, and they, too, will be allowed to bury wetlands, streams, and other waters with their wastes.

Also in the May *Voice*, the Conservancy's McFerrin, by now the polite master of declining invitations, wrote:

> The West Virginia Highlands Conservancy, the Ohio Valley Environmental Coalition, Coal River Mountain Watch, the West Virginia Rivers Coalition, the Appalachian Center for the Economy and the Environment, the West Virginia Citizen Action Group, the West Virginia Environmental Council, and the West Virginia Chapter of the Sierra Club have declined an invitation to appoint a representative to a Special Reclamation Fund Advisory Council established by the Department of Environmental Protection. The Department of Environmental Protection had originally invited citizen groups to nominate three

persons to the Council. The Governor would then select one of the nominees to serve on the eight-person Council.

The Special Reclamation Fund Advisory Council is a part of a proposed solution to the problem of inadequate performance bonds for coal mines. The proposed solution was agreed to by the coal industry and the Department of Environmental Protection and enacted by the West Virginia Legislature in 2001 as Senate Bill (SB) 5003.

Today thousands of acres of abandoned sites are not reclaimed, and hundreds of miles of polluted streams go untreated. One study found that the cleanup could cost more than $6 billion over the next fifty years.

In declining the invitation, the groups said, "For ten years, DEP and the federal Office of Surface Mining, along with the coal industry, have been loathe to fully tackle the issue of establishing a bonding program that will adequately and fully cover all present and future forfeited mine sites. We view the bonding program outlined in SB 5003 — and particularly the establishment of the special reclamation fund advisory council — as yet another avenue for agencies to let the program languish."

Citizen groups had previously objected to the inadequacy of the solution contained in SB 5003. They had also objected to the fact that it had been negotiated by the Department of Environmental Protection and the coal industry with no participation by any citizen organization. Had they been allowed to participate, their insights might have led to a Special Reclamation program that could have solved the problem of inadequate bonding. Having been excluded from the creation of the program, the groups could not now participate as part of an Advisory Council trying in vain to make a flawed system function.

In June, McFerrin summarized the past four years of Conservancy litigation on mining. In the first litigation, Bragg v. Robertson, the parties settled many of the claims in the case. On the claim of the legality of fills under the federal Clean Water Act and the extent of the environmental review that would be required, the parties agreed to an extensive environmental impact assessment of the practice of mountaintop removal and valley fills. The study was begun in early 1999 and was not yet complete, although a working draft had recently been made public.

On the second claim, namely returning mined land to its approximate original contour, the DEP agreed to change its practices to comply with the law. Judge Haden decided the third claim, the buffer zone issue. He decided that the law that prohibited valley fills within one hundred feet of streams included valley fills that buried streams. Unfortunately, the Fourth Circuit ruled Haden lacked jurisdiction, but it did not rule on the merits of the case. While his interpretation of the law may have been correct, the lack of jurisdiction left it with no binding effect. The agreed settlements otherwise remained in effect.

McFerrin continued. An entirely separate case, in which the Conservancy was involved, concerned the failure of West Virginia to have and enforce a mining regulatory program that complied with the federal Surface Mining Control and Reclamation Act. Although the state had received primacy in the early 1980s, OSM retained oversight authority, including an obligation to step in if the state's regulations or enforcement are not equal to or more stringent than the requirements of the federal law. OSM had identified weaknesses in West Virginia's program more than a decade earlier, but had taken no steps to correct them, other than calling the weaknesses to the attention of state regulators. McFerrin felt the inadequacy of the bonding program was a prime example.

In November 2000 the Conservancy had filed suit, seeking to force OSM to assume control of the regulation of mining in West Virginia. In August 2001 Judge Haden ruled that OSM had "unreasonably delayed" action to take over the West Virginia program. But the judge did not require OSM to take over the state program because both agencies promised to move promptly to correct the deficiencies.

Since then, West Virginia increased the payments to the Special Reclamation Fund from three cents per ton to fourteen cents per ton, although McFerrin felt the increase was still inadequate. OSM had also said that the tax increase was insufficient to provide a long-term solution.

Judge Haden had declined to order OSM to assume the state's regulatory program, based upon these signs of progress. McFerrin explained that as West Virginia made additional changes and OSM reviewed those changes, the Court would decide whether those changes were sufficient to bring the state into compliance with federal law.

Mining and logging did add to the flooding in 2001, according to a study released by the DEP in the summer of 2002. According to an article in the July *Voice*, the state flood study was part of the work of a task force appointed by Governor Wise.

In addition to its conclusions, the study contained supporting data that were informative. First, it brought together the rainfall data which various public agencies had collected at the time of the storm and which made clear that the widely held public perception about the amount of rain that had fallen was incorrect. The widely held perception was that this rain was of Biblical proportions, a rain that would have produced a major flood regardless of whether the area had been disturbed by mining or logging. Governor Wise encouraged this perception by referring to rainfalls of "6 to 9 inches of water." According to the study data, only one station (south of Beckley) recorded a rainfall of more than six inches on the date of the flood. Many of the reporting stations reported rainfall of less than two inches, and one Boone County station reported rainfall of less than an inch. While the rainfall was substantial by any measure, it was not the catastrophic deluge that many understood it to be.

In response to the study, the DEP made several recommendations for changes in mining methods. They included:

- Require a survey of man-made structures located near proposed strip mines to "determine the potential storm runoff impacts."
- Increase the size of sediment-control ponds at the bottom of valley fills to better contain runoff from those fills.
- Prohibit the construction of valley fills by dumping material from the tops of ridges down into valleys. Instead, fills would have to be built from the bottom up.

The Department also recommended changes in logging practices. These changes included limiting logging within watersheds based on acreage, area of timber removed, and type of logging used. The Department also recommended that logging companies improve their methods for disposal of treetops and branches left over from logging and increased inspection of logging operations.

Randy Dye, Director of the Division of Forestry, a separate agency which oversaw the logging industry, ignored the DEP's proposals.

The Conservancy and six other environmental groups were invited to meet with Interior Secretary Gail Norton during her visit to West Virginia on August 1. As a group, these organizations declined the invitation and, after thanking her, explained their reasons in a letter:

> Thirty minutes is simply not enough time for us to explain to you the day-to-day perils of living in the shadow of mountaintop removal operations. Additionally, we cannot meet with you on that day because the OSM, which you administer as Secretary of the Department of Interior (DOI), has chosen August 1 as the day it will commemorate the 25th anniversary of the federal Surface Mining Control and Reclamation Act (SMCRA).

It has been well publicized that, prior to your appointment to head the DOI, you maintained that SMCRA was unconstitutional. Many of our members have suffered immense hardship for over two decades because SMCRA has gone essentially un-enforced. Still, SMCRA and other laws that ought to rein in the excesses of the coal mining industry have afforded citizens the opportunity to attempt to force regulators to regulate, and to attempt to force the coal industry to obey laws written to protect the health and safety of people everywhere.

Now, the DOI, under your leadership, is bent upon weakening SMCRA. It is frankly a distasteful proposition to us to help you commemorate 25 years of slack enforcement of SMCRA, especially given your push to gut portions of SMCRA and your previous public stance on the Act itself.

For instance, the Bush administration proposes to remove the buffer from the buffer zone rule of SMCRA, a rule that currently says that no land within 100 feet of a perennial stream or an intermittent stream shall be disturbed by surface-mining activities. If you should decide to meet with us in the coalfields, you will see that this law is not well enforced, to state it politely. Yet, you would codify the outlaw behavior of the coal industry by eliminating this protection for both citizens and our life support system, that is, the environment.

A citizen lawsuit brought about because of the lax enforcement of coal-mining laws forced state and federal agencies to undertake an Environmental Impact Statement (EIS) on mountaintop removal. Thanks to a Freedom of Information request from the *Charleston Gazette*, citizens have access to the draft of this endlessly delayed EIS.

As you should know, in West Virginia alone, at least 1,000 miles of our biologically crucial headwater streams have been forever obliterated by valley fills. Already, nearly 400,000 acres of the world's most diverse temperate hardwood forests have been permitted for strip-mining operations.

Our communities and mountain lifestyles are in danger of extinction. The draft EIS shows that regulators expect mountaintop removal to destroy nearly 230,000 additional acres of our mountains and valleys. The study points out that many more miles of streams will be buried by valley fills, that streams not already buried could be seriously polluted, and that wildlife such as fish and songbirds in our biologically diverse area will likely be lost.

You have ignored the warnings of one of your agencies, the U.S. Fish and Wildlife Service, which state that "tremendous destruction of aquatic and terrestrial habitat" is already occurring as a result of mountaintop removal. Instead of following the true intent of the EIS, which was to seriously study and document the numerous social and environmental impacts of mountaintop removal, you have promoted the notion that the EIS should be used as a vehicle to centralize and streamline the permitting process.

The draft EIS shows us that OSM under DOI envisions one-stop shopping for SMCRA and Clean Water Act laws. We implore you to visit, on the ground, the result of the current permitting process. Southern West Virginia and eastern Kentucky have become the nation's energy sacrifice zones. Why then would you speed up the permitting process?

Of course, your participation in the administration's push for a Clean Water Act rule change on the definition of "fill" is of grave concern to us. With this rule change, the administration is rewarding the outlaw behavior of the coal industry, and is attempting to legalize what are currently illegal valley fills at mountaintop-removal operations. You essentially maintain that massive valley fills have minimal impact on the environment, including human communities. We, and the U.S. Fish and Wildlife Service, beg to differ. Take just the latest valley fill disaster on July 19, 2002.

A sediment pond overflow and resultant tidal wave of sediment-laden water churned down Winding Shoals Hollow, destroying two homes, damaging about ten others and hurtling 8–10 vehicles downstream. No one was killed, though there were some narrow escapes. In earlier floods in 2001 and 2002 people were killed and more homes, bridges, roads, and schools were destroyed. The DEP has concluded that mountaintop removal / valley fill coal mining has increased rainwater runoff, thereby exacerbating flooding. Minimal impact these valley fills are not. The rule change the administration has enacted is completely contrary to the intent of the Clean Water Act.

You also envision delegating MORE regulatory authority to the states. Incredibly, now that the "fill" rule change is finalized, you want to turn over to the states this aspect of permitting mountaintop-removal operations. Surely you know that for West Virginia, where politicians have longed been controlled by the coal industry, this would mean a warp-speed increase to the ecocide that is mountaintop removal. Lax as it has been, the federal government has offered us some enforcement help. Sadly and regrettably, you would strip us of even this flimsy safeguard for our property and our lives.

Furthermore, if you do in fact fly over mountaintop removal operations, you apparently will do so with the Army Corps of Engineers as your guide. The Corps is the very same agency that has publicly stated it "oozed" into issuing 404 permits for valley fills. The

Corps is the agency that suggests razing the most biologically diverse temperate forests on earth, blowing up mountains and then dumping the rubble into streams has only a "minimal" adverse impact on the environment. We suggest you need a different guide and also, we request that a representative chosen by our organizations would accompany you on your flyover.

As residents of the West Virginia coalfields who are greatly harmed by mountaintop removal / valley fill coal mining, and as representatives of organizations working in these areas, we invite you to visit us in the affected areas. We implore you to see first-hand the devastation from mountaintop removal — including the aftermath of recent catastrophic floods in West Virginia and the massive coal slurry impoundment spill in Kentucky in 2000.

The issue of the impact of mining and timbering on flooding, especially in southern West Virginia, continued to be discussed. The Conservancy had created the Timber Reform Research Project funded in part by a grant. Actually begun in 2000, a year ahead of the major floods, it examined watersheds in Fayette County, determining that "flooding was not caused by large rivers rising up and out, but by water running off steep slopes and ravines below cleared logging and mining sites." And later, "This flooding was a wake-up call. Manmade disturbance of steep forested slopes in southern West Virginia contributed to the deadly force of recent flooding." While the heavier blame was assessed against poorly regulated timber operations, mining was a contributing factor as well.

Longtime Board member Bob Gates, who with Penny Loeb, produced their own flood report, including more significant rainfall data than previously released. Governor Wise had yet to make any recommendations to the Legislature.

Cindy Rank Recognized Again

One of the Conservancy's hardest working members received something very special in late 2002. The story appeared in the November *Voice*:

> The Clean Water Network has named West Virginia Highlands Conservancy mining committee chair Cindy Rank one of thirty national Clean Water Act heroes as part of the celebration of the Clean Water Act's 30th anniversary. This award honors individuals who have made powerful contributions to the protection and restoration of America's rivers, lakes, wetlands, and coastal waters.

After reviewing the Ranks' history in West Virginia and describing their efforts to organize their neighbors into the Friends of the Little Kanawha, the recognition narrative continued:

In fact, Rank hasn't stopped since the 1970s. From the early days of the Clean Water Act, she engaged in state water quality standards development, clean water permitting, wetlands protection and more.

She remains active in the Friends of the Little Kanawha and volunteers for the West Virginia Highlands Conservancy. As mining chair for the Conservancy, Rank helped spearhead the first citizen lawsuit to protect West Virginia's streams from mountaintop-removal mining and valley fills. The effect of this lawsuit has been far-reaching — raising the issue with the national media, rousing congressional interest, and galvanizing a continuing legal battle. Cindy speaks out about mountaintop removal mining.

Anyone who works with Rank comments on the same thing — her amazing ability to dive into the nitty-gritty of the policy and legal issues surrounding clean water. What makes this all the more amazing is that all this work — all 25 years of it — has been done as a volunteer.

Why anyone would spend their free time reading statutes and regulations? According to Rank, the answer is simple: "That's where the decisions are made. You can yell and scream and cry until you're blue in the face, but it's all for naught if you can't back yourself up with the law. People forget that all the seemingly small changes made in the legislature and at the agencies are going to make such a difference in their own backyard."

"The importance of the Clean Water Act can't be overstated," Rank said. "Even though some rivers and streams in West Virginia have been cleaned up, we continue to get further and further and further away from the goals of the Act. The basic intention of the Act was to protect and restore the waters of the nation. Simply put, if water is clean, you are supposed to keep it clean. If it is dirty, you are supposed to clean it up."

Rank made her comments during a meeting reviewing studies for a long-overdue Environmental Impact Study on mountaintop removal / valley fill coal mining.

"It is very difficult to feel good about the 30th anniversary of the Clean Water Act when we are sitting in the middle of a meeting determining how many miles of streams we are going to bury based on profits for the coal industry.

"Probably the most egregious violation of the Clean Water Act in West Virginia today is the burying of thousands of miles of streams under millions of tons of coal-mining waste rock and slurry."

"Cindy is a Clean Water Act pioneer, an outstanding individual, and my personal environmental hero," says Margaret Janes, a fellow clean-water activist in West Virginia. The incredible wild streams of West Virginia and the communities nestled next to them rely on people who can speak out for their protection. Even corporate coal companies have to listen when people like Rank speak for the rivers.

Rank was one of thirty recipients of the national Clean Water Act Heroes ward. A few among them were: Wendell Berry, Kentucky; Senator Barbara Boxer, California; Representative John D. Dingell, Michigan; Robert F. Kennedy, Jr., New York; Senator Edmund S. Muskie and Senator John H. Chafee (joint award); and Pete Seeger, New York.

It was recognition well deserved!

By 2007 **Cindy Rank** might have been the most well-known member of the West Virginia Highlands Conservancy. Since 1979, when she first came to the Conservancy seeking help for the Friends of the Little Kanawha, until her most recent statement to the press, commenting on the latest lawsuit against the abuses of mountaintop-removal mining, to many she had become the face and voice of the Conservancy. Yet many of the Conservancy's own members really didn't know much about her background, or what had sustained her dedication to clean water and its enemy, coal mining, over the nearly thirty years.

Rank grew up in a middle class family in the East Liberty section of Pittsburgh, attended Catholic schools through high school, and enrolled in what was then Wheeling College, later Wheeling Jesuit University. After graduation, she attended Marquette University's Graduate School of Theology during the mid-1960s, an intense period of the civil unrest. She was greatly influenced by the passion for justice exemplified by Bernard Cooke, Father James Groppi, and other civil rights and anti-war leaders in Milwaukee.

After completing two years in the Masters Degree Program, she returned to Pittsburgh, taking a position as instructor in Theology and assistant in the Campus Ministry program at Duquesne University, where she also married Paul, a friend from Wheeling

College, who was on the Duquesne University staff as well. Together, they and several other young couples found their way to
southern Upshur County, West Virginia, in 1972, where they sought
a "personal retreat," a place of hard physical work and deep spiritual nourishment. That solitude ended a few short years later with
the noise of large drilling rigs on their little narrow country road,
and the drilling for oil, gas, and coal that would change her life
forever.

While at Wheeling College, she had known Davitt McAteer,
who by 1979 was an environmental attorney. It was McAteer who
referred the Ranks and their neighbors to Rick Webb of Mountain
Stream Monitors and to attorney Tom Galloway. In 2006 Rank
joined McAteer once again. He had become a vice president of
Wheeling Jesuit University and together they obtained funding to
work on a major study of water in the Appalachian Mountains.

Throughout this chapter Rank's writings have indicated the
depth of her research, the breadth of the issues, and the many times
she testified at public hearings, often facing down hostile miners
who saw her as a threat to their livelihood. Her compatriots have
written of her leadership and indeed she was honored with many
awards including the Mother Jones Award, the Clean Water Act
Hero, and even an Honorary Doctorate from Wheeling Jesuit
University, among others.

Within the Highlands Conservancy, she served three terms as
president (1988–1994), longer than any previous one, had been a
member of the Board of Directors continuously since 1984, and
chaired the Mining Committee since 1994, representing the Conservancy on numerous occasions. During many of these years she had
also been active in the leadership of other local, state, and regional
environmental justice organizations.

On a beautiful spring day in 2007 at their home in Upshur
County, the question of what kept Cindy so deeply engaged in this
tireless, thankless work as a volunteer seemed to defy a reasonable
answer. She said simply, "Because it is the right thing to do." Then
she asked, "Why are we here if not to do something with our lives?"

Voice Editor McFerrin opened 2003 with the headline, "Coal guys
want do-over on flooding rules." He wrote:

Coal industry officials have offered changes in proposed mining guidelines designed to reduce the contribution of mining operations to flooding.

These guidelines were prepared by the Department of Environmental Protection based upon the studies and recommendations of the task force which Governor Wise appointed to study the July 2001 flooding in southern West Virginia.

At the heart of the controversy is the Department's proposal that the coal industry use "constructed valley fills." Current practice is to shove the waste material (dirt and rock) into the valley. When the operator had disposed of what was previously the top of the mountain, it would plant grass on the fill.

Instead of shoving or blasting the rock and dirt into the valley, the mine operators would have to truck the material to the bottom of the area to be filled, deposit it in layers, and compact each layer. As each layer was added, grass would be planted on that layer. The result would be that less of the fill would be vulnerable to erosion at any one time.

A different view was taken by filmmaker and veteran Conservancy Board member Bob Gates, who asked a critical question, "Valley fills: How stable are they?" In a January 2003 article he wrote:

After the floods of July 2001, Penny Loeb and I did an extensive survey of causes of the flooding. Armed with mine maps we traveled thousands of miles taking photographs, shooting video, and talking to people. One mine map led us to the head of Armstrong Creek, where a well-traveled road crosses a sediment pond dam at the base of a valley fill. While we were there a guy on a four-wheeler comes by and we start up a conversation about the floods. He told us that one of his great concerns was that the big rocks stayed at the top of the valley fills and that over time the effects of water undercutting them would cause the valley fills to start to give way. A few weeks later when I was able to take a photograph of this valley fill I found that he was right — the little rocks go to the bottom.

One of my next travels took me to the base of a valley fill in Wyoming County. Here large bulldozers and trucks were shoving and dumping rock over the ledge at the top of the mountain. As I was filming this, I saw that a truck was going to back up and dump the mother of all big rocks over the hill. Naturally the photographer side of me was excited... this was going to be a great shot! The truck backs up with this huge rock, lifts its bed, and THUD. The rock lands a few feet below in a cloud of dust and that was it. In other video shots of rubble rolling down this fill it is clear — the smaller rocks bounce and tumble to the bottom, middle rocks tend to run out of steam at the middle, and many of the larger rocks are held up by all the loose dirt and stay at the top, only to wait for eons of rain to erode the soft material holding them up so that their momentum can carry them down the hill in the future.

This is not always true; it is a question of slope, fill material, and other factors. At one location that I would call a mountainside fill the rock is harder and the big rocks came rolling down to the bottom. I cannot quite describe the sounds of being below these things — the relentless sound of the rocks rolling down the hill sounds like a Jeep is coming up the gravel road behind you.

These are some of the factors that caused the Massey Energy valley fill at their Bandmill Mine at Lyburn to fail with 3½ inches of rain last July. Photographs show that the face of the valley fill gave way like an avalanche and sloshed all the water out of the pond, sending a tidal wave of mud and water downstream to wash away the community below. This is why the Department of Environmental Protection has come to its senses and wants to return to the practice of having the valley fills be constructed from the bottom up instead of following the myth of "end-dump durable rock fills" where rubble is dumped over the top of the hill. It does not take a mathematician to figure out why the coal industry will fight tooth and nail for a change in this policy; it certainly is cheaper to push stuff over the hill than truck it to the bottom and construct a huge fill from the bottom up.

Meanwhile, another important mountaintop-removal mining federal court case had been decided. This was the one brought by Kentucky groups, but heard by Judge Haden. On appeal to the Fourth Circuit, Haden was reversed again. *Voice* Editor McFerrin wrote:

Judge Haden had ruled that the filling of streams with waste from coal mining violated the Clean Water Act.

At issue was what material would be considered "waste" for purposes of the Act. When mining companies conduct mountaintop-removal mining, the result is that they have millions of tons of rock and dirt, the material which was previously the top of the mountain, which they must dispose of. In most, if not all, cases they dispose of this material by dumping it into an adjacent valley, creating a "valley fill." In a great many of those cases, the filling of a valley resulted in the filling of a stream that was in that valley.

Judge Haden decided that filling streams with waste from mountaintop-removal strip mines violated the federal Clean Water Act, which prohibits the disposal of waste in the nation's streams. Judge Haden's ruling considered the material blasted from above the coal seams to be waste material which could not be disposed of in streams. Judge Haden ruled that the prohibition upon the disposal of waste in streams prevented mining companies from dumping the mountaintops into valleys which contained streams.

Under Judge Haden's interpretation of the Clean Water Act, the mining companies could only classify the material as "fill" and fill the stream pursuant to a Section 404 permit if its purpose was to create dry land for some other purpose.

The Court of Appeals held that the fill could be disposed of in streams whether or not the filling had some other beneficial purpose. Its ruling relied in part upon the longstanding practice of the Army Corps of Engineers of allowing such fills. It assumed that if an agency had been doing something in a particular way long enough it must have been doing it legally.

As a result of the ruling, mining companies will be able to get permits to fill valleys with mining waste. The ruling does not affect the obligation of companies to refrain from extensively polluting the stream segments which remain below the valley fill.

The Highlands Conservancy had made the same claim in litigation begun in 1998 but agreed not to pursue that claim in exchange for an extensive environmental impact assessment of the practice of mountaintop removal and valley fills. The study was begun in early 1999 and was not yet complete. A working draft was made public during the summer of 2002.

In April 2003 McFerrin reported on the follow-up from the Task Force on flooding. He wrote:

> The West Virginia Legislature has passed most, if not all, of the coal-related recommendations of the Governor's Flooding Task Force. These new regulations were prepared by the Department of Environmental Protection based upon the studies and recommendations of the task force.
>
> The guidelines would require the coal industry to do runoff studies before they could obtain permits. They would have to show that their mining would not increase runoff during heavy rains. The new regulations would also require more rapid revegetation after mining so as to reduce the risk of erosion.
>
> In response to objections from the coal industry, the proposal to require constructed valley fills was dropped. In its place was a require-

ment that companies create a broad, flattened area immediately downstream from the fill. If the Department of Environmental Protection and the coal industry representatives are correct, then this would reduce the likelihood that a fill would cause or add to flooding.

The Task Force also recommended stricter oversight of logging operations. The Division of Environmental Protection had proposed that the Division of Forestry (which regulates logging) inspect all timber operations, not dispose of woody vegetation in stream channels, reseed logging roads when the logging ends, and limit logging in particular watersheds to limit runoff.

The recommendations by the Task Force concerning logging were not turned into law by the Legislature. They remain simply recommendations with no legally binding effect upon the logging industry.

Meanwhile, Congressmen Frank Pallone (D-NJ) and Christopher Shays (D-CT) had reintroduced legislation to amend the federal Clean Water Act to clarify that fill material could not be comprised of waste. The amendment would make clear that the dumping of mining waste and other pollutants into streams was prohibited.

Named the "Clean Water Protection Act," their bill had twenty-six cosponsors, though none from Kentucky or West Virginia where the legislation would have the greatest impact.

"Our bipartisan legislation is needed to ensure our streams and waterways aren't buried under millions of tons of mining and other industrial wastes," Pallone said. "While the legal debate continues, it is critical that we support the true intentions of the Clean Water Act and oppose the continued efforts of the Bush administration to use our waterways as dumping grounds for industrial wastes."

So as Congress was considering a more restrictive system, by closing the loophole within the Clean Water Act that had been so controversial, the state was busy easing restrictions on the mining industry and paving the way for future flooding. This epitomized what someone called, "the perpetual roller coaster of dealing with the mining industry." (The bill did not pass and was re-introduced every year through 2007.)

During this period, the Conservancy was consumed with at least three major campaigns. One was the new West Virginia Wilderness Campaign, focused on securing additional wilderness areas during the Monongahela National Forest Management plan revision (see Chapter 2). Another was the increasing controversy over wind energy and the huge turbines proposed for the highest peaks of the highlands (see

Chapter 8). The third was the campaign to save the Blackwater Canyon. Together these issues were bringing new members to the Conservancy, dominating Board discussions, and, frankly, offering a respite from the grinding work of trying to tame the political-mining complex.

The EIS

Finally the long-anticipated EIS on mountaintop-removal mining was officially released. McFerrin wrote in the June *Voice*:

> The United States Army Corps of Engineers, the United States Environmental Protection Agency, the United States Department of Interior's Office of Surface Mining and Fish and Wildlife Service, and the West Virginia Department of Environmental Protection have issued a long-awaited draft Environmental Impact Statement on mountaintop-removal strip mining. The agencies are now accepting public comment on that draft.
>
> The study is the result of litigation previously filed by the West Virginia Highlands Conservancy and several citizens of southern West Virginia. In late 1998 the plaintiffs in that case agreed not to pursue some of their allegations. In exchange, the various agencies agreed to conduct a comprehensive study of the environmental effects of mountaintop-removal strip mining and valley fills.
>
> The draft Environmental Impact Statement identified several effects of the practice:
> • Approximately 1275 square miles of land has been or will be affected by the practice in the area studied (southern West Virginia, eastern Kentucky, western Virginia, and scattered areas of Eastern Tennessee).
> • 1200 miles of headwater streams were directly impacted by mountain-top-removal strip mining. 724 miles of streams were covered by valley fills from 1985 to 2001.
> • Streams in watersheds where mountaintop-removal valley fills exist are characterized by an increase of minerals in the water as well as less diverse and more pollution-tolerant macroinvertebrates and fish species.
> • Streams with fills are less prone to flooding during smaller rains but more prone to flooding during larger rains.
> • Mining sometimes creates wetlands, either inadvertently or intentionally. These wetlands "provide some aquatic function, but are generally not of high quality."
> • Valley fills are generally stable. The study found fewer than twenty "reported slope movements out of more than 6800 fills constructed since 1985."

The draft study makes no recommendations and presents no alternatives that would restrict the practice or limit it. While earlier drafts had contained alternatives that would have restricted fill construction, this draft does not

The draft study's recommendations are largely for better coordination among agencies in streamlining of the process of evaluating applications for permits authorizing mountaintop-removal strip mining and valley fills. It says, "Cross-program actions include rulemaking; improved data collection, sharing and analysis; development of a joint application, harmonized public participation procedures, Best Management Practices and Advance Identification of Disposal Sites evaluations; and close interagency coordination. These actions would serve to further minimize the adverse effects on aquatic and terrestrial resources and protect the public."

The agencies who would be coordinating their efforts presided over the practices which resulted in the environmental damage described in the Draft. The Draft offers no explanation on how the same agencies doing the same thing would "minimize the adverse effects on aquatic and terrestrial resources and protect the public."

The draft does recommend that the agencies continue efforts to eliminate three barriers to mountaintop removal and valley fills. The first of theses barriers is the prohibition upon mining within one hundred feet of a stream, often called the "buffer zone rule." Under current law, mining within one hundred feet of a stream is prohibited. If mining within one hundred feet of a stream is prohibited, then one would assume that filling that stream with dirt and rock would also be prohibited. The federal Office of Surface Mining is currently pursuing a rule change that would eliminate this buffer zone rule so as to allow the filling of streams. The draft study recommends that these efforts continue.

The second of these barriers is status of the rock and dirt that is used to fill valleys and streams under the federal Clean Water Act. The discharge of waste material into the waters of the United States is prohibited by that Act. If the Act is interpreted in such a way as to include the rock, these site-specific permits require much more careful environmental review than does the nationwide general permit.

Historically, the Corps had approved valley fills under a nationwide permit. When mountaintop-removal strip mining became more controversial in recent years, the Corps indicated that it would begin doing some site-specific evaluations of proposed valley fills and issue site-specific permits.

The just issued draft Environmental Impact Statement endorses more extensive use of the nationwide general permit to approve valley fills. They would be approved under a general permit that assumes that they have limited environmental impact.

In summary, the draft Environmental Impact Statement documents the environmental destruction of mountaintop removal strip mining. It makes no recommendations to avoid that destruction. Instead, it recommends that the agencies carry on their currently ineffective regulation in a more coordinated manner. It does recommend that possible legal barriers to the continuation of the practice in its current form be eliminated.

President Frank Young summarized the feelings of many, when he wrote:

> What did this EIS find? Well, not unlike Congress found in 1977, the E.I.S. found that, among other things, mountaintop removal/ valley fill mining operations destroy forests and forest soils, decrease songbird and salamander (but not snake) populations, cover streams, and both intentionally and unintentionally create wetlands "that are not of high quality", and cause or promote the severity of flooding after rainfall.
>
> Duhh? Well, that was the predicate for the SMCRA legislation in the first place, in 1977, that surface mining disturbs and too often destroys ecological infrastructures.
>
> Why does it take the agencies of state and federal government charged with implementing the law 26 years, and then only after lawsuits and court orders, to come full circle and determine that the need to enforce the law does in fact exist after all?

In July the four federal and one state agencies held public hearings on the mountaintop EIS. Although it documented various adverse effects of mountaintop-removal mining, including 1,200 miles of obliterated streams, it made no recommendations nor presented any alternatives that would alter current practices. Coordination among agencies seemed to be its major recommendation. Left unsaid was the question of why those same agencies responsible for current adverse environmental impacts, would act differently under any new procedure.

Rank and Young testified on behalf of the Highlands Conservancy at the public hearing in Charleston. In their opinion, despite the 5,000 pages of research, the EIS seemed almost empty. During the long period of vetting, the four federal agencies and the state DEP had managed to remove most of the teeth found in earlier drafts and the remaining book would change little. One clue betraying its weakness was the high praise heaped upon the EIS by the West Virginia Coal Association.

The Conservancy's official written comments outlined its major objections and elaborated upon two major themes. The first was that the agencies involved had not conducted the kind of study to which they had agreed. It had been the Conservancy's position that mountaintop-removal mining had a substantial environmental impact even if nobody knew exactly how substantial that impact was. The point of doing the study was to determine the scope of the impact and identify ways to reduce that impact.

The comments continued:

The final Draft Environmental Impact Statement does not propose any actions by any agency that would result in minimizing adverse environmental impacts. Although it proposes changes designed to streamline the granting of permits for the mines and associated fills, it does not suggest any way in which the fills could be made smaller, the mining could be done differently, etc. It suggests ways to streamline the process of granting permits. It does nothing to suggest ways that the adverse environmental effects could be minimized.

Current practice is to not only fill ephemeral or intermittent streams but to fill perennial streams as well. Current law requires that all parts of the operation, including fills, be located at least one hundred feet from a stream (the "buffer zone rule"). The Conservancy has maintained in various proceedings that staying one hundred feet away from streams means that one cannot fill the streams. The West Virginia Department of Environmental Protection makes a contrary interpretation.

The final Draft Environmental Impact Statement drops all these actions as possibilities. Instead, it recommends that the buffer zone be "clarified" out of existence and that the permitting process be streamlined.

The Conservancy's comments on the final Draft Environmental Impact Statement point out that the change in direction of the Draft coincide with the change of administrations in Washington.

With the change of administrations, the emphasis of the Environmental Impact Statement went from seeking ways to reduce the impact of mountaintop-removal mining to seeking ways to streamline the process of permitting the operations.

In a nutshell, the first theme of the Conservancy's comments was that they agreed to drop some of their claims in the litigation in return for a study that sought alternatives that would reduce the environmental impact of mountaintop-removal mining. What it got was a study that recommended ways to streamline the process for getting a permit to do mountaintop-removal mining.

The second theme of the Conservancy's comments is more technical. Even were the Draft Environmental Impact Statement not in violation of the settlement agreement, it is in violation of the National Environmental Policy Act and the Clean Water Act.

The National Environmental Policy Act requires more than a process to justify a decision already made. It must be a fair consideration of alternatives for reducing or eliminating environmental damage.

The overall thrust of the Conservancy's comments is that the technical portions of the Draft recognize the environmental impacts of mountaintop removal operations. Yet the proposed alternatives only seek to improve the efficiency of issuing permits while not suggesting any alternatives that would reduce or eliminate these environmental impacts.

The EIS comment period eventually ended January 6, 2004 and EPA ultimately received 83,500 comments, mostly unfavorable.

On March 30, 2004, Conservancy President Young attended yet another public hearing on issues related to mining. He recounted his experience this way:

> I attended a public hearing on the Bush administration proposal to "clarify" (read "effectively eliminate") the stream protection regulation known as the "Buffer Zone Rule", which prohibits mining within 100 feet of a stream.
>
> I was heartened by the nothing less that spiritual outpouring of the three dozen or so folks who spoke against the buffer zone rule change. I spoke from my prepared notes. But many who spoke didn't use notes, and some of those who had notes got caught up in the emotion of the evening and of the issue, cast aside their notes and spoke directly from their hearts. The common thread was their heartfelt, honest concern about the streams, the critters that live there, and about the people negatively impacted by the proposed buffer zone rule change. As they spoke sometimes I wanted to laugh, other times to cry.
>
> Only Coal Association chief Bill Raney and coal industry lawyer Bob McLuskey spoke in favor of the rule change.
>
> I do not know what effect, if any, the sentiment expressed in Charleston on that Tuesday evening will ultimately have. But the message was unmistakable — "keep the buffer zone rule as it is".

One normally quite gentile lady declared, "The goddamn coal companies have taken it all except one hundred feet, and now they want that too"! Her outburst appeared to be considered and controlled, rather than from having lost control.

My own words follow:

Perhaps no environmental issue has more direct economic and quality of life impact on the people of West Virginia than that of water quality, including maintaining — as nearly as possible — the natural integrity of our streams, both of water quantity and water quality. The Clean Water Act and other laws have as their goal the preservation and improvement, not further degradation, of streams and underground aquifers — the natural conduits and storage basins for the water we must have to survive.

Yet we now see the federal government proclaiming, on the one hand, strong environmental protection policies, while on the other hand gutting the very rules and regulations designed to assure a good and decent environment for mankind and all of god's creatures.

Mountaintop (mountain range) removal mining and its associated valley fills destroy water storage aquifers, increase water runoff during rain events, and cause even lower water flow rates during times of little or no precipitation — because part of the reserve storage capacity has been depleted. The "evening out" of wet weather vs. dry weather water flow rates is significantly disrupted by mountaintop-removal mining.

And valley fills dump up-side-down concoctions and mixtures of various metallic elements into stream headwaters, mixtures which destroy the natural chemical and biologic balance of waterways throughout their length, and within the many aquifers they feed along their course.

Too, the political pretentiousness with which we proclaim the "protection of our streams" on the one hand, while allowing them to be filled to the brim with mining wastes, on the other, is nothing short of laughable. With this operating policy, "We protect the streams by destroying them" becomes the effective reality.

And the political hypocrisy inherent in being sworn to uphold the laws on the one hand, but arranging to allow subversion of those laws on the other, would be laughable were it not so tragically serious.

A Return to DLM

For the April 2004 *Highlands Voice,* Tim Higgins wrote an update on the DLM Mine that had been the focus of so much controversy in the 1970s. He wrote:

It was a bright day for November; temperature close to 60 degrees. I had invited Cindy Rank for a trip back through time, to a place we had traveled many times before, long ago. She had her camera and the taped-together multifolded, multi-colored, hi-lited topo-maps, now worn and torn from years of use.

We were headed to a forgotten part of Upshur County. On the Alexander Rd, County Route 11, the view toward the east is breathtaking at the turn. The mountains and trees reign still and beautiful.

We were now in the Buckhannon watershed, below Selbyville, above Beans Mill. With a quick left before the river and up the switchback road to the old church, we had our first view of the old DLM strip mine. At this point we had traveled about 12 miles from Cindy's home.

This was the second phase of the DLM strip-mining complex located on the western side of the Buckhannon River. It was here we began our picture-taking more that 20 years ago. Today some of the houses that were there before the mining took place remain — some in poor condition, others not. The water-holding ponds remain, close to the back door of some of these homes. There are a few new homes completed; one that caught my eye is a log cabin overlooking one of the holding ponds, still orange from the acid. One point to remember: Wherever they had gouged the earth for the coal, there are no trees.

Along the single lane gravel road, we passed another small pond that would run acid water all the time. It had been bulldozed open years ago. Up the hill to the ridge, we passed several small farms. The difference in the color of the pasture of these farms to the dry dead grasses of the stripped land is the difference between night and day. A turn to the right put us in the community of Alton.

Crossing the Buckhannon River, (Route 32) we are now close to no-man's land. A quick ascent through the woods opened up into the original DLM strip mining complex. Straight ahead lies a huge tank. Cindy informed me it was anhydrous ammonia, a new treatment for the water. "State of the Art", she had been told. Around the bend to the right were the multi-ponds of different colors. They were stair-stepped, one flowing into another until there was no place left to go but the creek and on to the Buckhannon River just above Alton. None of the ponds looked inviting.

Along the road bank, down toward the ponds, were several water seeps that stained the ground a bright orange. Ahead lay another tank 500 or more gallons in size filled with sodium hydroxide, the "State of the Art" water treatment we were told about many years ago. Both tanks had thousands of feet of hose running to the different ponds.

A treeless landscape lay ahead as we ascended to the ridge top, broken only by the several large oaks in a small fenced-in graveyard. We pulled out the torn and tattered topo maps. Besides the brown grasses blowing in the wind the only other movement was a white pickup truck with a green license plate. This is the person who has the thankless job of monitoring the water coming from this barren land. Keep in mind that the job is a secure one. Water treatment at this site will go on FOREVER at taxpayer's cost.

Once we had our bearings, we made a left turn at the equipment buildings run by the state that maintains this "Godforsaken" treeless land. Stopping at a gated road just before the road wound down to Panther Fork through the woods, we were greeted with a NO TRES-PASSING with a "Hazardous" warning sign. "Wonderful place', I thought to myself. Cindy informed me that this is the same area that she visited with the State personnel in a previous year, where this road leads to the three larger stair-step ponds, that are not visible from the public road system.

Continuing on down the hill on Rt. 32, is the only road that crosses Panther Fork on the valley floor for its full length, from Hemlock on the eastern border of Upshur County to Beans Mill on the Buckhannon River.

I have heard many stories of this river tributary and the treasures it held before the mining; hardly any one talks of it any more. Before the creek crossing on the left hand side of the road is THE POND. More like a toxic waste dump. The water from the mining ridge we just came off of is collected here for treatment before it is released into the lower end of Panther Fork.

The first time I saw this area was during active mining, with Rick Webb; it was my introduction to acid mine drainage. At that time, DLM, in an effort to abate THE PROBLEM, would routinely throw large bags of sodium hydroxide briquettes, split open with a knife, in the ditch on the right hand side of the road. Water from the active mine site ran through the split-open bags, neutralized the acid, and turned the rocks in the ditch bright orange.

"State of the Art Treatment," Rick Webb told me at the time. Sometime after semi-enforcement of water quality regulations, a little dam was constructed in this ditch to capture some of the water which feeds it into a pipe that goes under the road and into a barrel-shaped mechanical device that is rusted away and held lime. The remainder of the water from the ditch was measured for volume and flow, which was supposed to release a quantity of water from the pipe into this lime hopper. After the small amount of water had dissolved the proper amount of lime for the main flow rate, it was fed to the entire water flow to the pond.

This "State of The Art" device, named AQUAFIX, is now a rusting relic of another failed attempt to put the acid genie back in the bottle. Treatment now is by the West Virginia's monitoring of the ponds' water quality output and manually adjusting a valve connected to a line of anhydrous ammonia from the large tank we saw on the other side of the hill. The pond itself has a skimmer boom spread across it to keep the floating crud on top from reaching the discharge stand pipe. A well-worn small path leads to the discharge pipe on the downhill side of the ponds' lower end where the water sample is taken.

I could only imagine what it would be like to take a sample on a minus 20 degree day with 22" of snow on the ground analyze it then trudge to the other side of the pond and adjust the valve for the proper "State of the Art Treatment"

Is this what DLM meant when they said WE CAN PUT IT BACK BETTER THAN IT WAS BEFORE?

What's left on the DLM site that will grow are only spindly pines. Yes. They speak the truth. They can only whisper. All the trees cry for life. They don't want to die. Is any one able to hear their cries?

An accompanying article titled, "A Little History," reminded readers:

The current situation at DLM is only the latest in the long history of that site. In an earlier chapter, the West Virginia Rivers Coalition had petitioned to have the Buckhannon River watershed declared unsuitable for mining. Under both the federal and state Surface Mining Acts, one may petition to have an area designated as unsuitable for mining if some feature of the area makes it unsuitable for mining. The Rivers Coalition contended unsuccessfully that the Buckhannon drainage was so prone to produce acid that it should not be mined. The petition was rejected.

Another chapter took place in 1979 when Braxton Environmental Action Program filed complaints with the federal Office of Surface Mining and the Environmental Protection Agency about acid discharges from the property. At about the same time, Mountain Stream Monitors published a newsletter suggesting that the mining in Braxton County was destroying the trout streams.

While the article did not mention DLM by name, the permit numbers listed in the article were those of DLM. DLM decided it was being defamed, and sued Braxton Environmental Action Program, Mountain Stream Monitors, and WVHC member Rick Webb, a leader in both organizations.

That case was bounced out of the court system without even a trial by the West Virginia Supreme Court. It held that the defendants had a right to petition the government for redress of its grievances and, through its newsletter, seek to influence public sentiment concerning the passage and enforcement of laws.

The most recent event was the agreement that West Virginia made with DLM in 1985. West Virginia agreed to assume responsibility for treating the acid water that came from the DLM site. In exchange for assuming this responsibility, the state received $800,000 in cash, securities, and equipment. It also received the option on 4,000 acres of land in Upshur County.

At the time of the agreement, DLM was spending $300,000 per year on water treatment.

It was through this agreement that West Virginia became responsible for treatment of water at the site.

It had been twenty-five years since DLM had first been mentioned in *The Highlands Voice*. During that time the biggest issue in mining, that of perpetual treatment of acid-mine drainage in northern West Virginia, had given way to the issue of mountaintop-removal mining in southern West Virginia. Throughout this period the Highlands Conservancy — primarily though Rank, McFerrin, Martin, and Young — had remained a major player in the public debate. A few times it had won major victories, but often it had faced defeat, the victim of the combined forces of federal and state government officials serving as advocates for the mining industry. It had been, and would continue to be a lonely, but important battle.

The Passing of Judge Haden

Looking back, one of the most significant victories had been Judge Haden's landmark decision on mountaintop mining in 1999. Unfortunately, Haden would not be able to continue his help. The mountains of West Virginia lost a true friend when Judge Haden died on March 20, 2004. In a tribute titled "A Friend Remembered" in the April *Voice*, Martin, a college classmate, wrote:

> When the West Virginia Highlands Conservancy lawsuit against dumping mine waste in our streams came before federal Judge Charles Haden, I hoped he would go by the law. And that is what he did. The law is clear: mine waste cannot be dumped into intermittent and perennial streams. As a conservative, he believed in the law, and he ruled that the law meant what it said. People who love our mountains were overjoyed at his decision.

Judge Haden wrote that the destruction of the unique topography of Southern West Virginia by mountaintop removal is "permanent and irreversible" and that if the forest canopy is destroyed, our streams are exposed to extreme temperatures and aquatic life is destroyed — "these harms cannot be undone."

As a birdwatcher, he was concerned that "If the forest wildlife are driven away by the blasting, the noise, and the lack of safe nesting and eating areas, they cannot be coaxed back." Haden chastised administrators for trying to change the Clean Water Act behind the back of Congress. He wrote that amendments to the act "should be considered and accomplished in the sunlight of open congressional debate and resolution," and "not within the murk of administrative after-the-fact ratification of questionable regulatory practices."

To exclude dumping mine waste from the Clean Water Act would, in Haden's words, be an "... obviously absurd exception" that "would turn the Clean Water Act on its head and use it to authorize polluting and destroying the nation's waters for no reason but cheap waste disposal." Haden further observed that Congress "did not authorize cheap waste disposal when it passed the Clean Water Act."

Speaking to the question of whether dumping mine waste into streams had an adverse effect on the streams, Haden wrote that "When valley fills are permitted in intermittent and perennial streams, they destroy those stream segments" and "if there is any life form that cannot acclimate to life deep in a rubble pile, it is eliminated." Haden pointed out the obvious truth that "No effect on related environmental values is more adverse than obliteration. Under a valley fill, the water quality of the stream becomes zero. Because there is no stream, there is no water quality."

A mutual friend told me that Judge Haden was stunned when he was taken on a flyover and viewed mountaintop removal from the air. He observed in his ruling that "The sites stood out among the natural wooded ridges as huge white plateaus, and the valley fills appeared as massive, artificially landscaped stair steps."

"Some mine sites," he said, "were 20 years old, yet tree growth was stunted or nonexistent compared to the thick hardwoods of surrounding undisturbed hills, the mine sites appeared stark and barren and enormously different from the original topography."

It is ironic that Judge Haden died just 10 days before the Bush administration will conduct a hearing Tuesday in Charleston. They are proposing to change the buffer zone rule to make it legal to dump mine waste into the streams Judge Haden so valiantly tried to protect.

Long after the names of the people of limited vision, who are destroying our mountains and streams, are forgotten, the name of the very distinguished Judge Charles Haden II will live on. He is indeed an authentic West Virginia hero.

Ironically, the following month U.S. District Court Judge Joseph R. Goodwin issued a preliminary injunction preventing a subsidiary of Massey Coal from opening a mine under the Corps 404 nationwide permit. The suit, to which the Conservancy had not been a party, had challenged the Corps' practice of issuing a nationwide permit to cover valley fills, rather than considering them on a case-by-case basis. It was as if the ghost of Judge Haden was visiting the court.

On July 8, 2004, Judge Goodwin stopped the Corps of Engineers from issuing 404 permits to mines under the nationwide permit system. The Corps was ordered to revoke permits already issued to eleven mines where construction was yet to start. Goodwin's ruling affected only southern West Virginia. Until the order was changed or repealed, companies would need a permit determined on a site-specific basis.

In October the state Surface Mine Board rejected a Conservancy appeal 5-1 saying that the stream buffer rule did not apply to valley-fill waste sites. Conservancy lawyers expected to file an appeal in court that could eventually reach the West Virginia Supreme Court.

On the central issue in the case, Joe Lovett, Director of the Appalachian Center for the Economy and the Environment, and representing the Conservancy, wanted the board to conclude that the stream buffer-zone rule prohibited coal operators from burying certain streams with waste rock and dirt. This case followed directly from the 1999 case before Judge Haden. When overturned by the Fourth Circuit Court, it said the case should be heard in state court. The first step in that process was this case before the state Surface Mine Board, whose chairman was former Conservancy officer Tom Michael. His had been the minority vote of one.

The state DEP and industry lawyers had argued that, if applied to valley fills, the buffer zone rule would effectively outlaw most coal mining in West Virginia. That explained the significance of Judge Haden's initial decision, the Circuit Court's reversal, and this case. At stake was the future of mountaintop-removal mining.

Despite the 404 case, the Corps was continuing to issue permits under the nationwide general permit to mines where work had begun before Judge Goodwin's July 8 ruling. In February 2005, environmental groups in Kentucky had filed suit to apply Judge Goodwin's injunction against the Corps to its jurisdiction in Kentucky. If the first court case was lost, the appeal would move to a different appeals court, the Sixth Circuit in Cincinnati.

Following up on the Environmental Impact Statement on Mountaintop Removal Mining, forced by the Conservancy's litigation back in 1998, the EPA announced in June 2005 that approximately 83,500 comments had been received, including many e-mails, postcards, and letters.

McFerrin wrote in the June *Voice*:

> Prominent among the criticisms of the draft was that it identified adverse environmental effects of mountaintop removal but then made no recommendations other than shuffling agency responsibilities:
>
> What is the point of that? Why go through the entire NEPA process if all you can come out with is a reshuffling of agency responsibilities? There are no alternatives suggesting how we could do mountaintop removal in a more environmentally sound manner. There is no alternative that we not do it at all. The only alternatives proposed are that we keep doing it in the same way we always have, causing the same damage the Draft documents. The pseudo-alternatives offered are that we choose among different agencies to preside over the environmental devastation.
>
> If the agencies involved are not embarrassed by this, then I can only conclude that they have reached the point where they are beyond embarrassment.
>
> The only way the agencies can fix this Draft is to shred it. Having done that, they can try again, including proposing specific actions that would minimize the environmental effects of mountaintop-removal mining. The alternatives should include not doing it at all. By "actions" I do not mean more suggestions for paper shuffling or pondering on which agency should preside over the present course of environmental devastation. I mean real, on-the-ground actions that change the way we mine, including whether we mine by this method at all.
>
> So far as when the agencies involved will complete evaluation of the comments and respond, they say no more that the process will extend "well into 2005."

Here indeed was a stinging indictment of the process of citizens groups trying to change government policies through the environmental impact statement process. It had worked for the Conservancy when the law was new in the 1970s, but thirty-five years later it had proven worthless to control mountaintop removal mining.

Another Bush Initiative

Maybe it really was an embarrassment after all. In July, Ken Ward of *The Charleston Gazette* announced a "new" approach by the Bush Administration. He wrote:

> Bush administration officials have announced that they will conduct a detailed environmental study before they scrap a federal rule that prohibits coal mining within 100 feet of streams. The study could delay the rule change for two years or more. The change had been strongly pushed by the coal industry.
>
> In January 2004, the Office of Surface Mining had proposed to essentially eliminate the 20-year-old stream "buffer zone" rule, which generally prohibits mining activity within 100 feet of streams. Coal operators can obtain variances to mine within that buffer. To do so, companies must show that their operations will not cause water quality violations or "adversely affect the water quantity and quality, or other environmental resources of the stream."
>
> The announcement was a major reversal for the Office of Surface Mining. Originally, the agency argued that its buffer-zone rule changes would "not significantly affect the quality of the human environment."
>
> A more detailed study — called an Environmental Impact Statement — would not be needed, the Office of Surface Mining said. Environmental and citizen groups disagreed and urged the Office of Surface Mining during a comment period last year to perform an Environmental Impact Study.
>
> The Office of Surface Mining said it has "subsequently determined that the preparation of an EIS would be an appropriate mechanism to fully assess alternative approaches to these specific proposed actions and their potential impacts."
>
> In his 1999 ruling, Haden had said valley fills could never meet the strict test for a variance from the existing buffer zone rule.
>
> "When valley fills are permitted in intermittent and perennial streams, they destroy those stream segments," Haden wrote. "The normal flow and gradient of the stream is now buried under millions of cubic yards of excess spoil waste material, an extremely adverse effect," the judge wrote. "If there are fish, they cannot migrate. If there is any life form that cannot acclimate to life deep in a rubble pile, it is eliminated.

"No effect on related environmental values is more adverse than obliteration," Haden wrote. "Under a valley fills, the water quantity of the stream becomes zero. Because there is no stream, there is no water quality."

The Office of Surface Mining said it "believes there may be a need to clarify" the buffer zone rule. The agency cited "highly contradictory views on the application" of the rule. In its announcement, the Office of Surface Mining said it will accept public comments until mid-August on how to design the buffer zone study.

The Office of Surface Mining also said it will hold "scoping meetings" in Pittsburgh; Knoxville, Tenn.; Alton, Ill.; Denver; and Washington. None of the meetings was scheduled for any of the nation's top three coal-producing states — Wyoming, West Virginia and Kentucky. It had taken seven years, several major federal lawsuits, untold hours of research, public testimony, and national publicity to convince the major federal agency to re-examine its regulations under the law. It would remain to be seen if the re-examination would produce any meaningful changes.

Answering the question, "Why is this so important?" Rank wrote:

> Taking apart whole mountains hundreds of feet deep — as is done at mountaintop-removal and steep-slope mining operations across southern West Virginia and neighboring areas of Kentucky, Virginia and Tennessee — is possible only if millions of tons of waste rock can be dumped into the rich stream valleys below. The larger these fills, the larger and deeper the mining. The larger the operation, the larger and more severe is the impact on the water, forest, and human resources where mining is taking place. Had the Stream Buffer Zone Rule been enforced a major portion of the devastation that has occurred across the region would not have happened. A proper and thorough EIS should promote enforcement of the current rule and prevent the enactment of a change that threatens to legitimize the destruction of thousands more miles of headwater streams, hundreds more square miles of hardwood forest, and untold greater numbers of communities.

In her extensive comments presented to the scoping hearing on this new EIS, Rank reviewed the history leading to this re-evaluation. After extensive technical comments, she stated:

> The mental, emotional and physical scars to the people of the region as their ancestral mountains and homes are torn apart were not given adequate consideration in the MTM/VF DEIS [Mountaintop

Mining/Valley Fills Draft Environmental Impact Statement], but should rightfully be fully considered and analyzed during the SBZR [Stream Buffer Zone Rule] EIS.

ALTERNATIVES should be proposed to strengthen the SBZR and further protect the people and communities in and near the stream valleys where mining is proposed.

I end here and with this item — with the people — because it's damage to our families and friends and the heritage of the mountains that will have the last, greatest, and most long-lasting impact. The people may not be first on the priority list of technical and scientific considerations for OSM during this EIS, but the greatest loss attributable to lax enforcement of the SBZR may well be the loss of these communities and the rich mountain heritage that is disappearing with them.

Once again, as Nick Zvegintzov had written more than thirty years before, the abusive effects of mining on West Virginia's rural communities and their residents required a public outcry. For all those years in between, the Highlands Conservancy had tried with its limited resources to intervene in a system that ran on money and political support. Now in 2005 there were more activists, more national publicity, yet less political support. Mining operations that had been big at two hundred acres, were now small at three thousand acres. The story would continue. There would be no natural ending, happy or otherwise, at least by 2007.

In September 2005, three developments occurred involving the Corps of Engineers. On the 19th the Fourth Circuit Court heard oral arguments in the Bush Administration's appeal of Judge Goodwin's 2004 ruling that the Corps use individual permits for valley fills. On the 22nd another challenge was filed in District Court, this time against a Corps permit to Aracoma Coal Company in Boone County. On the 27th the Conservancy commented on yet another permit application, this one for Hobet Mining to extend its approximately 12,000-acre mine into new areas.

After Rank finished discussing these matter-of-factly, she explained her growing frustration this way:

> Long time readers of the *Voice* may remember a December '96 article in which I attempted to explain the maze of permitting that had allowed hundreds of miles of streams to be buried. The article highlighted Hobet 21's Westridge permit and the specifics of the seven valley fills proposed for tributaries of the Mud River — one of which would bury the entire length (2½ miles) of Connelly Branch.

Since that time Hobet has proceeded downstream with any number of modifications, incidental boundary revisions and relatively small permits — consuming every tributary of the Mud River as it goes. EPA noted the headwaters of the Mud River will be 42.2% disturbed by past, present, and future mining and other land disturbance activities.

I'll never forget taking the picture that appeared with that '96 VOICE article, or the ride through the small community of Mud and up the Connelly Branch hollow on a rickety bus with other members of the legislative interim committee on Mitigation before the Westridge permit was granted.

I visited the mine site on a number of occasions after that, during mining when Big John had been unleashed to feast on the deep mountain greenery — and have returned to the area several times since then.

Believe me, there is no combination of words from our 2,478 page Random House Dictionary that could even begin to describe the total annihilation that has taken place.

In that 1996 article I wrote that the state's reliance on industry's promises and the recuperative powers of mother nature to recovery after being put through the giant mixmaster of modern-day mining appeared to me to be crap shoot with the future of southern WV at stake.

Today, nearly ten years later, numerous studies have documented extensive harm to the streams, forests, and families where mountaintop removal and valley fills are permitted. Operations like Hobet 21, Samples, Marsh Fork, FOLA, etc., continue to turn the earth inside out. Homes and families in Mud and elsewhere continue to disappear, and stories of people from Delbarton, Van, Whitesville, Cow Run, Rock Creek, and so many other coalfield communities fill the airwaves.

I no longer view this activity as a crapshoot.— It's just plain crap.

For anyone who had ever met Rank, or heard her deliver one of her hundreds of public statements before hearing officers from state and federal agencies, this plain language told a story — a story of frustration, of heartbreak, of friends whose lives had been shattered, and of many forced to move from their homes. The social cost of mountaintop-removal mining had become overwhelming.

In November, *Voice* Editor McFerrin wrote that the Final EIS on mountaintop mining had finally been released. His subtitle was, " After Six Years of Labor, the Deck Chairs on the Titanic Are Satisfactorily Arranged." There was nothing new since the draft appeared, and no indication that the 83,000 comments had made any difference.

On November 23, 2005, the Fourth Circuit Court of Appeals partially overturned Judge Goodwin. It permitted the Corps to return to issuing a nationwide general permit for at least some valley fills rather than site-specific analysis. Once more the most conservative judges on the most conservative appeals court in the nation had opened the floodgates to the mining industry.

Cindy Rank Reflects

By February 2006, Rank had recovered from yet another court defeat and, perhaps for therapy, wrote about "coal and communities:"

> My articles in the *Voice* are most often attempts to make a fair and reasonable presentation about the illegal actions in the world of coal mining, and about various efforts by the West Virginia Highlands Conservancy and others to hold industry and the regulatory agencies accountable for their actions.
>
> What is often missing from those articles is the passion and outrage one feels when coming face to face with the blatant disregard for people and the environment as individual coal companies move into an area where mining is planned.
>
> One can only feel outrage when standing on the edge of Larry Gibson's family cemetery and witnessing the gradual disappearance of one ridge after another as far as the eye can see.... And to know that there are laws that are meant to prevent such widespread and complete devastation of our life-support system of mountains, forests and streams......
>
> However, what has always been even more infuriating is the cold and calculating way that the coal industry goes about dismantling communities while the company works its way through the legal hoops of permitting....
>
> Whether it was the Shaws or Zirkles or Russells at Tenmile on the Buckhannon River, or the Millers along the Mud, or the Barnetts in Artie, or the Weeklys and others in Blair, or the many other communities' folks like Bob Gates, Penny Loeb, etc. have captured in a multitude of visual documentaries, the story is still the same: communities are ripped apart, individuals harassed, property and the people who want to hang on to their property are devalued and cast aside like some worthless pieces of trash.
>
> I pass along the following message I received today. I've edited it a bit, but it comes from a friend who lives and works in the besieged coalfield communities. I realize it sounds very much like what we heard in 1997 from so many families in Blair when we filed suit to

stop the Spruce #1 Pigeonroost mine. …. But this was sent to me today, February 3, 2006.

Wal-Mart and other developers may see the need for the right to condemn property through "eminent domain", but the coal industry has no need of that …. It has more than enough ways to get rid of the people that might stand in their way.

The message referred to, follows:

I was in Blair yesterday. It's really something to see what they are doing there. They have moved in and they are taking it! No one is supposed to ask any questions when you put 6 treatment ponds above a community and move the roads and river. This is something you just have to see to believe.

The houses in the community have burnt, one after another. The last one was directly beside one family and the fire dept was just going to let it burn until their house started smoking. It was a house that the coal company had bought. It caught on fire in the middle of the night with no utilities hooked up. There have been 6 homes in this immediate area that have been bought and destroyed.

One house has a sign next to it that says "keep out we still live here" because of looters stealing from the other houses. Things like windows and doors cabinets, shower/tub units. Basically disassembling the houses and hauling them away. People call the law and they would not come. Someone was heard to say that the coal company had given this stuff away to get them torn down. When everybody got what they wanted, the coal company came in with backhoes and a dumpster and hauled what was left away.

During all of this the looters were stealing from people who still lived there. They actually stole a running air conditioner out of someone's window. What is going on here is bad.

They are even putting a double train track right down the middle of what is now a community. They are building the tracks with the homes there. They are offering rock bottom price for people's homes. They only pay for the square footage of the homes and say that the property is a part of the deal.

The historic road signs in Blair disappeared over night. They are gone….. someone came through and just took them. They are all gone there is not one left.

On January 2, 2006, the Sago Mine Disaster riveted the nation to its televisions. With her now-twenty years of sustained involvement in mining, Rank provided her reflections in the March 2006 *Highlands Voice*:

It seems every ten years some new and often unexpected chapter in the Tenmile saga unfolds.

Little did we suspect that the dawning of this new year would open another, even more tragic, chapter of the complicated story of this area along the Buckhannon River in Upshur County. This time it's a chapter of disastrous loss of life.

On January 2, 2006, the nation awoke to news about a mine explosion at the Sago mine, a deep mine maybe 3 miles downstream of the Tenmile strip operation. The mine is also owned and operated by ANKER — originally under the name of Hawthorne Coal and more recently as the International Coal Group (ICG). Thirteen miners had been trapped.

As events of the next 24 hours unfolded, the tragic death of 12 of the Sago miners caught and kept the nation's attention. Questions about Sago continue: — How could this happen? What went wrong? What caused the explosion? Could the miners have been saved if other safety measures had been available? Where was the Mine Health and Safety Administration? Were the laws enforced? Why was a mine with so many safety violations allowed to operate? Why was there so much misinformation during the rescue attempt? And why did the families have to suffer the pain of first being told their loved ones were alive only to learn hours later that all but one had died?

Senator Byrd was quick to call for Congressional hearings. The U.S. Senate heard testimony from current and former administrators of the Mine Safety and Health Administration (MSHA). After delivering his comments, acting MSHA director Dye left the hearing in defiance of Chairman Specter's request that he stay another hour in case other testimony prompted questions that only he could answer.

Formal investigations by both federal and state teams are underway.

Glowing news stories about the record low number of coal mining fatalities in 2005 quietly faded among subsequent stories of 2 more deaths just weeks after the Sago disaster, then one more just days after that, then 3 others in Kentucky, then one in Maryland.

By the end of February a whopping twenty-four mining fatalities had already been reported in the United States alone.

DLM — Tenmile — Grand Badger — Sago. — Efforts of the WV Highlands Conservancy, for the most part, have focused on real and potential problems associated with DLM and the 2,000-acre strip mine and sludge impoundment at Tenmile ......i.e. from the brave Zirkle family resisting a 90 ft high dam across their upper field to catch drainage from the next 12,000 acres of planned strip mining, the 1 mile long valley fill at Job #11, the acid and metals that have occasionally killed fish and deposited iron deltas in the Buckhannon River and its tributaries and passed along high treatment costs to the Buckhannon Water Department to maintain water potable enough for the ever-expanding numbers of thirsty communities served by their system, to inadequate bonding and ANKER's more recent plans for an eco-park and co-gen plant and more stripping and the use of coal ash in the mine backfills.

While the Highlands Conservancy's efforts have been focused on surface mining, these were not the only kinds of mines planned for the area. Overall plans of the Island Creek Coal Company in the early '80s always included a considerable amount of underground mining. ANKER — now ICG –continues to carry out those plans for more mining, both surface and deep, to extract their extensive mineral holdings along the Buckhannon and further downstream in the Buckhannon-Middle Fork-Tygart Valley river watershed. (e.g., 65,000 acres – yes, sixty-five thousand acres of longwall and traditional deep mining in the Grafton area of Taylor County.)

Coal industry claims about being "over regulated" ring hollow at a time like this, as do accusations about "frivolous" lawsuits and "radical" community groups going too far in their demands that mining laws be more carefully enforced.

Let us hope the lessons from January 2, 2006 are not soon forgotten. While our thoughts and prayers go with families of miners everywhere — whether their loved ones work hundreds of feet below ground in the bowels of the earth or far above ground in the cab of 25-story-high drag lines — let us also continue our work to ensure the safety of our environmental life support system so that we all may live full and fulfilled lives.

We must keep fighting for good law and the political will to enforce that law.

The following month, Rank returned to the topic of the MTR EIS. She wrote:

> It's difficult to tell just which regulatory agency is doing the least to minimize the damage from mountaintop-removal mining these days.
>
> A settlement agreement in our 1998 *Bragg v Robertson* lawsuit initiated the multi-year Environmental Impact Statement (EIS) that produced scientific studies documenting the intensive, extensive harm

that mountaintop removal and valley fills are doing to forest, stream, and human communities throughout the region.

The response to these EIS studies and ensuing court challenges has been under-whelming and contrary to all reason.

All agencies reneged on the original intent of the settlement agreement to recommend ways to reduce the impact of mountaintop-removal mining and valley fills. The Final Environmental Impact Statement instead recommended that the agencies join hands in streamlining the permitting process to allow more permits to flow more freely. — Go figure.

The Court hearing on the Conservancy's suit against the Corps was scheduled in October 2006. In December, Rank updated *Voice* readers on these ongoing battles:

As two District Court judges consider questions about the validity and adequacy of Clean Water Act fill permits in southern West Virginia, the twelve-thousand-plus acre Hobet 21 operation continues to expand further into Lincoln County, burying more of the headwaters of the Mud River.

The pleasant little community of Mud that I first saw in 1995 when visiting the area as a member of the Interim Legislative Committee on valley fills is gone now. Only the Miller's homeplace remains…(saved only after an appeal to the WV Supreme Court)

…..And the Caudill home, though it is no longer inhabited by those who cared for it for so many years. Homes along Berry Branch are gone too, the local church is burned, and the mining is expanding over into Big Ugly as well.

Driving down the road from Woodville and Cameo to Mud with Viv Stockman and Julian Martin the day after listening to final arguments in our litigation challenging the Army Corps' authorization of fills at four big mountaintop-removal mines, comments by the Justice Department lawyer representing the Corps echoed in my head…

Did she really say that remote, less developed areas of Appalachia deserve less consideration than more populated areas?

"Eleven percent of impacts may be significant in a national park" she stated. … "Whereas, a much greater percentage of impacts in an area of limited population and no alternative potential land use foreseeable, that may certainly be less significant."

I've long understood that many coal companies view any negative impacts from mines located in remote and undeveloped areas as just not very important. … But hearing that statement in the halls of justice as an excuse for picking and choosing what portions of the laws apply to what communities is mind-boggling, to say the least.

Visits to/through these huge mines, whether it be Kayford or the multitude of mountaintop removal sites I've been on since my first experience at Dal-Tex in 1994, are headache-producing events.

Our drive down county routes 8 & 46 the day after the court hearing in Huntington was particularly shattering. The once wooded drive is now merely a narrow slick goat path perched precariously between an unstable steep hillside above and a sheer drop below. Gone is the home and family who showed me the blasting damage they endured nearly ten years ago. Gone too are the trees that once lined the road and graced the hollow. In their place are drainage ditches below the road, and a pond further on down the hill that marks the toe of the future fill. A variety of saws and trucks and other machines are in the process of destroying and rearranging the geology of yet another section of God's good earth.

Company lawyers in the Huntington litigation wrote that the case is part of the environmental community's "ongoing war against one of the few economic engines left in West Virginia." But from where I sit, the ongoing war is one being waged by an industry bent on breaking the laws in order to garner the biggest profit in the shortest amount of time.

The goals of the Clean Water Act never included burying thousands of miles of valuable headwater streams. Nor were the goals of the Surface Mine Act ever intended to allow the total destruction of forest, soils, and water resources. And neither of those laws was written with the intention of harming the people and communities who depend on those resources.

War has always been hell, but it's particularly painful to see it being waged in our own backyards.

Again, as so many times before, the Conservancy was aligned with the rural residents against the overwhelming power of the coal industry and its political supporters. The only possibility of relief lay with the federal judicial system. Luckily for the environmental plaintiffs, including the Highlands Conservancy, a pro-bono legal team came together over the past decade. Most prominent was Joe Lovett, of the Appalachian Center, based in Lewisburg, joined on many cases by James Hecker, of Public Justice in Washington, D.C.

Federal District Judge Robert J. Chambers, who as Speaker "Chuck" Chambers of the West Virginia House of Delegates had been a friend to environmentalists, had recently heard some thirty-seven hours of testimony challenging this specific Corps permit. In a related case Judge Joseph R. Goodwin, also a well-connected state Democratic leader, was considering whether to block the Corps from using the nationwide valley-fill permit system. Unfortunately, even if environmentalists prevailed, any appeals went to the conservative Fourth Circuit. That had happened to Judge Haden on several decisions, and might be expected again.

As the West Virginia Highlands Conservancy began its celebration of its Fortieth anniversary in 2007, Rank wrote a front-page story in the February *Voice*, headlined "Sorrowful Days in Blair, WV":

> "WHO CAN FORGET BLAIR, WV?" I wrote in the November 2006 *Voice*. ...Well it appears the Army Corps of Engineers can. — And did.
>
> On January 22nd the Corps approved the 404 permit for the Spruce #1 Mine in Blair.
>
> My November article recalled our involvement in the landmark *Bragg v Robertson* litigation that began the day Jimmy Weekley walked into Joe Lovett's office, looking for help to fight off a huge mine that threatened his home in Pigeonroost Hollow.
>
> Joe had been reading Penny Loeb's 1997 *Newsweek* article "*Sheer Madness,*" the expose that first illustrated for the nation just what human toll was caused by the coal strip-mining method called mountaintop removal.
>
> The following ten years have been a seesaw of successes and painful setbacks.
>
> Now the tortuous road of litigation, Environmental Impact Statements, comments, and appealing permits appears to have broken through the last roadblock that had for so long delayed the devastation of Jim and Sibby's [Weekley] beloved hollow.
>
> The Individual Clean Water Act Section 404 Fill permit was granted just seven days after Sibby's death. As stated in lengthy comments on the Spruce #1 EIS last fall, we believe the permit should NOT have been granted because of many inadequacies.
>
> Joe Lovett (Appalachian Center) and Jim Hecker (Public Justice in DC) appealed the Corps decision to Judge Chambers on Friday February 2nd. The company has agreed to limit mining and grubbing that had already begun to just over 100 acres at the head of Seng Camp while Judge Chambers considers whether or not to include the Spruce permit as part of our 404 litigation now pending in his court.

A personal side note:

At 2,278 acres Spruce #1 remains the largest single strip mine permit to be granted in West Virginia.

In the 1998 *Bragg* court proceedings we used a large topographical map with mine permit boundaries hand drawn and highlighted in bright yellow to show the extent of mining proposed for Boone, Logan, and Mingo Counties. Industry lawyers went ballistic. .... Many of those permits had not yet been approved and several more were yet to be started.

Today I sit and look at that same faded map with a heavy heart. Nearly every one of those mines have received all their permits — mining, NPDES water discharge, and 404 fill permits. Many are underway, and even more have been applied for.

Spruce #1 may still be the largest single permit, but if you consider the expansions at Samples around Kayford, and the long arms of Hobet 21 in the Mud River and Big Ugly watersheds, and the Edwight mine on the ridges above the controversial sludge impoundment that looms over Marsh Fork Elementary School, and the Mingo-Logan operations around Stirrat and Cow Creek, the new impoundments planned for hollows not far from the mammoth Brushy Fork Impoundment, ...and Black Castle, Stollings, Elk Run, and so many more, the reality of the overall impact is far more devastating than the worst case scenario depicted in the Mountaintop Removal Environmental Impact Statement.

It's no longer a matter of connecting the dots. It's now a matter of finding space *between* the disturbances, of trying to see what — if anything — will be left from Raleigh and Greenbrier counties west to Mingo and Wayne.

Rank compared the recent death of Sibby Weekley with that of columnist Molly Ivins, who also died in January 2007:

Sibby Weekley died January 15, 2007.
Molly Ivins died January 31, 2007.
There have been many articles written about the popular author and columnist Ivins since she died ... And many tributes full of hilarious quotes and tender remembrances.
Sibby died and was buried quietly in the presence of family and friends.
The two women obviously lived worlds apart. But to me they will always stand together, side-by-side with a handful of strong women I've met and toiled with since moving to West Virginia some thirty-three years ago.

They shared the same clear-headed tenacity that gave them the courage and strength to face insurmountable odds with grace and dignity that would make any parent proud.

They embodied the true meaning of "speaking truth to power" ... Both in their individual and very different ways — one in the limelight and nationally known, one as daughter, sister, wife, mother, and grandmother in Logan County WV.

Both were admired and respected and provided inspiration to anyone looking for examples of good people hanging on no matter how rough the road they traveled....

Some ... may remember meeting Sibby during one of our Conservancy outings to Blair and the Weekley's home...or just know of Jim and Sibby from the multitude of stories about them, their home in Pigeonroost Hollow, and their crucial role in the 1998 *Bragg* litigation before the late Judge Haden that led to so many landmark actions in the pursuit of sanity in the coalfields now torn apart by the excesses of mountaintop removal.

Jimmy may be the firebrand in the news, but Sibby was always the supportive rock and anchor. She will be missed.

No doubt there would be more court suits filed, more court decisions, and more disappointing results. Occasionally there might even be victories, but the war against the devastation of mountaintop-removal mining would continue. Always the valiant struggle of the Sibby and James Weekleys, the Judy Bonds, the Larry Gibsons, and many others, were what kept Cindy Rank, Julian Martin, John McFerrin, Penny Loeb, Bob Gates, Viv Stockman, Joe Lovett, and so many others engaged. It certainly wasn't the untold personal sacrifices, the lack of remuneration, the threats to one's security, nor the devastated landscape. It was the inspiration of those whose mission was to "speak truth to power." They were the environmental heroes. Mother Jones had perhaps said it best, "Mourn for the dead and fight like hell for the living." No wonder several of these fighters had won the Mother Jones Award.

Readers are urged to use current technologies to stay informed. A wide variety of websites are now available, including the Highlands Conservancy's at www.wvhighlands.org. The continued struggle needs additional support.

Sources:

Abramson, Rudy, "A Judge in Coal Country," *APF Reporter*, vol. 20, no. 3, 2003, aliciapatterson.org

Caperton, W.Va. governor, reply to Cindy Rank's letter re: Larry George as Commissioner of the Department of Energy, 1990

Caudill, Harry, *Night Comes to the Cumberlands* (Boston: Little, Brown, 1963)

Close Up Foundation, videotape for Smithsonian Institution series, "Citizen Stories," profile of Cindy Rank, 1990

Corbin, David, *Life, Work and Rebellion in the Coal Fields, the West Virginia Miners, 1880-1922* (Urbana, Illinois: University of Illinois Press, 1981)

Fetty, Nathan, of W.Va. Rivers Coalition, on 2001 floods

Fout, Janet, of Ohio Valley Environmental Coalition, *Voice*, April 2002

Gates, Robert, *In Memory of the Land and People*, a 1977 film, available on DVD, from Omni Productions, Charleston, 2007

Gates, Bob, *Mucked: Man-made Disasters – Flash Flooding in the Coalfields*, a film (VHS and DVD), produced by Gates with Penny Loeb, available from Omni Productions, Charleston, 2003

Giardina, Denise, *Storming Heaven* (New York: Ballantine Books, 1987)

Giardina, Denise, *The Unquiet Earth* (New York: Ballantine Books, 1992)

Haden, Charles II, U.S. District Court judge, decision, October 20. 1999

The Highlands Voice articles by Gordon Billheimer, Perry Bryant, Bob Burrell, Skip Deegans, Richard diPretoro, Tom Dunham, Dave Elkinton, Linda Cooper Elkinton, Karen Farris, Judy Frank, Bob Gates, Larry George, Dave and Donna Haggerty, Bob Handley, Ron Hardway, Tim Higgins, Jason Huber, Jon Hunter, Doug Hurst, Carroll Jett, Carolyn Johnson, Tom King, Keith Kirk, Ed Light, Zip Little, Linda Mallet, Bob Marshall, Julian Martin, John McFerrin, Tom Michael, Ernie Nester, Mary Pat Peck (Cronin), Charles Peters, John Purbaugh, Dan Radmacher, Cindy Rank, Bill Reed, Tom Rodd, Dave Saville, Joan Sims, Wayne C. Spiggle, Vivian Stockman, Jenni Vincent, Rick Webb, Scottie Roberts Weist, David Wooley, Frank Young, Nick Zvegintzov, among others

Johnson, Skip, article in *The Charleston Gazette*

Kabler, Phil, article in *The Charleston Gazette*

Kennedy, Robert F., of Water Keeper Alliance, *Voice*, April 2002

Loeb, Penny, *Moving Mountains, How One Woman and Her Community Won Justice from Big Coal* (Lexington, Kentucky: University of Kentucky Press, 2007)

Loeb, Penny, "Shear Madness," *U.S. News and World Report*, August 11, 1997

Lovett, Joe, on Haden decision, *Voice*, April 2002

Marshall, Suzanne, *Lord, We're Just Trying to Save Your Water: Environmental Activism and Dissent in the Appalachian South* (Gainesville, Florida, University of Press of Florida, 2002)

Martin, Julian, article in *The Charleston Gazette*

Martin, Julian, interview, October 21, 2005, and correspondence

McFerrin, Joh, interview, January 27, 2007

McGraw, Darrell, W.Va. Supreme Court Justice, opinion on DLM and First Amendment rights, 2001

Niiler, Eric, article in *The Charleston Gazette*

Nyden, Paul, articles in *The Charleston Gazette*, March 30, 1990; April 19, 1991

Pancake, Catherine and Ann Pancake, *Black Diamonds*, a 95-minute film, available from www.blackdiamondsmovie.com/index.html, 2006

Patchwork Films, *Mountain Mourning*, a 30-minute film, available on DVD, with Look What They've Done - Maria's Backyard, 21-minutes, and Keeper of the Mountains, 18 minutes, available from www.patchworkfilms.com, 2006

Radmacher, Dan, article in *The Charleston Gazette*

Rank, Cindy, interview, March 28,2007, and correspondence

Riley, Bill, testimony in W. Va. Legislatiave committee meeting, 1971

Room 152 Productions, *Razing Appalachia*, a 55-minute film, available from Bullfrog Films, www.bullfrogfilms.com, 2002

Spadaro, Jack, testimony in U.S. House re Strip Mining Control Act, 1977

Toner, Robin, article in *The Charleston Daily Mail*

Udall, U.S. Rep., article in *The Charleston Gazette*, December 1979

Ward, Ken, article in *The Charleston Gazette*

Wetterich, Chris, article in *The Charleston Gazette*, July 2005(?)

Williams, Norman, quoted in *TheCharleston Gazette* and reprinted in *The Highlands Voice*, April 1971

Young, Frank, interview January 27,2007, and correspondence

Zvegintzov, Nick, correspondence

Chapter Eight
Blowing in the Wind:
An Answer, with Questions

The development of wind energy in the mountains of West Virginia produced more controversy within the environmental community than any other issue anyone could remember. Organizations with a long history of working together found themselves on opposing sides of several proposed wind energy projects. Individual environmentalists left organizations of which they had been leaders and new organizations sprung up, pitted against the older environmental groups. This chapter will tell a far different story than previous chapters and, as the Highlands Conservancy celebrated its fortieth anniversary in 2007, there was still no clear conclusion to the basic questions surrounding wind energy development in the highlands.

First, some history: *The Highlands Voice* published its first article on wind in February 1976, aptly titled "Whither the Wind?" The author, Gordon Hamrick, described the area near Bowden, east of Elkins, which was then under construction as part of the route of Corridor H (See Chapter 4). Hamrick analyzed wind speeds moving up valleys with an east-west orientation, and recorded frequent wind velocities through mountain gaps of 60 miles per hour. He noted that the removal of trees, such as that associated with highway construction, accelerated the wind flow. His article concluded with questions about the impacts of high winds on snowfall, pollination of fruit trees, and other biological impacts, but Hamrick never mentioned harnessing the wind for energy generation.

West Virginia's First Wind Farm Proposal

Sixteen years later, *Voice* readers read another discussion of wind and, once begun, the discussion went from a breeze to a gale. In the Summer 1992 issue of *The Highlands Voice*, coincidentally announcing the Conservancy's 25th Anniversary Gala Celebration at Cass, a reprinted Associated Press story from August 22 opened this way: "West Virginia environmentalists aren't sure if plans to build power-producing windmills in a scenic mountain region are a dream or a nightmare." (Fifteen years later, in 2007, the question still remained open.)

According to the AP story, Kenetech-U. S. Windpower, which operated similar facilities in Altamount Pass, California, proposed a wind farm to the Tucker County Commission in August 1992. The proposal was for 150–200 wind turbines to be located on mountains overlooking Canaan Valley and on a ridge north of the Dolly Sods Wilderness. These locations certainly grabbed the attention of environmental organizations, including the West Virginia Highlands Conservancy.

Cindy Rank, then-president of the Conservancy, summed up the conundrum that would plague the environmental community. "Wind power and the prospect of having it on line is very exciting to us," she wrote. "But the location — hundreds of windmills along the edge of Canaan Valley and the Dolly Sods and in the migratory flight path of hawks and songbirds — that location will be very difficult for us to swallow." Jim Kotcon, president of the West Virginia Chapter of the Sierra Club, added, "This is a divisive issue." That would turn out to be a gross understatement. He continued, "Many of our members believe in the establishment of alternative energy sources, but many also believe in protecting the area's wildlife and aesthetic qualities."

The issues were thus joined: the aesthetic beauty and wildlife of the mountaintops versus the desire to establish a sustainable alternative energy source and thus reduce the use of carbon-producing fossil fuel energy. Most environmentalists across the country could agree in principle to the need for green energy sources, but there would develop a fierce battle over the sites for such facilities. West Virginia would again become a major battleground in the nationwide (and soon global) war for sustainable energy.

It would be another two and one-half years before the Conservancy discussed wind energy. The November 1994 *Highlands Voice* contained three articles, focused on another Kenetech project, this time proposed for private timber lands in eastern Greenbrier County. The articles mentioned that the Tucker County proposal had been put "on the shelf" following "concern over the viewscape and the presence of a major migratory bird flyway."

The proposed Greenbrier County project included up to 1,200 wind turbines, capable of producing as much as 400 megawatts of electricity, located along Cold Knob Mountain, in an area between Richwood and

Rupert. As proposed, the project could become the largest wind-powered electricity generating plant in the East. Much of the land to be used had previously been strip-mined and belonged to timber companies Mead Westvaco and Georgia Pacific. The price tag was estimated at $400 million.

Of the 80,000 acres needed for the Greenbrier windfarm, half lay within the proclamation boundary of the Monongahela National Forest, but on private land. Within the boundary, the land could potentially be added to the Forest in the future. That eventuality would be unlikely if the land became an income-producing wind farm.

An article by Rick Steelhammer of *The Charleston Gazette* explained the sudden interest in wind energy production. The federal government would provide a 1.5 percent per kilowatt-hour production credit for the first ten years of a new wind plant's life. He also wrote that Kenetech would use towers containing three 33-meter blades each, producing electricity that could be sold for 3.5 to 5 cents per kilowatt-hour — about the same price as power from coal.

To any veteran Conservancy member viewing the map of the proposed wind farm, the community at the very center of the project area sounded familiar: Duo. This was the same rural community that twenty years earlier had been the subject of a strip mine fought by Conservancy Vice President Nick Zvegintzov, with financial support by the Conservancy (see Chapter 7). In 1994, Zvegintzov wrote a brief note to the *Voice* relating his visit to Altamount Pass and describing the huge size of each wind turbine he observed. He raised the question of whether wind farms would be fenced off for security reasons, noting, "It would sure make a total mess of bear-hunting."

Over the next six years, there would be rumored proposals, bird migration studies, and other discussions, but little evidence in *The Highlands Voice* of wind energy becoming a major environmental issue. That changed in the issue of August-September 2000. Conservancy President Frank Young reported that a wind farm proposal for Backbone Mountain in Tucker County was on a "fast track" before the state Public Service Commission. On behalf of the Conservancy, he had asked the PSC to conduct an independent Environmental Impact Study and to conduct a formal hearing on the project before approving the application.

Franklin D. Young, born in 1945, spent his early years on a farm in northern Kanawha County, West Virginia. In a family of six children, Frank quickly learned about farm work and became active in the 4-H program. He remembered both his dad and 4-H teaching him about the conservation of the earth's resources.

After graduation from Sissonville High School, he attended West Virginia State College, majoring in physics. Married and beginning his family, Frank became a salesman instead. He traveled 1200 miles a week, from Pikeville, Kentucky, to Morgantown, West Virginia. He encountered many different people and observed many different landscapes in the mountains. At age 33, Frank went into business in Ripley, building a successful tire and wrecker business over the next twenty-three years.

An old high school friend, Carroll Jett, had become a state trooper in the area, and one day Young and Jett were reunited when Young was called to tow Jett's truck. By April 1989, Jett and his family had invited Young and his family to attend a Highlands Conservancy Spring Review at Blackwater Falls. Both men became Conservancy board members in the fall of 1990.

Young had always been interested in politics and conservation, so the Conservancy seemed a logical place to become active. Very soon he was involved in organizing the West Virginia Environmental Council and in 1994, he became Conservancy Senior Vice President as John McFerrin became President. He succeeded McFerrin in 1998 and served three two-year terms.

In addition to dealing with the issue of wind power, discussed in this chapter, during Young's tenure as president the Conservancy addressed the issues of timbering in Blackwater Canyon, the beginning of a new wilderness campaign, and the acceleration of mountain-top removal mining. Because these issues were highly controversial and brought the Conservancy back into the news, it might be said that Young's six years were among the most contentious of any during the Conservancy's history.

When he stepped down in 2004, Young reflected on his presidency in *The Highlands Voice*. The Save the Blackwater Campaign had helped ignite a surge in membership. The Conservancy had spawned its first website, which would only grow in importance. And *The Highlands Voice* was by then composed and transmitted electronically to its printer. During his term, the Board had converted to communicating by email.

But Young saw his legacy in different terms. He wrote, "We successfully and earnestly maintained and grew the *credibility* of the Highlands Conservancy — in the eyes of our membership as well as those who see us from the outside — the media, regulatory agencies, and the general public." He had proven that the president of the West Virginia Highlands Conservancy was instrumental in building the organization, both internally and externally.

In the August-September 2000 *Highlands Voice*, Young wrote the first of a two-part series on wind power. The company proposing the Backbone Mountain project clearly hoped to gain the environmental community's support. Young wrote:

> When I learned that a meeting was proposed about the Tucker County project, and that the project's proponents wanted to "touch base with the environmental community," as they put it, I decided to be a part of that meeting. Early on I sensed that the project managers, through a company called Atlantic Renewable Energy, wanted my (our) blessings, not our money.
>
> With some trepidation, realizing that I could become an unwitting tool in the company's promotion of the project, I did attend their meeting at Blackwater Falls State Park on July 15th.
>
> It appears ...that 12 or 15 West Virginia environmental "leaders" were invited and that the company thought they would be attending. In actuality only four invitees attended. They were Jim Kotcon with West Virginia Environmental Council, Jim Sconyers with Sierra Club, Paul [Jim] Rawson with the Canaan Valley Institute, and myself.
>
> I went to this meeting armed with several pages of concerns some of our Conservancy members and Directors had about wind power. The concerns were about threats to birds, sight pollution, effects on esthetically sensitive landscapes, noise pollution, new roads for construction and maintenance of wind turbines, forest destruction during construction, oil and grease pollution during maintenance, and effects of power lines used to conduct electricity from the wind turbines to existing power grid input points.
>
> The project's promoters anticipated almost all our concerns. Their prepared presentation addressed most of the concerns before we even asked about them.

Young detailed each concern and the corresponding reply or mitigation arrangement. Among these were that the company's avian consultant believed that sufficient information on birds and habitat existed to permit a risk assessment and that the proposal represented no significant risk to birds.

Western Pocahontas Land Company owned nearly all the land proposed for the project. Lease payments were estimated to be approximately $2,000 per turbine per year, making a significant return to the company. As many as two hundred workers would be needed for construction but only as few as five to seven would be needed for permanent operation. West Virginia had been chosen by the company, Young continued, because it had the wind, compatible land uses, and was "cost effective."

He concluded that he felt that the company was open and receptive to his comments and questions. He continued that they had a timetable for permit approvals and for construction to begin. His hunch, he said, was that, while they'd like to have the blessing of environmental leaders and Tucker countians, they would aim to keep that time schedule and weren't going to let dissent deter them. He added that he thought the company wanted to try to blunt potential environmental objections before they became problems — either legal problems or public relations problems.

The following month, Young continued:

> When I learned in late spring that an eight-turbine wind farm was operating in nearby Pennsylvania and was supplying wind-generated electricity to the interstate electric power grid I was intrigued.
>
> When I learned a week or so later that a larger wind power project was on the drawing board for Tucker County, West Virginia, I decided to go see the Pennsylvania facility.
>
> For my wife, Becky, and me, finding and getting to the wind farm in Garret, a small town in Somerset County, Pennsylvania, was not difficult. That wind power facility is a mile or less off U.S. Rt. 219, about 10 miles north of Interstate Rt. 68 from the Grantsville, Maryland exit.
>
> Heading north on Rt. 219, coming around a bend just outside Garret, the Green Mountain Wind Farm looms almost intrusively to the motorist's immediate left. Upon seeing the large towers and turbines, I pulled to the roadside for a better look. To gawk, as it were.
>
> My first thought about the 30-story high machines I was looking at was "awesome"!

My next thought was "Imposing"! The turning blades, 90 feet long, three on each turbine hub, were an impressive sight, indeed. They were so large as to look like giant, unstoppable fans.

But two of the eight turbines and blades were not turning. For whatever reason, they were "parked". When these three bladed monsters are parked, two blades are at 10:00 and 2:00 o'clock, respectively, and the third blade is at 6:00 o'clock — straight down. Now this is a personal observation; but to me those parked blades looked eerily like the face of a dead elephant, its ears up a little, but its limp trunk just hanging there. Very "sad" looking, these two "dead" wind turbines.

We were still almost a mile from the formerly surface-mined mountain atop which these windmill towers were perched. We decided to try to get a closer look.

Young continued:

The tower and blade assemblies together reach the length of a football field in a vertical dimension. The towers are cylindrical and have a diameter of about 15 feet at the bottom. There are no outside ladders on the towers; they are perfectly round from bottom to top. Access to the generator units on top is by ladders on the inside of the supporting towers.

Three of the eight towers had a flashing white strobe light on top. It was not quite dark when we left. I presume that after dark the white flashing lights were replaced by red flashing lights.

The looming, intrusive appearance of these machines was probably accentuated by the treeless, grassy fields which surrounded them. I tried to visualize how they would look surrounded by a forest. They would still be looming, I think.

I don't know of any forests in the eastern United States nearly approaching 100 yards in height.

Initially, my shock at the size of these machines was shaking. As I spent more time there I tried to decide if I could ever get over the intrusive feeling about them. I decided that I could, after enough time and exposure to them. But even now, almost two weeks later, Becky still says, "They looked like something that's not supposed to be there." She admits that she feels the same way about the several Ohio Valley power-plant smokestacks we can see from a hilltop above Ripley.

Earlier in the day we had been told by a company representative that at winds speeds above about thirty miles per hour the blades gradually turn their narrow edges, instead of their broadsides, to the wind to maintain an even 20 RPM. We were also told that at wind speeds above about 56 miles per hour the blade and turbine brakes are applied and the unit totally stops and "parks" until the wind speed drops to below 56 miles per hour. This park operation is to prevent damage to the blades and transmission-generator units due to high winds and high RPMs.

A company representative had told us earlier in the day, "Aesthetics is a subjective judgment." I think this is probably true.

But my initial feelings about the imposing and intrusive nature of these mountaintop machines still sticks in my psyche. I could probably get over that feeling.

I felt the same way when I first saw a 1960s era coal-fired power-generating plant cooling tower and smokestack. I mostly got over that.

And I felt the same way when I first saw, from the valley floor of Cabin Creek, a drag line operating atop a surrounding mountain. I haven't gotten over that yet.

As we left the town of Garret we stopped near our first "stop and gawk" point for another look and a couple more pictures. We could see plainly only five of the wind power machines from this point. Then we saw a sixth. It was an ominous looking spinning blade, looping up over the horizon at about one second intervals. It was eerie. We could not see the supporting tower — only about 20 or 30 feet of a giant blade, looping - looping - looping - looping - looping up from the horizon. It was awesome, sort of scary, to be at a location where we could see only the turning blades but not the supporting tower, spinning, looping above the horizon. It reminded me of the first few scenes in Bob Gates' film "In Memory of Lands and People." The part where the top of the giant strip mining shovel, called "The Gem of Egypt", moves into and out of view and then back into view along Interstate 70 in Ohio. Of course, Gates' sound effects were not available at Garret, PA that July 15th. But the eerie feeling from seeing that giant looping blade swing - swing - swing - swing over the horizon is still with me.

I'm still trying to sort out what I feel about the prospect of 60 to 90 of these giant wind power machines spread along 7 miles of Backbone Mountain.

On one hand, I feel a need to see "us" change from coal-fired electrical production to something less polluting and less consuming of finite resources.

On the other hand, by going down the road of perhaps more benign but still somewhat problematic "wind farms" along scenic ridges, I wonder if we are maybe overlooking or otherwise bypassing even more benign and attractive power sources — or if we even need to change how we live to not need so much energy.

We can all think about this some more. Maybe wind power is a suitable "interim" power source to get us across the literal rivers of pollution until we develop technologies for the "perfect" power source, or the "perfect" lifestyle that doesn't require massive amounts of man-made power.

Indeed, Young and the environmental leaders in the Appalachian mountains as elsewhere across the nation would "think about this some more." This precisely was the contradiction for environmentalists. These towers, supporting looping blades, silently harnessing the natural wind, needed to be placed on the highest ridges of the West Virginia highlands. Their impact was certainly visual, but already biologists were beginning to worry about the mortality of birds and bats that flew into the path of these gigantic machines.

Young and the Conservancy primarily objected to the intrusion of the huge wind turbines into the semi-wilderness atmosphere of Blackwater Falls State Park and other special places. After negotiating with the company, in January 2001, Young announced a negotiated "win-win" agreement with Atlantic Renewable Energy and its subsidiary, Backbone Mountain Windpower. In a joint filing with the West Virginia Public Service Commission, the Conservancy and the company had agreed to project modifications that retained the majority of the original proposal, but imposed restrictions sought by the Conservancy. Specifically, the southernmost twenty turbines would be deleted from the proposal. The remaining turbines would not be observed from Blackwater Falls State Park.

Young added that the agreement created a technical committee to approve a post-construction avian monitoring program, to be developed by the wind-power developer's consultant. This technical committee, composed of stakeholders in the permitting process, included a representative of the company, the Highlands Conservancy, the U.S. Fish and Wildlife Service, the West Virginia Division of Natural Resources, a statewide avian organization, and a representative from a private or academic institution with a background in avian issues.

Young continued:

I am pleased that this agreement removes our objections to the project and that development of our wind resources in the West Virginia highlands can proceed. With this agreement on this, the first commercial wind-power project in West Virginia, we have set the precedent that wind power can be developed without seriously impacting existing developed recreational resources such as Blackwater Falls

State Park. Future wind-power projects will be on notice that we don't allow proposed "green energy" projects to diminish the value of existing "green" recreational assets. And the stakeholders committee that resulted from these negotiations is a model for future working relationships with wind power and perhaps even other industrial developments.

I thank the representatives of Atlantic Renewable Energy and its subsidiary, Backbone Mountain Windpower, LLC, for their willingness to negotiate and for accommodating our concerns in developing this project. The spirit of cooperation between the Highlands Conservancy and this company is a model for other commercial and industrial developers and citizen groups.

Young acknowledged the assistance of Conservancy attorney, William DePaulo, along with Wind Committee members and Conservancy vice presidents, Carroll Jett and Judy Rodd.

Unfortunately, the "win-win" negotiations Young thought would be a model for future wind development would not be sustained. Within a few short years, the Backbone Mountain project would end its willingness to permit outside technical advisers on the company's property. Rather than negotiate, other proposed wind farms would become a struggle between the developers and the environmentalists, often with well-organized local opposition groups involved.

But in its modified form, the Backbone Mountain Wind Farm was constructed, and its forty-four turbines became West Virginia's first wind farm. It would become famous a short time later for a major bird and bat "mortality event."

Mount Storm Proposals

Nearly a year later, on December 20, 2001, Paul Nyden, writing in *The Charleston Gazette*, announced another wind farm proposal, for the nearby Mount Storm area. To be built by Mount Storm Wind Force, the proposal would include 166 wind turbines, making it the largest wind farm in the state.

The new power plant would be built on 10,000 acres of land in Tucker and Grant counties, bordered by the Potomac River, Mount Storm Lake, and the town of Mount Storm. The new wind plant would generate 250 megawatts of electricity annually.

Judy Rodd, Conservancy Senior Vice-President, who also served as President of Friends of Blackwater, told Nyden:

I hope they [Mount Storm Wind Force] have done two years' worth of bird studies to make sure no migratory birds will be affected by their plan. And it should be out of the viewsheds of Canaan Valley and the Blackwater Canyon. On the whole, wind power is a very good thing. But finding the best sites is very important. It is better to use areas that are already disturbed, not areas used as flyways by migratory birds. Once they have assured us the new plant will not affect birds or the tourism value of that area, we think wind power is a good thing. It is clean energy. But it is very important to use areas that are already disturbed, and not areas that are flyways for birds.

Both cell [telephone] towers and the propellers on these wind turbines kill birds and bats. With the decline in migratory birds flying in our country, we have to be very cautious about creating new engines of destruction.

All the money from wind plants goes to out-of-state investors. They employ only two or three people after the wind farms are built. And the state Legislature recently exempted them from taxes.

In its application to the PSC, Mount Storm Wind Force stated it was not a public utility and asked the commission to exempt it from filing information about proposed rates, project construction cost, project financing, and estimates of operating revenues and expenses. The degree of oversight of wind farm developers and the ability of the PSC to regulate their projects would be an ongoing issue in the coming years.

Conservancy members and readers of *The Highlands Voice* had been regularly updated on the various wind farm proposals. Increasingly, there were disturbing reports of bird and bat deaths associated with the Backbone Mountain project. Many were asking a more general question: how many wind turbines would the highlands be able to absorb before the entire region looked from the air like one big windfarm. At the same time, the Friends of the Blackwater, which had grown out of the Conservancy's Blackwater Canyon Committee, was promoting the idea of the highlands as a potential national park. Its future could not be both.

In September 2002 *The Highlands Voice* reflected the growing interest and controversy about wind power development in West Virginia. A Wind Power Committee was listed for the first time among the standing Conservancy committees. The first President's column on wind appeared, Young's "There's Gold in the Wind Over Them There Hills." Peter Shoenfeld, Conservancy Vice President for Federal Affairs, summarized the wind farm proposals both approved and proposed. And George Beetham, Jr., wrote an insightful letter to the editor.

In Young's September 2002 commentary, he laid out the environmental contradictions. He wrote:

"I just love that mountain air", we often hear people say.

But the mountain air we so crave is mostly mixed with air blown across the continent, usually from the north and west, on high level "jet stream" winds, blowing from afar. These jet stream winds blow at speeds beyond 100 miles an hour at higher altitudes — 25,000 to 30,000 feet. At the level of the West Virginia "highlands", approximately 3500 to almost 5,000 feet, these winds, though reduced in speed, still are often quite brisk.

Energy is in demand. Therefore harnessed energy has value. The winds of the West Virginia highlands, when harnessed, are valuable. And the technology revolution of the 20th century has revolutionized the ability of mankind and machines to capture and harness the energy in the wind. Enter the age of commercial wind power.

We are familiar with the images of quaint little windmills used long ago to mechanically pump water from here to there, or to power a grain mill located adjacent to the energy-converting wind mill. But like Henry Ford's Model T, those quaint little windmills are mostly relegated to the pages of history. Today's "wind mills" often stand higher than the tallest electrical power transmission line support towers. Some are taller than the length of a football field. Giant rotating blades whirl and swish in the sky on the highest mountain ridges. Why there? Because usually that's where the wind blows strongest.

We are the West Virginia *Highlands Conservancy.* Our name suggests that we seek to *conserve* the mountain regions — presumably in their nature state. That means that we promote low impact, "sustainable" uses of the natural resources there. In doing so we encourage hiking, bicycling and a reasonable level of tourism, and modest commercial and human habitat infrastructure and institutions. We discourage mountain strip mining, excessive logging of trees, unneeded highway corridors, water resource degradation, and ugly intrusions upon nature.

The recent interest in constructing wind power towers and turbines, made relatively economical through technological achievements in electronics, plastics, and metallurgy, as well as governmental economic incentives, creates a dilemma for the WV *Highlands Conservancy* and other conservation advocates.

Theoretically, wind-generated electricity can replace that generated by mining and burning coal and other fossil fuels, avoiding the need for those processes. At first glance we are tempted to say, "Great! Clean power at last!"

Second thoughts, though, give us pause to think about potential problems with wind-generated electrical power, too. Do wind turbines create significant bird mortality hazards? Do they impact the habitats of endangered species? Do large wind turbine and tower assemblies, and their associated "aviation warming lights," mar majestic viewsheds? Are these impacts significant enough to warrant discouraging wind power development? Can these, and perhaps other potential problems, be mitigated and still keep wind power economically viable?

Will wind power be the yearned-for alternative to fossil fuel extraction and burning and the associated environmental detriments? Or will wind power simply be an added source for the nation's seemingly insatiable appetite for more and more "cheap" energy?

How should the West Virginia *Highlands Conservancy* approach wind-power issues in the West Virginia highlands? One of the West Virginia *Highlands Conservancy's* good friends recently cautioned against "squandering our good name" in challenging the wind power industry to make marketed "*green power*" really green.

Now we are trying to decide to what degree to engage with the project developer and the permitting state agency on a proposed 200-turbine wind-power project on the Allegheny Front in [Grant] County. This project may have a significant viewshed impact on the Dolly Sods North recreation area, as well as some possible migratory bird impact. We are trying to learn more about this project.

We need to have the discussion about how we will relate to ongoing and the many future wind power generation facilities that are certain to be forthcoming soon. In a separate article in this issue of *The Highlands Voice*, Peter Shoenfeld writes about the pending Allegheny Front wind power project. We are starting to have the discussion. We need to continue and expand the discussion.

Shoenfeld wrote:

Proposals for large-scale wind energy projects are proliferating in the West Virginia Highlands. This presents opportunity, responsibility and unusual challenges to the West Virginia Highlands Conservancy. Opportunity and responsibility exist because we can and must influence these projects. An unusual challenge is there because we must do so without the moral certainty with which we approach many issues — the environmental "goods" are not all on one side.

Wind energy is clean energy and must be supported, especially as an alternative to coal. On the other hand, there are undeniable adverse environmental impacts. These are very location sensitive, and, unfortunately, the locations that are most energy-productive are often also the most environmentally sensitive. Neither the State of West Virginia nor environmental organizations have established policies or procedures for certifying wind power proposals as environmentally sound.

Although no construction has yet taken place, two projects each are advancing in Grant and Tucker counties, and additional projects are rumored. The project of present great concern is the NedPower Mount Storm LLC proposal for a 200-unit, 300-megawatt development on Allegheny Front. The project would occupy a 14-mile by ½-mile strip along the Front, with southern boundary at Stack Rock, just a little over a mile north of Bear Rocks.

The Allegheny Front in Grant County is the eastern boundary of a broad plateau at the headwaters of Red Creek, Stony River, and several tributaries of the Blackwater and North Branch of Potomac rivers. When traveling west on Route 93/42 from Scherr, we ascend 2000 feet and stay high for many miles — this is a mountain with only one side. This windy plateau has been extensively strip-mined and is home to the massive Dominion Resources Mt. Storm power plant. At its southern extremity it also includes the spectacular resource we call North Dolly Sods.

The Allegheny Front is a unique geologic, meteorological, ecologic, and geographic landmark. It is the western boundary of the folds and uplifts that developed when North America and Northwest Africa collided 300 million years ago. The prevailing west wind is compressed and clouds drop their precipitation here, creating a rain shadow that results in much drier weather to the east. The winds, rain, snow, and rocks create unique boreal habit. The Front is a bird migration flyway, and, along most of its length, it is also the eastern continental divide, with waters to the east reaching the Chesapeake and those to the west reaching the Mississippi.

The Nedpower project would occupy a 14-mile by ½-mile strip along the Front, with southern boundary at Stack Rock, just a little over a mile north of Bear Rocks. The plans call for 200 units of 328-foot total height (tower plus blade). By way of comparison, the monstrous smoke stack at the Mt. Storm power plant is about 750 feet in height. The units will be distributed more or less linearly, generally in two rows about a thousand yards apart. Construction is planned in separate Central, Southern, and Northern phases, with the Central phase occupying the portion between Old Stony River Dam and a point just south of Route 93/42. Central phase construction is planned for 2003. Southern and Northern phase construction are planned for 2004.

In the days since this proposal surfaced, several Conservancy members have walked the North Dolly Sods area of Monongahela National Forest identifying locations providing scenic views of the Allegheny Front Ridge line. These exist along Raven Ridge, on Cabin Mountain, and on Allegheny Front outcrops south of Bear Rocks. There will also be major visual impact along the (presently) privately-held Divide north of Dobbin Slashings, at The Nature Conservancy's Bear Rocks Preserve, and possibly at their Greenland Gap Preserve as well.

The Allegheny Front is a major migratory flyway for both raptors and songbirds. The Brooks Bird Club conducts their annual bird-banding project along the Front near Red Creek Campground. Judy Rodd told *The Charleston Gazette*: "I'm concerned about the effect on bird populations — migratory neotropical birds that in certain weather conditions can get killed. The Allegheny Front lies along one of the primary routes followed by migrating birds. On foggy days and at night, birds can get confused by tower lights and fly into windmills." These issues should be addressed in the avian study, but they may not be easy or possible to mitigate.

The NedPower application promised local economic benefit and included several letters of local support, including one from the Grant County Board of Education. This is no surprise since the application specifically promised "annual educational contributions" to "two local schools."

Peter Shoenfeld was raised in the suburbs of Washington, D.C. He received a Ph.D. from the University of Maryland in mathematics. In the 1970s, using an early edition of the Conservancy's *Monongahela National Forest Hiking Guide*, he became an avid backpacker in the highlands. By 1973 he had bought a mountaintop lot in Pendleton County and, later, built a cabin. He joined the Conservancy, but it remained several years before he attended his first Fall Review.

In 1998 he accepted the responsibility of Vice President for Federal Affairs, watching national issues on behalf of the Conservancy. He remained on the Board of Directors thereafter, serving as Senior Vice President 2003–2005.

During the next decade, he was most involved in three specific areas. He re-invigorated the Conservancy's website, first established by *Voice* Editor Bill Ragettè in 1996. Shoenfeld designed a new home page, secured the domain name (www.wvhighlands.org),

419

added significantly to the content, and included several features that were quite advanced for a small non-profit organization site at the time. These included use of credit cards for ordering of merchandise and making donations, an inter-active forum, and a dynamic list of links to newspaper and other articles concerning West Virginia environmental issues.

Shoenfeld's second interest area was the Conservancy's outings program, re-established in 1999, and marketed a year later as "Mon-athon 2000, Celebrating Our Monongahela National Forest" (See Chapter 6).

His third area of interest came somewhat later as the Conservancy struggled to develop its policy on wind farm development.

In a 2000 interview with Tom Rodd, Shoenfeld commented:

"I'm a lifelong "woods person" who has been enjoying the Monongahela National Forest for over 20 years. I support the Conservancy's work generally, and I am particularly concerned with forest, wilderness, and backcountry preservation. I also help The Nature Conservancy of West Virginia.

"I worked as a Computer Programmer, Manager, and college teacher, before finishing graduate school. Since then my professional work has always included heavy computer usage, systems engineering and some programming. Since 1981, I've been an employee and officer of Science Applications International Corp, applying my math and science background to National Security projects. I never touched HTML or web programming before I took on the Highlands Conservancy site — learning this stuff was part of my motivation."

After 2000, Shoenfeld's involvement in the Highlands Conservancy continued to increase. He was appointed by President Young to the Wind Energy Committee and became its chair in 2003. Shoenfeld and his wife Marilyn, who was elected Vice President for Federal Affairs in 2005, eventually became residents of Timberline in Canaan Valley and in 2007 were active in the Friends of the 500th, a support group of the Canaan Valley National Wildlife Refuge.

George Beetham, Jr., a future Conservancy board member from eastern Pennsylvania, also shared his views on wind power development in a letter to the editor in the September 2002 *Voice*. He wrote that the developer, NedPower, had misled the public in saying that the proposed windfarm would not be visible from public viewing areas:

Bear Rocks and Stack Rocks along the Allegheny Front are owned by the Nature Conservancy and open to the public. Both are just south of the southern limits of the proposed project, as outlined to the Grant County Commissioners. Both are heavily visited by hikers, campers, backpackers, birders, nature photographers, and nature lovers. They are geologically and naturally unique microenvironments that have been preserved from development. The towers would ruin the view from both of these places.

The Monongahela National Forest, the crown jewel in West Virginia's natural areas, is located just south of the project area. Part of the plateau there is taken up by the Dolly Sods Wilderness, a congressionally declared wilderness, and the Dolly Sods Scenic area, set aside by the U.S. Forest Service as a unique natural area. Much of the remaining area on the plateau south of the eastern continental divide is either managed as wilderness or proposed for inclusion within the national forest. Both logging and mining are excluded in this area.

The Dolly Sods plateau is unique geologically. The Allegheny Front marks the western limit of the folded Appalachians, which were folded and uplifted when what is now North America collided with what is now Northwest Africa some 320 million years ago. To the west of the front, the force of that collision resulted in only mild ripples, in the case of the Dolly Sods, a shallow syncline or dipping valley.

It also is unique meteorologically. Prevailing winds from the northwest are compressed as they flow over the region, creating the winds that make the plateau so attractive to developers of wind power. But those same winds create a microclimate that is similar to parts of Canada many miles to the north.

The shallow dip of the underlying rocks also creates basins that are occupied by bogs — micro-habitats containing unique and somewhat rare plants. The plateau is also home to woodcocks, or timberdoodles, in season. Other birds and animals use the plateau as either a seasonal or permanent home.

Everything about the Dolly Sods is unique.

The NedPower project, if developed, would be highly visible from Cabin Mountain, the eastern continental divide, Raven Ridge, and other high points within the national forest down to and including Roaring Plains.

I spent the past week camping on the Dolly Sods and hiked through much of the area, including Raven Ridge, Cabin Mountain, and around Bear Rocks. This is a beautiful and pristine region with expansive views from extensive heath meadows. Although the Mount Storm power plant, 14 miles distant, is visible on clear days, it is at a remote distance. Placing wind turbines closer than that point would over-power the views.

My enjoyment of these wild places this past week was tempered by the realization that the view could be marred by windmill towers. I am extremely unhappy over that prospect. I have urged NedPower, in the interest of the many people who come to enjoy their national forest in all its natural glory, to modify its proposal and place the towers north of the existing power plant. My support of wind power is tempered by my feeling that natural lands are being encroached upon from every side and the realization that we must fight to protect them from unseemly development.

On any weekend one can drive up to the Dolly Sods. You will see a large number of cars parked at the parking lot near Bear Rocks and throngs of people walking and climbing them, picking blueberries, hiking, taking photos, looking at migratory birds, or just lounging. Farther south along the forest road you will find the trailhead for the wilderness area filled with cars of hikers and backpackers. Red Creek Campground will also be filled to capacity on most weekends.

I suggest a visit to these areas to see for yourself the impact the NedPower proposal would have on these natural places. They are precious. They are beautiful.

They are loved and used by countless people — destinations for tourists. The NedPower proposal would, if allowed to proceed as planned, ruin both the views and the wilderness experience.

I realize that I am not a West Virginian, but I have traveled to the Monongahela National Forest for three decades. In that time, I have met a number of West Virginians, wonderful people who are friendly and gracious. I understand the economic issues West Virginians face, and generally support efforts toward economic development.

But economic development should not come at the price of desecrating the natural wonders of the state, wonders that are, after all, a large part of West Virginia's heritage and tourism destinations. Windmill power is cheap, clean, and certainly a worthy goal ...but not in an area where wilderness rules and man is but a visitor ... and not where people go in search of the Earth's beauty.

These statements of fact and opinion captured the essence of the dilemma. It was a matter of balance. Could alternative energy sources such as wind be developed without jeopardizing unique natural areas in the highlands? Might places with somewhat less than optimum wind potential be found that would still generate energy, places that were not the very tallest peaks in the "mountain state?" Within a mix of regulatory agencies, could there be criteria for choosing wind farm sites and environmental safeguards established so every proposal would not re-open the issues all over again? And, adding together all the projects approved and proposed, what was the maximum number of wind turbines West Virginia should be asked to absorb to satisfy the nation's thirst for more energy?

The following month, October 2002, the *Voice's* headline read, "Between a Rock and a Hard Place?" Young continued his commentary from the previous month. He wrote:

> The West Virginia Highlands Conservancy's by-laws say that our GENERAL PURPOSES "shall be to promote, encourage and work for the conservation — including both preservation and wise use — and appreciation of the natural resources of West Virginia and the Nation, and especially of the Highlands Region of West Virginia, for the cultural, social, educational, physical, health, spiritual, and economic benefit of present and future generations of West Virginians and Americans."
>
> In keeping with those general purposes, we haven't had much reluctance to oppose strip mining of coal because strip mining is so anti-social, anti-environment, anti-democratic in practice and so contrary to concepts of good stewardship of the earth that there is no doubt in most of our minds about needing to oppose it.
>
> But I am increasingly troubled [by] this same "agin' it" attitude on the minds of some good and decent people relating to wind power. And it is especially disturbing that folks are suggesting that these wind projects should be opposed for virtually any reason that if one route of opposition does not work that we should work another route of opposition. Where is our objectivity? If an issue-specific, scientifically and legally rational case against windmills can't be made, then why go on interminably trying to litigate against or otherwise oppose them, as has been suggested?
>
> For years, decades really, there has been a strong sentiment from our members and our Board for "renewable" energy sources to replace the coal-fired electrical power sources we so despise. More recently, as the prospect of actually having wind electrical generation facilities on West Virginia hilltops becomes reality, we find ourselves in sort of a love-hate position with the developers of wind generated electricity.

From both within and outside the Conservancy I see an effort to discredit wind power with mostly a "not in my back yard" mindset. But if we can't vigorously support wind power, then I wonder why we individually even bother to collectively travel thousands of miles to meetings and if we've honestly been "Working since 1967 for the conservation and wise management of West Virginia's natural resources", as our letterhead tag line says.

Since my column and other wind articles appeared in last month's *Highlands Voice* I have had several contacts from *Voice* readers — people who appreciate our efforts, but who do not usually attend meetings and who are not on our Board of Directors.

One member, after considering the amounts of electricity a wind farm might produce, told me, "I'd opt for saving that many kilowatts by everyone cutting down on highway lights and clothes dryers. Then I'd tell myself we don't have to have the windmills after all. I suppose everyone could just move away from an ugly sight if they wanted to, but I think about NIMBY, and I guess I come down on the side against them."

Another told me, "At this time, however, I must say that I think the emphasis is in the wrong place. Our society will want energy. What is the least obnoxious way to get it? Is it better to have a windmill (rather pretty, though non natural in my view) in a viewshed or not to have a viewshed at all because it is dug up or smogged over? By all means find the best sighting for views, for birds, for ecology in general, but do not get in the way of windmills if you are serious about defeating mountaintop-removal mining."

I have contemplated the pros and cons of the several West Virginia windmill proposals that have been advanced over the past two years. I have come to believe that vigorously supporting wind power is a logical position for the West Virginia Highlands Conservancy. Any opposition we'd generate should be for specific reasons, scientifically and legally defensible, and directly relating to the preservation and protection of particular scenic, geologic, biologic, historic, wilderness, and/or recreational importance in West Virginia, as our SPECIFIC PURPOSES direct.

I have considered some of our history of fighting against strip mining, acid mine drainage from coal mines, acid rain, coal-fired power plant siting, and the air pollution and stream pollution attendant to mining and burning coal to produce electricity. These are good fights, and I am proud to have been associated with these battles. But I am not happy with the prospect of the West Virginia Highlands Conservancy needlessly squandering its good name by being 'agin' everything — even progressive energy technologies. What can we be for? If not wind power, then what? If not now, then when?

Reading his columns from both months, it was clear that Young was conflicted. Like many conservationists, he wanted to *conserve* the highlands region, yet he also wanted to support green energy production. He was struggling in his own mind to find a middle way if indeed one existed. The basic difference between Young and many other Conservancy members was that he was expected to lead the organization, articulate its positions, and negotiate with developers if that was appropriate. Everyone else could sit back and watch from the sidelines if they preferred.

It was not clear if Young's position was supported by a majority of the Conservancy membership or even by a majority of the Board of Directors. Over the next five years at least, the Board would continue the debate, often applying the general principles to a specific site of a proposed project, especially if the site was near one of the organization's cherished "special places" or if there was a local opposition group that sought the Conservancy's assistance.

In 2007, Shoenfeld recalled a memorable field trip in September 2002. Two of the Conservancy's Wind Power Committee members, Young and Shoenfeld — joined by former President Joe Rieffenberger, Sierra Club representative Frank Slider, and attorney Bill DePaulo — met at Nedpower's office. Nedpower President Jerome Niessen presented plans for its project and then they proceeded to the point where the power would join one of the inter-state lines taking electricity from the Mt. Storm power station east to Virginia. Except for Rieffenberger, the group then traveled to Cabin Mountain, Harman Knob, and east to Raven Ridge. Shoenfeld stressed that the purpose was to develop a reality-based impression of how bad the visual intrusion into Dolly Sods might be.

He wrote:

> A surprising and clear consensus emerged. All agreed that, at least from the places visited, the visual threat was not nearly as severe as had been feared. There were two reasons for this: (i) The prospective turbine locations lay to the north of the Dolly Sods public lands. The topography is such that mostly there is no view at all to the north. (ii) At places where there would be a view of the turbines, there is also a view of the very tall and ugly smoke stacks and plume of the Mt. Storm Power Station. This raises the aesthetic issue: How much uglier

are a power station plus the turbine than the power station alone? "Not much" was the consensus. The next week another location was analyzed and did show great visual vulnerability. This is the eastern-most of the outcrops, south of Bear Rocks and east of FS 175. But this location has no trail of any sort, is difficult to access, and is seldom visited.

For Shoenfeld, Young and the others who went to Raven Ridge, an impression was formed that would largely guide their actions as the controversy went forward. This was that the Nedpower development would not have serious visual impact in the Dolly Sods Wilderness, the Dolly Sods scenic area, or the "North Dolly Sods" area that extended north to Bear Rocks and Raven Ridge.

Unusual Board Action

The Board of Directors took an unusual action at the October 2002 meeting. It reversed its own officers. Shoenfeld reported in the November *Voice* that the Board meeting was dominated by discussions of wind power. The Wind Power Committee (Young, Carroll Jett, Shoenfeld, Judy Rodd, and Linda Cooper) had been responding to the 200-turbine project on Allegheny Front by NedPower. In a negotiated settlement reminiscent of the Backbone Mountain agreement two years earlier, Shoenfeld wrote:

> NedPower had offered the Highlands Conservancy an agreement, the main points of which included: (i) eliminating the southern-most mile of the project; (ii) a joint committee to design turbine lighting to minimize bird, bat, and viewshed impacts; (iii) additional jointly supervised avian studies, monitoring and pre-construction mitigation design; and (iv) work with landowners toward development of hiking trails accessing Stony River Reservoir.
>
> This agreement had been negotiated by committee members Young, Jett and Shoenfeld, but was opposed by Rodd and Cooper, who instead favored intervention before the PSC. An organization of nearby landowners, Friends of the Allegheny Front, has already filed to intervene.
>
> The board rejected the proposed agreement by a vote of 11 to 4 (with one abstention). Instead, resolutions were passed making the following points:
> 1. WVHC does not support permits for wind-power projects that would degrade scenic vistas from Canaan Valley, Dolly Sods, Seneca Rocks, Spruce Knob, and other special places in West Virginia.

2. WVHC insists that no permits be issued for wind power projects until siting criteria are in place including viewshed analysis and full environmental impact analysis.

3. The Wind Power Committee and the Executive Committee were authorized to intervene in both the Ned Power and Dominion cases after the Wind Power Committee consulted with legal counsel about further strategy.

President Young has written a letter to the Public Service Commission on siting criteria and expert analysis of wind power. Several other organizations have sent similar letters.

No one could remember the Conservancy's Board of Directors repudiating a position of its president and two vice presidents, certainly not by such an overwhelming margin. (One member called it "the BMFH," Board Meeting From Hell.) Clearly the issue of wind energy was more divisive within the Conservancy than any issue in memory.

Rather than retreating in defeat, Young began his fifth year as Conservancy president by sending the letter, mentioned by Shoenfeld, to the Public Service Commission, dated November 1, 2002. Called a "letter of conditional support," Young wrote:

> The Highlands Conservancy believes that wind power development is one of several technologies that can possibly provide reasonable alternatives to the many environmental and other societal costs of the mining, transportation, and burning of coal to generate electricity. Too, we realize that fossil fuels are a limited resource and that wind power and other "renewable" energy resources may be longer-term alternatives to fossil fuels.
>
> However, the Highlands Conservancy insists that your Commission, as the only existing permitting agency for West Virginia wind-power generating facilities, needs to develop and implement full, comprehensive, and objective siting criteria for wind turbines.
>
> Appropriate siting criteria should at least include consideration of visual and noise effects on certain public recreation areas and other recognized special places, consideration of the habitats and populations of rare and endangered species of plants and animals, consideration of the effects of wind power facilities on known flyways for local and migratory birds, and consideration of impacts on stream headwaters by earth disturbances caused by roads and other construction.
>
> Too, the Highlands Conservancy believes that before your Commission issues certificates of convenience and necessity for wind-power facilities that it should determine that the construction and operation

of these facilities will comport in all respects with the federal Endangered Species Act and Migratory Bird Act.

Further, we believe that your Commission should internalize the relevant expertise to conduct the appropriate ecological studies and reports needed to effect good wind turbine-siting recommendations. Such expertise should include the ability to conduct avian assessments, rare and endangered species and wetlands surveys, and sight and sound analyses.

We believe that this internal (or contracted) Commission scientific expertise is necessary because of the need to conduct credible studies and because of the dynamic of wind project developer's budgets available for these assessments *vis-à-vis* that of citizen environmental organizations.

The Highlands Conservancy has learned that the pool of local ornithologists and endangered species scientists is small; so small that when they are first retained by the wind power industry no one qualified and willing is available for review on behalf of the Commission or citizen environmental organizations. We believe that the Commission should internalize these scientific studies as perhaps either an attachment to your existing office of Consumer Advocate, or as adjunct capability to your existing engineering section.

Or as an alternative to internalizing this scientific expertise, we believe that the Commission should consider having wind power project applicants fund the required studies, but as studies commissioned by the *Public Service Commission,* rather than by the applicant. Without suggesting any disrespect whatsoever for the applicant in the case herein referenced, we believe that ecological studies and reports performed by either the Commission's internal experts or by independent scientists commissioned by your agency would perhaps have more credibility than would studies and reports commissioned solely by the wind power industry.

The Commission's existing engineering section is an example of publicly recognized internal expertise the Commission already has. We are suggesting that the Commission develop scientific expertise applicable to wind turbine project applications, either internally or contractually.

Further, the Highlands Conservancy believes that both the development of a general commission policy relating to wind turbine-siting criteria as well as application of that policy to specific wind-power projects should include a process for full public input and fair consideration of that input. The expedited procedural schedule the Commission allows for these wind-permit applications provides very limited opportunities for the public to learn about and consider the effects of these wind-power project proposals. A lengthened procedural schedule would allow for better public understanding of the project proposals.

Elsewhere in that same issue, Conservancy Secretary Hugh Rogers, who would succeed Young as president in 2004, reflected on the controversy within the Highlands Conservancy. Rogers asked:

> Why is this issue so contentious? Why was it so difficult to vote on every motion?
>
> Two years ago, we reached a compromise with the developers of the Backbone Mountain project and necessarily among ourselves. Moving the string of turbines north saved the view from Blackwater Falls State Park and some habitat for endangered species. However, those who support wind power as an alternative to coal did not change the minds of those who resent its increasingly flagrant occupation of the Highlands. The work we had to do on criteria for siting was left undone. Another argument was predictable.
>
> Our president, Frank Young, has been very active on the Wind Power Committee, which negotiated an agreement with Ned Power on its proposal for a "wind farm" on the Allegheny Front east of Snowy Point. The agreement was rejected by the board. (See Peter Shoenfeld's report in this issue.) In last month's *Voice*, Frank had asked, "If an issue-specific, scientifically and legally rational case against windmills can't be made, then why go on interminably trying to litigate against or otherwise oppose them?" He was expressing the frustration of a practical man. In the absence of clearly articulated and verifiable reasons to oppose these projects, the Highlands Conservancy would seem to be a bunch of NIMBY's.
>
> Opponents were equally frustrated. How could some people fail to see that the Highlands around Canaan Valley and Dolly Sods was the wrong place to put hundreds of three-hundred-foot-tall towers? For years, the Conservancy has worked to protect the area. We would betray the trust of our members if we agreed to this new threat.
>
> The practical negotiators used maps to show how the visual impact of the turbines would be almost nil in the Valley and on the Sods. The opponents scoffed at this nibbling around the edges. The negotiators showed how we could participate in studies of the impacts on migratory birds and other animals. The opponents said the studies would be too late.
>
> On the question of what other actions we should take, the positions were effectively reversed. Here, the opponents were the moving parties, asserting that we should protest the permits before the Public Service

Commission and possibly in the courts, while the negotiators put their feet down until we had a practical strategy with some hope of success. After all the votes on all the motions, we had reached a stalemate.

If I had to blame someone, I'd point the finger at myself. Not that I'm exceptional: somewhat practical, somewhat idealistic, sometimes confused. I have a lot of sympathy for Frank and Peter, who worked hard on the agreement with Ned Power.

On a different issue, Corridor H, I wore those shoes and wore out the seat of my pants, preferring to negotiate and get something rather than give nothing and get nothing. Purists have exasperated me too.

But I'm not gung-ho for wind power. In the editorial I quoted above, Frank wrote of "a strong sentiment from our members and our board for renewable energy sources to replace the coal-fired electrical power sources we so despise." Unfortunately, wind isn't replacing anything, it's only adding another source to supply our gluttony. The more we generate, the more we'll use. The same thing happens with water: when public water is extended to homes that had their own wells, average consumption triples. When I look at the towers on our skyline, I think of plug-in toothbrushes, shoe polishers, dishwashers, security lights, TV's in every room (I could go on). Wind won't help us unless it's part of a radically different energy policy.

I also share the opponents' frustration in expressing their objections. Beyond protecting birds and bats, we have spoken only of "viewsheds." What a mincing word. I think there's another reason, harder to get at, that we see three hundred-foot-tall towers as insults to our mountains. It's a spiritual as well as an aesthetic matter: in their gross disproportion, they assert human corporate dominion over the body of nature. But that spiritual value won't prevail — for the most part, won't even be recognized — in this aggressively unnatural society. Some practical people will see it as a word game.

According to an October 5 article by Jim Balow in *The Charleston Gazette*, the federal Department of Energy has estimated the potential for wind power in West Virginia at 5,000 megawatts. The turbines going up now can generate 1.5 megawatts. We could be looking at 3,333 towers. Wind power costs significantly more than coal power, a premium some purchasers are willing to pay for "green" power. That's our leverage. If it isn't "green" it won't sell. Can we keep it "green?" We'd better resume negotiations. At the same time, we'd better address the Legislature on siting criteria. We need a law more specific than, or in addition to, a ridge protection act.

Snowy Point, a Zen garden of white sand, stones, and rock islands at the tip of Cabin Mountain, ten miles north of Dolly Sods, is not on public land. Its view is not our business in the same way as the view from Dolly Sods or Canaan Valley or Spruce Knob. But all our views are bound to change.

Rogers had been the philosopher/activist on Corridor H (See Chapter 4). Now the Conservancy would need his mediation skills and clear thinking to help it forge its position on wind energy.

Between November 2002 and November 2004, the pace of wind-farm proposals accelerated greatly. The Conservancy leadership became consumed with how to meaningfully participate in the permitting process, monitor the bird and bat studies that were producing disturbing results, and mediate among the strongly held positions of its members.

- In January 2003, sixty-five turbines were proposed for Rich Mountain, near Harman. The Conservancy projected that they would be visible from Roaring Plains, Spruce Knob, Mt. Porte Crayon, among many other locations.

- Also that month, Dominion Mount Storm Wind, Inc., withdrew its application for a wind farm near Snowy Point, between the Mount Storm power plant and the town of Davis.

- In March Shoenfeld, now chair of the Wind Power Sub-committee, summarized the Conservancy's stand on wind energy in a *Voice* article. He specifically mentioned the publicly expressed, opposite positions of President Young and Senior Vice President Judy Rodd, Director of the Friends of Blackwater.

- The Spring Review in April 2003 focused on wind power, including a tour of the Backbone Mountain wind farm, followed by stops at three other proposed sites.

- On April 2, 2003, the state Public Service Commission conditionally approved the application by Nedpower Mount Storm for a 200-unit wind farm along the Allegheny Front, denying the southern third due to its proximity to Dolly Sods and Bear Rocks. The PSC also required bird and bat studies to meet concerns of the U.S. Fish and Wildlife Service.

- On the night of May 23–24, 2003, an "unusual mortality event" occurred at the Backbone Mountain wind farm. A total of 25–27 small songbirds were found dead at the base of turbine number 23 and at a nearby substation. A foggy night and six bright lights on the substation were attributed to be the causes. (This event was later used as an example of the risks wind energy posed to wildlife in the area.)

431

- Before August 1, 2003, Conservancy members were invited to nominate "special places" to the Public Service Commission as it began to implement new siting authority granted by the West Virginia Legislature.
- In November 2003 mortality figures at Backbone Mountain wind farm indicated sixty-nine dead birds during March–October, and 452 dead bats during a similar period.
- March 15, 2004, became the extended deadline for public comments to the PSC on proposed rules for wind power siting.
- On March 16, 2004, after repeated delays, the 39-page final report was issued on the Backbone Mountain avian study, including the "unusual mortality event" noted above.
- In April, Shoenfeld reported three additional wind farm proposals: one on Gauley Mountain on Forest Service land, another on Jack Mountain in Pendleton County, east of Spruce Knob, and a third on Red Oak Knob of Allegheny Mountain on the West Virginia-Virginia border.
- On June 22, 2004, Congress members Rahall and Mollohan requested a General Accounting Office study of the Fish and Wildlife Service's lack of enforcement of protection of migratory birds by wind farms. They specifically cited the rapid development of proposals along the Allegheny Front in West Virginia.
- In July 2004, Linda Cooper, past president of the Conservancy and more recently co-chair of the Blackwater Canyon Committee, now president of Citizens for Responsible Wind Power, sent a sharply-worded letter to the United States Fish and Wildlife Service about the Backbone Mountain avian study.
- During the summer of 2004 the Gauley Mountain wind project became inactive, but the Rich Mountain project erected meteorological towers, although no permit had yet been sought.
- An article in *The Charleston Gazette,* reprinted in the October 2004 *Voice,* reported that initial indications at Backbone Mountain were that at least as many bats were killed in 2004 as the surprising number found in 2003. The 2003 bat kill of 2,092 was called by one expert "by far the largest bat mortality event I know of worldwide."

These events created a whirlwind two-year period as the West Virginia highlands lived in the vortex of the wind energy industry. In November 2004 Shoenfeld, succeeding Judy Rodd as the Senior Vice President, provided *Voice* readers a "Wind Energy Update." As the Conservancy had agreed, it was addressing each project on a case-by-case basis. He wrote:

> The tax credit for wind-generated electricity producers has been reinstated after a year's hiatus. The credit lasts 10 years, but to get it projects must be in operation by the end of 2005. At this time, there are four major un-built projects in West Virginia that we know of. However, we've been told the Nedpower project is unlikely to begin construction before 2006 and that three more months of wind measurement are needed on Rich Mountain.
>
> NedPower and US Wind Force Mount Storm Projects — Both these projects have their permits. The Nedpower developer has completed the studies required by the WVPSC. Nedpower and US Wind Force are "development" companies. Such companies generally initiate these projects, then pick a location, secure the leases, obtain the permits, negotiate the needed agreements with power companies, plan the site, do the engineering, and order the equipment. Then the project is sold to a much larger company, such as FPL Energy, that will actually construct and operate it.
>
> The US Wind Force project is located in the heart of what is generally considered a "brown fields" area north of WV Route 93, and has attracted little opposition. The Nedpower project, on the other hand, is on the Allegheny Front and is very controversial. There will be dramatic visual impact from private lands to the east. Opponents allege that there will also be severe visual impact on Dolly Sods, but our own fieldwork and analysis does not bear this out.
>
> The Highlands Conservancy has not opposed either of these projects, although there was initial concern about the impact on Dolly Sods. The part of the planned project nearest Dolly Sods was eliminated in the terms of the permit.
>
> US Wind Force Liberty Gap Project — This is another large project, planned for Jack Mountain near the eastern edge of Pendleton County. Little interest in opposing this project has surfaced in Highlands Conservancy Board and Committee discussions. However, the visual impact will be severe at many beautiful locations in Pendleton County. Most of these are on private property, and are not widely known. Visibility from Spruce Knob is an issue we need to analyze.
>
> Greenwind Corp. Rich Mountain Project — This large project would be located on Rich Mountain, near Harman, on private land in the heart of the Mon National Forest. It would have devastating visual

433

impact on many special places, including four wilderness areas, Spruce Knob, and the Gandy-Dry Fork valley. The Highlands Conservancy has publicly opposed this project. It is going forward. The developer is doing wind measurements, and tells us these will continue for another three months. We do expect an application fairly soon and are trying to be proactive. In recent weeks we've been lobbying Congressional staff people and the leadership of the state Tourism Commission.

Actions by Other Groups — Congressmen Mollohan and Rahall asked the General Accounting Office to investigate the evolution of the wind industry in the U.S. The stated grounds were the need for a determination as to whether the USFWS "interim guidelines" are adequate to satisfy the government's obligations under the Migratory Bird Act. The GAO has responded that they will commence this investigation soon.

A group of organizations (Citizens for Responsible Windpower, Friends of Blackwater, Friends of Allegheny Front, and Stewards of the Potomac Highlands) has asked WVPSC for a moratorium on permits for wind facilities until the GAO investigation is finished.

Bird and Bat Mortality — Last year's Backbone Mountain bird study, projected only a few dead birds but thousands of dead migratory bats.

The *Gazette* quoted Merlin Tuttle [of Bat Conservation International] as predicting massive bat kills whenever a wind farm is sited on a "forested ridge." We've also heard that the kills appear not to be evenly distributed in time, but rather are concentrated in short time intervals often correlating with weather events. This would seem to indicate that the problem might be practically mitigated by curtailing operations during predicted high-risk periods.

If the "any forested ridge" thesis stands up, and effective mitigation can not be promised, this would provide a powerful argument against further wind power development at this time on many of our Highlands ridge tops.

West Virginia Public Service Commission Siting Rules — The development of rules for applicants for exempt power plant "Siting Certificates" has been underway over a year. There have been initial comments, draft rules, and comments on the rules. These rules generally cover what a developer is required to include in his application. Prescription of locations where projects may or may not be sited is addressed only by implication. Staff's comments have tended to agree with our own. Industry comments have tended to find the rules overly onerous, and to question the PSC's scope of authority. All of this has been under consideration by the commissioners for quite some time.

We've heard recently that the rules should be out and ready in time for the January 2005 legislative session. Legislature ratification is required.

Additional projects are moving forward on our doorstep in Maryland and Virginia. What is essentially an extension of the Mountaineer project is proposed on Backbone Mountain in Garrett County, Maryland. The Red Oak Knob/Tamarack Ridge project is proposed for Highland County, Virginia. Analysis of visibility for the latter project from West Virginia special places is needed.

In a relatively few short years the development of wind power in the highlands of West Virginia had assumed a major position in the list of critical issues facing the Highlands Conservancy. Other issues, such as saving the Blackwater Canyon, establishing additional wilderness areas, Corridor H, and always the consuming issue of mountaintop-removal mining, all remained important, too. But wind power brought the most controversy within the organization, and threatened to erase nearly forty years of the Conservancy's preservation and protection of "special places."

The December 2004 issue of *The Highlands Voice* continued the flurry of articles on wind power. The cover story by Shoenfeld reported on the 2004 bat kill at the Backbone Mountain site. "The 2003 event was severe enough," Shoenfeld wrote, "to threaten the future of wind energy in the Appalachian region." The statement sounded overly dramatic, but events would prove it prescient. As a result of the kill event, a major scientific research project was initiated, with representatives of the Bats and Wind Energy Cooperative, including Bat Conservation International, the U.S. Fish and Wildlife service, the American Wind Energy Association, and the National Renewable Energy Laboratory. He continued:

> While analysis is still pending, there is evidence for some important conclusions:
> - Massive bat kills appear probable whenever wind farms are sited on forested Appalachian ridges using current technology
> - The kill rate appears to be weather dependent, which suggests the possibility of mitigation by simply shutting turbines down at critical times.
> - The bats appear to actually be attracted by the spinning blades and the deaths are caused by collision with them. This suggests the possibility of mitigation by some alteration to blade design.
> - Much more work is needed and planned.

In another article, Shoenfeld reported:

On November 18, Liberty Gap Wind Force, LLC, a wholly owned subsidiary of US Wind Force, LLC, applied to the WV Public Service Commission (WV PSC) to build a wind farm on Jack Mountain, in southern Pendleton County east of the South Branch River. The application did not include any environmental or viewshed studies. These are being done, but are not yet complete.

The facility will include 50 turbines, distributed linearly along Jack Mountain, extending from the VA state line to the 3400 foot contour, above County Road 25 near Moatstown. The turbines may be slightly larger than those already constructed on Backbone Mountain.

The facility will also include a new 138 KV power line that will extend in a more-or-less straight line from the north end of the turbine string, near Moatstown, to the North Franklin sub-station located at the intersection of US 220 and US 33 W, just north of Franklin.

The Pendleton County Commission has signed an agreement with the developer to obtain the easements needed for the power line, by condemnation if necessary, in exchange for $450,000. The money is to be used to build a water line servicing the affected area.

The power line agreement already has aroused intense controversy in the affected area.

It is expected that the viewshed issue will engender this also. The Wind Farm was the subject of a long, top-of-front-page article in the December 2 issue of *The Pendleton Times*. This article relates the developer's story, and also the power line issue. The December 9 issue will include "local concerns, as well as the concerns of conservationist and environmental groups ..." The Highlands Conservancy has provided input.

WV PSC's formal comment period commenced after publication of the required newspaper notices on November 25, and runs for 30 days. Organizations and individuals commenting and requesting "Intervenor" status will become Parties of Record. If there are any protests, then a public hearing is required. Intervenors may additionally submit "pre-filed testimony," or offer themselves as witnesses, and are then expected to attend the hearing, where they may face questioning by the lawyers and Commissioners. The testimony and hearing record must all be reported and adequately addressed in the Commission's decision document. If not, this can become the basis of appeal.

The Highlands Conservancy has filed for Intervenor status in this case, citing concerns about viewshed and wildlife impacts, but has not thus far taken a position of outright opposition. A local citizens group

(Friends of Beautiful Pendleton County) has been formed to oppose the power line agreement and the wind farm application.

Meanwhile the *Voice* reported that Citizens for Responsible Wind Power had asked the West Virginia Public Service Commission to place a moratorium on wind developments in West Virginia until there had been more adequate study and siting regulations were in place. The Public Service Commission had taken no action on this request.

In another announcement:

> Time is running out to get new wind turbine projects up and running. In October 2004, Congress renewed a lucrative tax credit for wind energy projects. In order to get the tax credit, developers must have their projects up and running by the end of 2005.
>
> This has put the wind industry at odds with bat research. Recent research shows that wind turbines on forested ridgetops are killing large numbers of bats. While this research might indicate that a deliberate approach is called for, the current availability of the tax credit and its imminent expiration are pushing the industry toward construction as soon as possible.

Veteran mining activist and former Conservancy board member Rick Webb (See Chapter 7) provided an article on wind energy in Virginia. Reading Webb's piece, it was clear that all the same issues dividing the environmental community in West Virginia were having the same effect in Virginia. In fact, by the start of 2005, the debate was raging nationally, making news in places like the Adirondacks and Cape Cod, among others. Webb wrote:

> The current controversy over the proposed wind energy project in Highland County presents a dilemma for Virginia's conservation-minded citizens. On the one hand, we clearly need to develop clean, sustainable, and homegrown sources of energy if we are to solve our environmental problems and achieve independence from foreign sources. On the other hand, modern commercial wind development presents its own set of problems due to the massive scale and numbers of the turbines, the ecological sensitivity of mountain and coastal areas with high wind-energy potential, and the absence of any reliable pre-development assessment process.
>
> Wind energy advocates argue that the magnitude of the crisis we face is so great that all other issues are moot. They cite the significant ecological and human costs of an economy based on fossil fuel con-

sumption, including mountaintop-removal coal mining, air pollution, acid rain, and global warming. They point to the sacrifices of our armed forces in the Middle East. They assert a moral imperative that trumps other concerns.

Wind energy skeptics argue that wind development is not a real solution to our energy problems. They cite the ever-increasing use of electricity in Virginia, and observe that wind development cannot even keep pace with the growth in demand. They point out that wind is an intermittent resource and that we will still need the same fossil fuel generation capacity, up and running, to provide electricity when the wind isn't blowing. They point out that commercial wind energy requires taxpayer subsidies to be economically viable.

Wind energy advocates will argue that we have to do something, that every little bit helps, and that wind energy development should be viewed as part of a package that includes development of other renewable energy sources and energy conservation.

This is quite reasonable, up to a point. Certainly no one will argue with the need for conservation. We are simply not going to produce our way out our energy problem — at least not with the currently available options. And no one will argue that we shouldn't seriously address the need for clean sources of energy. But being serious shouldn't require indiscriminate support for any and all wind projects. If wind energy is indeed the green alternative that its well-meaning advocates claim, there is no reason not to require the same level of review and cost-benefit analysis that we would require for any other industrial-scale development in environmentally sensitive areas.

If we are serious about addressing our energy problem, and serious enough to invest our own time and energy to finding sustainable solutions, we will find a way to insure that each proposed wind project can be evaluated on its own merits. That will require a process for insuring objective site-specific assessments for each project. At present, there is no process in place to insure that reliable assessment will occur. The process provided by the National Environmental Policy Act only applies when federal decisions are involved. The process whereby the State Corporation Commission [or in West Virginia, the Public Service Commission] assesses the environmental effects of power plants has never been applied to wind projects, and the SCC and other state agencies do not have the resources to conduct meaningful assessments.

Yet now that federal tax subsidies for wind development have been extended and other states are requiring utilities to purchase renewable energy, we can expect a wave of wind development in Virginia. Surrounding states have already permitted projects involving hundreds of turbines. Wind development on our mountain ridges and in our coastal waters will happen whether we are prepared or not. We need, but do not have, a state-level process to insure that wind energy development will, in fact, be green energy development.

Webb could have changed the names of the state agencies involved and his article would have described the West Virginia situation. As 2004 ended, the Highlands Conservancy continued to be an active participant in the licensing process before the Public Service Commission. After all, in the scheme of things, wind energy development was only a small part of the PSC's workload, yet it represented the only arbiter available to decide this heated West Virginia issue. Maybe it really was time for a moratorium until more bat and bird studies and siting criteria could be developed.

For the next two years, the Conservancy struggled to find a rational position supporting wind and other sustainable sources of power, yet protecting the "special places," the wilderness areas and scenic vistas in the highlands. And the accompanying thought remained: every kilowatt produced from a source other than coal would be one less produced by mountaintop-removal mining with its onerous impacts.

Over the next few months, developments happened quickly. On December 23, 2004, Liberty Gap Wind Force withdrew their application for the Jack Mountain wind farm in the face of massive opposition and disclosure of a "secret" contract with the Pendleton County Commission, which both parties later repudiated. The commission had met with the developers and agreed to use its eminent domain power to purchase property for the wind farm. In this rural county, such an arrangement created a predictable political backlash. Conservancy veteran Young said he had "never before seen such swift capitulation by a public agency to citizen outrage."

The West Virginia PSC rejected the petition from Citizens for Responsible Wind Power for a moratorium pending a comprehensive environmental impact analysis, although both Congressmen Mollohan and Rahall had supported the moratorium. During the six-week study period in late summer 2004 between 1364 and 1980 bats were killed by the forty-four turbines at the Mountaineer (Backbone Mountain) facility and between 400 and 600 bats by the twenty turbines at Meyersdale, Pennsylvania. These estimates are among the highest ever reported and supported the contention that forested ridges were locations of especially high risk for bat fatality at wind facilities.

The August 2005 *Voice* reported that the Highland County, Virginia, supervisors granted a permit to a twenty-two turbine wind farm atop Allegheny Mountain. Meanwhile, Beech Ridge Wind Farm, a 130-tower, 200-megawatt wind farm, was announced near the town of Trout in Greenbrier County, on land owned by Mead Westvaco. Between August and December 2005 local opposition became strong. At its January 2006 meeting, the Conservancy Board voted to oppose the Beech Ridge project and provide financial support to the opponents of the Jack Mountain project.

In June 2006 President Hugh Rogers commented on a series of articles and commentaries that had been running in *The Highlands Voice*. He wrote:

> I received some blistering phone calls from readers who didn't appreciate David Buhrman's piece, "Greenbrier County Group Opposes Windfarm," in the April issue. What irked them most was Buhrman's references to coal, specifically his opinion that the most effective way to reduce air pollution and global warming would be to make coal "cleaner."
>
> In West Virginia, we should understand coal holistically. The trouble with the article on the Beech Ridge wind energy project in Greenbrier County was that it separated coal's air pollution from all its other evil effects.
>
> I had one other nit to pick from John's editorial in last month's *Voice*. He portrayed the Highlands Conservancy's board as "befuddled" about wind energy. I want to say that we have declared a position: we favor alternative energy production, including wind, where it does not kill wildlife or impinge on "special places." We went so far as to try to identify such places. And based on that experience we played a major role in the Public Service Commission's adoption of siting regulations.

In the same issue, Young wrote a thoughtful essay, titled, "Incredible Debate":

> To be perceived as credible, we must actually be credible.
> The first "local" utility scale wind energy facility (wind farm) in West Virginia was proposed for Backbone Mountain in Tucker County in the spring of 2000. Less than a year later it had been permitted. By the end of 2002 this wind turbine "farm", now called the Mountaineer

Wind Energy Center, was constructed and was putting electricity onto the power grid that serves much of eastern United States.

Although that first facility was permitted with little opposition, there was some limited and mostly honest objection to it. But cool heads, both within the WV Highlands Conservancy and with the wind power developer, prevailed and the "wind farm" became a reality.

Subsequent applications for wind farm siting permits have met stiffer, more organized opposition. Today it is more difficult to get a permit for a wind farm than for a mountaintop-removal mining operation.

And from my perspective, and from the perspective of many who have commented to me about it, the opposition to utility scale wind energy generation in West Virginia has taken on a tone of amazing incredibility.

Credibility means the quality of being believable or trustworthy, or of having a capacity for reasonable belief. To be credible means to be reliable, or plausible, or worthy of confidence.

Incredibility, on the other hand, means just the opposite. It means unreliable and not plausible, not worthy of confidence, or beyond reasonable belief.

More and more proposed wind farm proposals are being met with increasingly absolutely incredible lists of "facts" by opponents of the utility-scale wind energy industry.

One commenter told the West Virginia Public Service Commission that at the Backbone Mountain wind farm in Tucker County "the killing in just one day of some 4000 bats was verified". Well, as a part of the technical review committee that oversaw the bat mortality surveys at Backbone Mountain, I can assure you that no such numbers of bat kills have been verified for one day, *nor even for an entire year*. Actual dead bats located at Backbone Mountain in the summers of 2003 and 2004 were in the hundreds, with mathematical extrapolations of bat mortality for up to perhaps 2000 bats for the entire season. Yet, the alleged killing of 4000 bats a day is repeated as though it were a verified fact.

The most recent irresponsible claim I've seen put forth by wind farm opponents suggests that wind turbines do not actually produce any electricity. This claim is that wind turbines are turned, not by the wind, but by electricity taken FROM the power grid, and that any electricity produced is simply "recycled" electricity and does not actually represent any new energy being produced — but that by calling it "wind power" the facility is eligible for substantial production tax credits that would not otherwise accrue to the wind facility owner/

operator. That such a scam would include the cooperation of dozens of private and public entities in a conspiracy to commit monumental fraud by the wind power industry makes such a claim not reasonably credible in the absence of any confirming evidence.

Often it seems that the primary real objection to wind turbines is that some people simply don't want to see them at some proposed locations on mountain ridges. A more honest debate would be about the real primary objection — the visual intrusiveness of wind turbines — not unsubstantiated hype and innuendo about all manner of "facts" not really related to the primary concern.

But deception and misinformation is not limited to wind farm opponents. Wind farm developers can and do misrepresent the visual intrusiveness of wind turbines. For example, the Backbone Mountain wind power developers said that the facility there would not be visible from Blackwater Falls State Park. But it is almost always very visible from that park — both day and night. Wind industry assurances that wind turbines "fade into the haze" and are not seen past 4 to 5 miles distance simply do not ring true. I have observed wind turbines from perhaps 20 or more miles north of their Backbone Mountain location.

Too, the reluctance of Florida Power and Light [who bought the Mountaineer Wind Farm after production began] to allow further studies about bird and bat mortality at its Backbone Mountain facility calls into question the suggestion by wind industry consultants — who almost always suggest that effects of wind turbines on bats and birds are or will be "insignificant".

The wind industry needs to understand that, in order to continue to market "green" energy, it must maintain an open and honest appraisal of the actual effects of construction and operations of its facilities.

To be perceived as credible, we must actually be credible.

The issue of credibility, and especially the West Virginia Highlands Conservancy's credibility, meant everything to Young. In his final *Highlands Voice* commentary as he left the presidency in 2004, he hoped his legacy would be the protection of the Conservancy's credibility. In his participation before the Public Service Commission, the State Legislature, the Forest Service, and others, he had walked the fine line between strict principles of environmental protection and the understanding that society would always need energy. Admittedly conservation might slow down that appetite, but no one, especially Young, wanted to increase the pressure for more mountaintop-removal mining. Some degree of compromise would be inevitable, he felt, and total opposition to wind power was unrealistic, or to use his terms, incredible. He defined "incredible" as "unreliable and not plausible, not worthy of confidence, or beyond reasonable belief."

Later, on July 24, 2006, the PSC, acting in Shoenfeld's words, "in an unscheduled and unexpected development," dismissed the Liberty Gap wind farm application. In his report on the PSC decision in the August/September *Voice*, Shoenfeld wrote:

> If this case is not re-opened by the Commission and won by Liberty Gap, this will be the second loss on this project for U.S. Wind Force. At the end of 2004, they filed a similar application, which was withdrawn after just a few weeks. This was the first wind-energy case filed under the Commission's new legislative rule governing Siting Certificates for Exempt Wholesale Generating Facilities. Their application was quite thin and tainted by a much-criticized agreement with the [Pendleton] County Commission for Liberty Gap to compensate the County in exchange for use of the Commission's powers of condemnation to obtain transmission line easements.
>
> U.S. Wind Force has been in business since 2000 and has not yet brought any wind projects to the construction stage. Some of their projects have been permitted, development partnerships negotiated, and potential future energy sales contracts signed. Their prospects for ultimate success appear questionable.
>
> The Liberty Gap (Pendleton County) and Beech Ridge (Greenbrier and Nicholas Counties) were the first two cases fully litigated and decided under the new siting rule and were widely expected to establish precedent for the future of wind energy in West Virginia. However, in the Liberty Gap case, this has not occurred, since the dismissal was attributed more to the attitude and conduct of the applicants then the merits of their case.
>
> Rule 150-30 states requirements to the applicants regarding the information they must provide. It does not guide the Commissioners as to how this information should be weighed in reaching a decision. Attorney James McNeely, who represented the opponents in both cases, stressed applicant shortfalls in providing required information.
>
> The first three applications (Backbone Mountain, US Wind Force-Mt. Storm, Nedpower-Mt. Storm) were approved, with adjustments, by the PSC. Although there has been intense activist opposition (which still continues) in the Nedpower case, none of these three cases, in Tucker and Grant counties, attracted massive, local, publicly announced opposition.

However, the opposite is true for the current Liberty Gap (Pendleton County) and Beech Ridge (Greenbrier County) cases, where the numbers of opponents filing material with the PSC have been in the hundreds of thousands.

The Highlands Conservancy has not been very active organizationally in this case. Early on, the Commission ruled that the Conservancy and another organization could not submit testimony or participate in hearings, because legal representation would be required. Rather than assume this expense, the Conservancy decided to support Friends of Beautiful Pendleton County with resources available.

It was noted in that issue that, just before it went to press, the Beech Ridge Project had been approved by the PSC.

Young's summary of the Beech Ridge decision was amplified in the October 2006 *Highlands Voice*. He wrote:

Many PSC observers had predicted that, whichever of the parties prevailed at the PSC, the "other side" would challenge or appeal that order. Several parties on the "losing" side have done just that. The Greenbrier County citizen group *Mountain Communities for Responsible Energy* (MCRE), along with several individual intervenors against the project, asked the PSC to reconsider its action to grant the certificate.

The primary allegations asserted in the requests for reconsideration are that in its deliberations the PSC failed to comply with its own siting rules by accepting Beech Ridge's allegedly "flawed" maps that contained "glaring insufficiencies", and by accepting an incomplete cultural impacts assessment. The challengers further allege that the PSC failed to properly consider the impact of the project on communities within the local vicinity of Beech Ridge, and that it did not fairly appraise and balance the interests of the public, the general interests of the state and local economy, and the interests of the applicant, as state law requires.

MCRE asserts that, "the Commission exceeded its jurisdiction when it improperly considered the policies of other states and the need for sources of renewable energy in the region and weighed those factors against the interests of the citizens of West Virginia. It is clear that the renewable energy provided by Beech Ridge will be enjoyed by, and will fulfill the policies of, other states within the region serviced by PJM (regional power grid operator). It is equally clear that **all** of the negative impacts of this project will be endured by the citizens of West Virginia."

But in a footnote to its request for reconsideration, MCRE says, "To be clear, MCRE is not an advocate for the use and consumption of fossil fuels. MCRE proposes development of more efficient uses of existing energy sources consistent with protecting West Virginia's economy and environment. MCRE opposes this project because it seeks to prevent the destruction of yet another West Virginia mountain ridge for the purpose of providing a marginal amount of energy to consumers in other states."

The battle over the PSC consideration of the Beech Ridge wind farm had been long and heated and promised to get even longer. It was almost certain that the case would be appealed to the state Supreme Court.

The Beech Ridge proposal would mark a new stage in the environmental movement in West Virginia. The Sierra Club of West Virginia endorsed the wind farm project, although it asked the PSC to impose a set of restrictions. According to a *Charleston Gazette* article by Eric Eyre on August 19, 2006, the Sierra Club believed "wind power will someday provide America's energy needs at competitive prices." He quoted the Sierra Club's West Virginia Chairman Paul Wilson, "To some, yes, it's an eyesore, but [the wind turbines] don't produce more pollution. They don't cause global warming. They don't dump sulfur dioxide into the air. It would be nice to get some of those old coal-fired plants off line and replace them with green energy."

In May, Eyre had also reported that Coal River Mountain Watch, long a Conservancy ally against mountaintop-removal mining, had endorsed the Beech Ridge project as well. Coal River's Director Janice Nease told Eyre, "A wind farm may alter a viewshed, but mountaintop removal threatens our very survival."

The environmental community in West Virginia, as well as nationally, was fractured on questions relating to wind energy.

The October *Voice* provided an update on the Liberty Gap project:

> Despite hundreds of letters supporting the West Virginia Public Service Commission's July 24 decision to dismiss Liberty Gap LLC's application for the Jack Mountain wind facility, the PSC decided to give the company another chance.
> Liberty Gap, a subsidiary of U.S. Wind Force, seeks a state siting certificate for a 50-turbine industrial wind facility along several miles of Jack Mountain, abutting the border with Virginia's Highland County, along with a 200-kilovolt transmission line to carry the power to a substation in Franklin.
> In its latest order, the PSC is granting Liberty Gap's petition for reconsideration under certain conditions. [These included certain

financial and access issues to facilitate consultants working for Friends of Beautiful Pendleton County.]

The PSC stated, "These conditions will remedy the Commission's concern that Liberty Gap's actions prevented the presentation of relevant information to the commission at hearing."

However, it noted, "While the commission is not reversing its determination that Liberty Gap's conduct preceding dismissal was unreasonable, the commission concludes that by meeting the above conditions, the harm caused by Liberty Gap's conduct will be mitigated to the point that a fair litigation of the application can occur. In view of the considerable resources expended by all parties to date in this case, the case should proceed to a decision on the merits, provided the conditions above are met."

Wind Versus Coal

As 2006 drew to a close, *Voice* Editor John McFerrin offered a commentary on windmills and mountaintop removal. Both issues had dominated the Highlands Conservancy for the past few years. Both produced energy, yet threatened the environment. So far, they were concentrated in different parts of West Virginia, but no one could be sure that would remain true. McFerrin, a veteran opponent of mountaintop-removal mining (see Chapter 7) was a keen observer of the more recent struggle. In the November *Voice*, he wrote:

> An interesting, if ultimately unproductive, sidelight to the controversy over the proposed windfarm in Greenbrier County was the alignment of Coal River Mountain Watch on one side and the Greenbrier County citizen group Mountain Communities for Responsible Energy on the other. The Mountain Communities for Responsible Energy adamantly opposed the project. They like Greenbrier County the way it is and don't think that the electricity produced is worth the social costs of windmills.
>
> Coal River Mountain Watch's view is that the social costs of mountaintop-removal coal mining are so great, so high, that electricity from any other source would be preferable. They support the project. If we get the electricity at the cost of our streams, our air, and our mountains then it could never be worth the price.
>
> This controversy resulted in the parties sniping at each other at the public hearing and in letters to the editor. They seemed to frame the question as one of whether windmills or mountaintop-removal mining was the preferable method for producing the electricity that society

needs. Inherent in this debate was the question of who would suffer the most as a result of their living in an energy-producing area.

The question is not even close. It's me stepping in the ring with Mike Tyson. It's the 1976 World Series. It's the war with Grenada.

In Greenbrier County, the mountain ridges will be topped by windmills for the next twenty years. In mountaintop-removal areas, the mountain ridges will be gone. Forever.

In Greenbrier County, it is likely that the presence of the windmills will reduce some property values. Because the windmills are not in place, it hasn't happened yet. Since much of what makes that property valuable is its bucolic setting, even a relatively benign industrial use such as a windmill will probably reduce those values.

In southern West Virginia the mountaintop-removal mines are already there; we know what they do to property values. In Blair, West Virginia, the value of a piece of residential property near the mine is approximately zero.

In Greenbrier County, people have to look at windmills on the tops of distant ridges. There are places in West Virginia where the shadow of the boom of the giant dragline used in mountaintop-removal mining fell across people's houses.

From what we know, windmills in Greenbrier County will almost certainly result in the deaths of some wildlife, most notably birds and bats. In southern West Virginia the habitat that currently sustains wildlife, including those same birds and bats, will be gone. Of course, it won't be gone forever. Just a few centuries.

Beauty is, of course, in the eye of the beholder. Not even the shills from the Coal Association, who get paid to think that all aspects of mining are beautiful, contend that an active mountaintop- removal mine is pretty. After the mining is over, you could argue either way. For my money, even a post-mining mountaintop-removal site is uglier than a windmill. Others might think the windmills are uglier.

This is not to say, of course, that the citizens of Greenbrier County should not continue to object to the windmills. They moved there or, having been born there, stayed because they liked the particular kind of life that Greenbrier County offers. If they don't think that whatever tax, employment, or other benefits would come from the windmills is worth what they would have to give up, then they are free to take the bit in their teeth and fight the windmills as long and hard as they wish.

Any kind of electricity production imposes some sort of cost upon society. More sensible and efficient use of electricity would make the overall cost less but, unless we are going to forego the benefits of electricity altogether, society must choose some method or methods of producing electricity and be willing to endure the costs of those methods. We would still have a duty to assure that the methods we chose operated so that they had the least possible social cost and the costs were spread fairly. We do, however, have to recognize that any energy production has a social cost.

If the controversy over the proposed windfarm in Greenbrier County were merely a matter of looking at whether windmills or big strip mines resulted in greater social costs, the question would be easy. The social costs of big strip mines are so enormous that we would choose windmills every time.

Unfortunately, that is not what the controversy is. That is what makes the dustup between Coal River Mountain Watch and Mountain Communities for Responsible Energy unproductive.

The controversy is not over whether we have mountaintop-removal strip mining or windmills or, to put it another way, whether windmills will replace the mining. Mountaintop-removal mining will continue so long as it is economical. So long as the coal is here and someone can make money mining it, we will have mountaintop-removal strip mining. If the companies were forced to bear the social costs of the mining then it would be less economical and would end sooner, but as long as companies can make money doing it the practice will continue. The existence of windmills won't change that.

The economics of mining make it especially likely that the practice will continue whether we have windmills or not. In its early phase, any mountaintop-removal mine is a money pit. The company spends, spends, spends to get all the permits, build roads, build ponds, and do everything necessary to get ready to actually extract coal. These are essentially fixed costs; they will be about the same whether the company mines all the coal at the site or leaves some behind.

Once actual coal extraction begins, the mine turns from a money pit to a license to print money. With ruthless efficiency the coal comes out of the ground and goes to market. During this period, the companies make money hand over fist, enough to make up for the money-losing periods and make the mine as a whole profitable.

Unless we have enough windmills to replace an entire mine, their existence will not determine whether any mine goes forward. We are not even close to that point. Coal companies are not going to suffer through the money-losing start-up phase and then abandon some fraction of the coal because that coal can be replaced by windmills. They will still mine it, even if is not quite as profitable as it would have been had the mine not faced competition from wind energy. Windmills or not, the mining will go on.

This is what makes the debate between coal and wind power unproductive. Each will go ahead independent of whatever happens with the other. So long as somebody can make money doing it and our society, including the legal and political systems, concludes that producing electricity from strip-mine coal is worth the cost to society, we will have strip mining. So long as somebody can make money doing it and our society, including the legal and political systems, concludes that producing electricity from windmills is worth the cost to society, we will have wind farms.

Instead of debating the false choice of coal versus wind energy, we would all be better off spending our energy forcing the coal and wind industries to bear all the costs of their operations, including the costs to society. It would be more productive — –and more fun — than sniping at each other.

Would anyone have been surprised that there was a reaction to McFerrin's commentary? Indeed, over the next two months, there was a sharply worded exchange in the letters to the editor portion of *The Highlands Voice*. Judy Bonds, a veteran of and highly-respected leader of the Coal River Mountain Watch, a major voice against mountaintop-removal mining, took McFerrin to task for re-opening wounds that she thought had begun to heal. A month later, a Greenbrier County wind farm opponent, April Crowe, tried again to find common ground. She wrote:

> I have admired Judy's tenacity in fighting Mountaintop Removal over the years, but she is wrong on this issue — as are others who believe wind and other alternative energies alone will save us.
>
> Judy and her neighbors are understandably angry and grief stricken with the mining that is destroying their communities, but we have a lot to deal with here in Greenbrier County as well. We have had to watch the destruction of the gorgeous high mountain backcountry in the western end by the incessant huge strip mines in operation there, and are now facing the imminent erection of 450' turbines, AND a proposed coal-burning power plant!
>
> Our small community of Williamsburg and our group Mountain Communities for Responsible Energy are not just concerned for the mountains here in Greenbrier County, but for all of the Appalachians. If the giant turbines can't be stopped here in an influential county that has most people against them, what hope is there for the rest of West Virginia and other eastern mountain states? The mountains will be covered with thousands of these things.

We are not going to liey down and accept the wind turbines as some advocate we do. We too love the mountains, forests, streams, rivers and wildlife. We too want clean air and water and a decent place to raise our families. And we see the proposed turbines as a threat to these things that we hold dear.

We see as significant ...the costs of building and maintaining the wind projects ...and the loss of the millions of birds and bats being killed — at a time when the effects of global warming are already boosting insect populations that are eaten by these creatures ... permanent roads cleared through the forests to move and maintain the turbines ... connections to the power grid that will be kept clear of vegetation ... the huge 'footprints' needed to anchor the tall towers with tons of concrete and re-bar poured into the mountains — never to be removed. Nothing will ever grow on these sites again.

The Highlands Voice and John McFerrin are being thoughtful on this issue and shouldn't be denigrated for having and publishing differing views.

People are cognizant of the fact that we are about to lose the silent beauty and solace West Virginia's remaining mountains bestow, and even if that alone was all there was to lose it would be too much to bear.

We who love and want to protect and preserve the earth abhor the continuing nightmare that is mountaintop removal. In addition to our local struggles, many of us in Greenbrier County and elsewhere have been appalled by and fighting MTR over the long years it has been going on, in our own personal ways. We only wish that with its end those responsible for it will be appropriately held to account. Until that day comes — and it will, we must all treasure and fight for our mountains and our world because too many don't and won't.

It could not have been summarized better. The West Virginia Highlands Conservancy was actively involved on many fronts in trying to end the abuses of mountaintop-removal mining (see Chapter 7). Yet its history was one of protecting "special places," wilderness areas, wildlife refuges, and the Monongahela National Forest, among other places, from adverse impacts of development.

The battle over wind energy would continue as the Conservancy celebrated its fortieth anniversary, as would court suits to stop mountain top removal mining. As long as the mountains of West Virginia contained coal and produced high wind velocities, the nation's appetite for energy would force environmentalists who cared about West Virginia to fight for the highlands.

For further information or to follow wind energy developments after this book is published, go to the Highlands Conservancy web site at www.wvhighlands.org.

Sources:

The Charleston Gazette, articles by Jim Balow, Eric Eyre, Paul Nyden, Rick Steelhammer, Ken Ward

Cooper, Linda, interview, November 9, 2006, and correspondence

The Highlands Voice, articles by George Beetham, Jr., David Buhrman, Joe Carney, Linda Cooper, April Crowe, Gordon Hamrick, John McFerrin, Hugh Rogers, Peter Shoenfeld, Rick Webb, Frank Young

McFerrin, John, interview, January 27, 2007, and correspondence

Nyden, Paul, article in *The Charleston Gazette*,, December 20, 2001, quoting Judy Rodd

Shoenfeld, Peter, interview, April 23, 2007, and correspondence

West Virginia Highlands Conservancy, Minutes of Board of Directors, 2000-2004.

Young, Frank, interview, January 27, 2007, and correspondence

Young, Frank, letter to the Public Service Commission, November 1, 2002

West Virginia Wind Farm Projects

Name / Location	No. of Turbines	County	Date Proposed	Developer/ Owner	PSC Status	Conservancy Position	Other Groups
Beech Ridge/ Cold Knob Mt.	130	Greenbrier/ Nicholas	11- '94	Kenetech	applied '05 approved 8-'06 appealed to WV Supreme Court	intervenor - inactive	Mountain Communities for Responsible Energy Sierra Club Coal River Mountain Watch
Mountaineer/ Backbone Mtn constructed 2002	65/44	Tucker	7- '00	Atlantic Renewable Energy/Florida Light & Power	11-'00 approved '03 PSC study 3-'04 BWEC study	negotiated none South of U.S. 219 member Tech. Adv. Com until ended in '03 reviewer BWEC '04	—
Mt. Storm construction began '07	166	Grant	12- '01	Mt. Storm Windforce	8-'02 approved	—	no major opposition
Mount Storm/ Allegheny Front	200	Grant/ Tucker	8-'02	Nedpower/Shell	4-'03 approved w/o southern 1/3 appealed to WV Supreme Court	negotiated agreement, denied by Board 10-'02, 11-4-1	Friends of Allegheny Front
Rich Mountain	65	Randolph?	1-'03	Greenwind Corp.	—	opposed	—
Liberty Gap/ Jack Mountain	50	Pendleton	early '04 on web	U.S. Windforce	11-'04, 11-'05 applied, 4-'07 hearings on revised application	intervenor	Friends of Beautiful Pendleton County

West Virginia Wind Farm Projects, Inactive

Name / Location	No. of Turbines	County	Date Proposed	Developer/ Owner	PSC Status	Conservancy Position	Other Groups
Cabin Mountain/ Dolly Sods	150–200	Tucker	8-'92	Kenetech-U.S. Windforce	inactive		
Horseshoe Run		Tucker	summer '01	Mega-Energy	never applied		
Cabin Mtn./ Snowy Point	30–40			Dominion Resources	1-'03 withdrawn		Friends of Blackwater
Red Oak Knob/ Allegheny Mt. WV-Va border		Highland			7-'04 inactive		

Other projects mentioned but never seriously pursued. Data current as of May 1, 2007.
Sources: *The Highlands Voice*, Peter Shoenfeld and Frank Young

Chapter Nine
Continuing the Struggle:
Learning from the Past and Looking Ahead

The previous eight chapters have told the story of the first forty years of the West Virginia Highlands Conservancy. It has fought many struggles for protection and even preservation of special places within the highlands of West Virginia and has experienced both achievements and failures. Over this period the Conservancy distinguished itself by both which issues it chose to address, and how it engaged those issues. This chapter attempts to elaborate on the "how" and draw some conclusions that might be instructive in future struggles. Not only might the Conservancy itself learn from its own history, and it certainly has, but also other organizations, facing similar challenges, might profit from the experiences of this group of citizen-activists in West Virginia.

First, it needs to be said that much of the experience of the Highlands Conservancy was based on trial and error. At other times, various leaders were very cognizant that taking one path meant not taking an alternative path. Whether by chance or design, how and why most of these decisions were made will never be known. Records were only preserved when a leader later recalled the motivation.

A Multi-State Coalition

From the writings and interviews with some of the Conservancy's founders, several concepts were clearly articulated at the time of the founding and later became a set of principles as the fledgling organization came to life. One was that a partnership between West Virginia conservationists and like-minded individuals and organizations from nearby states would serve the interests of all. The "us versus them" friction that had so often characterized West Virginians' relations with outsiders was set aside at the outset. Instead, Lou Greathouse, Rupert Cutler, and the other early leaders solicited the names and leaders of a broad array of recreation user groups and invited them into the process. Bob Broughton, among others, discussed the advantages of forging a multi-state coalition that would maximize its political significance. Greathouse, however, was careful to establish enough of a West Virginia presence within the leadership circle to assure the president and a working majority of the board of directors would remain West Virginians.

That the organization was at first named the West Virginia Highlands Coalition revealed its intention. Indeed throughout virtually every campaign discussed in this book, coalition building remained a critically important strategy. Whether incarnated as the Shavers Fork Coalition, the West Virginia Rivers Coalition, the Buckhannon-Tygart River Coalition or, most recently, the West Virginia Wilderness Coalition, all were issue-focused coalitions composed of autonomous groups that came together for a common purpose. Others, not using the term "coalition," nonetheless served similar purposes. Some of these were the Corridor H Alternatives, the Canaan Valley Alliance, and the group of plaintiffs in the mountaintop-removal cases, among others. Historically, the stronger the effort at coalition building, the more likely were the chances of success on the issue.

Membership and Communication

As discussed in Chapter 1, it soon became apparent to the West Virginia Highlands Conservancy that it needed to develop its own membership structure in addition to the indirect membership derived from its constituent member organizations. No doubt, other coalitions have faced this same issue, but a second and closely related need arose, communication. A significant delay often occurred in the original two-step process as information went to constituent groups and then, through their channels, was communicated to their members. If announcements were time sensitive, they often arrived too late to be useful. *The Highlands Voice* was born out of a need for direct communication from the Conservancy officers and leaders to members.

Communication became another cornerstone of the Highlands Conservancy. By 2007, more than 6,400 articles had been published in the *Voice*, by then a 20-page monthly newspaper. In the earliest years, the *Voice* was a mimeographed newsletter, then in newsprint it grew from four to eight pages and eventually to its present size. It was no exaggeration to state that many members, especially those who lived longer distances from West Virginia, belonged to the Conservancy primarily to receive *The Highlands Voice*.

From the appointment of Bob Burrell as its first editor, *The Highlands Voice* has been deeply blessed with wonderful writers and editors. Each has developed a point of view, shared it eloquently and frequently, and together the *Voice* contributors helped to shape the policy perspectives of the organization. From the first, with only a few exceptions, the Conservancy presidents have maintained an editorial column, communicating directly to the membership.

Any list of the better writers in *The Highlands Voice*, many of whom have been reproduced in the previous eight chapters, would include: Tom King, Bob Burrell, Ron Hardway, Nick Zvegintzov, Linda Cooper Elkinton, Larry George, Hugh Rogers, Cindy Rank, Frank Young, Don Gasper, John McFerrin, Judy Rodd, Tom Rodd, Helen McGinnis, Dave Saville, Julian Martin, Bill Ragettè and Bill Reed. Brilliant photographs by Sayre and Jean Rodman and, recently, Jonathan Jessup, have enhanced the written words enormously.

How did these, and less frequent contributors, use communication to further the Conservancy's agenda? Sometimes the *Voice* was used to provide background information as an issue was emerging or changing. At other times members were urged through *Voice* articles to communicate directly with elected or administrative governmental leaders. At still other times, the communication was an announcement of a future event, perhaps the Fall Review or a pending public hearing. Occasionally the *Voice* reprinted newspaper articles that would not have been seen outside the papers' normal circulation areas.

In recent years, the use of the Internet has greatly changed communication. The Conservancy was one of the first small conservation groups to establish a lively website. By 2007, many visitors to the site were reading the *Voice* online, purchasing merchandise (including this book), and following links to other related sites.

All of these channels enabled the membership of the Highlands Conservancy, even members living hundreds of miles from West Virginia, to stay current and involved.

Show-Me Tours

Another technique used effectively from the beginning of, and even before, the Conservancy, was what Lou Greathouse called the "show-me" tour. There was no substitute for personal, first-hand observation of places in the highlands. In some cases the majestic and inspirational beauty of a waterfall, a wilderness area, or a sunset inspired observers to get involved. In other cases an inspection of a threatened area where a highway, a dam, a mine, or a wind farm was proposed led the observer to action. Either way, members saw for themselves what was at stake.

These tours and inspections were always a large part of a Conservancy Fall or Spring Review. As the outings program grew, especially after 2000, they too were opportunities to see those special places of concern to the Conservancy. As hiking guides to the three original wilderness areas were published, then through the nine editions of the *Monongahela National Forest Hiking Guide*, the Conservancy encouraged personal on-site observation by its members and the general public, secure in the knowledge that, once experienced, these sites would practically defend themselves.

Once in a while, a trip attracted an influential politician. West Virginia Secretary of State Jay Rockefeller and his wife Sharon toured Otter Creek in 1969, and Representatives Nick Rahall and Shelley Moore Capito both visited proposed wilderness areas in 2006. More often, other tour guests included congressional staffers, media members, state and federal agency officials, or documentary filmmakers. From Greathouse's trips with state officials even before there was a Highlands Conservancy to the Fall Review's invited guests, the outings spanning the last forty years provided a great opportunity to enjoy the natural environment and learn how to protect it.

Fall and Spring Reviews

The annual fall reviews, mid-winter workshops, and later, spring reviews also followed a well-established format. In addition to the "show-me tours," there was usually an evening program, often a single or panel presentation. The most famous would always be the "Sermon on the Mount" on Spruce Knob in 1965, when four hundred people heard Senator Byrd begin his talk and the lights went out. Other Conservancy forums were equally significant, as well. The Davis High School auditorium was filled with local residents at the height of the Davis Power Project controversy to hear from the power company and high state officials. At Seneca Rocks School, the local landowners finally had the chance to vent their opposition to the Forest Service's use of eminent domain to develop the Spruce Knob-Seneca Rocks National Recreation Area. On numerous occasions members of Congress and candidates for statewide office attended Conservancy events, seeking the members' input to assist in the formulation of important public policies.

On many other occasions the directors of the West Virginia departments of Natural Resources, Commerce, Highways, or Environmental Protection, and even more frequently the superintendents of the Monongahela National Forest, attended Conservancy gatherings to foster communication. In an echo of Senator Byrd being scheduled following a series of rousing conservation speeches in 1965, MNF Superintendent Clyde Thompson was subjected to a pro-wilderness slide show by wilderness guru Doug Scott in 2006. The Conservancy forums were always a combination of hearing from the featured guests, usually followed by a lively question-and-answer period, and often of subjecting them to a conservation presentation before letting them go.

Dialogue and communication were always considered essential both to developing a consensus Conservancy policy position and to advancing participation in public decisions. When any governmental agency or leader acted without providing an opportunity for public debate, the Conservancy would publicly criticize them and, occasionally, sue them to reconsider.

Litigation

The use of litigation in both the state and federal court systems became another hallmark of the West Virginia Highlands Conservancy. The Otter Creek case before U.S. District Judge Robert Maxwell led to the use of packhorses to haul drilling equipment into that proposed wilderness area. The courts also protected the wilderness characteristics of the Cranberry Backcountry. Several courts intervened to save the Shavers Fork from a variety of mining threats. Although the Conservancy was not lead plaintiff, Judge Maxwell's "Monongahela Decision" led to a nation-wide change in Forest Service planning and timbering practices.

The Conservancy preferred to work within the relevant agency's decision-making process and only went into court if that process failed. Examples of this strategy included the Davis Power Project case, Corridor H, and numerous mining appeals. Attending public hearings, presenting testimony, and appealing adverse decisions within the agency were required to establish "standing" in a later court challenge.

Throughout its history, the Conservancy had been blessed with the gift of many attorneys providing pro-bono legal assistance. From the young Washington attorneys, Jim Moorman and Fred Anderson, working with the new National Environmental Policy Act and applying it to Otter Creek with their local counsel Willis Shay, the combination of environmental and legal expertise provided the Conservancy a long record of success. Names like Paul Kaufman, Ray Ratliff, Davitt McAteer, Ron Wilson, Patrick McGinley, Tom Rodd, Hugh Rogers, Tom Michael, John Purbaugh, John McFerrin, Andrea Ferster, and others formed an impressive troupe of West Virginia advocates. In 1984, the Conservancy's officers and board members included six attorneys.

In the numerous cases to stop mountaintop-removal mining, Joe Lovett, Jim Hecker, and the staff of the Appalachian Center for the Economy and the Environment developed a specialized expertise and practice necessary to master the technical aspects of mining issues. Their arguments before U.S. District Judge Charles Haden brought about one of the most significant, if unfortunately short-lived, judicial victories for the Conservancy. Their later cases before federal judges Haden, Chambers, Goodwin, and others continued that battle even as these words were written.

NEPA and the EIS

A frequent line of argument by Conservancy attorneys was the failure of federal agencies to comply with provisions of the National Environmental Policy Act (NEPA), especially its requirements for an environmental impact statement (EIS). In virtually every earlier chapter, examples show the Conservancy requested, and if necessary litigated, to force a federal agency to comply with the EIS requirement of NEPA. It would be difficult to imagine the forty years of Highlands Conservancy legal battles without the protection this landmark law provided. In very recent years, the Conservancy even requested the West Virginia Public Service Commission establish a similar EIS process for wind farm proposals, although there was no federal requirement to do so.

Expertise Welcomed

Like the attorneys, the Conservancy had a long record of attracting professionals with expertise and encouraging them to apply their knowledge to Conservancy issues. Frequently a committee or task force formed to research the issue, often publishing a report. For the first three wilderness areas, a combination hiking guide and wilderness proposal provided a factual basis for wilderness advocacy. For Corridor H, the Markey-Green Report played a significant role in re-routing that highway. After

Burrell published *Voice* articles from several experts on the impact of the proposed Davis Power Project, a task force conducted additional research and presented a major report to the Conservancy. Later, the Shavers Fork Coalition provided a forum for scholars and other professionals to address its multiple issues. Most recently, the Wind Energy Committee struggled to forge a position that both endorsed green energy and protected the highlands. Collaborative and professional expertise was essential to developing public policy on these and other Conservancy issues.

Strong Leaders and an Active Board

Within the structure of the Conservancy itself, there were several principles that became important. For one, the president was given wide latitude to act and speak on behalf of the organization. Beginning with Tom King, and continuing through Bob Burrell, both the Elkintons, Larry George, Cindy Rank, Frank Young, and Hugh Rogers, all enjoyed the flexibility and exercised it responsibly. Only once, over the contentious issue of wind power, did the board reverse a president's action.

The board of directors has met regularly, once each quarter for more than forty years, to review reports from committees, check its financial condition, set its policies, and plan for coming events. Seldom was there a quorum problem, a considerable achievement considering the distance many members traveled and the location of meetings in the mountains. One snowstorm was memorable to Max Smith in 1966, and another in January 2007 kept only a very few away. Between these two meetings, blizzards, hurricanes, and floods have not deterred the volunteer board members from attending meetings.

Volunteers and Staffing

Although the Conservancy has always been volunteer-driven, for occasional projects it employed staff. Leslee McCarty was hired, for example, to provide extra energy to gain wilderness designation for Cranberry. On other occasions, student interns provided staffing. In the most recent campaign, the Wilderness Coalition hired project staff to coordinate all the volunteer efforts and provide needed expertise and continuity.

From the early years, the Conservancy provided an honorarium to its *Voice* editors and membership secretaries to ensure that these arduous tasks were completed on time. Gradually the duties of membership secretary grew into a position of administrative assistant. In 2003 Dave Saville became the first full-time employee of the Conservancy.

Throughout its first forty years, the Highlands Conservancy primarily relied upon its members as volunteers to lead the organization, support the committee functions, attend board meetings, plan fall and spring reviews, and otherwise be active on the issues. During most of these years, the Conservancy maintained a paid membership of approximately 500, but that number grew steadily after 2000. That growth resulted partly from high-visibility issues, such as Blackwater Canyon and Wilderness, from a re-energized outings program, and from a conscious effort by Saville and others to make membership development an organization priority. In January 2007 Saville reported a membership of more than 1600, virtually tripled from a decade earlier.

Board Re-Focusing

Along the way, there were periodic attempts to encourage the board of directors to restructure, develop a strategic planning process, and seek major grants for operations — in short, become more like other non-profit organizations. While some minor changes happened, the consensus often was that the structure and mode of operation that characterized the Highlands Conservancy worked for achieving its goals, even to the astonishment of outside observers. Lou Greathouse and Rupert Cutler, looking in forty years later, would have certainly recognized the organization in 2007.

Elizabeth "Buff" Rodman was born in 1964, three years before the founding of the Highlands Conservancy. Since her parents, Sayre and Jean Rodman, were active in the formation of the group and continued as board members over a forty-year period, Buff was literally raised in the Conservancy.

This was appropriate since her parents had helped form the Pittsburgh Climbers, both a recreational and a social group of Pittsburghers who spent the majority of their weekends each year in the highlands. The Climbers rented a series of small farmhouses, all within a few miles of Seneca Rocks, which served as base camps for a weekend of outdoor activities.

Except for the years she was in high school, college, and her early professional life, Rodman had been either dragged along to Conservancy meetings as a child or, later as an adult, chose to accompany her father as his health was failing. After his death in August 2004 at age 82, she became her mother's companion in attending Conservancy sessions. Jean was still a very active board member in 2007 and no doubt had been active longer than any other individual on the board.

The younger Rodman was elected as the first "second generation" Conservancy board member in 2005. In 2006 she was elected Senior Vice President. In this capacity her views of the current state of the Conservancy and, equally important, her outlook for its future were instructive. Rodman represented both the continuity of the first forty years and the potential for the future.

In a 2006 interview, Rodman shared several characteristics of the Conservancy that she considered unusual. As an organization, it was:

- volunteer-driven, with staffing on particular tasks only
- attracted people with a personal stake in issues, saying "come and lead us"
- encouraged participants to do more than they thought they could
- listened to each other
- fostered an encouraging environment for people to come into it

The picture she painted, she said, was "completely not how organizations run." Remembering a planning session a few years before when an outside consultant had been invited to help the board consider its future and its organizational development, Rodman said, "He had never met a group like this." He didn't expect that anyone would still be active over a thirty- or even a forty-year period." Obviously, there was something unusual about how this organization had been working.

Looking into the future, Rodman outlined issues she saw emerging or continuing. Mining would continue to challenge West Virginia's environment. Population growth, and especially second-home development, would add pressure on finite resources. Water, both quantity, but especially quality, would become more important. A lack of planning in West Virginia would handicap its ability to manage these issues. And, finally, the emergence of single-issue, local groups would necessitate broader coalitions to mobilize political and legislative change.

As one of those who would be leading the West Virginia Highlands Conservancy into its next decades, Rodman could use her lifetime perspective and her knowledge of many remote places in the highlands to continue the tradition her parents helped forge and lead.

In interviews for this book, each subject was asked to comment on reasons for the successes and failures of the Conservancy and to look ahead at issues the Conservancy might confront in the future. Some of the responses were interesting.

Many commented on the ability of the Conservancy to be flexible and react quickly to emerging issues. Since there was no national policy council, the board of directors could fashion a policy and implement actions in short order. Others lauded the Conservancy's appreciation of volunteers. In the Highlands Conservancy, Hugh Rogers said, "You can really make a difference." Others liked the fact that the Conservancy built its policy positions on well-researched information, often soliciting members with special expertise to help. Depending for support on its own financial resources, Saville mentioned, kept it independent. He remembered one major donation that was returned because of perceived strings attached. Certainly at least twice (see Chapter 7) the Conservancy had declined awards from, and high level meetings with, agencies it did not agree with.

But there were at least two potentially ominous challenges facing the organization. One was actually a function of its success. The Highlands Conservancy was steadily graying. From an organization founded by a group of recreational leaders mostly in their thirties, it had gradually matured into a group with many active members in or near retirement age. At the 2007 Spring Review, for example, one could count two very active eighty-year-olds, many board members in their fifties and sixties, a few in their thirties and forties, and an absence of anyone in their twenties. Yet West Virginians were actively involved in environmental organizations elsewhere, often on the same issues as the Conservancy. The challenge for the Conservancy would be to recruit, nurture, and support the next generation. Even Rodman was already in her forties, so she was only a bridge to the next generation.

The other challenge was one of competition. Over many years a proliferation of single-issue organizations had developed, focusing on such subjects as mountaintop- removal mining, river preservation, highways, and, more recently, wind energy. The Conservancy had consistently seen itself as a multi-issue organization and often combined forces with these groups when a common interest emerged. Local community-based organizations continued to be crucial on local issues such as wind-farm permits. In fact in 2007 the Wilderness Campaign was actively helping form county advocacy groups to promote wilderness areas.

Finally, there were signs of competition for the distinction of serving as advocate for the highlands. As the chapter closed on its first four decades, the Conservancy could see the Friends of Blackwater defining its mission to include not only Blackwater Canyon, but Dolly Sods, Cheat Canyon, and other areas of the highlands. One of their mailings touted, "We watch the highlands for you." Another group, Stewards of the Potomac Highlands, defined its purpose as preserving "open spaces, forests, farmland, rural communities, and towns, and foster stewardship of the Potomac Highlands of West Virginia, Virginia, and Maryland." Having more groups that shared common goals could make the total effort stronger. But it might also divide up a finite number of volunteers and financial resources. As the senior organization, the Conservancy needed to remain open to change, promote initiatives, and welcome newcomers. It didn't want to become a senior organization in the other sense.

As Conservancy leaders were interviewed, each was asked to define what made the Highlands Conservancy special. After the more predictable answers, several mentioned that a bond had developed among Conservancy activists, which some observers found unusual. A *Voice* 2006 column by Dave Elkinton, discussed the Conservancy's "Sense of Community":

> This is the most difficult to describe, but somehow seems to be the most meaningful to those who have mentioned it. We all understand how a family works. Even as adults, often living states apart, we make time to see each other. We are there for any crisis or blessed event. In communities, neighbors gather for a variety of occasions, cover for each other in emergencies, and join together for common activities or civic functions. The Highlands Conservancy shares some of these characteristics. A recent example has been the life-threatening medical crisis experienced by John McFerrin, our Past President, current

Secretary and *Voice* Editor. Thankfully John recovered, but others, especially Cindy Rank, have stepped forward to cover his duties until he is fully recovered. While John was hospitalized, I am sure John felt the support of the entire Conservancy community. In a lighter way, the general camaraderie experienced at each Spring and Fall Review, as old friends reunite and new friends are made, exemplifies the Conservancy as community. Without that spirit, and the enjoyment of each other's company, most first-time attendees would not return.

Conservancy members had always been optimistic, even when others thought that ridiculous. When there were no congressionally designated wilderness areas in the East, they said why not? When no one expected that the Davis Power Project could be stopped, they said why not? When core drilling was scheduled in Otter Creek or mining in the Cranberry, they said why? When Corridor H was already under construction, they asked why continue? When EPA, the Corps of Engineers, and OSM waived meaningful enforcement of mountaintop-removal mining, they said stop! When national conservation groups supported wind-farm development, they said wait a minute.

For their optimism and faith that their collaborative efforts could indeed change the world they lived in, Conservancy members had been pleasantly surprised on many occasions. Who would have guessed Judge Maxwell would have ended clearcutting and stopped road-building in Otter Creek? Who would have expected Administrative Law Judge Kaplan to deny the Davis Power Project license and recommend a smaller project? Who expected the Corps of Engineers District Engineer Janairo to deny a 404 wetlands permit? And who expected Judge Haden to rule against mountaintop-removal mining?

As the West Virginia Highlands Conservancy celebrated its fortieth anniversary in 2007, many of its founders were still around to see how it had matured. Newer members had contributed untold hours of volunteer effort and had identified and addressed new issues facing the highlands region, and *The Highlands Voice* was regularly delivering twenty pages each month to members, libraries, elected leaders, and agency officials.

The Conservancy might not be the oldest environmental organization in West Virginia, nor the most radical. But it claimed, without dispute, to be the oldest environmental *advocacy* organization in the state. Its reputation was one of credibility, based on well-researched policies, capable of mobilizing thousands of letters or emails when necessary. It had won some battles and lost some too. In 2007 it was as strong in membership and financial resources as ever in its history. As it looked ahead, it seemed to have been true to its original purpose: the preservation and conservation of the natural, scenic, and historic areas of significance within the West Virginia highland region. The highlands still needed it, and the Conservancy was ready.

Sources:

All interviews previously cited after each chapter

The Highlands Voice articles by Dave Elkinton, Judy Rodd, Dave Saville, Frank Young

Rodman, Buff, interview, June 22, 2006

Appendix

Presidents

1967–71	Tom King
1971–73	Bob Burrell
1973–74	Dave Elkinton
1974–75	Joe Rieffenberger
1975–77	Charles Carlson
1977–79	Linda Cooper Elkinton
1979–81	Joe Rieffenberger
1981–83	Jeannetta ("Tippy") Petras
1983–86	Larry George
1986–88	John Purbaugh
1988–94	Cindy Rank
1994–98	John McFerrin
1998–2004	Frank Young
2004–08	Hugh Rogers

Editors of *The Highlands Voice*

1969–71	Bob Burrell
1971–72	Ernie Nestor
1973–77	Ron Hardway
1978–80	Tom Dunham
1980–81	Judy Frank
1982	Paul Frank/Sally Keeney
1983	Brian Farkas
1984	Mary Ratliff
1985–86	Deborah Smith
1986–88	Gary Worthington
1988–90	Karen Farris
1990–93	Mary Pat Peck
1993–97	Bill Ragetté
1997–2005	Bill Reed
2005–	John McFerrin/Cindy Rank (2006–07)

Executive/Administrative Assistants

1984–85 .... Mary Ratliff
1985–86 .... Chris Leichliter
1994–98 .... Richard diPretoro
1998–2007 .... Dave Saville

Index

Entries have been grouped so as, we hope, to make this index user-friendly. For example, all references to courts, whether state or federal, are listed under courts, not under specific names such as District or Appeals. We have tried to be zealous in giving cross-references, and in identifying acronyms. Entries using proper nouns (i.e., as a name of someone or some thing) are listed before entries using the same word as a common noun.

A

C

D

F

H

I

O

P

Q

R

S

U

X

Y

Z